Lecture Notes in Computer Science 1021

Edited by G. Goos, J. Hartmanis and J. van Leeuwen

Advisory Board: W. Brauer   D. Gries   J. Stoer

Springer
Berlin
Heidelberg
New York
Barcelona
Budapest
Hong Kong
London
Milan
Paris
Santa Clara
Singapore
Tokyo

Michael P. Papazoglou (Ed.)

OOER '95: Object-Oriented and Entity-Relationship Modeling

14th International Conference
Gold Coast, Australia, December 13-15, 1995
Proceedings

 Springer

Series Editors

Gerhard Goos
Universität Karlsruhe
Vincenz-Priessnitz-Straße 3, D-76128 Karlsruhe, Germany

Juris Hartmanis
Department of Computer Science, Cornell University
4130 Upson Hall, Ithaca, NY 14853, USA

Jan van Leeuwen
Department of Computer Science, Utrecht University
Padualaan 14, 3584 CH Utrecht, The Netherlands

Volume Editor

Michael P. Papazoglou
School of Information Systems, Queensland University of Technology
2 George Street, GPO Box 2434, Brisbane Qld. 4001, Australia

Cataloging-in-Publication data applied for

Die Deutsche Bibliothek - CIP-Einheitsaufnahme

Object oriented and entity relationship modelling : 14th
international conference, Gold Coast, Australia, December 1995
; proceedings / OOER '95. Michael P. Papazoglou (ed.). -
Berlin ; Heidelberg ; New York ; Barcelona ; Budapest ; Hong
Kong ; London ; Milan ; Paris ; Tokyo : Springer, 1995
 (Lecture notes in computer science ; Vol. 1021)
 ISBN 3-540-60672-6
NE: Papazoglou, Mike [Hrsg.]; OOER <14, 1995, Gold Coast,
 Queensland>; GT

CR Subject Classification (1991): H.2, H.4, H.1, D.1.5, D.2.1-2, D.2.10,
D.3.2, I.2.4, I.6.5, J.1, J.4

ISBN 3-540-60672-6 Springer-Verlag Berlin Heidelberg New York

Typesetting: Camera-ready by author
SPIN 10512318   06/3142 – 5 4 3 2 1 0   Printed on acid-free paper

Foreword

Welcome to the Gold Coast and the fourteenth International Conference on Object-Oriented and Entity-Relationship Modelling. This is the first time this conference has been held in Australia. We thank the steering committee for its decision to hold the conference here and hope all of you find the venue conducive to technical, as well as social, interaction.

The Program Chair, Mike Papazoglou, has done a great job in maintaining the tradition of high quality in the conference presentations. I am sure that you will find the keynote talks by Gio Wiederhold and Julian Edwards to be both informative and thought provoking. I would like to thank them for agreeing to be part of the conference's technical program.

I would like to thank all of the sponsors who generously gave their support to this conference, especially Sun Microsystems, Information Industries Board - Queensland, Queensland University of Technology and the Australian Department of Industry Science and Technology.

I hope that you all enjoy your stay on the beautiful Gold Coast of Australia.

F.H. Lochovsky
General Conference Chair
O-O ER'95

October 1995

Preface

The fourteenth International Conference on Object-Oriented Entity-Relationship (O-O ER) Conference provides a forum for researchers and practitioners in the area of conceptual modelling to interact, present existing results and explore directions that affect the current and future generation of information systems. The conference has been renamed to encompass current technological thrusts and directions in the area of conceptual modelling and to provide a broader forum for researchers and practitioners to exchange ideas and report on progress.

This year's theme is the Application of Object-Oriented/Entity-Relationship Technologies to Information Systems Modelling.

The Entity-Relationship approach has been extensively used in many database system and information system design methodologies. Recently, Object-Oriented Technology has not only drawn tremendous interest from the research community but it has also moved into mainstream industrial software design and development.

The O-O ER conference provides an opportunity towards integrating these two technologies and opens new opportunities for modelling by promoting better understanding of applications, cleaner design practices, and more updatable and maintainable systems. It also provides a basis for re-using and retrofitting existing systems and technology.

The topic of the conference is of tremendous interest to both academia and industry. It is one where technological advances in conceptual modelling can have a profound impact on how organisations will model and meet future business objectives and cope with an evolving technology.

In response to the O-O ER'95 call for papers, approximately 120 papers were submitted from 26 countries around the world. 36 papers were accepted based on quality and originality. Each paper was reviewed by three reviewers and all papers were discussed at the program committee meeting held in Brisbane in July 1995. This volume contains in addition to all the papers selected by the program committee, the keynote address paper by Gio Wiederhold and summaries of papers accepted by the Industry Track Chair, Kit Dampney, and his subcommittee.

A conference such as O-O ER'95 depends on the volunteer efforts of a large number of individuals, and we are indeed very fortunate to to have been able to put together an excellent team. It has been a real pleasure working together with the members of the program committee and the additional reviewers, who devoted a considerable amount of their time to reviewing the submitted articles. I was privileged to work together with such highly gifted individuals as Fred Lochovsky (General Chair) and Zahir Tari (Organising Chair). Their commitment, enthusiasm, support, and continuous guidance are gratefully acknowledged.

Special thanks go to Leszek Maciaszek for coordinating the panels, to Makoto Takizawa for coordinating the tutorials, to Kit Dampney and Julian Edwards for coordinating the industrial stream, and Ed Lindsay for his efforts to publicize the Conference. Lastly, I wish to thank Michelle Taylor for her tireless efforts in maintaining the order of papers, and for handling correspondence and registration.

I hope that you will enjoy the conference and that you will find these proceedings a valuable source of information on conceptual modelling techniques and methodologies.

M.P. Papazoglou
Program Chair
O-O ER'95

October 1995

Conference Committees

General Conference Chair

Fred Lochovsky — Hong-Kong Univ. of Science & Technology

Program Committee Chair

Mike Papazoglou — Queensland Univ. of Technology

Organizing Chair

Zahir Tari — Queensland Univ. of Technology

Tutorial Chair

Makoto Takizawa — Tokyo Denki University

Panel Chair

Leszek Maciaszek — Macquarie University

Industrial Chair

Kit Dampney — Macquarie University

Publicity Chair

Edward Lindsay — Sun Microsystems, Australia

Demonstrations chair

Julian Edwards — Object Oriented Pty Ltd

Program Committee

Peter Apers — Twente Univ., Holland
Boualem Bentallah — Institute de Mathematiques de Grenoble
Janis Bubenko — SISU, Sweden
Athman Bouguettaya — QUT, Australia
Tiziana Catarci — Univ. of Rome, Italy
Sang Cha — Seoul National University, Korea
Chin-Wan Chung — KAIST, Korea
David Edmond — QUT, Australia
Opher Etzion — Technion, Israel
Joseph Fong — City Polytechnic of Hong-Kong

Terry Halpin	Univ. of Queensland, Australia
Jean-Luc Hainaut	Univ. of Namur, Belgium
Igor Hawryszkiewycz	Univ. of Technology, Sydney
Yahiko Kambayashi	Kyoto Univ., Japan
Ibrahim Kamel	Matsushita IT Laboratory, USA
Roger King	Univ. of Colorado, USA
Vram Kouramjian	Wichita University, USA
Qing Li	HKUST, Hong-Kong
Tok Wang Ling	NUS, Singapore
Peri Loucopoulos	UMIST, UK
Robert Meersman	Univ. of Tilburg, Holland
John Mylopoulos	Univ. of Toronto, Canada
Erich Neuhold	GMD-IPSI, Germany
Anne Ngu	UNSW, Australia
Oscar Nierstrasz	Bern Univ., Switzerland
Marian Nodine	Brown Univ., USA
Christine Parent	Univ. of Burgundy, France
Patrick Pfeffer	US West Advanced Technologies, USA
Niki Pissinou	Univ. of Southwestern Louisiana, USA
Sudha Ram	Univ. of Arizona, USA
Iztok Savnik	Jozef Stefan Institute, Ljubljana, Slovenia
Gunter Schlageter	Fern Univ. Hagen, Germany
Arie Segev	Berkeley Univ., USA
Graeme Shanks	Monash Univ., Australia
Amit Sheth	Univ. of Georgia, USA
Arne Solvberg	Univ. of Trondheim, Norway
Stefano Spaccapietra	EPFL, Switzerland
Kazumasa Yokota	ICOT, Japan
Kyu Whang	KIST, Korea
Carson Woo	Univ. of British Columbia
John Zeleznikow	La Trobe Univ., Australia

Additional Reviewers

S. Adali	T. Ajisaka	B. Bentallah	T. Berkel
A.J. Berre	O. Boucelma	P. Bruza	P. Buhrmann
S. Carlsen	S.D. Cha	L. C. Chan	C.M. Chen
D. Chiu	D.K. Chiu	L. C. Chan	C. M. Chen
N. Craske	H. Dalianis	A. Delis	P.K. Deo
T. D'Hondt	D.H. Eum	P. Fankhauser	B.A. Farshchian
D. Filippidou	A. Guessoum	E. Ho	G. Huck
M. Kajko-Mattsson	K. Karlapalem	E. Kavakli	F. Kemper
J.H. Kim	K.C. Kim	W. Klas	S. Konomi
J. Krogstie	M. Lanzerini	Q. LeViet	J. Lee
M. L. Lee	F. Lenzen	X. Li	N. Loucopoulos
P. Louridas	K. Makki	A. Massari	W. McIver, Jr.
J.A. Miller	S. Milliner	S. Mittrach	C. Nellborn
R. Ng	I. Ounis	M. Orlowski	D. Potter
H.A. Proper	G. Santucci	A. Schrerer	J. Shepherd
E. Smythe	W.W. Song	M. Straube	K. Subieta
K. Vanapipat	X.Y. Whang	X. Wu	J. Yang
S.M. Yang	S.B. Yoo	J. Yu	A. Zaslavski

Sponsoring Institutions

Contents

Industrial Stream Papers

Modeling and System Maintenance

Gio Wiederhold

Computer Science Department, Stanford University

Abstract:
This paper reports on recent work and directions in modern software architectures and their formal models with respect to software maintenance. The focus on maintenance attacks the most costly and frustrating aspect in dealing with large-scale software systems: keeping them up-to-date and responsive to user needs in changing environments.

We employ *mediators*, autonomous modules which create information objects out of source data. These modules are placed into an intermediate layer, bridging clients and servers. A mediated architecture can reduce the cost growth of maintenance to a near-linear function of system size, whereas current system architectures have quadratic factors.

Models provide the means for the maintainer to share knowledge with the customer. The customers can become involved in the maintenance of their task models without having to be familiar with the details of all the resources to be employed. These resources encompass the many kinds of databases that are becoming available on our networks.

1. Introduction

Maintenance of software amounts to about 60 to 85% of total software costs in industry. These costs are due to fixing bugs, making changes induced by changing needs of customers, by adaptation to externally imposed changes, and by changes in underlying resources [CALO:94]. Most maintenance needs are beyond control of the organization needing the maintenance, as new government regulations or corporate reorganizations, changes due to expanding databases, alterations in remote files, or updates in system services. Excluded from this percentage are actual improvements in functionality, i.e., tasks that require redesign of a program. However, often improvements in functionality are needed to keep customers and are difficult to distinguish from other forms of maintenance. Maintenance is best characterized by being *unscheduled*, because maintenance tasks require rapid responses to keep the system alive and acceptable to the customer. In operational systems, fixing bugs, that is, errors introduced when the programs were written, is a minor component of maintenance.

Traditional software engineering tools and methods, such as specification languages, verification, and testing, only address the reduction of bugs, and hence have had little impact on long-term maintenance costs [Tracz:95]. Due to the longlevity of software most maintenance is caused by change, namely that at the time of delivery, or in subsequent years, the expectations and the environment no longer are what they were when the program was specified. Efforts spent on specifications, to the extent that software delivery is delayed, actually increases maintenance costs, since delays obsolete the design specifications.

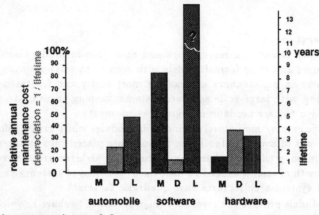

Figure 1. Maintenance is good for you

Why is software so much affected by change, apparently more so than hardware? The primary cause is that we expect software to be flexible and adaptable, while we expect hardware to be static. Maintenance of hardware is mainly performed to restore its original capabilities, and perhaps to add capacity in terms of storage or the number of users being served. Hardware is regularly replaced, preferably with equipment that is compatible with the existing software. For any system component where change is expected, we choose a software solution. If we are unsure about the use or eventual configuration or uitilization level of a system we maximize the software portion as well. The essence of software is its presumed ability to accomodate change, so that maintenance is a positive attribute of software, rather than a negative attribute to be avoided. Figure 1 aims to make that point.

Once maintenance is seen as a positive feature of software it becomes clear that we should invest to make software convenient to maintain, and not make software changes difficult by insisting on rigid adherence to specifications. However, maintenance must be planned for, so that it does not come as a surprise and a distraction. In long-lived systems most bugs are actually introduced during maintenance, making the issue of establishing maintainable architectures and models yet more important.

1.1 Maintenance cost

In large, multi-user systems maintenance costs are especially high because of two factors. First, the number of change requests increases in proportion to the number of types of users. Secondly, the cost of maintenance includes substantial efforts outside of the core application area. A change request to one module requires interaction with the owners of all other modules and finally orchestrating a changeover. These costs are universally much higher than the core cost of the requested change. The product of these two factors leads to an order squared cost in terms of system size for maintenance, as expanded in Section 3.2

A second order effect drives the cost of system maintenance yet higher. Since system changes become traumatic if they occur too frequently, all incremental requests are batched into periodic updates and performed perhaps twice a year. Composing and integrating the batch will take three months. Batching reduces responsiveness to the customer: it will take on the average at least a half year to have anything fixed. In practice responsiveness is much worse. Batching also increases the risk and the cost of failure, since some apparently independent changes introduced simultaneously may have interactions and these interactions will affect unsuspicious users. If the seriousness of the interaction errors requires a rollback to an earlier global version of the system, even users not affected by the failure will have to rollback their procedures.

1.2 Architectural effects

Taking these factors into account, it is not surprising that many data-processing organizations find that they lack the resources to advance the functionality of their systems. They may be bypassed by individual stand-alone systems, built by the customers themselves to gain the needed functionality. These systems will soon demand access to resources as corporate databases. *Open system* architectures respond to these demands and initiated the trend towards client-server architectures, now in full swing. Given stable and comprehensive servers, client applications can be rapidly constructed. However, the client-server architecture also fails to address the maintenance requirements outlined above. If a new client or a revised client application induces a need for a change in a server, then all other clients that use this server must be inspected and perhaps altered, as sketched in Figure 2. The problem has not changed, but might be more difficult now, since organizationally many clients are autonomous, and likely remote. In Example 1 we provide a simple problem case, and also its solution in a mediated architecture. Several alternatives exist for resolving this particular change. Most wii increase the complexity of the laboratory system and not deal with the case where the diagnosis support mediator also obtains information from other sources, as the medical record, say, to track the significance of any changes in the patients' cholesterol.

The mediated architecture uses an intermediate layer to provide isolation of one user application from other applications, even though resources are shared [ASK:95]. The use of formal, that is manipulable models, based on Entity-Relationship (E-R) concepts to create application objects, permits rapid regeneration of linkages to those resources. Figure 3 sketches modules in the three layers, and their linkages. An application can call on multiple mediators and each mediator, in turn, can invoke multiple resources, including other mediators.

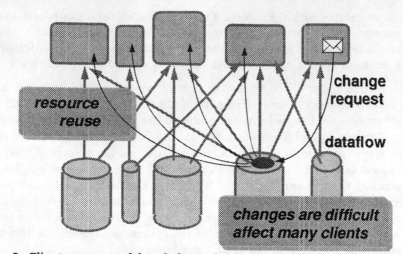

Figure 2. Client server model and the path of a client change request.

Example 1: A change mandated by scientific progress.

In a hospital many subsystems rely on information from the clinical laboratories. In addition to the treating physician's record, there will be charts to track progress, analysis for the quality of care, watching for iatrogenic incidents, information for billing, and evaluation of interaction with currently prescribed drugs. Recently the distinction of low-density and high-density cholesterol has become important. The clinic which surveys patients for cardiovascular risks needs these two values, instead of total cholesterol, and the server in the clinical laboratory is prepared to deliver such data. Without a mediator module every other client using cholesterol data will have to be changed. A synchronous switch has to be scheduled, and all clients are warned to have updated application programs ready at the cut-over date.

In a mediated environment the change in the laboratory server is only synchronized with the diagnosis support mediator and other mediators using laboratory data. That number will always be much smaller than the number of clients, as assessed in Section 2.4. Those mediators will sum the cholesterol values obtained from the laboratory and deliver the sum to the clients. As sketched in Figure 4, a new version of the mediator serving the cardiovascular clinic is created which delivers both values, and the clinic can switch over at any time. If the changes work reliably for their originators, any other clinic can switch over when it deems best. Since there is a cost to maintaining many versions of a mediator, there should be some inducement for all customers to convert, perhaps by increasing the price of obsolecent information over time. Figure 8 illustrates the concept.

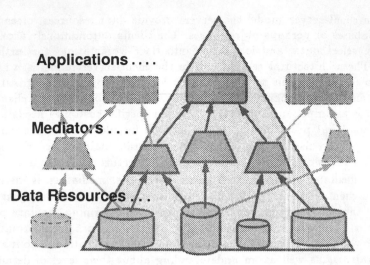

Applications....

Mediators....

Data Resources...

Figure 3. Modules in a mediated architecture and the scope of an application.

2. The Mediated Architecture

A mediated architecture is a departure from several prior architectures, which have implemented variations of two-layer separations for the last 30 years, as indicated in Figure 4. The boundary has moved up and down, as the capabilities of the hardware components evolved. Mediation inserts a third layer; its function is best described starting from a client-server model, as shown in Figure 5.

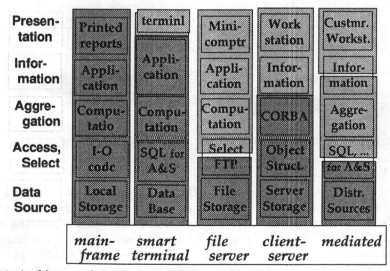

Presen-tation	Printed reports	terminl	Mini-comptr	Work station	Custmr. Workst.
Infor-mation	Appli-cation	Appli-cation	Appli-cation	Infor-mation	Infor-mation
Aggre-gation	Compu-tatio	Compu-tation	Compu-tation	CORBA	Aggre-gation
Access, Select	I-O code	SQL for A&S	Select / FTP	Object Struct.	SQL, ... for A&S
Data Source	Local Storage	Data Base	File Storage	Server Storage	Distr. Sources
	main-frame	*smart terminal*	*file server*	*client-server*	*mediated*

Figure 4. Architectural Evolution of Information Systems

In a client-server model the servers provide data resources, often derived from databases or perhaps object-bases. The clients autonomously access these resources, select data, and load them into their workstations for further processing. The architectural relationship in the client-server model is $n : m$ from clients to resources. This squared relationship leads to the steep growth curve for maintenance, as recognized in Section 1. Another problem in the client-server approach is an impedance mismatch between specific customer needs and general servers. That problem, and a solution will be addressed in Section 4. Our PENGUIN solution also helps in managing the internal maintenance of a mediator, but we first focus on the overall mediating architecture of Figure 3.

In a mediated architecture a layer of modules, *mediators*, is inserted between the client and server [W:92C]. Mediators provide more than just a *thick* interface; they provide significant functionality, transforming the data provided by a server to information needed by an application. Such transformations require knowledge, as knowing where the data are, specifications about the data representations, as well as an understanding about their level of detail versus the users' conceptual expectations [W:92I].

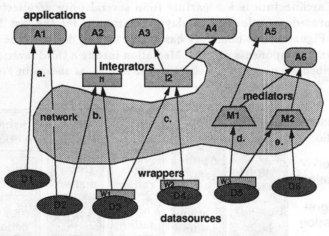

Figure 5. Mediator Evolution

2.1 Functions in mediation

Making computers understand and bridge the gap from server to customer may seem hard, but the job can be decomposed and executed in a logical flow of data from servers to clients. The resulting tasks select and access the relevant servers, integrate related data obtained from those servers, summarize, filter, and structure the result to match the customer's request [WG:95]. In a client-server architecture these tasks are primarily performed by client software. The mediator now acts as an information server with respect to the client module. The client software is still responsible for integrating information from multiple domain mediators and the user interface [ACHK:93]. Several ancillary tasks may be needed during mediation as well, for instance, processing to bring data from distinct servers to the same level of abstraction prior to integration, and resolving semantic mismatches [DeMichiel:89]. Once the job of mediation is decomposed, all of the tasks become manageable. The needed functions cited have all been demonstrated in other contexts. The contribution of the mediator concept is essentially the recognition and extraction of these tasks into an architecture that reduces their complexity. *Only simple systems work*. Figure 7 illustrates the task assignment within a mediator and Example 2 expands the diagnostic mediator.

2.2 Domain partitioning

We expect to have multiple mediators, partitioned by domain. Partitioning by domains provides a vertical partitioning, based on domains. Vertical or domain-specific or partitioning is crucial to maintenance, otherwise the middle layer will become the bottleneck. Formally, a domain is defined by having a coherent *ontology*. An ontology is comprised of the terms or vocabulary understood in the domain and the relationships among the terms [Gruber:91].

Having a single mediator would impose a volume of attendant knowledge which is too large for effective maintenance by a coherent group of individuals [W:95D]. Maintenance covering multiple domains requires meetings by committees. Committees are great to achieve compromise when there is a lack of coherence, but they are ineffective for software maintenance [W:86].

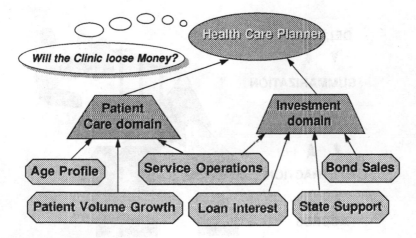

Figure 6. An application accessing multiple domains

2.3 Building mediators

Mediators can be hand-crafted, that is, built using available programming languages, as C++, or can use artificial intelligence techniques, where the operations are presented as rules. Rules can be used to compose the primitive operations in a mediator, and we make further gains in maintenance. Today most mediators are hand-crafted, and the gains in maintenance derive solely from the architecture.

The programmer writing a mediator will interact closely with domain experts, to assure that the models are accurate, that the functionality of the mediator is appropriate, and that the results are obvious to the client. Tools to build mediators are now being developed [Lehrer:94], so that the task in time can devolve upon individuals who are primarily domain experts, rather than programming experts. Crucial in mediation are interfaces which allow their composition. Interfaces from the mediator to the resources can be derived from client-server standards, as SQL, CORBA, DCE, OPENDOC, and OLE. Interfaces supplied by a mediator to the client need better facilities for multi-tasking, asynchrony, and task-sensitive representation, as well as provision for meta-information.

Within the ARPA Knowledge-Sharing Initiative [FCGB:91] a structure has evolved consisting of a Knowledge Query and Manipulation Language (KQML), which defines a transport layer [FFMM:94], and a Knowledge Interchange Formalism (KIF) [GK:94], which is a vehicle for transmitting first-order-logic rules. KQML specifies the operation or *performative*, the destination type, the vocabulary or the *ontology*, and the representation [W:89].

The mediator, acting as a server to its clients, does not provide a human-friendly interface. It provides the requested information and some meta-information, which can be used by the client to understand and display the information. Mediators, not having internal persistent databases nor extensive graphical user interfaces, can be kept small, further enhancing their maintainability.

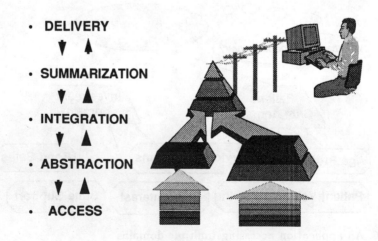

- **DELIVERY**
  ▼ ▲
- **SUMMARIZATION**
  ▼ ▲
- **INTEGRATION**
  ▼ ▲
- **ABSTRACTION**
  ▼ ▲
- **ACCESS**

Figure 7. Task and Flow in a Mediator

Example 2. Functions in the diagnostic mediator:

Information output: Current cholesterol level, trend lines, warning flag, ...

produced by:

Exception flagging: Provide meta-information to trigger a warning when cholesterol level has increased more than 5% per month.

Summarization: Compute trend line parameters from past medical record and recent data.

Integration: Combine past medical record data with current observations and standards for patient's in similar age/gender groups.

Representation change: Convert laboratory findings to UGS values.

Abstraction: Convert irregular observations to periodic (monthly) values.

Selection: Extract medical record data from past sites for current patient.

Search: Determine past treatment sites by navigation from current record.

2.4 Domain-specificity

As indicated earlier, mediators are domain-specific. This means that many mediators will inhabit the middle layer, each focused on one domain. A domain is often determined by existing organizational assignments. A financial mediator will be owned by the chief financial officer (CFO) of an organization, the diagnostic mediator by the chief pathologist, the drug mediator by the pharmacist, etc. Guidance to domain expertise may be obtained from their professional organizations, just as now professional organizations may proscribe minimal schemas for the collection of data in their field [McShane:79]. It is not a major step to move from data formats to the rules for interpretation. Technically such a move is supported by object-oriented approaches, where data structures are augmented by programmed, encapsulated methods to assure their consistent interpretation [Wegner:90].

2.5 Partitioned Maintenance

Figure 3 illustrated the mediated architecture. In Figure 8 we indicate how changes are handled in that architecture. We take the case of having a new or revised application, which demands new services from the data resources. The existing mediator in that path serves multiple applications. To accomodate the new application that mediator is revised to obtain and present the new data. If the data resources will no longer supply the old data, then the old mediator has to be adapted to supply surrogate information. In our cholesterol case this is simple; high-density and low-density cholesterol data are summed and reported as cholesterol to the old applications. The models for the two versions differ little.

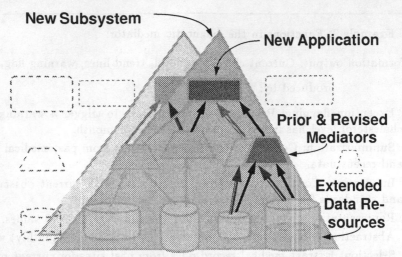

New Subsystem

New Application

Prior & Revised Mediators

Extended Data Resources

Figure 8. Changes induced by a client request in a mediated architecture.

All the required changes can be made by a domain specialist, in charge of the lipids mediator (seen in Figure 13). The cost of the change is linear, and the changeover can be scheduled at the convenience of the the new application alone. Any problems arising in the change are easily undone, only affecting the mediators and the new application. As other applications require specificity in cholesterol data, they can start using the new, proven mediator. The old version can be retired when all customers become up-to-date. The cost of the change is $\mathcal{O}(3)$, linear in the number of modules involved in the modernization.

Compare this cost with the cost of making changes in the traditional federated or client-server architecture, illustrated in Figure 2. We recognize 7 phases.

1 The application designer has to remind the resource provider to determine which other client applications will be affected by the proposed change. In an open systems architecture no records of resource utilization need to be kept, inducing delays in identifying clients.

2 To validate the proposed changes scaffolding must be built to check their effect on existing applications. It is risky and unacceptable to have failures that affect many customers beyond the requestor.

3 Agreements have to be worked out about the change with all identified applications. A mutually satisfactory time has to be negotiated.

4 The system change will be scheduled a few months in advance, and any other changes will be batched to occur at the same time.

5 The aggregated revision becomes a major task, requiring meetings of all parties to minimize problems due to possible interactions.

6 All involved programmers participate in the changeover, dealing both with their changes and with the changes induced by others.

7 Any failure in any of the batched changes will require a rollback of all changes, and a return to phase 3.

8 Changes which failed, or did not make it into the batch are now candidates for the next revision, at best three months hence. All bplanned enefits are delayed by the cyclic nature of batched system revisions.

The costs of traditional maintenance are dominated by the cost of inter-module interactions. These are then order $\mathcal{O}(m^2)$, where m is the number of modules. The mediated architecture will have more modules, at least one for every domain, but the cost of maintenance is $\mathcal{O}(\text{path length})$, or $\mathcal{O}(3)$ for systems with a single layer of mediation, and linearly more for more complex mediated systems. For all but small systems mediated maintenance will be less costly.

3. The Structural Model and Object Generation

Mediators should deliver information in a format that matches the customer's task model. Such a service is then semantically friendly, a deeper aspect of user-friendliness than having graphics, windows, point-and-click or drag-and drop interaction. Object-oriented systems provide information in a format which is organized to satisfy a specific programmed task; object-oriented approaches are in fact an outgrowth of programming concepts as abstract data types (ADT) [Liskov:75].

Servers have a problem satisfying the customers' desire for objects, since they must try to serve a variety of customers, and different customers need different object configurations. For instance, the pharmacist needs to be able to survey all patients receiving a certain drug, but a physician will want to know about all drugs one patient is receiving. We denote the relationship from root to dependent data as R ——⋆ D and show the conflicting models in Figure 9.

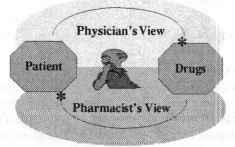

Figure 9. Conflicting Customer's Models

3.1 Relationships, relations, and objects

Relational data representations are general, but they demand from the user an understanding of possible relationships among the entities represented by the relations. An Entity-Relationship (E-R) model applied to such a database will describe all likely relationships. Most databases will be represented by a network more complex than a simple hierarchy. As stated above, we believe that a user working on a specific task will want an object-oriented representation of the data in the domains of current interest. There is an impedance mismatch of satisfying specific users' needs versus generality.

The approach we take here is to formalize the E-R model to match a relational infrastructure. We then can extend the relational algebra to operate on relationship representations as well as on relations that represent entities. In the structural model the relationships are represented by *connections* [WE:80]. The formalization of relationships leads to connections of five different types. Connections are characterized by semantics from which E-R relationship cardinalities can be derived. The structural model was described in an early Entity-Relationship conference. Four of these connections are significant within and among object classes. Two support inheritance and hence simplify the customer's world.

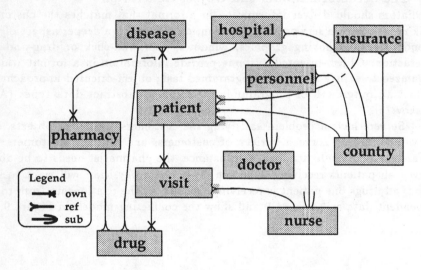

Figure 10. A structural model of a simple health-care setting

3.2 View-objects generation

A concept of view-objects can resolve this issue, by transforming base data into objects according to user needs [W:86]. Mediation provides an architectural bases to position this transformation in larger systems. The PENGUIN project [BSKW:91] demonstrated how object-oriented data structures can be automatically generated. Now only the model has to be maintained. PENGUIN applies the semantic knowledge embodied in the *structural model*, to data stored in a relational database.

The structural semantics permit not only the creation of objects, but the retention and transformation of relationships between objects. Although general methods are not supported, methods for retrieval and storage of objects are created. More general methods applicable to the generated object have to be provided by the customers. However, it is actually rare for persistent objects to have internal methods for functions other than for fetch, store, and update of data. Since the fetch, store, and update semantics are inherent in the relational model, we can guarantee the correctness of their mappings to the objects, while avoiding the complexity needed to deal with arbitrary methods.

We now define the four connection types of the structural model and how the PENGUIN implementation interprets their semantics in order to generate objects [BW:90]:

1 An *ownership connection* describes the relationship between a superior class and its members. For instance, an object class definition describes a potentially large set of object instances.

Different applications may incorporate the same elements in different models. For the pharmacy the administered instances fall within the drug object, while for a patient record the same instances fall within the patient or a visit object. Current object database systems, without this algebraic competence, can allow elements to appear in only one object configuration, limiting the practical size of objects.

2 Similar in structure are *part-of-hierarchies*. Conflicts between *class-of* and *part-of* object configurations are common.

3 A general type of connection is a *reference connection*; it is used to expand attributes by referencing foreign objects.

4 Divide-and-conquer is an essential approach in science, and in information systems as well. The *subset connection* defines such specialized groupings.

Three of the connections types define hierarchical $(1 : n)$ relationships of differing semantics [W:83]. Structures declared within objects in today's programming languages are restricted to hierarchies. More complex structures can be implemented by using programmed linkages within objects, but these will make algebraic manipulation difficult. PENGUIN creates hierarchies within objects, and uses external connections to link other objects needed in an application.

Note that the structural model has no connection with an $m : n$ cardinality. Such a relationship is described by two connections and one relation, since a relational implementation always requires a relation to define the subset of the $m \times n$ possible links. The composition extends to the semantics, giving $4^2 = 16$ different choices.

3.3 Relationship to the basic E-R model

Note that the semantics define relative cardinalities. Those cardinalities are presented in E-R Models. The additional semantics of the structural model convert the static E-R model to a dynamic structure.

A dynamic capability is essential if we wish to achieve associative access, since the transformations required to achieve optimization must maintain the correct semantics. The PENGUIN system constructs objects as needed out of relational databases, given the structural model of connections. A PENGUIN query identifies the root of the object hierarchy, the *pivot*, and object templates are generated automatically.

The same relational algebra operations, used to optimize queries, or to convert relations to achieve database integration, or to define user-based views, are also applicable to connections. The algebra used for relations maps directly to the structural connections. Specifications for the join operation can be simplified, since only one connection needs to be named, rather than the two endpoints. Figures 11 and 12 illustrate the extraction of an object model. The process starts by matching the root node of the object desired by the customer to the entities described by the structural model. This becomes the pivot, as applied to the database structure modeled in Figure 10. The algebraic transformations are applied to the model, so that the actual conversion is compiled, similar to the compilation of optimized database queries. Methods are created to automatically instantiate, select, and update object instances. We present the outline of the implemenation here because the work was published mainly in journals catering to the application areas; details are found in [B:90].

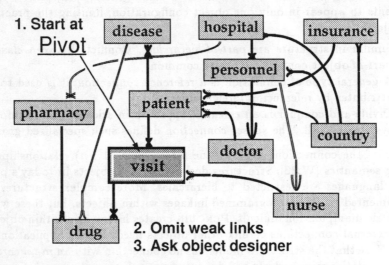

Figure 11. Applying the pivot and locating the object attributes

We give two examples of connections to illustrate the concepts:

Example 3. Two Connections in a Healthcare Setting.

Connection name	source	destination	type
Visit_made	Patient ———*	Visit	ownership
Drug_received	Visit ———*	Drug	ownership

To construct the hierarchy for a pivotal Visit object we can simply state

$$\texttt{Visit\_object} = \bowtie\texttt{Drug\_received};$$

to encapsulate the Drug data into the Visit object.

Transitive operations over connections that are of the same type retain their type semantics, so that we can bring the Visits, with the Drug data, into the Patient object.

When connection types are mixed, the semantics become complex, but remain formally manageable [WE:80].

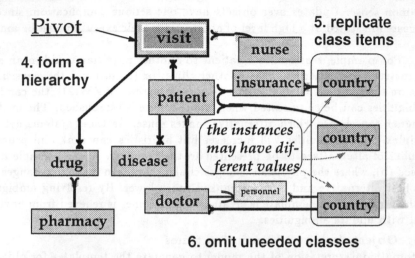

Figure 12. Restructuring and replicating shared leaves.

The mediator can now utilize the generated templates. When information about, say, a patient, is requested, all subsidiary data, say, the drug profile, identified in the template is included, as if a programmer had designed an appropriate object and written the code for it.

Distinct mediators can support distinct object configurations, as required by their domains. For example, the pharmacist can use a mediator for drugs and retrieve all patients receiving the drug as an object appropriate for the pharmacy, while the physician can obtain objects that use the patient as the pivot in another mediator. The conflict illustrated in Figure 9 has now been dealt with. Such flexibility rivals the capability of relational retrieval, but retains the constraints imposed by the semantic model and avoids possibly tricky programming. Having formal rules also permits checking of semantic consistency before any code generation occurs [KW:81].

The objects retrieved will obey the model, whereas a relational query can create nonsense; for example, one might join the daily dosage of a drug with the length of a patient's hospital stay. The lack of a documented connection (in a reasonable structural model) between dosage and length-of-stay makes it impossible to create such a template automatically. A determined programmer can, of course, retrieve drug and patient objects separately, and in the privacy of the mediator, compute anything that pleases the user.

3.4 Resolving the view-update Problem

Databases must also be updated. Here the templates must obey the constraints imposed by the structural model. No drug should be prescribed to a non-existing patient, and no drug class should be removed from the pharmacy that is still being given to an existing patient. In a relational database, the responsibility for maintaining correct program operation rests wholly on the programmer, augmented with some combination of foreign-key constraints, documentation, and common sense. Updates over objects have one serious complication: since the requests are stated at a high level of abstraction, their execution can be ambiguous.

For example, reassigning a patient to another physician could mean either (a) instruct the patient to visit another clinic, or (b) instruct the physician to take on the patient's current clinic. But as shown in [BSKW:91], the candidate ambiguities can be enumerated when the template is established. The mediator designer can choose which alternative makes sense. As these systems get more complex, the ambiguities will increase, but heuristics can rank and prune the number of alternatives to be presented to the manager. In the example above, choice (b), where the physician changes clinics, causes many more changes than the first alternative and is hence ranked much lower. By resolving ambiguities in the mediator, the template is created, the customer is relieved from having to deal with update ambiguities.

3.5 Object design and execution times

Automatic interpretation of the model to generate the templates for object instance generation and update the mediator greatly enhances maintenance. Since this work occurs at design time, the resulting templates can be compiled for fast execution. Rapid regeneration of mediator functions becomes feasible when the database models change.

3.6 Status

The PENGUIN technology has found its way into practice. For instance, it has been adopted by Persistence Software and is now part of the SUNSOFT Distributed Objects Everywhere (DOE) environment, operating with ORACLE, SYBASE, INGRES, and INFORMIX database systems [KJA:93]. It has also been used for some academic and commercial databases [RDCLPS:94].

The approach used also allows update of the underlying databases, typically disabled for relational views, as described in [BSKW:91]. The compilation takes place under management of an object administrator, typically the owner of the mediator in which the transformation code will reside. The customer is spared any need to resolve update problems.

4. Conclusion

We analyzed the factors leading to high software system maintenance cost: need for flexibility, unwarranted interaction among users from distinct domains, and the batching of system updates into periodic, traumatic events. None of these factors are effectively addressed by current exhortations in software engineering.

Implicitly we have clarified the difference between models and specifications. While specifications are developed initially, a program only ensues after a long sequence of transformational steps. No formal linkage from code to specification is provided within that process, although a current software engineering rule states that any section of code should have a documented audit trail to its origin. Comments giving such backward references to specifications are rarely found in programs, and their insertion delays the production of code.

The conflict between the generality of relational and E-R approaches versus object specificity can be resolved by transformations based on models. A model is intended to remain linked to the code objects, enable identification of the affected code, and aid in its regeneration. For example, PENGUIN keeps the models available to resolve hard issues, such as object-derived updates. To achieve such synergy requires a formal representation of the model and an algebraic capability over its components. Then the partitioning and layering into modules can be formally supported.

In general, mediation provides new level of scalability for large, distributed information systems. The economic benefits of system construction and maintenance under mediation are currently being analyzed for some of the early systems. In time customers will understand the tradeoff, and may place the induced costs of system maintenance due to alternate architectures as a parameter into the contracts they issue for new systems and applications. Of course, familiarity with mediation concepts and tools is a prerequisite to their implementation. Application Program Interfaces (APIs) for KQML are now available for a variety of platforms and programming languages.

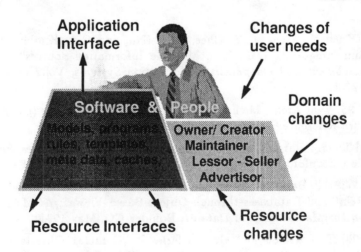

Figure 13. A Mediator Module and its Maintainer

Mediation does not eliminate maintenance, but it partitions the task it and allows its assignment to domain specialists. Every software designer agrees that modularization is essential for large scale software, but the rules have remained ad hoc [WKNSBBS:86]. The entity-relationship model provides a basis for such modeling, but until a better paradigm for software construction is adopted, the tools we have will be inserted in the manual approaches now in use, and the E-R model will be used as a specification rather than as a dynamic tool.

Within a module we benefit from the relational algebra. However, its operations assume the consistency which is only achievable in a coherent domain. The definitions that make objects coherent are also particular to a specific conceptual domain and its ontology. Scalability of software design and maintenance requires that we can build systems which encompass multiple disciplines and subdisciplines. The domain algebra sketched in this paper allows the defintion of articulation points among domains, so that we can maximize autonomy and minimize the cost of maintenance, while still providing interoperation.

Acknowledgement

This research direction would not have been feasible without the support of many students and colleagues. Most current work is performed in the context of the ARPA Intelligent Integration of Information (I3) program. Work on ontologies is supported through the Commercenet project at EIT, Menlo Park CA. Work in progress on these topics can be located via the World-Wide Web nodes http://www-db.stanford/pub, progress with KQML is documented in http://www.cs.umbc.edu/kqml/mail/, and http://www-ksl.stanford.edu/know-ledge-sharing.

References

[ACHK:93] Y. Arens, C.Y. Chee, C.N. Hsu, and C.A. Knoblock: "Retrieving and Integrating Data from Multiple Information Sources"; *Int.Journal of Intelligent and Cooperative Information Systems*, Vol.2 no.2, 1993, pages 127-158.

[ASK:95] Ygal Arens, Michael Siegel, and Larry Kerschberg (eds.): I3 Architecture Reference; http://isse.gmu.edu/I3_Arch/index.html.

[B:90] Thierry Barsalou: *View Objects for Relational Databases*; Ph.D. dissertation, Stanford University, March 1990, Technical Report STAN-CS-90-1310.

[BSKW:91]T. Barsalou, N. Siambela, A. Keller, and G. Wiederhold: "Updating Relational Databases through Object-Based Views"; *ACM SIGMOD Conf. on the Management of Data 91*, Boulder CO, May 1991.

[BW:90] T. Barsalou and G. Wiederhold: "Complex Objects For Relational Databases"; *Computer Aided Design*, Vol. 22 No. 8, Buttersworth, Great Britain, October 1990.

[CALO:94] Don Coleman, Dan Ash, Bruce Lowther, and Paul Oman: "Using Metrics to Evaluate Software Systems Maintainability"; *IEEE Computer*, Vol.27 No.8, Aug.1994, pp.44-49.

[CW:91] Stefano Ceri and Jenifer Widom: "Deriving Production Rules for Incremental View Maintenance"; *17th Int. Conf. on Very Large Data Bases*, Barcelona, Spain, September 1991, pages 577-589.

[DeMichiel:89] Linda DeMichiel: "Performing Operations over Mismatched Domains"; *IEEE Data Engineering Conference 5*, Feb.1989; *IEEE Transactions on Knowledge and Data Engineering*, Vol.1 No.4, Dec. 1989.

[FCGB:91] R. Fikes, M. Cutkosky, T.R. Gruber, and J.V. Baalen: *Knowledge Sharing Technology Project Overview*; Knowledge Systems Laboratory, KSL-91-71, November 1991.

[FFMM:94] Tim Finin, Richard Fritzson, Don McKay, and Robin McEntire: "KQML as an Agent Communication Language"; to appear in *The Proceedings of the Third International Conference on Information and Knowledge Management* (CIKM'94), ACM Press, November 1994.

[GK:94] Michael Genesereth and Steven Ketchpel: "Software Agents"; *Comm. ACM*, Vol.37 No.7, July 1994, pp.48-53,147.

[Gruber:91] T.R. Gruber: "The Role of Common Ontology in Achieving Sharable, Reusable Knowledge Bases"; in Allen, Fikes, Sandewall (eds): *Principles of Knowledge Representation and Reasoning*: Morgan Kaufmann, 1991.

[KB:95] A.M. Keller and Julie Basu: "A Predicate-based Caching Scheme for Client-Server Database Architectures"; *21st Int. Conf. on Very Large Data Bases*, Zurich, Switzerland, September 1995.

[KJA:93] Arthur M. Keller, Richard Jensen, and Shailesh Agarwal: "Persistence Software: Bridging Object-Oriented Programming and Relational Databases"; *Proceedings ACM SIGMOD*, 1993, pages 523-528.

[KW:81] Arthur M. Keller and Gio Wiederhold: "Validation of Updates Against the Structural Database Model"; *Symposium on Reliability in Distributed Software and Database Systems*, IEEE, July 1981, Pittsburgh PA, pages 195-199.

[Lehrer:94] Nancy Lehrer (ed.): Summary of I3 Projects; http://isx.com/pub/I3

[Liskov:75] Liskov,B.H. and Zilles, S.N.: "Specification Techniques for Data Abstractions"; *IEEE Transactions on Software Engineering*, Vol.SE-1, 1975, pp.7–19.

[McShane:79] D.J. McShane, A. Harlow, R.G. Kraines, and J.F. Fries: "TOD: A Software System for the ARAMIS Data Bank"; IEEE Computer, Vol.12 No.11, Nov.1979,pages 34–40.

[NFFGPSS:93] R. Neches, R. Fikes, T. Finin, T.R. Gruber, R. Patil, T. Senator, and W.R. Swartout: "Enabling Technology for Knowledge Sharing"; *AI Magazine*, Vol.12 No.3, pp.37–56, 1993.

[RDCLPS:94] B. Reinwald, S. Dessloch, M. Carey, T. Lehman, H. Pirahesh and V. Srinivasan: "Making Real Data Persistent: Initial Experiences with SMRC"; *Proc. Int'l Workshop on Persistent Object Systems*, Tarascon, France, Sept.1994, pp.194–208.

[Tracz:95] Will Tracz: *Confessions of a Used Program Salesman*; Addison-Wesley, 1995.

[W:83] Gio Wiederhold: *Database Design*; McGraw-Hill; Second edition, 1983; Third Edition http://www-db.stanford.edu/pub/gio/dbd/intro.html.

[W:86] Gio Wiederhold: "Views, Objects, and Databases"; *IEEE Computer*; Vol.19 No.12, December 1986, pp.37-44.

[W:89] Gio Wiederhold: KQML: Objectives for a Knowledge Query and Manipulation Language; Stanford Internal report, Nov.1989.

[W:92C] Gio Wiederhold:"Mediators in the Architecture of Future Information Systems"; IEEE Computer, March 1992, pp.38-49.

[W:92I] Gio Wiederhold: "'The Roles of Artficial Intelligence In Information Systems"; *Journal of Intelligent Information Systems*, Vol.1 No.1, 1992, pp.35-56.

[W:95A] Gio Wiederhold: Digital Libraries, and Productivity"; *Comm. of the ACM*, Vol.38 No.4, April 1995, pages 85-96.

[W:95D] Gio Wiederhold: "Value-added Mediation in Large-Scale Information Systems"; Proc. of the IFIP DS-6 Conference, Atlanta, May 1995; to appear in Meersman(ed): *Database Application Semantics*, Chapman and Hall, 1995.

[WCC:94] Gio Wiederhold, Stephen Cross, Charles Channell: *Information Integration*; IEEE Educational Videotape, 2 hours, October 1994, Robert Kahrman, sponsor. IEEE, Picataway NJ.

[WE:80] Gio Wiederhold and Ramez El-Masri:"The Structural Model for Database Design"; in Chen (ed.): Entity-Relationships Approach to Systems Analysis and Design, North-Holland, 1980, pages 237-257.

[Wegner:90] Peter Wegner: "Concepts and Paradigms of Object-Oriented Programming"; *OOPS Messenger*, August 1990.

[WG:95] Gio Wiederhold and Michael Genesereth: "Basis for Mediation"; *Proc. COOPIS'95 Conference*, Vienna Austria, available from US West, Boulder CO, May 1995.

[WKNSBBS:86] G. Wiederhold, A.M. Keller, S. Navathe, D. Spooner, M. Berkowitz, B. Brykczynski, and J.Salasin: "Modularizationof an ADA Database System"; *Proc. Sixth Advance Database Symposium*, Information Processing Society of Japan, Aug. 1986, pages 135-142.

Adaptive Schema Design and Evaluation in an Object-Oriented Information System

Ling Liu

University of Alberta, Department of Computing Science
615 General Service Building, Edmonton, Alberta, T6G 2H1 Canada

Abstract. This paper develops a formal framework for characterizing "normalization" in object-oriented schema design. We introduce style rules for achieving validity, minimality, and extensibility of an object-oriented schema, and the style rules that help to eliminate update anomalies and undesirable existence dependency loops. As a result, the adaptiveness of an object-oriented schema against future requirement changes is increased. This set of style rules can be used as not only a user-oriented method for designing the object-oriented schema, but also a means for validating quality of a schema and for transforming an object-oriented schema into a better style in terms of adaptiveness and robustness.

1 Introduction

An object-oriented information system, like any other software system, is seldom designed in "one shot", but rather explored through an iterative process of refinement, adaptation, and improvement. Change requirements may occur at various stages in the development cycle of the system and for a number of reasons [2,5,14,19]. For example, changes may be required (i)when experience shows how the system can be improved, (ii)when user needs a change and additional functionality has to be integrated, or (iii)when the universe of discourse modeled by the system changes and the system needs to be adapted. Due to the increased complexity in both schema design and development of application programs working with the schema, the robustness and adaptiveness of an object-oriented schema against future requirement changes become increasingly important. An object-oriented schema is *adaptive* and *robust* if it correctly uses the object-oriented modeling concepts, and can be easily adapted to changing requirements by encouraging as much information localization and data abstraction as possible, such that the overall impact of schema changes or database update can be minimized or reduced.

Most research on object-oriented design has so far been concentrated on how to use object-oriented concepts in logical design and conceptual modeling. However, there is surprisingly very little on evaluation of what constitutes a robust and adaptive schema in anticipation of future requirement changes. Many desired properties of a schema design (such as validity, extensibility, minimality, normality) [3] are only vaguely understood in the context of object-oriented models. Recall the relational database theory, quality design and evaluation of a schema is defined by the presence and absence of certain normal forms. Unfortunately, these normal forms have been developed only in the context of special classes of rules, namely functional and multi-valued dependencies, aiming at elimination of update anomalies implied in a relational schema. Therefore, the relational definition of schema quality is rather restrictive and excludes many other important issues, such as the complexity and extensibility of a schema, the normal form for subclass relationships, for existence dependencies, inclusion dependencies, and so on. We firmly believe that progress in quality design and evaluation of an object-oriented schema can only be made by methodologies that are able to integrate design rules with quality measures, and that clearly address the issues of adaptiveness and robustness of an object-oriented schema with important theoretical and practical implications.

In this paper we develop a formal framework for characterizing "normalization" in object-oriented schema design. Thank to the fact that schema transformation has been explored quite systematically, and many criteria have been introduced to ensure that a schema transformation preserves the nature and the validity of the original schema [1,4,9,11], this paper thus focuses more on how the desired properties of a schema design should be understood in the context of object-oriented models and what are the important design and evaluation rules for building highly adaptive object-oriented schema. Our primary goal is aimed to automate quality design and evaluation for building an adaptive object-oriented schema, which on the one hand eliminates the undesired dependencies and minimizes the impact of schema modifications, and on the other hand, is able to preserve all the necessary dependencies and thus the database integrity constraints required by applications during schema enhancement process and schema change management.

2 The Reference Object Data Model

Let O be an infinite set of objects, each has a unique, system-supplied identifier, and P denote an infinite set of property/role functions. The term **object** is used in its most general form. It may stand for a tuple (row) in a relational table, an entity (or a relationship) in the entity-relationship model, an entity in a semantic data model, or an object in an object-oriented data model. Objects are grouped into classes based on a set of common properties/roles, and only accessible through their property functions defined in their classes. A **property** function $p \in P$ can be a value of a primitive base type (e.g., String, Integer, Real, Boolean, etc.), an object instance of a class, a function of arbitrary complexity, or an object method. Each $p \in P$ has a name and a signature (i.e., domain types). In the sequel, for simplicity, we assume that every $p \in P$ has a unique property identifier. It is known that to determine the identity of two property functions is equally hard as to prove the equivalence of two programs.

The term **class** serves a dual purpose. A class imposes a *type description* which consists of a finite set of property functions as a common interface, and meanwhile represents a *set* of objects that conforms to its type. Each class is described by a unique class name, a type description, and a set membership. We use **type**(u) to denote the type of class u and **properties**(u) to denote the set of property functions defined in the type of class u, including both locally defined and inherited functions. For each $p \in$ **properties**(u), we refer to the domain class of p by **domain**(p,u) and the collection of objects that belong to class u by **content**(u) $=_{def} \{o \mid o \in u\}$. The membership predicate "$\in$" is defined based on object identities [18]. Let $X = \{p_i \mid p_i \in$ **properties**(u), $1 \le i \le n$ $\}$ be a set of properties of class u. Then, **domain**(X,u) $= \cup_{i-1,...,n}$ **domain**(p_i ,u).

Definition 1 Let u and v denote any two classes. We say that u is a **subset** of v, denoted as $u \subseteq v$, if and only if (iff) for any $o \in O$, if o is a member of class u, then o is a member of class v.

Definition 2 (subtype) Let u and v denote any two classes. We say that u is a **subtype** of v, denoted as $u \le v$, iff (i) **properties**(u) $\supseteq$ **properties**(v) and (ii) ($\forall p \in$ **properties**(v))(**domain**(p,u) $\subseteq$ **domain**(p,v)).

Definition 3 (subclass) Let u and v denote any two classes. We say that u is a **subclass** of v, denoted as u **is-a** v, iff $u \subseteq v$ and $u \le v$.

Definition 4 (construction relationship) Let u and v denote any two classes. If class u has property p defined by **domain**$(p,u)=v$, then we say that class u has a direct **construction** (composition) relationship labeled p with class v.

An object-oriented schema describes the logical structure of objects and classes. We formalize an object schema in terms of a class dictionary graph, so-called *schema graph*. Two kinds of relationships are distinguished among classes: inheritance relationships (called *specialization* edges) and object reference relationships (called *construction* edges). We refer to the set of *is-a* relationships of a schema as the **specialization hierarchy** and the set of *object construction* relationships as **construction hierarchy**. An object construction hierarchy may consist of several disconnected subgraphs with possibly multiple construction edges, and construction loops or self construction loops.

Definition 5 (schema graph) An object schema G is defined as a labeled, directed class dictionary graph or so-called **schema graph**, denoted as $G = (V, L, E)$ where V is a finite set of class vertices with a vertex **Object** as the *root* class; L is a set of labels, each described by a character string; and $E = EA \cup EC$ is a set of edges where EA is a binary relation on $V \times V$, representing *is-a* (*specialization*) edges; and EC is a ternary relation on $V \times V \times L$, representing object *construction* edges. Thus a schema graph may also be denoted by $G = (V, L, EA, EC)$.

Definition 6 (*specialization reachable*: $\Rightarrow^*$) Let $G = (V, L, EA, EC)$ be a schema graph. A class $u \in V$ is **specialization reachable** from class $v \in V$, denoted by $v \Rightarrow^* u$, iff one of the following conditions is satisfied: (i) $u = v$; (ii) $(v, u) \in EA$; (iii) $\exists w \in V$ s.t. $w \neq u$, $w \neq v$, and $v \Rightarrow^* w$, $w \Rightarrow^* u$.

Definition 7 (*construction reachable*: $\rightarrow^*$) Let $G = (V, L, EA, EC)$ be a schema graph. A class vertex $u \in V$ is **construction reachable** from class vertex $v \in V$, denoted by $v \rightarrow^* u$, iff one of the following conditions is verified:
  (i) $\exists l \in L$ s.t. $(v, u, l) \in EC$.
 (ii) $\exists w \in V$, $\exists l' \in L$ s.t. $v \Rightarrow^* w$ and $(w, u, l') \in EC$.
(iii) $\exists w \in V$ s.t. $w \neq u$, $w \neq v$, and $v \rightarrow^* w$, $w \rightarrow^* u$.

When a class vertex u is *specialization reachable* from class vertex v, then for any other vertex $w \in V$, if w is construction reachable from u, we may prove that w is also construction reachable from v (specialization inheritance) [18].

Definition 8 (construction closure operator of a class) Let $G = (V, L, EA, EC)$ be a schema graph and *Parts* : $V \rightarrow 2^V$ be a function defined as follows: For any $u \in V$,
  - If $u \in V$ is one of the primitive base classes, such as *String, Real, Integer, Date, Boolean*, then *Parts*$(u) =_{def} \emptyset$.
  - Otherwise, *Parts*$(u) =_{def}\{$ $w \in V \mid (u,w,l) \in EC$, $l \in L$ $\}$.
We define the construction closure operator *Parts** by *Parts*$^*(u) =_{def} \cup_{k=1,...,|V|}$ *Parts*$^k(u)$, where *Parts*$^1(u) =_{def}$ *Parts*(u) and *Parts*$^k(u) =_{def}$ *Parts*(*Parts*$^{k-1}(u)$) for $k>1$.

Informally speaking, *Parts*(u) identifies the set of class vertices anchored at vertex u through construction edges. It is the set of domain classes of those properties that are locally defined in class u. Whereas *Parts*$^*(u)$ computes the set of classes that are construction reachable from the vertex u. It includes all the classes that are used directly or indirectly in construction hierarchy of class u. A schema G is called construction *type-closed* if and only if *Parts*$^*(u) \subseteq V$ holds in G. We assume that all the schema graphs concerned in the sequel are *construction type-closed*.

3 Style Rules for Validity, Extensibility and Minimality

The validity of an object-oriented schema guarantees that it should have no-dangling class vertex, and satisfy the cycle-free specialization axiom and the unique construction label axiom. These are the baselines of the schema for correct use of the object-oriented modeling concepts [2,12,15,19].

Definition 9 (Validity Normal Form: V-NF)
Let G = (V, L, EA, EC) be a schema graph and V-NF denote a collection of valid schema graphs. The schema graph G belongs to V-NF iff G satisfies the no-dangling class axiom, the cycle-free specialization axiom, and the unique construction label axiom. We refer to this set of schema graphs as V-NF schema graphs.

Extensibility of a database schema is defined by the adaptiveness and the flexibility of the schema in anticipation of future schema changes. The crucial factor for extensibility is to reduce the impact of a schema modification on the entire structure of the existing schema [2,13], on the organization of the databases [14], and on the workload required for rewriting of the existing application programs [21]. The basic principle for achieving better extensibility in an object-oriented database system is to advocate minimal coupling between abstractions (e.g., methods, procedures, and modules) and to provide a certain degree of information hiding and information localization in order to reduce the cost of software changes [17]. Two axioms that we use for promoting extensibility are *information localization* and *minimization of multiple inheritance* (see [16] for detail).

Definition 10 (Inheritance Normal Form: I-NF)
Let G = (V, L, EA, EC) be any schema graph and I-NF denote a collection of adaptive schema graphs by making the best use of inheritance feature. A schema graph G belongs to I-NF if and only if (i) G belongs to V-NF and (ii) G satisfies the information localization axiom and the minimization of multiple inheritance axiom.

A schema is said to be semantically *minimal,* if no concept in the schema can be expressed through composition of the other concepts; more specifically, if no concept can be deleted from the schema without losing information. Redundancy in an object-oriented schema may occur for several reasons. One of the most common causes is due to the fact that application requirements often have an inherent redundancy and this redundancy migrates into the initial schema design. Redundancy can also be incurred when related concepts are expressed in different schemata and these schemata need to be merged such as required in the heterogeneous and distributed database environment [20]. Two types of redundancy are considered here: specialization redundancy and useless class.
   Specialization Redundancy is the redundancy that exists when a specialization edge between two class vertices has the same information content as a path of the specialization edges between these two classes. We may describe an specialization path from vertex u to vertex v by a list of vertices $<u, w_1, w_2, ...,w_n, v>$ $(n>1)$, satisfying that (u, w_1), (w_1, w_2), ..., $(w_n, v) \in EA$. The axiom for *specialization minimality* guarantees that schema G has no specialization edge that can be derived from any of the

others. It identifies a way of eliminating specialization duplicate by eliminating all the redundant specialization edges implied in specialization abstraction.

For any class vertex u, if it has no incoming specialization edge and $Parts(u)=\emptyset$, then it is desirable to consider vertex u as a *useless class*, because it contains no construction information at all. This style rule is refereed to as the axiom for elimination of useless specification. Most of the useless class specifications initially come from application requirements, and mostly caused by the difficulty in distinguishing between what should be modeled as classes and what are properties of a class in the logical design.

Definition 11 (Minimality Normal Form: M-NF)
Let $G = (V, L, EA, EC)$ be a schema graph and M-NF denote a collection of specialization minimal schema graphs. A schema graph G belongs to M-NF, iff (i) G is in V-NF, and (ii) G has neither specification redundancy nore useless classes.

4   Style Rules for Eliminating Update Anomalies

In the relational data model, normalization of relations is a commonly used means to eliminate database update anomalies [3,10,22]. The higher normal form a schema belongs to, the less update anomalies the schema would have. The intended schema can be obtained by applying progressive schema transformations.

Unlike the definition of relational normal forms, the definition of a normal form for object-oriented schemata should also take into account composite properties (components), multi-valued properties and special types of relationship sets, namely, *is-a* relationship, existence dependent relationship, Union relationship (if an object class is equal to union of some other object classes), Intersect relationship (if an object class is equal to intersect of some other object classes) and Decompose relationship (if an object class can be partitioned into several other classes). In this section we analyze how the theory of functional dependencies can be adapted to the normalization of object-oriented schemata and propose a normal form for object-oriented schema graphs.

4.1   The Problem

Definition 12 (Functional Dependencies)   Let C denote an object class and X, Y be two sets of single-valued properties of class C. If both X and Y are single-valued properties of C, then a **functional dependency** (FD) exists between X and Y, denoted as $X \rightarrow Y$, iff each object instance of **domain**(X, C) corresponds to precisely one object instance of **domain**(Y, C) at any time. I.e.,
$$X \rightarrow Y \Leftrightarrow \neg \exists o_1, o_2 \in C : o_1.X = o_2.X \text{ but } o_1.Y \neq o_2.Y.$$
When the right side of a FD is a set of properties, say $X \rightarrow A_1, ..., A_n$, then the original FD is equivalent to n individual FDs, i.e., $X \rightarrow A_1, ..., X \rightarrow A_n$.

A set K of properties (components) of C is said to be a **key** of C iff all properties of C are functionally dependent on K, and there exists no proper subset K' of K such that all properties of C are functionally dependent on K'. A property of C is called a *key property* if it is contained in a key of C; otherwise it is called *non-key property* of C.

Example 1. Assume we have an application, describing Supplier in terms of supplier's ssn, date of supply, item-no, price per unit, and quantity ordered for each item. We may model it as shown in Fig. 1. Suppose that we have the following constraints: properties ssn and item-no may together decide a Supplier object, but the `price` of one item is uniquely determined by its item number. We can describe them in terms of the following two functional dependencies:

$$\text{ssn, item-no} \rightarrow \text{quantity, date;} \quad \text{item-no} \rightarrow \text{price.}$$

```
Class Person                    Class Supplier inherit from Person
{   pname: String,              {   item-no: Integer,
    ssn: Integer,                   price: Real,
    birthday: Date }                date: Date,
                                    quantity: Integer }
```

Fig.1   An example schema violating normalization axiom

As every object in the object-oriented model has a unique (internal) identity, all the internal (system-supplied) identities of objects functionally determine the other single-valued properties (components). Thus we have the following FDs in class `Supplier`:

$$\text{oid(Person)} \rightarrow \text{pname, ssn, birthday.}$$

$$\text{oid(Supplier)} \rightarrow \text{pname, ssn, birthday, item-no, price, date, quantity.}$$

Given a class C, we call object identity the **primary key** of class C no matter whether it has more than one key or not. All the functional dependencies that correspond to object identities are referred to as "identity-based FDs".

Generally speaking, the identity-based dependencies do not incur problems. The other dependencies that exist in a class of objects, however, are often the cause of information redundancy and update anomalies, even in the context of object-oriented models. For instance, consider the example schema in Fig. 1, the functional dependencies below

$$\text{ssn, item-no} \rightarrow \text{quantity, date;} \quad \text{item-no} \rightarrow \text{price}$$

are actually the source of the following three anomalies.

(i) *Insertion anomaly*:

We cannot indicate the `price` of an item unless it has a supplier.

(ii) *Deletion anomaly*:

When we delete the last supplier object for an item in the class `Supplier`, we also lose the information about its `price`.

(iii) *Modification anomaly (potential inconsistency)*:

If the price of an item is changed, all suppliers referring to this item also need to change. Otherwise, we would not have a unique price for each item as we feel intuitively we should. Thus, the update operation has to be propagated to several `Supplier` objects. Similarly, if we need to add a new property regarding to item, e.g., `item-description`, we have to add it to the class `Supplier`. As a consequence, for each item, all the suppliers who supply the same item have to store its `item-description` repeatedly. Any change to this `item-description` would require to propagate the same change to all the `Supplier` instances in order to preserve the information consistency.

These anomalies are all related to the presence of an undesired functional dependency in the class type `Supplier`, namely, `item-no` → `price`. In this example, this FD is the actual cause for the problem of accidental loss of information, the difficulty of representing given facts, and the cause of some unnecessary work because the same changes must be applied to a number of object or data instances. Elimination of such insertion, deletion and update anomalies encourages the schema design to preserve the logical structure of objects in a clean and robust "normal form". This can be achieved by stepwise and dependency-preserving schema decomposition.

Recall the example in Fig. 1, if we decompose the class `Supplier` into two classes `Supplier` and `Item` (see Fig. 2), then all the above problems go away. The reason is simply because that the class `Item` in Fig. 2 presents the `price` of each item exactly once. Hence, there is no redundancy. Moreover, we can enter a `price` for an item even if it is currently no Supplier objects. We can also add new properties for each Item object without incurring any modification anomalies. It is interesting to note that this decomposition not only eliminates certain types of anomalies, but meanwhile also preserves all the original dependencies.

```
Class Person          Class Supplier            Class Item
  { pname: String,      { inherit from Person   {item-no: Integer,
    ssn: Integer,         item: Item,             price: Real }
    birthday: Date }      date: Date,
                          quantity: Integer }
```

Fig.2   Eliminating update anomalies of the example schema in Fig.1

Yet some questions remain. How do we recognize undesired functional dependencies for a given class type? Does the decomposition work in all the situations? How do we determine if the above replacement is beneficial? How do we find a better replacement for a "bad" object-oriented schema. We may answer these questions by introducing the concept of normalized object-oriented schema.

4.2   Normality of an Object-Oriented Schema

The process of normalization is a progressive detection and elimination of undesired functional dependencies. The main diffidence in extending the treatment of normalization from the relation realm to the object-oriented model arises from the different means of expressing identification. In this section we define a normal form for each class type in an object-oriented schema and the semantics of normalization of an object-oriented schema. The objectives for defining schema normality as such are mainly the following. First, it helps to capture and to preserve all the semantics of the real world which can be expressed in terms of functional dependencies in a database. Second, it ensures that all the relationships represented in the schema are non-redundant. Thirdly, it provides all the schemata with better adaptiveness towards future modification both at schema level and at database level.

Definition 13 (base functional dependencies)
Let C be a class and K denote a primary key (typically object identity) of instances of C. The set of **base dependencies** of C, denoted as BFD(C), is defined as follows:
  (i)   For each *one to one* property p of C, $K \rightarrow p, p \rightarrow K$ are FDs in BFD(C).
  (ii) For each *many-to-one* or *many-to-many* property p of C, $K \rightarrow p$ is a FD in BFD(C).
  (iii) For each one-to-many property p of C, $p \rightarrow K$ is a FD in BFD(C).
  (iv) For each key K_1 of C which is not the primary key of C, $K \rightarrow K_1, K_1 \rightarrow K$ are FDs in BFD(C).
  (v)   No other FDs are in BFD(C).

Axiom (elimination of undesired anomalies)   Let $G = (V, L, EA, EC)$ be an object-oriented schema graph . A class $C \in V$ is in a Class Normal Form (C-NF), iff all its functional dependencies that involve only properties of C, can be derived from the set of base FDs of C by using the Armstrong's axioms for functional dependencies [6, 22].

Interesting to note is that the FDs of class C that are not derivable from BFD(C) are the actual cause of update anomalies. If a class is not in C-NF form, then it must have such undesired FDs. Thus, the process of eliminating those undesirable FDs of C should, at the same time, automatically transform the class C to the C-NF form.

Example 2. Recall the schema graph in Fig. 1. Class Supplier has the following keys: (ssn, item-no), oid(Supplier) and two FDs in addition to its identity-based FDs. Note that SSN is a one-to-one attribute of Supplier and a key of Person but not a key of Supplier. The set of base dependencies for class Supplier is as follows:

BFD(Supplier) = { oid(Supplier) → pname, ssn, birthday,

item-no, price, date, quantity;

(SSN, item-no) → oid(Supplier) }.

Obviously, the FD "item-no→ price" is not logically implied by BFD(Supplier). According to Axiom 8, it is considered as a undesired FD in class Supplier. Therefore, class Supplier is not in C-NF form.

In the current style rule for normality, we do not consider *multi-valued* dependencies. However it should not be difficult to add them into the Axiom.

Definition 14 (Normality Normal Form: N-NF) Let $G = (V, L, EA, EC)$ be a schema graph, $\mathbf{FD}(G)$ be the set of FDs of G, and $\mathbf{BD}(G)$ be the set of **base dependencies** of G, which is the union of the sets of dependencies of all class vertices of G, i.e., $\mathbf{BD}(G) = \cup_{u \in V} BFD(u)$. We say the schema G belongs to a collection of normalized normal form (N-NF) schemata, if it satisfies the following conditions:

(i) G is in V-NF form, i.e., all property names are distinct and of different semantics.

(ii) Every class in the schema graph G is in C-NF.

(iii) All the functional dependencies are implied by the set of base dependencies of G.

$$\forall FD_i \in \mathbf{FD}(G), \exists FD_j \in \mathbf{BD}(G): FD_j \Rightarrow FD_i.$$

Recall the Supplier example in Fig.1. Since the FD for Supplier class, namely item-no—→ price, can not be derived (implied) by the set of base dependencies of Supplier. The class Supplier is not in a C-NF. The schema in Fig.1 is thus not a normalized normal form schema (N-NF) as well. A number of problems regarding update anomalies may occur as discussed in Section 6.2. In order to transform this schema to a N-NF schema, we decompose the Supplier class into the two classes as shown in Fig. 2.

5 Style Rules for Minimizing Existence Dependencies

An existence dependency between two classes depends on the existence dependency between their instance objects. A class C_1 exists dependently on a class C_2, if and only if every instance of class C_1 must have referenced to at least one instance of class C_2. It means that there is a total constraint on the relationship between their instance objects.

The main problem with existence dependencies is that a set of existence dependencies together may form a dependency cycle among a given set of classes. We call it a *construction dependency loop* of the schema. Such a loop can become a very dangerous cause for update inconsistency in an object-oriented database, and may often create difficulty and inefficiency during deletion, insertion and population of a database. In order to provide some control to certain types of existence dependencies, we develop a normal form for eliminating undesirable existence dependency loops.

Axiom (minimizing construction dependency loops)

Rule 1: The total number of edges involved in a construction dependency loop should be minimized.

Rule 2: The total number of construction dependency loops in a schema graph should be reduced.

It is indispensable to develop strategies and algorithms in order to break down the loops, because it is usually not very obvious how the minimization or reduction could be suggested or carried out to achieve a better compromise between the efficiency expected and the semantic richness required.

One way to destroy a construction dependency loop is to replace a mandatory construction edge in the loop by an optional one. Of course, consulting with users about the possibility and necessity of doing so is desirable and helpful. Another interesting issue related with the breaking down of construction dependency loops is then the choice of which construction edge could be replaced with less impact on the semantics of the original schema. We below propose a number of policies which can be used as a default choice or advice to the designer.

Policy 1: If there is only one edge involved in more than one construction dependency loop, then it is appropriate to relax the mandatory constraint on this edge by using an optional construction edge to replace the mandatory one.
Policy 2: If several edges are involved in more than one construction dependency loop, then the edge that is involved in the most of the construction dependency loops should be chosen first and be relaxed through replacing its mandatory constraint by an optional one.
Policy 3: Otherwise, chose any edge contained in a given construction dependency loop and relax it by using the optional constraint instead of the mandatory one.

Due to the space restriction, we here only present the cycle-free dependency normal form definition. Readers may refer to [16] for formal definitions of concepts and examples.

Definition 15 (cycle-free dependency normal form: D-NF)
Let $G = (V, L, EA, EC)$ be a schema graph and D-NF denote a collection of specialization minimal schema graphs. A schema graph G belongs to D-NF, iff (i) G is in V-NF, and (ii) G has minimal existence dependency loops.

6   Discussion

We have presented a framework for axiomatic characterizations of object-oriented schemata, aiming at enhancing the adaptiveness and robustness of object-oriented schema design. This framework consists of a selection of normal forms, i.e., valid NF, inheritance NF, minimal NF, normalized NF and cycle-free dependency NF (D-NF). We regard the valid NF as the baseline for every object-oriented schema design since it exhibits the basic assumption of object-oriented modeling.

It is interesting to note that a schema which belongs to, for example, inheritance-NF, may not be necessarily in the other normal forms (e.g., minimal NF, normalized NF, or cycle-free dependency NF). Fig. 3 shows the basic relationships among these five basic normal forms. By using this framework, many desired properties of a schema design, such as validity, extensibility, minimality, normality, etc., can be well understood under the context of object-oriented models. For example, a I-NF schema promotes maximum information localization so that the impact of schema changes can largely be reduced, a M-NF schema encourages that every aspect of the requirements should only appear once in the schema in order to enhance the maintainability of the schema, while a N-NF schema avoids update anomalies and therefore when a change happens to the database, the cost for database consistency maintenance is minimized. We use the D-NF to advocate cycle-free existence dependency so that any change to the population of the database can be performed more effectively. When a schema belongs to both I-NF and M-NF, it is certainly more adaptive and robust when changes occur to either specialization or construction structure of the schema. We evaluate those schemata that satisfy all the normal forms to be of mostly higher quality regarding adaptiveness and robustness of a schema in responding to future requirement changes at (schema level and database level).

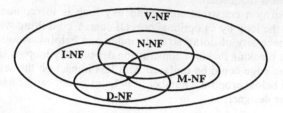

Fig. 3 Possible relationships among the five basic normal forms
object-oriented schemata

7 Concluding Remarks

The increased complexity of object-oriented models necessitates the enhancement of adaptiveness of an object-oriented schema design towards changing requirements. The understanding of what properties are critical for improving schema adaptiveness becomes increasingly important in schema design and evaluation. In this paper, we have formally presented a selection of style rules for building adaptive schema in an object-oriented data and knowledge base system. Many of them can also be regarded as basic mechanisms used during design validation stage for automatic transformation of a schema to be of better quality with respect to adaptiveness and extensibility. We believe that the framework developed in this paper presents an interesting step towards overcoming the potential problems hidden in many object-oriented schema designs.

The set of style rules we have introduced is not an exhaustive list. Many issues are still pending better solutions. For instance, it is interesting to study the interactions among the given style rules and the reasoning possibility by means of the proposed axioms. Our work on the present framework continues along with several lines. On the side of practical applicability, a prototype for the proposed framework is undergoing. It initially consists of three modules: object-oriented schema style evaluator, schema optimizer, and C++ code generator based on the Demeter system™[15]. On the side of theoretical justification, in addition to the ongoing research on studying the interactions among the given style rules and the reasoning possibility by means of the proposed axioms, we are also interested in exploring the basic set of primitive operations for both object-preserving and object-extending transformations. For example, we observe that a sequence of object-preserving transformations is also an object-preserving transformation. Using this property, we may formally prove that the schema transformations to inheritance-NF and minimal-NF are both object-preserving, whereas the transformation to Normality-NF is object-extending.

The work presented in this paper proposes a design and evaluation framework and not a new model or system. It is not be expected that the proposed framework be incorporated in a given system in its entirety. Instead, the designer may select a useful subset of the proposed style rules, taking into account a particular application domain and data modeling requirement. Furthermore, as is the case with most schema design and conceptual modeling concepts, the proposed framework is based on pragmatic ground and hence no rigorous proofs of its completeness can be given. Rather, its usefulness is demonstrated by concrete examples of situations that could not be handled adequately within other existing formalisms for object-oriented schema design and evaluation.

Acknowledgment The author would like to thank Roberto Zicari for the encouragement and Karl Lieberherr for the discussions on the Demeter system.

Reference

1. Batini C. and Battista G.Di, A methodology for conceptual documentation and maintenance. Information Systems 13 (3), pp297-320 (1988)
2. Banerjee J. Kim W. Kim H.J. and Korth H., Semantics and Implementation of Schema Evolution in Object-oriented databases. Proc. of ACM SIGMOD 1987
3. Batini C., Ceri S. and Navathe S., Conceptual Database Design: an entity-relationship approach. Benjamin/Cummings Publishing Company Inc. (1992).
4. Bergstein P., Object-preserving Class Transformations. Proc. of OOPSLA 1991.
5. Bersoff E.H. and Davis A.M., Impacts of life cycle models on software configuration management. CACM 34 (8) 1991.
6. Berri C., Fagin R. and Howard J.H., Complete Axiomatization for functional multivalued dependencies in database relations. in: ACM SIGMOD 1977.
7. Cardelli L., A semantics of multiple inheritance, in: Journal of Information and Computation 76 (1988).
8. Card L. and Wegner P., On understanding types, data abstractions and polymorphism, in: ACM Computing Surveys, 17 (4), 1985.
9. Grant J., Constraint preserving and lossless database transformations. Information Systems 9 (2) pp139-146 (1984).
10. Hull R. Relative information capacity of simple relational database schemata. SIAM J. Comput. Vol.15, No.3 (1986) pp857-886.
11. Jajodia S., Ng P. and Springsteel F., The problem of equivalence for Entity-Relationship Diagrams. IEEE Transactions on Software Engineering (Sept. 1983).
12. Kim W., A model of queries for object-oriented databases. Proc. VLDB 1989.
13. Lieberherr K., Bernstein P. and Silva-Lepe I., From Objects to Classes: Algorithms for object-oriented design. Journal of Software Engineering, 6(4) 1991.
14. Lerner B.S. and Habermann A.N., Beyond Schema Evolution to Database Reorganization. Proc. of OOPSLA 1990.
15. Lieberherr K., The Art of Growing Adaptive Software: Beyond Object-oriented Software. 1994
16. Liu L., Adaptive Schmea Design and Evaluation in an Object-oriented Information System. Technical Report TR-21-95, University of Alberta.
17. Liu L. and Meersman L. Extensibility in Object-oriented database systems. SPRITE - An integrated system for technical multimedia documentation, (eds.) J. Hoppe (Springer Verlag, 1992).
18. Liu L., Zicari R., Lieberherr K. and Hürsch W., The Role of Polymorphic Reuse Mechanisms in Schema Evolution in Object-oriented Database Systems. To appear in IEEE Transactions on Knowledge and Data Engineering.
19. Penney J. and Stein J. Class Modification in the GemStone Object-oriented DBMS. Proc. of OOPLSA 1987.
20. Sheth A. and Larson J.L., Federated Databases: Architecture and Integration. ACM Computing Survey (1990).
21. Skarra A. and Zdonik S., The management of changing types in an object-oriented database. Proc. of OOPLSA 1986.
22. Ullman J.D., Principles of database systems, CS press (1980).

Assertion of Consistency Within a Complex Object Database Using a Relationship Construct

Sven Thelemann

Universität Gesamthochschule Kassel, FB Mathematik/Informatik, D-34109 Kassel, Germany, e-mail: thele@db.informatik.uni-kassel.de

Abstract. We define semantic overlapping as the description of different points of view on the same application context in different parts of a database schema. E. g. type definitions may refer to each other and include the definition of the same "implicit" relationship type. We suggest another declarative element for schema definitions, called relationship, which supports detecting the manipulation of these relationship instances and triggering consistency-preserving update operations. In addition, cardinality and key constraints can be defined. The new construct stresses the ER-like nature of relationships and is more flexible than existing approaches.

1 Introduction

Nested structures like nested relations or objects with a complex valued state have proven to be a suitable representation of application data not only at the external level, where hierarchically structured query results and views are used, but also at the internal level, where access of complex objects is accelerated by nested storage structures [12]. At the conceptual or logical level many object-oriented data models define types in the same sense by using nested structures for the structural part, which leads to an object-centered view of an application context. The model presented in this paper belongs to this class of data models. It allows the definition of object types with arbitrarily nested state structure. Tables, which are usually defined as collections of values or objects, act as entry points to the instances. There are no implicit type extensions available at the user level.

Schema definitions based on nested structures may lead to severe problems due to what we call *semantic overlapping*: Type or table definitions may overlap in the sense that some of them contain the same information on user-defined relationships (in the sense of the relationship type known from ER modeling [4]) between sets of objects. In Fig. 1 it is shown how the structural descriptions of the two types Person and Course semantically overlap by offering two different "views" on a relationship Participation. Only type Person includes the relationship attribute points (indicated by the dotted line) for the result of a final course exam. At the instance level this kind of semantic overlapping leads to data redundancy. Thus manipulation of these "implicit" relationship instances will easily lead to data inconsistencies unless special precautions are taken. The manipulation of "implicit" relationship instances must be detected and consistency-preserving update operations must be triggered.

This paper focusses on the problem of controlling the described semantic overlapping due to "hidden" relationships. As a solution the paper introduces a relationship construct that becomes part of the building primitives for schema definition. In addition, the new construct allows to express a variety of semantic constraints such as cardinality and key constraints, which otherwise could not be captured within the schema. Throughout the paper we will call this new construct *relship* in order to distinguish it from the ER-concept *relationship type*.

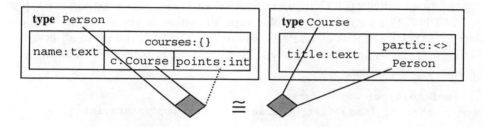

Fig. 1. Two object types `Person` and `Course` include a "hidden" relationship Participation

We argue that the new construct stresses the ER-like nature of the relationships appropriately and is more flexible than existing approaches, each of which has at least one of the following disadvantages:

- relationship information is spread over a number of type or table definitions,
- only binary relationships can be handled properly,
- relationship attributes are not supported adequately.

In Section 2 we outline the data model being used. In Section 3 the new *relship* construct as another element for schema definition is introduced. There we also introduce structure path expressions which prove to be an adequate means for describing correspondences within relship definitions. Furthermore cardinality constraints and key constraints are briefly mentioned. Section 4 compares the ideas with other approaches. Section 5 concludes the paper with a summary and final remarks.

2   The Data Model

In this section we present the basic notions of our data model as given in [16]. We refer to the model as the ESCHER data model, as it is the underlying data model for the database prototype ESCHER [7, 17, 18].

2.1 Structures and Types

The structural part of our model has its origin in the *Extended Non-First-Normal-Form* (eNF^2) data model [5, 10]. Starting from a predefined set of base types (integer, char, text, boolean etc.) and a set of constructors, complex types of arbitrary structure can be created. ESCHER provides the constructors [...] (tuple), {...} (set), ⟨...⟩ (list), and {*...*} (bag). With these building primitives *structural expressions* like

```
<[name: text, address: [zip: integer, city: text,
                        street: text], hobbies: {text}]>
```

can be constructed. With each structural expression a unique domain of complex values is associated. A user can build an application-specific set of *user-defined object types* called DEFTYPES. The set of all types including the base types is TYPES. The structural part of a type definition is given by the function $struct : \text{DEFTYPES} \rightarrow \mathcal{S}(\text{TYPES})$, where $\mathcal{S}(\text{TYPES})$ is the set of all possible structural expressions. Recursive type definitions are possible. The following two simple type definitions

```
define type{ name: Person
    struct: [name:text, courses:{[c:Course, points:int]}] }
```
(1)

```
define type{ name: Course
    struct: [title: text, participants: <Person>] }
```
(2)

specify the types shown in Fig. 1. In this paper we omit the behavioral part of type definitions. Operations (methods) would be defined in an ops-clause. See [9] for the introduction of a functional data type into ESCHER.

2.2 Instances and Tables

Database instances are pairs $(\omega, ['t_1 : v_1, \ldots, t_n : v_n'])$, where ω is an object from the abstract domain Ω of object identifiers. The second component describes the "state" of the object which is a finite set of types t_i together with a corresponding value v_i from the domain of $struct(t_i)$. Obviously an object may have more than one type by acquiring or loosing types during its lifetime. We will not elaborate on this mechanism in this paper. The state (*interpretation*) of an object with respect to a type t_i is accessed via a function $I(t_i)$, which returns the relevant value v_i. If $I(t)$ is defined for an object, we call it a *t-object*. A type definition does not imply the existence of an associated type extension that is accessible for the user. For the instance level we introduce special entry points called *tables*. The table definitions

```
define table{ name: Clients
    struct: {Person} }
```
(3)

```
define table{ name: OfferedCourses
    struct: [courses: <Course>, info: text] }
```
(4)

define a table called `Clients`, which maintains a subset of `Person`-objects, and a table `OfferedCourses`, which comprises a list of courses together with a (single) text with general information. Both types and tables are objects in the meta database. Via a table object ω we can access all values and objects in the table "state" $value(\omega)$, which is an element from the domain determined by the struct-clause of the table definition. An ESCHER *database schema* is given by a set DEFTYPES of type definitions and a non-empty set TABLES of table definitions. An ESCHER *database instance* is a set $Val(\text{TABLES}) := \{value(\omega) \,|\, \omega \in \text{TABLES}\}$ together with a set $Obj(\text{TABLES}) = \{(\omega, [' t_1 : v_1, \ldots, t_n : v_n \,']) \,|\, \omega \in \Omega$ reachable via $t \in \text{TABLES}\}$.

Example 1. Let us consider a small ESCHER database that is given by the definitions 1–3 and the following instances:

- $value(\omega_{\texttt{Clients}}) = \{\omega_1, \omega_2\}$
- $(\omega_1, [' \texttt{Person: [name: "Hugo", courses: \{[c:}\omega_3\texttt{, points:5],}$
  $\texttt{[c:}\omega_4\texttt{, points:3]\}]} \,'])$
- $(\omega_2, [' \texttt{Person: [name: "Anna", courses: \{\}]} \,'])$
- $(\omega_3, [' \texttt{Course: [title: "SQL", participants:<}\omega_1\texttt{>]} \,'])$
- $(\omega_4, [' \texttt{Course: [title: "UNIX", participants:<}\omega_1\texttt{>]} \,'])$

3 Relationships in Schema Definitions

3.1 The Need for Consistency Support

Consider the very small database from Example 1. It is intended that the two type definitions mutually correlate: Whenever a course appears in the `courses`-set of a `Person`-object then that person should also appear in the `participants`-list within the `Course`-object. If this is not the case the database is not consistent. If e. g. ω_3 was added to the `courses`-set of ω_2, but the `participants`-list in ω_3 remained unchanged, then consistency would obviously be violated. Note that this problem is different from the classical referential integrity problem. The latter is touched when e. g. the object ω_1 is removed from the database and consequently must be removed from the `participants` lists, otherwise we get a "dangling reference". Actually the consistency problem arises whenever corresponding spots of data redundancy caused by semantic overlapping cannot be identified by the system. We call this kind of data redundancy also *relationship redundancy*. Leaving the task of consistency control to the application programmer is clearly unacceptable. What we need is a mechanism that takes control on data manipulation functions like insert and remove operations in order to enforce consistency. For that purpose we introduce the *rlship* construct as another essential declaration primitive of the schema definition. First of all we need adequate syntactical means to identify relationship correspondences and to formulate various semantic constraints. For that purpose we will introduce structure path expressions.

3.2 Structure Path Expressions

Syntactically a *table* or *type path expression* (generically referred to as *structure path expression*) is a table or type name, called the *source*, followed by a structure path which is a (possibly empty) sequence of steps. There are three kinds of steps:

- "*.AttrName*" denotes a step from a tuple to the tuple component *AttrName*
- "*.#*" denotes a step from a collection (set, list, or bag) to the element structure
- "*.^*" denotes a step from a user-defined type *t* to its own structure *struct(t)*, thus enabling the traversal to a different structure tree

If the source of a path expression is a table *t* the sequence of steps describes a path starting at the root node of a tree representation for *struct(t)*, called the *structure tree* of *t*. If the source is a type *t* the path starts with an isolated node labelled *t*, then "*.^*" must be the first step of a non-empty path. Fig. 3.2 shows structure trees of table Clients and type Person. The table path expression Clients.#.^.name is shown with bold arrows.

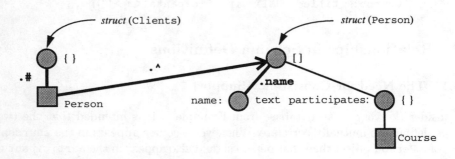

Fig. 2. Two structure trees and a table path expression

The syntax for structure path expressions allows a concise notation avoiding the explicit specification of "*.#*" or "*.^*" steps whenever no ambiguity arises. Thus Clients.name becomes a more convenient notation for Clients.#.^.name. We will frequently use this shorter notation.

The subtree (substructure) reached by a path expression *p* is the *structural semantics* of *p* and denoted by $\sigma_{struct}(p)$. Besides the structural semantics a path expression *p* also has a *value semantics* $\sigma_{val}(p)$, which is a set of values or objects. It is defined recursively:

- If $p = t$ for a table *t* then $\sigma_{val}(p) = \{value(t)\}$, which is a singleton set. If $p = t$ for a type *t* then $\sigma_{val}(p) = Ext(t)$, where $Ext(t)$ is the set of all objects that have the type *t* (Note that this extension is only used internally and is not part of the schema).

path expression p	structural semantics $\sigma_{struct}(p)$	value semantics $\sigma_{val}(p)$
table path expressions		
Clients	$struct(t_{\texttt{Clients}})$	$\{\{\omega_1, \omega_2\}\}$
Clients.#	t_{Person}	$\{\omega_1, \omega_2\}$
Clients.#.^	$struct(t_{Person})$	$\{[name : "\textbf{Hugo}", \ldots], [name : "\textbf{Anna}", \ldots]\}$
Clients.#.name	t_{string}	$\{"Hugo", "Anna"\}$
type path expressions		
Person	t_{Person}	$\{\omega_1, \omega_2\}$
Person.^	$struct(t_{Person})$	$\{[name : "\textbf{Hugo}", \ldots], [name : "\textbf{Anna}", \ldots]\}$

Table 1. Semantics of structure path expressions

- $\sigma_{val}(p.AttrName) := \{\omega.AttrName \mid \omega \in \sigma_{val}(p)\}$
- $\sigma_{val}(p.\#) := \{v \mid \exists \omega \in \sigma_{val}(p) : v \in \omega\}$, so .# acts as a "flattening" operator
- $\sigma_{val}(\text{p.}\hat{\ }) := \{I(t)(\omega) \mid \omega \in \sigma_{val}(p) \land \omega \text{ is a } t\text{-object}\}$

The structural and value semantics are naturally correlated: The sets which represent the value semantics are subsets of the domain of the corresponding structural semantics. In Table 1 further examples for path expressions and their semantics are shown.

3.3 Definition of Relationships

We introduce the syntax for a *relship* definition with an example.

Example 2. The relationship Participation from Fig. 1, which relates Person instances with Course instances, is added to the database schema by the statement

```
define relship{
   name: Participation
   comp: Person = Course.participants.# as P,
         Course = Person.courses.c as C
   attr: Person.courses.points as Result
   card: P = (0, *), C = (1, 15) }
```
(5)

In the comp-clause the components of the relationship are specified. They are identified by unique role names given after the as keyword. For a given role one or more path expressions denote corresponding substructures of the types. Path expressions connected by = are called *component equivalences*. They specify where semantic overlapping actually occurs.

Component equivalences assure a synchronisation between the states of Person-objects and Course-objects. Removal of a Person-object from the list of participants of a Course-object must lead to the removal of the Course-object from the set of courses within the Person-object (and analogously for insert operations).

The attr-clause specifies a relationship attribute called Result, which is accessible via the path Person.courses.points only.

The card-clause expresses cardinality constraints. For them the well-known (min,max) notation has been chosen, which covers many real world situations adequately [8]. Cardinalities refer to a "virtual" flat relation with the structure $\{[r_1 : t_1, \ldots, r_n : t_n, a_1 : s_1, \ldots, a_k : s_k]\}$ that records the relationship instances.

One notices that components are restricted to user-defined types. This is not just a coincidence: We argue that user-defined types provide the adequate level of abstraction for relationship participation. Therefore it is a general rule that the structural semantics of a path expression appearing in the comp-clause must denote a user-defined type.

More generally a *relship* definition consists of at least a name- and a comp-clause, and of optional attr-, card-, and key-clauses. The comp-clause specifies role names r_i and component equivalences. The number of role names determines the arity of the relationship. For an n-ary ($n \geq 2$) relationship the specification for role r_i ($1 \leq i \leq n$) has the general structure

$$p_{i1} = p_{i2} = \ldots = p_{im_i} \text{ as } r_i$$

where p_{ij} are type or table path expressions. For any i between 1 and n, $\sigma_{struct}(p_{ij})$ must be the same object type t_i, which is called the type of the role r_i. Relationship attributes are specified in the attr-clause, which has the same structure, but attribute names a_i ($1 \leq i \leq k$) occur in place of role names:

$$p_{n+i,1} = p_{n+i,2} = \ldots = p_{n+i,m_{n+i}} \text{ as } a_i$$

For any i between 1 and k, $\sigma_{struct}(p_{n+i,j})$ must be the same structure s_i, which must not be an object type, as attributes shall not contribute to relationship arity. Due to space limitations we cannot introduce the card- and key-clauses in detail, but the examples should sufficiently explain their usage.

3.4   Semantics of Relationships

For the following assume that we define a relship with the name R. We think of R as a "virtual" flat relation $rel(R)$ or equally as a table named R with the structure

$$\{[r_1 : t_1, \ldots, r_n : t_n, a_1 : s_1, \ldots, a_k : s_k]\} \tag{6}$$

Let $source(R)$ be the set of all sources of any p_{ij}. For $t \in source(R)$ let $roles(R, t)$ (resp. $attr(R, t)$) be the set of all roles r_i (resp. attributes a_i) where t appears as the source in any p_{ij} (resp. $p_{n+i,j}$). In the key-clause any subset of $\{r_1, \ldots, r_n\}$ can be specified as a key of (6), where the complete set is the default key. Let $paths(R, t)$ be the set of all path expressions in the comp- or attr-clause having source t. For every $t \in source(R)$ we can determine an expression called *relconfig*(R, t) by replacing the type information for the roles r_i and attributes a_i in the structure (6) by the corresponding path expressions from *paths*(R, t). If no path with source t reaches a given role or attribute, the type information is replaced by *null*. So we take into account that there might be a $t \in source(\text{R})$ that is indeed an incomplete view of the relationship and in that way we distinguish between *complete* and *incomplete* sources. The replacement yields a *relationship configuration relconfig*(R, t), which is an expression

$$\{[r_1 : q_1^t, \ldots, r_n : q_n^t, a_1 : q_{n+1}^t, \ldots, a_k : q_{n+k}^t]\} \tag{7}$$

with $q_i^t \in paths(\text{R}, t) \cup \{null\}$. This shows that the comp-clause has to obey an implicit constraint that forbids the specification of more than one path with the same source for the same role or attribute. *relconfig*(R, t) must be *well-defined*, i. e. there must be a unique sequence of restructuring/rewriting operations transforming (6) into (7). In other words: *relconfig*(R, t) must be a "sensible" view of R. We omit the details of this transformation, which is based on nest and projection operations.

Every elementary update operation o can be checked on whether it has any effect on R. An update operation o has an effect on R if it is applied to any node of a structure tree that is reached by a subpath p of any path p_{ij} specified in the comp-clause. The operation o modifies $\sigma_{val}(p)$, which implies a modification of $\sigma_{val}(t)$.

Preserving relationship consistency is enforced as follows: Let us first assume that t is a complete source. The operation o modifies the set $S_t^{old} = \sigma_{val}(p)$ to a set S_t^{new}. As *relconfig*(R, t) is well-defined the operation o can be translated into a sequence s_R of remove and/or insert operations in *rel*(R). For that purpose we consider the transformations that lead from (6) to (7). They induce "inverse" transformations at the instance level, which transform S_t^{old} and S_t^{new} into flat relations R_t^{old} and R_t^{new} with structure (6). The "difference" between R_t^{old} and R_t^{new} determines the sequence s_R to be applied to *rel*(R). For all $t' \in source(\text{R}), t' \neq t$, the sequence s_R is translated into a sequence $s_{t'}$ of update operations on $\sigma_{val}(t')$. This is possible due to the well-definedness of *relconfig*(R, t') for all $t' \in source(\text{R}), t' \neq t$.

If we allow t to be incomplete then R_t^{old} and R_t^{new} have the structure s', where s' is derived from *struct*(R) by discarding all tuple components not in *roles*(R, t) $\cup$ *attr*(R, t). If *roles*(R, t) $\cup$ *attr*(R, t) still contains a key of R there is no difference to the case where t is complete. Otherwise there are two possibilities: Either we consider the update as incomplete and reject it or there is a mechanism that asks for the missing information, which makes the update complete.

We leave it open whether another restriction should demand that tuples of *rel*(R) must not include any *null*-values: In Example 2 the insertion of another Person-object into a participants-list of a course does not provide a value for the Result attribute and must be rejected unless a default value is specified or *null* is allowed.

3.5 The Usage of Relationships

In this section further examples prove the usefulness of relationship definitions. The comp-clause in (5) is completely *type-based*, because it contains only type path expressions. The following example shows a *relship* definition with a completely *table-based* comp-clause.

Example 3. Let the definitions (1) through (4) be given. Consider the definition

```
define relship{
  name: Participation_2
  comp: OfferedCourses.courses.c = Clients.courses.c as C,
        Clients.# = OfferedCourses.courses.participants.#    (8)
                                                       as P,
  attr: Clients.courses.points as Result
  card: P = (0, *), C = (1, 12) }
```

Compared to the semantics from (5), (8) is a restriction to objects reachable via the tables Clients and OfferedCourses. Participation_2 could be defined without a prior definition of Participation according to (5). If both (5) and (8) are formulated then the logical conjunction of the integrity constraints from both *relships* must be enforced. Very often definitions like (8) will state a further restriction (above the maximal number of participants has been dropped to 12). In order to suspend constraints from a completely *type-based* relationship definition, as those found in (5), there is an optional redefines-clause. In (8) we could relax the cardinality constraint for the role C into C = (1, 20) and add the clause redefines: Participation. Now the constraints from (5) are no longer enforced for Persons in Clients and Courses in OfferedCourses. It should be mentioned that a "mixture" of type and table structure paths in a comp-clause is allowed, too.

Example 4. Consider a ternary relationship Teaching between objects of type Teacher, Class, and Subject. The relationship is "hidden" in the type definitions as follows:

- *struct*(Teacher) = [name: ..., tasks: {[c:Class, s:Subject]}]
- *struct*(Subject) = [title: ... ,plan: {[t:Teacher, c:Class]}]
- *struct*(Class) = [classid: ...,
                     schedule: {[s:Subject, t:Teacher, room:int]}]

The type definitions provide "views" on the relationship Teaching. In order to "integrate" the views we enter the definition

```
define relship{
   name: Teaching
   comp: Class = Teacher.tasks.c = Subject.plan.c as Class,
         Teacher = Class.schedule.t = Subject.plan.t
                                            as Teacher,   (9)
         Subject = Teacher.tasks.s = Class.schedule.s
                                            as Subject,
   attr: Class.schedule.room as Room,
   key: [Class, Subject] }
```

Based on this *relship* definition the system is able to synchronize object states and to detect incomplete updates (Note that the attribute information is part of only one type definition). The given key constraint states that the role combination Class and Subject determines a unique tuple in the "virtual" relation Teaching. Obviously the key constraint cannot be expressed using cardinality constraints only.

4 Related Work

The classical Entity-Relationship model [4] does not allow complex- or entity-valued attributes, so relationships between entity types can be expressed via the relationship construct only. ER supports a very "neutral" way of modeling by avoiding entity/object-centered "views" and stressing the symmetric nature of a relationship. This makes the addition of new relationships in a later phase very easy. There are extensions of the ER model that do allow complex- and/or entity-valued attributes, e. g. [6, 14]. However, experience shows that by frequently using the relationship construct the entity types themselves have a "flat" structure, because very often exactly the relationships are responsible for a nested structure.

In a number of object-based data models we find an inverse-clause that is part of a type definition and specifies relationship correspondences [13, 3]. In our syntax this would look like

```
define type{ name: Person,
   struct: ... courses: {Course} inverse Course.participants ...}
define type{ name: Course,
   struct: ... participants: {Person} inverse Person.courses ...}
```

Cardinalities are implied by the structure (collection-valued or single-valued) of the attributes and are only roughly classified by 1:1, 1:n, n:1, and m:n. A disadvantage is the fact that information on the relationship is split up into two type definitions. Besides that, only binary relationships can be identified in that way and relationship attributes cannot easily be integrated.

In the context of an object-oriented database programming language, [2] presents a language construct called *association* which is built after the relationship construct known from the ER model. However, if a schema is built up with type definitions like (1) and (2), there is no way to make an implicit relationship explicit and to add necessary constraints afterwards. So frequently the schema designer has to make a decision on whether to take advantage of the ER-like relationship construct or to do without it leaving integrity enforcement completely to the application programmer. A very similar technique that also borrows from ER modeling is described for the OMT-model [11] in the context of object-oriented modeling. Our approach turns out to be more flexible than [2, 11] in that it does not force the schema designer to choose between either the relationship construct or a nested table or type structure. Relationship information can be added to a schema at a later point of time.

A further comparison involves work in the area of schema resp. view integration. In [15] it is shown how different schemas based on the ERC+ data model [14] can be integrated into one global schema while not invalidating the use of the original schemas, which are then views on the complete schema. During the integration process new entity and relationship types may be automatically created. In our approach the type system is not changed. Besides that, we are able to integrate additional constraints into a *relship* definition.

5   Conclusions

We have shown how object type definitions are often biased in that they describe connections (relationships in the ER sense) among objects from a truely "object-oriented" point of view. The same applies to nested structures used in table definitions, which may also favor a specific point of view. Unless the complete application to be modeled is hierarchically structured, these points of view will almost necessarily overlap semantically. At the instance level this leads to a special kind of data redundancy, called relationship redundancy, which is a source for possible data inconsistency. We introduced an additional element for schema definition, called *relship*, which resembles the relationship type known from ER-modeling. The benefits of this construct are the following:

- Implicit (or hidden) relationships can be detected and set into mutual correspondence ensuring referential integrity and data consistency
- Relationship attributes, cardinality and key constraints can be appropriately expressed
- Incremental schema definition is supported, relships refering to existing types or tables can be added and modified at any time

Schema design and instance manipulation can be practically tested with the ESCHER database prototype, where research activities have primarily focussed on the development of a graphical user interface for the manipulation of nested structures.

References

1. S. Abiteboul, P. C. Fischer, and H.-J. Schek, editors. *Nested Relations and Complex Objects in Databases*. Number 361 in Lecture Notes in Computer Science. Springer, 1989.

2. A. Albano, G. Ghelli, and R. Orsini. A relationship mechanism for a strongly typed object-oriented database. In *Proc. 17th International Conference on Very Large Data Bases*, pages 565–575, 1991.

3. R. G. G Catell, editor. *The Object Database Standard: ODMG-93, Release 1.1*. Morgan Kaufmann, 1994.

4. P. P. Chen. The entity-relationship model - towards a unified view of data. *ACM Transactions on Database Systems*, 1(1):9–36, 1976.

5. P. Dadam, K. Küspert, K. Andersen, et al. A DBMS prototype to support extended NF^2 relations: An integrated view on flat tables and hierarchies. In *Proc. ACM SIGMOD Conf. Management of Data*, pages 356–366, 1986. Washington.

6. G. Engels, G. Gogolla, M. Hohenstein, et al. Conceptual modelling of database applications using an extended ER model. *Data & Knowledge Engineering*, 9:157–204, 1992.

7. K. Küspert, J. Teuhola, and L. Wegner. Design issues and first experience with a visual database editor for the extended NF^2 data model. In *Proc. 23rd Hawaii Int. Conf. System Science*, pages 308–317, 1990.

8. S. W. Liddle, D. W. Embley, and S. N Woodfield. Cardinality constraints in semantic data models. *Data & Knowledge Engineering*, 11:235–270, 1993.

9. Manfred Paul. *Typerweiterungen im eNF^2-Datenmodell*. PhD thesis, Universität Kassel, August 1994.

10. P. Pistor and P. Dadam. The advanced information management system. In Abiteboul et al. [1], pages 4–26.

11. J. Rumbaugh, M. Blaha, W. Premerlani, et al. *Object-oriented Modeling and Design*. Prentice-Hall, 1991.

12. H.-J. Scheck and M. H. Scholl. The two roles of nested relations in the DASDBS project. In Abiteboul et al. [1], pages 51–68.

13. M. Scholl, C. Laasch, C. Rich, et al. The COCOON object model. Technical Report 192, Dept. of Computer Science, ETH Zürich, 1992.

14. S. Spaccapietra and C. Parent. ERC+: an object based entity-relationship approach. In P. Loucopolous and R. Zicari, editors, *Conceptual Modelling, Databases and CASE: An Integrated View of Information Systems Development*. John Wiley, 1992.

15. S. Spaccapietra and C. Parent. View integration: A step forward in solving structural conflicts. *IEEE Transactions on Knowledge and Data Engineering*, 6(2):258–274, 1994.

16. S. Thelemann. A model for complex values with object identity. In *Technical Report 3-93, Universität Rostock, FB Informatik*, pages 117–121, 1993. in German.

17. L. Wegner. Let the fingers do the walking: Object manipulation in an NF^2 database editor. In *Proc. Symp. New Results and New Trends in Comp. Science*, number 555 in Lecture Notes in Computer Science, pages 337–358. Springer, 1991.

18. L. Wegner, M. Paul, and S. Thelemann. User interface techniques based on the non-first normal-form data model. Technical report, Universität Kassel, 1994.

A Cryptographic Mechanism for Object-Instance-based Authorization in Object-Oriented Database Systems

Ahmad Baraani-Dastjerdi   Josef Pieprzyk *

Reihaneh Safavi-Naini   Janusz R. Getta

Department of Computer Science
University of Wollongong
Wollongong, NSW 2522
AUSTRALIA

e-mail: [ahmadb,josef,rei,jrg]@cs.uow.edu.au

Abstract. *In this paper a mechanism for access control at the instance level of a class in object-oriented databases is suggested. The approach is based on the use of pseudo-random functions and sibling intractable functions. Each object-instance in the object-oriented model is associated with access keys that insure secure access to the object and all related objects. The security of the system depends on the difficulty of predicting the output of pseudo-random functions and finding extra collision for the sibling intractable function family. The authorization system supports ownership and granting/revoking of access rights.*

Keywords: Data Security, Database Security, Authorization System, Access Control, DAC, Object-Oriented Databases, Cryptography.

1 Introduction

Most of the current models for authorization in database systems are developed for relational databases [4, 10]. These models are not adequate for object-oriented databases (OODBs) which have a much richer and complex structure. Aspects such as inheritance and composite data structures allow expression of flexible and arbitrarily specific discretionary policies. Hence, authorization models for OODBs are more complex than their relational counterparts. Until now only a few authorization models for OODBs have been proposed [2, 3, 5, 7].

Inheritance and composite data create hierarchical structure in OODBs under *inclusion* and *is part of* relations, respectively [15]. An interesting question is how to extend the known cryptographic solutions for hierarchical access control to access control in OODBs. Two well-known solutions to hierarchical access control problem are based on RSA cryptosystem [11], and one way hash functions [14].

---
* Support for this project was provided in part by the Australian Research Council under the reference number A49530480.

The main drawback of the first solution is that it is only applicable to a fixed and known hierarchy with no provision for possible changes to the hierarchy. Moreover, the integer values associated with the nodes of the hierarchy become extremely large when the number of nodes is large. We use the second solution proposed by Zheng, Hardjono, and Pieprzyk [14] which is based on the sibling intractable function families (SIFF) to develop a cryptographic solution for discretionary access control in OODBs.

In [2], we proposed a similar approach to provide access control on the class-level and to manage user groups in a structurally OODB. The independent existence of object-instances in an OODB allows the object-instances to have their own access control (see [5]).

In this paper, we develop a mechanism to control the access in object-instance-level authorization. The access at the instance level of a class requires unique identification of instances; the user may refer to an instance by providing its unique identifier in the query. We use pseudo-random functions, SIFFs, and an authorization class, instead of access control lists (or protection matrix), to provide a cryptographic mechanism for object-instance-based authorization.

The organization of the paper is as follows. The next section discusses the basics of OODB model. In Section 3, we present the discretionary policy that our system supports and present the intuitive definition of SIFF (Section 4). In Section 5, we give the notations and assumptions that will be used in this paper. In Section 6, we describe the proposed solution and in Section 7, we consider the validation of access requests according to the proposed system. Next the security of the proposed system is discussed in Section 8. We conclude the paper in the last section by summarizing the results.

2 Review of Object-Oriented Concepts

The object-oriented model is based on number of basic concepts [8]. Here, we only describe those concepts that are relevant to the subsequent discussion.

In a general-purpose OODB system, all "real world" entities are modeled as objects. Every object encapsulates *a state* and *a behavior*. The state of an object is implemented by *attributes* (or instance variables), and the behavior of an object is encapsulated in *methods* that operate on the state of the object. The state and behavior are collectively called *properties of object*. Furthermore, an object is associated with a unique identifier called *object identifier* (OID) and may also be given a name.

A collection of the objects that share the same set of properties forms a class. An object belongs to only one class and is an instance of that *class*. Classes can be organized into hierarchy of classes. There are two types of hierarchies which are orthogonal to each other: *class-composition hierarchy and class-inheritance hierarchy* [13]. The class-composition hierarchy captures the *is-part-of* relationship between a parent class and its component classes, whereas a class-inheritance hierarchy represents the *is-a* relationship between a superclass and its subclasses.

A database system which provides mechanisms to define and to manipulate objects with complex internal structure is called *a structurally OODB system*. A database system which provides mechanisms to support the definition of class in a class-inheritance hierarchy and to define arbitrary methods is called *behaviorally OODB system*. A third type of OODBs called *fully OODB systems* is defined by Dittrich [6]. Fully OODB systems combine the properties of the first two OODB systems.

A mechanism for providing authorization for OODBs needs to address both the class-composition and the class-inheritance hierarchies. The mechanism presented here is designed to control access to a fully OODB system at the object-instance level.

3 Security Policy

An *authorization model* defines *who and how can access different data*. There are three different types of access control policy: *discretionary access control (DAC), mandatory access control (MAC), and role based access control (RBAC)*. A system may employ either DAC, MAC, RBAC, or combination of them for protection. In this paper, we consider discretionary access control policy (DAC) only.

As a coherent set of policies is needed as the guide for the design and use of a database system, we enumerate below the main aspects of an authorization system for OODBs.

1- Granularity of authorization- the smallest unit of authorization. This can be a class, an object-instance, and/or an attribute (instance variables) [5]. In *class-based authorization*, an authorized subject can access a class and all of its instances. In *instance-based authorization*, instances of a class are units of authorizations. A subject may have authorization for a subset of the instances of a class. Finally, in *instance-variable-based authorization*, access control on instance-variables or attributes is allowed. A subject can be limited to access only a part of an object. In this paper, we consider an instance-based authorization.

2- Access types- the specification of possible operations on the protected objects. We assume the following set of operations: *read, write, delete, execute,* and *create*. The operations are partially ordered: *read < execute < write < create,* and *read < delete.* This means that a subject who is authorized to an operation of a higher orders is also authorized to operations of the lower order. For example having authorization *execute* implies that the user has the authorizations *read* operation because the user must be able to read the values and definitions associated with the parameters of a method in order to execute a method.

3- Authorization types- full or partial (see [5]). The *full authorization* on a composite (class-hierarchy) object implies the same authorization on each component of the composite object (or on each class of the hierarchy). The *partial authorization* does not extend to the descendants of the composite (or class-hierarchy) object.

We assume that in the full authorization mode, *"read"* and *"execute"* rights are implicitly propagated to component objects of the object (or to the relevant object-instances of the superclasses) that a user is authorized to access. For other operations such as *"write"*, *"delete"*, and *"create"*, the user must be explicitly authorized by the owner of the component objects (or superclasses), unless the two objects have the same owner. However, users that are given access permissions to an object-instance of a class, will not be authorized to access the object-instances of subclasses (or ancestors) of that class unless they are authorized explicitly or are the owners of the instances of those subclasses.

6- Ownership- each object-instance has its owner. Every time, a user creates an object, (s)he will be its owner and have the full authority over it (the full authorization right). The owner is responsible for granting and revoking access rights for other users. The owner has only implicit *"read"* and *"execute"* authorization rights to the objects which related to the owner's object. The owner must get permission explicitly for other operations such as *"write"*, *"delete"*, and *"create"*. The ownership can also be granted and revoked by the creator of the object.

7- Group policy- a policy related to the definition of groups. Groups are not necessarily disjoint. A user may be a member of one group or more, and the groups again may become a member of other groups provided any groups does not belong (either directly nor indirectly) to any of its members. The resulting group hierarchy must be a directed acyclic graph. Each group has a sponsor who administers it. The sponsor can add new members to the group or remove members from the group. Any user who has sponsorship privilege may create a new group and may grant sponsorship privilege to other users. Note that the database administrator, duties include admitting new users to the database system, and revoking/replacing of the owners of the objects.

8- Open vs Closed system. Our authorization system is selected to be a closed system, i.e. each access right must be explicitly authorized. Hence, the absence of appropriate access rights is interpreted as *"access not allowed"*.

4   Sibling Intractable Function Families (SIFFs)

In this section, we give an intuitive definition of SIFF. See [14] for detailed discussion and formal definition.

Zheng, Hardjono, and Pieprzyk [14] introduced the notion of SIFF which is a generalization of the concept of the universal one-way hash function defined by Naor and Yung [9]. A universal one-way hash function is a class of hash function with the property that the number of functions that map any collection of r distinct input strings to the same hash value is fixed. SIFFs are universal one-way hash function families which have the added property that given a set of colliding sequences, it is computationally infeasible to find another sequence that collides with the initial sets. This means that if a hash function h maps the bit strings $x_1, x_2, \ldots, x_i$ to the same hash value, it must be computationally infeasible to find another string x' such that $h(x') = h(x_1) = \ldots = h(x_i)$. As shown in [14], the SIFFs can be constructed from any universal one-way hash function family.

5 Notations and Assumptions

1. $\aleph$ is the set of all positive integers. $n \in \aleph$ is the security parameter. $\sum$ is the alphabet $\{0, 1\}$. $x \in_R X$ means that an element x is randomly chosen from the set X. $\oplus$ is exclusive-or (XOR), and $\|$ is concatenation. K_{db} is the database key which is secret and is only accessible to a tamper-proof module (TM). $\{x\}_{K_{db}}$ is the ciphertext of x.

2. O_i, OID_i, U_j, $AOID_{j,i}$, and PS_j are: the name of the i-th object, the i-th object identifier, the j-th user's login-name, the authorization-instance identifier related to the user U_j for the object OID_i, and the login password of the user U_j, respectively. We use an n-bit string to represent OID_i, U_j, and $AOID_j$. The password is chosen by U_j after the database administrator admits him/her to the system. It should be long enough and kept secret by the user.

3. $F = \{F_n | n \in \aleph\}$ is a pseudo-random function family, where $F_n = \{f_K | f_K : \sum^n \to \sum^n, K \in \sum^n\}$. $H = \{H_n | n \in \aleph\}$ where $H_n = \{h | h : \sum^{2n} \to \sum^n\}$ is a k-SIFF mapping of a $2n$-bit input to an n-bit output string (k is the number of possible collisions).

4. The random n-bit strings K^r, K^w, K^e, K^d, K^c, corresponding to each of the operations *"read"*, *"write"*, *"execute"*, *"delete"*, and *"create"*, respectively are chosen and are only accessible to the TM.

5. An object is specified by (OID, OBJECT-NAME, CLASS-NAME, Values, SECURITY-INFO). OID is the identifier of the object. OBJECT-NAME is the name of the object given by the creator. CLASS-NAME indicates the name of the class. *"Values"* is the associated state of the object. SECURITY-INFO consist of OBJECT-KEY-LIST which is a pair of access keys (K_i^P, K_i^F) corresponding to partial and full authorizations, and H-FUNCTION which indicates the hash function that must be used by the related objects to derive the access key K_i^F of the object. The value of SECURITY-INFO is encrypted with the K_{db} by the TM.

6. There is an authorization class (AC) which is of the form (GRANTEE, OBJECT-ID, GRANTOR, MEMBER-LIST, DAC-INFO). GRANTEE indicates the user who is authorized to access this object. OBJECT-ID specifies the identifier of the object. GRANTOR specifies the user who has authorized the GRANTEE. MEMBER-LIST is the list of users who are the members of the group whose sponsor is the GRANTEE. DAC-INFO is of the form (ACCESS-TYPE-LIST, AUTH-TYPE, SPONSORSHIP, OWNERSHIP, H-FUNCTION, PSWORD). ACCESS-TYPE-LIST indicates the list of authorization rights which the GRANTEE has on the object. AUTH-TYPE (F or P) indicates full or partial authorization. SPONSORSHIP (YES or NO) indicates if the GRANTEE is the sponsor of a group (or groups) (indicated by the GRANTOR), and is able to propagate his/her access right to his group's members or not. OWNERSHIP (YES or NO) indicates if the GRANTEE has the ownership privilege or not.

H-FUNCTION specifies hash function which can be used to derive the grantor's password. PSWORD indicates the user's password. The value of the DAC-INFO is encrypted with the K_{db}.

6 Proposed Solution

As our main goal is to design a cryptographic mechanism for the discretionary access control in OODB, we will not consider other security issues such as authentication and secrecy of stored data. To enforce authentication and secrecy, the scheme proposed by Hardjono, Zheng and Seberry [12] for database authentication based on SIFF can be applied. We assume that the user authentication is done by the underlying operating system, and is secure. Also, we use a tamper-proof module (TM) to perform all necessary cryptographic operations, to generate needed cryptographic elements, and to verify the validity of access. The security of TM relies on the security of underlying operating system and DBMS. TM can be an intermediary between the user and the database system, or between the database and physical layer, or a separate function in the database system. The DBMS provides essential authorization information such as the object identifier and the operation in plain form and the user password, access key, and SIFF in encrypted form to TM. Then TM evaluates the request according to the algorithm described in this section and Section 7, and passes the result to the DBMS.

6.1 Access Key Generation Processing

To allow access to an object, we must be able to produce access keys K_i^P and K_i^F for the object OID_i, corresponding to the partial and the full authorization types, respectively. K_i^F can be derived from the access key of the related objects. The relationship can be either the inheritance *(is-a)* or the aggregation *(is-part-of)*. In the case of the inheritance, the access key K_i^F can be derived for the instances of subclasses of the object OID_i. Whereas in the case of the aggregation, the K_i^F can be computed for the object-instances of ancestors of the object.

Every time a user requests access to an object OID_i either K_i^F or K_i^P is computed and compared with the stored one by TM. If they match, the access is permitted otherwise denied.

When a user U_j (with login password PS_j) creates an object OID_i by running *create* command, the following two phases to generate access keys for the object will be completed.

Phase 1. Partial authorization.
Step 1. TM calculates the password $n_{j,i}$ of the user U_j to the object OID_i as $n_{j,i} = f_{PS_j}(U_j \oplus OID_i)$.
Step 2. TM selects at random the access keys K_i^P and K_i^F for OID_i (K_i^P and $K_i^F \in_R \sum^n$) for the full and the partial authorizations, respectively.

Step 3. TM selects at random hash function $h_i^P \in_R H_n$ for the partial authorization such that $h_i^P(n_{j,i}\|K^r) = h_i^P(n_{j,i}\|K^e) = h_i^P(n_{j,i}\|K^w) = h_i^P(n_{j,i}\|K^d) = h_i^P(n_{j,i}\|K^c) = K_i^P$. TM also encrypts DAC-INFO, { ("all", "F", "yes", "yes", h_i^P, $n_{j,i}$)}$_{K_{db}}$. The word "all" is used to indicated all possible operations.

Step 4. DBMS creates the object $(U_j, OID_i, U_j, \text{MEMBER-LIST}, \text{DAC-INFO})$ as an instance of the class AC.

Phase 2. Full authorization.

Suppose that objects $OID_{l_1}, OID_{l_2}, \ldots, OID_{l_p}$ with access keys $K_{l_1}^F, K_{l_2}^F, \ldots, K_{l_p}^F$ are related to the OID_i.

Step 1. TM selects at random a SIFF $h_i^F \in_R H_n$ for the full authorization such that $h_i^F(K_{l_1}^F\|K^r) = h_i^F(K_{l_1}^F\|K^e) = h_i^F(K_{l_2}^F\|K^r) = h_i^F(K_{l_2}^F\|K^e) = \ldots = h_i^F(K_{l_p}^F\|K^r) = h_i^F(K_{l_p}^F\|K^e) = K_i^F$. So in this way all objects which have a relationship with OID_i can access it directly by generating K_i^F from their $K_{l_s}^F$ $(1 \leq s \leq p)$ for "read" and "execute" operations only, by using h_i^F. Note that in the case of the inheritance OID_{l_s} $(1 \leq s \leq p)$ are instances of subclasses of OID_i. Whereas in the case of the aggregation OID_{l_s} $(1 \leq s \leq p)$ are object-instances of ancestors of OID_i.

Step 2. DBMS appends the hash function $\{h_i^F\}_{K_{ab}}$ in the H-FUNCTION of OID_i.

It is worth noting that if the owner of an object is replaced by a new one or if the login password of the owner has been changed, then in both cases the process described must be done.

6.2 Authorization Administration

To be complete an authorization system must include mechanism for administration of authorizations. Here, we present algorithms to perform authorization operations *grant, revoke,* and *transfer ownership* operations.

Granting Process. Suppose the grantor U_j has the password $n_{j,i}$ for OID_i. U_j can be the owner (or sponsor) of OID_i and wants to give m grantees $U_{l_1}, U_{l_2}, \ldots, U_{l_m}$ (with their login passwords $PS_{l_1}, PS_{l_2}, \ldots, PS_{l_m}$, respectively) access rights to OID_i by executing the *grant* command. The following steps must be completed.

Step 1. TM calculates the password $n_{l_s,j,i}$ of grantee U_{l_s} for OID_i granted by the grantor U_j as $n_{l_s,j,i} = f_{PS_{l_s}}(U_j \oplus OID_i)$, $s = 1, \ldots, m$.

Step 2. TM selects at random a hash function $h_{j,i} \in_R H_n$ such that $h_{j,i}(n_{l_1,j,i}) = h_{j,i}(n_{l_2,j,i}) = \ldots = h_{j,i}(n_{l_m,j,i}) = AOID_{j,i}$. This step ensures that all grantees are members of the group whose sponsor is U_j can directly compute $AOID_{j,i}$ of U_j and access the authorization-instance related to U_j. After the above steps are completed, TM also encrypts the DAC-INFO, { ("list-of-operations", "P/F", "yes/no", $h_{j,i}$, $n_{l_s,j,i}$)}$_{K_{db}}$.

Step 3. DBMS creates the object $(U_{l_s}, OID_i, U_j, \text{MEMBER-LIST}, \text{DAC-INFO})$ as an instance of the class AC for all $s = 1, \ldots, m$.

Step 4. DBMS updates the MEMBER-LIST of the authorization-instance related to the grantor U_j.

Revoking Process. Deletion of a user's authorization U_j is done by the *revoke* command.

Step 1. DBMS deletes the associated authorization-instance with U_j from the AC.

Step 2. TM selects new SIFF with one degree less collision accessibility property for the group which the user belongs to.

Step 3. TM replaces the old SIFF in the authorization-instance associated with users in the MEMBER-LIST of the sponsor with the new one.

Step 4. DBMS updates the MEMBER-LIST associated with the sponsor of the U_j.

See [1] for detailed discussion of the impact of the group updating on the authorization system.

Transferring the Ownership. An object can have several owners who may act independently. Suppose that the previous owner of the OID_i is U_j and (s)he wants to grant the ownership of the OID_i to users U_r and U_s by executing *transfer-own* command. The following steps must be completed.

Step 1. For new owners, TM chooses passwords as $n_{r,i} = f_{PS_r}(U_r \oplus OID_i)$ and $n_{s,i} = f_{PS_s}(U_s \oplus OID_i)$

Step 2. TM selects a new SIFF such that

$$h_i^P(n_{j,i}\|K^r) = h_i^P(n_{j,i}\|K^e) = h_i^P(n_{j,i}\|K^w) = h_i^P(n_{j,i}\|K^d) = h_i^P(n_{j,i}\|K^c) =$$
$$h_i^P(n_{r,i}\|K^r) = h_i^P(n_{r,i}\|K^e) = h_i^P(n_{r,i}\|K^w) = h_i^P(n_{r,i}\|K^d) = h_i^P(n_{r,i}\|K^c) =$$
$$h_i^P(n_{s,i}\|K^r) = h_i^P(n_{s,i}\|K^e) = h_i^P(n_{s,i}\|K^w) = h_i^P(n_{s,i}\|K^d) = h_i^P(n_{s,i}\|K^c) =$$
$$K_i^P$$

Step 3. DBMS updates tha instance of the U_j in the AC and creates new instances for U_r and U_s.

7 Validation of Access Requests

The processing of a user query starts by checking if the user has appropriate access rights to the objects specified in the query. This is done by the authorization system. In OODBs, the hierarchical structure of an object may or may not be included in the evaluation of the query and hence there are two forms of query: *simple queries* and *hierarchical queries.* A query can have the following form:

- **retrieve** Target-clause[*] [**from** Entry-clause] [**where** Qualification-clause];

Target-clause denotes target object names which must be retrieved. "*" indicates that the hierarchy must be included in the evaluation of the query (**hierarchical query**) i.e., the value of all properties of all objects of the hierarchical structure of the target object which are are object-instances of superclasses (or descendants) of the inheritance (or composition) hierarchy must be retrieved. Entry-clause (**from**) denotes sets of objects through which the target object can be accessed. In the case that the target object is a complex object, the Entry-clause may denote any of the ancestors of the target object. Whereas in the case of inheritance hierarchy, the Entry-clause may denote instances of subclasses of the target object. It is worth noting that if a user does not have an explicit right to the target object then it is essential that the Entry-clause be specified. Qualification-clause (**where**) specifies Boolean combination of predicates that must be satisfied by the retrieved objects.

The access validation of a query is done in two phases. First, the authority of the user who issues the query is checked i.e., it must be checked whether the user has proper authorization rights to objects which are requested (**user validation phase**). Second, the specified access rights to the objects retrieved by the query are forced. So no outsiders or illegal insiders cannot access the objects (**access validation phase**). In the following discussion, we assume that the user U_l issues the query: **retrieve O_j^* from O_i;**

Phase 1. User validation.

Step 1. Retrieve authorization instance related to U_l for OID_j or OID_i.

retrieve AC where (GRANTEE $= U_l$ **and** OBJECT-ID $= OID_j$ **and** PSWORD $= f_{PS_l}(GRANTOR \oplus OID_j)$) **or** (GRANTEE $= U_l$ **and** OBJECT-ID $= OID_i$ **and** PSWORD $= f_{PS_l}(GRANTOR \oplus OID_i)$);

The check PSWORD $= f_{PS_l}$(GRANTOR $\oplus OID_i$)), or (PSWORD $= f_{PS_l}$ (GRANTOR $\oplus OID_j$) is done by TM. If there is no such instance in the AC then the system rejects the request and exits. Suppose the query has been successful and the extracted instance is $(U_l, OID_k, U_{l'}$, MEMBER-LIST, { ("list-of-operation", "F", "yes"/"no", "yes"/"no", $h_{l',k}, n_{l,l',k})\}_{K_{db}})$ where k is j or i.

Step 2. Derive the password of the owner of OID_k, say U_w, i.e.

retrieve $h_{l',k}(PSWORD)$ where GRANTOR $\neq$ GRANTEE **and** OWNERSHIP $\neq$ "yes";

For new values of the SIFF and PSWORD, TM first obtains $AOID_{l',k} = h_{l',k}(PSWORD)$. Then until the check GRANTOR $=$ GRANTEE or OWNERSHIP $=$ "yes" is satisfied, the query is evaluated by DBMS . Suppose the derived password and SIFF for the owner U_w of OID_k are $n_{w,k}$ and h_k^P, respectively (k is j or i). Then we enter the access validation.

Phase 2. Access validation.

Step 1. retrieve OID_j where $(h_j^P(n_{w,j}\|K^r) = K_j^P)$ **or** $(h_i^P(n_{w,i}\|K^r) = K_i^P$ **and** AUTH-TYPE $=$"F" **and** $h_j^F(K_i^F\|K^r)=K_j^F)$;

Step 2. Retrieve the objects which are in relation with OID_j (either inheritance or aggragation). Let OID_s denote such an object.

retrieve OID_s where (AUTH-TYPE $=$"F" **and** $h_s^F(K_j^F\|K^r)=K_s^F)$;

After all OID_s have been retrieved, the process will finish. In the above steps, all checks must be evaluated by TM.

Note that since the access key of instances of descendants in the case of the composite object, or the instances of superclasses in case of the inheritance hierarchy, can only be derived by the the access key of the object, then it is ensured that the access to the instances of ancestors or subclasses of the object is not occurred. Furthermore, in the case of the partial authorization, because the checks for mapping in Steps 1 and 2 are not satisfied, the request for indirect access will fail.

8 Security of the Authorization System

The authorization system is considered secure if it is computationally infeasible for an insider/outsider to have an unauthorized access.

Proposition 1. *Assume that the tamper-proof module (TM) is secure and is only run by DBMS and the computational power of an outsider is polynomially bounded. If the authorization system can be broken, then either the SIFF scheme or the pseudo-random functions or the user authentication scheme or the cryptosystem used for encryption is insecure.*

The sketch proof of that is given in [1]

9 Conclusion

The paper proposes a cryptographic mechanism for discretionary access control at object-instance level in a fully OODB system. The mechanism is based on creating unique and secure access keys for each object, and unique passwords for owners and user groups, using pseudo-random functions and SIFF. The necessary access keys can be derived from other access keys (of related objects) or from the users' passwords (if the users belong to the same group). We use an authorization class to specify security and then apply the query processing to evaluate access request and enforce the security policy. The advantages of our approach compared to the traditional methods of access control (based on the protection matrix and supporting implicit rights) are as follows.

□ The maintanence and handling of protection matrices at the granularity of object-instances become extremely hard and time consuming whan the number of object-instances is large. Finding implicit rights will be even harder. Employing an authorization class (instead of access control lists or protection matrices) to modify authorizations and using SIFF to derive authorization-instance identifiers associated with users, results in a system that is more efficient and practical. This is true because any alterations of the organization of user groups requires manipulation of the authorization class only rather than checking through all access control lists in the database. Moreover, because of data structure consistency, database system operation can be used to manipulate the authorization class. Hence, access request may be checked during query processing.

□ The security of the system relies on the indistinguishability of the output of pseudo-random functions from truly random functions and the difficulty of finding collisions for SIFF. Both of which are known to be difficult.

□ Other operations such as grant, revoke, propagation of rights, and the required changes due to the alterations of the user groups and/or the class structure are relatively easier.

□ Allowing multiple owners for an object.

In this paper due to the space limitation, we do not address the effect of object restructuring, group updating, and the complexity of implementation of the system. For a detailed discussion of these issues, the reader is directed to [1].

References

1. A. Baraani-Dastjerdi and J. Pieprzyk and R. Safavi-Naini and J. R. Getta. A Cryptographic Mechanism for Object-Instnace-Based Authorization in Object-Oriented Database Systems. Technical report, TR-95-1, Department of Computer Science, The University of Wollongong, Wollongong, Australia, 1995.
2. A. Baraani-Dastjerdi and J. R. Getta and J. Pieprzyk and R. Safavi-Naini. A Cryptographic Solution to Discretionary Access Control in Structurally Object-Oriented Databases. In *Proceedings of the 6th Australian Database Conference (ADC'95)*, volume 17(2), pages 36–45, 1995.
3. D. B. Faatz and D. L. Spooner. Discretionary Access Control in Object-Oriented Engineering Database Systems. In *Database Security IV: Status and Prospects*, pages 73–83, 1991.
4. E. B. Fernandez and R. C. Summers and C. Wood. *Database Security and Integrity*. Addison-Wesley Publishing Company, 1981.
5. F. Rabitti and E. Bertino and W. Kim and D. Woelk. A Model of Authorization for Next-Generation Database Systems. *ACM Transactions on Database Systems*, 16(1):88–131, March 1991.
6. K. Dittrich. Object-Oriented Database Systems: The Notations and Issues. In *Proceedings of the First International Workshop on Object-Oriented Database Systems*. IEEE Computer Society Press, September 1986.
7. K. R. Dittrich and M. Hartig and H. Pfefferle. Discretionary Access Control In Structurally Object-Oriented Database Systems. In *Database Security II: Status and Prospects*, pages 105–121, 1989.
8. M. Atkinson and D. DeWitt and D. Maier and F. Bancilhon and K. Dittrich. The Object-Oriented Database System Manifesto. In *Proceeding of First International Conference on DOOD89*, pages 223–240, December 1989.
9. M. Naor and M. Yung. Universal one-way hash functions and their cryptographic applications. In *Proceedings of the 21st ACM Symposium on Theory of Computing*, pages 33–43. ACM, 1989.
10. P. P. Griffiths and B. W. Wade. An Authorization mechanism for a Relational Database System. *ACM Transactions on Database Systems*, 1(3):242–253, 1976.
11. S. G. Akl and P. D. Taylor. Cryptographic Solution To A Multilevel Security Problem. In *Advances in Cryptology Proceedings of CRYPTO'82*, pages 237–250. Plenum Press, 1982.
12. T. Hardjono and Y. Zheng and J. Seberry. A New Approach to Database Authentication. In *Research and Practical Issues in Databases:Proceedings of the Third Australian Database Conference (Database'92)*, pages 334–342, 1992.
13. Won Kim. Object-Oriented Databases: Definition and Research Directions. *IEEE Transactions on Knowledge and Data Engineering*, 2(3):327–341, September 1990.
14. Y. Zheng and T. Hardjono and J. Pieprzyk. The Sibling Intractable Function Family (SIFF): Notation, Construction and Applications. *IEICE Transactions, Fundamentals*, E76-A(1):4–13, January 1993.
15. Yair Wand. A Proposal for a Formal Model of Objects. In *Object-Oriented Concepts, Databases, and Applications*, pages 537–559. Addison-Wesley, Reading, ACM Press, 1989.

Unifying Modeling and Programming through an Active, Object-Oriented, Model-Equivalent Programming Language

Stephen W. Liddle
School of Accountancy and
Information Systems

David W. Embley
Scott N. Woodfield
Department of Computer Science

Brigham Young University, Provo, UT 84602

ABSTRACT

The intricate and complex structure of existing advanced database applications results in part from poor integration of existing models and languages. This complexity is a barrier to effectively understanding and developing advanced applications. We can significantly reduce the complexity of advanced-application specification and implementation by using a model-equivalent language (a language with a one-to-one correspondence to an underlying, executable model as defined herein). In this paper we explain the difficulties encountered in making models and languages equivalent, and we resolve these difficulties for a particular language and model.

Key Words: Database programming languages, model-equivalent languages, semantics of models and languages, impedance mismatch.

1 Introduction

One of the formidable barriers to effective understanding and development of advanced applications is the poor integration of model and language. We use semantic models to facilitate our understanding, but we implement our systems using languages that are neither fully integrated nor fully compatible with our models. This causes numerous problems, the foremost of which are 1) difficult and lossy transformations between models, languages, and tools, and 2) needless complexity.

In this paper we propose the concept of a model-equivalent language to help solve these problems. By "model" we mean a software model for systems analysis and design (e.g., ER, NIAM, OMT); and by "language" we mean a programming language (e.g., Pascal, Ada, Eiffel, C++). In this context, a language L is *model-equivalent with respect to a model M* if for every model instance I_M of M, there exists a program I_L of L whose semantics are one-to-one with I_M, and conversely, for every program I_L of L, there exists a model instance I_M of M whose semantics are one-to-one with I_L. By "semantics are one-to-one with" we mean that for every construct in the program, there is a corresponding construct in the model instance and vice versa. Consequently, a program written in a model-equivalent language is nothing more than an alternative view of some model instance and vice versa. Hence, every program written in a model-equivalent language is fully integrated with and fully compatible with a model instance.

The primary advantage of a model-equivalent language is that it eliminates the need for transformations when moving between different aspects of system development. For example, the shift from analysis to implementation using a model-equivalent language does not require that the system be transformed from data-flow diagrams to COBOL code. Since transformations are merely shifts in point of view, model-equivalence should lead to faster and smoother application development with correspondingly fewer problems and higher quality results.

We are not aware of any existing language that fits our definition of model-equivalence, though there are systems that move in this direction. For example, IEF [10] provides both analysis/design tools and code generators, but only for a narrow application domain, and object-oriented database systems such as O_2 [1] provide a general language and implementation model, but support no analysis and design models. In practice, either the language does not support all the features of an underlying software model, or the software model is not sufficiently general or fails to satisfy the needs of the entire lifecycle of advanced-application development from analysis through implementation. In general, the current state of the art in software and data engineering combines too many distinct models that have overt and subtle incompatibilities.

There are many roadblocks to achieving model equivalence. As a first challenge, we must make models Turing complete, and we must do so without losing a natural correspondence to the real world, for otherwise we lose the analysis and simulation features of our model (we address this in Section 2). Secondly, we must overcome a number of so-called impedance mismatches, including: variable/type/class conflicts, persistent/transient data conflicts, textual/graphical notational conflicts, imperative/declarative processing conflicts, and object-interaction/operator-invocation conflicts (this is the topic of Section 3). Finally, we must not lose the advances made in programming-languages with regard to style and notation, ease of compilation, and optimization (we discuss this in Section 4).

In this paper, we show how to overcome these problems and obtain a model-equivalent language by giving a specific example: our language is Melody, and our model is the Object-oriented Systems Model (OSM) [6]. Our purpose is to explore the issues behind the design of a model-equivalent language and to address these issues. Whether the language is Melody and the model is OSM, or whether some other language and model are investigated, the principles, issues, and major challenges are largely the same.

2 The OSM Model

The Object-oriented Systems Model (OSM) is a derivative of OSA, which was originally developed for systems analysis [4]. OSM is a non-traditional object-oriented model because there are no attributes — only objects and relationships — and because behavior is active, driven by events and conditions, rather than being passive and driven by method invocation. OSM represents structure as objects and relationships among objects. OSM captures object behavior in two ways: individual object behavior and interaction among multiple, collaborating objects. Fig. 1 shows a simple OSM model instance that highlights many of the features of OSM.

In OSM, objects have unique identity and are grouped into sets called object classes. In Fig. 1, rectangles represent object classes, and there are six in our example: Person, Patient, Doctor, Patient ID, Name, and Address. Object classes with a dashed border contain objects that can be printed or read (e.g., numbers, strings, images). An object class may be a generalization and/or a specialization of other object classes. For example, Person is a generalization of Patient and Doctor. We also say that Patient and Doctor are specializations of Person. Other lines between object classes represent relationship sets, of which there are four in our example: Person has Name, Person has Address, Doctor treats Patient, and Patient has Patient ID. The text items near the relationship-set connections are participation constraints that indicate how many times an object from a particular class can participate in the corresponding relationship set. For example, the 1:* near Address indicates that each address object in the Address class must relate to one or more Person objects through the Person has Address relationship set. OSM has other cardinality constraints, general constraints, and additional forms of relationship sets that we do not illustrate here.

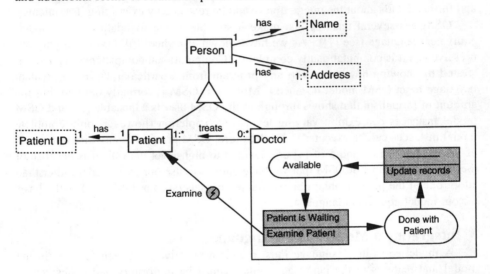

Fig. 1. Simple OSM Model Instance.

OSM models object behavior with state nets, so-called because behavior is represented in terms of transitions among states. An object may have one or more threads of control associated with it. A thread is either in a state or firing a transition. Threads may be created or destroyed in the process of firing transitions. States and transitions in a state net pertain to object classes in an OSM model instance. When a thread is in a state or firing a transition, then the object owning the thread is considered to be a member of the object class to which the particular state or transition pertains. Fig. 1 shows part of the state net for the Doctor class. The state net has two states (represented by ovals), named Available and Done with Patient, and two transitions (represented by divided rectangles). Transitions consist of a trigger (written in the top half) and an action (written below the trigger). A transition can fire when its trigger is true and a thread is in the prior state(s) of the transition. When a transition fires, its thread leaves the prior state(s), and it performs the transition action. After firing, the thread enters one or more subsequent states. Since the two transitions in Fig. 1 are shaded, we understand that they are high level, and that we could discover more detail by examining their currently hidden contents.

An interaction is a point of synchronization and communication between two or more threads. When an interaction occurs, the associated threads are synchronized, and information may be distributed from the sender to the receiver(s). Interactions may be broadcast to multiple receivers. A special form of interaction, called a two-way interaction, also allows information to be returned from the receiver to the sender. In a two-way interaction, the sending thread blocks until the receiving thread has finished firing its transition, signaling that the two-way interaction is complete. Fig. 1 shows one interaction between Doctor and Patient. This interaction is named Examine, and is represented by an arrow with a circled lightning bolt at the center. The shading in the circle again indicates that this interaction is high level, and further details about the interaction would be revealed by examining its contents.

OSM has several features that make it suitable as the foundation for a model-equivalent language (see [7]). As we have shown elsewhere [6], OSM is highly expressive and it is computationally complete. (Computational completeness is demonstrated by showing how to convert any program from a particular Turing-equivalent language to an OSM model instance.) Moreover, OSM is formally defined, but the amount of formalism that shows through to the OSM user is adjustable [3], and OSM model instances can exhibit varying levels of completion (however, only complete model instances can be executed). Furthermore, OSM provides many different kinds of views (Chapters 4 and 5 of [4] are devoted to high-level views). It is because of these unique features of OSM that we have chosen to use our own model rather than adopt one of the more popular object-oriented models (such as OMT [8]) as the basis for our model-equivalent language.

3 Integrating a Model and a Language

A model-equivalent language must maintain bijectivity between features in the model and features in the language — there must be uniformity and cohesiveness between both views. This section describes how we addressed these issues in the design of Melody. We organize our discussion in terms of structure, behavior, and interaction.

3.1 A Uniform Structural Model

With the advent of object-oriented models and languages, we have seen more opportunity to consolidate elements from programming languages and database systems. However, most object-oriented systems have a physical (implementation-oriented) definition of what an object is. It is typical, for example, to define an object as an instantiation of a class, and a class as a record structure (or collection of attributes) together with a set of methods to operate on the structure members. This creates a direct conflict with the desire to be free from physical concerns at the model level.

Thus, there is an "impedance mismatch" between the semantics of a general, non-physical model, and a more-specific, physical type system [9].

In Melody, we resolve this conflict by providing language elements that are logical, and yet look like their traditional counterparts. The key to our approach is the substitution of *object class* for the concept of *variable*. In OSM an object class is a collection of objects, the membership of which can change over time; this idea is similar to the concept of a container. Thus, a variable in Melody is an object class. For us, a variable is a container that represents a *set* of objects. (Variables containing a single element can be considered to be scalar values.) Types in Melody are restrictions on class membership as constrained by the generalizations of a class. To be a member of a class, an object must also be a member of all generalizations of that class. Thus, if we fix the membership of one or more generalizations, we can restrict the set of objects that are candidates for membership in a class. This achieves the same effect as typing a variable in a standard programming language.

Suppose we have two read-only object classes named **real** and **integer**, and we have two specialization object classes, x and y, where x is a specialization of **real** and y is a specialization of **integer**. The effect of this model instance is to create two containers (x and y) whose members can change over time. However, the members are restricted by the definitions of **real** and **integer**, whose members are fixed. This would be similar to defining variables x and y of type real and integer in a programming language. Indeed, in Melody we allow the following textual representation of the model instance just described:

```
x: real;
y: integer;
```

Observe, however, that this does not quite give the traditional declaration semantics because x is a *set* of reals and y is a *set* of integers. We can achieve scalar semantics by associating an OSM object-class cardinality constraint of 1 with an object class. For example, x[1]: **real**; forces x to have exactly one member.

In addition to the *variable* concept, there is the related concept of *type constructor*. For example, programming languages usually provide record and array type constructors that allow the physical combination of data types to form new aggregate types. In Melody, relationship sets play the role of type constructors. Any logical structure can be modeled in OSM using object classes and relationship sets, and so any physical structure, such as an array, can be emulated. For those bulk structures that are common, we provide optimized physical structures in the implementation of Melody. However, the optimized form of a particular structure does not show through to the Melody program. Only the logical structure is available to a Melody programmer.

Melody defines persistence by declaring that object classes and relationship sets persist for the duration of their scope. When a thread enters a nested scope, a nested model instance associated with the scope is instantiated. Objects and relationships in such a model instance exist as long as a thread is inside the corresponding scope. When a thread leaves a scope, associated object classes and relationship sets (together with their members, as appropriate) are destroyed. Thus, transient objects in Melody are those defined within a nested scope. Fully persistent objects are those defined in the outermost (global) scope of a model instance, which like a database can exist for an arbitrary length of time. This approach to persistence is uniform and type-complete, meaning that any kind of data (i.e., any object or relationship) may persist.

3.2 A Uniform Behavior Model

Another aspect of the impedance mismatch problem is that database systems are usually declarative while programming languages are usually imperative [9]. How do we ensure that our behavior model will adequately span the declarative/imperative spectrum? Our approach incorporates elements of both imperative and declarative programming paradigms. A state net is essentially an imperative system, though it is not restricted to a single thread of control like traditional programming languages. Also, a state net incorporates declarative elements, such as its triggers and real-time constraints. On the other hand, OSM structure (object classes and relationship sets) is essentially declarative, though its instances are dynamic. Furthermore, OSM general and cardinality constraints are also declarative. Thus, OSM inherently incorporates both imperative and declarative paradigms.

Melody builds on this multi-paradigm foundation, integrating programming features from imperative, logic, and constraint paradigms. Basically, Melody programs can be thought of as having an imperative skeleton, with logic elements fleshing out the structure. The imperative skeleton acts by evaluating constraints and triggers and executing transition actions. Using OSM-equivalent statements, a transition action can be thought of as a sequence of statements, with flow-control constructs for repeated and conditional execution, and, indeed, it can be written textually using familiar if-then-else, while, and for-each statements [6].

Within this imperative framework, Melody provides a mechanism for deriving high-level object classes and high-level relationship sets, and this provides the means to integrate logic within the imperative-paradigm skeleton. Indeed, OSM and Melody support predicate cal-

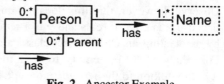

Fig. 2. Ancestor Example.

culus and a form of Datalog directly. Consider, for example, the problem of finding a person's ancestors, given the recursive relationship set Person has Parent, shown in Fig. 2. We can define a derived high-level relationship set, Person has Ancestor, as follows:

```
hlrs Person[0:*] has Ancestor[1:*] derivation
    Person(x) has Ancestor(y) :- Person(x) has Parent(y);
    Person(x) has Ancestor(y) :- Person(x) has Parent(z),
                                 Person(z) has Ancestor(y);
end;
```

This simple logic program provides a derived (intensional) relationship set that is accessible in the same way as any non-derived (extensional) relationship set (but it cannot be updated like an extensional relationship set). Chapter 5 of [5] describes the formal semantics of our logic components.

3.3 A Uniform Interaction Model

The third area of model/language integration we must consider is the OSM interaction model. In order for a model-equivalent language to be successful, the object interaction mechanism must be equally suited to analysis and implementation. While interaction perspectives such as data flows are common in modeling, function calls are ubiquitous in languages. We find the foundation for a harmony between the two in object orientation, where message passing is the predominant concept. The OSM version of object interaction is general enough to use in various development phases.

As a basic principle, threads may send interactions within transition actions, and threads may receive interactions within transition triggers. To support this, Melody needs a way to specify send and receive events. The following two examples show interaction-send statements:

```
Deposit(Account Number, Deposit Amount);
to all Subscriber.Report Score(Current Game Score);
```

Corresponding interaction-receive expressions are:

```
@Deposit(AcctNum: Account Number, Amt: Dollar Amount)
@Report Score(score: Game Score)
```

While one-way interactions, like those above, are powerful enough to accomplish any desired communication, they are not necessarily convenient for accomplishing two-way communication. For example, one thread could send a one-way interaction to another, and the sender could listen for a message from the receiver. However, it is difficult in the presence of multiple independently behaving objects to specify appropriate constraints to guarantee that the return message is causally linked with the original interaction. To overcome this difficulty, we provide a two-way interaction, which is similar in several ways to the concept of function call found in traditional languages.

Let us consider an example. Suppose we have the following two-way-interaction-send statement:

```
im: Image;
...
Compress Image(img)->(cimg: Compressed Image);
```

and the receiving transition's trigger is the following:

```
@Compress Image(im: Image)->(cim: Compressed Image)
```

When the interaction occurs, objects from `img` in the sending thread are added to the class `im` in the receiving thread. When the interaction completes, objects from the class `cim` in the receiving thread are added to the `cimg` class in the receiving thread. In this way, information can be transferred in both directions between threads communicating via a two-way interaction.

4 Preserving Advances of the Past

It would be unwise to propose an entirely new language that radically departs in every way from existing technology. To the extent possible, we should preserve those structures, techniques, and concepts that have proven their worth over the years. Function call and variable assignment, for example, are ubiquitous in traditional languages because they are useful abstractions and are easy to use and understand. With some "syntactic sugar" added to our OSM interaction mechanism, for example, if we choose "+" as an interaction name, write its send parameters using infix notation, and assume an anonymously named return parameter, we have the familiar x + y expression for addition. Similarly, Melody's dot operator subsumes attribute selection and pointer de-referencing found in traditional programming languages, and lets us write, for example, `Person.Name` to retrieve the name. This could either be a query traversing from the `Person` class to find a related `Age` class, or it could be an interaction with `Person` as the destination, and `Age` as the interaction activity description.

As a larger example, we consider the traditional programming language assignment statement, which generally takes the form *variable* := *expression*. The effect of an assignment statement is to replace the contents of a memory cell of fixed size and type with a new value. In Melody, we do not have fixed-sized cells holding data values; rather, we have object classes as containers holding zero or more objects. Furthermore, these objects may be involved in relationships with other objects. Because we have generalized the concept of data storage, we also need to generalize the concept of assignment statement for Melody. The full details are extensive, so we only give several examples here.

Consider again the model instance of Fig. 1, and suppose we have the following Melody code:

```
p: Patient; d: Doctor;
p := Patient ID(126892).Patient;
d := p.Doctor;
p.Address := "123 Elm Street";
```

The first assignment statement has the effect of removing any current members of `p`, then selecting and assigning to `p` the `Patient` object that is related to the `Patient ID` object whose value is `126892`. Note that in general, we cannot guarantee the cardinality of a variable after an assignment statement; it may be empty, or it may contain one or more objects. However, in this case we know that the cardinality of class `p` after the first assignment statement is either 0 or 1, because the participation constraints on the `Patient has Patient ID` relationship set guarantee that patient objects and patient-ID objects are in a one-to-one correspondence. In the case of the second assignment statement, which assigns to d the doctors who are treating patient p, we do not know what the cardinality of d will be, because there may be many doctors treating a patient. The third assignment statement is more complex. Because the left-hand side has a dot operator, the assignment relates each object in p to the Address object "123 Elm Street", replacing any existing relationships between p objects and Address objects. If "123 Elm Street" is not a member of the Address class, it is added, and any address that is no longer associated with a person is deleted.

5 Conclusion

The advantages of a model-equivalent language are compelling. Because the application never leaves its single, unified model/language, there is no need to translate from one language or model to another. Thus, there is no loss of information or added complexity due to these transformations. Furthermore, the semantics of the analysis of a system are directly observable in its implementation. This makes communication easier because an object and its behavior in the model mean the same thing as an object and its behavior in the language, and because all parties are operating from the same lexicon and with the same set of definitions.

We have shown how a number of model/language impedance mismatches (integration challenges) can be resolved, by removing physical, implementation-oriented details from our model and language. Moreover, we can recast a number of traditional constructs in more general forms that apply to all phases of the software lifecycle.

As we consider the ramifications of our approach, however, one question comes to the forefront. Will a model-equivalent language necessarily be rather complex, bulky, and inefficient? The answer, at least initially, appears to be affirmative. However, we need to view a model-equivalent language with proper perspective, comparing a single model and language with the multiple models, languages, and tools brought together in other approaches. We claim that a model-equivalent language approach is less complex and bulky, on balance, than an approach that uses disparate models and languages.

Efficiency, however, is still in question. Yet as the database community in particular has shown, we can turn this challenge into an opportunity, using principles of design together with the principle of data independence (the idea of separating a logical data model from physical data-structure implementation) to achieve satisfactory efficiency. Eventually, perhaps we can achieve even greater efficiency than has hitherto been realized. High-level languages met initial resistance for the same reason — initially, compilers were not as efficient as assembly-language programmers — however, this eventually changed. Yet we recognize that a number of important optimization issues currently remain open.

Our implementation has been underway for some time now. We have created an OSM diagramming tool, called the OSM Composer, that forms the basis for our OSM/Melody programming environment (see [11]). With the OSM Composer, a user can create OSM model instances for systems analysis, specification, design, and implementation. The Composer also provides a platform for integrating other tools to assist in the development of OSM-based systems. For example, we have a rapid-prototyping component, a graphical query language, and a database normalization assistant. We have implemented a subset of the Melody language, and we are continuing to enlarge the implementation. Other related projects are also planned or under way (see [11]).

References

[1] F. Bancilhon, C. Delobel, and P. Kanellakis (eds.), *Building an Object-Oriented Database System: The Story of O_2*, Morgan Kaufmann, San Mateo, Calif., 1992.

[2] R.G.G. Cattell (ed.), *The Object Database Standard: ODMG-93*, Morgan Kaufmann Publishers, San Mateo, California, 1994.

[3] S.W. Clyde, D.W. Embley, and S.N. Woodfield, "Tunable Formalism in Object-oriented Systems Analysis: Meeting the Needs of Both Theoreticians and Practitioners," *OOPSLA '92 Conference Proceedings*, pp. 452-465, Vancouver, British Columbia, Canada, October 1992.

[4] D.W. Embley, B.D. Kurtz, and S.N. Woodfield, *Object-Oriented Systems Analysis: A Model-Driven Approach*, Yourdon Press Series, Prentice-Hall, Englewood Cliffs, New Jersey, 1992.

[5] N.H. Gehani, H.V. Jagadish, and O. Shmueli, "Event Specification in an Active Object- Oriented Database," *Proceedings of the 1992 ACM SIGMOD International Conference on Management of Data*, pp. 81-90, San Diego, California, June 1992.

[6] S.W. Liddle, "Object-Oriented Systems Implementation: A Model-Equivalent Approach," *Ph.D. Dissertation*, Computer Science Department, Brigham Young University, June 1995.

[7] S.W. Liddle, D.W. Embley, and S.N. Woodfield, "A Seamless Model for Object-Oriented Systems Development," *Proceedings of the International Symposium on Object-Oriented Methodologies and Systems, ISOOMS 94*, pp. 123-131, Palermo, Italy, September 1994.

[8] J. Rumbaugh, M. Blaha, W. Premerlani, F. Eddy, and W. Lorensen, *Object-Oriented Modeling and Design*, Prentice Hall, Englewood Cliffs, New Jersey, 1991.

[9] S.B. Zdonik and D. Maier, "Fundamentals of Object-Oriented Databases," in *Readings in Object-Oriented Database Systems*, ed. S.B. Zdonik and D. Maier, pp. 1-32, Morgan Kaufmann, San Mateo, California, 1990.

[10] *A Guide to Information Engineering Using the IEF*, 2nd Edition, Texas Instruments, Dallas, Texas, Part Number 2739756-0001, 1990.

[11] *OSM Lab Home Page*, World Wide Web URL http://osm7.cs.byu.edu/.

A Declarative Query Approach to Object Identification

Martin Gogolla*
Bremen University, FB 3, Informatics
Postfach 330440, D-28334 Bremen
Germany
e-mail: gogolla@informatik.uni-bremen.de

Abstract. Object identification in data models, especially in semantic, Entity-Relationship, and Object-Oriented data models is studied. Various known approaches to object identification are shown, and an alternative proposal to the topic is put forward. The main new idea is to attach to each object type an arbitrary query in order to observe a unique, identifying property of objects of the corresponding type.

1 Introduction

One of the central issues in object-orientation [ABD+90] is object identity. In object models with identity, objects can exist independent of the values of their attributes. Advantages of such identities are object sharing and object updates. The importance of the identity concept with different perspectives from programming and database languages [KC86] and philosophy [WJ91] has also been emphasized.

Object identity has been studied intensively in recent literature. In [AK89] the significance of object identity w.r.t. data base query languages is pointed out. The proposed query language IQL employs object identities to represent data structures with sharing and cycles, to manipulate sets, and to express any computable database query. Object identities from the deductive databases point of view are treated in [HY90]. Logic databases are also considered in [KLS92] with special emphasis on updates, a topic which seems to be one of the mayor problems in this field [Abi88]. An approach to object identity from the functional programming perspective by the use of categorical monad structures is given in [Oho90]. For the special purpose of databases, a functional language incorporating parametrized set types is introduced. Different kinds of (not necessarily

---

* Work reported here has been partially supported by the CEC under Grant No. 6112 (COMPASS).

66

formal) object equality definitions are studied in [Mas90]. The implementation of
the proposed concepts in the database management system OMEGA is also discussed there. In [VD91], algebraic query processing was the main motivation for
given a set-theoretic semantics for object identities in the presence of multiple-
inheritance. The paper also discusses implementation issues in the context of
the EXTRA/EXCESS system. [SSW92] treats object identity from the data
type point of view by providing a special identifier data type for this purpose. A
similar framework like ours but with emphasis on integrating different databases
and with attention to the instance level has been put forward in [LSPR93]. Our
approach differs from the cited ones because we establish a connection between
abstract object identities and concrete data values in order to identify objects.

Our paper is organized as follows. In Sect. 2 we introduce an example schema
which will be used throughout the paper, and in Sect. 3 the interpretation of
object schemas is sketched in an informal way. Several known and our new
proposal (the so-called observation term approach) to object identification are
studied in Sect. 4. The advantages of our new proposal are discussed in Sect. 5.
The paper ends with some concluding remarks in Sect. 6.

2 An Example Schema: Town-Country-River

Let us start with a simple example application where real world objects like
towns, countries, and rivers are of interest. Towns and countries both possess
the data-valued properties 'Name' and 'Pop' (for population), rivers also have a
'Name' and a 'Length' of flow. Towns possess an object-valued property 'LiesIn'
which gives the country object the town object lies in; towns also have a set- and
object-valued property 'LiesAt' yielding the set of rivers the town lies at. Finally,
rivers are assumed to 'FlowThrough' a set of country objects. The schema for
this application can be represented graphically as given in Fig. 1 (following the
notation of [GH91]).

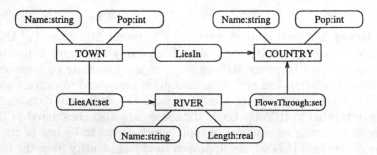

Fig. 1. Town-Country-River OO-like

In order to round off the discussion of the representation of the considered schema
we explain how the above would have been modelled in the classical Entity-
Relationship [Che76] approach. Here, the object-valued attributes would have

been expressed as general relationships as denoted in Fig. 2. In order to simplify matters we refrain from adorning the arcs of the relationships with cardinality specifications typically found in many Entity-Relationship approaches.

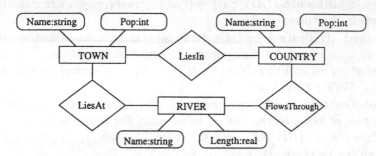

Fig. 2. Town-Country-River ER-like

It is amazing to see how similar these schemas are. In fact, in our comprehension it is only a matter of taste – as far as structural modelling is concerned – to use the term "Entity-Relationship" or "Object-Oriented" database schema. Indeed, the relation between Entity-Relationship and Object-Oriented modelling has always been in the center of interest on the Entity-Relationship conferences (see for example [Dit87, NP88, KS88, LBSL90, RS91, ADD+92, PKB94, LT94], among many other interesting papers).

3   Interpretation of Database Schemas

We now turn to the compelling question of how single elements of the given object domains are identified. But before going into details concerning this point, we have to clarify how we formally interpret schemas like the above ones. We recognize that the following items must have an interpretation: Data sorts and data operations, object sorts, data-valued attributes, type constructors, and object-valued attributes. We explain the interpretation of these notions by examples from the above schema.

Data sorts: Each data sort like string is associated with a corresponding set of values denoted by $I(string)$.[1]

Data operations: Each data operation like the string concatenation operation concat : string string -> string is associated with a function with respective domain and target like $I(concat) : I(string) \times I(string) \rightarrow I(string)$.

---

[1] Here, we give formal semantics to syntactic domains by applying the function I which returns for the parameter the corresponding interpretation.

Object sorts: Each object sort is connected with a infinite universe of object identities[2] for this object sort like $U(RIVER) = \{river_n \mid n \in \mathbf{N}\}$ for the object sort RIVER. In each database state there is an "active" finite subset of object identities like $I(RIVER) = \{river_2, river_4, river_8\}$ representing the objects in the current state.

Data-valued attributes: In each database state a data-valued attribute is seen as a function from the appropriate active object domain into the associated set of values like $I(Name) : I(TOWN) \rightarrow I(string)$ for the attribute Name : TOWN -> string.

Type constructors: Each type constructor builds over its argument a new collection of items corresponding to its task. For example, for set(RIVER) we have $I(set)(I(RIVER)) = \{\ \emptyset, \{river_2\}, \{river_4\}, ..., \{river_2, river_4\}, ..., \{river_2, river_4, river_8\}\ \}$.

Object-valued attributes: In each database state an object-valued attribute is connected with a function from the respective active object domain into the appropriate target. For example, for the attribute LiesIn : TOWN -> COUNTRY we have $I(LiesIn) : I(TOWN) \rightarrow I(COUNTRY)$, and for the attribute LiesAt : TOWN -> set(RIVER) we have $I(LiesAt) : I(TOWN) \rightarrow I(set)(I(RIVER))$. Thus, in a concrete state we could have for instance $I(LiesAt) : town_{42} \mapsto \{river_2, river_8\}$.

4   Approaches to Object Identification

After we have given an impression how to interpret schemas like the above ones, in particular how to interpret object sorts by object identities, we can now proceed and discuss the topic of object identification. In principle, all occurring questions originate from the freedom and flexibility offered by the above interpretation for object sorts and, in consequence of this, from the freedom for the interpretation of attributes. The following situation can occur: There may be objects which have different identities, say $country_2$ and $country_4$, but for which the interpretation of both attributes $I(Name)$ and $I(Pop)$ coincides. Thus we cannot distinguish between the objects $country_2$ and $country_4$ wrt. their characteristics, but assume we would like to do so. The object identities are of no help in this case because both identities tell us nothing about the properties of the objects. Therefore, there must be some other means to distinguish them. In the following we discuss several approaches to achieve this distinction, namely data-valued key attributes, data- and object-valued key attributes, data- and object-valued key attributes with additional contributions from other attributes having the respective object sort as target sort, identity observing formulas, and identity observing terms and queries.

---

[2] Object identities have appeared under the name surrogates in [Cod79], l-values in [KV84], and object identifiers in [AH87].

Data-valued keys: In the relational model it is usual to mark some of the attributes of a relation as keys. This means that tuples in the relation are already uniquely identified by the values of the key attributes. This is also possible in our object model. For example, we could require that the attribute 'Name' is the key for the object type 'COUNTRY'. By doing this, we would state a restriction on the interpretation of 'Name' and 'Pop' saying that the value of 'Name' already determines the rest of the object. However, we have to be careful with the formalization of this requirement. At least two different possibilities exist:

(A) $\forall(c_1, c_2 : COUNTRY)$
$$(Name(c_1) = Name(c_2)) \Rightarrow (Pop(c_1) = Pop(c_2))$$
(B) $\forall(c_1, c_2 : COUNTRY)$
$$(Name(c_1) = Name(c_2)) \Rightarrow (c_1 = c_2)$$

The first formula (A) requires that whenever two COUNTRY objects coincide in their 'Name' attribute, then they must also have equal values for the 'Pop' attribute. The second formula (B) states that under the same precondition as in (A) the two *objects* must be identical not only their 'Pop' *data values*.[3] The difference can be explained best by the sample state mentioned above where two different COUNTRY objects exist which have identical values for their 'Name' and 'Pop' attributes: This state would be accepted as valid by formula (A) but not by formula (B). Following the arguments from above stating that different objects with indistinguishable properties should be avoided we cannot accept (A) as a proper solution but must prefer the stronger[4] formula (B) as the right formulation for the problem.

Perhaps it is instructive to explain how the above formulas contribute to object identification. Let us first re-formulate formula (B) equivalently by employing the simple logical law $(\alpha \Rightarrow \beta) \Leftrightarrow (\neg\beta \Rightarrow \neg\alpha)$.

(B') $\forall(c_1, c_2 : COUNTRY)(c_1 \neq c_2) \Rightarrow (Name(c_1) \neq Name(c_2))$

This formulation now clearly states that two different countries must have different names.

Data- and object-valued keys: What we have done for data-valued attributes above can also be done for object-valued attributes. For example, we could require that 'Name' and 'LiesIn' are the key for TOWN allowing that different towns in different countries can have the same name. The restricting formula then reads as follows:

(C) $\forall(t_1, t_2 : TOWN)$
$$(Name(t_1) = Name(t_2) \wedge LiesIn(t_1) = LiesIn(t_2)) \Rightarrow (t_1 = t_2)$$

Data- and object-valued keys plus other attributes: The above achievement can even be extended by allowing not only attributes of the considered object type to contribute to object identity but also attributes of other object types which have the considered object sort as their target sort. Consider the slight modification of Fig. 1 presented in Fig. 3.

---

[3] The distinction between values and objects is discussed, for instance, in [Bee90].

[4] 'Stronger' in the sense that (B) implies (A).

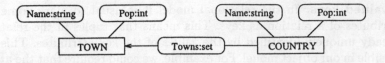

Fig. 3. Town-Country-River OO-like (modified)

We have replaced the single-valued attribute 'LiesIn : TOWN → COUNTRY' by the inverse, set-valued attribute 'Towns : COUNTRY → set(TOWN)'. Now consider the same requirement for towns as above, namely that different towns in different countries with the same name are allowed to exist. Expressing this requires to refer to an attribute not belonging to the object type 'TOWN'. The respective formula reads as follows:[5]

$(D)\ \forall(t_1, t_2 : TOWN)$
$\qquad (Name(t_1) = Name(t_2) \land$
$\qquad (\forall(c : COUNTRY)(t_1\ in\ Towns(c) \Leftrightarrow t_2\ in\ Towns(c))))$
$\qquad \Rightarrow (t_1 = t_2)$

Identity observing formulas: All above axioms had a very particular form. Speaking in general terms, they were instances of the following axiom schema where os refers to an object sort and φ is a formula with two free variables o_1 and o_2.

$(E)\ \forall(o_1, o_2 : os)\ \varphi(o_1, o_2) \Rightarrow (o_1 = o_2)$

For instance in the case of formula (C) we had $\varphi(t_1, t_2) \equiv (Name(t_1) = Name(t_2) \land LiesIn(t_1) = LiesIn(t_2))$ which is a precondition analogously to the precondition of key constraints in the relational model. But if we take a broader view and allow not only these special key constraints, the formula $\varphi(o_1, o_2)$ can be any formula (with free variables o_1 and o_2) which then serves as an object identification mechanism. One such alternative choice could be for instance $\varphi(t_1, t_2) \equiv (Name(t_1) = Name(t_2) \lor LiesIn(t_1) = LiesIn(t_2))$ which would require that two different towns must have different names and must lie in different countries.

Although such general preconditions offer a great amount of flexibility and look attractive, there are some difficulties which can arise when we employ such formulas for observing the identity of objects. Consider the following schema in Fig. 4 in which each town (apart from having a 'Name') has a direct 'Link' to its nearest neighbour town.

Furthermore assume that different towns must have different names or must be linked to different towns, which can be formulated as follows:

$(F)\ \forall(t_1, t_2 : TOWN)$
$\qquad (t_1 \neq t_2) \Rightarrow (Name(t_1) \neq Name(t_2) \lor Link(t_1) \neq Link(t_2))$

We re-formulate the formal requirement equivalently and obtain the equation $t_1 = t_2$ as the conclusion.

---

[5] Requirements (B) and (C) look like requirements for well-known functional dependencies, however, this requirement (D) and the ones to follow cannot be expressed in this way.

Fig. 4. Schema for towns linked to nearest neighbours

$$(F')\ \forall(t_1, t_2 : TOWN)$$
$$(Name(t_1) = Name(t_2) \wedge Link(t_1) = Link(t_2)) \Rightarrow (t_1 = t_2)$$

Although this seems to be some kind of observable inequality there is a problem with this formula. Consider the following state with three different TOWN objects $town_1$, $town_2$ and $town_3$ which have identical 'Name' attribute values and are linked as depicted in Fig. 5.

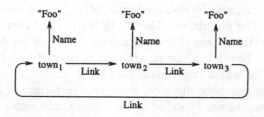

Fig. 5. Database state with cyclic links

The formula (F) accepts the state in Fig. 5 as a valid state but due to the cyclic 'Link' structure there is no possibility to distinguish between, say, the town objects $town_1$ and $town_2$, by taking data observations only. Therefore all towns in the state cannot be observed to be different although the formula is valid.

Identity observing terms and queries: The above obstacle will be removed when one employs not only formulas for identification purposes but data terms which can be looked at and which can really generate object identities. Therefore the general idea for identity observing terms and queries is to have axiom schemas of the following form where τ is a term with a sort built over data sorts and type constructors and with one free variable of object sort os.

$$(G)\ \forall(o_1, o_2 : os)(\tau(o_1) = \tau(o_2)) \Rightarrow (o_1 = o_2)$$

Let us examine the above examples again in the light of this new perspective. We specify the observation terms τ which have to be substituted in the above axiom schema in order to yield the desired constraints.

(B): The formula (B) can be achieved if we actualize the above axiom schema with the term $\tau(c) \equiv Name(c)$ which has the free variable $(c : COUNTRY)$ and is of sort *string*. Of course, we obtain a formula equivalent to formula (B') from above.

(*C*): Requirement (*C*) from above is gained by substituting the term $\tau(t) \equiv tuple(Name(t), Name(LiesIn(t)))$ with free variable (*t* : *TOWN*). The term has the sort $tuple(string, string)$. $tuple$ is assumed to be a type constructor which takes a collection of single values and returns the tuple value which consists of the given values.[6]

(*D*): Constraint (*D*) may be seen as an instantiation of the above schema with the following observation term:

$$(H)\ \tau(t) \equiv tuple(Name(t), (select\ Name(c)$$
$$from\ \ (c : COUNTRY)$$
$$where\ t\ in\ Towns(c)))$$

The term has exactly one free variable (*t* : *TOWN*) and is of sort $tuple(string, bag(string))$. It employs a query term which is evaluated for the free variable (*t* : *TOWN*) as a kind of parameter. The query follows the well-known select-from-where structure proposed in SQL. In our approach, the result of a query is a bag of values retaining duplicates; sets can also be obtained by applying an operator eliminating the duplicates (for details, see [Gog94, HG94]). The 'where' part is a formula which returns true if the parameter town *t* is an element of the set $Towns(c)$. The 'select' terms are only evaluated and returned for those countries for which the 'where' part yields true.

(*F*): The most complex situation was given in formula (*F*) where a cyclic 'Link' structure was specified in the schema, and also a cyclic state structure was given in the counter example state in Fig. 5.

$$(I)\ \tau(t) \equiv tuple(Name(t), Name(Link(t)), Name(Link(Link(t))))$$

This term is again a tuple term and has one free variable: (*t* : *TOWN*). It is of sort $tuple(string, string, string)$ and selects the name of the 'parameter' town and the names of the first and second towns linked to the parameter town. Thus the above state (with three towns named 'Foo') would not be accepted by the constraint generated by the axiom schema if we actualize it by this observation term.

Let now us focus on the most important point of identity observing terms and queries. We assume that each object sort *os* in the database schema is attached to such an observation term τ_{os} of (data) sort s_τ and that this attachment induces the constraint given hereafter.

$$(J)\ (\forall o_1, o_2 : os)(o_1 \neq o_2) \Rightarrow (\tau_{os}(o_1) \neq \tau_{os}(o_2))$$

We assume further that this constraint is enforced during the whole lifetime of the database. This means that two different *os* objects with the same τ_{os} value of sort s_τ cannot exist. This value can be computed for an *os* object by applying the term τ_{os} to the object and the other way round: An *os* object can be computed from an s_τ value. Or, to say it in other words, we have described the concept of a partial function $f_{\tau_{os}} : s_\tau \to os$ which will be

---

[6] If want we to very precise we have to distinguish syntactically between the type constructor *tuple* (for example to construct the sort $tuple(string, int)$) and an operation mk_{tuple} constructing an appropriate value (for example $mk_{tuple} : string \times int \to tuple(string, int)$). However, we use the notation *tuple* in both positions.

bijective in all database states (on the part where it yields defined values) and can therefore serve for object identification purposes. The function will be given an s_τ value as a parameter. It will respond by either returning a uniquely determined object with that s_τ value, or it will say that there is no object in the current database state with the respective property. Because of the possibility of this negative answer, the function will be partial.

In the total, we achieve with observation terms an approach which seems to be more general than and thus can be refined to the well-known "deep equality".[7]

5   Advantages of the Observation Term Approach

Our observation term approach to object identification embodies a number of features that distinguishes it from other ways to handle the problem and offers a greater amount of flexibility. We shortly explain how to define the approach formally, how to retrieve objects, how to treat multiple observation terms, how to apply the approach to other data models, how to dynamically use observation terms, and how to handle updates on the attributes involved in observation terms.

Formal definition: Our approach is defined on a formal mathematical basis. Thus, comprehension and implementation is supported without any ambiguities. Due to space limitations we have to refer to [Gog94, HG94] for a more elaborate treatment.

Retrieving abstract objects by concrete values: Within the observation term approach it is possible to retrieve abstract objects, which are internally identified by surrogates, with the help of concrete data values. After retrieving an object in this way one can access other properties which are different from the identifying ones.

Multiple observation terms: It is also possible to have more than one observation term for a single object sort. Consider the case that we have for COUNTRY objects in addition to a 'Name' observation (i.e., 'Name' is a key for COUNTRY) also an attribute for the country's geometry. In order to keep things simple we assume this geometry is given by the country's border represented by a polygon: 'Geo : COUNTRY $\rightarrow$ polygon'. Now clearly two different countries will have different geometries, i.e., different polygons, and therefore the attribute 'Geo' can serve as a second observation structure for a COUNTRY object ($c : COUNTRY$): $\tau(c) \equiv Geo(c)$. Such multiple observation terms and their implementation by some sort of index are helpful from the conceptual point of view, because different identification mechanisms for one object sort are supported. Such multiple observation terms

---

[7] "Deep equality" again refines to "shallow equality" and the "identity predicate" as pointed out in [KC86].

are also useful from the implementation point of view in terms of query optimization, because these 'query' indexes can be employed for faster query evaluation and constraint enforcement.

Observation terms for other data models: Clearly, the applicatibility of the observation term approach is not restricted to the object-oriented world. The underlying idea originated from keys in the relational model, and therefore, this approach is applicable to the relational model per se.

Dynamic observation terms: Yet another distinguishing feature of the observation term approach is that it can be employed dynamically during the lifetime of a database. It is not necessary to specify all observation terms at the time when the database schema is fixed. Initially, only one such term should be given. Afterwards, other such observations may be added and dropped as it is needed. This is analogously to the relational model where indexes on different attributes for a relation may be created and deleted dynamically.

Updates on observation contributing attributes: The observation term approach generalizes key attributes of the relational model, and there has been a debate in the database field whether to allow for updates on key attributes or not. Formally, we do not have key attributes but we can coin the notion of an *observation contributing attribute* for an attribute which is needed for calculating the τ_{os} value for an object o of sort os. And then we can ask the same question as in the relational model, namely, whether to allow updates on these attributes or not. Our answer to this is very simple: Yes, we allow for such updates as long as the integrity of the database is respected.

6 Conclusion

We have studied object identification in the context of Entity-Relationship and Object-Oriented data models. The new idea of our proposal, the so-called observation term approach, was to associate with each object type a query in order to observe an identifying property of objects. This proposal seems to be more general than the well-known "deep equality" approach [KC86]. We have argued that the advantages of our approach are its formal definition, the employment of multiple observation terms, dynamic observation terms, and updates on observation contributing attributes.

We have not taken into account implementation issues, for example index and clustering techniques which could be of use here. Such techniques are advantageous in terms of query optimization, because 'query' indexes induced by observation terms can be employed for faster query evaluation and constraint enforcement.

References

[ABD+90] M. Atkinson, F. Bancilhon, D. DeWitt, K. Dittrich, D. Maier, and
S. Zdonik. The Object-Oriented Database System Manifesto. In W. Kim,
J.-M. Nicolas, and S. Nishio, editors, *Proc. Int. Conf. on Deductive
and Object-Oriented Databases (DOOD'89)*, pages 223–240. North-Holland,
Amsterdam, 1990.

[Abi88] S. Abiteboul. Updates, a New Frontier. In M. Gyssens, J. Paredaens, and
D. van Gucht, editors, *Int. Conf. on Data Base Theory (ICDT'88)*, pages
1–18. Springer, Berlin, LNCS 326, 1988.

[ADD+92] A. Auddino, Y. Dennebouy, Y. Dupont, E. Fontana, S. Spaccapietra, and
Z. Tari. SUPER-Visual Interaction with an Object-Based ER Model.
In G. Pernul and A.M. Tjoa, editors, *Proc. 11th Int. Conf. on Entity-
Relationship Approach (ER'92)*, pages 340–356. Springer, Berlin, LNCS 645,
1992.

[AH87] S. Abiteboul and R. Hull. IFO – A Formal Semantic Database Model.
ACM Trans. on Database Systems, 12(4):525–565, 1987.

[AK89] S. Abiteboul and P. Kanellakis. Object Identity as a Query Language Primitive. *ACM SIGMOD Record*, 18(2):159–173, 1989. *Proc. ACM SIGMOD
Conf. on Management of Data (SIGMOD'89)*.

[Bee90] C. Beeri. A Formal Approach to Object-Oriented Databases. *Data &
Knowledge Engineering*, 5(4):353–382, 1990.

[Che76] P.P. Chen. The Entity-Relationship Model – Towards a Unified View of
Data. *ACM Trans. on Database Systems*, 1(1):9–36, 1976.

[Cod79] E.F. Codd. Extending the Database Relational Model to Capture More
Meaning. *ACM Trans. on Database Systems*, 4(4):397–434, 1979.

[Deu91] O. Deux et. al. The O2 System. *Communications of the ACM*, 34(10):34–
48, 1991.

[Dit87] K.R. Dittrich. Object-Oriented Database Systems: A Workshop Report.
In S. Spaccapietra, editor, *Proc. 5th Int. Conf. on Entity-Relationship Approach (ER'86)*, pages 51–66. North Holland, Amsterdam, 1987.

[GH91] M. Gogolla and U. Hohenstein. Towards a Semantic View of an Extended
Entity-Relationship Model. *ACM Trans. on Database Systems*, 16(3):369–
416, 1991.

[Gog94] M. Gogolla. *An Extended Entity-Relationship Model – Fundamentals and
Pragmatics*. Springer, Berlin, LNCS 767, 1994.

[HG94] R. Herzig and M. Gogolla. A SQL-like Query Calculus for Object-Oriented
Database Systems. In E. Bertino and S. Urban, editors, *Proc. Int. Symp.
on Object-Oriented Methodologies and Systems (ISOOMS'94)*, pages 20–39.
Springer, Berlin, LNCS 858, 1994.

[HY90] R. Hull and M. Yoshikawa. ILOG: Declarative Creation and Manipulation
of Object Identifiers. In D. McLeod, R. Sacks-Davis, and H.-J. Schek, editors, *Proc. Int. Conf. Very Large Data Bases (VLDB'90)*, pages 455–468.
Morgan Kaufmann, 1990.

[KC86] S.N. Khoshafian and G.P. Copeland. Object Identity. *ACM SIGPLAN
Notices*, 21(11):406–416, 1986. *Proc. ACM Int. Conf. on Object Oriented
Programming Systems, Languages and Applications (OOPSLA'86)*.

[KLS92] M. Kramer, G. Lausen, and G. Saake. Updates in a Rule-Based Language
for Objects. In L.-Y. Yuan, editor, *Proc. 18th Int. Conf. on Very Large
Databases (VLDB'92)*, pages 251–262. Morgan Kaufmann, 1992.

[KS88]   G. Kappel and M. Schrefl. A Behaviour Integrated Entity-Relationship Approach for the Design of Object-Oriented Databases. In C. Batini, editor, *Proc. 7th Int. Conf. on Entity-Relationship Approach (ER'88)*, pages 175–192. ER Institute, Pittsburgh (CA), Participants' Proceedings, 1988.

[KV84]   G.M. Kuper and M.Y. Vardi. A New Approach to Database Logic. In *Proc. 3rd ACM Symp. Principles of Database Systems (PODS'84)*, pages 86–96. ACM, New York, 1984.

[LBSL90]   K.J. Lieberherr, P. Bergstein, and I. Silva-Lepe. Abstraction of Object-Oriented Data Models. In H. Kangassalo, editor, *Proc. 9th Int. Conf. on Entity-Relationship Approach (ER'90)*, pages 81–94. ER Institute, Pittsburgh (CA), Participants' Proceedings, 1990.

[LSPR93]   E.-P. Lim, J. Srivastava, S. Prabhakar, and J. Richardson. Entity Identification in Database Integration. In *Proc. 9th Int. Conf. Data Engineering (ICDE'93)*, pages 294–301. IEEE, 1993.

[LT94]   T.W. Ling and P.K. Teo. A Normal Form Object-Oriented Entity Relationship Diagram. In P. Loucopoulos, editor, *Proc. Int. Conf. on Entity-Relationship Approach (ER'94)*, pages 241–258. Springer, Berlin, LNCS 881, 1994.

[Mas90]   Y. Masunaga. Object Identity, Equality and Relational Concept. In W. Kim, J.-M. Nicolas, and S. Nishio, editors, *Proc. 1st Int. Conf. on Deductive and Object-Oriented Databases (DOOD'89)*, pages 185–202. North-Holland, Amsterdam, 1990.

[NP88]   S.B. Navathe and M.K. Pillalamarri. OOER: Toward Making the E-R Approach Object-Oriented. In C. Batini, editor, *Proc. 7th Int. Conf. on Entity-Relationship Approach (ER'88)*, pages 55–76. ER Institute, Pittsburgh (CA), Participants' Proceedings, 1988.

[Oho90]   A. Ohori. Representing Object Identity in a Pure Functional Language. In S. Abiteboul and P.C. Kanellakis, editors, *Proc. 3rd Int. Conf. on Database Theory (ICDT'90)*, pages 41–55. Springer, Berlin, LNCS 470, 1990.

[PKB94]   M.P. Papazoglou, B.J. Kraemer, and A. Bouguettaya. On the Representation of Objects with Polymorphic Shape and Behaviour. In P. Loucopoulos, editor, *Proc. 13th Int. Conf. on Entity-Relationship Approach (ER'94)*, pages 223–240. Springer, Berlin, LNCS 881, 1994.

[RS91]   E. Rose and A. Segev. TOODM - A Temporal Object-Oriented Data Model with Temporal Constraints. In T.J. Teorey, editor, *Proc. 10th Int. Conf. on Entity-Relationship Approach (ER'91)*, pages 205–230. ER Institute, Pittsburgh (CA), Participants' Proceedings, 1991.

[SSW92]   K.-D. Schewe, J.W. Schmidt, and I. Wetzel. Identification, Genericity and Consistency in Object-Oriented Databases. In J. Biskup and R. Hull, editors, *Proc. 4th Int. Conf. on Database Theory (ICDT'92)*, pages 341–356. Springer, Berlin, LNCS 646, 1992.

[VD91]   S.L. Vandenberg and D.J. DeWitt. Algebraic Support for Complex Objects with Arrays, Identity, and Inheritance. *SIGMOD Record*, 20(2):158–167, 1991. *Proc. ACM SIGMOD Conf. on Management of Data (SIGMOD'91)*.

[WJ91]   R. Wieringa and W. De Jonge. The Identification of Objects and Roles – Object Identifiers Revisited. Technical Report IR-267, Faculty of Mathematics and Computer Science, Vrije Universiteit Amsterdam, 1991.

Versatile Querying Facilities for a Dynamic Object Clustering Model

Chi-Wai FUNG

Qing LI

Department of Computing Studies
Vocational Training Council
Tuen Mun Technical Institute
Tsing Wun Road, Hong Kong

Department of Computer Science
University of Science and Technology
Clear Water Bay
Kowloon, Hong Kong

E-mail: {cwfung, qing}@cs.ust.hk

Abstract. The conceptual clustering model (CCM) that we have defined in [19] is an extension to current object-oriented models; it facilitates the modeling of dynamic, evolving, and/or ad hoc object clusters through a well-devised clustering mechanism that incorporates "roles". To support general definition and access of clusters (and roles), associated query language facilities have been defined and are presented in detail in this paper. An experimental prototype of the CCM and its associated query language are being implemented on top of a persistent object storage manager.

1 Introduction

Conventional OODB systems take a static, classification-based approach (through classes) to model and structure data objects; hence, objects within the same class are restricted to be "*homogeneous*" (i.e., they share the same structural and behavioral definitions). While such an approach has the advantage of being efficient, it falls short of supporting those applications involving objects and inter-object relationships that are by nature tentative, irregular, ill-structured, evolving, or simply unpredictable. In particular, the abilities to model and manipulate dynamically both homogeneous and non-homogeneous (viz., "heterogeneous") objects collectively can be extremely useful and important for many types of applications. As exemplified by GIS and DSS applications [18,19], new (composite) objects may arise dynamically as "clusters" of existing ones in some ad hoc fashion. In the processes of interest, the objects evolve and undertake numerous periodic or ephemeral roles within the clusters. Unfortunately, current object-oriented technologies, particularly object-oriented database management systems (OODBMSs), do not provide adequate facilities to model and support such *application dynamics*: while it is in theory possible to introduce new classes to accommodate such new types of objects, it is infeasible as this may result in many *ad hoc* classes with a small number of objects, and may frequently incur expensive structural evolution changes as these objects are highly dynamic and evolving. Extensions to OODBMS models are therefore needed in order to accommodate such advanced applications effectively.

In [19], we have defined such a basic conceptual clustering model (CCM) with a taxonomy of 12 kinds of clusters (see Table 1 in Section 2); necessary cluster operators at the base level which facilitate cluster creation, deletion, modification, and retrieval have also been defined, and a "proof-of-concept" prototype of CCM was developed on top of a persistent object storage manager [20]. While these primitive CCM facilities provide basic means for accommodating the application dynamics imposed on the OODBMS, they are not intended nor suitable for end-users to directly use. To support general definitions and manipulations of clusters and their associated features (such as roles), higher-level language (preferably declarative) facilities are desired to be introduced and incorporated into the system. Such high level language facilities are particularly useful and important to those advanced applications requiring advanced yet efficient query capabilities. This paper thus presents such high level (SQL-like) language facilities which can be implemented based upon the primitive ones.

The rest of the paper is organized as follows. In section 2 we review some key aspects of CCM in terms of its basic constructs and associated role facilities; we also examine different kinds of hierarchies in an OODB extended with clusters. In section 3 we detail the query language facilities that we have been developing; in doing so, we provide necessary examples and show how these introduced language facilities can be used for various purposes. These query language facilities are currently being incorporated into a new endeavor of an experimental prototyping system. In section 4 we examine some of the related work in extended object modeling and object query languages. Finally, conclusions and further research directions are given in section 5.

2 Basic Features of the Conceptual Clustering Model

2.1 Motivations and Key Concepts

The conceptual cluster model as defined in [19] is one facilitating dynamic creation, deletion and manipulation of ad hoc cluster objects, which complements existing object class mechanism for accommodating generic application dynamics. In this model, existing objects can be dynamically grouped to form homogeneous or heterogeneous collections, namely cluster objects. Depending on the following three perspectives: *source of derivation, source of certainty* and *behavior interaction*, a taxonomy of 12 kinds of clusters has been established. Table 1 shows the complete taxonomy of clusters with their derivations. (The detailed specification of the taxonomy can be found from [19], and is beyond the scope of this paper.) Such a CCM model complements the classification-based approach of current OODBMS models in capturing more dynamic semantics, and it allows object individuality to be adequately captured and accommodated (rather than to be suppressed as in the class case).

Table 1. A Taxonomy of Clusters and Their Derivations

Source of Derivation	Infixed	Adaptive	Source of Certainty	Obscure		Explicit	
Deep	DIC	DAC	⟶	ODIC*	ODAC*	EDIC*	EDAC*
Shallow	SIC	SAC	⟶	OSIC	OSAC	ESIC	ESAC
Remarks: (1) Deep clusters are always Loosely-coupled; (2) Asterisked combinations constitutes the taxonomy			Behavior Interaction	⇓	⇓	⇓	⇓
			Loosely-coupled	LOSIC*	LOSAC*	LESIC*	LESAC*
			Tightly-coupled	TOSIC*	TOSAC*	TESIC*	TESAC*

To a great extent, cluster can be regarded as enriched "virtual classes" parallel and/or complementary to classes in modeling additional application semantics. Like a class, a cluster also has a set of attributes and methods which defines the properties and behaviors. However, unlike a class, it does not create or delete any object of any existing class in the database. Instead, it only include-in or exclude-out objects from database classes and assign them to some specific roles (hence these class objects are also called "role players"). Besides, clusters can be created, deleted or modified dynamically, and their role players can be sets of homogeneous or heterogeneous class objects. Thus users can have greater flexibility in grouping different kinds of objects together.

In a nutshell, a cluster differs from a class in the following fundamental aspects [19]: (i) it is an extended aggregate/composite object consisting of a collection of (typically heterogeneous) objects, rather than a warehouse holding a set of uniform objects; (ii) it supports the notion of dynamic roles, and is a dynamic construct useful for transient, tentative, and/or irregular situations, whereas a class is a statically defined construct for stable/regular sets of objects; (iii) it only includes/removes existing objects to itself, and does not create "new" objects (except for new roles and the cluster itself); (iv) it allows individuality of its constituent/member objects to be expressed (partially through the roles), whereas a class emphasizes the commonalities of its objects; (v) it supports behavioral interactions between the cluster and its constituent/member objects (and possibly among the constituents themselves) -- another feature not supported by a class-based system.

2.2 Three Different Types of Constructs and Links

In an OODB model extended with CCM, there are three kinds of constructs, namely, classes, clusters and roles. These in turn introduce three different types of semantic links: *ISA link, RoleOf link*, and *MemberRoleOf link*. As in a conventional object-oriented model, the ISA links are used to form an inheritance hierarchy between two or more modeling constructs of the same type. In general, a sub-type will inherit all the instance variables, methods and/or roles (if applicable) from its super-type. In our model, these types can be class, cluster and role types.

The RoleOf link connects a role type to a class or another role type. A role type contains information about some aspects/behaviors (in the forms of attributes, methods and/or roles) of its role instance. Unlike the ISA link, a "sub" type in the RoleOf link does not automatically inherit any instance variable, role or method from its "super" type. Rather, role hierarchies apply specialization and inheritance at the instance level rather than at the role type level. This is more appropriate when objects change their type dynamically. The main difference with respect to the class hierarchy is that a "sub" type in a role hierarchy does not inherit the definitions of instance variable, role and method from its "super" type, but leaves that to individual role instance. The main purpose of using RoleOf link is to represent evolving behaviors and multi-faceted objects.

The MemberRoleOf links are for modeling clusters' behaviors. In particular, we introduce the MemberRoleOf relationship between a cluster type and a role type. A cluster type can define any number of role types as its components through the MemberRoleOf relationship.

3 OQL/race - Associated Query Language Facilities

In this section, we describe a set of associated query language facilities of our conceptual clustering model (CCM). This set of querying facilities (collectively called Object Query Language with role and cluster extensions (OQL/race)) supports *declarative* definitions and manipulations of objects, roles and clusters.

3.1 An Example Schema of a Real-world Application

Before we start the description of various OQL/race facilities, we introduce an example CCM schema (along with an example occurrence) of a real-world banking application, as a necessary "context" for subsequent discussions. This real-world example is to illustrate the use of inheritance hierarchy through ISA links, class/role hierarchy through RoleOf links and cluster/role hierarchy through MemberRoleOf links; it also demonstrates the use of *intersecting roles* - roles that are shared by clusters and/or classes. Suppose the bank is going to organize a public function -- a seminar about its new telebanking services. As usual, a seminar represented as cluster may have roles of host, speaker, guest and helper (c.f. figure 1). These roles may be played by different classes of objects, and are connected with the classes through RoleOf links. In the bank, assume a manager can usually play the role of host of the seminar, clients are invited as guests of the seminar, and the manager (who is also the host) may give a short talk in the seminar (and so he is also a speaker). The bank may as well invite clients to give a talk about some topics in the seminar, and company employees (e.g. programmers and clerks) may be invited to the seminar as helper to decorate the venue and to do some preparation works (like preparing drinks).

An example occurrence of the real-world situation is also shown in figure 1 where it is recorded that the Telebanking seminar is to be held on 7/7/95 at 2-5 p.m. in the City Hall, the seminar contains one host member role played by a manager called Mark, and it also has two speaker member roles played by the client David and the (same) manager Mark (whose topics of talk are "Trends in Telebanking" and "Recap of Seminar", respectively). Furthermore, the seminar has a guest member role played the same client David (whose seat number is 888), and finally it contains two helper member roles played by a programmer named Henry who helps in decorating the venue and a clerk named Mary who helps in preparing drinks.

Observe in this example that an object can play many different roles, e.g., David as an object of the *Client* class plays the roles of *Speaker* and *Guest* at the same time. (So does the *Manager* Mark who plays the roles of *Host* and *Speaker.*) Also in this example, we see a role can be played by objects from different classes, i.e., heterogeneous class objects, as in the case of *Speaker* and *Helper* roles. The common roles that are shared by different hierarchies are linked by dotted lines as "virtual links". (Note that these virtual links are not part of the database and are not actually stored, they are shown merely for highlighting the case in the figure.)

3.2 Object Definition and Manipulation Facilities

OQL/race is an object-oriented extension of SQL coupled with advanced cluster and role facilities. First, we introduce some *conventions*: (1) all capital letters are reserved word in OQL, e.g., CREATE, SELECT (2) strings starting with capital letter, then lower case letters or "_" denote class/cluster/role type names, e.g., Person, Office_worker (3) all lower case letters denote instance variable names (e.g. dob) or method name (e.g. check_venue) (4) strings starting with "_", followed by either capital or lower case letters denote class/cluster/role instance identifiers, e.g., _ClientDavid. (This is similar to the OID in conventional object-oriented systems.) (5) all OQL statements end with a ";".

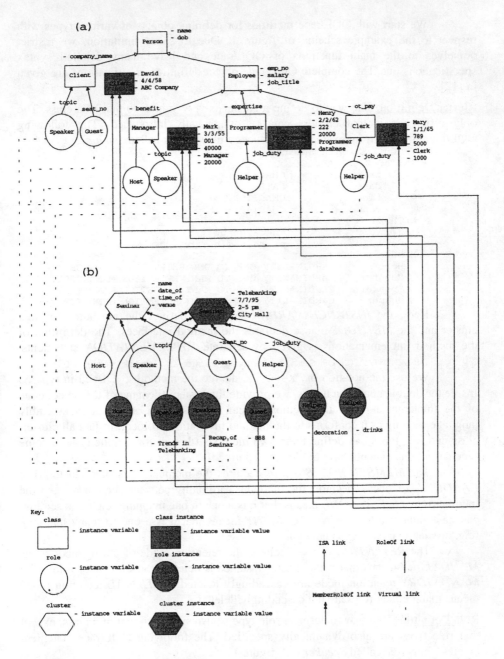

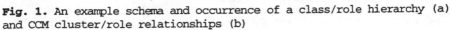

Fig. 1. An example schema and occurrence of a class/role hierarchy (a) and CCM cluster/role relationships (b)

We start with OQL/race facilities for defining objects of various types with respect to the example schema of figure 1. Due to space limitation, we restrict ourselves to the main functions of OQL/race and leave many detailed syntax specifications out. The complete OQL/race object definition specifications are given in [12].

Cluster Definition: The way to define a cluster is very similar to that of a class. The only difference is that clusters can be dynamically introduced. The following OQL/race statement, for example, introduces a new cluster called *Seminar*.

```
INTRODUCE CLUSTER Seminar (
    INSTANCE VARIABLES (
        name                CHAR(40),
        date_of             DATE,
        time_of             CHAR(10),
        venue               CHAR(40))
    METHODS (
        VOID                check_venue(),
        VOID                print_seminar_programme())
    MEMBER ROLES (
    Host      CARDINALITY ONE_TO_ONE RETENTION MANDATORY,
    Guest     CARDINALITY ONE_TO_MANY RETENTION MANDATORY,
    Speaker   CARDINALITY ONE_TO_MANY RETENTION MANDATORY,
    Helper    CARDINALITY ONE_TO_MANY RETENTION MANDATORY));
```

Here, the *INSTANCE VARIABLES* clause defines the attributes for that cluster and the *METHODS* clause declares the method interfaces. The definition of the method implementations is given by separate *IMPLEMENTATION* statements, e.g., `IMPLEMENTATION OF Seminar->check_venue IS "check_venue.obj";`

We use the notation of "X->Y" to denote the method Y defined in type X. Inside the double quotation marks, we provide the system filename of the object code of the implementation of the method. It can be in C++, C or even in assembly language, as long as it conforms to the method invocation protocol. In fact all cluster, class and role types can define their own methods (though for simplicity here some type definitions may not have any method defined).

The *MEMBER ROLES* clause declares the member roles of a cluster. The *CARDINALITY* clause declares the mapping cardinality between the cluster and the member role. *ONE_TO_ONE* means that it is a one to one mapping (e.g., one seminar can have only one host). *ONE_TO_MANY* means that it is a one to many mapping (e.g. one seminar can have many guests).

The *RETENTION* clause declares the retention mode of the member roles. *MANDATORY* means that if the cluster instance is deleted, those member roles with *MANDATORY* retention mode are cascadingly deleted. *OPTIONAL* retention mode means that member roles are not cascadingly deleted.

Role Definition: The way to define a role type is also similar to that of a class, except that role types are also dynamically specified. The following OQL/race statement creates a new role called *Speaker* (c.f. figure 1).

```
CREATE ROLE Speaker
        ROLE OF Client OR Manager
        MEMBER ROLE OF Seminar (
            INSTANCE VARIABLES (
                topic   CHAR(40)));
```

Note that because a role is evolving and/or temporary in nature, the class hierarchy designer may not know beforehand what role an object from the class will play, so the role definition is not encapsulated inside the class definition (unlike the case in cluster definition). In the above definition, the *ROLE OF* clause forms an initial simple role hierarchy between a class type and the role type, the *MEMBER ROLE OF* clause also forms an initial simple role hierarchy between a cluster type and the role type. Furthermore, the combined usage of both *ROLE OF* and *MEMBER ROLE OF* clauses indicates that the role is an intersecting role.

While roles can be linked/attached to both classes and clusters, there are some subtle differences. In particular, in the case of a class, the *CARDINALITY* for role can be regarded as always *ONE_TO_MANY* and the *RETENTION* for roles is always *MANDATORY*. This is because the role instances are always dependent upon the corresponding class instances' existence. On the contrary, in the case of clusters the *RETENTION* mode for member roles can be *OPTIONAL* or *MANDATORY*, and it is up to the designer when considering the real-world situation. Another difference lies in the fact that a cluster definition must have the *MEMBER ROLES* clause (but not for a class). This is because clusters are conceptually "derived" objects composed of member roles, whereas classes are not.

3.3 Versatile Query Facilities
3.3.1 Property Access and Type Variable

In OQL/race , "X.Y" means to access the value of instance variable Y: it returns the set of values of the instance variable Y defined in type X. Here, X can be of any class/cluster/role type. For example, "Client.company_name" returns the set of values of the instance variable *company_name* of all *Client* objects. X can also be an object identifier. For example, "_ClientDavid.company_name" returns the value of the instance variable *company_name* of the object identified by the identifier *_ClientDavid*. Similarly X can be a cluster/role type or one of their instance identifiers.

Type variable

The type variable is similar to the tuple variable in relational databases. A type variable always starts with a "~" then followed by capital letters (e.g. "~X"). The type variable stands for an unknown class/cluster/role type name ("~X" is also called a wild card, or "don't care" type name). Depending on the context, the database system may or may not able to figure out the unknown class/cluster/role type name. In the latter (negative) case, "~X" effects an empty type.

3.3.2 Traversing between Different Kinds of Constructs

OQL/race offers several "link" operators for accessing the classes, clusters, and/or roles in some "associated" manner. These are useful when traversing from one class/cluster/role type to another class/cluster/role type becomes necessary or significant. There are two groups of such link operators, as described below.

<1> RoleOf link

• "X:Y" returns the set of role instances (of role type Y) played by X. X can be a class, a role type or one of the instance identifiers. For example, "Client:Guest" returns the set of *Guest* role instances played by all *Client* objects. Note that X can also be a wild card (e.g., denoted by ~X), in which case it can be any class or role type, but not an instance. Consider an example: "Find the seat number of guest David":

```
SELECT seat_no
FROM ~X:Guest
WHERE ~X.name = "David";
```

Here, we use the "`:`" operator to access the role *Guest* of some class/role type, though we don't know exactly who David is.

• Inversely, "`Y!X`" returns the set of instances (of type X) that play the role Y. Here, X can be a class, a role type, or simply a wild card. For example, "`Guest!Client`" returns the set of *Client* objects that play the role *Guest*. In case X is a wild card (e.g., ~X), "`Y!~X`" will return any class or role type in which the role Y is involved.

<2> MemberRoleOf link

• "`X$Y`" returns the set of member role instances (of role type Y) that are contained in the cluster X. Here, X must be of a cluster type, or a wild card that can match any cluster type. For example, "`Seminar$Speaker`" returns the set of *Speaker* role instances contained in every *Seminar* cluster instance. Consider an example: "Get all seat numbers of all guests in the Telebanking seminar":

```
SELECT seat_no
FROM Seminar$Guest
WHERE Seminar.name = "Telebanking";
```

Here, we use the "`$`" to access the member role *Guest* of the cluster type *Seminar*. If in the above example we replace *Seminar* by ~X, then the query becomes of listing all seat numbers of all guests in any cluster that contains the role *Guest*, and has name called "Telebanking".

• Inversely, "`Y#X`" returns the set of cluster instances (of type X) that contain the member role Y. Again, X needs to be a cluster type, or a wild card that can match any cluster type. For example, "`Speaker#Seminar`" returns the set of *Seminar* cluster instances that contain the member role *Speaker*, whereas "`Helper#~X`" will return any type of cluster instances that contain the member role *Helper*.

3.3.3 Queries with Complex Role Chains

When the above different kinds of link operators are used jointly in a query, we are essentially traversing a "complex role hierarchy" through *complex role chains*. Consider the following example: "List all ot_pay of all clerk helpers in the Telebanking seminar":

```
SELECT ot_pay
FROM Seminar$Helper!Clerk
WHERE Seminar.name = "Telebanking";
```

Here, we use the "`Seminar$Helper!Clerk`" to obtain the set of all *Clerk* objects that play the role of *Helper* in the *Seminar* cluster. Such kinds of "link" operator combinations are called *complex role chains*, which are useful for traversing the complex role hierarchy. In this example we are traversing from cluster type (*Seminar*) to a class type (*Clerk*) via a role type (*Helper*); the *Helper* role type is used as an intersecting role.

Complex role chains can also involve "wild card" type variables, which are useful when we don't know or don't care what types the objects of interest may be of. Consider the following example: "List the names of any attendants in the Telebanking seminar" (i.e., any person involved in the Telebanking seminar, irrespective of their role or class):

```
SELECT ~Y.name
FROM Seminar$~X!~Y
WHERE Seminar.name = "Telebanking";
```

In this example, the "~X" in "Seminar$~X!~Y" refers to any member role type contained in the *Seminar* cluster. With respect to figure 1, "~X" can be any member role type contained in the Telebanking seminar cluster instance, i.e., *Host*, *Speaker*, *Guest* and *Helper*. The "~Y" similarly can be any class type that has some roles in the *Seminar* cluster. With respect to figure 1, "~Y" can be any class type that is related with the *Seminar* cluster instance (i.e., *Client*, *Manager*, *Programmer* or *Clerk*) via some intersecting roles.

3.4 Meta-level Querying Facilities

Besides the various querying facilities at object instance level, OQL/race also supports the capabilities to query CCM data at meta-level. In general, the schema of a CCM database consists of a collection of class, cluster and role type definitions. A system catalog is maintained to store the information about these definitions. Some invariant information about each type definition includes: (1) TYPE_NAME -- it stores the name of that type (2) CATEGORY -- it represents the category of that type, possible values: CLASS, CLUSTER or ROLE (3) SET_OF_INSTANCE_VARIABLES -- it is a collection of all instance variables defined in that type, the definition is consisted of pairs of variable name and variable type (4) SET_OF_METHODS -- it is a collection of all methods defined in that type, the definition is consisted of pairs of method name, parameter list and return type.

Depending on the CATEGORY value, the type definition may further have other components such as: SET_OF_SUPER_CLASSES, SET_OF_SUB_CLASSES, SET_OF_SUPER_CLUSTERS, SET_OF_SUB_CLUSTERS, SET_OF_ROLES, SET_OF_SUPER_ROLES, SET_OF_SUB_ROLES, SET_OF_MEMBER_ROLES, SET_OF_PLAYER_CLASSES, SET_OF_PLAYER_ROLES and SET_OF_OWNER_CLUSTERS. All such "meta-data" information is maintained in the catalog, which allows various kinds of meta-level queries to be accommodated with the help of a meta-level operator, namely the "^" operator which is used specifically for accessing the meta-data as illustrated below.

(1) get all roles played by an object.

E.g.: Retrieve all role type names played by manager Mark.

```
SELECT TYPE_NAME
FROM Manager^SET_OF_ROLES
WHERE Manager.name = "Mark";
```

In this query, the meta-level operator "^" in "Manager^SET_OF_ROLES" accesses the meta-data defined in the class *Manager*, namely the SET_OF_ROLES, which causes the set of all roles played by the manager Mark to be returned.

(2) get all clusters/classes/roles that a role is involved in.

E.g.: Get all clusters names that the role *Speaker* is involved in.

```
SELECT TYPE_NAME
FROM Speaker^SET_OF_OWNER_CLUSTERS;
```

In this query, the meta-data "Speaker^SET_OF_OWNER_CLUSTERS" is used to access the clusters in which the role Speaker is contained. Similarly, if we use the meta-data "SET_OF_PLAYER_CLASSES" we get the player classes as result.

4 A Discussion of Related Works

To better understand the strength and weakness of our work vis-a-vis others, we examine in this section several existing works that are relevant to our research. The comparison with such related works are grouped into two categories: the first concerns the work on extended object modeling and advanced object-oriented facilities, and in the second category, our focus is on representative object query languages supported by influential object-oriented database systems.

4.1 Related Works on Advanced Object Modeling Facilities

The work on conceptual clustering support described in this paper falls into the general category of devising dynamic capabilities into an object database system. There has been some extensive research in this category on more conventional topics such as schema evolution [8,23,17], object migration [11,10], and object (updatable) views [1,26]. Clearly, our work on conceptual clustering contributes (yet differs from) each of these aspects one way or the other. More closely, there has been an increasing interest in the OODB research community on extending conventional OODB models by incorporating the (same) notion of "roles" into the models directly. The earliest example was the work by Bachman and Daya [6], in which "roles" were defined and used for network data modeling approach. Recently, the concept has been refined and applied to office/semantic modeling [28,24,29], object-oriented analysis [27,18,22], and database (persistent programming) languages [25,3,13]. Of these related works, some (e.g. [27,13]) facilitate "bottom-up" design, prototypical for AI-related database applications, whereas the rest are more suitable for "top-down" design applications. Our approach can be used in both bottom-up and top-down designs, but departs dramatically from all these works by providing one more level of abstraction besides roles, namely clusters which can be regarded, at the application level, as "contexts" through which objects acquire/relinquish roles dynamically.

4.2 Related Works on Object Query Languages

While the objectives of a query language are commonly accepted, in the case of object-oriented database systems a wide range of approaches have been taken in an attempt to achieve those objectives. These can be classified into two approaches: (i) *Extending a programming language with appropriate persistent data structuring facilities* and (ii) *Extending an existing relational database query language*. Examples of the first approach includes OPAL - the query language of the GemStone system [9] (which extends the Smalltalk programming language with a declarative notation for set expressions), and the COP query language of VBASE [4], which is an extended version of the C programming language augmented with object-oriented features. Another example is the O++ [2], an extended C++ database language, as found in the Object Database and Environment (ODE). The mainstream of research has been on the second approach, and most of the work has been in the context of extending the SQL language with "object-oriented" properties. Examples are the various Object-SQL query languages found from, e.g., ORION [16] , Iris [11] and ONTOS [14], and O_2SQL language from O_2 [7]. Our approach also belongs to the second category, but we have further enhanced the query model with role and cluster types support. Other unique features of our work include the introduction of type variables, and the capability of query at meta-level. The latter is usually rather tedious in conventional object-oriented languages and systems, but we have shown how this can be done uniformly through OQL/race facilities in a concise and declarative manner.

5 Summary and Future Research

We have described in this paper a set of versatile object querying facilities (viz, OQL/race) associated with a conceptual clustering model (CCM) as defined in [19]. By offering dynamic and flexible clustering capabilities, CCM extends the conventional OODB models and systems by facilitating the modeling and representation of tentative, evolving, and/or ad hoc object collections (called clusters) and their relationships that may arise dynamically in many data-intensive applications. To support general definition and access of clusters (and their associated roles), corresponding high-level querying facilities have been defined and presented in detail. These querying facilities are currently being incorporated into a successor prototype system of CCM that we have built, which utilizes EOS [5] - a persistent object storage manager from AT&T Bell Lab.

Analysis, testing, and evaluation of the research described in this paper is currently under study. On the query language side, we are currently working on the issues of formalization of the object query model that supports role clusters, and the applicability of utilizing a graphical user interface (GUI) to fully support the various querying facilities and capabilities. On refining the model and prototype of CCM side, we are investigating the application of the model and the system to several real life applications, including computer supported cooperative work, decision support systems and multimedia database applications. For instance, we are in the stage of applying the newly developed CCM prototype to a video information management system [15] in order to support a wide range of video manipulation activities including semantic indexing, video editing, and content-based retrieval [21]. The query facilities described in this paper shall, in particular, provide an advantageous and immediate support for facilitating semantic-based video retrieval. It is conceivable that such application exercises will bring us with further insight to the requirements and thus possible refinement to the CCM model and prototype.

References

1. S. Abiteboul and A. Bonner, "Objects and views", in Proceedings of the ACM SIGMOD International Conference on Management of Data, pages 238--247. ACM SIGMOD, 1991.
2. R. Agrawal and N. H. Gehani, "ODE (Object Database and Environment): The Language and the Data Model", in Object-Oriented Databases with Applications to CASE, Network, and VLSI CAD, (edited by R. Gupta and E. Horowitz), Prentice-Hall, 1991, pages 365--386.
3. A. Albano, R. Bergamini, G. Ghelli and R. Orsini, "An Object Data Model with Roles", in Proceedings of the 19th International Conference on Very Large Data Bases, pages 39--51. Dublin, Ireland, 1993.
4. T. Andrews, "Programming with VBASE", in Object-Oriented Databases with Applications to CASE, Network, and VLSI CAD, (edited by R. Gupta and E. Horowitz), Prentice-Hall, 1991, pages 130--177.
5. AT&T Bell Lab, "EOS User's Guide (Release 2.1)", Murray Hill, New Jersey 07974, 1994.
6. C. W. Bachman and M. Daya, "The role concept in data models", in Proc. Intl. Conf. on Very Large Data Bases, pages 464--476, 1977.
7. F. Bancilhon and D. Maier, "Introduction to Languages, in Building an Object-oriented Database System", in The Story of O_2 , edited by F. Bancilhon, C. Delobel and P. Kanellabis, Morgan Kaufmann Publishers, 1992, pages 185--186.
8. J. Banerjee, W. Kim, H-J. Kim, and H. Korth, "Semantics and implementation of schema evolution in object-oriented databases", in Proceedings of the ACM SIGMOD International Conference on Management of Data, pages 311--322. ACM SIGMOD, May 1987.
9. R. Bretl et al., "The GemStone Data Management System", in Object-oriented Concepts, Databases, and Applications, W. Kim and F.H. Lochovsky (editors) ACM Press, 1989.

10. G. Dong and Q. Li, "Object Migrations in Object-Oriented Databases", Proc. of the 4th International Workshop on Foundations of Models and Languages for Data and Objects, Volkse, Germany, pages 81--92, October 1992.

11. D. H. Fishman et al. "Iris: An object-oriented database management system", ACM Transactions on Office Information Systems, 5(1), pages 48--69, 1987.

12. C.W. Fung, "OQL/race : An Object Query Language with Role And Cluster Extensions", M.Sc. Project Report, Department of Computer Science, Hong Kong University of Science and Technology, June, 1995.

13. G. Gottlob, M. Schrefl, and B. Rock, "Extending Object-Oriented Systems with Roles", ACM Trans. on Information Systems, to appear.

14. C. Harris and J. Duhl, "Object-SQL", in Object-Oriented Databases with Applications to CASE, Network, and VLSI CAD, (edited by R. Gupta and E. Horowitz), Prentice-Hall, 1991, pages 199--215.

15. L.S. Huang, C.M. Lee, Q. Li and W. Xiong. "Developing a Video Database Management System with Extended Object-Oriented Techniques", Technical Report HKUST-CS95-11, Dept of Computer Science, Hong Kong Univ. of Science & Technology, 1995.

16. W. Kim, Introduction to Object-oriented Databases, MIT Press, 1990, pages 55--89.

17. Q. Li and D. McLeod, "Conceptual Database Evolution through Learning", in Object-Oriented Databases with Applications to CASE, Network, and VLSI CAD, (edited by R. Gupta and E. Horowitz), Prentice-Hall, 1991.

18. Q. Li, M. Papazoglou, and J.L. Smith, "Dynamic object models with spatial application", In Proceedings of the 15th Int'l Computer Software and Applications Conference. IEEE Computer Society, Tokyo, Japan, September 1991.

19. Q. Li and J.L. Smith, "A conceptual model for dynamic clustering in object databases", in Proceedings of the International Conference on Very Large Data Bases, pages 457--468. Vancouver, Canada, 1992.

20. Q. Li and M.S. Yuen, "Developing a dynamic mechanism for conceptual clustering in an object database system", Technical Report, HKUST-CS93-15, Department of Computer Science, Hong Kong University of Science and Technology, December, 1993.

21. Q. Li and C.M. Lee. "Dynamic Object Clustering for Video Database Manipulations", Proc. of IFIP 2.6 Third Working Conf. on Visual Database Systems (VDB-3), Lausanne, Switzerland, pages 125-137, 1995.

22. M.P. Papazoglou, "Roles: A Methodology for Representing Multi-faceted Objects", in Proc. of the Int'l Conf. on Database and Expert Systems Applications, pages 7--12, 1991.

23. D.J. Penney and J. Stein, "Class modification in the GemStone object-oriented DBMS", in Proceedings of the Conference on Object-Oriented Programming Systems, Languages, and Applications, pages 111--117, 1987.

24. B. Pernici, "Objects with roles", in Proc. of ACM Conferences on Office Information Systems, pages 205--215. ACM, 1990.

25. J. Richardson and P. Schwartz, "Aspects: Extending objects to support multiple, independent roles", in Proceedings of the ACM SIGMOD International Conference on Management of Data, pages 298--307. ACM SIGMOD, May 1991.

26. M.H. Scholl, C. Laasch, and M. Tresch, "Updatable views in object-oriented databases", in Proceedings of the 2nd Int'l Conference on Deductive and Object-Oriented Databases. Munich, Germany, Dec. 1991.

27. E. Sciore, "Object specialization", ACM Transactions on Information Systems, 7(2):103--122, April 1989.

28. D. Tsichritzis and S. J. Gibbs, "Etiquette specification in message systems", in Office Automation, D. Tsichritzis (ed.), Springer-Verlag, 1985.

29. R. Wieringa and W. de Jong, "The identification of objects and roles", Faculty of Mathematics and Computer Science, Vrije Universiteit (working manuscript), 1992

Reverse engineering of relational database applications

Mark W.W. Vermeer and Peter M.G. Apers

Department of Computer Science
University of Twente
Enschede, The Netherlands
{*vermeer, apers*}*@cs.utwente.nl*

Abstract. This paper presents techniques for reverse engineering of relational database applications. The target of such an effort is the definition of a fully equipped object-oriented view of the relational database, including methods and constraints. Such views can be seen as a full specification of the database semantics, aiding for example in the identification of semantic heterogeneity among interoperable databases.

The general problem of translating from an imperative programming language environment to a declarative context such as provided by our target OODML is very hard. However, we show that the specific features of database application software allow for the development of a framework geared towards the particular problems encountered in this context.

1 Introduction

With the success of object-orientation in complex application domains, an interest in reverse engineering of legacy relational databases into object-oriented specifications has been risen. Such a specification can be seen as defining a *view* of the relational database in terms of an object-oriented data model. The derivation of such a view has received considerable attention in literature. However, current work (e.g. [2,3,7]) is concerned with the structural side of such views only, i.e. the translation of a relational schema into a corresponding object structure. While such views are adequate as an interface for data interchange, they neglect the additional possibility of the object-oriented model to specify *behaviour* as well, thus obtaining a high-level specification of both the relational database and its application software.

In [10] we proposed to equip object-oriented views of relational databases with methods and constraints extracted from application programs on these databases, thus making semantics embedded in these applications explicitly available at the view level. As a first step in achieving this, we presented an algorithm for translating SQL-statements on a relational schema to object methods on the corresponding object-oriented schema. To fully satisfy the demands defined above, however, we need to address the issue of reverse engineering general database application code. This is the subject of the present paper.

Views thus obtained may serve various purposes. They may serve as a gradual migration mechanism to an OODBMS, storing new data in the object database, but obtaining old values from the legacy database; they may ease maintenance of the legacy database; they may encourage re-use of code by developing new applications on top of this view; and they may serve as a means of identifying *semantic heterogeneity* among legacy databases for which interoperability mechanisms are developed. Semantic heterogeneity arises when data stemming from different modelling environments should be brought into a uniform semantical context. It is then often hard to determine whether data from different sources has a comparable meaning. In the words of [5], 'The extraction of semantics from application programs is central to the practical identification and resolution of semantic heterogeneity. Much of the meaning of data in existing data-intensive systems is embedded in code; a prerequisite to solving semantic differences is specifying them in a manner conducive to resolution.' (....) There is a need for 'approaches that capture the semantics and integrity constraints currently embedded within applications that may also need to be integrated for access by other applications.' [5]

Obtaining declarative specifications from imperative programming language constructs is a very hard problem. For general-purpose application code, this problem may be next to unsolvable in an automatic way. This is probably the reason why work on database application program analysis has been very scarce, and the semantic information extracted by approaches like the one of [9] is rather limited. In this paper, we present techniques for attacking the problem anyway, in which we exploit the particular characteristics of relational database application software. Due to space limitations, our discussion is brief. For details, the reader is referred to [11]. Although we will show that there exist sufficient application features that can be dealt with generically to justify the formulation of a translation framework, the general reverse engineering problem remains very hard and can be dealt with only semi-automatically. As we are dealing with a relatively unexplored problem, we use a case-based approach to illustrate the problem itself and the possibilities offered by our techniques.

The remainder of this paper is organised as follows. In Section 2, we review earlier work exploited in our approach. In Section 3, we discuss techniques for deriving object methods from relational application code. Section 4 demonstrates how such methods can be reorganised into actual operations and constraints embedded in the original operation code. Section 5 presents our conclusions.

2 Cornerstones

2.1 The TM language

The target model of our reverse engineering effort should be a specification language with a rich and formal semantics. Such a language will enable us to both model and reason about the semantics of database software. As will be shown in Section 5, these features will for example enable us to infer class constraints from class methods obtained through reverse engineering. The TM [1,

6] object-oriented database specification language meets these requirements. It has a formal semantics based on set-theory. TM allows the specification of data structures in terms of Classes and Sorts (the latter being abstract data types without object identity). Both methods and constraints may be defined on these data structures, using a computationally complete, functional data manipulation language, which is also capable of expressing set-oriented queries in a declarative way. This DML will be used as the target language of our translation. A large and well-defined subset of TM-specifications is executable; the mapping to an OO-PL is performed at the implementation stage. However, our approach is sufficiently general to be geared towards any language with comparable expressiveness.

2.2 Schema translation

Below we present the schema for the example relational database used throughout this paper. It describes a concession database registering the ownership of concessions to exploit certain pieces of, say, oil-containing surfaces. The location of a concession is determined by a set of boundary points. Additional information is provided on keys and inclusion dependencies for attribute values.

```
CONC-HOLDER(chno, name, address)
CONCESSION(concno, name, chno)
BOUND-POINT(id, lat, lon)
CONC-BOUND(concno, bound-id)
```

```
CONCESSION.chno ⊆ CONC-HOLDER.chno
CONC-BOUND.concno ⊆ CONCESSION.concno
CONC-BOUND.bound-id ⊆ BOUND-POINT.id
```

The definition of an object-oriented view of a relational database is based on schema translation methodologies, which have been described extensively in literature (e.g. [2,3,7]). Applying such a translation methodology may lead to a corresponding TM-schema as in Figure 1. The object-valued attributes and the constraints defined on them are derived from the inclusion dependencies of the relational schema. The $\mathbb{P}$-symbol denotes a set-valued attribute.

The schema translation induces a relationship between classes and tables. Table 1 illustrates this relationship.

Class	Table
ConcessionHolder	CONC-HOLDER
Concession	CONCESSION
Concession	CONC-BOUND
BoundaryPoint	BOUND-POINT
BoundaryPoint	CONC-BOUND

Table 1. The relationship between classes and tables

```
class ConcessionHolder
attributes   chno           : int,   name          : string,
             address        : string
end ConcessionHolder

class Concession
attributes   concno         : int,   owner         : ConcessionHolder,
             name           : string,bounded-by    : PBoundaryPoint
object constraints
o1: forall x in bounded-by | self in x.bounds
end Concession

class BoundaryPoint
attributes   id             : int,   lat           : real,
             lon            : real,  bounds        : PConcession
object constraints
o1: forall x in bounds | self in x.bounded-by
end BoundaryPoint
```

Fig. 1. TM-translation of the relational schema

2.3   Translation of SQL-statements

In [10], we presented an algorithm for the translation of individual SQL-statements to TM- methods. The algorithm is comparable to, but more powerful than the algorithm described in [8]. The algorithm exploits the additional semantics acquired in the translation from the relational to the object-oriented schema. Thus, typical relational features like specifying joins, semijoins and antijoins in a query [4] are translated by navigating through the inheritance and aggregation structure of the object schema.

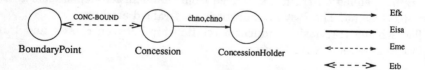

Fig. 2. The Join Materialisation Graph for the example object schema

The algorithm is based on *matching* the join structure specified in an SQL-query to the *materialised joins* available through the isa-relations and object references in the object schema. Figure 2 shows the so-called Join Materialisation Graph of the object schema, a graph-based representation of the joins materialised in the object schema through object references obtained from either foreign keys (fk) or relationship tables (tb), through the identification of missing entities (me) from the relational schema, or through isa-relationships. This graph is subsequently matched to a comparable representation of an SQL-query, the Query Join Graph [4]. A QJG may consist of joins, semijoins and antijoins. The matching of the two graphs leads to the identification of the *complex object definition* implicit in the query. The translation TM-method is then defined on the root class of this complex object definition. Figure 3 presents a query translation example. Note that in certain cases, the semantics of the object schema allows for disposing of constructs like **exists**. For details we refer to [10].

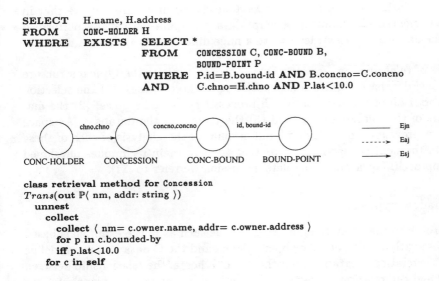

```
SELECT     H.name, H.address
FROM       CONC-HOLDER H
WHERE      EXISTS     SELECT *
                      FROM     CONCESSION C, CONC-BOUND B,
                               BOUND-POINT P
                      WHERE    P.id=B.bound-id AND B.concno=C.concno
                      AND      C.chno=H.chno AND P.lat<10.0
```

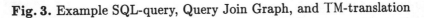

```
class retrieval method for Concession
Trans(out ℙ⟨ nm, addr: string ⟩)
   unnest
     collect
        collect ⟨ nm= c.owner.name, addr= c.owner.address ⟩
        for p in c.bounded-by
        iff p.lat<10.0
     for c in self
```

Fig. 3. Example SQL-query, Query Join Graph, and TM-translation

3 Translation of object behaviour

In the relational context, object behaviour is encoded in application software. Such application software is typically written in a general-purpose language such as C, using embedded SQL for the database interaction. Figure 4 shows a possible definition of C-data structures contained in an application program on the relational database. In Figure 5, a C-function implementing a database operation is listed. The operation NewConc inserts a new concession into the database. Before the actual insertion, however, it is checked if the concession to be inserted overlaps a concession owned by a different concession holder. If this is the case, the insertion is not performed.

Based on this example, we discuss the possibilities of deriving object methods from relational application code. As an illustration of our eventual goal, consider

```
struct{ long concno;  char name[strsize];  char owner_name[strsize];
        long owner_chno; BoundaryPoint **bounded_by;
} Conc;

struct{ long id;  double lat;  double lon;
} BoundaryPoint;
```

Fig. 4. C-data structure of the application

the TM-translation for the procedure NewConc listed in Figure 6. Note that in an object-oriented environment, general data manipulation can be performed within the database context, leading to a huge difference in code volume.

Structure of relational applications Our approach exploits the typical structure of relational database applications, consisting of three phases: (1) the selection and importation of the data on which processing is to take place; (2) the manipulation of this buffered data; and (3) the update of the database. As space limitations prevent us from giving a full account of the analysis of each of these phases, in the next subsections we present the two main techniques developed in our approach. For a more complete discussion we refer to [11].

3.1 Shadow types

Our approach to the reverse engineering of code such as in the example is based on the observation that both the object schema and the C-data structures define *views* of the relational database. For the object schema, the relationship between the view and the relational schema is determined by the schema translation, as was illustrated in Table 1.

Table(atts)	C-structure(vars)	(Variable)	Query
CONCESSION(concno,name)	Conc(concno,name)	(list_of_concs)	cons
CONC-HOLDER(chno,name)	Conc(owner_chno,owner_name)	(list_of_concs)	cons
BOUND-POINT(id,lat,lon)	BoundaryPoint(id,lat,lon)	(list_of_concs->bounded_by)	pts

Table 2. The relationship between tables and C-structures

For the C-data structures, this relationship is established by the FETCH statement featured by embedded SQL, which binds a C-variable to the result of an SQL-query. The C-variable can then be seen as materialising the view defined by the query.

Table 2 lists the relationships between C-structures and relational tables induced by the FETCH statements in the NewConc operation. Note that different queries may establish different views, materialised into different C-variables. Note furthermore that the relationship between the variables materialising the

```
int NewConc( Conc *newconc, int num_points)
{ Conc         **list_of_concs=malloc(...), *ccursor;
  BoundaryPoint *bcursor;
  int           i,j,num_cons=0;

  /* Does newconc overlap existing concessions owned by others? */
  /* Retrieve existing concessions */
  ccursor = *list_of_concs; sql_nm = *newconc->owner_name;
  EXEC SQL DECLARE cons CURSOR FOR    /* Q1 */
       SELECT C.concno, C.name, H.name, H.chno,
       FROM   CONCESSION C, CONC-HOLDER H
       WHERE  C.chno = H.chno AND H.name <> :sqlnm;
  EXEC SQL OPEN cons;
  while( sqlca.sql-code == 0)
  {   EXEC SQL FETCH cons INTO *ccursor;
      ccursor++;
      num_cons++; }
  /* Retrieve associated boundary points */
  for( i=0;i<num_cons;i++)
  {   sql_cno= *list_of_concs[i]->concno;
      EXEC SQL DECLARE pts CURSOR FOR   /* Q2 */
          SELECT B.id, B.lat, B.lon
          FROM   CONC-BOUND C, BOUND-POINT B
          WHERE  C.concno = :sql_cno AND B.id=C.bound-id;
      bcursor = *list_of_concs[i]->bounded_by;
      while( sqlca.sql-code == 0)
      {   EXEC SQL FETCH pts INTO *bcursor;
          bcursor++; } }
  /* Calculate overlap */
  i=0; while( i<numcons && !Overlap(newconc, *list_of_concs[i])
        {   i++; }
  /* If no overlap, enter concession */
  if( i == numcons)
  { sql_cno=newconc->concno; sql_nm=newconc->name;
    sql_chno=newconc->owner-chno; sql_tp=newconc->type;
    EXEC SQL INSERT INTO CONCESSION       /* I1 */
             VALUES ( :sql_cno, :sql_nm, :sql_chno, :sql_tp);
    for( j=0; j<num_points; j++)
    {   sql_id=newconc->bounded_by[j]->id;
        EXEC SQL INSERT INTO CONC-BOUND      /* I2 */
                VALUES (:sql_cno, :sql_id); } }
  /* Assume points and owner already exist in the database */
  return(SUCCESS);
}
```

Fig. 5. Example C-function implementing a database operation

```
class update method for Concession
Trans(in conc: Concession)=
if
    forall x in
      collect y
      for y in self
      iff y.owner.name ≠ conc.owner.name
    | not conc.Overlap(x)
then self union conc
else self
```

Fig. 6. The translation TM-method

queries cons and pts suggests a correlation between these queries. This is indeed the case, as discussed in the next subsection.

C-Variable	Class
list_of_concs->(cons,name)	Concession
list_of_concs->(owner_chno,owner_name)	ConcessionHolder
list_of_concs->bounded_by->(id,lat,lon)	BoundaryPoint
newconc->(cons,name)	Concession
newconc->(owner_chno,owner_name)	ConcessionHolder

Table 3. The relationship between C-variables and classes

Having determined these relationships, a relationship between C-variables appearing in the application code and classes from the object schema may now be derived. Such a class is then called the *shadow type* of the C-variable. The shadow-types of the C-variables storing the result of embedded SELECT-statements can easily be determined by performing a 'natural join' of the relationship between classes and tables induced by the schema translation (Table 1), and the relationship between tables and C-variables induced by the primary application view definition phase (Table 2). The result is shown in the upper part of Table 3.

For other variables v introduced in the application code we introduce the following rules:

- If a statement v=v1 occurs in the code, where v1 has shadow type C, assign C as the shadow-type of v.
- If a statement v=f(v1,v2,...,vn) occurs in the code, where vi has shadow-type Ci, assign f(C1,C2,...,Cn) as the shadow-type of v.
- If none of the rules above apply, and the type of variable v is associated to a shadow-type C through another variable w, assign C as the shadow-type of v.

The lower part of Table 3 shows the resulting relationship for the variable newconc. Note that these entries result from applying the last of the rules above.

Shadow types provide a means of organising the translation code into object methods. Consider for example the C-function Overlap(c1,c2: Conc), called in NewConc. The shadow-types of c1 are Concession and ConcessionHolder. Thus, the function describes an operation on the complex object rooted at class Concession. Therefore, the function should be translated into a **class method** for Concession *Overlap*(c: Concession).

3.2 Translating embedded SQL statements

An important feature of embedded SQL is the possibility to execute multiple, *related* statements, using SQL-variables to relate attributes occurring in different queries.

In Figure 5 for example, the SQL-variable sql_cno is used to relate H.chno from query cons (Q_1) and C.concno from query pts (Q_2). Note that we need to lookup Table 2 indicating the attribute associated with list_of_cons->concno to discover this relationship. As Q_2 is executed once for each value of H.chno returned by Q_1, the effect of such a construction is the *nesting* of the result of Q_2 in the result of Q_1, based on the *nesting equality* H.chno=C.concno.

Update statements may be related through SQL-variables as well. Again referring to Figure 5, the insert statements marked I_1 and I_2 are related through the variable sql_cno. By inserting identical values for CONCESSION.chno and CONC-BOUND.conco, a relationship between these tables is *established* which may later be reconstructed using a query containing a join on these two attributes.

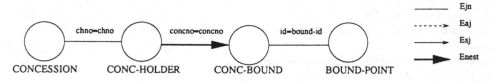

Fig. 7. The aggregate join graph for Q_1 and Q_2

Aggregate Join Graphs To cope with such relationships, we extend the concept of a query join graph associated with an SQL-query as defined by Dayal [4] to an *aggregate join graph* associated with several embedded SQL-queries or update statements.

Figure 7 shows the aggregate join graph for Q_1 and Q_2. Note that we introduced a new kind of edge into the graph: a *nesting edge*, annotated with the nesting equality.

Figure 8 shows an aggregate join graph for the two insertion statements I_1 and I_2. Here we introduce a type of edge to represent common update values, a *join establishment edge*, annotated with the attributes on which a join is established.

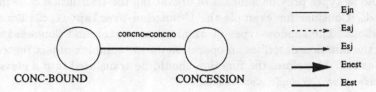

———	Ejn
- - - ->	Eaj
——>	Esj
➤	Enest
———	Eest

Fig. 8. The aggregate join graph for I_1 and I_2

Analogous to [10], the translation is based on *matching* the AJG of the queries to the MOG of the object schema. A nesting required by the queries is available in the schema iff there exists an object reference in the object schema that was based on an inclusion dependency in the original relational schema involving exactly the attributes in the nesting equality. [1] Analogously, a join establishment edge matches an object reference that was based on that particular join.

The matching of an AJG and a MOG results in a set of complex object definitions. The SQL-statements are subsequently translated to a TM-method on the root of each of these complex object definitions. The translation depends on the cardinality of the object reference matching the nesting or join establishment edge, respectively. Due to lack of space, we here only present the translations of Q_1/Q_2 and I_1/I_2, respectively:

class retrieval method for Concession
Trans1(**in** conc: Concession)=
  collect x
  for x **in** self
  iff x.owner.name $\neq$ conc.owner.name

class update method for Concession
Trans2(**in** conc: Concession)=
  self = self **union** conc

Note how the shadow-types of C-variables were used in this translation. Note furthermore that join establishment edges are translated to simple updates of complex objects identified by the matching of these edges.

Complete translation The complete translation consists of putting the results of the analysis of each of the three application phases together. The analysis of the first phase yields a complex object structure upon which the application acts, using our SQL translation algorithm. The analysis of the second phase identifies function evaluations performed on this complex object structure. Note

---

[1] If there is no such match, we have to resort to a 'blunt', quasi-relational translation of the SQL-query. See [10].

that updates made to the data buffered in the application need not be translated unless they are eventually effectuated on the database through SQL-statements issued in the database update phase. These effects can be accounted for by again applying our SQL translation algorithm.

As an illustration, note how the translation method of Figure 6 is composed from the translations of Q_1/Q_2 and I_1/I_2 given above. For more details, refer to [11].

4 Database operations and constraints

The constraint definition facilities provided by relational DBMSs are usually inadequate for definition of integrity constraints in complex application domains. Therefore, the enforcement of such constraints is typically implemented by application software. However, TM offers the possibility of defining arbitrarily complex first-order constraints on the database state. Therefore, the translation of database operations of the nature described above can be taken one step further to extract integrity constraint *definitions* from operations implementing their *enforcement*.

The operation NewConc is a typical example of such an integrity checking operation. The actual insertion of new data into the database takes place only if a certain condition holds. Once these operations have been translated into TM, such conditions can easily be rewritten to class constraints. In the example of Figure 6, the condition *Insert(o)* under which a Concession object is added to the class extent (represented by the keyword **self**), is the following:

$$Insert(o) : \forall x \in \{y \in self \, | y.owner.name \neq o.owner.name\} | \neg o.Overlap(x)$$

This can be rewritten to the following class constraint:

$$\forall x \in self \, |\forall y \in self \, | y.owner.name \neq x.owner.name \land y \neq x \Rightarrow \neg x.Overlap(y)$$

Since $y.owner.name \neq x.owner.name \Rightarrow y \neq x$, this can be rewritten to the TM-constraint

class constraint for Concession
  forall x **in self** |
    not exists y **in self** |
      y.owner.name $\neq$ x.owner.name **and** x.Overlap(y)

The translation of the operation NewConc itself then reduces to the translation of the insertion statements.

Note that by first translating the entire operation to TM, and only then extracting the integrity constraints, we benefit from the formal semantics of TM expressions, making the actual extraction relatively easy.

5 Conclusion

This paper described the translation of database operations from a relational to an object-oriented context. We dwelled upon the necessity of such a translation as a means of describing the semantics of interoperable databases, to support data migration, to ease code maintenance, and to enable code reuse.

We described two main reverse engineering techniques, based on the typical view defining and manipulating structure of relational database applications: a translation algorithm for embedded SQL, and the notion of object classes as shadow types of program variables. These are the basis for a more complete framework described in [11]. We showed that constraint definitions that were hidden in the application software in the relational context can be discovered and made explicit in the object-oriented translation.

It is clear that further research on this subject is needed. The framework could be refined and additional code analysis techniques developed.

References

[1] H. Balsters, R. A. de By & R. Zicari, "Typed sets as a basis for object-oriented database schemas," in *Proceedings Seventh European Conference on Object-Oriented Programming, July 26–30, 1993, Kaiserslautern, Germany*, LNCS #707, O. M. Nierstrasz, ed., Springer–Verlag, New York–Heidelberg–Berlin, 1993, 161–184, See also http://wwwis.cs.utwente.nl:8080/oodm.html.

[2] M. Castellanos, "A methodology for semantically enriching interoperable databases," in *Advances in Database - BNCOD 11*, Springer-Verlag, New York–Heidelberg–Berlin, 1993, 58–75.

[3] R. H. L. Chiang, T. M. Barron & V. C. Storey, "Reverse engineering of relational databases: Extraction of an EER model from a relational database," *Data & Knowledge Engineering* 12 (March 1994), 107–142.

[4] U. Dayal, "Of nests and trees: A unified approach to processing queries that contain nested subqueries, aggregates, and quantifiers," in *Proceedings of Thirteenth International Conference on Very Large Data Bases, Brighton, England, September 1–4, 1987*, P. M. Stocker, W. Kent & P. Hammersley, eds., Morgan Kaufmann Publishers, Los Altos, CA, 1987, 197–207.

[5] P. Drew, R. King, D. McLeod, M. Rusinkiewicz & A. Silberschatz, "Report of the workshop on semantic heterogeneity and interoperation in multidatabase systems," *SIGMOD RECORD* 22 (September 1993), 47–55.

[6] J. Flokstra, M. van Keulen & J. Skowronek, "The IMPRESS DDT: A database design toolbox based on a formal specification language," in *Proceedings ACM-SIGMOD 1994 International Conference on Management of Data*, ACM Press, New York, NY, 1994, 506.

[7] P. Johannesson, "A method for transforming relational schemas into conceptual schemas," in *Proceedings Tenth International Conference on Data Engineering*, IEEE Computer Society Press, Los Alamitos, CA, 1994, 190–201.

[8] W. Meng, C. Yu, W. Kim, G. Wang, T. Pham & S. Dao, "Construction of a relational front-end for object oriented database systems," in *Proceedings Ninth International Conference on Data Engineering, Vienna, Austria, April 19–23, 1993*, IEEE Computer Society Press, Washington, DC, 1993, 476–483.

[9] S. Y. W. Su, H. Lam & D. H. Lo, "Transformation of data traversals and operations in application programs to account for semantic changes of databases," *ACM Transactions on Database Systems* 6 (June 1981), 255–294.

[10] M. W. W. Vermeer & P. M. G. Apers, "Object-oriented views of relational databases incorporating behaviour," in *Fourth International Conference on Database Systems for Advanced Applications (DASFAA'95), Singapore, April 10–13 1995*, T. W. Ling & Y. Masunaga, eds., World Scientific Publishing Co., 1995, 26–35.

[11] M. W. W. Vermeer & P. M. G. Apers, "A framework for reverse engineering of relational database applications," Universiteit Twente, 95–24, Enschede, The Netherlands, 1995, Memoranda Informatica.

A Rigorous Approach to Schema Restructuring

Vânia M.P. Vidal[1] and Marianne Winslett[2]

[1] Universidade Federal do Ceará, Fortaleza, Ceará, Brazil
[2] University of Illinois, Urbana, Illinois, U.S.A.

Abstract. A problem of schema integration is that one cannot directly merge concepts that are intuitively the same but have different representations. This problem can be solved by performing schema transformations to conform the views being integrated so that merging of classes and attributes becomes possible (schema restructuring). Previously, researchers have approached schema restructuring in an informal manner, offering heuristics to guide practitioners during integration; thus a formal underpinning for schema restructuring has not yet been established. To establish a formal underpinning, one must extend current methodologies for schema integration to be able to express the equivalence of concepts that have nonidentical representations. Such expressive power is needed to be able to formally justify the correctness of the transformations that are used during schema restructuring. Our work addresses this problem by supporting more general forms of existence dependency constraints which allow the formal definition of the most common types of transformations that are required during schema restructuring. In this paper we formally define a *decomposable normal form* for schemas that specifies which properties a schema should have so that certain technical problem of concept merging do not occur. We also present an algorithm to transform a schema into an equivalent schema which is in decomposable normal form.

1 Introduction

View integration or, as it is often called, schema integration, is a process that takes a set of views designed by separate user groups, and integrates them into a global conceptual schema for the entire organization. We propose to divide view integration into three steps: combination, restructuring, and optimization. View combination consists of defining new constraints that capture similarities between views. The restructuring step is devoted to normalizing the views so that merging becomes possible. The optimization step tries to reduce redundancy and the size of the schema. The main focus of this paper is the restructuring step. The other steps are discussed in [Vidal94a,Vidal94b].

Schema restructuring is required when one cannot directly merge concepts that are intuitively the same but have different representations. This problem can be solved by performing schema transformations to conform the views so that merging of the common parts becomes possible. For example, consider the

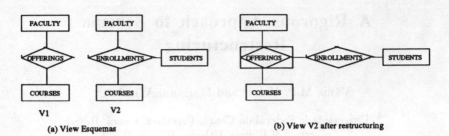

(a) View Esquemas   (b) View V2 after restructuring

Fig. 1. ER schemas.

ER diagrams of the views V_1 and V_2 shown in the figure 1(a). In view V_1, *OFFERINGS* describes the relationship of a faculty member offering a course. In view V_2, *ENROLLMENTS* describes the relationship of a student enrolled in a course with a faculty member. *OFFERINGS* and *ENROLLMENTS* are related, since the existence of a relationship between a student "s", a course "c" and a faculty member "f" in *ENROLLMENTS* requires the existence of a relationship between "c" and "f" in *OFFERINGS*. To make possible the merge of information about *OFFERINGS* that is repeated in V_2, the view V_2 should be restructured as shown in figure 1(b). In the ER schema of figure 1(b), the relationship *ENROLLMENTS* is no longer made up of the entities types *FACULTY*, *COURSES*, and *STUDENTS*, but of the relationship type *OFFERINGS* and the entity type *STUDENTS*.

Current view integration methodologies [Batini84, Navathe86, Gottard92] omit a rigorous treatment of schema restructuring. This is partly due to the fact that the model used by those methodologies cannot express the equivalence of concepts that have nonidentical representations. In the case of the views V_1 and V_2 the relation between *ENROLLMENTS* and *OFFERINGS* cannot be explicitly specified by the ER model. Therefore, they cannot formally define transformations where those constraints must be preserved. Our work addresses this problem by supporting more general forms of *existence dependency constraints* which allow the formal definition of the most common types of transformations that are required during schema restructuring. In this paper we propose a *decomposable normal form* for schemas that specifies which properties a schema should have so that the problem of "merge incompatibility" captured by certain existence dependency constraints does not occur. We also present an algorithm to transform restricted class of schemas into equivalent schemas which are in decomposable normal form.

Our methodology defines a set of transformation primitives that allows schema restructuring to be realized in a safe and algorithmic way. In the proposed transformation primitives, the relationship between the original and transformed schema is formally specified by the *instance mapping* and *update mapping*. The instance mapping specifies how instances of the original schema are mapped to instances of the transformed schema and vice-versa. The update mapping specifies how each update operation defined under the original schema is transformed into an update operation defined under the transformed schema. In our approach, a transformation must be *information* and *update semantics preserving*. A transformation is *information preserving* when the original and transformed schemas are of equivalent information capacity [Miller93]. A transformation is *update semantics preserving* when any update specified against the transformed schema has the same effect as if the user had performed the update directly on the original schema. The formal guarantee of preservation of update semantics is the focus of our work in [Vidal94a]. One advantage of this approach is that the view definition mappings and the view update translators can be directly defined from the instance mapping and update mappings between the different intermediate schemas generated during the view integration process. In [Vidal94a], we have showed that since schema transformation under our methodology is information and update semantics preserving, we can formally prove that a view update translation defined from the update mappings is a valid translation. In the current paper, we extend [Vidal94a] by including algorithmic specification of the schema restructuring process.

This paper is divided into six sections as follows. In section 2, we present a semantic data model for use in view modeling and view integration. In section 3, we propose a decomposable normal form for schemas and discuss the problems that it overcomes. In section 4, we specify the transformation primitive "Decompose" which is used during the normalization process. In section 5 we present an algorithm to transform restricted class of schemas into equivalent schemas which are in decomposable normal form. Section 6 contains conclusions and directions for future research.

2 The Semantic Data Model

In this section we present the semantic data model for use in view modeling and view integration. We have adopted a model that is heavily influenced by SDM [Hammer81], the Functional Model [Shipman81] and TAXIS [Mylopoulos80]. In our model the conceptual objects are modeled as entities. The model supports the notion of *class*, which allows one to group entities according to perceived similarities. In our model, a schema is a triple $S = (\mathcal{C}, \mathcal{A}, \mathcal{R})$ where $\mathcal{C}$ is a set of classes, $\mathcal{A}$ is a set of attributes of the classes in $\mathcal{C}$, and $\mathcal{R}$ is a set of integrity constraints over the classes in $\mathcal{C}$ and the attributes in $\mathcal{A}$. Attribute definitions are functional relationships between entities in a class and other entities that are instances of the attribute's range. Attributes can be expressed as $f : A \rightarrow B$, where f is the name of the attribute whose domain consists of entities in the class A and whose range consists of entities in the class B. For example, the attribute *department* : *STUDENTS* $\rightarrow$ *DEPARTMENTS* relates entities of the class *STUDENTS* with entities of the class *DEPARTMENTS*. In the graphical notation of figure 2, rectangles represent classes, circles represent built-in classes, and labeled arcs represent attribute definitions.

An *instance* $\mathcal{D}$ of a schema $S = (\mathcal{C}, \mathcal{A}, \mathcal{R})$ is a function defined on the sets $\mathcal{C}$

Constraint	Notation	Condition for validity in $\mathcal{D}$
Key Constraint	$\{f_1,\ldots,f_n\} \in keys(C)$, where $f_1,\ldots,f_n \in rel(C)$	$\forall e_1, e_2 \in C$, if for all $1 \le i \le n$ $\mathcal{D}(f_i)(e_1) = \mathcal{D}(f_i)(e_2)$, then $e_1 = e_2$.
Functional Constraint	$C([f_1 \ldots f_n] \to f)$, where $f_1,\ldots,f_n,f \in rel(C)$	$\forall e_1, e_2 \in C$, if for all $1 \le i \le n$ $\mathcal{D}(f_i)(e_1) = \mathcal{D}(f_i)(e_2)$, then $\mathcal{D}(f)(e_1) = \mathcal{D}(f)(e_2)$
Union Functional Constraint	$\langle C_1([f_{1,1},\ldots,f_{1,m}] \to f_1),\ldots,$ $C_n([f_{n,1},\ldots,f_{n,m}] \to f_n)\rangle$, where $C_i \in C, f_{i_k} \in rel(C_i), 1 \le i,k \le n$	$\forall i,j \in [1,n], \forall e \in \mathcal{D}(C_i)$ and $\forall e' \in \mathcal{D}(C_j)$, if for all $1 \le i,k \le n, \mathcal{D}(f_{i,k})(e) = \mathcal{D}(f_{i,k})(e')$, then $\mathcal{D}(f_i)(e) = \mathcal{D}(f_j)(e')$.
Referential	$f : A \to B$, where $f \in \mathcal{A}$ and $A, B \in C$	$\forall a \in \mathcal{D}(A)$ if $b \in \mathcal{D}(f)(e)$ then $b \in \mathcal{D}(B)$.
Totality	$f : A\bullet \to B$, where $f \in \mathcal{A}$ and $A, B \in C$	$\forall b \in \mathcal{D}(B) \; \exists a \in \mathcal{D}(A)$ such that $b \in \mathcal{D}(f)(e)$.

Table 1. Formal definitions of several constraints.

and $\mathcal{A}$ as follows: (i) For any class $A \in C$, $\mathcal{D}$ assigns a specific set of entities to A (denoted $\mathcal{D}(A)$). Thus, $\mathcal{D}(A)$ is referred to as the extension of A in the instance $\mathcal{D}$. (ii) For any attribute $f : A \to B \in \mathcal{A}$, $\mathcal{D}(f)$ is a function from $\mathcal{D}(A)$ to $\mathcal{D}(B)$, where: For any entity $a \in \mathcal{D}(A)$, $\mathcal{D}(f)$ assigns a specific set of entities in $\mathcal{D}(B)$ (denoted $\mathcal{D}(f)(a)$). Thus, $\mathcal{D}(f)(a))$ is referred to as the value of $f(a)$ in the instance $\mathcal{D}$.

The set of relationships of class A in the schema $S = (C, \mathcal{A}, \mathcal{R})$, denoted $rel(A)$, is the smallest set such that: (i) If the attribute $f : A \to B \in \mathcal{A}$ then $f : A \to B \in rel(A)$. (ii) If the reference attribute $f : B \to A \in \mathcal{A}$ then $f^{-1} : A \to B \in rel(A)$, where for any instance $\mathcal{D}$ of S, and any $a \in \mathcal{D}(A)$, $\mathcal{D}(f^{-1})(a) = \{b | b \in \mathcal{D}(B) \text{ and } a \in \mathcal{D}(f)(b)\}$. (iii) If $f : A \to B \in rel(A), g : B \to C \in rel(B)$ then $g \circ f : A \to C \in rel(A)$, where for any instance $\mathcal{D}$ of S, and any $a \in \mathcal{A}$, $\mathcal{D}(g \circ f)(a) = (\mathcal{D}(g)(\mathcal{D}(f)(a)))$.

The model supports the following types of integrity constraints: key constraints, functional dependency constraints (FDs), union-functional-dependency constraints (UFDs), referential constraints, totality constraint, structural constraints, equivalence-of-relationships constraints and existence dependency constraints (EDs). Additional constraint types could be added if desired. In this section, we describe the constraints used in our example in section 5. Table 1 shows the formal definition of several constraints.

Existence dependency constraints (EDs) are used to express how the existence of entities in a class depends on the existence of entities in other classes. The existence dependency constraint $A[f_1,\ldots,f_n] \subset B[g_1,\ldots,g_n]$ where $A, B \in C, f_1,\ldots,f_n \in rel(A)$, and $g_1,\ldots,g_n \in rel(B)$, is valid in $\mathcal{D}$ iff for every $a \in \mathcal{D}(A)$, there is a $b \in \mathcal{D}(B)$ such that $\mathcal{D}(f_i)(a) = \mathcal{D}(g_i)(b)$ for $1 \le i \le n$. Our model supports five other types of EDs not discussed here [Vidal94b].

Structural constraints are a special case of existence dependency constraints where the classes have been identified as referring to the same real world concept.

The structural subset constraint $A \subset B$ where $A, B \in C$, is valid in $\mathcal{D}$ iff for every $a \in \mathcal{D}(A)$ we have $a \in \mathcal{D}(B)$, that is $\mathcal{D}(A) \subseteq \mathcal{D}(B)$. Our model supports five other types of structural constraints not discussed here [Vidal94b].

Equivalence_of_relationships constraints, or synonym constraints, are used to indicate that 'relationships' are synonyms. The synonym constraint $f \equiv g$ where $f \in rel(A), g \in rel(B)$, and $A, B \in C$, is valid in $\mathcal{D}$ iff for all $a \in \mathcal{D}(A)$, if $a \in \mathcal{D}(B)$ then $\mathcal{D}(f)(a) = \mathcal{D}(g)(a)$.

Integrity constraints impose constraints on the allowable database states (instances). Any operation modifying the database must preserve consistency. When an update violates a constraint, the update may be rejected or else other updates may be triggered in order to maintain consistency. In our model, for those integrity constraints for which several alternative corrections are possible, the designer can extend the declaration of the integrity constraint with extra information to indicate which option should be used (update semantics). In [Vidal94a] we defined a notation to specify the update semantics of constraints.

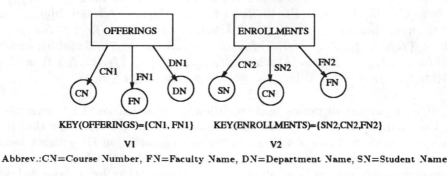

KEY(OFFERINGS)={CN1, FN1}   KEY(ENROLLMENTS)={SN2,CN2,FN2}

V1   V2

Abbrev.:CN=Course Number, FN=Faculty Name, DN=Department Name, SN=Student Name

Fig. 2. Example view schemas.

3 The Decomposable Normal Form

Schema restructuring is required when one cannot directly merge concepts that are intuitively the same but have different representations. Consider for example the views V_1 and V_2 in Figure 2. Combining the views V_1 and V_2 in figure 2, we obtain the combined schema CS which contains the views V_1 and V_2, plus the following new existence dependency constraint:

$$\psi = ENROLLMENTS[CN2, FN2] \subset OFFERINGS[CN1, FN1].$$

ψ specifies that for any instance $\mathcal{D}$ of CS, ψ is valid in $\mathcal{D}$ iff for every $e \in \mathcal{D}(ENROLLMENTS)$, there is a $o \in \mathcal{D}(OFFERINGS)$ such that $\mathcal{D}(CN2)(e) = \mathcal{D}(CN1)(o)$ and $\mathcal{D}(FN2)(e) = \mathcal{D}(FN1)(o)$. The redundancies captured by ED ψ cannot be directly integrated. This problem can be solved by performing schema transformations to conform the views so that merging of classes and attributes becomes possible.

Another problem that is also solved with schema restructuring is the problem of redundancy and anomalies caused by certain FDs. The process of normalization that solves this problem in relational databases was originally defined in [Codd 72]. In this section we formally define a *decomposable normal form* for schemas that specifies which properties a schema should have so that the problem of "merge incompatibility" captured by certain EDs and the problem of redundancy and anomalies caused by certain FDs do not occur.

In the rest of this section, let $S = (\mathcal{C}, \mathcal{A}, \mathcal{R})$ be a schema. We assume without loss of generality that $\mathcal{R}$ is a minimal cover. Informally, we say that the schema S is in decomposable normal form if the only functional constraints (FDs) in $\mathcal{R}$ are those implying key constraints, the only existence constraints (EDs) in $\mathcal{R}$ are those implying structural constraints and the only UFDs in $\mathcal{R}$ are those implying equivalency_of_relationships constraints. This can be formalized as follows:

Definition 3.1: We say that $S = (\mathcal{C}, \mathcal{A}, \mathcal{R})$ is in decomposable normal form iff: (i) If $C([f_1, \ldots, f_n] \rightarrow g)$ is a FD in $\mathcal{R}$ then $\{f_1, \ldots, f_n\} \in S\_keys(C)$. [3] (ii) If $C([f_1, \ldots, f_n] \rightarrow g)$ is a member of an UFD in $\mathcal{R}$, then $\{f_1, \ldots, f_n\} \in S\_keys(C)$. (iii) If ψ is a ED in $\mathcal{R}$, such that $A[f_1, \ldots, f_n]$ and $B[g_1, \ldots, g_n]$ occur in ψ, then a) $\{f_1, \ldots, f_n\} \in S\_keys(A)$, b) $\{f_{k_1}, \ldots, f_{k_m}\} \in S\_keys(A)$ where $\{f_{k_1}, \ldots, f_{k_m}\} \subseteq \{f_1, \ldots, f_n\}$ iff $\{g_{k_1}, \ldots, g_{k_m}\} \in S\_keys(B)$, and c) If $\{f_{k_1}, \ldots, f_{k_m}\} \in S\_keys(A)$ where $\{f_{k_1}, \ldots, f_{k_m}\} \subseteq \{f_1, \ldots, f_n\}$ then $\mathcal{R} \models \langle A([f_{k_1}, \ldots, f_{k_m}] \rightarrow f_j), B([g_{k_1}, \ldots, g_{k_m}] \rightarrow g_j) \rangle$,for $1 \leq j \leq n$. $\Diamond$

It is important to notice that condition (i) of definition 3.1 is equivalent to the condition imposed by the BCNF normal form. We can show that it is always possible to bring a schema to satisfy the condition (i) without losing the ability to preserve constraints. As we show in [Vidal94], when an schema is in decomposable normal form, all existence constraints can be transformed into structural and synonym constraints so that merging becomes possible. From now on, we will concentrate on a restricted class of schemas for which we can always find an equivalent schema that is in decomposable normal form. It is important to notice that the class of restricted schemas includes most schemas that are likely to need merging in practice.

Definition 3.2: We say that the schema $S = (\mathcal{C}, \mathcal{A}, \mathcal{R})$ is *restricted* iff (i) If $C([f_1, \ldots, f_n] \rightarrow g)$ is a FD in $\mathcal{R}$ or a member of an UFD in $\mathcal{R}$, then $\{f_1, \ldots, f_n, g\} \subseteq attributes(C)$. (ii) If ψ is a ED in $\mathcal{R}$, such that $C[f_1, \ldots, f_n]$ occur in ψ, then $\{f_1, \ldots, f_n, g\} \subseteq attributes(C)$. (iii) For any ED ψ in $\mathcal{R}$ such that $A[f_1, \ldots, f_n]$ and $B[g_1, \ldots, g_n]$ occur in ψ, if $\mathcal{R} \models A([f_{k_1}, \ldots, f_{k_m}] \rightarrow f_j)$ where $f_{k_1}, \ldots, f_{k_m}$ and f_j are distinct members of $\{f_1, \ldots, f_n\}$, then $\mathcal{R} \models B([g_{k_1}, \ldots, g_{k_m}] \rightarrow g_j)$ and $\mathcal{R} \models \langle A([f_{k_1}, \ldots, f_{k_m}] \rightarrow f_j), B([g_{k_1}, \ldots, g_{k_m}] \rightarrow g_j) \rangle$. $\Diamond$

---

[3] $S\_keys(C)$ denotes the set of superkeys of class C.

4 The Transformation Primitive Decompose

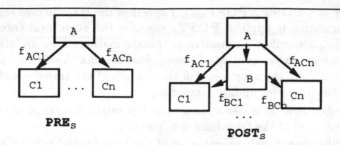

$$\text{PRE}_S \qquad\qquad \text{POST}_S$$

PRE_{const}:

$\{f_{AC_1}, \ldots, f_{AC_n}\} \subseteq Attributes(A)$

$\forall k \in keys(A), k \not\subseteq \{f_{AC_1}, \ldots, f_{AC_n}\}$

POST_{const}:

(i) add constraints:

- $f_{AB} : A \to B$; $f_{AB} : A\bullet \to B$
- $f_{AC_i} \equiv f_{AB} \circ f_{BC_i}$; $constraints(f_{BC_i}) = constraints(f_{AC_i}), 1 \leq i \leq n$,

(ii) Replace every FD $\gamma = A(f_{AC_{i_1}}, \ldots, f_{AC_{i_m}} \to f_{AC_i})$ where $i_k \in [1, n]$ and $i \in [1, n]$, by FD $B(f_{BC_{i_1}}, \ldots, f_{BC_{i_m}} \to f_{BC_i})$ (γ becomes redundant)

(iii) Replace every UFD ψ such that $A(f_{AC_{i_1}}, \ldots, f_{AC_{i_m}} \to f_{AC_i})$ is in ψ, $i_k \in [1, n]$, and $i \in [1, n]$, by UFD ψ' where ψ' is obtained from ψ by replacing $A(f_{AC_{i_1}}, \ldots, f_{AC_{i_m}} \to f_{AC_i})$ by $B(f_{BC_{i_1}}, \ldots, f_{BC_{i_m}} \to f_{BC_i})$

(iv) Replace every ED ρ such that $A[f_{AC_{i_1}}, \ldots, f_{AC_{i_m}}]$ is in ρ, $i_k \in [1, n]$, by ED ρ' where ρ' is obtained from ρ by replacing $A[f_{AC_{i_1}}, \ldots, f_{AC_{i_m}}]$ by $B[f_{BC_{i_1}}, \ldots, f_{BC_{i_m}}]$.

Fig. 3. The transformation primitive *Decompose*: $Decompose(A, \{f_{AC_1}, \ldots, f_{AC_n}\}, B, f_{AB}, \{f_{BC_1}, \ldots, f_{BC_n}\})$.

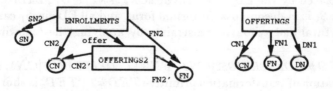

Fig. 4. Schema S_1, obtained by decomposing schema CS.

Our methodology defines a set of transformation primitives that allows schema transformations to be realized in a safe (information preserving) and algorithmic way. A transformation primitive is a 5-tuple (**PRE, POST**, ϕ, σ, τ) where:

- **PRE** = (**PRE**$_s$, **PRE**$_{const}$) specifies under which pre- conditions the transformation is applicable. **PRE**$_s$ specifies the conditions in terms of the original structure and **PRE**$_{const}$ specifies further constraints that are not represented in **PRE**$_s$.

- **POST** = (**POST**$_s$, **POST**$_{const}$) specifies the transformed schema when the transformation is applied. **POST**$_s$ specifies the structural transformation and **POST**$_{const}$ specifies the constraint transformations. The update semantics of the constraints in the context of the original schema should be "mapped" to update semantics of the constraints in the context of the transformed schema in a manner that preserves update semantics.

- ϕ specifies how database instances of the original schema are mapped to database instances of the transformed schema.

- σ specifies how database instances of the transformed schema are mapped to database instances of the original schema.

- τ specifies how each update operation defined under the original schema is translated to update operations defined under the transformed schema (update mapping).

As shown in [Vidal94a], the instance mappings (ϕ and σ) and the upadate mapping (τ) are needed to prove that a transformation is information and update semantics preserving. Figure 3 shows the specification of the transformation primitive "*Decompose*" which is used during the normalization process. To allow us concentrate on the structural aspects of the transformation, in figure 3 we omit the mappings ϕ, σ and τ and the update semantics of the constraint. The complete specification of the transformation primitive "*Decompose*" is given in [Vidal94a].

In our example, the combined schema CS, obtained by combining the views V_1 and V_2, can be transformed into an equivalent schema which is in decomposable normal form by applying the following transformation:

$T_1 = Decompose(ENROLLMENTS, \{CN2, FN2\}, OFFERINGS2, offer, \{CN2', FN2'\})$.

These transformations are needed in our example so that we can merge information about *OFFERINGS* that is repeated in different places in the combined schema. Applying the transformation T_1 to CS, we obtain the schema S_1 shown in figure 4 where the ED $ENROLLMENTS[CN2, FN2] \subset OFFERINGS[CN1, FN1]$ of CS is replaced by the ED $OFFERINGS2[CN2', FN2'] \subset OFFERINGS[CN1, FN1]$. The schema S_1 is in decomposable normal form, and all EDs in S_1 can be rewritten as structural and synonym constraints by applying the following transformation:

$T_2 = TED\#2(OFFERINGS2[CN2', FN2'] \subset OFFERINGS[CN1, FN1])$.

The specification of transformation primitive $TED\#2$ ('TED' is short for 'transformation of existence dependency') is ommited here due to space limitations. The only transformation resulting from applying T_2 to S_1 is the replacement of the ED $OFFERINGS2[CN2', FN2'] \subset OFFERINGS[CN1, FN1]$ by the following constraints: $OFFERINGS2 \subset OFFERINGS, CN2' \equiv CN1, FN2' \equiv FN1$. Notice that after the above transformations the redundancies are expressed by synonym constraints and merging becomes possible.

5 The Decomposition Algorithm

In this section, we present an algorithm to transform a restricted schema into an equivalent schema which is in decomposable normal form. But first, we present several preliminary concepts. In this section, let $S = (C, A, R)$ be a schema where R is a minimal cover.

Definition 5.1: Let C be a class of S. C is in *Decomposable Normal Form*(DNF) iff: (i) If $C([f_1, \ldots, f_n] \to g)$ is a FD in R then $\{f_1, \ldots, f_n\} \in S\_keys(C)$. (ii) If $C([f_1, \ldots, f_n] \to g)$ is a member of an UFD in R, then $\{f_1, \ldots, f_n\} \in S\_keys(C)$. (iii) If ψ is an ED in R such that $C[f_1, \ldots, f_n]$ occur in ψ, then $\{f_1, \ldots, f_n\} \in S\_keys(C)\Diamond$.

In [Vidal94b] we prove that if all classes of a restricted schema S are in DNF then S is in decomposable normal form. Therefore, the problem of transforming a restricted schema into an equivalent schema which is in decomposable normal form can be reduced to the problem of transforming a schema into an equivalent schema where all classes are in DNF. To determine the set of transformations required to normalize a class, we use the decomposition graph of the class defined as follows.

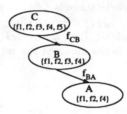

Fig. 5. Decomposition Graph D_c for the class C.

Definition 5.2: A *decomposition graph* of a class C in S is a directed acyclic graph (V, A), where V is a set of classes, $C \in V$, and A is a set of directed edges. For each class F in V, $attributes^*(F)$ [4] $\subseteq attributes^*(C)$, and the set of FDs over F is the projection of the FDs over C onto $attributes^*(F)$. If the edge a from E to F, denoted by $a = \langle E, F \rangle$, is in A then $attributes^*(F) \subset attributes^*(E)$ *The transformation defined by the graph D_c* is the transformation obtained by traversing the decomposition graph D_c. $\Diamond$. Figure 5 shows a decomposition graph for the class C where $attributes^*(C) = \{f_1, f_2, f_3, f_4, f_5\}$. The transformation T defined by the graph D_c is given by $T = T_2 \circ T_1$ where:

T_1 : $Decompose(C, \{f_1, f_2, f_3, f_4\}, B, f_{CB}, \{f_1, f_2, f_3, f_4\})$
T_2 : $Decompose(B, \{f_1, f_2, f_4\}, A, f_{BA}, \{f_1, f_2, f_4\})$.

Definition 5.3: Suppose that $D_c = (V, A)$ is the decomposition graph of the class C in S. Let T be the transformation defined by the graph D_c, and $S_1 = T(S)$. D_c *defines a normalized decomposition of C* iff for any class F in S_1 if $F \in V$ then F is in DNF. $\Diamond$.

---

[4] $attributes^*(F)$ is the set of names of the attributes of F.

Input:

$S = (\mathcal{C}, \mathcal{A}, \mathcal{R})$ - A restricted schema, where R is a minimal cover.

C - A class in S

Output:

(V, A) - A decomposition graph of C that defines an optimal normalized decomposition of C.

Begin

/* *Create vertices*(V) */

- Set $V := \{C\}$;
- <u>For all</u> FDs $C([f_1, \ldots, f_n] \rightarrow g)$ in $\mathcal{R}$ <u>do</u>
  - create class E and set $attributes^*(E) := \{f_1, \ldots, f_n, g\}$;
  - define the set of FDs over E as the projection of the FDs over C onto $\{f_1, \ldots, f_n, g\}$;
  - add E to V ;
- <u>For all</u> UFDs ψ in $\mathcal{R}$, where $C([f_1, \ldots, f_n] \rightarrow g)$ is a member of ψ <u>do</u>
  - create class E and set $attributes^*(E) := \{f_1, \ldots, f_n, g\}$;
  - define the set of FDs over E as the projection of the FDs over C onto $\{f_1, \ldots, f_n, g\}$.
  - add E to V ;
- <u>For all</u> EDs ψ in $\mathcal{R}$, where $C[f_1, \ldots, f_n]$ is in ψ <u>do</u>
  - create class E and set $attributes^*(E) := \{f_1, \ldots, f_n\}$;
  - define the set of FDs over E as the projection of the FDs over C onto $\{f_1, \ldots, f_n\}$;
  - add E to V ;
- <u>For all</u> classes E and F in V where there is $\{f_1, \ldots, f_n\} \subseteq attributes^*(E)$ such that $\{f_1, \ldots, f_n\} \in keys(E)$ and $\{f_1, \ldots, f_n\} \in keys(G)$ <u>do</u>
  - create class G and set $attributes^*(G) := attributes^*(E) \cup attributes^*(F)$;
  - define the set of FDs over G as the union of the set of FDs over E with the set of FDs over F;
  - add G to V;
  - remove E and F from V;
- <u>For all</u> classes E and F in V where there is $\{f_1, \ldots, f_n\} \subseteq attributes^*(E)$ such that $\{f_1, \ldots, f_n\} \in keys(E)$ and $\{f_1, \ldots, f_n\} \subset attributes^*(F)$ <u>do</u>
  - set $attributes^*(F) := attributes^*(E) \cup attributes^*(F)$;

/* *Create edges* (A) */

- set $A := \emptyset$;
- <u>For all</u> classes E and F in V where $attributes^*(E) \subset attributes^*(F)$ and there is no D in V such that $attributes^*(E) \subset attributes^*(D)$ and $attributes^*(D) \subset attributes^*(F)$ <u>do</u>
  - add $\langle E, F \rangle$ to A.

end algorithm.

Fig. 6. Algorithm 5.1

For example, suppose that C is a class of S, where $\{C([f_1] \rightarrow f_2), C([f_1] \rightarrow f_4), C([f_1, f_2, f_3] \subset E([g_1, g_2, g_3])\}$ is the set of all EDs and FDs in $\mathcal{R}$ over C. Applying the transformation T defined by the decomposition graph D_c in figure 5 to the schema S, we obtain the schema $S_1 = (\mathcal{C}_1, \mathcal{A}_1, \mathcal{R}_1)$ where $\{A([f_1] \rightarrow f_2), \{A([f_1] \rightarrow f_4), B([f_1, f_2, f_3] \subset E([g_1, g_2, g_3])\}$ is the set of all EDs and FDs in $\mathcal{R}_1$ over the classes in V. Based on definition 5.3, we observe that all classes in V are in DNF. Therefore D_c defines a normalized decomposition of C. In

[Vidal94b]we show that there may exist more than one decomposition graph for a class C that defines a normalized decomposition of C. We are interested in the one that defines an *optimal normalized decomposition* of C, defined as follows.

Definition 5.4: Suppose that $D_c = (V, A)$ is a decomposition graph of the class C in S. Let T be the transformation defined by the graph D_c. D_c defines an *optimal normalized decomposition of* C iff : (i) D_c defines a normalized decomposition of C. (ii) For any classes E and G in V, if $E \neq G$ then if $\{f_1, \ldots, f_n\} \in keys(E)$ then $\{f_1, \ldots, f_n\} \notin S\_keys(G)$. (iii) For any classes E and G in V, if $\{f_1, \ldots, f_n\} \in keys(E)$ and $\{f_1, \ldots, f_n\} \subseteq attributes(G)$ then $E \in references(G)$.◊

Based on definition 5.4 the decomposition graph D_c in figure 5 defines an optimal normalized decomposition of C. In Figure 6 we present an algorithm to obtain a decomposition graph for a class C that defines an optimal normalized decomposition of C. The proof of the correctness of the algorithm appear in [Vidal94b].

6 Conclusion

In this paper, we have examined the problem of schema restructuring and we have proposed a formal underpinning for schema restructuring. We have proposed a *decomposable normal form* for schemas that specifies which properties a schema should have so that the problem of "merge incompatibility" captured by certain existence dependency constraints do not occur. We also have presented an algorithm to transform restricted class of schemas into equivalent schemas which are in decomposable normal form.

With the general forms of existence dependency constraints supported by our model, we have formally specified the most common types of transformations that are required during schema restructuring. The proposed framework allows schema restructuring to be realized in a safe and efficient way, and eliminates the problem of the anomalies that may arise with the use of methodologies that are not able of justifying the correctness of their transformations. Further work should be directed towards extending the proposed framework to support other forms of structural dissimilarity which cannot be expressed with the use of existence dependence constraints supported by our model.

References

[Bancilhon81] Bancilhon, F., Spyratos, N., "Update Semantics and Relational Views," ACM Transactions on Database Systems, vol. 6, No. 4, Dec. 1981.

[Batini84] Batini C., Lenzerini M., "A Methodology for Data Schema Integration in the Entity Relationship Model," IEEE Trans. on Software Eng., SE-10(6):650-664, November 1984.

[Chen76] Chen P. P., "The Entity-Relationship Model: Towards a Unified View of Data," ACM Transaction on DAtabase Systems, 1, 1,1976.

[Codd 72] E. F. Codd, "Further Normalization of Data Base Relational Model," in Data Base Systems, edited by Randell Rustin, Prentice Hall, 1972.

[Cosmadakis84] Cosmadakis S. S., Papadimitriou C. H., "Updates of Relational Views," J. ACM, Vol. 31, No. 4, Oct. 1984.

[Dayal82] Dayal, U., Bernstein, P., "On the correct Translation of Update Operations on Relational Views," ACM Transactions on Database Systems, vol. 7, No. 3, Sept. 1982.

[Eick91] Eick, C. F., "A Methodology for the Design and Transformation of Conceptual Schemas," Proceedings of 17th International Conference on Very Large Databases, Barcelona, Sept. 1991.

[Hammer81] Hammer, M. and McLeod, D., "Database Description with SDM: A Semantic Database Model," ACM TODS, vol. 6, no. 3, pp. 351-387, September 1981.

[Jajodia83] Jajodia, S., Ng, P. A., Springsteel, "Entity-Relationship Diagrams which are in BCNF," International Journal of Computer and Information Sciences 12,4 (1983).

[Keller86] Keller, A.M., "The Role of Semantics in Translating View Updates," IEEE Computer, vol. 19, no. 1, pp. 63-73, Jan. 1986.

[Larson89] Larson, J. A., Navathe, S. B., Elmasri, R., "A Theory of Attribute Equivalence in Databases with Application to Schema Integration," IEEE Transactions on Software Engineering, vol. 15, no. 4, April 1989.

[Ling81] Ling, T. W., Tompa, F. W., Kameda, T., "An Improved Third Normal for Relational Databases," ACM Transactions on Database Systems 6 2, June 1981.

[Ling85] Ling, T. W., "A Normal Form For Entity-Relationship Diagrams," Proceeding of the International Conference on Data Enginineering, pp. 24-35, 1985.

[Miller93] Miller, R. J., Ioannidis, Y. E., Ramakrishman, R., "The Use of Information Capacity in Schema Integration and Translation," Proceedings of 19th International Conference on Very Large Databases, Ireland, 1993.

[Mylopoulos80] Mylopoulos, J., Bernstein, P. A., and Wong, H. K. T., "A Language Facility for Designing Database-Intensive Applications," ACM Transactions on Database Systems, vol. 5, no. 2, pp. 185-207, June 1980.

[Navathe86] Navathe, S. B., Elmasri, R., and Larson, J., "Integrating User Views in Database Design," IEEE Computer, vol. 19, no. 1, pp. 50-62, Jan. 1986.

[Rochfel92] Rochfeld, A., Negros, P., "Relationship of relationship and other interrelationship links in E-R model," Data & Knowledge Engineering 9, Norh-Holland, 1992.

[Spaccapietra] S., Parent, C.,"View Integration: A Step Forward in Solving Structural Conflicts," IEEE Transaction on Knowledge and Data Engineering, vol. 6, no. 2, April 1994.

[Shipman81] Shipman, D.W., "The Functional Data Model and the Data Language DAPLEX," ACM TODS, vol. 6, no. 1, pp. 140-173, 1981.

[Vidal94a] Vidal, V. M. P., Winslett, M., "Specifying View Update Translation in Schema Integration," Third International Conference on Information and Knowledge Management (CIKM'94), Gaithersburg, 1994.

[Vidal94b] Vidal, V. M. P., "Specifying View Update Translation in Schema Integration." PhD Thesis, Department of Computer Science, Federal University of Rio de Janeiro, 1994.

Managing Schema Changes in Object-Relationship Databases

Mohamed Bouneffa and Nacer Boudjlida

Centre de Recherche en Informatique de Nancy (CRIN-CNRS)
Campus scientifique B.P. 239 54506 Vandoeuvre-lès-Nancy
E-mail: {Mourad.Bouneffa, Nacer.Boudjlida}@loria.fr

Abstract. Changing a database schema may affect existing data and application programs. *Immediate data restructuring* is a first usual strategy that transforms the existing database to render it conform to the modified schema, but it does not deal with program adaptation to the changes. An other approach allows the existence of several schema versions for a single database: *emulation mechanisms* are then used to achieve program adaptation but they cannot avoid data redundancy. Furthermore, both the approaches only considered atomic schema changes. This paper proposes a combination of both the approaches: several facets of the database are virtually maintained: every facet represents the database in conformance to a schema version and only one "reference facet" may be physically stored. Mapping functions among the facets are also maintained: they deliver data items (to a user or to an application program) according to their definitions in a given version of the database schema.

1   Introduction

Full schema evolution is the ability of a DataBase Management System (DBMS) to support schema changes and to propagate the changes on the current DataBase (DB) state and on application programs. At least three strategies may be followed to make the DB meet the new schema: *(i)* immediate migration, *(ii)* deferred migration and *(iii)* opportunistic migration. Deferred migration and opportunistic migration assumes the availability of, at least, two versions of the schema: prior and after the change. To enable the implementation of any of these strategies and considering atomic as well as complex schema changes (like schema restructuring while integrating schemas), we suggest the management of *multi-facetted data* where every facet is the representation of the objects in the DB as defined in version of the schema. Relationships among the facets are expressed as *homomorphic functions* and serve to map pieces of data under a representation in a facet into a representation in an other one. The mapping functions may also help in program adaptation. Indeed, the data representation model we fixed to support our study has an object-oriented flavour where objects are manipulated by means of methods (or operations) through message passing. The mapping functions may be used either to rewrite a message or to convert its parameters prior to the application of the method: this way, we attempt to achieve a kind of *ad hoc polymorphism with coercion*. The presentation of the proposal is detailed as follows: related work is reviewed and discussed in section 2, the

Generic Object-Relationship Data representation Model is briefly introduced in section 3, section 4 contains the unformal and the formal presentation of multi-facetted data. Implementation considerations and concluding remarks are the matter of sections 5 and 6, respectively.

2 Related work

Five approaches to instances and/or programs adaptation are considered here-after.

(1) Instance *conversion* was introduced by *Gemstone* [12] and *Orion* systems. In *Gemstone*, all the affected instances must be restructured *"off line"*, as a result of a DBMS administrator request. This leads the database to be unusable during the restructuring time. In contrast, *Orion* allows data restructuring *"on line"* by hiding deleted attributes or enlarging the bounds of a newly generalised domain. In fact, schema change operations allowed by *Orion* do not affect the already stored data, except attributes deletion. Thus, *Orion* does not provide user-defined conversion procedures, limiting then, schema changes to a restrictive predefined list[3]. The conversion as used in both *Orion* or *Gemstone* does not allow programs compatibility : there is in fact, no explicit relationship between different versions of a schema [7].

(2) *Emulation* [14] provides schema versioning and programs compatibility by means of a class versioning scheme. Every class change produce s a new version of this class. Each instance or program is then, related to a particular class version. Mapping between an instance of a new class version and methods defined in the old ones is performed by a set of system routines implemented as exception handlers. Like conversion, emulation only deals with a restrictive and predefined list of atomic class changes.

(3) *The use of the polymorphism.* Polymorphism has been used to achieve program compatibility without data instances restructuring. In [11], a polymorphic algebra was defined by a set of operators which can be executed under different representations of the same piece of data. Polymorphic algebra is more interesting to support transformations from atomic structure to an aggregation one, or to a set, and from an aggregation to a set. However, it can't be used in the case of class or attribute deletion.

(4) *Temporal and historical models* often consist in an extension of the relational data model to manage the time as an attribute associated with the real world entities[2, 9]. Thus, time can be used as a relevant parameter in queries. This approach only allows data retrieval in several versions of a schema. It does not deal with data sharing problems between schema versions nor with programs compatibility. Thus, data redundancy may occur and old programs must be explicitly transformed by introducing the convenient time values in the old DB queries.

(5) *Dynamic classification* has been introduced in [10] to support incremental database schema design. In this approach an instance is dynamically related to a class and each class change can make instances migrate to other more relevant classes. Such an approach doesn't deal with schema versioning nor programs compatibility. In fact, managing several versions of a DB schema in presence of

instances migration is a very hard problem. Since, generally, data instances are referenced by their classes, then the migration of an instance leads to update all the relationships in which the instance participates.

Discussion: These approaches may be considered as special cases of two more general strategies: *database restructuring* and *schema versioning*.

Following the database restructuring strategy, data instances must be converted to be conform to the modified schema. Such a conversion can be made by some atomic operations or by more complex ones like the dynamic classification, atomic domains to tuples conversions, etc. Restructuring a database leads, naturally, to transform the affected programs operating on its instances. These transformations have rarely been considered in the studied approaches. In [15] a method using λ-calculus has been developed to compare two behavioural components (object methods) of two distinct OODB schemas. Such a comparison gives a significant knowledge about what must be done in order to adapt a method defined for one schema version to another one. Using the polymorphism of DB programs is an alternative way to achieve programs adaptation to schema changes. However, polymorphism can only be used for a limited set of changes. Another important question that should be addressed, with databases restructuring strategy, is how to share the data instances between all the schema versions? In *Orion* a data instance can be shared by several schema versions, avoiding then data redundancy. However, this sharing is possible because the schema changes considered are quite simple and do not require an effective restructuring. To reduce data redundancy, some approaches [1] limit schema versioning to only specific parts of a database schema.

Emulation is a special case of the strategy allowing the coexistence of multiple schema in the same database. This strategy tries to avoid the database restructuring and to provide schema versioning by associating each data instance and each program to a specific schema version. Such a strategy increases the data redundancy and may, then, cause some semantical problems in real world data interpreting. In fact, there is no relationship between two pieces of data representing the same real object into two distinct schema versions.

To avoid inconvenient of both databases restructuring and the coexistence of multiple schemas, we define an approach combining these two strategies. Our approach allows each piece of data to be viewed as an instance of more than one DB schema: data instances are multifaceted and each facet corresponds to one DB schema. Since only one facet may be physically stored, all the facets are related by means of mapping functions. Such functions are used by the programs operating on them to achieve programs compatibility.

The following section introduces the data model underlying to our approach.

3   The GORM data model

GORM (Generic Object-Relationship Data Model) has been defined in order to manage complex data generally used in advanced database environments, like CASE databases[4]. GORM has been defined as a synthetic model of the more relevant semantic and object oriented data models. GORM encompasses basic types of objects as well as classical semantic constructors and relationships among objects. The concepts of the data model are briefly exposed.

There are three kinds of object types: *(1) Basic types* are used for Input/Output operations. Such types may be atomic (integers, boolean, string, ...) or structured like arrays, lists or tuples. No identifier is associated with basic types values. *(2) Entity types* are interpreted as entities in the Entity/Relationship data model or as abstract types in semantic data models. Each entity is identified by an internal identifier in its entity-set. *(3) Relationship types* represent semantical associations between entity types (e.g. the relationship type *Module* in the right part of figure 1). *Participants* to a relationship type are (e.g. *Specification* and *Body*) are labelled by their respective roles (e.g. *spec* and *body*) and a cardinality: single (single arrow for one-to-one) or multiple (double arrow for one to many). Relationships are also identified by internal symbols.

There are *three additional means* to link different data types. *(1) The attribute* relationship is a function $a : T_1 \longrightarrow T_2$ where T_1 may be an entity or relationship type and T_2 an entity or basic type. When T_1 is a relationship type, T_2 may only be a basic type. *(2) Composition* relationships or links defined between two entity types can be viewed as a combination of classical aggregations (tuples) and grouping. The figure 1 shows a module as an aggregation of a specification and many bodies (or implementations). A composition link is defined giving a composite entity type (e.g. *Module*) and the components (e.g. *Specification* and *Body*) which are designated by their roles (*spec* and *bodies*) and their cardinalities. *(3) Sub-type* relationship among two entity types is the classical IS_A relationship restricted to single inheritance.

4 The use of multiple facets in schema evolution

We propose to promote data sharing between several schema versions and programs compatibility by considering every instance i of a piece of data as a sequence of facets $\{f_1(i), \ldots, f_n(i)\}$. Each facet $f_j(i)$ represents the value of the instance i in a version V_j of the DB schema. We first give an example that, intuitively, introduces the notion of facets and then present these facets in a formal way. Finally we show how these facets must be used in presence of schema changes.

4.1 Informal presentation

Figure 1 shows two versions of the entity type *Module*. Version V_2 of the schema results from changes performed on version V_1 :

- the module's attribute *name* is unchanged. So, it can be shared by the two versions without any database restructuring,
- the entity type *Module* has been transformed into a relationship type with, as its participants, the entity types *Specification* and *Body*,
- the attribute *Body.author* was a string value representing a programer's name: it is represented, in V_2, by an entity type *Programer* and the attribute *Body.author* "corresponds" to attribute *Programer.name*,
- the domain of the attribute *Module.date_update* is restructured from a string value (in V_1) into a tuple in V_2. Further, the domain of *Body.size* is changed

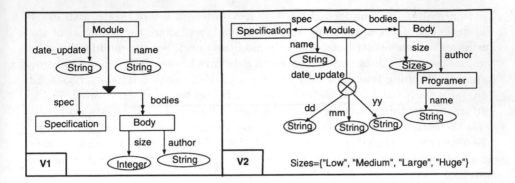

Fig. 1. Example of schema changes

from integer to the set $\{"Small", "Medium", "Large", "Huge"\}$.

Figure 2 illustrates the notion of facets. In its left part (Facet f1) a graphical instance of a module identified by m is shown. The "object" m refers to a body identified by b in the *Body* entity-set. In the right part of the figure, the represen-

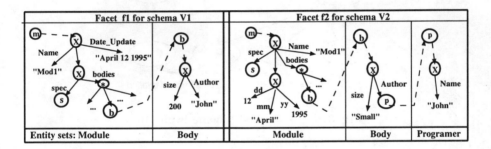

Fig. 2. Multifaceted instances

tation is conform to the version V_2. Facets are virtual representations: in fact, we intend to physically store only one facet as a synthesis of the various facets. The stored facet is labelled with the adopted representation and with mapping functions. For instance, $f2$ could be chosen as the synthetic facet and the attribute *date_update* would be derived from its representation in $f2$ under its representation as a string. Similarly, every access to *Module.bodies.author* is transformed into an access to *Module.bodies.auhtor.name*. Unfortunately, mapping functions may not exist (e.g. one cannot derive the integer value of the attribute *size* from a value in the set $\{$ *"Small", "Medium", ...* $\}$). Then the synthetic facet may encompass representations coming from different schema versions (in our example, the attribute *size* would be represented as an integer and labelled by a formula like *"if size ≤ 200 then "Small" else if size ≤ 500 then "Medium" ..."*).

Informally, our approach consists in associating a set of facets with every database (one facet per schema version). Such facets share the identifier of the instances and some attribute values (unmodified ones). For the modified properties, mapping functions may be defined as gateways between the different schema versions. Mapping functions may be used to achieve both data conversion and programs compatibility. Such functions may be automatically generated during the schema evolution process or may be user defined. The following section, defines the notion of multiple facets and mapping functions in a more formal way. We also explain the strategies which may be followed to achieve schema reuse and data and programs adaptation. We then illustrate the application of the approach to the most relevant schema changes.

4.2 Formal definition of multiple facets

Over time, a database D may be viewed as a sequence of schemas S_i and database states D_i^j where every state is conform to the corresponding schema S_i (figure 3). D_i^j transitions are performed through database updates while S_i transitions re-

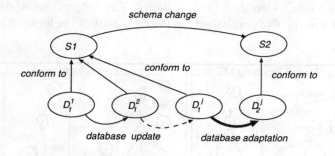

Fig. 3. Database and schema evolution

sult from schema changes. A first problem is how to make a database state D_i^j conform to a database schema S_{i+1}? A data item that has different definitions in the schema versions is associated with a function that maps its value according to its definition in a schema version into its value according to its definition in another schema version. An item who has the same definition in the schema versions has the identity function associated with it. Thus, mapping functions help in restructuring D_i^j into a database D_{i+1}^j conform to the new schema version. An additional usefulness of the mapping functions is in program restructuring. Indeed, some functions can be used to re-write method invocations (ie. operations that are addressed to the objects in the database) while others can be used to make some methods polymorphic. Instead of storing every facet, to avoid data redundancy data may be stored following a synthetic schema version. Thus, mapping functions will be used to derive a data value for a given schema version from the synthetic one.

Multiple facets are defined only for entity and relationship types instances.

Atomic and constructed values are "mandatorily" related to entities (respectively relationships) by means of attribute links, so their facets are defined inside the entities (respectively the relationships).

An entity e is formally defined as a tuple $[id; vp_1; ... ; vp_n]$ where id is the entity identifier and vp_i ($i = 1, ... , n$) the attribute or components values of e. These values may be atomic or constructed. They also may be entity identifiers or sets of entity identifiers (representing the mono-valued and the multivalued components).

In the same way, a relationship a of type type ta is formally defined as a tuple $[id; vp_1; ... ; vp_n]$ with the same semantics. However, the values vp_i ($i = 1, ... , n$) must be atomic or constructed.

A facet f_j of an entity e or a relationship a is then defined by the homomorphism f_j such that:

$$f_j(e) = f_j([id; vp_1; ... ; vp_n]) = [id; f_j(vp_1); ... ; f_j(vp_n)]$$
and
$$f_j(a) = f_j([id; vp_1; ... ; vp_n]) = [id; f_j(vp_1); ... ; f_j(vp_n)]$$

Applying such an homomorphism to vp_i may return:

1. an error code if the type of vp_i is not defined within the facet f_j,
2. a null value if the type of vp_i is not yet instantiated in the database,
3. a stored constant value which may be an atomic value, a constructed value, an entity's identifier or a set of entity identifiers, depending on the type of vp_i,
4. a constant that results from the application of a mapping function.

A mapping function between two facets f_i and f_j is formalised by an homomorphism $G_{f_i \to f_j}$ defined by:

$$G_{f_i \to f_j}([id; f_j(vp_1); ... ; f_j(vp_n)]) = [id; G_{f_i \to f_j}(f_j(vp_1)); ... ; G_{f_i \to f_j}(f_j(vp_n))]$$

Both facets and mapping functions are formalised by homomorphisms. The ideal situation happens when $G_{f_i \to f_j}$ in an isomorphism.

4.3 Mapping functions in presence of schema changes

This section defines mapping functions for the more significant schema changes. Our approach has been applied to a list of schema changes that can be found in [6]. This list has been defined considering a schemas and every data type in it as abstract data types. The list of changes includes the restructuring of the sub-type relationship together with various schema changes like changing the domain of an attribute, changing an entity type composition, adding or deleting an entity type or a relationship type and so on. In this paper we only consider the most common schema modifications. These changes have a real side effect on data instances and programs.

i) Attribute deletion or migration This change is shown in the figure 4. The attribute $T_1.a$, in the version V_1 of the DB schema, is first deleted and migrates to $T_2.a$ in the version V_2.

The mapping functions associated to such a change are defined by:

$$G_{f_1 \to f_2}(f_1(T_1.a)) = f_2(T_2.a') = f_1(T_1).a'.a \text{ and } G_{f_2 \to f_1}(f_2(T_2.a)) = f_1(T_1.a)$$
with $f_1(T_2.a) = f_2(T_1.a) = nil$

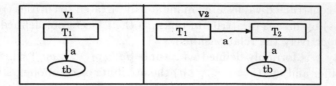

Fig. 4. Attribute migration

As an example, consider the migration of the attribute *Body.author* to *Programer.name* (figure 1):

$G_{f_1 \to f_2}(f_1(b.author)) = f_2(p.name)$ and
$G_{f_2 \to f_1}(f_2(p.name)) = f_1(b.author)$ and
$f_1(p.name) = f_2(b.author) = nil,$

where m and b are instance identifiers of the entity types *Body* and *Module*. That means that the message *b.author* is rewritten into *p.name* in the all programs defined for the version V_1.

ii) Restructuring the domain of an attribute Restructuring the domain of an attribute consists in transforming a domain from atomic values into tuples, or from tuples into sets, etc. As an example, the mapping functions associated with the restructuring of the domain of the attribute *Module.date_update* from a string to a tuple of strings (figure 1) are:

$G_{f_1 \to f_2}(f_1(m.date\_update)) = disaggregate(f_1(m.date\_update))$
$G_{f_2 \to f_1}(f_2(m.date\_update)) = aggregate(f_2(m.date\_update))$

We assume that *aggregate*() and *disaggregate*() are generic functions which transform an atomic value to an aggregation and conversely. So, if the attribute *Module.date_update* is physically stored as a string (according the version V_1) then the disaggregate functions is applied to it whenever it is accessed as a 3-uple.

iii) Arbitrary transformation of an attributes' domain In some domain changes there is no mapping between the old and the modified domain. We call such a modification "an arbitrary domain change". For example, consider the transformation of the domain of the attribute *Body.size* from integer values to the set {"*Small*", "*Medium*", "*Large*", "*Huge*"}. In this case, the user must define an explicit function which retrieves a qualitative range for the attribute *Body.size* ("Small" etc.) given the integer value of their sizes. The reverse function does not exist, this case shows undecidable situations.

iv) Transforming an entity type into a relationship type Transforming an entity type into a relationship type is quite specific to schema integration process. As an example, consider the *Module*'s transformation from an entity type to a relationship type (figure 1). In this case, there is no real restructuring needed because the path expressions which retrieve components are identical to those retrieving relationship participants. Mapping functions are only needed to translate the names of modules properties. They will be expressed by:

$$G_{f_1 \to f_2}(f_1(m.spec)) = f_2(m.sp) \quad \text{and } G_{f_2 \to f_1}(f_2(m.sp)) = f_1(m.spec)$$
$$G_{f_1 \to f_2}(f_1(m.bodies)) = f_2(m.bod) \text{ and } G_{f_2 \to f_1}(f_2(m.bod)) = f_1(m.bodies)$$

The following section gives some ideas leading to an effective implementation of our proposals.

5 Implementation issues

We consider the facets and mapping functions as basic services which may be used to implement all the strategies dealing with the impact of schema evolution on the existing databases and programs. Mapping functions may be used to just implement data conversion. They also may be used in order to use a same databse through several schema versions. A multifaceted data instance is then manipulated by polymorphic methods. Thus, for a same message selector we associate a set of method bodies (one body for each facet).

Let's assume the existence of a synthetic schema version according to which data is physically stored. To implement methods' polymorphism three cases must be considered:

i) a mapping function exists and can be automatically extracted. This case concerns especially all schema changes which consist in properties migration or domains restructuring. For such cases we assume the existence of a library of operation translator schemes. We then choose a translator scheme and instantiate its parameters which can be extracted from the specification of the schema change.

ii) A mapping f may be provided by the user. So, we replace the operation acceding to the property concerned by the user-defined procedure. This case is similar to the modification of $Body.size$ attribute from integer values to qualitative ones.

iii) We cannot define a mapping: data redundancy cannot be avoided.

6 Concluding Remarks

Every database schema change may affect both data instances contained in the database and the programs operating on them. The two general strategies developed to deal with the impact of schema changes on instances and program consist in restructuring the database or allowing the coexistence of several schema versions into a single database. Using the database restructuring allows instances conformity to the modified schema. However, there isn't any strategy to transform programs in the same manner. Furthermore, the current approaches that use the strategy of databases restructuring, only consider the atomic changes of a schema which consist in attribute deletion or generalisation. In contrast, the coexistence of several schema versions in a same database may lead to programs adaptation by means of the emulation mechanism. However it is only used for some atomic changes. Such a mechanism causes also data redundancy.

We have proposed an approach consisting in a combination of both database restructuring and the emulation mechanism. Where each instance can be viewed as set of facets, each one representing its state in one schema version. Thus an instance can belong to more than one schema version. To eliminate data redundancy, only one facet is physically implemented, the others are derived by means of mapping functions. Such functions are also used to adapt programs to the schema changes.

References

1. Jose Andany, Michel Leonard, and Carole Palisser. Management of schema evolution in databases. In *17th International Conference on Very Large Data Bases (VLDB)*, 1991.
2. Gad Ariav. Temporally oriented data definitions: managing schema evolution in temporally oriented databases. *Data and Knowledge Engineering*, 6:451–467, 1991.
3. J. Banerjee, H.-T. Chou, H.J. Kim, and H.F. Korth. Semantics and implementation of schema evolution in object-oriented databases. *ACM SIGMOD conference, SIGMOD Record*, 16(3):311–322, 1987.
4. Philip A. Bernstein. Database system support for software engineering– an extended abstract–. In *9th Internat. Conf. on Software Engineering*, pages 166–178, 1987.
5. Nacer Boudjlida and Olivier Perrin. A formal framework and a procedural approach for data interchange. In *Third Int. Conf. on Systems Integration*, pages 476–485, Sao Paulo, Brazil, August 1994.
6. M. Bouneffa. *Gestion des Objects Complexes: Modélisation, Intégration et Évolution*. PhD thesis, Université Henri Poincaré (Nancy I), May 1995.
7. W. Kim and H.-T. Chou. Versions of schema for object-oriented databases. In F. Bancilhon and D.J. DeWitt, editors, *ACM SIGMOD Int. Conf. Very Large DataBases*, pages 148–59, Los Angeles, CA, 1988.
8. J.A. Larson, S.B. Navathe, and R. Elmasri. A theory of attribute equivalence in databases with application to schema integration. *IEEE transactions On Software Engineering*, SE-15(4), 1989.
9. E. McKenzie and R. Snodgrass. Schema evolution and the relational algebra. *Information Systems*, 15(2):207–232, 1990.
10. G.T Nguyen and D. Rieu. Schema evolution in object-oriented database systems. *Data and Knowledge Engineering*, 4(1):43–67, 1989.
11. S.L. Osborn. The role of polymorphism in schema evolution in an object-oriented database. *IEEE Transactions on Knowledge and Data Engineering*, 1(3):310–317, 1989.
12. D.J. Penney and J. Stein. Class modification in the gemstone object-oriented dbms. *SIGPLAN Notices (Proc. OOPSLA '87)*, 22(12):111–117, 1987.
13. Amit Sheth and Vipul Kashyap. Sofar (schematically) yet so near (semantically). In D.K. Hsiao *et al.*, editor, *Interoperable Database Systems, IFIP Transactions A-25*. North-Holland, 1993.
14. Andrea H. Skarra and Stanley B. Zdonik. *Type evolution in an object-oriented database*, volume Research directions in object-oriented programming, pages 393–416. B. Shriver, Cambridge, MA, mit press edition, 1987.
15. Christian Thieme and Arno Siebes. Schema integration in object-oriented databes. In *Proc. of CAISE 93, LNCS 685*, June 1993.

Behavioural Constraints:
Why Using Events Instead of States

Maguelonne Teisseire[1,2]

[1] Institut des Sciences de l'Ingénieur de Montpellier (ISIM)
[2] LIRMM UMR 9928 CNRS, Montpellier II,
161 rue Ada, 34395 Montpellier Cedex 5, FRANCE.
E-mail: Maguelonne.Teisseire@lirmm.fr

Abstract. This paper focusses on the behavioural constraints of the IFO$_2$ model, an extension of the semantic model IFO defined by S. Abiteboul and R. Hull [1]. IFO$_2$ provides a "whole-event" approach for the dynamic modelling of applications (any fact is modelled as an event). As regards the behavioural conditions constraining event triggering, IFO$_2$ also provides an event approach, based on traces. In fact, operators are proposed to manipulate traces and can be combined in order to express varied behavioural conditions.

1 Introduction

Various models for abstracting behaviour of applications have been proposed for software, real-time systems or databases [2, 3, 5, 8, 9, 10, 11, 13, 14, 15]. One of the issues in representing the behaviour of complex systems is expressing conditions constraining the triggering of operations. These conditions can be particularly precise and can apply on the past history of the system. To meet this need, most of the proposed approaches make use of the notion of state (even if they are not based on state-transition diagrams). However expressing such conditions in terms of states is not necessarily natural because states can be artificial from a structural view point. In fact, they can correspond to attributes or even objects which are not identified in the real world during the structural analysis, but which are necessary for the behavioural description [15].

In proposing the IFO$_2$ model, we have already shown in earlier papers that a "whole-event" approach works fine when modelling the behaviour of applications [19]. By "whole-event", we mean that events are the single elementary description units. They can be combined or related by causality links within an IFO$_2$ event schema which can be implemented in an automatic way by using active rules [20].

In this paper, our aim is to show that events can also be used, instead of states, to express conditions constraining the possible behaviours of an application. Such constraints complement the overall description of the application dynamics offered by the IFO$_2$ event schemas. These event-based constraints are an alternative to state-based conditions. We believe that they resemble more closely to real-world constraints than expressions with states, and they avoid to handle artificial objects. The paper is organized as follows. The second section summarizes the IFO_2 dynamic model[3]. The third section addresses the expression of behavioural conditions. In this section our aim is to give an illustrated overview of the IFO_2 facilities provided to express behavioural constraints. More precisely, we present a set of operators which can be combined in order to specify varied behavioural conditions (the formal definitions of a few primitives can be found in [18]).

2   Overview of the IFO_2 dynamic model

The main feature of IFO_2 [12, 20] is to provide a uniform framework for both structural and behavioural modelling. In fact, the dynamic concepts introduced mirror the structural concepts of the model and by this way, IFO_2 reconciles the static and dynamic representations. These representations are closely related but nevertheless clearly distinct and it is not necessary to complement the structural specifications to take into account dynamic description needs. Actually, the fewer effects on structural representation that the dynamic modelling has, the more likely this static description will stay faithful to the modelled real world.

As in other approaches, an event in IFO_2 is characterized by its instant of occurrence and its parameters representing the objects which react to the considered event. But furthermore, an event is identified (exactly like an object in the structural part of the model) and it has a value, depending on the type of the event in question. Of course, different categories of events are usually distinguished not for a representation issue but rather as an aid for designers. IFO_2 places much more emphasis on defining event types than current behavioural approaches. The proposed basic types (their graphic formalism is given figure 1) are the following:

- The *simple* event type represents the events triggering a method. This method is considered as the event value and its specification is included in the structural representation of the application.
- The *abstract* event type symbolizes external or temporal events, stemmed from the outside world. It is also used to represent internal events which are interesting only through their consequences by triggering other events. The value of abstract events is null.
- The *represented* event type stands for any other type, described elsewhere which can be used without knowing its precise description. Its value depends on the symbolized type.

Example 1 The borrowing management in a library serves as an example throughout the paper. In this application, a simple event type could be "Reminder". The associated method edits a reminder letter if the loan period is completed and the borrowed book not returned. "Borrowing-Request" is an abstract event type which represents the external events occurring when users request the borrowing of a book. The abstract type "End" symbolizes internal events happening when a loan is completed and "R-Loan" is a represented type, introduced in the dynamic description to re-use the type "Loan" (described later because it is complex).

---

[3] Comparisons between IFO_2 and related work have been discussed in [20]

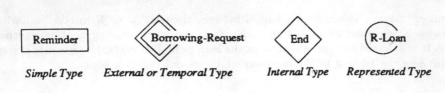

Fig. 1. Basic Event Type Examples

To model the behaviour of a system, it is necessary to express event synchronization conditions, i.e. different variants of event conjunction and disjunction. To answer this need, we choose to represent complex events by using *constructors*. With this approach, we provide not only the required expressive power but also the uniformity with respect to the IFO$_2$ structural modelling. The event constructors (their graphic formalism is given in figure 2), which can apply recursively, are the following:

- The *composition* reflects the conjunction of events of different types.
- The *sequence* is defined as the previous constructor but with a chronological constraint on the occurrences of the component events.
- The *grouping* expresses conjunctions of events of the same type. It is close to the HiPAC closure constructor [4].
- The *union* expresses a disjunction of events of different types.

Example 2 When a loan is performed, the borrowed book becomes unavailable and then a new loan is actually created. Loan events can thus be described through a sequence of two simple types "Unavailable" and "Create-Loan" (Cf. figure 2).

Apart from synchronization conditions, the relations between events can also express the chaining of events. These causality links are expressed with functions. In fact, the event types are interconnected by functions through the *event fragment* concept, focused on a principal type called *heart*. Functions of event fragments express general conditions on the event chaining since they can combine the following features: *simple* or *complex*, i.e. multivalued; *partial* or *total*, i.e. an event of their type origin can or must trigger an event of their target; and *deferred* or *immediate*, if there is a delay or not between the occurrences of the origin and target events. In addition, we make a distinction between *triggering* and *precedence functions*, which roughly express the fact that an event of the fragment heart triggers the occurrence of other events or that it is preceded by the occurrence of other events. In order to emphasize this, let us consider an external or temporal event. By its very nature, it cannot be triggered by another event, therefore it is sometimes necessary to express that its occurrence is necessarily preceded by other events.

Example 3 The fragment of heart "Loan", in Figure 2, describes the reactions of the system when a loan is performed. The simple type "Inc-nb-loan" corresponds to a method incrementing the number of current loans of a borrower. It is related to the heart of the fragment by a function which is simple, total and immediate. This means that a single event of "Inc-nb-loan" stems, automatically and immediately, from an event of "Loan". The function, defined between the heart and "Reminder" is partial because a reminder event is triggered only if the corresponding book is returned late. It is deferred to take into account the loan period. It is complex because several reminders can be sent to the borrower who does not return a book.

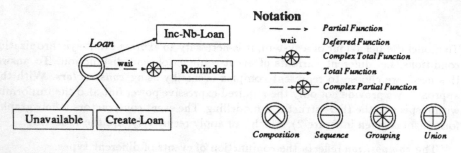

Fig. 2. The "Loan" Fragment

An original feature of IFO$_2$ is to offer the synchronization of operations. Actually, a complex event type, target of a triggering function, can represent such synchronizations. This is particularly interesting to express an alternative between operations or the repeated triggering of an operation.

The partial views provided by fragments are grouped together within an event schema which offers an overview of the behaviour. More precisely represented types are related to heart of fragments by means of IS_A links. These links introduce a behavioural hierarchy and multiple inheritance is possible: a represented type can inherit from several fragment hearts. Thus the behaviour part, modelled through a fragment, can be re-used as a whole.

Example 4 Apart from the fragment "Loan", the schema, illustrated figure 3, encompasses the fragments "Return", "Borrowing-Request" and "End". The first one describes the system behaviour when a borrower returns a book. The heart of the fragment is the external type "Return". When a book is returned, it becomes available. This fragment includes a precedence function between the represented type "R-Loan" which stands for the loan and the heart. This function captures the causality and chronological constraint between the return of a book and its borrowing. "Borrowing-Request" describes what happens when a user wants to borrow a book. In fact, if the requested book is already checked out, a reservation can be performed, else a "New-loan" event (which is a loan) is triggered. The last fragment in the schema specifies in which way a loan is completed. When an event of the heart "End" occurs, it triggers a method "End-Loan" which performs an archival storage of the considered loan. Then an event of "Termination" happens. It can be either the withdrawal of the borrowing privileges if the user has not returned a book or the decrementation of the number of current loans for the user. Let us note that a loan can be concluded only if it has happened. This obvious constraint is captured through the precedence function between the type "S-Loan" (standing for "Loan") and the internal event type "End".

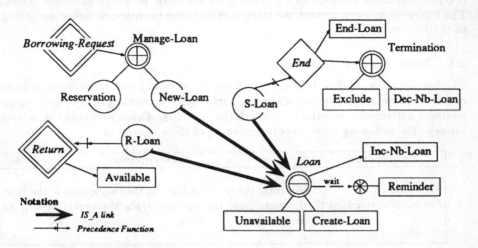

Fig. 3. The "Librairy" Schema Example

3 Expressing behavioural conditions

The fragment functions express general conditions constraining event triggering. Nevertheless, they must be refined because they cannot capture very precise details. For instance, it is necessary to describe under which conditions a borrowing request is satisfied or the borrowing privileges are revoked.

In fact, such behavioural conditions concern object values or the past behaviour of the system. Generally, these conditions are expressed in terms of object properties. Of course, the corresponding attribute and object must exist in the structural representation and if not, some artificial element must be added in the static description. Thus the dynamic modelling alters the faithfulness of the structural description. Furthermore, we believe that this need of artificial elements increases the difficulties of dynamic modelling. The designer has to wonder what is to be stored, what must be revised in the structural representation instead of only focussing on the dynamic modelling.

In IFO$_2$, behavioural conditions can be expressed in terms of existing object values but also in terms of events. Event-based constraints are used everytime the knowledge of the past behaviour is necessary to determine the future behaviour. In fact, any needed information about the past behaviour is captured in the event trace of the system. A trace is just the sequence of the occurred events. This concept, introduced in [7], is widely used in dynamic approaches [3, 13, 21, 22] and IFO_2 also uses it. Then the major issue is to manipulate traces in order to yield any information. Let us note that a few approaches includes some trace manipulation facilities to complement state-based conditions [16, 17].

IFO_2 boosts these capabilities by defining an algebraic language based on traces. The following sections present the trace manipulation facilities, classified according to their objective.

3.1 Event type operators

The two operators of this class apply on a trace and yield a new trace encompassing events of some given type(s). They are particularly interesting to capture events having a particular semantics or to check the existence of such events in the system history. The following table gives the meaning of these operators.

Operators	Description
Restriction $\lceil$ *Fragment restriction* $\lceil\lceil$	Restricts the specified trace to the only events of the type. Extracts from the operand trace the events of a given fragment.

Example 5 Let $Tr_{Library}$ be the trace representing the application history. It is possible to focus on the loans by using the following restriction:

$$Tr_{Library} \lceil Loan.$$

Furthermore, among these loans, we can consider the loans which have been completed by using another restriction:

$$(Tr_{Library} \lceil Loan) \lceil S\text{-}Loan.$$

3.2 List Operators

This class provides facilities to merge or at least compare two traces. The associated operators, presented in the following table, have the usual semantics when manipulating lists.

Operators	Description
Union	Creates a new trace encompassing the events of the two operand traces.
Intersection	The resulting trace only includes the common events of the two specified traces, if any.
Difference	Extracts a new trace from the first operand by removing possible common events between the two operand traces.
Concatenation .	Concatenates two traces.

Example 6 The following expression yields the loans for which no return has occurred:

$$(Tr_{Library}\lceil Loan) - (Tr_{Library}\lceil R\text{-}Loan).$$

3.3 Parameter operators

The manipulation primitives of this class operate on events according to their parameters. More precisely, it is possible to extract from a trace events having a given object among their parameters, or an object of a given type. The simplest way to specify this object or this object type is to give its identifier or its name. But the most interesting way is to specify them through an event by referencing its own parameters. Thus it is possible to focus on the behaviour of a single object or a set of objects (an object type in IFO$_2$ [12]) sharing a common semantics. The following table summarizes the mentioned possibilities.

Operators	Description
Select-Parameter	Extracts from the operand trace events which have a given object of a given type as being one of their parameters.
Same-Parameter	Yields the events of the specified trace having the same parameter object than a given event.
Select-Type-Parameter	The resulting trace includes events of the operand, each of which having a given object type within their parameters.
Same-Type-Parameter	Extracts the events of the operand trace having at least a common object type with a given event.

Example 7 Let us imagine that when a borrowing request occurs, we would like to examine the whole behaviour of the concerned user. This user represents a parameter of the external event in question, e_{BR_1}. The type of this object is "Borrower". Then, the following expression yields the history of the user:

$$Same\text{-}Parameter(Tr_{Library}, e_{BR_1}, Borrower).$$

3.4 Temporal Operators

This class addresses the expression of temporal constraints. Its major concern is to provide comparisons between traces by considering the occurrence instants of their events. Other possibilities merge temporal conditions and type constraints. The proposed operators limit the scope of searches in a trace, thus it is possible to focus on a precise part of the system history.

Operators	Description
Before	Yields the events of the first trace which have occurred before the events of the second specified trace.
After	The resulting trace encompasses the event of the first operand trace occurred after the events of the second operand trace.
Between	Creates, from the system history, a new trace, each event of which has occurred after the events of the first trace and before the events of the second trace.
First-of-Type	Yields the first event of a given type which has ever occurred in the operand trace.
Last-of-Type	Plays the same role than the previous operator but considers the last event of a given type.
Before-First	Restricts the operand trace to the events happened before the first event of a given type.
Before-Last	Is similar to the previous operator but the considered event is the last event of a given type.
After-First	Creates a new trace with the events of the operand trace occurred after the first event of a given type.
After-Last	Equivalent to After-First but for the last event.

Example 8 Let us consider the following question which is to be asked whenever a user requests a borrowing: "Has a return occurred since the last reminder sent to this user ?". It could be expressed as follows:

$$After(Tr_{BR_1}, Last\text{-}of\text{-}Type(Tr_{BR_1}, Reminder))$$

where Tr_{BR_1} is the trace capturing the history of the considered user.

3.5 Causality Operator

For an event, this operator yields the event which has caused it. Thus, this operator exhibits causality relationships between events. External and temporal events are a particular case, since they are considered as being their own cause. This operator is particularly useful whenever the cause of an event must be traced back through the application history.

Example 9 To illustrate this operator, let us consider the example of an exclusion decision for a user. We imagine that, in spite of repeated reminders, a borrower has not returned a book. When the maximal number of reminders (for instance three) is reached, his borrowing privileges will be revoked. In fact, such a decision is captured in the specification of the precedence function between "S-Loan" and "End" (Cf. Figure 3). This function is denoted by f and its specification is the following:

$\forall e_L$ of type "S-Loan", $f(e_L) = e_E$ of type "End" if and only if (the book was returned by the user):
$\exists e_{Re}$ of type "Return" | $Cause(e_{Re}) = e_L$
else (The book has not been returned by the user since the final reminder)
$\exists e_{R1}, e_{R2}, e_{R3}$ of type "Reminder" | $\forall i \in [1..3], Cause(e_{Ri}) = e_L$.

The benefits resulting from the use of the presented operators are significant. The expression of behavioural constraints is frequently the style to address conditions in the real world. Furthermore, the dynamic modelling does not influence the way in which the designer views the structural part of the application. Furthermore, even for different designers, identified events are likely to be the very same, contrary to states.

4 Conclusion

The IFO$_2$ dynamic model, presented in this paper, proposes a "whole-event" approach for both the overall description of the system behaviour and the expression of behavioural constraints. IFO$_2$ provides a uniform way for specifying dynamics by only considering events. Events are characterized by their type which can capture not only their usual semantics but also synchronization conditions. These conditions are expressed by using event constructors. The IFO$_2$ modelling is modular since specifications can be divided into fragments. Each one is devoted to the system reactions in a particular situation. A fragment can be re-used as a whole through the concepts of represented type and event IS_A link. These links define a behavioural inheritance hierarchy which offers the same features than the structural specialization.
The causality relationships between events are represented by functions. These functions can capture particularly precise conditions constraining the event triggering. To express such conditions, an algebraic language is proposed. It is based on the trace concept. The defined operators express constraints including temporal conditions, semantics-driven restrictions or trace comparison. A powerful operator is provided in order to retrieve the cause of any event. Furthermore, by using parameter operators it is possible to consider events through the objects which react to them. These operators permit to meet the object-driven vision of the behaviour which is widely used in dynamic modelling, in particular in state-based approaches.
Event-based conditions are an alternative to state-based conditions. We have shown that they resemble more closely to real world constraints. But above all, they avoid the need of introducing new attributes and objects in the structural description when a past behaviour must be reminded. Thus the IFO$_2$ behavioural modelling has no effect on the structural representation of the system.

References

1. S. Abiteboul and R. Hull. IFO: A Formal Semantic Database Model. *ACM Transactions on Database Systems*, 12(4):525–565, December 1987.

2. G. Booch. *Object-Oriented Design with Applications*. Benjamin/Cumming Company, 1991.

3. J. Carmo and A. Sernadas. A Temporal Logic Framework for a Layered Approach to Systems Specification and Verification. In *Proceedings of the Temporal Aspects in Information Systems Conference (IFIP 88)*, pp 31–46. Elsevier Science, 1988.

4. S. Chakravarthy, B. Blaustein, A. P. Buchmann, M. Carey, U. Dayal, D. Goldhirsch, M. Hsu, R. Jauhari, and al. HiPAC: A Research Project in Active, Time-Constrained Database Management. Technical report, Xerox Advanced Information Technology, Cambrige, MA, August 1990.

5. P. Coad and E. Yourdon. *Object-Oriented Analysis*. Yourdon Press Computing Series, 1990.

6. D. Harel. On Visual Formalisms. *Communications of the ACM*, 31(5):514–530, 1988.

7. C. Hoare. *Communicating Sequential Processes*. Prentice-Hall, 1985.

8. P. Loucopoulos and R. Zicari. *Conceptual Modeling, Databases and CASE: An Integrated View of Information Systems Development*. Wiley Professional Computing, 1992.

9. Z. Manna and A. Pnueli. Specification and Verification of Concurrent Programs by ∀-Automata. In *Proceedings of the Temporal Logic in Specification Conference*, LNCS Vol 398, pp 124–164, Altrincham, UK, April 1987.

10. J. Ostroff. *Temporal Logic for Real Time Systems*. Wiley and Sons, 1989.

11. J. Ostroff. A Logic for Real-Time Discrete Event Processes. *IEEE Control Systems Magazine*, pp 95–102, June 1990.

12. P. Poncelet, M. Teisseire, R. Cicchetti, and L. Lakhal. Towards a Formal Approach for Object-Oriented Database Design. In *Proceedings of the 19th VLDB Conference*, pp 278–289, Dublin, Ireland, August 1993.

13. G. Reggio. Event Logic for Specifying Abstract Dynamic Data Types. In *Proceedings of 8th Workshop on Specification of Abstract Data Types and the 3rd COMPASS Workshop*, LNCS Vol 655, pp 292–309, Dourdan, France, August 1991.

14. C. Rolland and C. Cauvet. Modélisation Conceptuelle Orientée Objet. In *Actes des 7ièmes Journées BDA*, pp 299–325, Lyon, France, Septembre 1991.

15. J. Rumbaugh, M. Blaha, W. Premerlani, F. Eddy, and W. Lorensen. *Object-Oriented Modeling and Design*. Prentice-Hall, 1991.

16. A. Sernadas, C. Sernadas, and H. D. Ehrich. Object-Oriented Specification of Databases: An Algebraic Approach. In *Proceedings of the 13th VLDB Conference*, pp 107–116, Brighton,UK, August 1987.

17. R. Smedinga. Locked Discrete Event Systems: How to Model and How to Unlock. *Discrete Event Dynamic Systems: Theory and Applications*, pp 265–297, 1993.

18. M. Teisseire and R. Cicchetti. An Algebraic Approach for Event-Driven Modelling. In *Proceedings of the 5th DEXA Conference*, LNCS Vol 856, pp 300–309, Athens, Greece, September 1994.

19. M. Teisseire, P. Poncelet, and R. Cicchetti. Dynamic Modelling with Events. In *Proceedings of the 6th CAiSE Conference*, LNCS Vol 811, pp 285–295, Utrecht, The NetherLands, June 1994.

20. M. Teisseire, P. Poncelet, and R. Cicchetti. Towards Event-Driven Modelling for Database Design. In *Proceedings of the 20th VLDB Conference*, pp 285–296, Santiago, Chile, September 1994.

21. R. Wieringa. Steps Towards a Method for the Formal Modeling of Dynamic Objects. *Data & Knowledge Engineering*, 6:509–540, 1991.

22. R. J. Wieringa. A Formalization of Objects Using Equational Dynamic Logic. In *Proceedings of the 2nd DOOD Conference*, LCNS Vol 566, pp 431–452, Munich, Germany, December 1991.

Behavior Consistent Extension of Object Life Cycles

Michael Schrefl[1] and Markus Stumptner[2]

[1] Department of Information Systems, University of Linz, Austria
e-mail: schrefl@dke.uni-linz.ac.at
[2] Christian Doppler Laboratory for Expert Systems, TU Wien, Austria
e-mail: mst@vexpert.dbai.tuwien.ac.at

Abstract. Various notions of conformance between operations of a subtype and operations of a supertype have been proposed (e.g., contravariance and covariance). Similarly, different notions of "consistent extension" of object life cycles can be defined to meet various objectives.
This paper treats inheritance of object life cycles in the realm of behavior diagrams that identify legal sequences of states and activities (operations). It presents necessary and sufficient rules for checking three different kinds of conformance (observation consistency, weak invocation consistency, and strong invocation consistency) between a behavior diagram of a subtype and that of its supertype.

1 Introduction

Several object-oriented design methods, such as OMT [16], OOSA [7], OOAD [2] and OBD [8] model the behavior of object types at two interrelated levels of detail: at the activity level and at the object type level. For example, behavior diagrams [8] specify at the activity level the signature of an activity by identifying types and preconditions of input parameters as well as the type and the postcondition of the return value. At the object type level, object behavior is specified in terms of object life cycles that identify legal sequences of states and activities.

Inheritance of activities corresponds to inheritance of operations in programming languages, which is fairly well understood [4, 21, 23]. Inheritance of object-life cycles has received less attention although some recent work begins to address the problem how the life cycle of a subtype should relate to the life cyle of its supertype. Inheritance of object life cycles has been discussed in the area of object-oriented specification methods (e.g., OMT [16] and OOSA [7]), but without providing a set of complete rules. The articles by Ebert and Engels [6], and by Saake et. al. [17] provide inheritance rules for object life cycles, which are similar to our approach, but in the realm of state diagrams. Their work is based on graph (homo-)morphisms, similar to the work of Ehrich and Sernadas [20] and Lopes and Costa [10]. An informal treatment of inheritance of state machines is provided in [11]. More recently, Paech and Rumpe have studied inheritance in the context of automata [13].

This paper continues and extends our previous work on the design of object-oriented databases using Object/Behavior diagrams [8, 18, 1]. We discuss inheritance of object life cycles in the realm of behavior diagrams which are based on Petri Nets. A behavior diagram of an object type represents the possible life cycles of its instances by activities, states, and arcs corresponding to transitions, places, and arcs of Petri Nets. Subtypes may specialize the behavior diagram of supertypes in two ways: by refinement and by extension. Refinement means expanding inherited activities and states into subdiagrams. Extension means adding activities, states, and arcs. Refinement of behavior diagrams has been treated in [18] already. Extension of behavior diagrams is the topic of this paper. We also presented initial results on the consistent extension of behavior diagrams in [9], but there we considered only one facet of the problem (what is called "observation consistency" in this paper.)

As behavior diagrams are based on Petri Nets, we hoped to be able to use directly some result already published about Petri Nets. Indeed, many papers have been published on behavior and equivalence preserving refinements of Petri Nets (cf. [3] for an excellent survey). These results, however, apply mainly to refinement of behavior diagrams and not to extension. The net morphism by Winskel [24], mentioned but not discussed in [3], comes closest to our research. We will refer to it, as well as to other relevant literature, in more detail later.

2 Behavior Diagrams

Object/Behavior diagrams are an object-oriented graphical design notation for the design of object-oriented databases [8]. Object/Behavior Diagrams represent the structure of object types in object diagrams and their behavior in behavior diagrams. For the scope of this paper we restrict our attention to behavior diagrams.

Behavior diagrams depict the behavior of instances of an object type by a set of states, a set of activities, and a set of arcs connecting states with activities and vice versa. Each of the states represents a particular period, each of the activities an event in the life cycle of the instances of the object type. All possible life cycles of instances of an object type have a single start state called the *initial state* and a common set of completion states called *final states*. The principal idea behind behavior diagrams stems from Petri Nets [14]. States correspond to places of Petri Nets, activities to transitions.

Definition 1 Behavior Diagram.
A *behavior diagram* $B_O = (S_O, T_O, F_O, s_O^\alpha, \Omega_O)$ of an object type O consists of a set of states $S_O \neq \emptyset$, a set of activities $T_O \neq \emptyset$, $T_O \cap S_O = \emptyset$, and a set of arcs $F_O \subseteq (S_O \times T_O) \cup (T_O \times S_O)$, such that $\forall t \in T_O: (\exists s \in S_O: (s,t) \in F_O) \wedge (\exists s \in S_O: (t,s) \in F_O)$ and $\forall s \in S_O: (\exists t \in T_O: (s,t) \in F_O) \vee (\exists t \in T_O: (t,s) \in F_O)$. There is a distinguished state in S_O, the *initial state* s_O^α, where for no $t \in T_O$: $(t, s_O^\alpha) \in F_O$; and there is a set of distinguished states of S_O, the *final states* Ω_O, where for no $s \in \Omega_O$ and no $t \in T_O : (s,t) \in F_O$.

Instances of an object type which reside in states correspond to individual tokens of a Petri net. We say an activity $t \in T_O$ *consumes* a token (or object) from a state $s \in S_O$ iff $(s,t) \in F_O$, and $t \in T_O$ *produces* a token into $s \in S_O$ iff $(t,s) \in F_O$. In addition, we say a state $s \in S_O$ is a *prestate* of an activity $t \in T_O$ iff $(s,t) \in F_O$, and $s \in S_O$ is a *post state* of $t \in T_O$ iff $(t,s) \in F_O$. Due to the underlying Petri net semantics a behavior diagram determines the legal sequences of states and activities, and thus the legal sequences in which activities may be applied: an activity may be applied on an object if the object is contained in every prestate of the activity. If an activity on some object has been executed successfully, the object is contained in every post state of the activity but in no prestate unless that prestate is also a post state. Unlike Petri nets, where a transition is automatically fired if every prestate contains a token, an activity in a behavior diagram must be explicitly invoked for an object which is in every prestate of the activity. In addition, and unlike Petri nets, activities take time. Therefore, during the execution of an activity on an object, the object resides in an implicit state named after the activity. This state is referred to as *activity state*. Thus, we can say that every instance of an object type is at any point in time in one or several (activity) states of its object type, which are jointly referred to as *life cycle state*.

Definition 2 Life cycle state. A *life cycle state (LCS)* σ of an object type O is a subset of $S_O \cup T_O$. We denote the *initial* LCS $\{s_O^\alpha\}$ by α_O.

Definition 3 Start and completion of an activity. An activity $t \in T_O$ can be *started* on a life cycle state σ, if the set of prestates of t is contained in σ. The start of activity t on LCS σ yields the life cycle state $\sigma' = \sigma \setminus \{s \in S_O \mid (s,t) \in F_O\} \cup \{t\}$. An activity $t \in T_O$ can be *completed* on a life cycle state σ, if t is in σ. The completion of activity t on σ yields the life cycle state $\sigma' = \sigma \setminus \{t\} \cup \{s \in S_O \mid (t,s) \in F_O\}$.

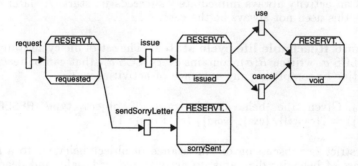

Fig. 1. Behavior diagram of object type RESERVATION

Example 1. Figure 1 shows the behavior diagram of object type RESERVATION. Activities are depicted by vertical bars. States are depicted by rectangles which are labeled by the name of the object type they describe at the top and the name of the state at the bottom. For simplicity, the initial state alpha is not shown. Also, final states are not marked visually. It is assumed that every activity for which no prestate is shown has the initial state as prestate and that every state from which no activity consumes is a final state. □

A behavior diagram of an object type specifies all legal sequences of life cycle states. A particular sequence of life cycle states of an object type is referred to as *life cycle occurrence* of that object type.

Definition 4 Life cycle occurrence. A *life cycle occurrence* (LCO) γ of object type O is a sequence of life cycle states $\sigma^1, \ldots, \sigma^n$, such that $\sigma^1 = \alpha_O$, and for $i = 1 \ldots n-1$ either $\sigma^i = \sigma^{i+1}$, or there exists an activity $t \in T_O$ such that either t can be started on σ^i and the start of t yields σ^{i+1} or σ^i contains t and the completion of t yields σ^{i+1}. Any subsequence of γ is called *partial LCO*. A LCO γ is called *complete*, if $\sigma^n \subseteq \Omega_O$.

Example 2. A possible life cycle occurrence of object type **RESERVATION** is
[{request}, {requested}, {issue}, {issued}, {cancel}, {void}] (cf. Figure 1).   □

It is often more convenient to denote the sequence of starts and completions
of activities that cause a life cycle occurrence than to denote the life cycle states
of a life cycle occurrence.

Definition 5 Activation sequence. An *activation sequence* μ of object type
O is a sequence of statements $\tau^1, \ldots \tau^n$ $(n \geq 0)$, where $\tau^i = start(t)$ or $\tau^i =$
$completion(t)$ for some $t \in T_O$; μ is *valid* on some LCS $\sigma \in R(\alpha_O)$ if there is
some partial LCO $\gamma = \sigma^1 \ldots \sigma^{n+1}$ of O where for $i \in \{1 \ldots n\}$ σ^{i+1} results from
performing τ^i on σ^i and we say μ yields the *trace* γ. If $n = 0$, the activation
sequence is called *empty*. An empty activation sequence can be applied on every
LCS σ and yields trace σ.

Example 3. A possible activation sequence for object type **RESERVATION** is
[s(request), c(request), s(issue), c(issue), s(cancel), c(cancel)], where s stands for start
and c for completion. Note: due to lack of parallelism in this example, the completion of an activity always immediately succeeds its start. As later examples
will show, this need not always be the case.   □

Definition 6 Reachable life cycle states. The set of life cycle states reachable from LCS σ, written $R(\sigma)$, contains every LCS σ'_O that can be reached from
σ by starting or completing any sequence of activities in T_O.

Example 4. Given the behavior diagram of object type **RESERVATION**,
$R(\{issued\}) = \{\{cancel\}, \{use\}, \{void\}\}$ (cf. Figure 1).   □

We restrict our discussion of inheritance of object behavior to a meaningful subclass of behavior diagrams, to activity-reduced, safe, and deadlock-free
behavior diagrams.

Definition 7 Safe, activity-reduced, deadlock-free. A behavior diagram
$B_O = (S_O, T_O, F_O, \sigma_O^\alpha, \Omega_O)$ is *safe*, if there exists no LCS $\sigma \in R(\alpha_O)$ such
that some activity $t \in T_O$ can be completed on σ and σ contains already some
post state of t. B_O is *activity-reduced* iff every $t \in T_O$ is potentially applicable.
An activity $t \in T_O$ is *potentially applicable* if there exists a life cycle occurrence
$\gamma = \sigma^1 \ldots \sigma^n (n > 0)$ such that t can be started on σ^n. B_O is *deadlock free* iff for
every $\sigma \in R(\alpha_O)$ either some $t \in T_O$ can be started on σ or $\sigma \subseteq \Omega_O$.

To restrict our discussion to activity-reduced, safe, and deadlock-free behavior diagrams is meaningful in practice. First, activities which are not potentially
applicable have no influence on object behavior. Such activities correspond to
program statements never reached. Second, unsafe nets contradict the intention
of behavior diagrams to identify by a state or an activity a single, specific processing state of an object. Third, freedom from deadlocks ensures that, unless
processing has finished (i.e., a set of final states has been reached), there is at
least one possible way to continue.

Activities of behavior diagrams can be further described by activity specification diagrams, activity realization diagrams, and activity scripts. These diagrams
are not needed in this paper; the interested reader is referred to [1, 8].

3 Kinds of Behavior Consistency

Intuitively, one expects the behavior diagram of a subtype to be "consistent" with the behavior diagram of a supertype. In this section, we define precisely what "consistent" means with respect to extension of behavior diagrams. Similar to inheritance of operations, for which several types of conformance have been defined, several possibilities exist to relate the behavior diagram of a subtype to the behavior diagram of a supertype.

For inheritance of operations, possibilities proposed range from no restriction at all, called *arbitrary inheritance*, to allowing no changes to operation interfaces, called *strict inheritance*. The first extreme is too unrestricted in order to be used for building reusable and reliable systems as no general properties about the relationship between operations of a subtype and operations of a supertype are known. The second extreme is too restrictive as it prohibits adding new parameters and redefining inherited ones. In between, two alternative notions of conformance prevail: *covariance* and *contra-variance*. Covariance requires that input and output parameters of operations are restricted to subtypes when operations are redefined at a subtype. Contra-variance requires that input parameters are generalized to supertypes and output parameters are restricted to subtypes. Covariance is favored by object-oriented design methods as it supports the concept of specialization in the tradition of semantic networks of artificial intelligence. Contra-variance is favored by type theoreticians as it supports static type checking in the presence of type substitutability [5, 23], which allows using an instance of a subtype whenever an instance of a supertype is expected.

For inheritance of behavior diagrams, we have, as we will see later, similar choices. If we reject, for reasons mentioned above, the extremes of allowing arbitrary changes and of allowing no changes, the idea immediately emerges to borrow from Petri Nets the notions of "subnet" and "embedding" in order to define the notion of "consistent extension" of behavior diagrams.

A behavior diagram $B_O = (S_O, T_O, F_O, s_O^\alpha, \Omega_O)$ is a *subnet* of behavior diagram $B_{O'} = (S_{O'}, T_{O'}, F_{O'}, s_{O'}^\alpha, \Omega_{O'})$, if $S_O \subseteq S_{O'}$, $T_O \subseteq T_{O'}$, $F_O \subseteq F_{O'} \cap ((S_O \times T_O) \cup (T_O \times S_O))$, $s_O^\alpha = s_{O'}^\alpha$, and $\Omega_O \subseteq \Omega_{O'}$. B_O is *embedded* in $B_{O'}$, if there exists an injective function, called *embedding*, $h : (S_O \cup T_O) \to (S_{O'} \cup T_{O'})$, such that $h(e) \in S_{O'} \Leftrightarrow e \in S_O$, $h(e) \in T_{O'} \Leftrightarrow e \in T_O$, $(h(e), h(f)) \in F_{O'} \Leftrightarrow (e, f) \in F_O$, $h(s_O^\alpha) = s_{O'}^\alpha$, and $h(s) \in \Omega_O \Leftrightarrow s \in \Omega_{O'}$. As an example consider behavior diagram RESERVATION which is embedded in the behavior diagrams RESERVATION_PLUS, FRIENDLY_RES, and RESERVATION_WITH_PAYMENT (cf. Figures 1, 2, 3, and 4).

It is natural to call $B_{O'}$ an "extension" of B_O only if B_O is a subnet of $B_{O'}$ and it is reasonable to call an extension "consistent" only if the identity function on states and activities is an embedding of B_O in $B_{O'}$. However, as we will see, this is not sufficient to ensure that B_O and $B_{O'}$ exhibit "comparable behavior".

In Petri Net literature, two approaches are common for comparing the behavior of two Petri Nets (cf. [15] for a comprehensive survey of equivalence notions for net-based systems): (1) Abstracting from actions, one can compare the possible sequences of sets of states in which tokens reside and (2) abstracting from states, one can compare the possible sequences in which transitions can be fired. These approaches are usually followed alternatively (cf. [15]).

Comparing life cycle occurrences of behavior diagrams, both approaches coincide as activities are included next to states in life cycle states, and, thus, we can denote a life cycle occurrence either by the sequence of its life cycle states or by the activation sequence generating it, whichever is more convenient (see above).

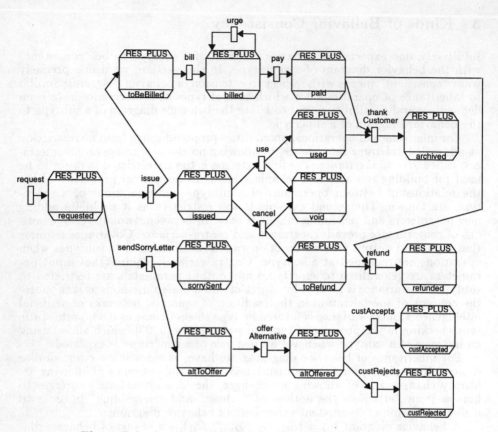

Fig. 2. Behavior diagram of object type RESERVATION_PLUS

We are now ready for describing three kinds of behavior consistency, each pursuing a different reasonable objective.

3.1 Observation consistency

It is common in semantic data models and object-oriented systems to consider each instance of a subtype also an instance of the supertype. Then, each instance of a subtype must be observable according to the structure and behavior definition given at the supertype, if features added at the subtype are ignored. We follow this approach, which is in the line of covariant inheritance (see above), when we define observation consistency for life cycle occurrences.

A life cycle occurrence of a subtype can be observed at the level of the supertype, if activities and states added at the subtype are ignored. This is expressed by the following definition of the restriction of a life cycle occurrence.

Definition 8 Restriction of a life cycle occurrence. The *restriction of a life cycle state* $\sigma_{O'}$ of an object type O' to object type O, written $\sigma_{O'}/O$, is defined as $\sigma_{O'}/O = \sigma_{O'} \cap (S_O \cup T_O)$. The *restriction of a life cycle occurrence*

$\gamma_{O'} = \sigma_{O'}^1, \ldots, \sigma_{O'}^n$, of object type O' to object type O, written $\gamma_{O'}/O$, is defined as $\sigma_O^1, \ldots, \sigma_O^n$, where for $i = 1 \ldots n: \sigma_O^i = \sigma_{O'}^i/O$.

Example 5. A possible life cycle occurrence of object type RESERVATION_PLUS (cf. Figure 2) is [{request}, {requested}, {issue}, {issued, toBeBilled}, {issued, bill}, {issued, billed}, {issued, pay}, {issued, paid}, {cancel, paid}, {void, toRefund, paid }, {void, refund}, {void, refunded}]. The restriction of this life cycle occurrence to object type RESERVATION yields [{request}, {requested}, {issue}, {issued}, {issued}, {issued}, {issued}, {issued}, {cancel}, {void }, {void }, {void }]. □

Observation consistent extension of behavior requires that each possible life cycle occurrence of a subtype is, disregarding activities and states added at the subtype, also a life cycle occurrence of the supertype.

Definition 9 Observation consistent extension. We refer to a behavior diagram $B_{O'} = (S_{O'}, T_{O'}, F_{O'}, s_{O'}^\alpha, \Omega_{O'})$ as an *observation consistent extension* of a behavior diagram $B_O = (S_O, T_O, F_O, s_O^\alpha, \Omega_O)$, if for every life cycle occurrence $\gamma_{O'}$ of object type O', $\gamma_{O'}/O$ is a life cycle occurrence of B_O.

Example 6. The behavior diagram depicted in Figure 2 is an observation consistent extension of the behavior diagram depicted in Figure 1. Thus every life cycle occurrence of object type RESERVATION_PLUS restricted to object type RESERVATION is also a life cycle occurrence of object type RESERVATION. This is shown for a particular life cycle occurrence in example 5. □

Observation consistency ensures that all instances of an object type (including those of its subtypes) evolve only according to its behavior diagram. This property is especially important for modeling workflows, where, for example, the current processing state of an order should always be visible at the manager's abstraction level defined by some higher-level object type. The example below, which violates observation consistency, illustrates this.

Example 7. The behavior diagram of object type FRIENDLY_RESERVATION depicted in Figure 3 is no observation consistent extension of the behavior diagram of object type RESERVATION depicted in Figure 1. The restriction of life cycle occurrence [{request}, {requested}, {offerAlternative}] of object type FRIENDLY_RESERVATION to object type RESERVATION yields [{request}, {requested}, {}], which is no life cycle occurrence of object type RESERVATION. □

3.2 Weak invocation consistency

Type substitutability in object-oriented programming languages allows using an instance of a subtype whenever an instance of a supertype is expected. Thus, any operation invocable on instances of a supertype must under the same precondition also be invocable on instances of any subtype and executing the operation on instances of a subtype meets the postcondition for the operation specified at the supertype. We follow this principle of programming by contract [12], which is supported by contra-variant inheritance (see above), when we define invocation consistency for behavior diagrams.

We distinguish two forms of invocation consistency: weak invocation consistency, which corresponds to the notion of "invocable behavior" of Engels and Ebert [6], and strong invocation consistency.

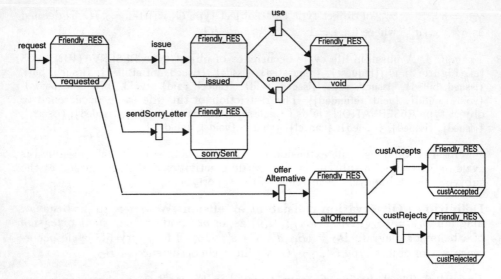

Fig. 3. Behavior diagram of object type FRIENDLY_RESERVATION

Weak invocation consistency is satisfied, if one can use instances of a subtype in the same way as instances of the supertype: Any sequence of activities that can be performed on instances of a supertype can also be performed on instances of subtypes, thereby, producing the effect expected at the supertype. This is expressed by the following definition of weak invocation consistency.

Definition 10 Weak invocation consistent extension.
A behavior diagram $B_{O'} = (S_{O'}, T_{O'}, F_{O'}, s_{O'}^{\alpha}, \Omega_{O'})$ is a *weak invocation consistent specialisation* of a behavior diagram $B_O = (S_O, T_O, F_O, s_O^{\alpha}, \Omega_O)$ if every activation sequence μ valid on α_O in B_O is also valid on $\alpha_{O'}$ in $B_{O'}$ and for their respective traces γ_O and $\gamma_{O'}$ it holds that $\gamma_O = \gamma_{O'}/O$.

Example 8. The behavior diagram of object type RESERVATION_PLUS depicted in Figure 2 is a weak invocation consistent extension of the behavior diagram of object type RESERVATION depicted in Figure 1. □

Weak invocation consistency ensures that if an object is extended with new features, e.g., a television set with video text, the object is usable the same way as without the extension. This property is violated in the example below.

Example 9.
The behavior diagram of object type RESERVATION_WITH_PAYMENT depicted in Figure 4 is no weak invocation consistent extension of the behavior diagram of object type RESERVATION depicted in Figure 1. The activation sequence [s(request), c(request), s(issue), c(issue), s(use)] is valid for object type RESERVATION, but not for object type RESERVATION_WITH_PAYMENT, as s(use) cannot be applied on the LCS {toBeBilled, issued} reached by executing [s(request), c(request), s(issue), c(issue)]. □

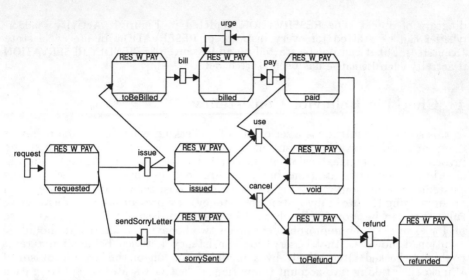

Fig. 4. Behavior diagram of object type RESERVATION_WITH_PAYMENT

3.3 Strong invocation consistency

Strong invocation consistency goes beyond weak invocation consistency in that it requires additionally that activities added at a subtype do not interfere with activities inherited from the supertype. Strong invocation consistency is satisfied, if one can use instances of a subtype in the same way as instances of the supertype, despite using or having used new activities of the subtype. This is expressed by the definition of strong invocation consistency below.

Definition 11 Strong invocation consistent extension.
A behavior diagram $B_{O'} = (S_{O'}, T_{O'}, F_{O'}, s_{O'}^\alpha, \Omega_{O'})$ is a *strong invocation consistent extension* of a behavior diagram $B_O = (S_O, T_O, F_O, s_\alpha, \Omega_O)$ if
(1) every activation sequence ν valid on α_O in B_O is valid on $\alpha_{O'}$ in $B_{O'}$, and
(2) every activation sequence ν valid in B_O on $\sigma_{O'}/O$ ($\sigma_{O'} \in R(\alpha_{O'})$) is valid in $B_{O'}$ on every life cycle state $\hat{\sigma}_{O'}$ that results from performing any activation sequence κ of activities in $T_{O'} \setminus T_O$ on $\sigma_{O'}$, and for the traces γ_O and $\gamma_{O'}$ generated by performing ν in B_O on $\sigma_{O'}/O$ and by performing ν in $B_{O'}$ on $\hat{\sigma}_{O'}$, respectively, it holds that $\gamma_O = \gamma_{O'}/O$. (Note: ν and κ may be empty).

Example 10. The behavior diagram of object type RESERVATION_PLUS depicted in Figure 2 is a strong invocation consistent extension of the behavior diagram of object type RESERVATION depicted in Figure 1. □

Strong invocation consistency ensures that if an object is extended with new features, e.g., a television set with video text, the object is usable the same way as without the extension despite new features being used. E.g., using any video text function will not invalidate the loudness button of the TV. This property is violated in the example below.

Example 11. The behavior diagram of object type FRIENDLY_RESERVATION depicted in Figure 3 is no strong invocation consistent extension of the behavior diagram of object type RESERVATION depicted in Figure 1: Activity sendSorryLetter can be started for every instance of RESERVATION in life cycle state {requested}, but it can not be started on an instance of FRIENDLY_RESERVATION if activity offerAlternative has been started before. □

4   Checking Behavior Consistency

In this section we introduce a set of rules for checking whether a given behavior diagram is an observation consistent, a weak invocation consistent, or a strong invocation consistent extension of another behavior diagram. Whereas approaches in the realm of state transition diagrams (e.g., [6]) base such checks on the existence of a homomorphism (for observation consistency) or the existence of an embedding (for weak invocation consistency), we present a set of constructive rules that can be more easily checked by a system designer than the existence of, for example, a homomorphism between two behavior diagrams. It should be mentioned, however, that observation consistency between behavior diagrams could be checked alternatively by a modified version of the net morphism of Winskel [24] taking into account the notion of "activity state" by splitting each activity in an instanteous start event, an explicit activity state, and an instanteneous completion event. The existence of an embedding between two behavior diagrams (see above) is a necessary but not a sufficient condition for satisfying weak and strong invocation consistency.

4.1   Observation consistency

Rules to check whether a behavior diagram $B_{O'}$ is an observation consistent extension of another behavior diagram B_O are the rule of *partial inheritance*, the rule of *immediate definition of prestates and post states*, and the rule of *parallel extension* (cf. Figure 5).

The rule of *weak inheritance* requires that (a) the initial state of $B_{O'}$ is identical to the initial state of B_O, and (b) every activity of $B_{O'}$ which is already in B_O has at least the prestates and at least the post states as the activity has in B_O. Note: Although it is meaningful to speak of an "extension" only if all activities of B_O are also present in $B_{O'}$, this is not a necessary condition for observation consistency.

The rule of *immediate definition of prestates and post states* requires that (a) no arc is added in $B_{O'}$ between a state and an activity which belong already to B_O and are not connected by an arc in B_O, and conversely (b) no arc is added in $B_{O'}$ between an activity and a state which belong already to B_O and are not connected by an arc in B_O. The rule of *parallel extension* requires that an activity added in $B_{O'}$ does not consume from a state already present in B_O and does not produce into a state already present in B_O.

Theorem 1. *$B_{O'}$ is an observation consistent extension of B_O if and only if rules 1, 2, and 3 of Figure 5 are obeyed. (Proof: see [9].)*

4.2   Weak invocation consistency

Rules to check whether a behavior diagram $B_{O'}$ is a weak consistent extension of a behavior diagram B_O are the rule of *partial inheritance*, the rule of *immediate definition of pre- and post states*, the rule of *full inheritance*, and the rule of *alternative extension* (cf. Figure 5). The first two have already been explained.

1. Partial inheritance
   (a) $s^\alpha_{O'} = s^\alpha_O$
   (b) $t \in T_{O'} \wedge t \in T_O \wedge (s,t) \in F_O \Rightarrow (s,t) \in F_{O'}$
   (c) $t \in T_{O'} \wedge t \in T_O \wedge (t,s) \in F_O \Rightarrow (t,s) \in F_{O'}$
2. Immediate definition of prestates and post states
   (a) $(s,t) \in F_{O'} \wedge s \in S_O \wedge t \in T_O \Rightarrow (s,t) \in F_O$
   (b) $(t,s) \in F_{O'} \wedge s \in S_O \wedge t \in T_O \Rightarrow (t,s) \in F_O$
3. Parallel extension
   (a) $(s,t) \in F_{O'} \wedge t \in T_{O'} \wedge t \notin T_O \Rightarrow s \notin S_O$
   (b) $(t,s) \in F_{O'} \wedge t \in T_{O'} \wedge t \notin T_O \Rightarrow s \notin S_O$
4. Full inheritance
   $T_{O'} \supseteq T_O$
5. Alternative extension
   $(s,t) \in F_{O'} \wedge s \in S_{O'} \wedge s \notin S_O \Rightarrow t \notin T_O$

Fig. 5. Rules for checking behavior consistency

The rule of *full inheritance* requires that the set of activities of $B_{O'}$ is a superset of the set of activities of B_O. The rule of *alternative extension* requires that an activity in $B_{O'}$ which is already present in B_O consumes in $B_{O'}$ at most from those states from which the activity consumes in B_O.

Theorem 2. $B_{O'}$ *is a weak invocation consistent extension of B_O if rules 1, 2, 4, and 5 of Figure 5 are obeyed. (Proof: see [19].)*

We call a behavior diagram $B_{O'}$ a *substantial* extension of a behavior diagram B_O, if a state added in $B_{O'}$ is not both prestate of an activity already present in B_O and post state of an activity already present in B_O. Adding merely a new state between two old activities is not a substantial extension as an intermediate new activity is missing.

Definition 12. Behavior diagram $B_{O'} = (S_{O'}, T_{O'}, F_{O'}, s^\alpha_{O'}, \Omega_{O'})$ is a *substantial extension* of $B_O = (S_O, T_O, F_O, s^\alpha_O, \Omega_O)$ if for every $s \in S_{O'} \setminus S_O$, $t \in T_{O'}$, $\hat{t} \in T_{O'}$ it holds that $(t,s) \in F_{O'} \wedge (s,\hat{t}) \in F_{O'} \wedge \hat{t} \in T_O \rightarrow t \notin T_O$.

In the case of substantial extensions, the rules introduced above are also necessary to check for weak invocation consistency.

Theorem 3. *Providing $B_{O'}$ is a substantial extension of B_O, then $B_{O'}$ is a weak invocation consistent extension of B_O if and only if rules 1, 2, 4 and 5 are obeyed. (Proof: see [19].)*

4.3 Strong invocation consistency

Sufficient rules to check whether a behavior diagram $B_{O'}$ is a strong invocation consistent extension of a behavior diagram $B_{O'}$ are all rules of Figure 5.

Theorem 4. $B_{O'}$ *is a strong invocation consistent extension of B_O if rules 1 to 5 of Figure 5 are obeyed. (Proof: see [19].)*

Strong invocation consistency implies observation consistency and weak invocation consistency. The converse does not hold.

Theorem 5. *If $B_{O'}$ is a strong invocation consistent extension of B_O then $B_{O'}$ is an observation consistent extension of B_O and $B_{O'}$ is a weak invocation consistent extension of B_O. (Proof: see [19].)*

Theorem 6. *If $B_{O'}$ is an observation consistent extension and a weak invocation consistent extension of B_O, then $B_{O'}$ need not be a strong invocation consistent extension of B_O. (Proof: see [19].)*

In the case of substantial extensions, rules 1 to 5 are not only sufficient but also necessary for checking strong invocation consistency, and strong invocation consistency is equivalent to observation consistency and weak invocation consistency.

Theorem 7. *Providing $B_{O'}$ is a substantial extension of B_O, then $B_{O'}$ is a strong invocation consistent extension of B_O if and only if rules 1 to 5 of Figure 5 are obeyed. (Proof: see [19].)*

Corollary 1. *Providing $B_{O'}$ is a substantial extension of B_O, then $B_{O'}$ is a strong invocation consistent extension of B_O iff $B_{O'}$ is an observation consistent and a weak invocation consistent extension of B_O. (Proof: follows from Theorems 1, 3, and 7.)*

5 Conclusion

We have presented a set of constructive rules which can be used during system design to check whether a behavior diagram $B_{O'}$ is an observation consistent, or a weak invocation consistent, or a strong invocation consistent extension of a behavior diagram B_O. *Observation consistency* guarantees that every life cycle of an instance of a subtype is observable as a life cycle of the supertype if states and activities added at the subtype are neglected. *Weak invocation consistency* guarantees that a sequence of activities performable on instances of a supertype can also be performed on instances of a subtype. And, *strong invocation consistency* guarantees this property even if activities added at the subtype have been inserted arbitrarily in that sequence. We believe the decision about which kind of consistency to follow is application dependent. Observation consistency may be the right choice in a workflow environment in which the behavior diagram of an object type is used to track the processing of instances of the object type and, also, of instances of its subtypes. Weak invocation consistency may be the right choice in situations when an instance of a subtype may be used as a substitute for an instance of a supertype. Strong invocation consistency implies both, observation and weak invocation consistency, but may be too restrictive in many practical situations. Nevertheless, the rules introduced in this paper can assist the designer to recognize and identify situations that violate a particular kind of consistency. If the designer detects a consistency violation, he/she may adjust the design (e.g., by replacing the behavior diagrams of Figures 3 and 4 by the behavior diagram of Figure 2) or, if this is not possible due to the problem statement (e.g., a reservation may only be used if it has been paid, cf. Figure 4), he/she may mark the involved states and activities to avoid a behavior diagram to be read erroneously.

References

1. P. Bichler, M. Schrefl "Active Object-Oriented Database Design Using Active Object/Behavior Diagrams", in *IEEE RIDE-ADS'94*, 1994.
2. G. Booch, *Object-Oriented Analysis and Design with Applications (2nd edition)*, Benjamin Cummings, 1994.
3. W. Brauer and R. Gold and W. Vogler, "A Survey of Behaviour and Equivalence Preserving Refinements of Petri Nets," Springer LNCS 483, pp. 1-46, 1991.
4. P.S. Canningen, W.R. Cook, W.L. Hill and W.G. Olthoff, "Interfaces for Strongly-Typed Object-Oriented Programming," in *Proc. OOPSLA'89,*, ed. N. Meyrowitz, pp. 457-467, 1989.
5. L. Cardelli, "A Semantics of Multiple Inheritance," in *Information and Computation*, vol. 76, Academic Press, 1988.
6. J. Ebert and G. Engels, "Observable or Invocable Behaviour - You Have to Choose!" *Technical Report*, Koblenz University, 1994.
7. D.W. Embley, B.D. Kurtz and S.N. Woodfield, *Object-Oriented Systems Analysis - A Model-Driven Approach*, Yourdon Press, 1992.
8. G. Kappel and M. Schrefl, "Object/Behavior Diagrams," in *Proc. 7th Int. Conf. IEEE Data Engineering*, pp. 530-539, 1991.
9. G. Kappel and M. Schrefl, "Inheritance of Object Behavior - Consistent Extension of Object Life Cycles," in *Proc. East/West Database Workshop*, pp. 289-300, Springer, 1995.
10. A. Lopes and J.F. Costa, "Rewriting for Reuse," in *Proc. ERCIM Workshop on Development and Transformation of Programs*, pp. 43-55, Nancy (F), 1993.
11. J.D. McGregor and D.M. Dyer, "A Note on Inheritance and State Machines," *ACM SIGSOFT Software Engineering Notes*, 18 (4) pp. 61-69, 1993.
12. B. Meyer, "Applying Design by Contract", *IEEE Computer*, 25(10), 1992, pp. 40-51.
13. B. Paech and P. Rumpe, "A new Concept of Refinement used for Behaviour Modelling with Automata," *Proc. FME'94*, Springer LNCS 873, 1994.
14. J.L. Peterson, "Petri nets," in *ACM Computing Surveys*, pp. 223-252, 1977.
15. L. Pomello and G. Rozenberg and C. Simone, "A Survey of Equivalence Notions for Net Based Systems," Springer LNCS 609, 1992.
16. J. Rumbaugh, M. Blaha, W. Premerlani, F. Eddy and W. Lorensen, *Object-Oriented Modelling and Design*, Prentice-Hall, 1991.
17. G. Saake, P. Hartel, R. Jungclaus, R.Wieringa and R. Feenstra, "Inheritance Conditions for Object Life Cycle Diagrams," in *EMISA Workshop*, 1994.
18. M. Schrefl, "Behavior Modeling by Stepwise Refining Behavior Diagrams," in *Proc. 9th Int. Conf. Entity-Relationship Approach*, pp. 113-128, 1990.
19. M. Schrefl and M. Stumptner, "Behavior Consistent Extension of Object Life Cycles," *Institutsbericht 95.03, Inst. für Wirtschaftsinformatik, Universität Linz*, Austria, 1995.
20. A. Sernadas and H.-D. Ehrich , "What is an Object, After All?," in *Proc. IFIP WG 2.6 Working Conference on Object-Oriented Databases: Analysis, Design and Construction (DS-4)*, ed. R. Meersman et. al., pp. 39-70, North-Holland, 1991.
21. A. Snyder, "Inheritance and the Development of Encapsulated Software Components," in *Research Directions in Object-Oriented Programming*, ed. B. Shriver and P. Wegner, pp. 165-188, The MIT Press, 1987.
22. P. Wegner, "Dimensions of Object-Based Language Design," in *Proc. OOPSLA'87* pp. 168-182, Dez. 1987.
23. P. Wegner and S.B. Zdonik, "Inheritance as an Incremental Modification Mechanism or What Like Is and Isn't Like," in *Proc. ECOOP'88*, ed. Gjessing S. and Nygaard K., pp. 55-77, Springer LNCS 322, 1988.
24. G. Winskel, "Petri nets, algebras, morphisms, and compositionality," in *Information and Computation*, vol. 72, pp. 197-238, 1987.

C$^{\text{OO}}_{\text{L}}$R-$\mathcal{X}$ Event Model: Integrated Specification of the Dynamics of Individual Objects

J.F.M. Burg* and R.P. van de Riet

Department of Computer Science
Vrije Universiteit
Amsterdam, The Netherlands
{jfmburg,vdriet}@cs.vu.nl

Abstract. In this paper we show that specifying the dynamics of a system as a whole requires more information than just the combination of the dynamics of the individual objects of the system. The introduction of yet another additional model, often called something as the object interaction diagram, does not bridge the gap completely. We propose a linguistically based dynamic modeling technique, the C$^{\text{OO}}_{\text{L}}$R-$\mathcal{X}$ Event Models, which defines the system dynamics in an overall fashion, and from which the individual object dynamics are automatically retrieved. A comparison with existing approaches in dynamic modeling is included.
Keywords: C$^{\text{OO}}_{\text{L}}$R-$\mathcal{X}$ Event Model, Dynamic Model, Linguistics, CPL, Information and Communication Systems, Lexicon, OMT, CASE

1 Introduction

The name of our current project, COLOR-X, is an acronym for the **CO**nceptual **L**inguistically based **O**bject oriented **R**epresentation Language for Information and Communication Systems (**ICS** abbreviated to **X**). In the COLOR-X project we are using the logical conceptual modeling technique CPL (Conceptual Prototyping Language) [Dig89], which is linguistically based, as a formal foundation for graphical modeling techniques. This approach is chosen to facilitate the process of conceptual modeling and which leads to more consistent and complete models that are linguistically correct. COLOR-X is the first phase of a larger project which has as objective the generation of object-oriented programming code from a natural language based modeling technique, which brings, as a side-effect, the conceptual models closer to programming code. In addition, by using a modeling technique based on linguistic notions, we are narrowing the gap between requirements documents, written in natural language, and conceptual models as well. The COLOR-X project is divided into several parts, analog to existing conceptual modeling methods, like OMT [RBP+91]. [BR95a] focuses on the dynamic part, whereas [BR94] and [BR95b] describe the COLOR-X *Static*

---

* Supported by the Foundation for Computer Science in the Netherlands (SION) with financial support from the Dutch Organization for Scientific Research (NWO), project 612-123-309

Object Model (CSOM), in which the static aspects of the *Universe of Discourse (UoD)* are contained.

One of the main reasons to use linguistic knowledge is to make the use of words appearing in the models consistent, and thus making the models as a whole more meaningful. Earlier projects conducted in our group have shown the profitability of this approach, [BR92b], [BR92a], [VR94], [BR94], [BR95b], [BR95a] and [BR95c]. Another reason to use linguistic knowledge in modeling techniques is to give more expressive power to them. An additional nice feature of a linguistically based modeling technique is that it is relatively easy to generate natural language sentences from it, in order to give some feedback to the system designers and to the end-users as well, see also [Dal92]. This feedback consists of generated sentences during the modeling phase, in order to check if the model is consistent with the requirements and on the other hand this feedback consists of explanation facilities, like [Gul93]. The first kind of feedback is already incorporated into COLOR-X. As a source for this linguistic knowledge we use WordNet [MBF+93].

In this paper we will focus on specifying the dynamics of a UoD in a correct and adequate way, such that the specification of the behaviour of the individual object participating in this UoD can be generated automatically. Our approach sticks as closely as possible to existing methods that have proven their usefulness, but differ from them at the points we think they should be improved or adjusted. We will start with retrieving the information necessary to model the dynamics of a system from a requirements document. Instead of specifying the dynamics of the individual objects after that we will concentrate on the system as a whole, and introduce a linguistically based event model, called COLOR-X *Event Model* (CEM). Then, we will return to the specification of the individual behaviour of the objects, but it will be generated, in several well-known representations, automatically.

2 Retrieving System Dynamics

To retrieve the system dynamics, stated in an informal way in a requirements document, we follow Rumbaugh's approach, the Object Modeling Technique (OMT) [RBP+91]. Our choice for this method was directed by the fact that OMT supported a static as well as dynamic view on the same Universe of Discourse (UoD), and that OMT relates closely to other well-known and accepted methods (as State-Transition Diagrams (STD) for example). Finally, OMT is also widely accepted as being an effective and useful method. On the other hand, the OMT approach to retrieve the system and object dynamics, are universally and well-known, so we can use them, without any commitment to the OMT method.

To retrieve the dynamics of a system, we have to look at the actual *events* that take place in the UoD. Events, which represent external stimuli, occur at a point in time and are in fact a one-way transmission of information from one object to another. In OMT, a *scenario* is a sequence of events that occur during one particular execution of a system. These scenarios can be augmented with the objects exchanging the events. Augmented scenarios are called *Event Traces* in OMT. An example of such a event trace can be found in Figure 1(a). Concentrating on the objects and putting all the events occurring between two objects on one arc, an *Event Flow Diagram* is created (Figure 1(b)), which shows possible control flows of the system.

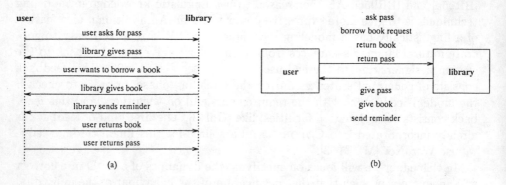

Fig. 1. Rumbaughs Event Trace (a) and Event Flow (b)

Exactly at this point, we disagree with the common opinion (e.g. [RBP+91], [Wie93], [FW93]) to focus on individual objects and their behaviour without getting a real grip on the system dynamics. Up to now, the events, the scenarios, the traces and the event flow, are created and specified in an informal way, and hence missing any meaning and semantics, which makes working with them impossible in the next steps of the modeling process.

We propose a new step to be taken after creating the event traces and flows, mentioned above, which formalizes the events individually and their mutual dependencies. In the next section we will introduce COLOR-X EVENT MODELS (CEMs), which are merely a trace of the events that could and should be performed in the Universe of Discourse (UoD). This way of modeling the dynamic aspects of the UoD links up very well with the way these aspects are described in the requirements document.

For clearness sake, we do *not* think that individual object dynamics should not be modeled at all. On the contrary, we think that the encapsulation of object properties and behaviour is one of the major achievements of the object oriented paradigm in the area of modeling and programming. We just think that it is too early to focus on individual objects when the overall dynamics are not understood well. In a following section we will show that the dynamics of individual object can be generated out of the formalized system dynamics automatically.

3   Formalizing System Dynamics

Formalizing the system dynamics consists of two parts:

1. defining the events individually in a formal linguistically based manner
2. defining dependencies between events

The first part, defining the individual events, is supported by WordNet, a lexical database that is the result of an ongoing research program at Princeton University in the representation of lexical information [MBF+93]. When all the events occurring in the UoD have been identified in event scenarios and traces, the exact meaning and instantiation of these events should be captured. By retrieving information about the verb, indicating the event, from WordNet, the *meaning*, the *occurrence* and the *objects* playing a role in the event are determined. This leads to event descriptions that are linguistically correct (i.e. structure and type of involved objects) and that correspond to the UoD.

The (CPL-) syntax of the terms building a formal event description is: *[<cardinality>] role = [variable in] noun* [2]. The (semantic) roles are retrieved from the linguistic theory called *Functional Grammar* [Dik89] and define the exact role objects play in a certain relationship. The semantic roles are based on the occurrence frame of the specified verb, that is retrieved from WordNet. For example, WordNets verbframe "somebody ---s to somebody" is formalized in one of the following CPL-structures:

1. verb(ag) (dir), e.g. walk
2. verb(ag) (rec), e.g. apologize

This is done for all the verbframes occurring in WordNet.

As a result, after the objects and the *semantic roles*, like ag(ent), go(al) and rec(ipient), have been instantiated, the event description becomes for example:

sell(**ag** = boss) (**go** = car) (**rec** = customer)

Advantages yielded by this formalization are:

- the number of objects involved in a certain event is defined,
- the type of the objects is restricted,
- the objects are identified,
- the role the objects play in the event is formalized.

This leads to event specifications that reflect *exactly* the meaning that is intended and that is as complete as possible. The fact that the specification is founded in a linguistic formalism, gives opportunities to paraphrase these event specifications in natural language sentences in an unambiguous way.

The other aspect of formalizing the event scenarios and traces is to define the dependencies between the events. Up to now, we have accomplished to express sequential, parallel and conditional occurrences of events. Topic of research is still the incorporation of *rhetorical relations* (e.g. causal) [MT87] to augment the general conditional *if...then* construct with more advanced ones.

The graphical notation to depict these formalized event traces, is called COLOR-X *Event Models* (CEM) [BR95a]. We will introduce this modeling technique by an example that corresponds to the following requirements:

---

[2] everything between square brackets ([..]) is optional [Dig89]

A user can borrow a book from a library. If a user has borrowed a book he has to return it within three weeks, before he is allowed to borrow a book again.

Figure 2 shows the corresponding CEM. It is fairly easy to read and corresponds very closely to the natural language sentences.

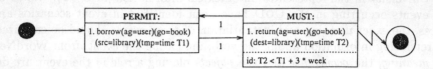

Fig. 2. Example of a COLOR-X Event Model

Informally, a box represents an event that could, should or has to take place (depending on the modality, i.e. **PERMIT, MUST** or **NEC** respectively), a straight arrow represents the actual occurrence of that event (i.e. the event referenced to by the number attached to the arrow) and a 'lightning'-arrow represents the fact that the specific event did not take place.

The graphical notations of CEMs can be found in Figure 3. An event box, Figure 3(a), consists of a modality, one or more event descriptions and zero or more constraint descriptions. An event description consists of a verb denoting an event, which is either an action (an event controlled by some agent) or a (not controlled) process, and one or more terms. An example clarifies this abstract formulation:

one user borrows four books ⇔ borrow(<1> ag = user) (<4> go = book)

This formal event representation expresses exactly what the modeler wants, which is not always true when using ambiguous natural language sentences. Another advantage of this approach is that it is now possible to use automatic tools to support the modeling process. It is always possible to generate natural language sentences automatically out of the CPL constructs.

A constraint description constrains the value of one or more terms (through the use of variables) absolutely (*age* > *21*) or relatively (*age father* > *age son*). The syntax used to express these constraints is the same as the one used in CPL: (**id:** $V_1 > 21$) and (**id:** $V_1 > V_2$).

Besides the event-nodes there are two special nodes that denote start and final points (Figure 3(b) and (c), respectively).

Because of the fact that there are three modalities to use (permit, necessary and must), there are three different kinds of event-boxes (Figure 3(d) - (f)).

In this way a certain degree of completeness is accomplished. When a **MUST**-box is used there are always two succeeding events to be specified. After finishing the model the remark "the model does not specify what has to be done when event X has not taken place" will not occur! One has always to specify a relative or absolute *expiration-time*, which may be infinite, when using a **MUST**-box, in order to verify whether the obligation has been violated or not. The event-boxes

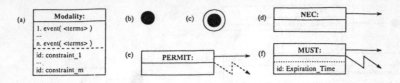

Fig. 3. CEM Notation, (a) general event, (b) start node, (c) final node, (d) necessary, (e) permitted, (f) obligatory

are connected with arrows which denote the fact that one more events are performed (depicted by a straight arrow with one or more event-numbers) or are not performed at all (depicted by a lightning-arrow).

The CEM corresponding to the event trace and event flow, showed before in Figure 1, is depicted in Figure 4(a).

4 Object Dynamics

We have developed several algorithms that generate the dynamics of individual objects automatically out of a CEM expressing the system dynamics. The dynamics of individual objects are necessary in order to generate object-oriented programming code automatically. The actual code generation is still a topic of research. Among the representations generated are *State Transition Diagrams* [RBP+91, BR95a], *Jacksons Entity Life Cycles* [Jac83], *Wieringa's Object Life Cycles* and *Wieringa's Communication Diagrams* [Wie93]. Both Jackson and Wieringa distinguish between modeling the UoD and modeling the database itself. According to Wieringa:

> A life cycle is the dialog, a process involving a system and some systems in its environment that has a logical completion, that an object in the UoD has with its surrogate in the database system.

This means that the life cycle of an object is the behaviour of the object as seen by the database system. In this paper, however, we fully concentrate on modeling the UoD in a complete and adequate way. We use life cycles to represent the actual life of the object in the UoD without looking at any database system at all. In the next sections we will treat each of the representations mentioned.

Note: In section 2 we left the traditional path of creating diagrams expressing the dynamics of the objects in the UoD out of informal system descriptions (like event traces). Instead, we suggested a formalization of the system dynamics in section 3. After modeling these formalized system dynamics in CEMs, we return to the traditional path and model the object dynamics. The difference is that now this is supported by generating (parts of) the individual models automatically.

4.1 State Transition Diagrams

The exact algorithm to generate STDs is published in [BR95a], but we will summarize it briefly:

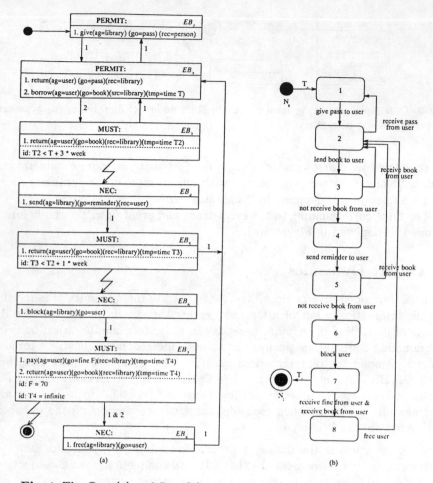

Fig. 4. The CEM (a) and STD (b) of a Library Book Circulation System

The generated STDs, of which an example is shown in Figure 4(b), satisfy the following rules:

- Every STD belongs to exactly *one* active object occurring in the UoD. Active objects are nouns that play the *agent*-role in one or more CEM-events.
- A state is represented by a box, identified by a unique number. A verbal label can be added manually, but has no semantic meaning in the model. This decision is made because it is really hard to find meaningful labels for every state, and to maintain a certain degree of conformity among the labels.
- A transition is represented by a uni-directional arrow labeled with a verbal phrase, describing the event(s) that causes the state-transition. This verbal phrase is created as follows (for each event):
  - if the object, described by the STD, is the agent of the CEM-event, the CEM-event is copied into the transition-label

- otherwise, the sentence is transformed into a new one in which the object is the linguistic subject of it. To achieve this the perspective antonym of the verb describing the event is retrieved from WordNet. This new sentence becomes the transition-label. E.g. the transition label in the library-STD corresponding to the CEM-event "*a user borrows a book from a library*" will become "*a library lends a book to a user*".

Constraints can be attached to a transition as an optional component of it.

- There exist two special states: the *start*-state and the *final*-state, that are connected with the first 'real' state (i.e. the state before the first event) and the last state, respectively, by empty transitions. These states correspond to the creation and destructions, respectively, of the object.

4.2 Life Cycles

Another representation for object dynamics are *life cycles*, which are used by [Jac83] and [Wie93]. Both representations contain almost the same information, and hence we will focus on JSD life cycles in the next discussion.

For every function a certain active object performs, a branch in the entity life cycle is created. Figure 5(a) shows one of the branches of the library life cycle that corresponds to the document circulation function, that is actually generated with the algorithm we have developed.

The algorithm generating JSD entity life cycles [Jac83] is stated in a rather informal, but understandable way:

1. This algorithm should be repeated for every function of every active object, that has to be implemented.
2. For each object, create a standard top of the graph, containing a box with the name of the object as topmost node, and three second-level nodes representing the *birth*, *life* and *death* of that object.
3. Find cycles in the CEM, say $EB_{j_1}, \cdots, EB_{j_m}, EB_{j_1}, j \geq 0$.
4. Keep the most general cycles, i.e. cycles that are contained in other ones.
5. Traverse the CEM, starting with EB_0. The current event box is EB_i. For each EB_i-action (on outgoing arrow):
   - EB_i is the begin of a cycle:
     (a) add box with label: <label_of EB_i >-LIFE
     (b) add iteration box (below) with label: ITER
     (c) add box (below) with label: <label_of EB_i >
   - EB_i is the end of a cycle (i.e. EB_{j_m}):
     (a) add box (on same level) with label: <label_of EB_i >
   - EB_i is a MUST- or a PERMIT-BOX with an outgoing lightning-arrow:
     (a) add box (below) with label: POSSIBLE- <label_of EB_i >
     (b) add choice box (below) with label: <label_of EB_i >
     (c) add choice box (on same level) with label: NILL (if the lightning-arrow ends up in an CEM end node) or ALTERNATIVE
   - EB_is outgoing arrow consists of several actions (its label contains a '&'):
     (a) add box (below) with label: SEQUENCE

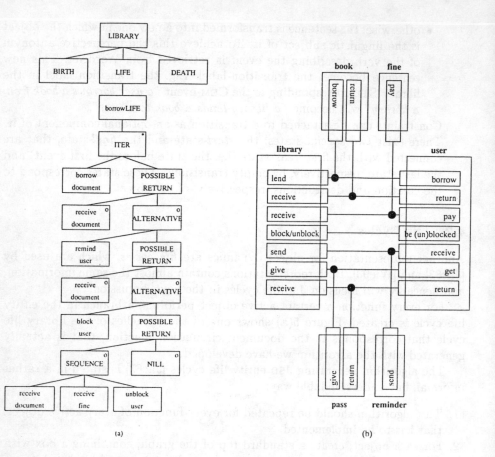

(a) (b)

Fig. 5. (a) Jacksons Life Cycle and (b) Wieringa's Communication Diagram

    (b) for every EB_i-action add box below SEQUENCE in sequence with as labels their corresponding actions.

    – for each other EB_is: add box (on same level) with label: $<$label_of_$EB_i>$

6. As Figure 5(a) shows, life cycles expand rather. quickly. We are developing some heuristics in order to shrink the life cycles to an appropriate size:

    (a) The leftmost action occurring in one of the LIFE sub-nodes corresponds probably to the BIRTH of the object. In some cases the label of this leftmost node can be carried back linguistically to a *creative verb*, by using the taxonomy information from WordNet.

    (b) The same sort of heuristic can be applied to the rightmost node, which could correspond to the DEATH of the object.

Note: Because we transform action descriptions into linguistic equivalents (perspective antonyms) in which the object has the agent-role, our notion of *common actions* is slightly different, than Jacksons original definition. E.g. *library lends book to user* and *user borrows book from library* are common actions.

4.3 Communication Diagrams

Because traditional modeling methods focus on the dynamics of individual objects, i.e. without formalizing the overall dynamics as suggested in this paper, the communication between objects is hardly modeled. JSDs life cycles have included the notion of common actions to model communications between objects. This approach has several drawbacks because it is based solely on two or more matching strings. Two fundamental different actions with the same name (e.g. *library receives book from publisher* and *user receives reminder from library*, both occurring as *receive* actions) are not necessarily common actions!

Other approaches that model the communication between objects, often introduce a so called *object communication diagrams*, e.g. [Wie93], [SM92]. An example, using Wieringa's notation, is shown in Figure 5(b).

This kind of models is redundant, because it shows exactly the same information as the informal event traces with which we started. In CEMs the information is implicitly present, because the formalized event specifications contain all the involved objects. Furthermore, they contain the roles they play in the 'communication', which is lost again in most of the communication diagrams. It is therefore very straightforward to generate communication models out of CEMs:

1. create a box for each object playing a role in an event
2. for each event, draw a line between the objects involved in that event

Again, we do not pay attention to any database system, but focus solely on modeling the dynamics of the UoD.

4.4 Paraphrasing CEMs into Natural Language

To verify if the modeled CEM reflects the information stated in the requirements document, natural language sentences could be generated out of the dynamic models. This facilitates the communication about the rather complex dynamic models. Some NL-sentences (generated by our tool CPL2NL) that are generated out of Figure 4(a), are listed below:

1. [a,library,is,permitted to,give,a,pass,to,an,user]
2. [if,a,library,gave,a,pass,to,an,user,
      then,an,user,is,permitted to,borrow,a,book,from,a,library]

5 Conclusions

In this paper we suggest an approach to model the dynamics of individual objects in a global and integrated way. Due to the fact that the dynamic behaviour of individual objects cannot be seen in isolation, because they interact intensely and the combination of their behaviour determines the dynamics of the system in which they participate, the top-down approach as we propose is a more natural one, than the bottom-up approach. This statement is in fact supported by the traditional methods themselves, because they also start with modeling event traces and flows for the overall system, but they do not incorporate it formally into their method. The algorithms presented have been tested for some applications, but are still preliminary and have to be adjusted, probably. We are still working on them, and are incorporating new insights in modeling dynamic behaviour as much as possible (e.g. Jacobson's Use Case approach [Jac92]). As mentioned before, the use of rhetorical relations is still a topic of research, as well as the expressive power of the COLOR-X Event Models and the integration of the dynamic (CEM) and static information (CSOM) about one UoD. Future extensions include event disjunctions and global system constraints. Formalizing the events themselves by reusing knowledge from a lexicon, e.g. WordNet, and the formal integration of the events into CEMs seems to be a viable approach, because the dynamics of the system as a whole are captured in a clear, consistent and correct manner. Furthermore, the underlying representation language, i.e. CPL, is also used to represent the static aspects of an UoD [BR95b], which leads to a formal integration of both aspects of the UoD. By logical inferences, a certain degree of consistency and completeness of the information can be verified. The generation of natural language sentences out of the, dynamic as well as static, models facilitates the communication about the models and the informal verification of the consistency between the requirements document and the models.

References

[BR92a] P. Buitelaar and R.P. van de Riet. A Feasibility Study in Linguistically Motivated Object-Oriented Conceptual Design of Information Systems. Technical Report IR-293, Vrije Universiteit, Amsterdam, 1992.

[BR92b] P. Buitelaar and R.P. van de Riet. The Use of a Lexicon to interpret ER Diagrams: a LIKE Project. In *Proceedings of the ER Conference*, Karlsruhe, 1992.

[BR94] J.F.M. Burg and R.P. van de Riet. COLOR-X: Object Modeling profits from Linguistics. Technical Report IR-365, Vrije Universiteit, Amsterdam, 1994.

[BR95a] J.F.M. Burg and R.P. van de Riet. COLOR-X: Linguistically-based Event Modeling: A General Approach to Dynamic Modeling. In J. Iivari, K. Lyytinen, and M. Rossi, editors, *The Proceedings of the Seventh International Conference on Advanced Information System Engineering (CAiSE'95)*, Lecture Notes in Computer Science (932), pages 26–39, Jyvaskyla, Finland, 1995. Springer-Verlag.

[BR95b] J.F.M. Burg and R.P. van de Riet. COLOR-X: Object Modeling profits from Linguistics. In N.J.I. Mars, editor, *Towards Very Large Knowledge Bases: Knowledge Building & Knowledge Sharing (KB&KS'95)*, pages 204–214, Enschede, The Netherlands, 1995. IOS Press, Amsterdam.

[BR95c] J.F.M. Burg and R.P. van de Riet. The Impact of Linguistics on Conceptual Models: Consistency and Understandability. In *First International Workshop on Applications of Natural Language to Data Bases (NLDB'95)*, pages 183–197, Versailles, France, 1995. AFCET.

[Dal92]   H. Dalianis. A Method for Validating a Conceptual Model by Natural Language Discourse Generation. *Proceedings of the 4th International Conference on Advanced Information Systems Engineering*, 1992.

[Dig89]   F.P.M. Dignum. *A Language for Modelling Knowledge Bases. Based on Linguistics, Founded in Logic.* PhD thesis, Vrije Universiteit, Amsterdam, 1989.

[Dik89]   S.C. Dik. *The Theory of Functional Grammar. Part I: The Structure of the Clause.* Floris Publications, Dordrecht, 1989.

[FW93]   R.B. Feenstra and R.J. Wieringa. LCM 3.0: A Language for Describing Conceptual Models – Syntax Definition. Technical Report IR-344, Vrije Universiteit, Amsterdam, 1993.

[Gul93]   J.A. Gulla. *Deep Explanation Generation in Conceptual Modeling Environments.* PhD thesis, University of Trondheim, Trondheim, 1993.

[Jac83]   M Jackson. *System Development.* Prentice-Hall, 1983.

[Jac92]   I. Jacobson. *Object-Oriented Software Engineering: A Use Case Approach.* Addison-Wesley, 1992.

[KM93]   K. Koskimies and E. Makinen. Inferring State Machines from Trace Diagrams. Technical Report A-1993-3, University of Tampere, 1993.

[MBF+93] G.A. Miller, R. Beckwith, C. Fellbaum, D. Gross, K. Miller, and R. Tengi. Five Papers on WordNet. Technical report, Cognitive Science Laboratory, Princeton University, 1993.

[MT87]   W.C. Mann and S.A. Thompson. Rhetorical Structure Theory: Description and Construction of Text Structures. In G. Kempen, editor, *Natural Language Generation: New Results in Artificial Intelligence, Psychology and Linguistics*, pages 85–95. Martinus Nijhoff Publishers, 1987.

[RBP+91] J. Rumbaugh, M. Blaha, W. Premerlani, F. Eddy, and W. Lorensen. *Object-Oriented Modeling and Design.* Prentice-Hall International, Inc., Englewood Cliffs, New Yersey, 1991.

[RP92]   C. Rolland and C. Proix. A Natural Language Approach for Requirements Engineering. In P. Loucopoulos, editor, *Proceedings of the 4th International Conference on Advanced Information Systems Engineering.* Springer-Verlag, Manchester, 1992.

[SM92]   S. Shlaer and S.J. Mellor. *Object Life Cycles, Modelling the World in States.* Prentice Hall, 1992.

[vGO94]   Nederlands Gebruikersgroep van Gestructureerde Ontwikkelingsmethoden. *13 Methoden voor object-georienteerde systeemontwikkeling.* Uitgeverij Tutein Nolthenius, 1994.

[VR94]   A.J. van der Vos and R.P. van de Riet. A First Semantic Check based on Linguistic Information for State Transition Diagrams. Technical Report IR-372, Vrije Universiteit, Amsterdam, 1994.

[Wie93]   R.J. Wieringa. A Method for Building and Evaluating Formal Specifications of Object-Oriented Conceptual Models and Database Systems. Technical Report IR-340, Vrije Universiteit, Amsterdam, 1993.

Database Design with Behavior and Views Using Parameterized Petri Nets

Padmini Srinivasan Hands[1], Anand Srinivasan[2] and Gerard M. Vignes[1]

[1] Computer Science Department &
[2] The Center for Advanced Computer Studies,
University of Southwestern Louisiana, Lafayette, LA 70504, USA

Abstract. We propose a method and a modeling tool for the design of relational databases. This conceptual design technique incorporates, from the earliest design stages, both database behavior and the existence of multiple user views of the database. It utilizes the structure and capabilities of parameterized Petri nets (PPNs) described in [2]. Petri nets are traditionally found useful for describing conditions and events that constitute a dynamic system. Parameterized Petri nets are (non-strictly) heirarchical or multi-level, and have a parameterization capability which is used to develop differing useful system views (PPNviews) of the relational database structure and dynamics.

Using Petri nets in general and PPNs in particular, users may create models that describe the flow of work or the transformations that take place in the system at an intuitive, comfortable level of detail. This produces one view of the system (PPNview). Different users with detailed knowledge about particular segments or aspects of the system will be able to design PPNviews showing those sections in great detail while leaving the less familiar segments less detailed. A set of normalized relations produced by traditional methods is the basis (parameterization descriptor) for a different PPNview. This PPNview depicts the transactions that occur in the system connected to the normalized relations that participate in the transaction.

1 Introduction

It is our purpose in this paper to describe the use of parameterized Petri nets (PPNs) in the design of relational databases. This method is offered as a way to help system designers and users (who help generate requirements and system descriptions) to construct descriptions of the system. These system descriptions are Petri nets, or bipartite graphs with nodes representing conditions or system state (places) and nodes representing system dynamics (transitions). Various descriptions may be created of the same system, depending on level of abstraciton and point of view. The multiple system views described are supported by the definition of PPNs, and the views are called PPNveiws. The PPN approach applied for database design results in the following advantages: First, the behavior or dynamic aspect of the database is captured directly in the design as the transitions of the Petri net. Second, multiple views or levels of abstraction of the system (tables and transactions) are supported including a view that shows normalized relations. Transition dynamics are maintained across PPNviews.

The rest of this paper is organized as follows: Section 2 presents a review of related literature. Section 3 contains an overview of Petri nets in general and PPNs in particular. Section 4 contains an example to demonstrate modeling using PPNs. Section 5 contains the mappings between PPNs, PPNviews, PPN transitions and database tables, views, and transactions. In section 6 is an example that illustrates the design of a database using PPNs, using its parameterization capability to view normalized database and transactions as well as other more or less detailed useful views. Section 7 concludes the paper.

2 Literature Review

Over the past decades there has been an increased interest in directly modeling the dynamics or "behavior" of database systems. This is a fundamentally different direction from most "ER-like" languages which represent static relationships between relations or record types. [4] has described a number of modeling tools, including ordinary Petri nets, for the purpose of conceptual modeling. A class of high-level Petri nets, the colored Petri nets (CPN) [1], have been proposed as a modeling tool for active databases [7]. However, any CPN which models complex behavior tends to produce complicated nets that are difficult to decipher and analyze. The formal definition of CPNs is similarly non-trivial to learn and apply. The PPN appproach is aimed at overcoming these limitations through its abstraction or parameterization capability.

The theory of PPNs is described in detail in [2]. This theory was not originally devised for the purpose of database design. Rather, it was devised for handling complexity in the modeling and analysis of manufacturing systems and control systems in general. In this paper, the PPN definitions are detailed along with manufacturing examples, and a discussion of properties and analysis of PPNs. Applying this theory to the design of databases had brought a richer interpretation of place and parameterized place (database view).

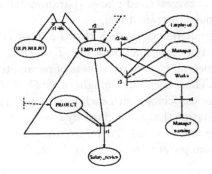

Fig. 1. Example on modeling aDBS [6]

We now give a detailed summary of a related effort applying PPNs in the modeling of active database systems (aDBS) described in [6]. This technical report explains the definitions of PPNs from [2], and also describes active databases. A database example from the literature is used to depict the PPN modeling technique. The authors propose to use PPNs for design in view of the inherent complexity in the application of contemporary non-heirarchical CPNs and of the relative ease with which PPNs handle this complexity through a heirarchy of parameterizations. The report indicates that cyclic firing or loops can be detected in PPNs by mapping them to ordinary PNs and analyzing the latter for cycles or loops. Thus the analysis of PPN models aids in detecting infinite loops, and at the same time, reducing the complexity of the analysis through its parameterization capability, without loss of accuracy of the model. This has been demonstrated in [6] with the aid of the example. Figure 2 from this report is included for completeness.

Another related effort worthy of mention [3] applies a version of PPN to the modeling of behavior in fuzzy object-oriented databases. PPN definition is extended to include fuzzy transitions that can take partial effect, defined on objects with fuzzy membership in classes. Object-oriented databases are inherently multilevel structures with their classification heirarchies, and the multi-level capabilities of PPNs are utilized to capture classes and to associate methods or transactions with the classes.

3 PPN Definitions

The structure of a standard Petri net (PN) is [5]: $PN = (P,\ T,\ I,\ O)$ where
P is a set of places,
T is a set of transitions,
I is an input function $I : T \mapsto P^\infty$, and
O is an input function $O : T \mapsto P^\infty$.
of the PPN model described in [2] is: $PPN = (C,\ D,\ P_p,\ T,\ I,\ O)$ where
C is the set of all parameter values
D is the set of all patterns
P_p is the set of all parameterized places (parameterization descriptor),
T is the set of all pattern transitions,
I is the set of all input functions such that $I : T \mapsto D^\infty$, and
O set of all output functions such that $O : T \mapsto D^\infty$.

The set of all parameters, C, consists of sets of parameter values that describe a give relation or type. Thus, C can be thought of as: $C = \{CV_1,\ CV_2, \ldots, CV_{|C|}\}$ where CV_i is some value associated with each parameter. These values are known as the pattern of information that are defined by a vector $x = (x_1,\ x_2,\ \ldots, x_{|C|})$. Each x_j portrays a parameter value. Therefore, the set of all patterns, D, is the Cartesian product of the parameter values (i.e., $D = CV_1 \times CV_2 \times \ldots \times CV_{|C|}$).

The parameterization descriptor, P_p is defined in [2] as:
$P_p = \{PP_1,\ PP_2,\ \ldots PP_{|P_p|}\}$

Thus, P_p is the set of all parameterized places with a parameter vector, x. The parameterization descriptor is an identifier for the set of parameterized places such that the union of the parameterized places yield D, and are mutually disjoint.

Additionally, the set of all pattern transitions, T, exhaustively specifies all actions that may take place in a system modeled by a PPN. This set is defined in the following manner: $T = \{pt_1, \ldots pt_{|T|}\}$ where
pt_i is a pattern transition, and
$pt_i : I(pt_i) \mapsto O(pt_i)$ for
$I(pt_i)$ a set of consumed patterns, and
$O(pt_i)$ a set of produced patterns.

A pattern transition, then, is a description of information to produce other patterns, and the set of all parameterized transitions, PT, is uniquely determined by the parameterization descriptor, P_p, and the set of transitions, T. Thus, there is a mapping such that $P_p \to T$.

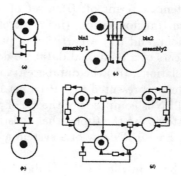

Fig. 2. A static "low level" structure of a simple assembly process

Parameterized input and output functions (i.e., $PI(t)$ and $PO(t)$ respectively) are defined in the following manner:
$$PI(t) = \{PP_{i1}, \ldots, PP_{i|PI(t)|}\} \subseteq P_p$$
$$PO(t) = \{PP_{j1}, \ldots, PP_{j|PO(t)|}\} \subseteq P_p$$

4   Examples

A single assembly line is used as an example to illustrate parameterizations or the procution of PPNviews. First, the order of the assembly line in figure 3(d) is a static structure consisting of holding bins containing parts a and b as well as an assemblage of those parts that produces s. If a pattern appears in B_1a and correspondingly a pattern appears in B_1b then a pattern will appear in B_1s. In this manner, an item, s, is assembled from parts a and b.

The assembly is modeled with a PPN as follows. The assembly can be viewed in its "most abstract" form that is shown in figure 3(a) where the initial marking reflects the assemblage of one part with another part to create a third. Beginning with figure 3(a), a parameterization can be made where: $(C, D, P_{p1}, T, I, O) \rightarrow \{(C, D, P_{p2}, T, I, O)\}$. In this case, $P_{p1} = \{D\}$ and P_{p2}

$$= \{(bin_1, part_1), (bin_1, part_2), (bin_2, part_1), (bin_2, part_2)\},$$
$$\{(assembly_1, part_3), (assembly_2, part_3)\}.$$

As shown in figure 3(b), *PP1* contains all patterns present in the parts bin (i.e., $\{(bin_1, part_1), (bin_1, part_2), (bin_2, part_1), (bin_2, part_2)\}$ and *PP2* contains all patterns present in the assembled bin (i.e., $\{(assembly_1, part_3), (assembly_2, part_3)\}$. In figure 3(c), the patterns are separated according to a desired parameter (i.e., in this case a spatial view with respect to the bin) where $(C, D, P_{p2}, T, I, O) \rightarrow \{(C, D, P_{p3}, T, I, O)\}$.

5 PPN Design Methodology and Database Mapping

A PPN models the system in terms of: (i) a set of all possible patterns, (ii) a set of rules for pattern transformation, (iii) a set of patterns describing the current state of the system, and (iv) a partition of patterns into classes based on properties. The elements of a relational database design include (i) the data elements, (ii) the 3NF relations, (iii) the database transactions, and (iv) views.

The state of any system represented in a Petri net is contained in its "marking". The marking of a PPN is composed of the set of patterns actually existing in the system. These patterns are the tuples that constitute an "instance" of the corresponding database. Each PPNview of a system at one instant contains the same tuples or patterns.

Each parameterized place in the PPN is a database view, containing some subset of the tuples in the database. The 3NF PPNview contains places that are 3NF relations. The hightest level abstraction or PPNview contains all the tuples that exist in the database, or all the patterns that exist in the PPN into one place, or a database view that contains all the tuples.

The methodology applied is as follows: First, an intuitive Petri net model of the system is developed, focusing on the dynamics of the system and "how it works." Next, each place in this first model is examined to define the pattern attributes or parameters that correctly describe the objects/patterns in that place. Third, each transition in this PPNview is defined as an input/output rule. Fourth, various other parameterizations or PPNviews are developed, which are simpler depictions for clarity and to ease Petri net analysis. Fifth, the attributes of all the patterns, or the set C, is normalized by traditional RDB design methods based on functional dependencies (FDs). The set of 3NF relations produced is translated back into a PPNview, which incorporates the dynamics of the system.

The correspondence between a PPN model and a database design is summed up as follows: The set C contains all the data elements. The patterns of information that occur in the Petri net constitute the records or tuples in the database. Each PPN place corresponds to a database view or table. A PPNview can be constructed with places corresponding to 3NF tables. Each PPN transition or rule corresponds to a data manipulation on the database, either an update or a transaction or multiple transactions. The PPN does not illustrate relationships that can be depicted in an Entity-Relationship (ER) diagram.

6 A Database Design Example

In this section, we present an example design of a database. PPNs are used to model a database for managing a generic multi-user database with a focus on transaction processing. The generic multi-user database system has a number of users and a number of ports for them to log in. When a user enters an ID and password from a free port, the entries are verified and, if the entries are valid, a session begins. During a session, the port is said to be "occupied", and the user begins terminal entries identified by the port of entry. These entries are identified with the user on that port and given an InputID as they are received by the system. These terminal inputs can be any one of queries, updates, commits, rollbacks, logout request or one with an error. The system parses and interprets the input. Queries generate query data if valid and a diagnostic if not. An update attempts changes to the users database and results in diagnostics and deltas. Deltas represent information about changes to the users database that are stored till a commit is received and the changes are made permanent. A rollback undoes an earlier update. Commits, rollbacks and input errors result in diagnostic output. All types of outputs are formated, and sent to the appropriate terminal (port). A logout request results in the termination of the session and the freeing of the occupied port.

A database to support the operations of the above system contains data about users, ports, sessions, etc., and incorporates the behaviors or actions that occur in it(e.g. start of a session, processing of various inputs and logout). We show a series of PPN parameterizations for this database. In each parameterization, or PPNview, the places represent database tables or database views. The transitions in the PPNview represent behaviors or transactions of the database.

Parameter Definition : Based on the description of the above system, the parameters and their domains are enumerated as follows:

1. UserID: $CV_1 = Set\ of\ all\ user\ IDs$.
2. Password: $CV_2 = Set\ of\ all\ user\ passwords$.
3. PortID: $CV_3 = Set\ of\ all\ port\ IDs$.
4. SessionID: $CV_4 = Set\ of\ all\ session\ IDs$.
5. InputID: $CV_5 = Set\ of\ all\ input\ IDs$.
6. InputType: $CV_6 = \{Query, Update, Commit, Rollback, Error, Logout\}$.
7. OuputType: $CV_7 = \{Data, Diagnostic, Delta\}$.
8. InputValue: $CV_8 = Set\ of\ all\ inputs$.
9. OutputValue: $CV_9 = Set\ of\ all\ outputs$.

The Transition Firing Rules : The transition rules are:
Rule 1: A valid terminal login is received from a free port and a user who was not logged in is now logged in. The port now becomes an occupied port and a

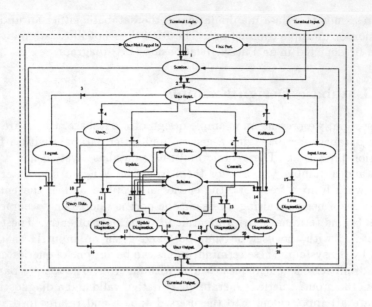

Fig. 3. System at the intuitive level of detail/parameterization.

session begins.
$$\{\{UserID, Password\}, \{UserID, Password, PortID\}, \{PortID\}\} \Rightarrow$$
$$\{\{SessionID, UserID, PortID\}\}$$
Rule 2: During a session, a terminal input is received and is associated with the corresponding user information.
$$\{\{SessionID, UserID, PortID\}, \{PortID, InputType, InputValue\}\} \Rightarrow$$
$$\{\{SessionID, UserID, PortID\},$$
$$\{UserID, InputID, InputType, InputValue\}\}$$
$$InputType \in \{Query, Update, Commit, Rollback, Error, Logout\}$$
Rule 3: The received user input is parsed and found to be a logout request.
$$\{\{UserID, InputID, Logout, InputValue\}\} \Rightarrow$$
$$\{\{UserID, InputID, Logout, InputValue\}\}$$
Rule 4: The received user input is parsed and found to be a query.
$$\{\{UserId, InputID, Query, InputValue\}\} \Rightarrow$$
$$\{\{UserId, InputID, Query, InputValue\}\}$$
Rule 5: The received user input is parsed and found to be an update.
$$\{\{UserId, InputID, Update, InputValue\}\} \Rightarrow$$
$$\{\{UserId, InputID, Update, InputValue\}\}$$
Rule 6: The received user input is parsed and found to be a commit.
$$\{\{UserId, InputID, Commit, InputValue\}\} \Rightarrow$$
$$\{\{UserId, InputID, Commit, InputValue\}\}$$
Rule 7: The received user input is parsed and found to be a rollback.
$$\{\{UserId, InputID, Rollback, InputValue\}\} \Rightarrow$$
$$\{\{UserId, InputID, Rollback, InputValue\}\}$$

Rule 8: The received user input is parsed and found to be an erroneous entry.
$\{\{UserId, InputID, Error, InputValue\}\} \Rightarrow$
$\qquad \{\{UserId, Input\dot{I}D, Error, InputValue\}\}$

Rule 9: The logout request is processed by terminating the session. The user now becomes not logged in and the port becomes free.
$\{\{SessionID, UserID, PortID\}, \{UserId, InputID, Logout, InputValue\}\} \Rightarrow$
$\qquad \{\{UserID, Password\}, \{PortID\}\}$

Rule 10: Process valid query to generate the query-data. In this process, the data-stores and schemas are referred to.
$\{\{UserId, InputID, Query, InputValue\}\} \Rightarrow$
$\qquad \{\{UserId, InputID, Data, OutputValue\}\}$

Rule 11: Generate the query-diagnostic upon error. In the process of doing so, the schemas of the users database are referred to.
$\{\{UserId, InputID, Query, InputValue\}\} \Rightarrow$
$\qquad \{\{UserId, InputID, Diagnostic, OutputValue\}\}$

Rule 12: Attempt the database update and generate the appropriate diagnostic. An additional Delta output is also generated if the update is successful.
$\{\{UserId, InputID, Update, InputValue\}\} \Rightarrow$
$\qquad \{\{UserId, InputID, Diagnostic, OutputValue\},$
$\qquad\qquad \{UserID, InputID, Delta, OutputValue\}\}$

Rule 13: The commit operation is performed, consuming the deltas.
$\{\{UserID, InputID, Commit, InputValue\},$
$\{UserID, InputID, Delta, OutputValue\}\} \Rightarrow$
$\qquad \{\{UserID, Commit, Diagnostic, OutputValue\}\}$

Rule 14: The rollback operation is performed with the required reference to the schemas and the corresponding changes to the data-stores and the appropriate diagnostic is generated.
$\{\{UserID, InputID, Rollback, InputValue\},$
$\{UserID, InputID, Delta, OutputValue\}\} \Rightarrow$
$\qquad \{\{UserId, InputID, Diagnostic, OutputValue\}\}$

Rule 15: A diagnostic depending on the input-error is generated.
$\{\{UserId, InputID, Error, InputValue\}\} \Rightarrow$
$\qquad \{\{UserId, InputID, Diagnostic, OutputValue\}\}$

Rule 16: The query-data is formated.
$\{\{UserId, InputID, Data, InputValue, OutputValue\}\} \Rightarrow$
$\qquad \{\{UserId, InputID, Data, OutputValue\}\}$

Rule 17: The query-diagnostic is formated.
$\{\{UserId, InputID, Diagnostic, OutputValue\}\} \rightarrow$
$\qquad \{\{UserId, InputID, Diagnostic, OutputValue\}\}$

Rule 18: The update-diagnostic is formated.
$\{\{UserId, InputID, Diagnostic, OutputValue\}\} \Rightarrow$
$\qquad \{\{UserId, InputID, Diagnostic, InputValue, OutputValue\}\}$

Rule 19: The commit-diagnostic is formated.
$\{\{UserId, InputID, Commit, Diagnostic, InputValue, OutputValue\}\} \Rightarrow$
$\qquad \{\{UserId, InputID, Commit, Diagnostic, InputValue, OutputValue\}\}$

Rule 20: The rollback-diagnostic is formated.

$$\{\{UserId, InputID, Diagnostic, InputValue, OutputValue\}\} \Rightarrow$$
$$\{\{UserId, InputID, Diagnostic, InputValue, OutputValue\}\}$$

Rule 21: The error-diagnostic is formated.

$$\{\{UserId, InputID, Diagnostic, OutputValue\}\} \Rightarrow$$
$$\{\{UserId, InputID, Diagnostic, OutputValue\}\}$$

Rule 22: The user's output is sent to his/her login terminal.

$$\{\{UserId, InputID, OutputType, OutputValue\}\} \Rightarrow$$
$$\{\{PortID, OutputValue\}\}$$

$$InputType \in \{Query, Update, Commit, Rollback, Error, Logout\}$$
$$OutputType \in \{Data, Diagnostic, Delta\}$$

PPNviews of the Generic Multiuser Database : We show a series of PPN parameterizations for the database modeled. In each parameterization, or PP-Nview, the places represent database tables or database views. The transitions in the views represent behaviors or transactions of the database. In an event-driven system input conditions to the transitions determine the conduct of the transactions. In other cases, a transaction is invoked by a pattern that enters from outside the system. The starting point of the PPN model of the system is an intuitive level PPNview of the database operation. In this view, shown in figure 3, focus is on the dynamics of the multi-user database. The various processes taking place in the system, viz. users logging in, presenting inputs and receiving data, diagnostics, etc., as outputs, are represented. This system description is most effective in defining behavior (transitions). Note that *each transitions' input and output places can be considered in relation to the database as views or RDB views of one or more relations*. The patterns that affect the behavior of the system are shown in table 1 along with their corresponding places. Some pattern entries in table 1 contain parameter values in parentheses next to the corresponding parameter name to signify the particular value (in parentheses) of the parameter named, e.g. the pattern entry for Query. The most detailed view of the system is the one containing patterns with all possible combinations of all values of all the parameters. The view in figure 3 is a higher level PPN than this one in that all possible values for the parameters UserID, Password, SessionID, InputID, InputValue and OutputValue are not considered separately. PPNs allow the design process to start at any convenient level of abstraction of the modeled system and allow a specialization or generalization from thereon. We mention here, that the Data Stores and Schemas are not considered in detail in our model though they participate in determining the transitions. Any changes/parameterization done on them is assumed to be understood. Higher level views can be obtained from a current PPN by combining "like" places on the latter, based on similar connectivity or other properties.

A PPN at a level that is of specific interest in the present context, appears in figure 4. This view is of interest here because of its correspondence with the 3NF relations of the example database. The ER-diagram of the 3NF relations and the functional dependencies used to arrive at them are shown in figure 5. This "nor-

Place	Pattern
Terminal Login	$\{UserID, Password, PortID\}$
User Not Logged In	$\{UserID, Password\}$
Free Port	$\{PortID\}$
Session	$\{SessionID, UserID, PortID\}$
Terminal Input	$\{PortID, InputType, InputValue\}$
User Input	$\{UserID, InputID, InputType, InputValue\}$
Logout	$\{UserID, InputID, InputType(Logout), InputValue\}$
Query	$\{UserID, InputID, InputType(Query), InputValue\}$
Update	$\{UserID, InputID, InputType(Update), InputValue\}$
Commit	$\{UserID, InputID, InputType(Commit), InputValue\}$
Rollback	$\{UserID, InputID, InputType(Rollback), InputValue\}$
Error	$\{UserID, InputID, InputType(Error), InputValue\}$
Query Data	$\{UserID, InputID, OutputType(Data), OutputValue\}$
Query Diagnostics	$\{UserID, InputID, OutputType(Diagnostic), OutputValue\}$
Update Diagnostics	$\{UserID, InputID, OutputType(Diagnostic), OutputValue\}$
Deltas	$\{UserID, InputID, OutputType(Delta), OutputValue\}$
Commit Diagnostics	$\{UserID, InputID, OutputType(Diagnostic), OutputValue\}$
Rollback Diagnostics	$\{UserID, InputID, OutputType(Diagnostic), OutputValue\}$
Error Diagnostics	$\{UserID, InputID, OutputType(Diagnostic), OutputValue\}$
User Output	$\{UserID, InputID, OutputType, OutputValue\}$
Terminal Output	$\{PortID, OutputValue\}$

Table 1. Place-Token association for initial parameterization.

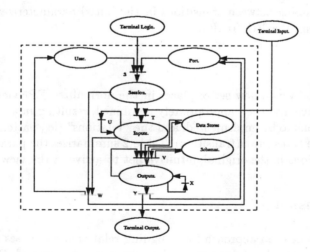

Fig. 4. PPNview of the 3NF Tables.

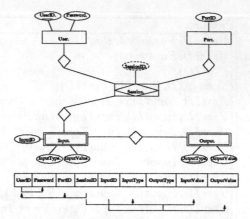

Fig. 5. The ER Diagram of the 3NF Relations and the Functional Dependencies.

Transitions in figure 3	Transitions in 3NF Net
{1}	S
{2}	T
{3, 4, 5, 6, 7, 8}	U
{10, 11, 12, 13, 14, 15}	V
{9}	W
{16, 17, 18, 19, 20, 21}	X
{22}	Y

Table 2. Mapping between transitions in the initial parameterization and the net representing the 3NF Tables.

malization" delivers a new set of places in the normalized PPNview. The PPN transitions have also been appropriately combined, resulting in a description of the transactions to be implemented, and the "relations" (ie., patterns) that participate in the transaction(transition). Table 2 summarizes the parameterization of the transitions in the original, intuitive net to arrive at the view in figure 4.

7 Conclusion

We have presented an approach for designing relational databases using PPNs. A detailed example has been presented to illustrate the method. Petri nets are intuitive tools that can be used even by non-technical users to describe the state and dynamics of a system. By using the parameterization operations the user can deal with the subset of states that is of interest, and the transitions affecting that subset of states. The combining of PPNviews to create a complete and correct PPN model of a large system, as well as analysis of properties, will need a more significant understanding of the PPN theory. A normalized set of relations is the information needed to produce a PPNview that shows the transactions as related to the 3NF relational schema.

The use of PPNs for database design as described provides a way for users and designers to describe database dynamics in terms of system dynamics. It provides a useful communication means for reviewing the database design as well as the system model, and enables the design of databases with a high degree of coherence with the system whose state is stored in the database. It allows the design of database dynamics based on the model of system dynamics.

We have presented the PPN as a database modeling mechanism mainly for its ability to model events or dynamics and the abstraction capability for designing views. However, we have observed three additional pervasive benefits through actually employing PPNs as information system design tool: First, the parameterization capability can be used to handle the design at a high level of abstraction while working on others, thus allowing a view of the entire system at all times. Second, the systems designed tend to exhibit an extraordinary degree of coherence with the systems that they represent and support. Third, in modeling the patterns and transitions that occur in real-life process or situation, multiple potential improvements (or opportunities for reengineering) of the real-life system or process were revealed. These improvements, would be incorporated into the design of the physical system and simultaneously reflected in the information system.

References

1. S. Gatziu and K. R. Dittrich. Events in Active Object Oriented Database System. In *Proceedings of the First International Workshop on Rules in Database Systems*, Edinburgh, Great Britain, 1993.
2. D. Gračanin, P. Srinivasan, and K. P. Valavanis. Parameterized Petri Nets and Their Application to Planning and Coordination in Intelligent Systems. *IEEE Transactions on Systems, Man and Cybernetics*, 24(10):1483–1497, October 1994.
3. K. Keith, P. Srinivasan, and R. George. Modeling Behavior in Fuzzy Object-Oriented Databases. In *Proceedings of the North American Fuzzy Information Processing Society Conference*, 1993.
4. C.-H. Kung and A. Solvberg. *Information System Engineering : An Introduction*. Springer-Verlag, Berlin, New York, 1993.
5. J. L. Peterson. *Petri net Theory and the Modeling of Systems*. Prentice-Hall, Englewood Cliffs, NJ, 1981.
6. N. Pissinou, A. I. Kokkinaki, and D. Gračanin. On Modeling Active Databases using Parameterized Petri Nets. Technical Report TR-94-6-1, CACS, University of Southwestern Louisiana, Lafayette, LA, 1994.
7. A. K. Tanaka. *On Conceptual Design of Active Databases*. PhD thesis, Georgia Institute of Technology, 1992.

This work has been supported by the National Textile Council through their grant S95-27.

SEER: Security Enhanced Entity-Relationship Model for Secure Relational Databases

Yong-Chul Oh and Shamkant B. Navathe

College of Computing
Georgia Institute of Technology
Atlanta, GA 30332

E-mail:{oh,sham}@cc.gatech.edu

Abstract. In this paper we propose extensions of the ER modeling concepts to address the conceptual modeling of security features and authorization histories in a database. It is designed to serve as the global conceptual model in a federated database environment. In such databases, data belonging to a variety of users under different constraints and security policies is subject to sharing. For the purposes of this paper, we assume that the local databases are relational. We propose a two-layered representation of data, one of which is the traditional ER model, whereas the other layer deals with the history of authorizations. We propose a methodology for dealing with relational databases by first analyzing the local database schemas and then mapping the security constraints appropriately while transforming/integrating each local data model into the global data model. We believe that the proposed conceptual model provides a useful common framework for dealing with the modeling and enforcement of security schemes in federated database environments.

1 Introduction

The increased use of information systems technology by a variety of users in all walks of life will become much more dependent on the proper functioning of the systems and their security features in the near future. Even when only a single database management system is involved, the security aspect in databases is quite a complex problem and subject to national and international evaluation and standardization work [21].

In the case of open systems technology, the security aspect becomes even more complex because besides having heterogeneity of data, the participating systems may enforce security by using different data protection techniques. This makes a global security model and a supporting mapping policy from the local models to that model necessary. Most of the research during the 1970-1980 was devoted to the relational data model [3] [4]. Semantic data models [7] [17] and systems supporting the object-oriented paradigm have dominated the modeling of new applications in the eighties and nineties. It is expected that most database research in the next decade will be influenced by providing access to existing autonomous databases and related issues such as modeling, design, querying, and transaction processing in the federated environments[19]. Our present research is aimed at addressing the security aspect of autonomous databases in the above context.

A federated database system is a collection of cooperating database management systems (DBMSs) that are autonomous and possibly heterogeneous [19]. To support users with access to remote databases that are part of the federation, a common data model is necessary. However, most of the federated database work has focused on problems such as view integration, development of common query languages, and global transaction processing. The security aspect in a federated environment has not been given enough attention. In this paper we show how the Entity-Relationship (ER) model [2] extended by security constraints can serve as a common data model taking into account the different access control mechanisms supported by the participating DBMSs. It needs to be further enhanced by additional security related information. Such a conceptual model of security can then be used by the federated database security manager to administer the security constraints. It can further be used by a federated DBMS to enforce authorization control while processing queries and transactions.

Database security is concerned with the ability of a computer system to enforce a security policy governing the disclosure, modification, or destruction of information. Two access control policies are frequently discussed in the literature: namely *Discretionary* and *Mandatory* Security Policies. Both policies should be supported in a system trying to meet a satisfactory barrier against unauthorized disclosure or modification of information.

Discretionary security policies define access restrictions based on the identity of users or user groups, the type of access, the specific object being accessed, and perhaps other factors. Discretionary access control (DAC) models can be represented by the access matrix model developed by Lampson [10]. A restrictive data protection is based on mandatory access controls (MAC). The mandatory access control requirements are formalized by two properties:

- simple property : read access is allowed when level (Subject) dominates level (Object).
- *-property : write access is allowed when level (Object) dominates level (Subject).

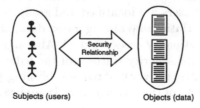

Fig. 1. Security Relationship

The security mechanism can be explained with a relationship between two groups: subject and object (see Figure 1). In discretionary access control, this relationship may be access types, and in mandatory access control, this relationship may be dominance of classifications. Conventional E-R model is only able to represent passive data which are called *objects* in security community. Any user information related to *subjects* in the security community as well as the concept of *security relationships* cannot be represented.

In order to concentrate on the security issue we assume homogeneity of the supported data model of the participating DBMSs (i.e. all support the relational data model) but heterogeneity in the supported access control mechanisms. This situation is very likely because of the different security schemes even in relational databases. Our assumption regarding heterogeneity of local security models are the support of DAC and MAC. Thus, the security representation problem for a global database becomes one of mappings from local database to the global schema. The global data model will be the Entity-Relationship model and the security requirements of each participating system need to be adequately mapped and represented into the global ER model. Given this scenario, we will first map from one data model (the relational model) to the common data model (the ER model). In addition to translating one schema into another schema, we need to include the individual access control mechanisms of the local DBMSs in our translation. Therefore, in such an environment we must integrate the security systems as well as the database schemas.

2　Relevant Literature

Database security requirements often start with the concepts associated with the Trusted Computing Base (TCB) that emerged from research on secure operating systems; it is summarized in the US Department of Defense Trusted Computer System Evaluation Criteria [13] and its interpretation for databases [21]. Recently, the importance of design methodologies for the development of secure databases has been discussed [8][11][20] .

Several efforts to extend database security to other data models have been reported recently. Preliminary reports have been published regarding development of security models for object-oriented databases, entity-relationship databases, and knowledge-based systems. In [6],[16], and [18] security features were added to the ER model. There has been some work on access control in FDBS environments. Templeton et al. [22] discuss the issue of installing a new user into the federation, and how users are identified and grouped into classes. All above works are based on the relationship among users, data, and operations, which is related to only the discretionary access control. Although current access control models of FDBS study the security features of the federation itself, there is, to the best of our knowledge, no work about establishing global security models based on the heterogeneity of the security models applicable to the participating DBMSs.

A number of schema analyses and schema translations between the relational and the ER model have been reported in [5][9][12]. All these mappings are well explained in Batini et al. [1].

3 Proposed Extended E-R Model for Modeling Security Schemes and Authorization Histories

We propose an extension to the entity-relationship model as follows: Two layers are proposed - one for data (the conventional E-R schema) and one for modeling security schemes and authorization histories. These layers are shown graphically on the right side of Figure 2 which is an abstract representation of some hypothetical secure database. In order to completely specify the security relationship information, it is necessary to represent, in addition to the above two layers, information about the subjects or user information which is modeled on the left side of Figure 2 under the heading of *USER GROUPS*. The security model on the right, particularly, the authorization history, can only be defined on the basis of these user groups. The hexagonal object called *SECURITY RELATION* in the center is a *meta-relationship* that relates the user groups to the two-layered security model.

A user group is a set of user entities. Any collection of active agents may be called as a user group if they are treated together for the purposes of security, e.g., granting and revoking of access privileges.

The meta-relationship called the security relationship would contain information pertaining to the current status of the security scheme as it relates to users and data objects—entity types or relationship types. Consider a relational implementation of this abstract model shown in Figure 2. The user groups will be described in one relation schema called USER_GROUPS giving details of each user group per tuple, as shown below. The security relationship will give rise to another relational schema called SECURITY_RELATION that includes security related information for each user group. The attribute of the latter relation called user_vs_data_dominance is related to the idea of user's security classification exceeding the data object's security classification as we discussed under mandatory access control in section 1.

```
USER_GROUP (usergroup#, usergroup_name,
            usergroup_description, .....)

SECURITY_RELATION (usergroup#, data_object_id,
            authorization_type,
            site_information,user_vs_data_dominance, .....)
```

The security information layer (shaded layer in Figure 2) consists of an information propagation tree (IPT) for each object, which will be explained in the next section.

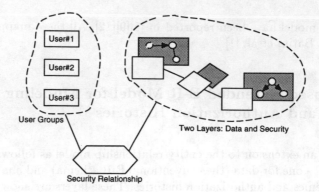

Fig. 2. Security Model of a hypothetical database

4 Information Propagation Tree for a General Representation of Security

In this section, the Information Propagation Tree (IPT) which models security scheme in a general manner is introduced. This general framework can give a broader and general view of current control mechanisms and we can extend an existing access control mechanism to one which satisfies complex security requirements. This tree can be changed dynamically, according to the propagation of authorization information from one subject to any other subject. Therefore, it is called the information propagation tree (IPT).

As described above, access controls can be explained by an access matrix in one type of database security models. In other words, we can explain the access control with a set of dynamically updated access matrices, if there are a number of propagations of access rights, we need to keep a history of access matrices to explain how the access rights are propagated among subjects.

Traditionally database system security is managed by a grant/revoke mechanism. In the following we illustrate the use of the GRANT and GRANT OPTION facilities with actual SQL commands against data objects o_1 and o_2 for the set of users s_1, s_2, s_3, and s_4.

```
DBA: GRANT CREATTAB TO S1;
```

The DBA grants create authorization to user s_1. Then, the user s_1 can create the object o_1 and the object o_2. (At this point the system is supposed to generate an access matrix - let us call it copy #0)

```
S1: GRANT SELECT, UPDATE ON O1 TO S2 WITH GRANT OPTION;
S1: GRANT UPDATE ON O1 TO S3 WITH GRANT OPTION;
```

As shown above, user s_1 grants the select and update authorizations on both the object o_1 and o_2 to user s_2. User s_1 wants user s_2 to have the ability to

	o_1	o_2
s_1	all	all
s_2	select,update	select,update
s_3	select,update	select
s_4	select	-

Fig. 3. Final Access Matrix (Copy #4 according to above operations)

propagate this access type to other users, so the grant option is included. User s_1 also grants the update authorizations on the object o_1 to user s_3 with grant option. (Access matrix copy#0 gets modified into copy#1).

S2: GRANT SELECT ON O1 TO S3 WITH GRANT OPTION

In the above, user s_2 grants the select authorization on the object o_1 to the user s_3 User s_2 wants user s_3 to have the ability to propagate this access type to other users, so grant option is included. (Access matrix copy#1 gets modified into copy#2)

S2: GRANT SELECT ON O2 TO S3;

The user s_2 grants the select authorization on the object o_2 to the user s_3. User s_2 does not want the user s_3 to have the grant option. (Access matrix copy#2 gets modified into copy#3)

S3: GRANT SELECT ON O1 TO S4;

Similarly as shown above, user s_3 grants the select authorization on object o_1 to the user s_4. User s_3 does not want the user s_4 to have the grant option. (Access matrix copy#3 gets modified into copy#4). The final access matrix is shown in Figure 3.

Note that the access matrix went through updates which we referred to as copies zero through four. It is possible to represent these dynamically updated access matrices in the form of a tree. We call this as the information propagation tree (IPT). This tree can be changed incrementally at each update without losing the existing information. It portrays how the access rights held by one subject keep propagating to other subjects for a given object. In order to represent this information, we define IPT as the following.

Definition 1. Information Propagation Tree (IPT) is a rooted tree whose root is the creator of that information, and IPT = (V, E) where V is a set of subjects, E is a set of transitions from a subject s_1 to a subject s_2 and (s_1, s_2) has a label a. The label a represents a type of access rights given.

Definition 2. Nodes in IPT are V = {non-terminal, terminal}. A terminal node is represented by a double lined circle and it does not have any GRANT privileges. A node that has the GRANT privilege is non-terminal, because it can propagate its access rights.

Definition 3. A vertex split occurs when a vertex is split into two vertices: v-nonterminal and v-terminal; this happens when one subject is granted different grant options for different types of access.

For example, if s_1 grants select to s_2 with grant option and s_1 grants update to s_2 without grant option, then should s_2 be a terminal or non-terminal? In this case, s_2 is split into s_2-n and s_2-t, and then select is applied to s_2-n, whereas the update is applied to s_2-t. The o_2 tree in Figure 4 shows the result of splitting.

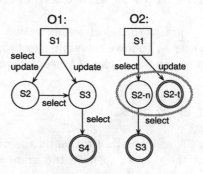

Fig. 4. Information Propagation Tree

Each object has its own tree. In the case of the object o_1, the creator is s_1, so s_1 is the root, s_1 is also the root of tree o_1. The creator of the information is represented in a square box as shown in Figure 4. Subjects except a creator/owner are represented in circles. The subject who is not allowed to propagate the information is represented as terminal node in a double lined circle. The arrow from one node to another node means that the information is propagated from one subject (the grantor) to another (the grantee). A label associated with the arc represents the access type that is allowed to the grantee.

In mandatory access control, a conventional access matrix is not enough to explain the access control. Every subject needs an additional attribute, the *security clearance level*, and every data object needs an additional attribute, the *security sensitivity level*. Any subject cannot transfer their authorizations to someone else. In IPT, subjects are represented in circles. The subject who is not allowed to propagate the information is represented as a terminal node. In modeling MAC with IPT for a given object, we introduce the notion of a *virtual owner* who grants read/write access for that object to the actual users. All nodes must be represented as terminal nodes and the length of every arc is 1.

Claim 1 *The length of each arc in mandatory access control is 1.*

Explanation 1. In Mandatory Access Control, access controls are managed by two properties: the simple-property and the *-property listed in section 1. Authorizations are granted by dominance rules. Dominance rules are evaluated by comparison at two levels: subject's security clearance level and object's security sensitivity level. The allowable accesst type can be inferred by comparing two levels; the clearance level of subject and the classification level of the object. Also no user can grant any access right to other user even if he/she has the proper access right on that object or he/she is the creator of the object. The authorization cannot be propagated at all. In other words, all nodes except the root node in IPT are terminal nodes. As we can see in the Figure 5, the length from the root to terminal nodes is always 1.

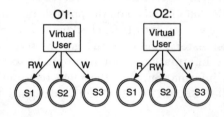

Fig. 5. Information Propagation Tree in MAC

4.1 Advantages of IPT

We briefly summarize the advantages of the second layer of the model consisting of the IPT.

1. Security schemes of MAC and DAC can be distinguished. According to Claim 1, every length of path in MAC is 1, and every node in MAC is terminal.
2. We can keep track of the entire history of authorization propagation. If we use the access matrix only, we can evaluate the valid authorization by the last matrix. However, we do not know how the information is propagated. We do not have the information about who gave which authorization to whom. This problem is solved with the IPT.
3. Evaluation is possible by keeping track of the access type label.

5 Developing an SEER Model from underlying relations

In this section, we propose the use of reverse engineering algorithms for translating the relational data model either using mandatory access control or discretionary access control policy. In general, we could have a system with an access matrix that may be the result of any *local* security scheme. The target data model is a two layer extended entity-relationship data model as we have described before. There are several schema analysis and schema translation proposals (for example, see Chapter 12 in [1]). Most studies have involved two models from among the following: relational, hierarchical, network, and E-R [5][12]. To the best of our knowledge, there has been no explicit schema analysis or schema translation between two data models that includes database security requirements.

Steps for developing an SEER schema from an underlying relation schema:

1. Relational schema analysis.
2. Constructing E-R from existing models. Our methodology deals with the use of various keys [14][15] in relations and *reverse* engineers an ER model.
3. Constructing USER GROUPS based on the possible information of active agents,
4. In each step of conversion into E-R, checking possible security information and authorization history, and constructing the second layer (security layer with IPT). If the information is not appropriate to these two layers, such as instance level information, then the meta relationship between subjects and objects, called SECURITY RELATION is designed to store this type of information.

We present the example a simplified hypothetical hospital database elsewhere [14] in order to show the methodology of developing an SEER schema design from underlying relations having different security schemes.

6 Conclusion and Future Work

We discussed the handling of security schemes and constraints as well as of the history of authorizations at a conceptual level in the extended ER model called SEER. We expect the model will prove useful in dealing with component databases that come from different underlying environments with their own security schemes and authorization histories. In translating from the relational data model, we considered two different security policies: Discretionary Access Control and Mandatory Access Control which are predominantly in use today. We proposed the notion of information propagation tree (IPT) to capture the history of propagation of access rights among user groups. The resulting conceptual schema in SEER thus has two layers - the traditional ER schema, and the IPT structure.

We have elsewhere [15] proposed the algorithm to translate a relational database with an access matrix mechanism to the entity-relationship data model with some extension. To do this translation, we first analyze the relational database schema, and categorize relation types, primary key types, and attribute types. We have also proposed an algorithm to translate a multilevel relational data model to the extended entity-relationship data model. In this paper we focused on dealing with these two different security policies as well as any other instance-specific security information into one global conceptual data model in a federated database environment. Once the global extended E-R model is constructed, the resulting information will have to be stored in some auxilliary database. That meta-database would aid in the process of enforcing security in a federated database environment. We are presently dealing with the problem of how this enforcement should work coupled with a federated database management system.

This research is continuing by developing a testbed environment that would allow the capture of security information and would enable query processing against underlying secure databases. The meta-data may be stored in an Object-Oriented global model at the logical level. As immediate extensions of the current work, attribute level granularity will have to be incorporated for security modeling over and above the relation and instance level security that we considered in this paper. Views and materialized relations also need to be considered. We plan to keep the SEER model at the present level of detail and incorporate these issues into the run-time query processing environment. We hope that the representation in SEER would still be useful for conceptually understanding the security related information regarding the underlying databases.

References

1. C. Batini, S. Ceri, and S. Navathe. *Conceptual Database Design: Entity-Relationship Approach*. Benjamin Cumings, 1991.
2. P Chen. The entity-relationship model: Toward a unified view of data. *ACM Transactions on Database Systems*, 1(1), 1976.
3. E. Codd. A relational model of data for large shared data bank. *Communications of ACM*, 13(6), 1970.
4. E. Codd. Extending the database relational model to capture more meaning. *ACM Transactions on Database Systems*, 4(4), 1979.
5. S. Dumpala and S. Arora. Schema translation using the entity-relationship approach. *Entity-Relationship Approach to Information Modeling and Analysis*, 1983.
6. G. Gajnak. Some results from the entity-relationship multilevel secure dbms project. In *the 4th Aerospace Computer Security Application Conference*, 1988.
7. R. Hull and R. King. Semantic database modeling: Survey, applications, and research issues. *Computing Surveys*, 19(3), 1987.
8. S. Jajodia and R. Sandhu. Database security: current status and key issues. *SIGMOD Record*, 19(4):123–126, 1990.
9. P. Johannesson and K. Kalman. A method for translating relational schemas into conceptual schema. In C. Batini, editor, *the 7th International Conference on Entity-Relationship Approach*, pages 279–294. North-Holland, 1988.
10. B. Lampson. Protection. In *the 5th Princeton Symposium on Information Science*, 1971.
11. T. Lunt and Fernandcz E. Database security. *SIGMOD Record*, 19(4):90–97, 1990.
12. S. Navathe and A. Awong. Abstracting relational and hierarchical data with a semantic data model. In *the 6th International Conference on Entity-Relationship Approach*. North-Holland, 1987.
13. Department of Defense. Trusted computer system evaluation criteria, 1985.

14. Y. Oh and S. Navathe. Seer : Security enhanced entity-relationship model for modeling and integrating secure database environments. Technical Report GIT-TR-95-29, Georgia Institute of Tecnology, 1995.

15. Y. Oh, S. Navathe, and G. Pernul. Entity-relationship modeling of global security in a federated database environment. Technical Report GIT-TR-91-57, Georgia Institute of Tecnology, 1991.

16. B. Patkau and D. Tennenhouse. The implementation of secure entity-relationship databases. In *IEEE Sympo. on Security and Privacy*, 1985.

17. J. Peckham and F. Maryanski. Semantic data models. *ACM Computing Surveys*, 20(3), 1988.

18. G. Pernul and A. Tjoa. A view integration approach for the design of mls databases. In *10th Int'l. Conf. on the Entity-Relationship Approach*, 1991.

19. A. Sheth and J. Larson. Federated database systems for managing distributed, heterogeneous, and autonomous databases. *ACM Computing Surveys*, 22(3), 1990.

20. G. Smith. Multilevel secure database design: a practical application. In *5th annual Computer security applications conference*, 1990.

21. Trusted Database Management System. Interpretation of the trusted computer system evaluation criteria, 1990.

22. M. Templeton, E. Lund, and P. Ward. Pragmatics of access control in mermaid. *In special issue on Federated Database Systems, Quarterly Bulletin of the IEEE-CS TC on Data Engineering*, 10(3), 1987.

Neural Network Technology to Support View Integration

Ernst Ellmer[1], Christian Huemer[1], Dieter Merkl[2], Günther Pernul[3]

[1] University of Vienna, Institute of Applied Computer Science
Liebiggasse 4, A-1010 Wien, Austria
[2] Vienna University of Technology, Institute of Software Technology
Resselgasse 3, A-1040 Wien, Austria
[3] University of Essen, FB 5 - Information Systems
Altendorfer Str. 97, D-45143 Essen, Germany
`<lastname>@ifs.univie.ac.at`

Abstract-The most difficult and time consuming activity to perform during view integration is to find correspondences between different view specifications. Such correspondences may be the source for conflicts when integrating the views and thus must be detected and resolved. A manual inspection of the class definitions in each view and a comparison with each class definition in the other views may result in an almost endless process. To support a designer we propose a computerized tool to extract the semantics from view definitions, to transform them into a unique vector representation of each class, and to use the class vectors to train a neural network in order to determine categories of classes. The output of the tool is a 'first guess' which concepts in views may be overlapping or which concepts do not overlap at all. This may be of tremendous value because the designers are relieved from manual inspection of all the classes and can direct their focus on classes grouped into the same category.

1. Introduction

For the development of large databases it is difficult to design the whole conceptual database schema at once. Schema integration, i.e. the process of deriving an integrated schema from a set of component schemata, is generally understood as an important activity during database design. This activity may be necessary in two design scenarios. The first is *database schema integration* for building database federations where a uniform canonical database schema is derived from existing, possibly heterogeneous, information systems and necessary to support interoperable access. The second is *view integration*, a process in classical database design, which derives an integrated schema from a set of user views. In general, if requirements on a database were developed by different design teams and are stated on the basis of individual requirements documents and schema specifications, there is a need for integration. Although related to all aspects our main focus in this paper is on the view integration process.

The view integration process can be divided into three main phases, namely view comparison, conflict resolution, and actual view integration. *View comparison* involves analysis and comparison of schemes to determine correspondences, in particular different representations of the same concept. *Conflict resolution* involves modifying one or more of the schemes to be integrated until each conflict is resolved and the conflicting concept is represented equally in each schema. The *actual view integration* generates the integrated schema by merging the individual view schema representations.

The most difficult part of the schema integration process is view comparison. The fundamental problems here lie in the fact that one concept of reality can be modelled in different views differently. This may be because the same phenomenon may be seen in different views from different levels of abstraction or may be represented by using different properties. The key in detecting such conflicts is proper understanding of the intended meaning of object classes and based on certain criteria to identify semantic similarity between classes from different views.

In this paper we try to solve the view comparison problem by assuming that concepts in different views that refer to the same real world semantics will have similar features, such as their names, attributes, domains, links, functions, or occur in similar contexts. Our assumption is that similarities may exist, yet we do not pretend to know them. We make use of this assumption and train a neural network to recognize common patterns in different views and to deliver a 'first guess' to the designer which concepts may be overlapping with other concepts in other views. For view comparison we use neural networks because of two reasons: First, neural networks are robust in the sense of tolerating 'noisy' input data (overlapping classes represented by similar features) and as a second reason, we refer to their ability of generalization. Pragmatically speaking, a neural network learns conceptually relevant features of the input domain and is thereby able to structure the various concepts accordingly.

This paper is organized as follows: In the remaining part of Section 1 we give an overview of the proposed architecture for view comparison based on neural network technology. Section 2 presents related work performed in the area of view integration. Section 3 contains a description of a case study. Section 4 shows how the view specifications to be compared are transformed in neural net input data and is devoted to the analysis of the neural network, its learning process, and to a discussion of the experimental results achieved. Section 5 contains our conclusions and hints on future research.

1.1 Overview of the proposed architecture for view comparison

For view comparison we propose an architecture consisting of four main building blocks (see Fig. 1) and several major design activities. The main goal of the proposed tool is to minimize human activities during view comparison. In our methodology only manual input of view specifications and human interpretation of results is required. Individual user views are specified using the object model of OMT [17]. The first computerized activity is a translation of the OMT schema definitions into C++-like database class definitions. The class definitions serve as an input to a specific parsing activity during which the semantic meaningful and relevant information for view comparison is extracted from the C++ class definitions. This completes building-block 1 which we call the *data extraction* phase. Building-block 2 is called *data transformation* and is responsible for determining the input vector to train the neural network. We refer to each semantically meaningful unit that is determined while performing building-block 1 as a classifier, and each classifier will serve as an element within the vector representation of a class. The next activity is instantiating the vector and consists of parsing the meta-data to determine for each class which of the classifiers are satisfied. This completes building-block 2. During building-block 3, *training process*, the resulting class vectors are used to train the neural network to recognize categories of classes. Human intervention is again necessary in building-block 4, *cluster interpretation*, to check and confirm the results.

2. Related work

View integration has been a research topic for more than fifteen years. A survey of the area can be found in [2] in which the authors discuss twelve methodologies for database or view integration. Early work has been done in the context of the relational model [3], the functional model [15] or more recently in the context of the Entity-Relationship model [5] (see for example [12], [19], [8]). Early work has focused on how to merge a given number of schemes by using a given set of correspondences. More recently, the interest of researchers has changed and more work is done for providing assistance during the view comparison phase. [16] was the first who developed a tax-

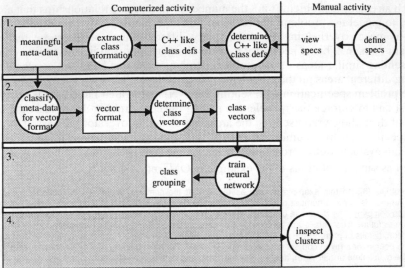

Fig. 1: Proposed architecture for view comparison

onomy for types of conflicts that might occur by integrating different schemes. [1] compares by means of a unification process concepts in different schemes by analysing similarities among names, structures, and constraints. In [18] a method for identifying schema similarities based on using a semantic dictionary and a taxonomy structure is proposed while [9] uses conceptual graph theory to support schema integration. Another idea is to use linguistic tools, such as thesauri and information retrieval techniques to build dictionaries and to support the view comparison. In [4] such experiences are reported. In [7] fuzzy and incomplete terminological knowledge together with schema knowledge is used to determine the similarity of object classes. An innovative and new approach is reported by [13] in which semantic integration in heterogeneous databases is achieved by using neural networks. Although their work is related to the approach reported in this paper there are fundamental differences. While [13] focus on the integration of existing databases we do focus on view integration. Their goal was to find equivalencies between fields in different existing databases while we address to capture a much higher level of real world semantics. Their input into the neural net is driven by data content and a flat table file structure while we use conceptual database structures expressed in a high level data model as input to train the net. Their results may be applicable to develop a canonical data model for a database federation while the results of our efforts may be seen as a 'first guess' which concepts in user views may be overlapping in other views. In large design teams and in database environments with a large set of heterogeneous users this information may be of tremendous value because the designers are relieved from manual inspection of a great variety of different object classes.

3. A view comparison case study

In order to evaluate our approach to view comparison, we carried out a case study. Usually, view comparison is necessary if a number of analysts model partly overlapping areas of a large real world domain containing hundreds of classes and relationships. The problem we faced was to find an example which first is complex and large enough to show the usefulness and applicability of our approach to view comparison and second is small enough to be presented in this paper. We feel that the central point of such an example problem is not the number of classes and relationships that are necessary to model the problem, but rather to find an example allowing a number of analysts to model overlapping as well as very different areas of the same real world problem domain. This is necessary to show that our approach is able to find concepts representing similar areas of the problem domain on the one hand and concepts representing different areas on the other hand. We used the well-known Date example [6] as a core problem specification representing the overlapping area) to be modeled by each analyst and to enforce the modelers to extend the core problem by at least three concepts of their choice representing the areas which do not overlap. We passed the problem specification to a number of experts and undergraduate students and used their results to evaluate our approach. Fig. 2 shows the core problem specification from [6] as well as sample solutions to the example in OMT notation [17].

Core problem [6]: "In this example we are assuming that the company maintains an education department whose function is to run a number of training courses. Each course is offered at a number of different locations within the company. The database contains details both of offerings already given and of offerings scheduled to be given in future. The details are as follows: For each course: course number (unique), course title, course description, details of prerequisite courses (if any), and details of all offerings (past and planned); For each prerequisite course for a given course: course number and title; For each offering of a given course: date, location, format (e.g., full-time or half-time), details of all teachers, and details of all students; For each teacher of a given offering: employee number and name; For each student of a given offering: employee number, name, and grade"

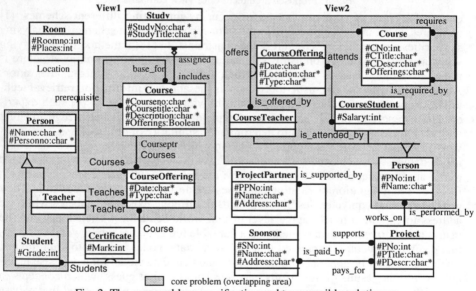

Fig. 2: The core problem specification and two possible solutions

4. A 'neural' tool supporting view comparison
4.1 Data Extraction
Determine C++-like class definitions.
As mentioned in Section 3 we use the OMT technique for the description of the data schema, or more specific the OMT object model, which describes the static structural and relationship aspects of a system. The utilities which the object model provides to capture those concepts from the real world that are important to the system have to be mapped into C++-like constructs: Each class of the OMT model is expressed as a C++ class. The names and types of attributes are expressed as data member names and types in the C++ header file. A generalization is converted according to the C++ syn-

tax for the definition of super- and subclass relationships. Associations and aggregations are both resolved in C++ by pointers if the number of participating classes is 1 or by a set of pointers to the related class otherwise. If a link attribute is attached to a relationship the pointers do not reference to the related class, but to the class which is built from the link attribute. Note, at the moment our approach is based on the static structure of the data model and thus, we do not use the notation of operations.

The two view definitions presented in Fig. 3 include a subset of the classes depicted in Fig. 2. Both views include among others a class CourseOffering. View 1 includes the class Student, whereas view 2 includes a similar class CourseStudent. Furthermore, view 1 includes the class Certificate and view 2 the class Project. Consider the classes of view 1 for a closer inspection. CourseOffering directly adopts the attribute names and types from Date and Type of the OMT model. Since the number of the related Code, Room and Teacher is 1 in each case, pointers to these classes are established and designated by the relationship attribute. Note, the class instance specifying the room is termed Location in both views, but is a pointer to a separate class Room in view 1 and a simple char* in view 2. The same rules are applied to the class Student, but since it is a subclass of Person the statement 'public Person' is added at the beginning of the class definition. Since a certificate is issued for each course the link attribute Certificate is added to the n:m relationship between Student and CourseOffering. Therefore, Students and CourseOffering do not have a set of pointers referencing each other, but each one has a set referencing to Certificate. Each Certificate includes exactly one pointer to each Student and to each CourseOffering. The n:m relationship is split up into two 1:n relationships via the link attribute Certificate.

View 1:

```
class CourseOffering {
    protected:
    char* Date;
    char * Type;
    Course* Courseptr;
    Room* Location;
    Teacher* Teacher;
    Set<Certificate*> Students; };
```

```
class Student : public Person {
    protected:
    int Grade;
    Set<Certificate*> Course; };
```

```
class Certificate {
    protected:
    Student* Students;
    CourseOffering* Course;
    int Mark; };
```

View 2:

```
class CourseOffering {
    protected:
    Course* offers;
    CourseTeacher*
        is_offered_by;
    char* Date;
    char* Location;
    char* Type;
    Set<CourseStudent*>
        is_attended_by; };
```

```
class CourseStudent :
        public Person {
    protected:
    int Salary;
    Set<CourseOffering*> attends; };
```

```
class Project {
    protected:
    int PNo;
    char* PTitle;
    char* PDescr;
    Set<Person*>
        is_performed_by;
    Set<ProjectPartner*>
        is_supported_by;
    Set<Sponsor*> is_paid_by; };
```

Fig. 3: C++-like class definitions

Extract class information.

It is difficult to identify and resolve all the semantic heterogeneity among components. In our approach we use three features to classify semantic similarity and dissimilarity: the names of the classes, the names of the attributes and the types of the attributes.

It is assumed that some classes or at least some of their attributes and/or relationships are assigned with meaningful names. Therefore, the knowledge about the terminological relationship between the names can be used as an indicator of the real world correspondence between the objects. However, similar classes and attributes might have different synonyms, which are not detected by inspection. This shifts the problem to building a synonym lexicon. A general purpose synonym lexicon cannot be specified, the synonyms must rather be specified according to the semantics of the problem description. Thus, such a lexicon cannot be generated automatically and is expensive to build. Consequently, we omitted a synonym lexicon in our approach. Furthermore, it is assumed that given a database design application, different designers tend to produce similar schemata because they use the same technology and have comparable knowledge about designing a 'good' database. Thus, information about the types of attributes used within a class can be regarded as a discriminator to determine the likelihood that two classes describe similar real world objects.

To extract the semantic meaningful meta-data all C++ header files including the class definitions have to be parsed. The result of the parsing process are sets containing all meta-data: class names set, attribute names set, data types set. Each element of these sets serves as a so-called classifier to characterize a class according to the above mentioned criteria. Fig. 4 shows these sets, if only the views of Fig. 2 were parsed.

class names:	attribute names:			attribute types:	
study	studyno	name	is_supported_by	char*	set<sponsor*>
course	studytitle	personno	is_paid_by	set<course*>	project*
courseoffering	includes	date	works_on	boolean	set<project*>
room	courseno	type	ppnr	set<study*>	
teacher	coursetitle	courseptr	supports	set<courseoffering*>	
student	description	location	sno	int	
certificate	offerings	teacher	address	student*	
person	assigned	teaches	pays_for	courseoffering*	
courseteacher	base_for	grade	cno	course*	
coursestudent	prerequisite	offers	ctitle	room*	
project	roomno	is_offered_by	cdescr	courseteacher*	
projectpartner	places	is_attended_by	is_required_by	set<certificate*>	
sponsor	courses	pno	requires	teacher*	
	students	ptitle	salary	set<coursestudent*>	
	course	pdescr	attends	set<person*>	
	mark	is_performed_by		set<projectpartner*>	

Fig. 4: Classifiers

4.2 Data Transformation
Classify meta data for vector format.

Training a neural network with the class information requires the creation of the format of the vectors describing the classes. In particular, each of the different class names, attribute names and attribute types used as a classifier will be an element of the vector. The classifiers 1 to n (n represents the number of different class names) are used to mark the class name. The elements n+1 to n+m (m represents the number of different attribute names) indicate the use of the corresponding attribute names within the corresponding class. The elements n+m+1 to n+m+p (p represents the number of different attribute types) are used to describe the types of attributes used in the class at hand. Fig. 5 depicts the vector formats resulting from the classifiers in Fig. 4.

1	2	3	...	13	14
study	course	courseoffering	...	sponsor	studyno

...	27	...	32	33	34
...	students	...	date	type	courseptr

35	36	...	60	61	...
location	teacher	...	attends	char*	...

69	70	71	72	...	79
course*	room*	teacher*	set<certificate*>	...	set<project*>

Fig. 5: Vector format

Determine class vectors.

An additional parsing of the C++ class definitions creates a vector for each class. The vector elements describing the class name are set to 1, if the class is specified with the name in question or left 0 otherwise. Similarly, the elements describing the attribute names are set to 1, if the class includes an attribute with the corresponding name or are left 0 otherwise. The elements describing the attribute types are set to the number of occurrences of the corresponding type in the class. Fig. 6 shows the transformation of the semantics included in OMT to the corresponding vector representation of the class by using class `CourseOffering` of view 1 as an example. Note, the vector elements not explicitly depicted in Fig. 6 are set to 0.

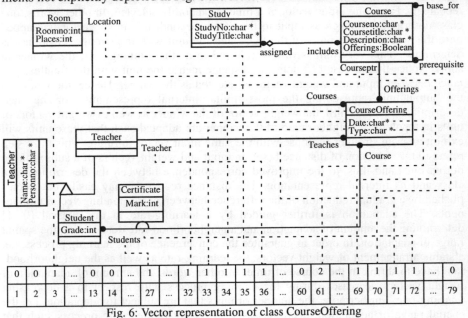

0	0	1	...	0	0	...	1	...	1	1	1	1	1	...	0	2	...	1	1	1	1	...	0
1	2	3	...	13	14	...	27	...	32	33	34	35	36	...	60	61	...	69	70	71	72	...	79

Fig. 6: Vector representation of class CourseOffering

4.3 Training process

We selected the self-organizing map (SOM) [10], [11] as the architecture to represent similarities within the classes obtained from different designers. The motivation to use exactly the SOM is mainly due to its unsupervised learning rule. Unsupervised learning refers to adaptation of the neural network's structure in order to enable the construction of internal models capturing the regularities of the input domain without any additional information. With additional information we refer to concepts such as a desired output that has to be specified with supervised learning models. For an overview of neural networks in general we refer to [14].

The utilization of neural networks is justified in that they are robust, i.e. they tolerate noisy input data. This fact is of essential importance during view comparison since different designers tend to model the same fact of reality slightly different, e.g. names of classes, names of attributes, types of attributes. These at first sight minor differences constitute major obstacles for conventional approaches, e.g. keyword matching. Moreover, we feel that an adequate representation of these differences for a knowledge-based system is not achievable with satisfactory generality and in reasonable time.

Basically, the SOM consists of a layer of n input units and a grid of output units each of which has assigned an n-dimensional weight vector. The task of the input units is to propagate the input vectors as they are onto the grid of output units. Each output unit computes exactly one output value which is proportional to the similarity between the current input vector, i.e. the description of one class in our application domain, and the unit's weight vector. This value is commonly referred to as the unit's activation (the unit's response). Commonly, similarity is measured in terms of the Euclidean distance between the two vectors. In terms of our application domain we may regard the activation of an output unit as the degree of correspondence between the description of a class, i.e. the input vector representing the class, and the internal representation of that very class, i.e. the weight vector of the output unit.

The SOM learning rule may be described in three steps which are to be performed repeatedly. First, one input vector at a time is randomly selected. In other words, one class description is taken as input to the SOM. Second, this input vector is mapped onto the grid of output units of the SOM and the unit with the strongest response is determined. This very unit is further referred to as the winning unit, the winner in short. Notice that in case of Euclidean distance metric the unit with the smallest distance between input and weight vector is selected as the winner. Hence, the winner is the output unit representing the most similar internal representation of the class description at hand. Third, the weight vector of the winner as well as weight vectors of units in topological neighborhood of the winner are adapted such that these units will exhibit an even stronger response with the same input vector in future. This third step refers to the reduction of distance between input and weight vectors of a subset of the output units and thus, to the improved correspondence between the description of a class and its internal representation. The distance reduction may easily be accomplished by a gradual reduction of the difference between corresponding vector components. The adaptation is further guided by a learning-rate in the interval [0, 1] determining the amount of adaptation and a neighborhood-rate determining the spatial range of adaptation. In order to guarantee the convergence of the learning process, i.e. a stable arrangement of weight vectors, the learning-rate as well as the neighborhood-rate have to shrink in the course of time. In other words, the amount of adaptation of weight vectors decreases during the learning process with respect to a decreasing learning-rate. Furthermore, the number of units that are subject to adaptation, i.e. the spatial range of adaptation, decreases as well during the learning process such that towards the end of learning only the winner is adapted. Given these two restrictions it is obvious that the learning process will converge towards a stable arrangement of weight vector entries. Moreover, the SOM will assign highly similar input data, i.e. classes that have a highly similar description, to neighboring output units thanks to the inclusion of a spatial dimension to the learning process. It is the spatial dimension that distinguishes the SOM the most from other unsupervised learning architectures and thus makes it suitable for an application such as view comparison.

4.4 Cluster interpretation

Based on the description of the various classes as described above we trained a SOM to structure the classes according to their similarity. In the following we will present one typical arrangement of the classes in Fig. 7. The figure represents the result obtained from a 3×3 SOM. In other words, we mapped the class description onto a square of nine output units. For each unit we provide the list of classes that are represented by the unit. Additionally, each unit is further designated by a number. Please note that there is no formal justification to use a SOM of exactly that size. This size rather turned out to be useful in a number of training runs.

Just to start the description of the result with the units representing only one input, i.e. units 2, 5, 8, and 9, we may arrive at the following conclusion. As described in Section 3 we asked all designers to specify additional classes that may be relevant to the basic example but are not contained in the core problem specification. It is obvious that these classes represent a highly subjective view of the various designers on the problem at hand and thus no correspondence to other designers may be found. As expected, the SOM successfully identifies these classes and assigns them exclusively to output units. With a simple 'manual' analysis of the problem description we may realize that the most important aggregations of classes refer on the one hand to persons, be it teachers or students, and on the other hand to courses. The latter group is represented by units 1 and 4. Thus, the person who has the responsibility of performing view comparison is pointed to a reasonable subset of the modelled classes that are all related to the real-world concept of a course. Turning now to the 'human aspect' of the problem description, most of the classes that model the real-world concept of a person are mapped onto units 3 and 6. Moreover, unit 3 comprises mostly students whereas unit 6 represents mostly lecturers. However, some distortion in the mapping may be observed. In this sense it is only unit 7 that represents a mix of rather unrelated concepts, namely some course classes and some person classes. Yet, such a distortion is still negligeable since the intention of the classification is to provide the designer with a 'first guess' on classes that may be integrated. Pragmatically speaking, due to the fact that the only alternative is manual inspection of all classes our classification provides substantial assistance to the designer.

CourseOffering.1, PlannedCourse.5, CourseOffering.2, CourseHeld.3, COffering.4 1	Room.1 2	Student.1, CourseStudent.5, CourseTeacherExtern.3, CourseStudent.3, CourseStudent.2 3
Course.1, Course.5, Course.3, Course.2, Course.4 4	Project.2 5	Study.1, Person.1, CourseTeacher.5, Registration.5, CourseRoom.5, CourseTeacher.3, Location.3, Person.2, ProjectPartner.2, Sponsor.2, Person.4 6
Certificate.1, Teacher.1, HeldCourse.5, CoursePlanned.3, CourseTeacherIntern.3, CourseTeacher.2, Contents.4, Workshop.4, Teacher.4 7	Vehicle.4 8	Department.3 9

Fig. 7: Arrangement of classes within a 3×3 self-organizing map

The advantages of using neural network technology are obvious from a data modelling point of view. The SOM was able to group the potentially overlapping input classes that originate from different view specifications into categories of related object classes. Each category represents a cluster of similar object classes referring to closely related concepts of the real world. Hence, a tool for view comparison is now available that facilitates the determination of classes referring to similar real world objects. This apparently is of considerable value because the designers can direct their attention on classes grouped into the same category by the SOM. Please note, the main manual effort involved during view comparison is uncovering the correspondences between various view specifications and this process is now reduced to a subset of all possible inspections. By using the tool, the designer is able to distinguish between reasonable and unreasonable candidates for integration and thus, integration can be performed with less manual interference and consequently at less time and cost.

5. Conclusion and further work

In this paper we reported on a novel approach to view comparison by means of neural network technology. As an illustrative example we used the description of an education department modelled by a number of people. Hence, the task of view comparison may be paraphrased as determining the correspondences between the views of different designers onto the same reality. The distinguished features of our approach are an automated transformation of an OMT-style class description to a vector based class representation that is further utilized as the input to an unsupervised neural network. The neural network performs a classification of the various input classes based on their mutual similarity. In other words, classes referring to the same real world concept are grouped within the same cluster. As a consequence, the process of view comparison may now be regarded as the manual inspection of a subset of the input classes instead of the whole range of classes that are modelled by various designers. We were able to show that such a classification was performed to a highly promising degree.

Future work will concentrate on improved vector representation of the various input classes. At the moment we achieved the results provided in this paper on the basis of the static structure of the OMT data model. We may arrive at further improvements by an inclusion of the dynamic structure as well. Currently, we are investigating the possibilities to enlarge the vector representation to cover methods that are defined for the various classes as well.

References

[1] M. Bouzeghoub, I. Comyn-Wattiau. View Integration by Semantic Unification and Transformation of Data Structures. *Proc. 9th Int. Conf. on the Entity-Relationship Approach*, North Holland, 1990.

[2] C. Batini, M. Lenzerini, S. B. Navathe. A Comparative Analysis of Methodologies for Database Schema Integration. *ACM Computing Surveys*, Vol. 18, No 4, pp. 323-364, 1986.

[3] J. Biskup, B. Convent. A Formal View Integration Method. *Proc. ACM Int. Conf. on Management of Data (Sigmod)*, Washington, DC, 1986.

[4] W. Bright, A Hurson. A Taxonomy and Current Issues in Multidatabase Systems. *IEEE Computer*, Vol 24, No. 10, 1990.

[5] P. P. Chen. The Entity-Relationship Model - Toward a Unified View of Data. *ACM Trans. on Database Systems (ToDS)*, Vol. 1, No. 1, pp. 9-36, 1976.

[6] C. Date. *An Introduction to Database Systems*. Addison-Wesley, 1991.

[7] P. Fankhauser, M. Kracker, E. Neuhold. Semantic vs. Structural Resemblance of Classes. *ACM Sigmod Record*, Vol. 20, No. 4, Dec. 1991.

[8] P. Johannesson. A Logical Basis for Schema Integration. *Proc. 3rd Int. Workshop on Research Issues in Data Engineering (RIDE)*, IEEE Comp. Society Press, 1993.

[9] P. Johannesson. Using Conceptual Graph Theory to Support Schema Integration. *Proc. 12th Int. Conf. on the Entity-Relationship Approach*, Springer Verlag, LNCS 823, 1994. (R. Elmasri, V. Kouramajian, B. Thalheim, Eds.).

[10]T. Kohonen. The Self-Organizing Map. *Proceedings of the IEEE* 78(9). 1990.

[11]T. Kohonen. *Self-Organizing Maps*. Berlin: Springer-Verlag. 1995.

[12]J. A. Larson, S. B. Navathe, R. Elmasri. A Theory of Attribute Equivalence in Databases with Applications to Schema Integration. *IEEE Trans. on Software Engineering (ToSE)*. Vol. 15, No. 4, pp. 449-463, 1989.

[13]W.-S. Li, C. Clifton. Semantic Integration in Heterogeneous Databases Using Neural Networks. *Proc. 20th VLDB Conference*, Santiago, Chile, 1994.

[14]P. Mehra and B. J. Wah (Eds.). *Artificial Neural Networks: Concepts and Theory*. Los Alamitos, CA: IEEE Computer Society Press. 1992.

[15]A. Motro. Superviews: Virtual Integration of Multiple Databases. *IEEE Trans. on Software Engineering (ToSE)*. Vol. 13, No. 7, pp. 785-798, 1987.

[16]S. B. Navathe, S. G. Gadgil. A Methodology for View Integration in Logical Database Design. *Proc. 8th Int. Conf. on the Entity-Relationship Approach*, North Holland, 1982.

[17]J. Rumbaugh, et al. *Object-Oriented Modeling and Design*. Prentice Hall, 1991.

[18]W. W. Song, P. Johannesson, J. Bubenko. Semantic Similarity Relations in Schema Integration. *Proc. 11th Int. Conf. on the Entity-Relationship Approach*, Springer Verlag, LNCS 645, 1992. (G. Pernul, A M. Tjoa, Eds.).

[19]S. Spaccapietra, C. Parant, Y. Dupont. Model Independent Assertions for Integration of Heterogeneous Schemes. *The VLDB Journal*, Vol. 1, No. 2, pp. 81-126, 1992.

Database schema transformation and optimization

T. A. Halpin[1] and H. A. Proper[2]

[1] Asymetrix Corporation, 110 110th Ave NE, Bellevue WA 98004, USA
(on leave from Dept of Computer Science, University of Queensland)
email: terryh@asymetrix.com

[2] Department of Computer Science, University of Queensland, Australia 4072
(partly supported by an Australian Research Council grant, titled "An expert
system for improving database design")   email: erikp@cs.uq.oz.au

Abstract. An application structure is best modeled first as a conceptual
schema, and then mapped to an internal schema for the target DBMS.
Different but equivalent conceptual schemas often map to different internal
schemas, so performance may be improved by applying conceptual transformations prior to the standard mapping. This paper discusses recent advances in
the theory of schema transformation and optimization within the framework of
ORM (Object-Role Modeling). New aspects include object relativity, complex
types, a high level transformation language and update distributivity.

1 Introduction

When designing an information structure for a given universe of discourse (UoD), it
is best to model first at the conceptual level. This helps us to capture semantics from
users and to implement the model on different platforms. Conceptual modeling may
include process and behavior specification, but this paper focuses on data modeling.

Although heuristics may be used to elicit UoD descriptions from users, the
same UoD might be described in many different ways. By adhering to one modeling
method, the variation in description is reduced but not eliminated. This paper adopts
the *Object-Role Modeling (ORM)* approach, because of its advantages over Entity-
Relationship (ER) modeling (e.g. ORM facilitates communication between modeler
and client, is semantically rich, and its notations are populatable). ORM pictures the
UoD in terms of objects that play roles (either individually or within relationships),
thus avoiding arbitrary decisions about attributes. ER views may be abstracted from
ORM models when desired [3].

ORM versions include BRM (Binary-Relationship Modeling [27]), NIAM
(Natural language Information Analysis Method [29]), MOON (Normalized Object-
Oriented Method [10]), NORM (Natural Object-Relationship Model [8]), PSM
(Predicator Set Model [22]) and FORM (Formal Object-Role Modeling [15]). An
overview of ORM may be found in [16], and a detailed treatment in [15].

At the conceptual level, the basic structural unit is the elementary fact type
[14], which stores information in simple units. For implementation, a conceptual
schema is mapped to a logical schema, where the information is grouped into

structures supported by the logical data model (relational, hierarchic, network, object-oriented etc.). For instance, the conceptual fact types might be partitioned into sets, with each set mapped to a different table in a relational database schema.

The conceptual schema also records constraints which limit the allowable fact populations, as well as derivation rules to declare how some fact types may be derived from others. These constraints and derivation rules should be mapped to corresponding constraints (e.g. foreign key clauses) and derivations (e.g. views) in the logical schema. Additional non-logical details (e.g. indexes, clustering, column order, final data types) may now be specified to complete the internal schema for implementation on the target DBMS. External schemas (e.g. form and report interfaces) may also be defined for end-users, but we ignore these in this paper.

We use the term "optimization" to describe procedures for improving the performance of a system, whether or not this is optimal in the sense of the "best possible". There are three basic phases: "conceptual optimization"; logical optimization; internal optimization. A correct conceptual schema may often be reshaped into an equivalent (or nearly equivalent) conceptual schema which maps via the standard mapping algorithm to a more efficient logical schema. We call this reshaping "conceptual optimization" since it is done at the conceptual level—of course, optimization is not a conceptual issue. At the logical level the schema may be reshaped into an equivalent logical schema giving better performance (e.g. controlled denormalization may be applied to improve query response). Finally the internal schema may be tuned to improve performance (e.g. by adding indexes).

The optimization depends on many factors, including the logical data model (relational, etc.), the access profile (query/update pattern for focused transactions), the data profile (statistics on data volumes) and the location mode (centralized, distributed, federated etc.). Although a vast literature exists on internal and logical optimization, research on conceptual optimization is still relatively new, and most of this assumes the mapping will be to a relational model. A detailed ORM-to-relational mapping procedure (Rmap) is described in [32]. Similar though less complete mapping algorithms from ER to logical models exist (see, e.g. [1]).

A formal approach to ORM was introduced in [11] and extended in [12, 13, 15]. For related work on ORM schema transformations see [9, 21, 22]. Other researchers have examined schema equivalence within the relational model [23] and the (E)ER model [7, 1, 19]. The optimization history of a schema may be seen as an evolution-worm through a model space via successive transformations. In [25] the predicate calculus-based language used in [11] to specify ORM transformations is used as a metalanguage to specify transformations between ORM and relational schemas. A general ORM-based optimization framework is specified in [2] which exploits data and access profiles as well as choices of different logical data models.

While schema transformations have many uses (e.g. to compare or translate models) in this paper we focus on their use in optimization. In section 2, a simple example illustrates conceptual optimization in ORM. Section 3 outlines some recent extensions, including object relativity, visualization choice and complex types. Section 4 introduces a high level language for specifying schema transformations, and examines a basic restriction on the derivation and update rules. Finally, section 5 summarizes the contributions and outlines future research directions.

2   A simple example of schema optimization

Figure 1 is a simple ORM schema. Here "hor", "vert", "loc", "nat", "CD" and "FD" abbreviate "horizontal", "vertical", "local", "national", "compact disk" and "floppy disk". Entity types are shown as named ellipses, with their reference schemes in parenthesis. Logical predicates are displayed as box-sequences (one box for each role), with their name in mixfix notation starting at their first role-box.

An arrow-tipped bar across a role sequence indicates an internal *uniqueness constraint* (e.g. each advertisement is for at most one position, and each advertisement in a given direction spans at most one length). A circled "u" denotes an external uniqueness constraint. For example, each advert-coverage pair is associated with at most one newspaper (each advert is placed in at most one local and at most one national newspaper).

A dot where *n* role-arcs (*n* > 0) connect to an object type indicates the disjunction of the roles is *mandatory* (each object in the database population of that type must play at least one of those roles). For example, each advertisement is for at least one position, and each wordprocessor is stored on CD or FD. A number or number range written beside a role is a *frequency constraint* (e.g. each advertisement was designed by at most two employees). A list of values in braces depicts a *value-constraint* (e.g. each direction is either horizontal or vertical).

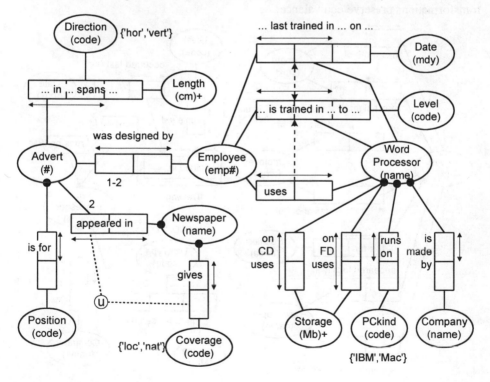

Fig. 1.   An unoptimized ORM schema

194

A dotted arrow from one role-sequence to another is a *subset constraint*. (e.g. each employee who uses a wordprocessor is trained in it to some level). A double-headed arrow denotes an *equality constraint* (e.g. we record an employee's training if and only if we record when this training last occurred).

Suppose the conceptual schema of Figure 1 is to be mapped to a relational schema. To avoid redundancy, the Rmap procedure [24, 15] maps each fact type with a composite internal uniqueness constraint to a separate table. Hence Figure 1 maps to twelve relation schemes, one for each fact type. For example, the top-left ternary fact type maps to the relation scheme: *AdvertSize* (advert#, direction, length). In practice a schema normally has many functional fact types which can be grouped together, but we have omitted these to demonstrate optimization with a small example. Regardless, the 12-table relational schema would typically be inefficient for most plausible query/update patterns on this UoD.

Without data and access profiles, a default optimization procedure can still be specified mainly based on reducing the number of tables (and hence joins). Figure 1 may be reshaped into Figure 2. A *predicate specialization* transformation absorbs the object types Direction, Coverage and PCkind into the relevant predicates, specializing them into separate cases, one for each value in the associated value constraint. The inverse transformation *predicate generalization* extracts the object type DiskType. A *nesting* transformation objectifies the Training relationship type. These transformations preserve equivalence.

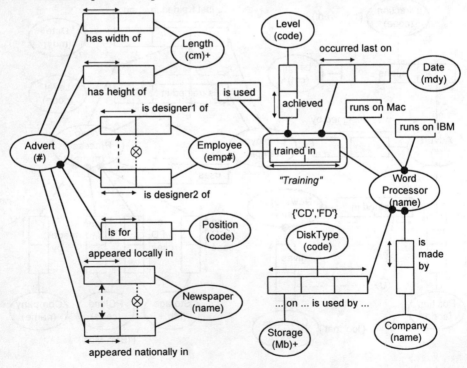

Fig. 2. An "optimized" version of Figure 1

Another predicate specialization transformation specializes the was designed by predicate into two cases, one for each frequency in the associated frequency constraint: this transform strengthens the schema (the original schema does not tell us which of the designer1 and designer2 fact types to use for some designer).

Each of the original constraints has re-appeared as a corresponding constraint in the new schema. For example, the uniqueness constraint that each newspaper gives only one coverage (local or national) is now captured by the exclusion constraint (marked "⊗") between the newspaper roles in the second schema. The basic ORM transformation theorems include corollaries to specify the effect of additional constraints. The list of ORM transformation theorems and the associated optimization procedure to fire transformations are extensive (e.g. see ch. 9 of [15]).

Figure 3 shows the relational schema obtained by mapping the optimized schema. There are now just four tables, instead of twelve. Queries that previously involved multiple joins will now run much faster. The constraint pattern is also simplified, so updates will often be faster too. In Figure 3, keys are underlined and optional columns are placed in square brackets, as for BNF. Subset and equality constraints are marked with arrowed lines. The inequality constraint applies within the same row, while the exclusion constraint applies between the column-sets. The codes "y" and "n" are used for "yes" and "no", since many systems do not support Booleans. The mapping and optimization can be automated, but names generated for the new predicates, object types, tables and columns are not always as intuitive as those in Figures 2 and 3. The modeler should be prompted to provide better names.

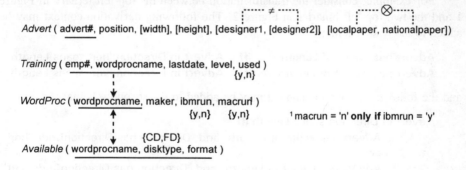

Fig. 3. The relational schema obtained by Rmapping Figure 2

3 Schema equivalence and modeling choices

The notion of reshaping one schema to another via an equivalence transformation is fundamental not only to optimization procedures, but also to the general problems of schema re-engineering, schema evolution and full or partial schema integration (see e.g. [4, 6, 26]). Although some rigorous treatments of schema equivalence and transformations exist for relational and ER schemas (e.g [23], [18], [28]), analyses of this notion at the conceptual level have often suffered from obscurity, limited scope or lack of rigor. It is indeed a challenge to present a theory of transformations which is sound, expressive in terms of constraint classes, and easy to understand.

Within the ORM community, the main formal contributions to schema transformation theory have been either set-based (e.g. [20]) or logic-based (e.g. [11, 9]). The approach introduced in [11] is distinct in that it specifies the precise isomorphism mappings in a way that can be proved using first order logic: its central notion is that of *contextual equivalence*. We briefly outline this approach and then refine it by introducing the notion of object relativity.

Let CS1 and CS2 be conceptual ORM schemas (possibly subschemas), each of which is expressed as a conjunction of first order sentences (an algorithm for translating any ORM schema to such a formula is specified in [11]). Let D1 be a conjunction of first order sentences defining the symbols unique to CS2 in terms of the symbols of CS1. Similarly, let D2 provide the context for defining extra symbols of CS1 in terms of CS2. Using "&" for conjunction and "⇔" for necessary equivalence, we say that CS1 is contextually equivalent to CS2 (under D1/D2) if and only if CS1 & D1 ⇔ CS2 & D2. The first order theories CS1 & D1 and CS2 & D2 provide a conservative extension ([5]) to the theories CS1 and CS2 respectively, since no new primitives are added.

The creative aspect of discovering transformation theorems is now reduced to providing the derivation rules or contexts (D1, D2) which allow the symbols in one representation to be translated into those of the other. If the two schemas are already declared it is first necessary to resolve any naming conflicts (e.g. the same symbol may have different connotations in the two schemas). For the purposes of generating a new, more optimal schema from a given schema, this problem does not arise.

For example, consider the transformation between the top-left ternary in Figure 1 and the two top-left binaries in Figure 2. The following derivation context may be added to the first schema:

Advert has width of Length   **iff**   Advert in Direction 'hor' spans Length
Advert has height of Length   **iff**   Advert in Direction 'ver' spans Length

and the following derivation context may be added to the second schema:

Advert in Direction spans Length **iff**
     Advert has width of Length **and** Direction has DirectionCode 'hor'
     or
     Advert has height of Length **and** Direction has DirectionCode 'ver'

The second schema requires the introduction of the object type Direction, along with its reference scheme. In [11] any object type unique to one schema is explicitly introduced into the other schema before the equivalence test is conducted. This was because the equivalence proofs were conducted using a first order technique (deduction trees, i.e. semantic tableaux amenable to natural deduction). At that time, proofs were done manually. Later a theorem-prover was built which enabled typical equivalence proofs or counterexamples to be generated in under one second. In rare cases, the expressibility of ORM encroached on some undecidable fragments of predicate logic. A modified logic is currently under development in which it is hoped to avoid these problems by incorporating some finiteness axioms.

In revising the underlying logic, it has been decided to abandon, in one sense, the normal requirement of classical logic that equivalent theories must match in their domain of individuals. This domain-matching requirement is unrealistic, since it presumes an absolute theory of objects. For modeling purposes, objects rather lie in the eye of the beholder. Consider a UoD populated by a single advertisement of length 3 cm and height 5 cm. Ignoring the values (e.g. numbers) used to reference entities, how many entities are in this UoD? A person who models this world in terms of the two binary fact types will "see" three entities: one advertisement and two lengths. But a person who models this same world in terms of the ternary fact type will "see" five entities: one advertisement, two directions, and two lengths.

It is thus relative to the observer whether directions are to be thought of as objects. This is what we mean by *object relativity*. Seen in this light, objects that occur explicitly in only one schema (viewpoint) may always be implicitly introduced in the other schema. After this is done, classical proof techniques may still be used.

We now sketch some of our recent work on "conceptual" optimization. Previously, we simply replaced the original conceptual schema by the optimized version. However, practical experience has shown that sometimes a conceptual transformation used for optimization may make the conceptual schema harder for a modeler to understand. This tends to be more dependent on the modeler than the transformation, though nesting transformations often appear to be involved. For example, some modelers would prefer to see the three fact types which associate Employee and WordProcessor in Figure 1 just like that. To them, the nested version shown in Figure 2 seems more awkward. We now believe it is best to present the modelers with the optimized version of a schema fragment and allow them to adopt or reject this as a way of visualizing the UoD. If they retain the previous version, they should be given the option of having the optimization step being performed "under the covers" before the schema is passed to the standard mapper. So one "truly conceptual" schema may be used for clarity and another for efficiency.

Annotations may be used to declare all "non-conceptual" decisions which impact on the ultimate mapping (e.g. overriding of default mapping choices for 1:1 cases and subtyping, controlled denormalization decisions etc.), allowing an exact correspondence with the resulting logical schema. As the modeler will not always wish to view these annotations, their display should be toggled.

Recent extensions to ORM include join-constraints and constructors for complex object types [15, 21]. Join constraints allow set-comparison constraints to be specified between compatible role-sequences spanning any number of predicates. Apart from the need to cater for these constraints, it is possible to use this notation to specify many derivation rules, including portions of various translation contexts. Work is also underway to refine the textual version of the ORM language. The textual version is more expressive than the graphical version, and sometimes a graphic constraint is transformed into a textual constraint, or vice versa.

Complex types allow compound fact types to be specified directly on the conceptual schema. For example sets, lists and bags may now be modeled directly. New classes of transformations arise. In [17], we discuss a simple example of modeling choices involving set constructors. Apart from the extra transformation theorems needed to license the shift between viewpoints, the schema design discipline needs to be extended to guide modelers in their use of constructors.

4   A transformation language

In previous work, individual transformation theorems were specified in a combined graphical/textual language based on predicate-calculus, but for compact communication of transformation classes, an informal metalanguage was used. As a foundation for automated support, we now sketch a formal language to define schema transformations, with appropriate attention to update aspects.

A general format is introduced in which classes of schema transformations can be defined using a *data schema transformation scheme*. When applying such a transformation scheme to a concrete data schema, the transformation scheme is interpreted in the context of that schema, leading to a concrete transformation. A schema transformation scheme is typically centered around a set of parameters that have to be instantiated with actual components from the particular application data schema that is to be transformed.

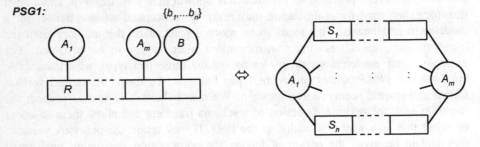

where $m \geq 1$, and each S_i corresponds to R where $B = b_i$

Fig. 4.   A basic schema equivalence theorem

Figure 4 depicts one equivalence theorem which allows a predicate to be specialized by absorbing an enumerated object type (transform to right), or for compatible predicates to be generalized by extracting this object type (transform to left). The transformation of the advertisement ternary in Figure 1 to two binaries was one application of this theorem. Another application is shown in Figure 5. The binaries in (b) may be generalized into one ternary by extracting MedalKind.

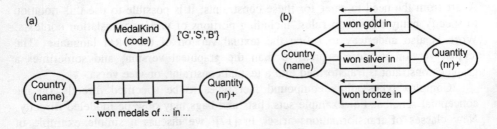

Fig. 5.   Three binaries (b) transform to a ternary (a) by extracting object type MedalKind

It is easy to verify that this holds for our example with: f_1 = won-gold-in; f_2 = won-silver-in; f_3 = won-bronze-in; g = won-medals-of-in. The EntityType statement requires y to be an entity type with label type l and domain d. In our example we require that MedalKind is an entity type identified through value type MedalKindcode, where this value type has the domain char. In the example this is indeed the case.

With the Constraints statements we capture the requirement that there exists a constraint $c1$ in the universe with definition: each l is in $v!m$. In our example case this becomes: each MedalKindcode is in {'G', 'S', 'B'}. Then there is a listing of components that are to be replaced (From) by the transformation; in our case: won-gold-in, won-silver-in, and won-bronze-in. Similarly the To statement lists the components added by the transformation. In our example these components are: MedalKind, MedalKindcode, char, won-medals-of-in.

Finally, the UpdRules and DerRules provide the translation of populations between the schema before and after the transformation. We have specified these rules in a relational algebra like language. In this article we are not concerned with a concrete language for these purposes. The completely substituted transformation is shown in Table 2.

Table 2. The example transformation

TransSchema OTExtraction;
Type:	Country, Quantity;
RelType:	won-gold-in = Country:won-gold-in-1, Quantity:won-gold-in-2;
	won-silver-in = Country:won-silver-in-1, Quantity:won-silver-in-2;
	won-bronze-in = Country:won-bronze-in-1, Quantity:won-bronze-in-2;
	won-medals-of-in = Country:won-medals-of-in-1, Quantity:won-medals-of-in-3,
	MedalKind:won-medals-of-in-2;
EntityType:	MedalKind(MedalKindcode:char);
Constraints:	c1: each MedalKindcode is in 'G', 'S', 'B';
From:	won-gold-in, won-silver-in, won-bronze-in
To:	MedalKind, MedalKindcode, char, won-medals-of-in, c1;
DerRules:	

won-gold-in = **proj**[won-gold-in-1 = won-medals-of-in-1, won-gold-in-2 = won-medals-of-in-3]
    sel[won-medals-of-in-2 = 'G'] won-medals-of-in

won-silver-in = **proj**[won-silver-in-1 = won-medals-of-in-1, won-silver-in-2 = won-medals-of-in-3]
    sel[won-medals-of-in-2 = 'S'] won-medals-of-in

won-bronze-in = **proj**[won-bronze-in-1 = won-medals-of-in-1, won-bronze-in-2 = won-medals-of-in-3]
    sel[won-medals-of-in-2 = 'B'] won-medals-of-in

UpdRules:

won-medals-of-in = **proj**[won-medals-of-in-1 = won-gold-in-1, won-medals-of-in-3 = won-gold-in-2,
        won-medals-of-in-2 = 'G'] won-gold-in
    union
    proj[won-medals-of-in-1 = won-silver-in-1, won-medals-of-in-3 =
        won-silver-in-2, won-medals-of-in-2 = 'S'] won-silver-In
    union
    proj[won-medals-of-in-1 = won-bronze-in-1, won-medals-of-in-3 =
        won-bronze-in-2, won-medals-of-in-2 = 'B'] won-bronze-in

End TransSchema.

The transformation from right to left in Figure 4 may be set out textually as in Table 1. The parameters to this transformation schema are $x!n$; $(r!n)!m$; $s!n$; u; y; l; d; $v!m$. This is a set of parameters with a variable size.

Table 1. An example transformation scheme (transforming right to left in Figure 4)

TransSchema OTExtraction $(x!n; (r!n)!m; s!n; u; y; l; d; v!m)$;
    Type: $x!n$;
    RelType: $(f = [(x : r)!n])!m$; $h = [(x : s)!n; y : u]$;
    EntityType: $(l : d)$;
    Constraints: $c1$: **each** l **is in** $v!m$;
    From: $f\,!m$;
    To: y; l; d; h; $c1$;
    DerRules: $(f = \textbf{proj}\ [(r = s)!n]\ \textbf{sel}[u = v] h)!m$;
    UpdRules: $h = \textbf{union of } (\textbf{proj}\ [(s = r)!n; u = v]f\,)!m$;
End TransSchema.

The expression $x!n$ denotes the list of parameters $x_1,...,x_n$, where n is not *a priori* known. Analogously, $(r!n)!m$ denotes the sequence of parameters: $r_{1,1},...,r_{n,1},...,...,r_{1,m},...,r_{n,m}$. So this transformation scheme takes $n + nm + n + 4 = n(m + 2) + 4$ parameters, where n and m are determined at application time. A concrete example is set out below. This depicts the transformation from (b) to (a) in Figure 5 (ignoring uniqueness constraints).

OTExtraction ([Country; Quantity],
  [[won-gold-in-1, won-gold-in-2], [won-silver-in-1, won-silver-in-2], [won-bronze-in-1, won-bronze-in-2]],
  [won-medals-of-in-1, won-medals-of-in-3], won-medals-of-in-2, MedalKind, MedalKindcode, char,
  ['G', 'S', 'B'])

We use the convention that won-gold-in-1, won-gold-in-2 refer to the first and second roles of the fact type labelled won-gold-in respectively. In the example we have $n = 2$ and $m = 3$. In this paper we ignore the introduction of names for newly introduced object types or predicates, or with mixfix predicate slots. For the example we have the following instantiations to the transformation scheme: $x_1 =$ Country, $x_2 =$ Quantity, $r_{1,1} =$ won-gold-in-1, $r_{2,1} =$ won-gold-in-2, $r_{1,2} =$ won-silver-in-1, $r_{2,2} =$ won-silver-in-2, $r_{1,3} =$ won-bronze-in-1, $r_{2,3} =$ won-bronze-in-2, $s_1 =$ won-medals-of-in-1, $s_2 =$ won-medals-of-in-3, $u =$ won-medals-of-in-2, $y =$ MedalKind, $l =$ MedalKindcode, $d =$ char, $v_1 =$ 'G', $v_2 =$ 'S', $v_3 =$ 'B'.

This allows us to further fill in the transformation scheme. The Type statement simply requires that $x_1,...,x_n$, y are some kind of type in the ORM schema. In our case we have to verify that Country and Quantity are some kind of types, which they indeed are. A RelType statement requires the presence of a proper fact type in the universe of ORM schemes. In our case we have:

1. For each $1 \le i \le m$ there is a relationship type f_i in the ORM universe such that $\text{Roles}(f_i) = \{r_{1,i},..., r_{n,i}\}$ and $\forall_{1 \le j \le n}$ [Player$(r_{j,i}) = x_j$]. The function Roles returns the roles in a fact type, whereas Player returns the player of the role.
2. There is a relationship g in the ORM universe such that $\text{Roles}(g) = \{s_1,...,s_n\}$ and $\forall_{1 \le j \le n}$ [Player$(s_j) = x_j$].

The transformation scheme does not cater for the transformation of the uniqueness constraints on the relationships involved in the transformation. In [11] and [15] constraint transformation was covered by corollaries to the basic schema transformations. While useful, this approach leads to many corollaries to deal with different classes of constraints and it currently ignores most textual (non-graphical) constraints that must be formulated in some formal textual language. Our approach for now is to enforce the (uniqueness) constraints on the transformed relationships on the (now) derived relationships. For example, in schema (a) of Figure 5 the won-gold-in relationship is derivable, and we enforce the uniqueness of its first role on this derived relationship. Currently we are researching ways to develop a general constraint re-writing mechanism to (as much as possible) re-write constraints enforced on derivable relationships to constraints on the non-derivable base types.

Although we do not provide a formal semantics of the language used to specify the transformation schemes, we do presume the existence of three functions providing these semantics. When a precise language is defined these functions would become concrete. The (partial) functions are: From: TransSchema × ParList ↦ SCH; To: TransSchema × ParList ↦ SCH; Schema: TransSchema × ParList ↦ SCH.

Here TransSchema is the language of transformation schemes, and ParList is the set of parameter lists that can be built from the roles and types in the ORM schema SCH. The three functions are partial since some combinations of transformation schemes and lists of parameters may define incorrect transformations. The From function returns the schema components that will be changed by the transformation. What exactly happens with these schema components depends on the aim with which the transformation is applied—for example: (1) select a conceptual schema alternative as a preferred way of viewing the UoD; (2) enrich an existing schema with an extra view; (3) optimize a final conceptual schema.

In case (1) the components listed in the From statement need to be removed from the existing schema. In case (2) none of the components nominated by the From statement need to be removed. In case (3) the components in the From statement will not be removed as they remain part of what the user sees as the conceptual schema. They will, however, be marked as derivable (using the specified derivation rules).

The result of the From statement is given as a (sub) schema. As this usually is a subschema without a proper context, this is not likely to be a complete and correct ORM schema. In our example the schema resulting from the From function contains only the three fact types from the (b) variation of the Olympic games schemas, without the Country and Quantity entity types.

The To function returns the added schema components as a subschema. This is usually incomplete since it misses the proper context. The To function returns the components listed by the To statement, and also returns the derivation and update rules (in the resulting schema these rules are required to derive the instances of the transformed types and translate the updates of the transformed types to updates of the new types). Finally, the Schema function yields all schema components listed in the transformation scheme, and returns this as the schema. However, the update rules are ignored. The resulting schema is the context of the schema transformation.

When transforming a conceptual schema to another data schema, the user will still want to perform the updates and queries as if they are done on the original conceptual schema (not the optimized schema). This is why we added the derivation and update rules—they allow us to define the official conceptual schema as an updatable view on the actually implemented schema. In supporting this approach however, we must avoid the view update problem. To allow the user to specify updates directly on the conceptual level, the update rules must be *update distributive*. The update rules can be regarded as function μ : POP $\rightarrow$ POP that transforms a population of the original schema to a population of the actually stored data schema. The derivation rules perform the opposite function μ^{-1}, and for an equivalence preserving schema transformation this μ^{-1} is the inverse function of μ.

Let p_1, p_2 be populations of an ORM schema. We can generalize each binary operation Θ on sets (of instances) to populations as a whole by: $(p_1 \Theta p_2)(x) = p_1(x) \Theta p_2(x)$. A function μ: POP $\rightarrow$ POP is *update distributive* if and only if for $\Theta \in \{\cup, -\}$ and a correct schema SCH we have: IsPop(p, SCH) & IsPop($p \Theta x$, SCH) $\Rightarrow$ $\mu(p \Theta x) = \mu(p) \Theta \mu(x)$. Here IsPop($p$, SCH) means that p is a correct population of schema SCH. If μ is the population transformation function following from the update rules from a given transformation scheme t, then μ must be update distributive. With such a μ we can safely translate any update of the population of the original schema to an update of the transformed schema.

5 Conclusion

Schema transformations at the conceptual level may be used to improve the clarity of a conceptual schema or the efficiency of the final database application. This article surveyed the state of the art on conceptual optimization, and then discussed several new contributions, including object relativity, visualization choices, complex types, a formal language for transformation schemes, and update distributivity. Though couched in terms of Object-Role Modeling, the approach may be adapted to Entity-Relationship Modeling so long as a supplementary textual language is available to specify domains, as well as ORM constraints and derivation rules.

We are developing a constraint re-writing mechanism to re-write constraints enforced on derivable types to constraints on fundamental types. This is needed to optimize the enforcement of constraints and to support the mapping of data schemas to internal schemas. Further heuristics and algorithms are being developed to cater for transformation and optimization of additional constructs at the conceptual level, and mapping to different logical data models. The ideas presented in this article will be implemented in a prototype schema transformation and optimization tool.

References

1. Batini, C., Ceri, S. & Navathe, S.B. 1992, *Conceptual database design: an entity-relationship approach*, Benjamin/Cummings, Redwood City CA, USA.
2. Bommel, P. van & Weide, Th.P. van der 1992, 'Reducing the search space for conceptual schema transformation', *Data and Knowledge Engineering*, v.8, pp. 269–92.
3. Campbell, L. & Halpin, T.A. 1994a, 'Abstraction techniques for conceptual schemas', *ADC'94: Proc. 5th Australasian Database Conf.*, World Scientific, Singapore.
4. Campbell, L. & Halpin, T.A. 1994b, 'The reverse engineering of relational databases', *Proc. 5th Workshop on Next Generation CASE Tools*, Utrecht, The Netherlands (June).

5. Chang, C.C. & Keisler, H.J. 1977, *Model theory*, 2nd edn, North-Holland, Amsterdam.
6. Dupont, Y. 1994, 'Resolving fragmentation conflicts in schema integration', *Proc. 13th Entity-Relationship Conf.*, Springer-Verlag LNCS vol. 881, pp. 513–32.
7. D'Atri, A. & Sacca, D. 1984, 'Equivalence and mapping of database schemas', *Proc. 10th Int. Conf. On Very Large Databases*, VLDB, Singapore, pp. 187–95.
8. De Troyer, O.M.F. 1991, 'The OO-Binary Relationship Model: a truly object-oriented conceptual model', *Proc. CAiSE-91*, Springer-Verlag LNCS, no. 498, Trondheim.
9. De Troyer, O.M.F. 1993, 'On data schema transformations', PhD thesis, University of Tilburg (K.U.B.), Tilburg, The Netherlands.
10. Habrias, H. 1993, 'Normalized Object Oriented Method', in *Encyclopedia of Microcomputers*, vol. 12, Marcel Dekker, New York, pp. 271–85.
11. Halpin, T.A. 1989, 'A Logical Analysis of Information Systems: static aspects of the data-oriented perspective', PhD thesis, University of Queensland, Brisbane, Australia.
12. Halpin, T.A. 1991, 'A fact-oriented approach to schema transformation', *Proc. MFDBS-91*, Spinger-Verlag LNCS, no. 495, Rostock, Germany.
13. Halpin, T.A. 1992, 'Fact-Oriented Schema Optimization', *Proc. CISMOD-92,* pp. 288–302, Indian Institute of Science, Bangalore, India.
14. Halpin, T.A. 1993, 'What is an elementary fact?', *Proc. First NIAM-ISDM Conf.*, eds G.M. Nijssen & J. Sharp, Utrecht, The Netherlands (Sep).
15. Halpin, T.A. 1995, *Conceptual Schema and Relational Database Design*, 2nd edn, Prentice Hall, Sydney, Australia.
16. Halpin. T.A. & Orlowska, M.E. 1992, 'Fact-Oriented Modelling for Data Analysis', *Journal of Inform. Systems*, vol. 2, no. 2, pp. 1-23, Blackwell Scientific, Oxford.
17. Halpin, T.A. & Proper, H.A. 1995, 'Subtyping and polymorphism in Object-Role Modeling', *Data and Knowledge Engineering*, vol. 15, pp. 251-281, Elsevier Science.
18. Hainut, J-L 1991, 'Entity-generating schema transformation for entity-relationaship models', *Proc. 10th Entity-Relationship Conf.*, San Mateo (CA), North-Holland, 1992.
19. Hainaut, J.-L., Englebert, V., Henrard, J., Hick, J-M., Roland, D. 1994, 'Database evolution: the DB-MAIN approach', *Proc. 13th ER Conf.,* LNCS vol. 881, pp. 112–31.
20. Hofstede, A.H.M. ter, Proper, H.A. & Weide, Th.P. van der 1993, 'A note on schema equivalence', *Tech. Report 92-30*, Dept of Inf. Systems, University of Nijmegen.
21. Hofstede, A.H.M. ter, Proper, H.A. & Weide, Th.P. van der 1993, 'Formal definition of a conceptual language for the description and manipulation of information models', *Information Systems*, vol. 18, no. 7, pp. 489–523.
22. Hofstede, A.H.M. ter & Weide, Th.P. van der 1993, 'Expressiveness in conceptual data modelling', *Data and Knowledge Engineering*, vol. 10, no. 1, pp. 65–100.
23. Kobayashi, I. 1986, 'Losslessness and semantic correctness of database schema transformation: another look at schema equivalence', *Information Systems*, 11 (41–49).
24. Ritson, P.R. & Halpin, T.A. 1993, 'Mapping Integrity Constraints to a Relational Schema', *Proc. 4th ACIS*, Brisbane, Australia (Sep.), pp. 381-400.
25. Ritson, P.R, 1994, 'Use of conceptual schemas for a relational implementation', PhD thesis, University of Queensland, Brisbane, Australia.
26. Shoval, P. & Shreiber, N. 1993, 'Database reverse engineering: from the relational to the binary relational model', *Data and Knowledge Engineering*, vol. 10, pp. 293–315.
27. Shoval, P. & Zohn, S. 1991, 'Binary-relationship integration methodology', *Data and Knowledge Engineering*, vol. 6, no. 3, pp. 225–50.
28. Thalheim, B. 1994, 'State-conditioned semantics in databases', *Proc. 13th Int. Conf. On the Entity-Relationship Approach*, Springer-Verlag LNCS, vol. 881, pp. 171–8.
29. Wintraecken, J.J.V.R. 1990, *The NIAM Information Analysis Method: Theory and Practice*, Kluwer, Deventer, The Netherlands.

Mapping an Extended Entity-Relationship Schema into a Schema of Complex Objects

Rokia Missaoui[1] Jean-Marc Gagnon and Robert Godin

Département d'Informatique, Université du Québec à Montréal
C.P. 8888, Succursale "Centre-Ville", Montréal, Canada, H3C 3P8

Abstract. With the advent of object-oriented database systems, there
is an urgent need to define a methodology for mapping a conceptual
schema into an object-oriented one, and migrating from a conventional
database to an object-oriented database containing complex objects.
This paper deals with an important step of the migration process by
describing a technique for complex entity formation which involves recursively grouping entities and relationships from an extended entity-
relationship schema, using semantic abstractions such as aggregation,
generalization and association. The abstract schema produced by the
clustering technique at a given level of grouping can then be converted
into a structurally object-oriented schema allowing the explicit expression of complex entity types, relationships and integrity constraints. The
overall methodology is implemented within the environment of INTER-
SEM, a prototype for semantic object-oriented modelling.

1 Introduction

Most of present database (DB) applications are based on traditional (conventional) database management systems (DBMS). With the advent of object-
oriented (OO) systems in the market and the increasing popularity and utilization of the entity-relationship model [5], the following related questions need
to be addressed: (i) how to map an extended entity-relationship (EER) schema
into a corresponding object-oriented schema? (ii) how to re-engineer the old conventional applications to produce object-oriented databases instead of designing
them from scratch? The second question (which includes the first one) can be answered by dealing with the three consecutive steps [2]: (i) *backward step*: map the
existing logical (i.e., relational, hierarchical, or network) schema of the database
into a semantic (conceptual) one, (ii) *forward step*: map the resulting semantic schema into an OO schema, (iii) *loading step*: migrate the existing data to
the new schema. Since the entity-relationship model is a very commonly used
and continuously improved semantic model, the first step of this process can be
undertaken by mapping a conventional logical schema to a corresponding EER
diagram. Such a mapping has been extensively studied and handled by many
researchers [11, 13].

Our main concern in this paper is to deal with a part of the issue of re-
engineering database applications. More specifically, our objective is to deal with

the second step of the whole process of re-engineering by providing a methodology for converting an extended entity-relationship into a structurally OO schema. This methodology is mainly based on the observation that (i) in many database modelling applications, several types of entities are related to each other, and (ii) such a set of related components should be perceived and described as a unit. An important step of this methodology is inspired by the clustering technique proposed by Teorey et al. [17].

The article is organized as follows. First, we show how the clustering technique described in [17] can be adapted to convert an EER schema into a schema of complex objects. Rules for mapping complex object types into a semantic object-oriented schema are also described. We provide a practical example to illustrate the application of the clustering technique.

We assume the reader is familiar with the key notions of object-oriented models and semantic modelling [1, 2, 4, 6, 9].

2 Complex Entity Type Formation

In many real-world applications, designers tend to constitute classes of objects such as concepts, chunks and clusters according to some similarity criteria. The clustering technique proposed by [17] is basically suggested to be an aid in user communication and documentation. It consists in recursively grouping entities and relationships from an extended entity-relationship schema, using semantic abstractions such as aggregation, generalization and association. In this paper, we shall show that some variations of this clustering technique can be useful not only to improve the understanding of the DB conceptual schema and master its complexity, but also to contribute to the formation of complex entities, and therefore could be used as an important step in the mapping process of an initial EER diagram into an object-oriented schema.

2.1 The clustering Technique

The procedure [17] is performed iteratively in a bottom-up manner by starting from atomic entities in an EER and building more complex entities (entity clusters) out of them until the desired level of abstraction n is reached or until no more clustering operation can be applied. The level n of clustering represents the desirable depth of aggregation hierarchies in the resulting complex object schema. It can be set based on the peculiarities of the application under consideration.

To ensure a high semantic cohesion within complex entities, the grouping operations are done in a precedence (priority) order. This order is defined in terms of the concept of cohesion, to represent the strength of the relationship among entities in an entity cluster. The weakest cohesion appears in the last grouping (see below) since there is no dominant entity in ternary and higher-degree relationships.

2.2 Grouping operations and Priority Order

The four grouping operations and their priority order are slightly different from the ones proposed in [17]. The priority order applies as follows: when a given entity E is both involved in a relationship of priority order k and a relationship of priority order $k + 1$, then the grouping of order k is chosen. When a given entity E is candidate to two groupings of a same priority (except for weak entity absorption), then we decide which one to use based on additional rules defined later.

1. *Weak entity absorption*

   A strong entity E is collapsed with all its direct dependent entities to form a single complex entity whose label corresponds to the name of the strong entity. The weak relationships as well as any one-to-many relationship and its corresponding related (member) entity associated with E are also absorbed in the complex entity. In the presence of a sequence of weak entities and relationships, the grouping starts with the most dependent entity and assembles entities in cascade (see below) as illustrated by the example in Section 2.4.

2. *Dominance Grouping*

   We define a dominant entity as the one which is in a binary association with at least two entities by a one-to-many relationship. Dominance grouping consists in assembling a dominant entity with its related entities and relationships. The name of the clustered entity is identical to the name of the dominant entity.

3. *Generalization and Categorization Grouping*

   The generalization/categorization grouping consists in creating a complex entity whose name is identical to the name of the supertype/category [1] and whose components are the immediate subtypes/supertypes of the generalized entity or category. A category is defined as a subset of the union of some classes [6].

4. *Relationship Grouping*

   The n-ary relationships of any degree can be grouped into an entity cluster, reflecting the semantics of the relationship as a whole. As opposed to [17], the name of the entity cluster is not necessarily identical to the name of the relationship. It corresponds to the name of the relationship especially when the association is either a many-to-many binary relationship or n-ary relationship. In the mapping process (see Section 4 for more details), the translation of an entity cluster obtained by relationship clustering takes into account the nature of the entities in relationship: key entities, mandatory/optional participation, and the number of other associations in which an entity is involved in.

---

[1] when there exists only one specialization/categorization of the generalized/category entity

2.3 Additional Rules

In order to preserve the logical and natural sequence of viewing a database at different levels of abstraction, to maintain the whole semantics of data, and handle some conflicting situations, we use the following four rules which will be illustrated with an example in Section 2.4. The first two rules are borrowed from [17].

Step-by-step grouping

- Whenever a new grouping is to be done on a schema C_i (schema with a clustering level i), the output is a schema C_{i+1} as long as at least one grouping operation is achieved on C_i. The initial schema is assigned level 0.
- If the n-th clustering operation within level i is achieved around the entity E, then it leads to an entity cluster with a label, and a level expressed by $< i.n >$. The label of the complex entity depends on the kind of clustering: it is the name of the dominant (or strong, or generalized or category, or owner) entity, or the name of the relationship if it is a many-to-many binary relationship or a ternary relationship.
- A grouping operation cannot be achieved at level i if it involves a complex entity recently formed at that same level, and therefore has to be postponed to the next level.

Consistency

To avoid the possibility of losing the semantics associated with data, and in order to preserve the initial relationships between entities inside and outside a complex entity, we do the following. Whenever a component (or subcomponent) E_i of a complex entity E_j is in a relationship (IS-A, or association) with another entity, the appropriate side of this relationship will be labeled by $E_{j-1}.....E_i$ representing the path needed to reach the component E_i inside E_j (see Figure 2).

Cascading

If an entity E_i is both a candidate to a clustering operation of any kind (weak entity absorption, dominance, generalization/categorization, or relationship grouping) as a `slave` entity (i.e. a component of a potential complex entity E), and a candidate to another clustering operation as a `master` entity (i.e. an entity whose name is identical to the name of a potential cluster such as dominant/strong entities, generalized entities, and one-side entities in a one-to-many relationship), then the inner clustering operation (i.e. the one involving E_i as a master) is applied before the outer grouping (i.e the one involving E_i as a slave). As a special case, in the presence of a sequence of weak entities with their corresponding relationships, the absorption grouping starts from the most dependent entity and relationship, and then iteratively forms a complex entity until the strong entity is encountered.

Visibility/Unvisibility of Entities

In any information system, there are some entities that are relevant to many procedures and needs of users. We think that these key entities have to be quite visible at any level of abstraction of the initial schema, and not hidden inside a complex entity. Therefore, any grouping that encapsulates a key entity has to be prohibited.

2.4   An Illustrative Example

Let the EER schema of the database be the one illustrated by Figure 1 indicating that an employee has dependents who are either adult or non-adult, he/she works for a department, and is involved in one or many projects. Each department controls projects. Dependents benefit from social services, may have a driver's license (if they are adult) and toys (when they are non-adult). Assume also that *Employee* and *Department* are key entities. Therefore, any grouping in which these entities have to be components of a complex entity is prohibited. Figure 1 shows a chain of weaks entities *Dependent* and *Soc_service*. At the clustering level 1, the weak entities *Soc_service*, *Toy* and *Project* are absorbed by *Dependent*, *Non_adult* and *Department* respectively. For the entity *Driver* which is a union/category of *Employee* and *Adult_dependent*, there are two candidate groupings: one by categorization, and the other as by 1 : 1 binary relationship grouping. Even though the former has priority over the latter, it is in conflict with the visibility principle. Then, *Driver* is assembled with *License*. At the next level, the new complex entity *Dependent* is candidate to three kinds of grouping: weak entity absorption by *Employee*, generalization grouping where *Dependent* acts as a slave entity, and generalization grouping where *Dependent* is a master entity. Then, using the cascade rule, the clustering by generalization in which *Dependent* is a master entity is performed at the level 2 to hide the specialized entities *Adult* and *Non_adult*. We cannot undertake an additional grouping operation at level 2 because each potential grouping involves either the complex entity *Dependent* recently clustered at that level, or a key entity. At level 3, *Employee* absorbs its weak entity *Dependent*. To maintain the semantic consistency of the schema, relationships (association, ISA, and union) that involve a component of a complex entity must exhibit the path needed to reach that component. For example, Figure 2 indicates that the relationship *involved_in* connects the entity *Employee* to the entity *Project* which is a component of the complex entity *Department*.

Our clustering approach is based on [17]. However, it diverges from Teorey's paper in the following way:

- It aims mainly at complex object formation even though it can be a useful technique for documentation and abstraction.
- Additional rules and refinements are proposed to handle multiple choices, and preserve the logical sequence of DB schema abstract views.
- Once the appropriate grouping is retained by the user, there is an additional step aimed at converting the clustered EER into an object-oriented schema.

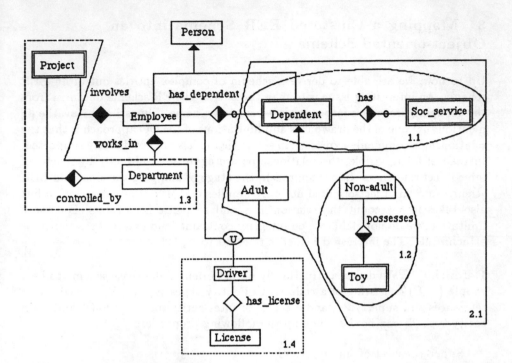

Fig. 1. A two-level clustering

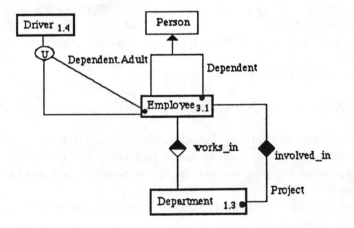

Fig. 2. Complex entities for a three-level clustering

3 Mapping a Clustered EER Schema into an Object-oriented Schema

Up to now, we are able to derive a schema of complex entities out of an EER schema. An interesting issue is to map the clustered EER schema obtained from the grouping procedure into an object-oriented schema. Elmasri and Navathe [6] mention that one of the drawbacks and limitations of the OO approach is that the relationships commonly expressed in semantic models are not directly supported. Instead of being visible, the relationships are expressed indirectly by means of interobject references. In our approach, the stage of mapping the clustered EER schema into an object-oriented not only handles complex object description but also takes into account the relationships and semantic constraints. For space limitation, we do not elaborate on integrity contraints and external relationships attachments. The interested reader is referred to [8, 12].

Definition 1. We define a structurally object-oriented database scheme to be a couple (S, Σ) consisting of a collection of entity types $E_1, \ldots, E_m$ closed under references and supertypes, and a set Σ of inter-entity integrity constraints. An entity type E_i can be described by the following properties:

- Supertypes: set of supertypes of E_i,
- Structure: aggregation of (atomic or complex) attributes A_j belonging to either built-in or user-defined types,
- Relationships: set of associations in which E_i participates,
- Specializations: set of specializations $< Sub, CD, Inherit >$ where E_i is the generalized entity,
- Category: description of the supertypes that participate to the union (if applicable), and
- Constraints: set of intra-entity constraints.

Generalized entities are defined by the triplet $< Sub, CD, Inherit >$, where:

* Sub represents the entities that specialize the supertype,
* CD is a couple of two boolean values indicating whether the generalization is complete or not, and whether the instances of the subtypes overlap or not (see [2, 6]).
* $Inherit$ indicates how the subtypes are formed [1] (e.g. user-defined or predicate-based specialization).

Since a same entity can be a generalization for more than one specialization criterion, there are as many triplets as there are kinds of specialization for that entity.

The extension of E_i is the set of objects $O_{i1}, \ldots, O_{ip}$ whose type is E_i. A database extension D of a schema S is a set of all the instances of the entities in S which verify the whole set of intra and inter-entity integrity constraints.

3.1 Transformation Rules

Once the diagram for complex objects is produced, the OO schema description can then be produced. There are at least two kinds of mapping of an ER diagram into an OO schema [16]: the first type, called **stable translation**, consists in converting each entity and each relationship into an object as in [14] while the second one, called **mapped translation**, consists in integrating a relationship into an object class using references, and creating an object class for each ternary relationship [10].

We define an entity E_j in the initial (i.e, non clustered) schema as *a potential candidate to absorption* by another entity E_i when one of the following cases occurs:

- E_j is in only one 1:1 or one 1:N relationship or only one ternary relationship involving E_i, and E_j has no other associations in the schema under consideration.
- E_j is a weak entity with respect to E_i and participates only to weak relationships (if any) as a strong entity.
- Each specialized entity E_j of E_i does not have specific properties by its own and does not participate to any relationship.

The translation process we adopt is a little bit similar to the mapping of an ER schema into a relational one [2]:

- Each entity of the clustered EER diagram is mapped into an object type. The structure of the complex object type depends upon the grouping operation used for complex entity formation. Except for entities that are candidates to absorption, each component of the complex object is recursively mapped into an object type. Multivalued attributes are expressed using the set or list constructors. Aggregate attributes are expressed using the tuple constructor.
- Depending on the arity of the relationship and the (minimal and maximal) cardinalities of the associations, each relationship is mapped onto either new attributes (either references to object types or actual attributes) added to the appropriate entities, or new entities making reference to the concerned entities.

It is important to note that during the translation process and independently of the way the complex entity E_i has been formed, the reference to an entity E_j inside E_i can take one of the following forms:

- *the actual structure* (attributes) of E_j when E_j is a candidate to absorption by E_i,
- *a reference* attribute (pointer) otherwise.

Weak entity absorption and dominance grouping. For this type of grouping, a complex type is created as an aggregation of the strong/dominant entity and the weak/related entities. Each relationship inside the grouping is mapped to a reference attribute whose name is the label of the relationship, and whose type conforms to the weak/related entity type. Curly braces {} are used whenever there are many occurrences of the weak/related entities for one occurrence of the strong entity.

Relationship grouping. There are two approaches for relationship translations in the literature [3]: one which explicitly describes the relationship as a class structure [14, 15]. The second approach maps the relationship into a pair of direct and inverse references as described in [4, 10]. In the last case, reference attributes are used to express the relationships between objects and ensure the navigation in one or both directions. To describe the inverse relationships, inverse reference attributes are used.

- *Translation of One-to-one Relationships*
  The translation of one-to-one relationships depends on the kind of the two entities (key or non-key) and their minimal cardinalities in the relationship (optional versus mandatory participation), and on the number of other associations in which each of the two entities is involved in (see [12] for more details). As an illustration, let *Office* be (i) a non-key entity, (ii) in an optional participation to the one-to-one relationship *occupies* with the entity *Employee*, and (iii) with no other associations in the schema under consideration. In such a situation, it may be wise to make the actual attributes of *Office* be components of the entity *Employee* and destroy the entity *Office*, especially if no new relationships are expected between *Office* and other entities of the schema.
- *Translation of One-to-many Relationships*
  For one-to-many binary relationships grouping, we have to aggregate the entity on the "one side" part together with the entity on the "many side" part placed inside curly brackets, followed by the attributes attached to the relationship, if any.
- *Translation of Many-to-many and Ternary Relationships*
  For many-to-many relationships and ternary relationships, a new structure is created by aggregating the references to the participating entities as well as the attributes associated with the relationships.

Generalization/Categorization. The definition of a generalized entity includes the specification of the generalization relationship described by the triplet $< Sub, CD, Inherit >$ as well as its structure. The mapping of a generalized entity and its related specialized entities can be perceived as a translation of a 1 : 1 relationship between the generalized entity and each of its subtypes.

A category is described in an OO schema mainly by means of two properties: its structure and its superclasses. The structure is the aggregation of the name of the appropriate superclass together with a reference attribute to the instance of that superclass. The second property enumerates the participating superclasses.

The choice of a given mapping depends also upon:

- **The expected usage patterns.** For example, if there are queries that ask for employees of a given department as well as requests for departments having some kinds of employees, then it is required to have both direct and inverse reference attributes connecting departments to their employees.
- **The expected evolution of the DB schema.** For example, if we expect that the entity *Office* can very likely participate to a new relationship with another entity, say *Floor*, then it may be wise to keep *Office* as an independent object type instead of pushing it inside *Employee*.
- **The peculiarities of the OODBMS** under consideration. For example, the database designer is allowed in ObjectStore© to declare two attributes as inverse of one another. This feature is interesting since it offers a way to maintain the consistency of relationships, as opposed to a need for an explicit declaration of directional relationships as in some other OO systems.

3.2 An Example

The OO schema corresponding to the clustered EER in Figure 2 can be expressed partly by the following definitions. For the description of class structures and constraints, we make use of the object-oriented language TQL [7].

Class Person
Superclasses Nil
Structure
　$[name : string, age : integer\ ]$
Relationships Nil
Specializations
　$< \{Employee, Dependent\}, (F, T), User >$
Category Nil
Constraints
　$IC_1 : this.age < 110$
end Person

Class Employee
Superclasses Person
Structure
　$[ssn : integer, works\_in : Department, has : \{Dependent\}_{0,4},$
　$involved\_in : \{Project\}_{1,2}, personal\_data : Person\ ]$
Relationships
　$works\_in : Department$ **inverse** $has\_worker,$
　$involved\_in : Department.Project$ **inverse** $involves$
Specializations Nil
Category Nil
Constraints
　$IC_2 : this.ssn \neq Employee.ssn$
　$IC_3 : this.involved\_in \leq this.works\_in.controls$
end Employee

Class Department
Superclasses Nil
Structure
  $[name : string, floor : (1 \ldots 9), head : Employee, staff : \{Employee\}_+,$
  $controls : \{Project\}_{0,5}$]
Relationships
  $controls : Project$ **inverse** $controlled\_by$
Specializations Nil
Category Nil
Constraints
  $IC_4 : this.name = this.head.works\_in.name$
end Department

The definition of *Person* specifies that this entity is a generalized class for *Employee* and *Dependent* with a partial coverage (e.g. a consultant is a person who is neither an employee nor an employee's dependent), and without overlapping between instances of the two classes (i.e., the dependent of an employee is not allowed to be an employee). The specialization is user-defined.

In the description of *Employee*, the cardinality constraint stating that an employee has at most four dependents is expressed by $\{Dependent\}_{0,4}$. The keyword "this" in the syntax of TQL denotes the current object, while a type name indicates the class of objects (minus the current object if the key-word "this" also appears). IC_2 is then a uniqueness constraint. IC_3 means that an employee works on a project only when the latter is under the control of the department in which this employee works. The comparison symbol stands for inclusion when applied to sets. IC_4 expresses the idea that if an employee is a head of a department, he/she also works in that department.

4   Conclusion and Further Research

In this paper, we have presented an adaptation of the clustering technique proposed in [17] to complex entity formation which is an important step in the mapping process of an EER schema into an object-oriented schema.

The overall methodology is implemented within the environment of the prototype called INTERSEM (*Interface sémantique*) [12]. INTERSEM is intended to reduce the semantic gap between the conceptual modelling of OODBs and the modelling tools by providing a framework and an environment for semantic data modelling, OODB design and interfacing, reverse engineering, generic model extraction, and DB schema querying.

We are currently studying the validity of the mapping procedure for a real-life application within an industrial project called IGLOO. We are also investigating its potential as a physical object clustering technique when the database usage patterns are closely related to the semantic relationships between object types.

Acknowledgements. This work was supported in part by the Natural Sciences and Engineering Research Council of Canada, and by the Ministry of Industry, Commerce, Science and Technology, Quebec, under the IGLOO project organized by the *Centre de Recherche Informatique de Montréal*.

References

1. Atkinson, M. et al.: *The Object-oriented Database System Manifesto.* Technical Report #30-89, GIP ALTAIR, LeChesnay, France, 1989.
2. Batini, C., Ceri, S., and Navathe, S.B.: *Conceptual Database Design. An Entity-relationship Approach.* The Benjamin/Cummings, New York, 1992.
3. Bertino, E., Martino, L.: *Object-Oriented Database Systems. Concepts and Architectures.* Addison-Wesley. 1993.
4. Cattell, R.G.G.: *The ODMG-93 Standard.* Morgan Kaufmann, San Mateo, 1993.
5. Chen, P.: The Entity-Relationship Model: Toward a Unified View of Data. ACM Transactions on Database Systems. 1(1), 1976, 9–36.
6. Elmasri, R., Navathe, S.B.: *Fundamentals of Database Systems*, Second edition, Benjamin/Cummings, Redwood City, 1994.
7. Formica, A., Missikoff, M.: Adding Integrity Constraints to Object-Oriented Databases, *Proceedings International Conference on Information and Knowledge Management.* Baltimore, MD, 1992, 593–601.
8. Gagnon, J-M, *Représentation et exploitation de la sémantique dans un mod'ele orienté objets.*, Master's thesis, Université du Québec à Montréal, August 1995.
9. Gray, P.M.D., Kulkarni, K.G., Paton, N.W.: *Object-Oriented Databases: Semantic Data Model Approach*, C.A.R. Hoare Series Editor. New York/London, Prentice Hall, 1992.
10. Hughes, J.G.: *Object-Oriented Databases.* Computer Science. Prentice Hall. 1991.
11. Johannesson, P.: A Method for Transforming Relational Schemas into Conceptual Schemas, *Proceedings Tenth International Conference on Data Engineering*, IEEE Computer Society Press, Los Alamitos, CA, 1994, 190-201.
12. Missaoui, R., Gagnon, J.M.: *Mapping an Extended Entity-Relationship Schema into a Schema of Complex Objects.* Technical Report, IGLOO Program, Centre de Recherche Informatique de Montréal, 40 pages, 1994.
13. Navathe, S.B., Awong, A.M.: Abstracting Relational and Hierarchical Data with a Semantic Data Model. In *Proceedings of Sixth International Conference on Entity-Relational Approach*, 1987.
14. Navathe, S.B., Pillallamarri, M.K.: OOER: Toward Making the ER Approach Object Oriented. *Proceedings of the 8th International Conference on Entity-Relationship Approach*, 1989, 55–76.
15. Rumbaugh, J.E.: Relations as Semantic Constraints in an Object-Oriented Language, *Proceedings of the International Conference on Object-Oriented Programming Systems, Languages, and Applications (OOPSLA).* Orlando, Florida, 1987, 466–481.
16. Song, I.Y.: A Survey of Object Oriented Database Design Methodologies, *Proceedings of the International Conference on Information and Knowledge Management.* Baltimore, MD, 52–59, 1992.
17. Teorey, T.J. et al.: ER Model Clustering as an Aid for User Communication and Documentation in Database Design. CACM. 32(8), 1989, 975–987.

Binary Representation of Ternary Relationships in ER Conceptual Modeling

Trevor H. Jones[1] & Il-Yeol Song[2]

Abstract

Our paper seeks to provide an analysis of ternary relationship logic with an objective of identifying whether they can be decomposed given only the constructs and constraints provided during conceptual entity relationship (ER) modeling.

Our paper investigates which ternary relationship cardinality combinations can be losslessly decomposed, which combinations preserve functional dependencies, and whether the logic involved in these processes is sufficient to provide a model which is rigorous at the physical or practical level. We show that if ternary relationships can be explicitly constrained by binary cardinalities, some ternary/binary cardinality combinations have legitimate equivalencies in a binary decomposed form, but that certain other combinations cannot be decomposed without creating additional implementation concerns.

1. Introduction

No research, to date, has completely answered the question of which ternary relationship constructs can be represented by binary projections in entity relationship modeling. Some methodologies have been suggested to provide binary "translations" of the ternary construct (e.g. Hawryszyiewycz, 1988; McFadden and Hoffer, 1994). No complete analysis has been undertaken to test the ability of these alternatives to fully model ternary relationships or otherwise attempt to logically decompose the various ternary relationship cardinalities into binary structures. Consequently, the different methods of dealing with ternary relationships continue to be used, in classrooms, by practitioners and in CASE tools, without any attempts to reconcile the differences. In this paper, we provide some insight into these differences, adding a logical analysis of the ability to decompose certain cardinality combinations into equivalent binary projections.

Elmasri and Navathe (1994) have stated that if a ternary relationship contains a 1:1 relationship, it can be decomposed into an equivalent binary format. Previous work (Song et al., 1993; Song and Jones, 1993) has expanded on the basis of this statement, identifying specifically when a ternary/1:1 combination can occur. Teorey (1994) has indicated that under certain conditions ternary relationships may be decomposed. Ling (1985) when discussing the ability to conceptually model, relationally correct, ternary relationships, questions the applicability of the higher normal forms, but does not complete the argument. Jones and Song (1993) have additionally demonstrated that ternary relationships can be losslessly decomposed in situations other that when a 1:1 relationship exists. Lossless decompositions, however, do not provide a complete basis on which to judge equivalent modeling capabilities. This paper further explores the allowable combinations of ternary and binary relationship combinations in the context of the potential to reduce them to a simpler binary *equivalent* form including all requirements for

---

[1] A. J. Palumbo School of Business Administration, Duquesne University, Pittsburgh, PA 15282

[2] College of Information Studies, Drexel University, Philadelphia, PA 19104

full representation of data, constraints and practical issues. The term equivalence is explored in this paper, but briefly, it is used in the context of testing the ability of binary projections to fully represent all data, information and constraints contained in any particular ternary relationship. The decomposition findings and equivalence testing are also supported with the functional dependency analysis and proofs for each combination. In discussing decompositions of a structure, certain implicit considerations are important to ensure equivalency between the alternatives. In the case of ternary relationships the two important considerations we research are the requirements of lossless joins and updates.

Lossless joins refer to the necessity to correctly re-establish a relationship between three entities from any combination of binary relationships, without missing or spurious tuples. We investigate lossless joins through two formats of relationships: those without explicit binary constraints, and those which are explicitly constrained by binary relationships. Update considerations refer to the requirements of maintaining equivalent integrity in a binary format as opposed to the original ternary structure. This means enforcement of constraints during insertions, deletions and modifications to the database model. The paper includes full consideration of decomposition strategies on join and updates when equivocating binary and ternary relationships.

One concept which is central to the findings presented here, is that of the Semantically Constraining Binary (SCB) Relationship. A full explanation of this concept is provided in Song and Jones (1993). A SCB relationship defines a binary constraint between two entities participating in a ternary relationship, where the semantics of the binary relationship are associated with those of the ternary and therefore affect potential ternary combinations of entity instances. A SCB relationship is distinguished from a Semantically Unconstrained Binary (SUB) relationship, which is a relationship between two entities participating in a ternary relationship, but where the binary relationship is semantically unrelated to that of the ternary and therefore modeled independently. Song and Jones (1993) use the notation of a broken line for the SCB relationships as opposed to a solid line used for the more common, independent SUB relationships. That notation is also used in this paper.

2. Ternary Decomposition

The decomposition of any modeling structure assumes that the resulting structure(s) possesses all the implicit attributes of the original structure. That is, the alternatives are at least equal to the original structure, and *may* be more acceptable. When considering ternary relationships, we have identified three areas which we investigate to identify whether this equivalency is preserved. These are:

1. Whether the decomposition is lossless
2. Whether the decomposition preserves functional dependencies
3. Whether the decomposition can equivalently deal with the practical

requirements of the physical database resulting from the model i.e. insertions, deletions and updates.

2.1 Lossless Decompositions / Joins

Jones and Song (1993) and Song and Jones (1995), have provided an analysis of which ternary/binary cardinality combinations can be *losslessly* decomposed and the structures resulting from those decompositions. They have identified that all cardinalities of ternary rleationships can be decomposed provided that at least one SCB relationship exisits.

2.2 Functional Dependency Preserving Decompositions

The consideration of whether all lossless decompositions maintain all the implicit functional dependencies and whether any potential loss of functional dependencies would make a difference to the representation, has not yet been considered. In this section we look at the exhaustive list of lossless decompositions and consider whether implicit functional dependencies are preserved. Additionally, we investigate how the impact of functional dependency preservation, or loss, affects the usefulness of such decomposition strategies.

2.2.1 Insertions and Ternary Relationship Decomposition

Dealing with a ternary decomposition in isolation, we could assume that we would *always* be provided *three* participating entity values (since we are dealing with a relationship that by definition requires three values). In the spirit of the universal role assumption (Markowitz & Shoshani, 1992) in an entity relationship model, putting a decomposed structure back into context, forces us to deal with the requirement of independent update of each relationship derived in the decomposition. Following the breakdown of a ternary relationship into its component binary projections, the two binary relationships are now viewed as independent and we must deal with problems of independent modification of either relationship whilst at the same time ensuring the integrity of the original ternary relationship.

Some theoretical work has contributed to this investigation of this problem (e.g., Rissanen, 1977; Date, 1994). Part of the solution entails consideration of preserving the full set of functional dependencies of the original ternary structure. However, previous work concentrated on optimal decompositions in situations of Boyce-Codd normal form, and did not take into account the combinations of functional dependencies found in ternary relationships. However, it does indicate that retention of the implicit functional dependencies provides that:

"...the join of the two projections after update will always be valid". (Date, 1994)

Consequently, with those decompositions that preserve all functional dependencies, certain modifications to any specific entity instance can be accommodated without further consideration. The question remains; which cardinality combinations preserve functional dependencies following any specific decomposition.?

When we consider the decomposition of a ternary relationship into a binary relationship equivalent, we are actually considering whether the equivalent model has the ability to represent, and enforce, all constraints which were present in the original structure. The desired constraints in entity relationship modeling are explicitly identified through the cardinality constraints associated with each relationship, or set of relationships. Consequently, we can test the equivalency of ternary formats against binary formats simply by comparing the implicit and explicit functional dependencies found with each. The first question we test is whether it is necessary to require *total* equivalency of functional dependencies between the two models in order to ensure complete constraint enforcement. In later sections, we assess whether there are other issues which must be considered before we declare full modeling equivalency.

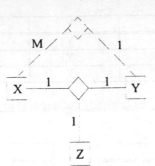

Figure 1. 1:1:1 Ternary Relationship with M:1 (XY) Constraint

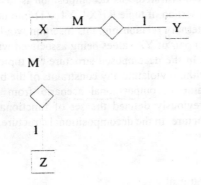

Figure 2. Suggested decomposition for Figure 1

Consider a ternary relationship R(X, Y, Z) with cardinality 1:1:1 and an imposed binary constraint of M:1 between X:Y. Using the notation identified previously, we can diagrammatically represent this structure as shown in Figure 1.

The explicit constraint between X/Y implicitly requires the following set of functional dependencies:

$$XY \rightarrow Z \qquad XZ \rightarrow Y \qquad YZ \rightarrow X \qquad X \rightarrow Y \qquad X \rightarrow Z$$

[X → Z is implicitly (logically) required as a function of X → Y. The relationship Y:Z remains M:N (IBC rule).]

We can use a binary decomposition of (XY)(XZ), as shown in Figure 2.

Also consider a set of instances complying with the same cardinality requirements and subsequent decomposition strategy.

X	Y	Z
X1	Y1	Z1
X2	Y1	Z2
X3	Y2	Z1

This relation may be losslessly decomposed to :

X	Y
X1	Y1
X2	Y1
X3	Y2

X	Z
X1	Z1
X2	Z2
X3	Z1

As previously demonstrated, this decomposition is lossless. But consider further the act of requesting an insertion of tuple R1(X4, Y1, Z1) into the database. In the original format of structuring the ternary relationship, this insertion would be disallowed because it violates the constraint of a pair of YZ values being associated with a single value for X (in this case Y1 Z1 → X1). In the decomposed structure the tuple would be inserted in the form (X4, Y1)(X4, Z1) without violating any constraints of the binary structure.

Consider the same decompositional scenario from a functional dependency perspective. We have previously defined the set of functional dependencies that were present in the original structure. In the decompositional structure, we identify the following functional dependency set:

$X \rightarrow Y$

$X \rightarrow Z$

$XY \rightarrow Z$ (pseudotransitivity)

$XZ \rightarrow Y$ (pseudotransitivity)

In this decomposition strategy, we lose the functional dependency of $YZ \rightarrow X$, and there is no way to recover it through reconstruction based on Armstrong's Axioms (Armstrong, 1974). This supports our hypothesis that a binary decomposition is not always able to enforce functional dependency constraints, even though the decomposition may be lossless. This observation indicates that when considering binary decompositions which may be equivalent to an original ternary structure, we must ensure that all functional dependencies found in the ternary relationship model are also implicitly or explicitly reflected in the binary model. We can then be sure that any insertion is required to comply with all constraint requirements, even though the representative storage structure is different.

In scrutinizing all potential cardinality outcomes we find that applying the same functional dependency and decomposition analysis identifies that three combinations cannot be decomposed without losing some level of functional constraint enforcement. Table 1 shows the unique combinations possible together with their decompositional status regarding functional dependency preservation. This table is then an extension of the decompositions presented in Jones and Song(1993), where only the join, and losslessness, was considered and every combination of cardinalities qualified. We also notice in comparing the two sets of outcomes, that some of the alternate decompositions allowed

Ternary Cardinality (X:Y:Z)	Binary Impositions	Potential Decomposition	Preserves FD's?	Enforces constraints on insertions	Enforces constraints on deletions
1:1:1	(X:Y) = (M:1)	None	No		
1:1:1	(X:Y) = (1:1)	(XY)(XZ) -or- (XY)(YZ)	Yes	Yes	Yes
1:1:1	(X:Y) = (M:1) (Z:Y) = (M:1)	(XY)(XZ) -or- (XZ)(ZY)	Yes	Yes	Yes
1:1:1	(X:Y) = (M:1) (X:Z) = (1:1)	(XY)(XZ) -or- (XZ)(ZY)	Yes	Yes	Yes
M:1:1	(X:Y) = (M:1)	(XY)(XZ)	Yes	Yes	Yes
M:1:1	(Y:Z) = (M:1)	None	No		
M:1:1	(Y:Z) = (1:1)	(XY)(YZ)	Yes	Yes	No
M:1:1	(X:Y) = (M:1) (Y:Z) = (1:1)	(XY)(YZ) -or- (XZ)(ZY)	Yes	Yes	No
M:1:1	(X:Y) = (M:1) (Y:Z) = (1:M)	(XZ)(ZY)	Yes	Yes	No
M:N:1	(X:Z) = (M:1)	(XY)(XZ)	Yes	Yes	No
M:N:1	(X:Z) = (M:1) (Y:Z) = (M:1)	None	No		
M:N:P	Not Allowed	None	None		

Table 1. Lossless *and* FD Preserving Decompositions

when considering only losslessness, do not preserve all functional dependencies and are therefore disqualified in the more restrictive Table 1. These findings can be supported through functional dependency proofs.

2.2.2 Deletions and Ternary Relationship Decomposition

The consideration of deletions is similar to that of insertions. Can we remove a ternary relationship from a binary (decomposed) structure which is capable of losslessly (and FD preserving) storing a ternary relationship. Consider the following example ternary relationship R(X, Y, Z) with cardinality M:1:1, and binary impositions M:1 (X, Y) and 1:1 (Y, Z). According to Section 2.2.1 this relation can be losslessly and FD preserving decomposed to its binary equivalent of S(X, Y) and T(Y, Z). An example of this decomposition is shown in Table 2 and Table 3.

Relation_R

X	Y	Z
X1	Y1	Z1
X2	Y1	Z1

Table 2. M:1:1 Ternary Relationship with Binary Impositions

Relation_S

X	Y
X1	Y1
X2	Y1

Relation_T

Y	Z
Y1	Z1

Table 3. Lossless and FD Preserving Decomposition of Table 2

In this example, we have stored two tuples, $R_1(X1, Y1, Z1)$ and $R_2(X2, Y1, Z1)$. If we now delete tuple $R_1(X1, Y1, Z1)$, the ternary storage structure dictates that we have tuple R_2 remaining. However, if we delete the same tuple, $R_1(X1, Y1, Z1)$, from the equivalent binary storage format, we delete tuples $S_1(X1, Y1)$ and $T_1(Y1, Z1)$, based on the projections of R_1. We have now deleted the only reference to $(Y1, Z1)$ when it is needed as part of the remaining relationship $R_2(X2, Y1, Z1)$. We therefore see that although the decomposition is equivalent from the point of view of those constraints considered in entity relationship modeling theory (i.e., preservation of data and functional dependencies), from a practical standpoint, the binary structure does not have the implicit practical constraint checking properties of the ternary structure. We have no ability to preserve the necessary binary relationships without some additional mechanism (application program) to check reference requirements. The binary structure does not automatically provide the storage requirements to allow deletions without potential loss of data.

Is this phenomena applicable only to this, or a restricted, combination of ternary/binary cardinalities? We notice from the above example that the problem stems from the collapse of redundant binary pairs into a single representation. In the above case, it is the collapse of two occurrences of $(Y1, Z1)$ into a single representation in the decomposition, which creates the problem for subsequent deletion actions.

Consider the requirements of a unique binary instance pair to occur. For the complete binary tuple to be non-redundantly stored, the third participating instance must be different than all others. For example, to see the binary pair $(X1, Y1)$ multiple times, following a decomposition, the pair must have existed only in combination with different Z values as part of the original ternary relationship, e.g. $(X1, Y1, Z1)$ and $(X1, Y1, Z2)$. We can deduce from this that the relationship between (XY) and (Z) must be M. If the relationship must always be singular (1), logically we cannot have duplicate sets of the X/Y value combinations. We can therefore conclude that the possibility of losing data through binary decomposition exists in any decomposition structure derived from an original ternary possessing a many relationship. Conversely, we can say that the only decompositional solution which will not be subject to data loss, are those derived from ternary relationships where either of the binary pairs used in the decomposition have singular cardinalities with their corresponding entity in the original ternary relationship. Any decomposition of a ternary relationship which contains a binary pair of entities which was originally associated with a cardinality of M in the ternary relationship, has the potential to suffer from this removal of redundancy, and therefore, a potential loss of implicit constraint checking. On researching all functional dependency preserving decompositions, we find that four of the decompositions fall into this category of "redundancy removal" and must therefore be disqualified as valid equivalents of their ternary counterparts. Table 1 includes two columns indicating the ability of the decompositions to correctly allow insertions and deletions. Section 2.2.1 explained that functional dependency preservation automatically enforced correct insertions, which accounts for that columns' entries. We note however that only four of the potential FD preserving decompositions allow correct deletion enforcement.

2.2.3 Modifications and Ternary Relationship Decomposition

Within our terminology, the update process refers to the overall process of inserting, deleting and changing (modifying) data values. We are then left with questioning our ability to alter the values of existing data in a binary format structure as opposed to the original ternary structure. In section 2.2.2, we identified that it was possible to collapse several redundant pairs following decomposition. From this standpoint, the binary format appears beneficial since it addresses the problem of update anomalies, or multiple modifications for a single data value, providing a lesser number of data instances to modify in any given situation. However, considering the findings of section 2.2.2, the benefits of this finding are in direct conflict with the potential loss of data caused by collapsing redundant binary pairs. Consequently, we note that the binary decomposition poses no problems to data modification, and can be beneficial by reducing data redundancy; we qualify this in the context of the potential data loss impact of the same redundancy reduction process (section 2.2.2).

3. Conclusion

In this paper we have continued the analysis of ternary relationships with an objective of determining the ability to represent them through binary projections. In analyzing ternary relationships with no implicit binary constraints, we developed the UTD rule which identifies that a ternary relationship cannot be decomposed, regardless of cardinality unless some explicit binary constraint (related to the semantics of the ternary relationship) is recognized. Associated with this finding, we acknowledge the theory behind MVD's and JD's in a corollary to the UTD rule, and conclude that these dependencies cannot be modeled at the conceptual ER level, but are essentially logical, or instance based constraints. Consequently, the UTD rule and all subsequent analysis presented regarding ternary relationship decomposition, is completed in spite of these relational theory issues.

Following a review of previous work identifying lossless decompositions we included an analysis and need for functional dependency preservation during decomposition. We identify that not all lossless decompositions have the ability to preserve functional dependencies. The ternary cardinalities of 1:1:1, M:1:1 and M:N:1 when combined with certain binary cardinality impositions, cannot be modeled as binary projections without loss of functional dependency. We explicitly identify which of these cardinality combinations can be modeled as binary projections, and provide proofs of their functional dependency equivalence.

We further extend the arguments of functional dependency preservation by considering the practical implications of this type of decomposition (or projection) modeling. We find that the preservation of functional dependencies provides for correct constraint checking during insertions, but does not provide the checking requirements during deletion operations. We have shown that only four of those decompositions which are lossless and preserve functional dependencies have the ability to correctly allow deletion operations and therefore the binary decompositional structure is inadequate to preserve the constraint checking that is possible through the original ternary relationship.

If we now consolidate these facts, we see that of the 8 cardinality combinations that are eligible for decomposition (by virtue of losslessness and FD preservation), only 4 qualify as being fully equivalent to the ternary relationship structure from which they were derived. These findings should allow further insight into whether the current *binary* modeling methodologies fully represent the underlying ternary relationship. In terms of modeling power we must keep in mind the equivalent inclusions of constraint representation and the abilities to represent practical requirements of derived physical database models.

4. References

Armstrong, W.W. (1974) "Dependency Structures of Data Base Relationships". In *Proc. IFIP Congress*, 1974.

Date, CJ. *An Introduction to Database Systems*. Addison--Wesley Publishing Company, Menlo Park, CA., 6th Edition, 1994.

Elmasri, R., and Navathe, S. (1993). *Fundamentals of Database Systems*. 2nd Edition, Benjamin/Cummings, Redwood City, CA. 1993.

Hawryszyiewycz I. T. *An Introduction to Systems Analysis and Design*. Prentice Hall, Englewood Cliffs, NJ, 1988

Jones, T.H. & Song, I.Y. (1993). "Binary Imposition Rules and Ternary Decomposition". In *Proceedings of InfoScience '93, Conference on Information Science and Technology*, Korea Information Science Society, Seoul, Korea, October 21 -- 23, 1993, pp. 267 -- 274.

Ling, T.W. (1985b). "A Normal Form for Entity-Relationship Diagrams". In *Proceedings of 4th International Conference on the Entity-Relationship Approach (Chicago)*. IEEE Computer Society Press, Silver Springs, MD., 1985.

Markowitz, V.M. & Shoshani, A. (1992). "Representing Extended Entity-Relationship Structures in Relational Databases: A Modular Approach". *ACM Transactions on Database Systems*, 17(3), September, 1992, pp. 423 -- 464.

McFadden & Hoffer. *Database Management*. 4th Edition, Benjamin/Cummings, Redwood City, CA. 1994.

McKee, R.L. & Rodgers, J.(1992). "N-ary Versus Binary Data Modeling: a Matter of Perspective". *Data Resource Management*, 3(4), Fall 1992, pp. 22 -- 32.

Rissannen, J. (1977). "Independent Components of Relations". *ACM TODS*, 2(4), December 1977.

Song, I.Y. & Jones T.H. (1993). "Analysis of Binary Relationships within Ternary Relationships in ER modeling". In *Proceedings of 12th International Conference on Entity-Relationship Approach*, Dallas, TX., December, 1993, pp. 265 -- 276.

Song, I.Y. & Jones T.H. (1995). "Ternary Relationship Strategies Based on Binary Imposition Rules". In *Proceedings of 11th Intl. Conference on Data Engineering (ICDE '95)*, Taipei, Taiwan, March 1995.

Song, I.Y., Jones T.H. & Park, E.K. (1993). "Binary Relationship Imposition Rules on Ternary Relationships in ER Modeling". In *Proceedings of 2nd International Conference on Information and Knowledge Management*, Washington, D.C., October, 1993, pp. 57 -- 66.

Teorey, T.J. *Database Modeling and Design: The Fundamental Principles*. 2nd Edition. Morgan-Kauffman, 1994.

Variable Sets and Functions Framework for Conceptual Modeling: Integrating ER and OO via Sketches with Dynamic Markers

Zinovy Diskin*   Boris Cadish*

Frame Inform Systems, Riga, Latvija
E-mail: diskin@frame.riga.lv

Abstract. In the paper a graph-based specification language for semantic modeling is proposed. It is as handy as conventional graphical languages but, in contrast to them, possesses a precisely formalized semantics based on certain ideas of the mathematical category theory. In particular, it provides mathematically correct semantics for formerly somewhat mythical notions of object identity and weak entity type.

Among other benefits of the approach there are provable (!) universality w.r.to simulation of any other formal data specification, flexibility and unification in treating various kinds of associations and relationships, precise semantic basis for the familiar distinguishing between the specialization and generalization ISA-relationships, intrinsic object-orientedness.

1 Introduction

It appears that currently there are two central questions in the area of conceptual modeling and design: the first one is how to handle heterogeneity of semantic data models, and the second consists in integrating ER and OO paradigms into a consistent unified framework. It will be shown in this paper that adaptation of two simple ideas taken from categorical logic (a standard reference is [2]) provide a concise framework for conceptual modeling in which both problems can be resolved simultaneously in a coherent way.

Indeed, in spite of the vast diversity of semantic data models (in which OO has contributed greatly and continues to contribute), three fundamental issues of conceptual modeling can be identified: modeling object identity (with distinguishing objects and values), modeling relationships (with distinguishing arbitrary associations from aggregations when some objects are somehow "built" from others considered as their parts or components), modeling ISA-relationship (with distinguishing between specialization and generalization) (see [4, 5, 7, 1, 8] and for more recent references [9, 11, 10, 12] and elsewhere). Correspondingly, any model should be classified and evaluated according to what mechanisms it provides for explanation and specification of these phenomena.

* Supported by Grant 94.315 from the Latvian Council of Science

In this paper we will demonstrate that semantics of the constructs above can be consistently explained in precise formal terms of *variable (or dynamic) sets* and *functions*. On this ground a substantial comparison of ER and OO can be fulfilled providing a framework for their integration. Moreover, having an accurately defined formal semantics, a denotational mechanism for specifying ER and OO constructs can be developed and, thus, we obtain a powerful specification language with precisely formulated semantics. [2]

Following the terminology tradition of categorical logic, we will call specifications of the language *sketches*. Incorporation of the sketch methodology into the conceptual modeling area is the first general idea we have mentioned above, the variable set semantics for sketches is the second one. These two concepts determine the name *SkeDM* (abbreviated from 'Sketches with Dynamic Markers') for both the language and the approach as a whole.

2 Semantic modeling via sketches, I : arrow specification of internal structure of objects and classes

Even an overall glance at graphical images currently used in semantic modeling shows an abundance of various kinds of conventional graphical constructs, symbols, labels and markers. Every specialist in semantic modeling and every DB designer uses that kind of semantic schemas which (s)he finds more suitable and convenient for her/his purposes. This is natural as well as reasonable, however, some problems arise.

First of all, a natural theoretical question is whether the existing collection of modeling constructs is sufficient for specifying all possible semantic constructions, i.e., whether it is complete in some sense, and what 'sense' should we mean here? Another problem is the universality of conceptual design methodologies and techniques (in particular, for view integration), *ie*, their independence on specific data models: it seems that the field strongly needs design techniques where *data model would be a parameter*. At last, the field needs a data definition/manipulation language combining evidence and user-friendliness of graph-oriented object semantic models together with formal rigor and clearness of relational models.

In the paper we will demonstrate that the sketch machinery just provides a proper universal framework for developing specification languages satisfying the requirements above. By suggesting this idea we do not wish to force all practitioners and researchers to use the same universal language – let everyone use that collection of markers (s)he likes. What we actually suggest concerns *what should be marked* in semantic schemas.

Let us consider a familiar issue of structural conflicts between different views. In the majority of semantic schemas in use, particularly, in ER-diagrams, in order

---

[2] We assert that none of the conventional powerful semantic models possesses this property. Moreover, a great advantage of the language we suggest is that general results of category theory make it possible to prove (!) that *any* formal data specification can be replaced by a semantically equivalent specification of the language.

to specify the intended semantic meaning of a given node N of a schema, one labels the very node N by a corresponding marker. For instance, to specify a node as a relation, *ie*, as a set of relationship objects (tuples), one labels it by a diamond. However, if another user perceives the same data objects as entities, (s)he labels the corresponding node in his schema by a rectangle. How should the node N of an integrated schema be labeled?

One can observe that structural conflicts like above are caused by determining internal structure of a set via determining the structure of its elements: a relation is a set of tuples, a powerset is a set of subsets *etc.* Contrariwise, in the mathematical category theory there was developed the paradigm of *arrow thinking* which consists in characterizing internal structure of objects through mappings between classes of these objects.

For example, instead of saying that a set X consists of n-tuples over a list of domains $D_1, \ldots, D_n$, one can equivalently say that there is a *separating* family of functions, $f_i \colon X \longrightarrow D_i$ $(i = 1, ..., n)$, that is,

$$\forall x, x' \in X, \ x \neq x' \text{ implies } f_i(x) \neq f_i(x') \text{ for some } i.$$

Indeed, in such a case the function $f = [f_1 \ldots f_n] \colon X \longrightarrow D_1 \times \ldots \times D_n$ (determined by $fx = [f_1x, \ldots, f_nx]$) is injective so that X is actually a relation up to isomorphism and its elements can be identified with tuples. In the classical ER-terminology ([4]), if domains D_i's are entity sets then f_i's are *roles* and any $x \in X$ is a relationship between entities $f_1(x), \ldots, f_n(x)$. What we would like to emphasize here is that any relationship set determines the corresponding separating family of functions and conversely so that the very notions of a relationship set and *a separating source* (of functions) are equivalent. Correspondingly, on the syntax level, to specify a node as a relation one can safely leave the node without any marking but label instead the corresponding source of outgoing arrows by some marker (say, an arc) denoting a separating family of functions. (Actually, this is nothing but a well known idea of designating a key of a relation).

Similar arrow treatments of other conventional semantic constructs (*eg*, grouping) are presented in Table 1 (over the bold line). Then, for example, the following five pictures (sketches) on Fig. 1 specify the node X as a relation, disjoint sum (coproduct), union, the image of a given function and a subset of the powerset (of Y) respectively.

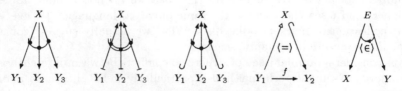

Fig. 1. Several simple sketches

So, in contrast to thinking in terms of elements, the paradigm of arrow thinking suggests to specify internal structure of both elements of a given set and the very set by characterizing (labeling) the corresponding diagram of functions adjoint to the set. The corresponding specifications, sketches, are graphical constructs consisting of three kinds of items: (i) nodes, to be interpreted as sets, (ii) arrows, to be interpreted as functions between corresponding sets, and (iii) diagram markers, to be interpreted as constrains imposed on diagrams labeled by these markers. A simple example of using sketches for semantic modeling is presented on Fig. 2 (the sketch in the left lower corner is an instance of static modeling explained above, dynamic sketches will be explained in the next section).

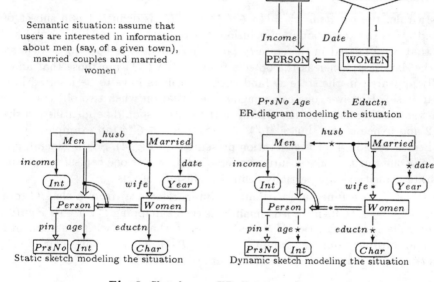

Fig. 2. Sketches vs. ER-diagrams: An example

3 Semantic modeling via sketches, II: dynamic constraints

It is easy to see that the static sketch on Fig. 2 does not capture some important semantic properties of the situation, *eg*, such as the weak entity type of the node '*Women*'. Moreover, some of these properties are not specified in the ER-model at all, *eg*, the essential distinction between attributes *Income* (whose value for a given object can change) and *Date* (whose value is a constant).

To explain these and similar semantic phenomena in a precise formal way we will develop *the variable set and functions semantics* for the sketch specifications (the idea also has its origin in category theory). To begin with, we consider a simple example. Let S be a semantic schema of some institution, and one of the nodes is named '*Employee*'. The intended semantics of this node is not a concrete static set of employees of the institution but rather *a concept* of the employees, that is, a sequence of sets of employees indexed by time moments. Indeed, let $\mathcal{O}$ denotes some universe of objects (determined by some context $\mathcal{W}$) and $\mathcal{T}$ denotes some set of logical (rather than physical) time moments (also connected with $\mathcal{W}$) which are partially ordered by logical precedence. Then, for a class name C (*eg*,'*Employee*') its semantics is a mapping $C^* : \mathcal{T} \longrightarrow Set(\mathcal{O})$ into the collection of finite sets over $\mathcal{O}$ s.t. for any time moment $t \in \mathcal{T}$ the set $C^*(t) \subset \mathcal{O}$ (called the *state* of C at the moment t) is the extension of C at this moment.

In addition, and this is the crucial point, for any pair $t_1, t_2 \in \mathcal{T}$ s.t. $t_1 \leq t_2$ there is defined a certain partial *state transition* mapping $\tau_C^{t_1,t_2} : C^*(t_1) \longrightarrow C^*(t_2)$ which traces the evolution of objects (we will write it shortly by $\tau_C^{12} : C^{*1} \longrightarrow C^{*2}$).

As a rule, the set $dom\tau_C^{12} \stackrel{def}{=} \{o \in C^{*1} : \tau_C^{12}(o) \text{ is defined }\}$ is a subset of C^{*2} and τ_C^{12} is the corresponding inclusion: the objects from $(C^{*1} \setminus dom\tau_C^{12})$ are those that disappeared in the state t_2 (and their identifiers have to be deleted from the database) whereas the objects from $(C^{*2} \setminus C^{*1})$ are those that additionally appeared in the state t_2 (and their identifiers have to be inserted into the database). However, one can imagine the situation when two objects o', o'' which were distinguished by the DBMS in the state 1 should be identified in the state 2 and hence $o' \neq o'$ but $\tau_C^{12}(o') = \tau_C^{12}(o'') = o \in C^{*2}$ (an example will be described in section 4 for the situation presented on Fig. 4). So, in general, τ_C^{12} is not one-one but to make intuitive understanding easier one can safely assume that state transitions are partially defined inclusions of sets.

Now, let f be a function (attribute, pointer, reference) from a class C to a class D, $f : C \longrightarrow D$. Its intended semantics is then a mapping $f^* : \mathcal{T} \longrightarrow Fun(\mathcal{O})$ into the collection of functions between $\mathcal{O}$-sets so that for each time moment t $f^*(t)$ is an ordinary function from $C^*(t)$ into $D^*(t)$. Thus, for any pair of moments $t_1 \leq t_2$ we have the following diagram of functions over $Set(\mathcal{O})$:

$$
\begin{array}{ccc}
C^{*1} & \xrightarrow{\tau_C^{12}} & C^{*2} \\
{\scriptstyle f^{*1}}\downarrow & & \downarrow{\scriptstyle f^{*2}} \\
D^{*1} & \xrightarrow{\tau_D^{12}} & D^{*2}
\end{array}
$$

This *variable (*or *dynamic) function transition diagram* is not necessarily commutative, *ie*, there can be an object $o \in C^{*1}$ s.t. $\tau_D^{12}(f^{*1}.o) \neq f^{*2}.\tau_C^{12}(o)$ (here the attribute-like notation for function values is used).

This means that during the evolution from t_1 to t_2 the state of the object o changed. For example, if D is a value domain (say, **Integer**) and, hence, τ_D^{12} is the identity function, whereas C is an object class (say, '*Person*'), the inequality above means a change of the f-attribute (say, '*Salary*') of the person o.

On the other hand, the diagram *can be constrained* to be commutative and actually two commutativity conditions can be imposed as follows.

3.1 Definition of dynamic commutativity constraints

(i) *Weak dynamic commutativity constraint*:

if $o \in dom\tau_C^{12}$ then $f^{*1}(o) \in dom\tau_D^{12}$ and $f^{*2}.\tau_C^{12}(o) = \tau_D^{12}(f^{*1}.o)$, whereas nothing is said for the case when $\tau_C^{12}(o)$ is undefined;

(ii) *Strict dynamic commutativity constraint*:
if $o \in dom\tau_C^{12}$ then as in (i) whereas if $\tau_C^{12}(o)$ is undefined then $\tau_D^{12}(f^{*1}.o)$ is also undefined.

A dynamic arrow is called *static/strictly static* (or just *strict*) if it satisfies the corresponding weak/strict commutativity condition above. In graphical schemas these arrows will be marked by two different stars (see Table 1). □

It can be shown that these dynamic constraints imposed on arrows in combination with structural static constraints of function injectivity/surjectivity provide quite natural yet precise formalized treatment of the following familiar conceptual modeling constructs:

- weak entity type, existence dependency, identification dependency;
- association reference, aggregation reference, composition association *etc*;
- specialization and generalization ISA-relationships,

which are usually treated informally or semiformally (or, what is the worst, pseudoformally) and, therefore, ambiguously.

Moreover, while the constructs listed above can be specified by different combinations of the appropriate arrow markers (expressing the corresponding constraints), actually much more combinations are logically possible, and each of them corresponds to a distinguishable semantic situation. Some of these situations occur frequently in the real world and therefore were explicitly identified in the conceptual modeling area. Other are more characteristic for rapidly changing programing environments and were identified in the OO programing framework. However, it seems that there are combinations of markers capturing semantics of practically possible situations which yet were not identified (at any rate, explicitly). In particular, a novel, SkeDM-based, taxonomy of object classes will be developed in the next section. In addition, the complete taxonomy of associations between object classes which can be expressed by different combinations of markers appears very involved and deserve a special exploring – this is the goal of a forthcoming paper. (However, main principles of the SkeDM-approach to this problem can be seen from the examples on Fig. 2,4).

Thus, to summarize, the chief semantic modeling principle underlying the SkeDM-approach can be formulated as follows: *the world consists of variable sets and variable functions between them subjected to certain constant constraints*.

Sketches with Dynamic Markers is just the specification language built upon this principle. A simple example of using sketches (with dynamic markers) for semantic modeling is presented on Fig. 2 (right lower corner). A bit more involved example will be described in section 4 (Fig. 4).

4 Types and classes

In this section we will make a distinction between types and classes in a formal way and then introduce a new taxonomy of classes. In particular, our considerations provide a precise formal semantics for the "mythical" object identity.

4.1 Basic and complex value domains. Let C be a node name in a semantic schema and $C^*: \mathcal{T} \longrightarrow Set(\mathcal{O})$ be its dynamic extension.

If C^* is a constant set (that is, all sets $C^*(t)$ coincide and all state transition mappings are identity functions), and DMBS *a priori* knows how to store and manipulate the elements of C, then C will be called *a value domain* or just *domain* and $C^*(t)$ will be denoted by $DomC$. Thus, if C is a domain node then $C^{*1} = C^{*2} = DomC$ and τ_C^{12} is the identity function of $DomC$ for any $t_1, t_2 \in \mathcal{T}$. For every domain known to the DBMS we introduce a special marker, for example, `Int`, `Char` *etc* so that if a node C is marked, *eg*, by the marker `Int` then, for any $t \in \mathcal{T}$, $C^*(t)$ is the set of all integers.

More formally, we assume a collection $\mathcal{B} = \{\texttt{B1}, ..., \texttt{Bk}\}$ of *basic domain markers* is given, and each such a marker is coupled with a certain set of values, $DomBi$, *a priori* known to the DBMS. If a node named C is labeled by a basic domain marker $\texttt{B}$ then it is common to suppress the name C and consider $\texttt{B}$ as a marker and a name simultaneously. This is reasonable since different nodes labeled by the same domain marker have the same constant extension.

It is also common to assume that besides a predefined collection of basic domains there is a predefined collection Ω of operation for building new domains. A node C is called *a complex (value) domain* if its extension $DomC$ is a constant set composed from basic domains in a way *a priori* known to the DBMS, *ie*, for any $t \in \mathcal{T}$, $C^* = DomC = \omega(DomB1, ..., DomBn)$ for some $\omega \in \Omega$ of arity n and $Bi \in \mathcal{B}$.

If C^* is a variable set whose extension is not *a priori* known and hence has to be stored in the database, then C is called *an object class* or just *class*.

4.2 Regular sketches. As it was stated above, sketches are directed multigraphs some of whose diagrams are labeled by special markers.

A sketch is called *regular* if its nodes are marked as either classes or value domains and, in addition, the graph has terminal nodes, each terminal node is a domain, any node has a path from the node to a domain, and the entire graph satisfies a certain condition of acyclicity (which is outside the scope of the paper). Further we will assume that all sketches are regular.

4.3 Definition. Let S be a sketch. For any arrow f, $\Box f$ and $f\Box$ denote the source and target of f respectively.

With any class node C of the sketch there are correlated the following *types*:

- *immediate value type*, $\tau_{val}^{imm}(C) \overset{\text{def}}{=} \{f \in ArrsS : \Box f = C$ and $f\Box$ is a domain $\}$

- *immediate object type*, $\tau_{obj}^{imm}(C) \overset{\text{def}}{=} \{f \in ArrsS : \Box f = C$ and $f\Box$ is a class $\}$

- *immediate type*, $\tau^{imm}(C) \overset{\text{def}}{=} \tau_{val}^{imm}(C) \cup \tau_{obj}^{imm}(C)$

- *full (value) type*, $\tau(C) \overset{\text{def}}{=} \{p \in PathsS : \Box p = C$ and $p\Box$ is a domain $\}$

where *a path* is a sequence of arrows $p = (f_1, \ldots, f_n)$ s.t. $f_i\Box = \Box f_{i+1}$ for all $i = 1, \ldots, n - 1$; $\Box p$ and $p\Box$ denote $\Box f_1$ and $f_n\Box$.

A sketch S can be extended with derived arrows, *eg*, by taking inverse arrows where is possible. The extended sketch will be denoted by $\overline{S}$ and, correspondingly, we obtain three notions of *extended* or *derived types*: $\overline{\tau}_{val}^{imm}(C)$, $\overline{\tau}_{obj}^{imm}(C)$, $\overline{\tau}(C)$.

4.4 Definition. Let C be a class node of a given sketch.

A *key* of C is a set of (derived and basic) arrows $K = (p_1, \ldots, p_n) \subset \overline{\tau}(C)$ s.t. for any $t \in \mathcal{T}$ the set of functions $\{p_1^*(t), \ldots, p_n^*(t)\}$ is separating whereas its any proper subset is not separating. A key is called *static* if all its arrows are static.

Static keys will be also called *(external) identifiers* or *surrogates*. □

Note, for any moment $t \in \mathcal{T}$, the elements of $C^*(t)$ should be considered either objects (material or conceptual) from the real world or *internal object identifiers* representing them in the DBMS. These internal identifiers are not visible to users which are allowed to refer to objects via values of the corresponding class key.

Thus, we have three kinds of object identification: (i) through internal oids which are in one-one correspondence with real world entities and actually constitute extensions of classes; (ii) through external identifiers (surrogates) which provide tuples of values uniquely characterizing real world entities; (iii) through keys which provide tuples of values uniquely characterizing object within a given state only.

Note, with any key K, $K = (p_1, \ldots, p_n) \subset \overline{\tau}(C)$, there is correlated the product monic function (to simplify notation we will suppress the time argument):

$$p_K^* \stackrel{\text{def}}{=} [p_1^*, \ldots, p_n^*]: C^* \longrightarrow Dom\mathrm{K} \stackrel{\text{def}}{=} Dom(p_1^*\square) \times \ldots \times Dom(p_n^*\square)$$

and then the cover $p_K^{*+}: C^* \longrightarrow Img^*(\mathrm{K})$, where $Img^*(\mathrm{K})$ denotes the image of p_K^* in $Dom\mathrm{K}$, is actually an isomorphism for any time moment. So, $Img(\mathrm{K})$ is a class whose instances are "printable" and are in one-one (but dynamic!) correspondence with objects of C.

Furthermore, it is easy to see that if K is static, then the cover above is a strict isomorphism of C onto $Img\mathrm{K}$. Hence, the printable instances of the latter class are in static one-one correspondence with the objects of C, that is, these instances are values which can serve as surrogates for objects of C (note, classes like $Img(\mathrm{K})$ with static K Codd called *E-domains* in his RM/T model [5]).

The consideration above motivates the following dichotomy of collections of objects (Fig. 3) built in a fully formalized way.

A sketch illustrating some of the notions just introduced is presented on Fig. 4 (in this example we assume that rules of some company do not allow married couples among employees).

REMARK. It is worthwhile to examine semantics of the attribute *children* as is specified by the sketch.

With each employee e (represented in the DB by a certain unique object identifier (oid), say, e) there is strictly (!) connected the object $g = children.\mathrm{e}$ (of the type '*Set − of − Objects*') which in its turn is dynamically (!) connected with the set of objects $fam^{-1}(g)$ of the class '*Child*' (the same is for oids representing real world objects in the DB). Then, for example, if in the family of an employee e a child was born then $children.\mathrm{e}$ is not changed but $fam^{-1}(children.\mathrm{e})$ should be changed.

Now let us suppose the possibility of married couples among *Employees* and consider the following situation. In the state 1 an employee e with $sex.\mathrm{e} = \mathrm{M}$ is single but has children, and another employee e' with $sex.\mathrm{e}' = \mathrm{F}$ is also single but has children. Further, if in the state 2 employees e and e' happily became a married couple, then the variable-set-semantics description of the situation is as follows (C denotes the class *Group − of − Children*):

$$\tau_C^{12}(children^{*1}.\mathrm{e}) = \tau_C^{12}(children^{*1}.\mathrm{e}') = \text{ a new object } g \in C \text{ with}$$

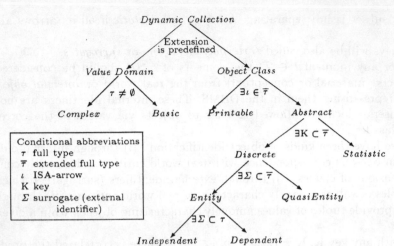

Each dichotomy is determined by the condition written under the corresponding node of separation. The left term of the separation satisfies the condition

Fig. 3. Taxonomy of classes

$(fam^{-1})^{*2}(\mathbf{g}) = (children^{*1}.\mathbf{e}) \cup (children^{*1}.\mathbf{e}')$ and $children^{*2}.\mathbf{e} = children^{*2}.\mathbf{e}' = \mathbf{g}$.

It seems that the example demonstrates the great flexibility of the SkeDM-framework for semantic modeling.

5 Modeling ISA-relationships via dynamic inclusion arrows

Definition. Let a context $\mathcal{W}$ with its object universe $\mathcal{O}$ and logical time $\mathcal{T}$ are given. A dynamic function $f: C \longrightarrow D$ (over $Set\mathcal{O}$) is called an *inclusion* if, for any $t \in \mathcal{T}$, $C^*(t) \subset D^*(t)$ and $f_t^*: C^*(t) \to D^*(t)$ is the corresponding inclusion, *ie*, $f_t^*(c) = c$ for all $c \in C^*$.

Note, just dynamic notion of inclusion captures properly semantics of the ISA-relationship in a formal way; we will call dynamic inclusions also ISA-arrows.

It follows readily from the definition that any inclusion is static but not necessarily strict. Then, an arrow will be called a *strict inclusion* if it is simultaneously an inclusion and a strictly static arrow. Thus, we have two kinds of dynamic inclusions and it appears that this formally specified difference captures semantics of the well known distinction between specialization ISA-relationship and generalization ISA-relationship in a proper way. For space limitations we omit examples.

6 Conclusion

In the paper a graph-based specification language, SkeDM, was proposed for semantic modeling. It is as handy as other conventional graph-based languages like

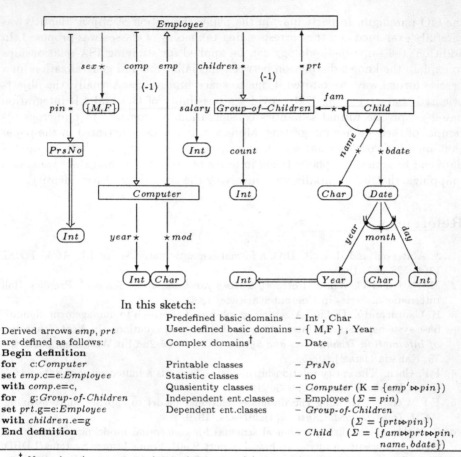

In this sketch:

Predefined basic domains	– Int , Char
User-defined basic domains	– { M,F } , Year
Complex domains†	– Date
Printable classes	– PrsNo
Statistic classes	– no
Quasientity classes	– Computer (K = {emp′⋈pin})
Independent ent.classes	– Employee (Σ = pin)
Dependent ent.classes	– Group-of-Children
	(Σ = {prt⋈pin})
	– Child (Σ = {fam⋈prt⋈pin, name, bdate})

Derived arrows *emp*, *prt*
are defined as follows:
Begin definition
for   *c:Computer*
set *emp.c=e:Employee*
with *comp.e=c*,
for   *g:Group-of-Children*
set *prt.g=e:Employee*
with *children.e=g*
End definition

---

† Note, domain names are also markers constraining extensions of the corresponding nodes to be, *eg*, the set of integers, or, for a node named {M,F} , to be the two-element set consisting of the character M and the character F

Fig. 4. An example of semantic modeling via sketches with dynamic markers

---

ER-diagrams but, in contrast to them, possesses a precisely formalized semantics based on certain ideas of the mathematical category theory.

A great advantage of the SkeDM-language is that it is provably (!) universal: it follows from some general results of categorical logic that any formal data specification can be replaced by a semantically equivalent sketch. This provides a real possibility of handling semantic models heterogeneity via SkeDM. Moreover, as it was shown in [3], the sketch language makes it possible to develop a practically effective approach to automated heterogeneuos view integration built upon formal algebraic manipulations with sketches. Application of the approach to conceptual modeling is also discussed in [6].

Another advantage of the SkeDM-approach to semantic modeling is that it is inherently object-oriented and actually provides a precise formal semantics for the OO paradigm. In particular, in the paper the notion of object identity was carefully examined and the corresponding taxonomy of classes was proposed. In addition, the same methodology can be applied for studying ISA-relationships to explain the known distinction between specialization and generalization in a precise formal way; we omited it due to space limitations. Actually, the object-oriented character of SkeDM provides a possibility of OO and ER integration based on precise formal semantics considerations in contrast to numerous attempts of their *ad hoc* integrating. Moreover, it was demonstrated in the paper that many of conventional semantic constructs for specifying the structure of data can be actually explained only in terms of variable sets and state transition mappings, that is, essentially with involving the concept of object identity.

References

1. S. Abiteboul and R. Hull. IFO: a formal semantic database model. *ACM TODS*, 12(4):525–565, 1987.
2. M. Barr and C. Wells. *Category Theory for Computing Science*. Prentice Hall International Series in Computer Science, 1990.
3. B. Cadish and Z. Diskin. Algebraic graph-based approach to management of multi-base systems, I: Schema integration via sketches and equations. In *Next Generation of Information Technologies and Systems,NGITS'95*, 2nd Int.Workshop, pages 69–79, Naharia (Israel), 1995.
4. P.P. Chen. The entity-relationship model – Towards a inified view of data. *ACM Trans.Database Syst.*, 1(1):9–36, 1976.
5. E.F. Codd. Extending the database relational model to capture more meaning. *ACM Trans.Database Syst.*, 4(4):397–434, 1979.
6. Z. Diskin. Formalizing graphical schemas for conceptual modeling: Sketch-based logic vs. heuristic pictures. Technical Report 95-01, Frame Inform Systems/LDBD, Riga, Latvia, 1995. To appear in Proc. of Int. KRUSE Symp. *"Knowledge Retrieval, Use and Storage for Efficiency"* (Santa Cruz, CA), 1995 (On ftp: //ftp.cs.chalmers.se/pub/users/diskin/Rep9501.*).
7. M. Hammer and D. McLeod. Database description with SDM: A semantic database model. *ACM Trans.Database Syst.*, 6(3):351–386, 1981.
8. R. Hull and R. King. Semantic database modeling: Survey, applications and research issues. *ACM Computing Surveys*, 19(3):201–260, 1987.
9. L. Liu. Exploring semantics in aggregation hierarchies for object-oriented databases. In *Int.Conf. on Data Engineering, ICDE'92*, pages 116–125, 1992.
10. V. Markowitz and A. Shoshani. An overview of the Laurence Berkeley Laboratory extended entity-relationship database tools. Technical report, 1993.
11. C. Parent and S. Spaccapietra. ERC+: an object-based entity-relationship approach. In *Conceptual modeling, databases and CASE: An integrated view of Information System Development*, 1992.
12. S. Spaccapietra, C. Parent, M. Sunye, and K. Yetongton. Object orientation and conceptual modeling. Technical report, 1993

Name	Arity Shape and Designation	Denotational Semantics
Separating Source	X $Y_1 \ldots Y_n$	$(\forall x, x' \in X)\ x \neq x'$ implies $f_i(x) \neq f_i(x')$ for some f_i
Monic Arrow †	$X \xrightarrow{f} Y$	$(\forall x, x' \in X)\ x \neq x'$ implies $f(x) \neq f(x')$
ISA-Arrow or Inclusion	$X \xRightarrow{f} Y$ or $X \xhookrightarrow{f} Y$	$X \subset Y$ and $f(x) = x$ for all $x \in X$
Covering Flow	Y $X_1 \ldots X_n$	$(\forall y \in Y)(\exists i < n)y \in f_i(X_i)$
Cover †	$X \xrightarrow{f} Y$	$Y = f(X)$
Inversion	$X \xrightarrow[g]{f} Y$ (-1)	$(\forall y \in Y)f(g(y)) = y$
Maximal Separating Source	X $Y_1 \ldots Y_n$	$(\forall x, x' \in X)\ x \neq x'$ implies $f_i(x) \neq f_i(x')$ for some f_i, and $(\forall y_1 \in Y_1, \ldots, \forall y_n \in Y_n)\ \exists x \in X$ s.t. $f_1(x) = y_1, \ldots, f_n(x) = y_n$.
Disjoint Covering Flow	Y $X_1 \ldots X_n$	$(\forall y \in Y \exists i < n)y \in f_i(X_i)$ and $i \neq j$ implies $f_i(X_i) \cap f_j(X_j) = \emptyset$
ϵ-relation	X $Y_1 \qquad Y_2$	$(\forall y, y' \in Y_1)\ y \neq y'$ implies $\{f_2 x : x \in f_1^{-1}y\} \neq \{f_2 x : x \in f_1^{-1}y'\}$, ie, there is an embedding $Y_1 \longmapsto \mathbf{Powerset} Y_2$.
Static Arrow	$X \xrightarrow{f} Y$	weak commutativity (definition 3.1(i))
Strictly Static Arrow	$X \xrightarrow{f} Y$	strict commutativity (definition 3.1(ii))

†The construction is a trivial case of the previous one.

Table 1. A collection of static and dynamic diagram constraints (over and below the bold line respectively)

A Logic Framework for a Semantics of Object Oriented Data Modelling

O. De Troyer
Tilburg University , Infolab
P.O.Box 90153
NL-5000 LE Tilburg
The Netherlands
Phn: +31-13-662432
e-mail: detroyer@kub.nl

R. Meersman
Free University of Brussels (VUB)
Computer Science Department
Pleinlaan 2   --Bldg. FG/10
B-1050 Brussels, Belgium
Phn: +32-2 629 3819
e-mail: meersman@vub.ac.be

Abstract

We describe a (meta) formalism, called Data Modelling Logic (DM logic), for defining a variety of (object oriented) data models in a unified framework based on first-order logic. Using NORM, an OO model, we illustrate how essential OO properties such as *information hiding, encapsulation, inheritance* and *behavior* may be generically described, as well as the fundamental distinction with object-oriented programming, namely *persistence*. A *formal semantics* for these concepts can so be given independently of the chosen data model. DM logic has been demonstrated in earlier work to adequately support "classical" data models such as (E)ER, NIAM, and the Relational Model, and so-called *lossless* transformations between them. By "programming" an OO data model in DM Logic, it should become possible to arrive at objective relationships between (OO and other) data modelling techniques.

1   Introduction

As it becomes increasingly important to connect heterogeneous information systems with the purpose of interoperation, it becomes necessary to deal within the same context with different specification techniques and methodologies. This in turn indicates the need for a common formalism in which one can define *different* and *multiple* modelling and representation languages.

The approach we follow is based on a first-order logical formalism, called DM-Logic (Data Modelling Logic), an extension and refinement of the one used in [3]. There it is shown how one may describe NIAM [12], (E)ER [9] and the "vanilla" relational data model within this same representation. In this paper we extend the formalism with a specification method for the "dynamics" of a conceptual schema and demonstrate that it is possible to express encapsulation and information hiding.

We have deliberately adopted a model-theoretic approach [10] although a proof-theoretic approach could perhaps have yielded a simpler and more uniform notation as is e.g. apparent in F-logic [7]. We felt however the extra mile was justified as classical databases and information systems almost exclusively adopts a model theoretic approach; this is appreciated in general as more intuitive because of the "natural" distinction of schema and "data". For the same reason the description of behaviour through *methods* is done using an imperative language involving "classical" instruction such as assignment, choice, loops, etc.. But we shall pay only token attention to these instructions as we want to concentrate rather on the distinction between instructions that cause a state transition and those that do not.

To illustrate the formalism, we describe it by means of an existing object-oriented specification language NORM [2]. It is not our goal here to (re)define NORM but rather to illustrate the descriptive power and principles of DM-Logic. Therefore a number of simplifications will be adopted.

We also do not have the ambition, at least within the scope of this paper, to either achieve deep results in logic or fundamental new results in OO modelling itself. Rather we pursue what we believe is a new and consistent approach in (meta-) modelling that allows to describe exactly and in a comprehensive manner the many complex aspects of "real-life" data modelling, especially object oriented, in a unifying framework that is semantically sound.

The paper is organized as follows. First we give a small introduction to NORM. Then we describe NORM in terms of DM Logic and give the semantics of a NORM-schema as well as an OT-schema; in particular the concept of *state* is introduced as the locally defined realization of persistency. Finally an OB-schema is defined as an "application-dependent" schema having a "global" state and which "uses" OT-schema's in a well-defined *aggregation*; we show that the local states can be made to behave properly in this aggregation, without losing information hiding.

2 A Tourist's Introduction to NORM

NORM is intended for conceptual modelling and is an object oriented version of the binary Object Role Model (ORM) (e.g. [6], [4], also known as NIAM [12]). NORM combines the assets of ORM with the advantages of object orientation.

Contrary to most OO models which define the state of an Object Type (OT) by means of attributes, the state of an OT is defined by a complete schema, the so-called *Object Type schema* (*OT-schemas*). The OT defined by this schema is called the *focus*. As an example consider the OT-schema with focus Document, its graphical representation is given in fig. 1 and reads as follows: Each Document has a Size and may have a Title. A Document may contain several Keywords. A Document also has a maximal Size which is the same for all Documents. The Size is expressed in bytes (ByteSize). ByteSize and Title are lexical types. Document, Size and Keyword are non-lexical types. Size is a *local type* while Keyword refers to the OT-schema with focus Keyword. Fig. 2 gives the graphical representation of the Keyword-schema. This schema also refers to a third OT-schema Topic which is not shown here.

Behavior is specified by means of *methods*. Example 1 shows the (type-)method create_empty for Document. NORM uses pre- and post-conditions to express the semantics of a method. A body may also be given to express the procedural semantics but this is not needed. NORM allows to construct methods using role names and type names in a well-defined way, e.g. Keyword-appearing_in to obtain all instances of Keyword which are related to a Document instance by means of the role appearing_in. NORM also supports *relation methods* and *triggers*. Relation methods are methods which are defined for relations instead of for object types. The corresponding messages are sent to relation instances. *Triggers* allow to express dependencies between the activation of messages. Due to lack of space, they are not treated in this paper.

To make methods and possibly also relations visible outside the OT-schema in which they are defined, they should explicitly be *exported*. Exported concepts may be *imported* and used in other schema's (e.g. Keyword is imported in the OT-schema Document).

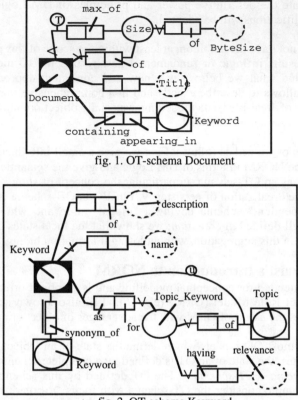

fig. 1. OT-schema Document

fig. 2. OT-schema Keyword

```
Object type Document method create_empty
out o_document: a Document ;
Description
creates a new Document object with Size=0 and without Keywords.
Preconditions True
Postconditions
P1: o_document is in Document ;
P2: Keyword-appearing_in o_document is empty;
P3: ByteSize-of Size-of o_document = 0 ;
Internal
Let o_document be New Document;
add-Size-of (with-ByteSize 0) o_document
end
```

Example 1: method create_empty

OT-schemas constitute general building blocks. The conceptual schema of a particular application is given by means of an *OB-schema* (Object Base schema). An OB-schema describes an application using OT-schemas as building blocks. Usually, it contains also its own types, methods and binary relations expressing application specific concepts and behavior. Syntactically, an OB-schema is an OT-schema without a focus. A fragment of an OB-schema for the document example is given in fig. 3. `Person`, `Document` and `Product` refer to OT-schemas Person, Document and Product.

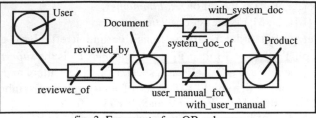

fig. 3. Fragment of an OB-schema

NORM supports the "is-a" variety of subtyping, i.e. each instance of a type is also an instance of a supertype of this type. E.g. a `Manual` can be defined as a subtype of a `Document`. As a consequence, overriding should only be used to specialize, i.e. adding more constraints or specialize the type of the inherited relations.

3   Syntax of NORM Expressed in DM-Logic

We define in the classical manner of first-order logic the syntax of a NORM language **L** and the syntactic rules to construct the terms, well formed formulas and instructions. NORM-schema's are then defined as theories, 3-tuples (**L**, Γ, Δ) where Γ is a set of closed well-formed formulas expressing integrity constraints, and Δ is a set of methods. To enhance the descriptive power of first-order predicate logic we use a many-sorted logic ([8], [11]) where *sorts* or *types* can be attached to individuals and predicates. We also allow to define a partial order on the set of types (*order-sorted logic*), for representing the "is-a" subtype relationship between types and which will enable to support inheritance. Although distinction between lexical and non-lexical types, and roles are essential for the (linguistically inspired) methodology that underlie NORM, we omit them here. This will not influence the results.

DM-Logic makes an explicit distinction between predicate symbols describing the persistent relationships, called *Relations*, and "ordinary" predicate symbols which denote other properties and relationships between data and objects, e.g. the "less-than" predicate. In NORM, Relations have to satisfy certain conditions. We omit these here. NORM also supports functions and sets. However, to simplify the notation, and since they are not essential for our purpose, sets and functions are omitted here.

Methods are associated with an OT. To activate a method, an activation message is sent to an instance of this OT (or the OT itself in case of a so-called *type-method*). To simplify the notation, each method comes with at most one *in* and one *out* *parameter*, but this is not a real restriction. The language only defines the headings of the methods, called *signatures*. We distinguish between *inspections* and *updates*. The latter may change the persistent state, the former not. There is also a distinction between *own signatures*, *built-in signatures* and *external signatures*. The built-in signatures include the usual update primitives *New* for instantiation, *Kill* for the removal of instances and *Make* to qualify an instance as an instance of a subtype.

A NORM language defines a set of symbols and constructs of various plumage. In addition to the usual (typed) *constant -*, *variable -*, *predicate -*, *truth -* and *logical symbols*, *punctuation signs* and (typed) *quantifier*s, a *NORM-language* consists of:

(1) A number of non-empty, finite and disjoint sets of names:
$T = \{T_1, ..., T_n\}$ is the set of *type names*;
$\mathbf{Rel} = \{R_1, ..., R_m\}$ is the set of *relation names*;
$\mathbf{Meth} = \{M_1, ..., M_l\}$ is the set of *method names*.

(2) $\prec$ a strict partial order relation (transitive and irreflexive), called *subtype relation*, on T. If $T_1 \prec T_2$ then T_1 is the *subtype*, T_2 is the *supertype* .

(3) For each type name $T \in T$, $\mathbf{self}_T$ is a special variable symbol and there is unary relation symbol T of type (T). The set of unary relation symbols is denoted *Type*, and partitioned into *ExtType* and *OwnType* (*external* and *own types*).

(4) A finite set *Rel* of binary *relation* structures of the form $R(T_1, T_2)$, where $R \in \mathbf{Rel}$, $T_1, T_2 \in T$.

(5) A finite set *Sig* of (*Method*) *Signatures* of the form $T \leftarrow M(\mathbf{in}\ p_i:T_i, \mathbf{out}\ p_o:T_o)$ where $M \in \mathbf{Meth}$; $T_i, T_o \in T$, $T \in Type$ and p_i, p_o are variables respectively of type T_i, T_o.
$p_i:T_i$, is the *formal in parameter*, $p_o:T_o$ the *formal out parameter*. The signature M is called a *T-signature* of type (T, T_i, T_o).
The primitive update T-signatures are as follows:
$T \leftarrow New_T(\mathbf{out}\ p_o:T)$, $T \leftarrow Kill_T(\mathbf{in}\ p_i:T)$ and $T \leftarrow Make_T(\mathbf{in}\ p_i:T', \mathbf{out}\ p_o:T)$ for each $T' \in Type$, such that $T \prec T'$.

For reasons of simplicity the relation methods are omitted here; their definition is similar to (5). The only exceptions are the *primitive* update operations *add* and *delete* for updating the (persistent) relations: these methods each have two input parameters, their signatures are $R \leftarrow Add(\mathbf{in}\ p_1:T_1, \mathbf{in}\ p_2:T_2)$ and $R \leftarrow Delete(\mathbf{in}\ p_1:T_1, \mathbf{in}\ p_2:T_2)$.

The syntactic rules for terms and for well-formed formulas (wffs) are rather standard, except that terms are typed. We only mention the rule to realize the *inheritance*:
any T'-term, such that $T' \prec T$ is a T-term;
A term of a subtype may be used wherever a term of the supertype is expected. Therefore all properties of the supertype are also applicable to the subtype. The additional property which we require for is-a subtyping (i.e. subset populations) will be expressed by the semantics. However, note that type-inheritance cannot be realized in this way. This is why in rule (3) of definition 3.1 (which follows) type-inheritance is handle explicitly.

The meaning of *closed* wff (a wff without free variables) is the usual one. We now define *instructions* as needed to program method bodies. They include the primitive operations *Add* and *Delete* for updating the persistent relations but also other classical imperative programming instructions such as assigment, sequence, test, loop may be defined as instruction. We omit them here, for a standard definition see e.g. [11]. An Add, a Delete or a (type) activation message of an update signature are called *update instructions*, the others are called *inspection instructions*.

Definition 3.1
For a NORM-language L, *instructions* are defined as follows:
(1) If $T \leftarrow M(\mathbf{in}\ p_i:T_i, \mathbf{out}\ p_o:T_o)$ is an instance signature and t and t_i are terms respectively of type T and T_i, x is a variable of type T_o then $t \leftarrow M(t_i, x)$ is an instruction, called an *activation message* of the given signature;

(2) If $T \leftarrow M(\textbf{in } p_i:T_i, \textbf{out } p_o:T_o)$ is a type signature and t_i is a term of type T_i, x is a variable of type T_o, $T' = T$ or $T' \prec T$, then $T' \leftarrow M(t_i, x)$ is an instruction, called a *type activation message* of the given signature;

(3) If $R(T_1, T_2) \in \textbf{\textit{Rel}}$ and t_1, t_2 are terms of type T_1, T_2 respectively, then $R \leftarrow$ Add (t_1, t_2) and $R \leftarrow$ Delete(t_1, t_2) are instructions;

(4) Other instructions, left unspecified, for assignment, loop, choice, etc.. $\quad\square$

Method signatures may be bracketed with pre- and post-conditions, expressed by means of wffs: if s is a signature, w_{pre} and w_{post} are wffs then $\{w_{pre}\}$ s $\{w_{post}\}$ is *an asserted signature*, w_{pre} is the *pre-condition* and w_{post} the *post-condition*. If Π is an instruction then s : Π is *a method* with *method body* Π. If s is asserted $\{w_{pre}\}$ s $\{w_{post}\}$: Π is an *asserted method*. Note that for the primitive update signatures Add, Delete, New, Kill and Make, proper pre- and post-conditions have to be defined. Due to lack of space they are omitted here. Also note that all variables in the body of a method are treated as local variables, we ignore global variables.

Definition 3.2

A *DM-schema* Σ is a logical theory (L, Γ, Δ) where L is a DM-language, Γ is a set of closed wffs of L, called the *integrity constraints*, and Δ is a set of asserted methods for L, such that there is exactly one asserted method for each own method signature in L. A DM-schema is a *NORM-schema* if its DM-language is a NORM-language. $\quad\square$

Only for the own signatures of the language there must be an asserted method. External signatures will have their definition "elsewhere" (e.g. in another NORM schema). Built-in signatures do not have a body, their interpretation is defined by the semantics of the model (see definition 4.3). The integrity constraints as defined here correspond to the so-called *static* integrity constraints. *Dynamic* integrity constraints which restrict possible successor state(s) of a given state are not treated here.

4 Semantics of NORM expressed in DM Logic

A classical declarative semantics for data models (see e.g. [10]) is based on a mapping of the language elements to values, mathematical relations and functions. In our case each type T is interpreted by a non-empty set, called the *domain* of T, Dom(T), constants are mapped to domain values, predicate symbols to relations. The subtype relation is interpreted by the subset relationship, i.e. If $T \prec T'$ then Dom(T) $\subseteq$ Dom(T') holds. This realizes a clean *is-a* meaning of the subtype relation.

An important difference with a classical interpretation is the distinction we introduce between the "algebra" and the "state". The *algebra* contains the domains, the interpretation of the constants and the predicates. The *state* contains the interpretation of the relations and represents the *persistent* information stored in a database. The algebra is state-invariant and is usually fixed for a given database implementation.

Definition 4.1

Let A be an algebra for a NORM-schema $\Sigma = (L, \Gamma, \Delta)$. A *state* S over A consists of:
- A binary relation $R_E \subseteq$ Dom(T_1) $\times$ Dom(T_2) (i.e. a set of binary tuples), for each Relation $R \in \textbf{\textit{Rel}}$ of type (T_1, T_2). R_E is called the *extension of* R in S.

- A unary relation $T_E \subseteq \text{Dom}(T)$ (i.e. a set of instances), for each $T \in OwnType$. T_E is called the *extension of* T in S.
- If $(a, b) \in R_E$ with R of type (T_1, T_2) then $a \in T_{1E}$ and $b \in T_{2E}$. □

The last rule avoids *dangling oids* (object identifiers) since (a, b) is in the extension of a binary relation R only if both a and b are in the extensions of its types.

As usual, an *environment* or *variable assignment* is a mapping γ from variables of **L** into **U**, i.e. for each variable x of type T, $\gamma(x) \in \text{Dom}(T)$. The combination of a state S and an implicit environment γ, called *state environment* and denoted by S, completely determines evaluation of the terms and consequently the truth values of the wffs. $S(x/d)$ denotes a state environment identical to S except that it maps the variable x into d. $S(E/\!\!/E')$ denotes a state environment identical to S except that the (value of the) extension E is substituted by E'.

Term evaluation is standard, the *evaluation* of a term t is denoted by $[t]$ (or sometimes $S[t]$ or $S[t]_A$ if we want to make algebra and/or state environment explicit). Also the truth value of a wff is defined in the standard manner (see e.g. [5]). The notation $A \models_S w$ is used when the truth value of the wff w is TRUE in the state environment S over an algebra A. If $A \models_S w$ for all possible environments γ, then w is *valid in the state S over the algebra A*, notation $A \models_S w$. A state S over an algebra A is a *valid state* iff each wff of Γ is valid in S.

The following definition gives the evaluation or execution of an instruction in a state environment. In general, an instruction may change this state environment.

Definition 4.2
For a given algebra A and state environment S, an instruction Π of **L** *transforms* S into S', denoted $S[\Pi]S'$ (or $S[\Pi]_A S'$ if the algebra needs to be explicit), as follows:
(1) $S[R \leftarrow \text{Add } (t_1, t_2)]S'$ iff $S' = S(R_E /\!\!/ R_E \cup \{([t_1], [t_2])\})$;
(2) $S[R \leftarrow \text{Delete } (t_1, t_2)]S'$ iff $S' = S(R_E /\!\!/ R_E \setminus \{([t_1], [t_2])\})$;
(3) $S[T \leftarrow \text{New}(x)]S'$ iff $S' = S(x/d, T_E /\!\!/ T_E \cup \{d\})$ where $d \in \text{Dom}(T)$ and $T(x)$ is FALSE in $S(x/d)$;
(4) $S[T \leftarrow \text{Kill}(t)]S'$ iff $S' = S(T_E /\!\!/ T_E \setminus \{[t]\})$;
(5) $S[T \leftarrow \text{Make } (t, x)]S'$ iff $S' = S(T_E /\!\!/ T_E \cup \{[t]\}, x/S[t])$;
(6) $S[t \leftarrow M(t_i, x)]S'$ iff $S_1[\Pi_M]S_2$ where Π_M is the method body of the signature $T \leftarrow M(\textbf{in } p_i: T_i, \textbf{out } p_o: T_o)$ in Δ, and where $S_1 = S(\textbf{self}/S[t], p_i/S[t_i])$ and $S' = S_2(x/S_2[p_o])$;
(7) $S[T \leftarrow M(t_i, x)]S'$ iff $S_1[\Pi_M]S_2$ where Π_M is the method body of the signature $T \leftarrow M(\textbf{in } p_i: T_i, \textbf{out } p_o: T_o)$ in Δ, and where $S_1 = S(p_i/S[t_i])$ and $S' = S_2(x/S_2[p_o])$; □

Rules (1) to (5) above define the state transitions caused by the elementary update messages of *Add*, *Delete*, *New*, *Kill* and *Make*. E.g. the update *Add* "adds" a new tuple to the extension of a relation, more precisely switches to a new state that reflects this change. *New* adds a new instance to the extension of a type. The value of this instance is returned as value of the output parameter. *Make* requires some care. Remember (rule (6) of NORM language) that its signature is such that the output parameter's type is a subtype of the input parameter's. *Make* adds the value obtained by evaluation of the input parameter t, a term of type T', to the extension of T (a subtype of T'). This same value is returned as value for the output parameter x (which is of type T). This is needed before we can manipulate it as a legal term also of the subtype T. The result of a message activation is a new state obtained by executing the method body (including proper parameter binding) of the corresponding method.

An activation message $t \leftarrow M(t_i, x)$ of an asserted method is *applicable* in a state environment S over an algebra A, iff the precondition is satisfied after its formal parameters (including **self**) are substituted by actual parameters, i.e. $A \models_{S1} w_{pre}$ where $S_1 = S(self/S[t], p_i/S[t_i])$. This activation message is *safe* iff the postcondition is satisfied in its "result" state, i.e. $A \models_{S2} w_{post}$ where $S_1[\Pi]_M S_2$.

An (update) instruction Π is *valid* in S, iff $[\Pi]$ transforms the valid state S into another valid state S', and in addition if Π is a (type) activation message of an asserted method of Δ, then it must be both applicable and safe in S

A simple but fundamental notion that will allow us to glue NORM schema's together is that of *agreement* between algebra's and between states.

Definition 4.3
An algebra A for a DM-language L and an algebra A' for a DM-language L' *agree* if they are equal for the concepts of $L \cap L'$. Similarly, states *agree* if the algebra's agree and the states are equal for the concepts of $L \cap L'$. For state environments, the states must agree and the environments must be equal for the variables of $L \cap L'$. $\qquad\square$

5   OT-Schemas and OB-Schemas
In this section we formally define the concepts of OT-schema and OB-schema as described in section 2. An OT-schema is modelled as a NORM-schema where one of its types is selected as focus. As explained in section 2, an OT-schema may "refer" to other OT-schemas. This is modelled by means of an *Import* list, which explicitly lists all external types and signatures. OT-schemas also have an *Export* list that lists the externally visible types and signatures (which may be imported by other schema's), thereby achieving information hiding. An OB-schema is also defined as a NORM-schema. As for an OT-schema, an OB-schema also has a Import list but in addition it also specifies the actual OT-schema's used to resolve (directly as well as indirectly) this Import list. This is needed because in general an import list may be resolved in more than one way (as there may be more than one OT-schema for a focus (e.g. different versions)).

We also define the state of an OB-schema which consistently aggregates the states of the different OT-schema's (as "local" states). To achieve this, states and algebra's are required to agree as defined in Definition 4.2. We show that the notion of state transformation of NORM-schema's in that case correctly generalizes in a natural way to the corresponding notion for OB-schemas, i.e. with preservation of information hiding in the "local" OT-schemas.

Definition 5.1
An *OT-schema* is a 4-tuple $\Sigma_F = (\Sigma, F, \texttt{Import}, \texttt{Export})$, where
(1) Σ is a NORM-schema $\Sigma = (L, \Gamma, \Delta)$;
(2)   F is an element of *OwnType* and is called the *focus* of Σ_F;

(3) `Import` equals the set of external types and external signatures of the language **L**, denoted by `Import.T` and `Import.Sig` (*imported type names* and *imported signatures*);

(4) `Export` is a subset of the language **L**, `Export.T` (disjoint from `Import.T`) is the set of *exported type names*, and `Export.Sig` the set of *exported signatures*.

To keep it simple we only allow to export the focus and (some of) its signatures (the exact specification of this is omitted in the definition). It may also be useful to allow to export other types or even relations together with their related signatures.

Definition 5.2

An *OB-schema* is a 3-tuple $\Sigma_B = (\Sigma, \text{Import}, \Sigma)$, where

(1) Σ is a NORM-schema $\Sigma = (\mathbf{L}, \Gamma, \Delta)$;

(2) `Import` equals the set of external types and external signatures of the language **L**, denoted by `Import.T` and `Import.Sig` (*imported type names* and *imported signatures*);

(3) Σ is a (possibly empty) set of OT-schema's. □

Informally, we say that an OB-schema is *completely specified* iff all imported concepts are 'resolved' by Σ. This means that for each imported type name T and associated imported signatures, there is exactly one OT-schema in Σ which *fits*, i.e. of which T is the focus, and which is capable of handling the message activations of the associated imported signatures. However, as these OT-schema's may also have sets of `Import`, these imported concepts must also be resolved by Σ. Formally, this can be defined by defining the set `Import*` as a kind of transitive closure over `Import`.

In what follows we will (implicitly) use only completely specified OB-schemas. We also suppose that the sets of own symbols of the different OT-schemas are pairwise disjoint.

We define an *algebra*, *state* and *state environment* for an OT-schema respectively as an algebra, state and state environment for its NORM-schema Σ. Algebra's and states for OB-schemas are straightforward but somewhat more complex since we need one algebra (and state) for each imported OT-schema, as well as an algebra (and state) for Σ itself. So if Σ_B is an OB-schema as defined above, then an *algebra* for Σ_B is a 2-tuple $(A, \mathcal{A})$ such that A is an algebra for Σ and $\mathcal{A}$ is a set of algebra's, one for each Σ_T in Σ (denoted A_T). All algebra's must agree. Likewise a *state* over an algebra $(A, \mathcal{A})$ for Σ_B is a 2-tuple $(S, \mathcal{S})$ such that S is a state over A for Σ and $\mathcal{S}$ is a set of states, one for each A_T for Σ_T (denoted S_T). $\mathcal{S}$ is called the *external states* of Σ_B. All states must agree. A *state environment* for an OB-schema is analogous and denoted $S_B = (S, \mathcal{S})$.

Lemma 5.1

For an OB-schema $\Sigma_B = (\Sigma, \text{Import}, \Sigma)$ and a state environment $(S, \mathcal{S})$, all states S_T and state environments S_T over A_T for Σ_T in $\mathcal{S}$ are disjoint.

Proof (sketch)

A state only contains the extension of own symbols. Therefore all states are disjoint. Since there are no global variables the state environments are also disjoint. □

We now show how state transitions work for an OB-schema. Except for a message activation of an imported signature, terms and instructions can be evaluated resp. executed in the OB-schema own NORM-schema. A message activation of an imported signature is sent for execution to the OT-schema from which it is imported. This may cause a state transition for the state of this OT-schema. Note however, that a message activation may cause a chain of message activations (activated in the body of the corresponding method). If (some of) these methods are imported from other OT-schema's, the states of these OT-schemas may change as well. Therefore, the effect of a single message activation may be a state transition for several of the external states.

As the activations of imported messages are executed in the OT-schema from which they are imported, we first have to define term evaluation and instruction execution for an OT-schema Σ_T within the OB-schema. The definition of term evaluation is trivial, i.e. the evaluation within Σ_T of a term t, denoted $[t]^T$, is the evaluation of t in Σ_T for the algebra A_T and state environment S_T. The definition of an instruction execution, denoted $[\Pi]^T$, is a recursive one. As explained above, $[\Pi]^T$ may results is a change of $\boldsymbol{S}$, the external states of the OB-schema.

Definition 5.3

Let Σ_B be an OB-schema with algebra $A_B=(A, \mathcal{A})$ and state environment $S_B = (S, \boldsymbol{S})$, let Σ_T be an OT-schema of Σ with algebra A_T of $\mathcal{A}$ and state environment S_T of $\boldsymbol{S}$. An instruction Π of L_T *transforms* $\boldsymbol{S}$ into $\boldsymbol{S'}$ denoted by $\boldsymbol{S}[\Pi]^T\boldsymbol{S'}$ as follows:

(1) if Π stands for a (type) activation message of an imported T'-signature,
   $t\leftarrow M(t_i, x)$ or $T'\leftarrow M(t_i, x)$, imported by T from the OT-schema $\Sigma_{T'}$ of Σ, and
   if $\boldsymbol{S}[\Pi]^T\boldsymbol{S''}$ then $\boldsymbol{S'} = \boldsymbol{S''}$ ($S''_T /\!/ S''_{T'}(x/S''_{T'}[x])$
   $\boldsymbol{S'} = \boldsymbol{S''}$ ($S''_T /\!/ S''_{T'}(x/S''_{T'}[x])$);

(2) otherwise $\boldsymbol{S'}= \boldsymbol{S}$ ($S_T /\!/ S'_T$) iff $S_T[\Pi]S'_T$ in Σ_T for the algebra A_T and state environment S_T. $\qquad\square$

In general the instruction will only change the OT-schema own state environment (rule (2)). However, if it a message activation of an imported method (rule (1)), the instruction is executed for the OT-schema T' from which the method is imported, $\boldsymbol{S}[\Pi]^T\boldsymbol{S''}$, which results in the new set of external states $\boldsymbol{S''}$. Next, the value of x, the actual output parameter, in the state environment of T' must be carried over to the (possible new) state environment of T.

This now permits the definition of term evaluation and instruction execution within an OB-schema itself. Again, the definition of term evaluation is trivial, i.e. the *evaluation* of a term t in the algebra A_B and state environment S_B, denoted $[t]^B$, is the evaluation of t in Σ for the algebra A and state environment S. Imported messages are executed in the local state of their corresponding OT-schema, other terms and instructions are evaluated resp. executed in the "own" schema Σ of the OB-schema Σ_B.

Definition 5.4

Let Σ_B be an OB-schema as above, with algebra $A_B=(A, \mathcal{A})$ and state environment $S_B = (S, \boldsymbol{S})$, an instruction Π of L *computes* S'_B from S_B or *transforms* state S_B into $S'_B = (S, \boldsymbol{S'})$, denoted by $S_B [\Pi]^B S'_B$ as follows :

(1) if Π stands for a (type) activation message of an imported T-signature, $t \leftarrow M(t_i, x)$ or $T \leftarrow M(t_i, x)$, imported from the OT-schema Σ_T of Σ, then $S_B [\Pi]^B S'_B$ iff $\boldsymbol{S}[\Pi]^T \boldsymbol{S'}$ and $S'_B = (S(x/S'_T[x]) , \boldsymbol{S})$;

(2) otherwise $S_B [\Pi]^B S'_B$ iff $S [\Pi]S'$ in Σ for the algebra A and state environment S and $S'_B = (S', \boldsymbol{S})$. $\square$

We now show that definition 5.4 indeed transforms a state environment of a OB-schema into another state environment of this OB-schema. First we prove that this is true for "its" OT-schemas. For OB-schema's the proof is omitted but similar.

Lemma 5.2
An instruction Π of $\mathbf{L}_T$ transforms (according to def. 5.3) a set of state environments $\boldsymbol{S}$ for an OB-schema Σ_B into another set of state environments $\boldsymbol{S'}$ for Σ_B.

Proof
If rule(2) of def. 5.3 applies, then clearly, $\boldsymbol{S'} = \boldsymbol{S} (S_T \,/\!/\, S'_T)$ is a set of external states for Σ_B because the state environment S_T over A_T for Σ_T in $\boldsymbol{S}$ is replaced by a state environment S'_T over A_T for Σ_T (namely $S_T[\Pi]S'_T$). Also all states agree since they are disjoint by Lemma 5.1.
If rule(1) of def. 5.3 applies, then $\boldsymbol{S'} = \boldsymbol{S''}(S''_T \,/\!/\, S''_T(x/S''_{T'} [x]))$ where $\boldsymbol{S}[\Pi]^T \boldsymbol{S''}$.
First we show that $\boldsymbol{S''}$ is a state environment. Indeed, for $\boldsymbol{S}[\Pi]^T \boldsymbol{S''}$ we can apply the rule (2) of def. 5.3 because Π is now the activation message of an own signature. By the definition of $\boldsymbol{S'}$, $\boldsymbol{S'}$ will be a set of external states for Σ_B when $\boldsymbol{S''}$ is. $\square$

Theorem 5.1
An instruction Π of $\mathbf{L}$ transforms (according to def. 5.4) a state environment S_B of the OB-schema Σ_B into another state environment S'_B of Σ_B. $\square$

The next theorem, which we give without proof here, states that it is possible to transform each OB-schema losslessly into a NORM-schema, i.e. into a "flat" schema. A *lossless schema transformation* is pair of mappings; the first maps the source schema into the target schema and the second is a total, one-to-one and onto correspondence (i.e. a bijection) between the (sets of) valid states of the two schema's (for a more precise definition, see [3]). This result is important since it makes it possible to carry over to OB-schemas the work done for "flat" (NORM)-schema's, more in particular the results about lossless schema transformation towards conventional data models, such as the Relational Model and (E)ER.

Theorem 5.2 (Universal OB-schema theorem)
Each OB-schema $\Sigma_B = (\Sigma, \texttt{Import}, \Sigma)$ can be transformed by means of a lossless schema transformation into an OB-schema Σ'_B of the form $(\Sigma, \emptyset, \emptyset)$. $\square$

6 Conclusion, Ongoing and Future Work

We have shown that an OO information system specification model possessing generic properties of encapsulation of structure and behavior, inheritance, aggregation and information hiding, may be described adequately in terms of a generic logic-based meta-specification language called DM-logic. This language is also capable of describing non-OO models such as EER or the relational model and has been shown in [3] to allow a consistent description of the lossless transformations between data models mentioned.

We model persistence using the concepts of state, and we have shown that the semantics of DM-logic may be described completely declaratively, allowing a model-theoretic treatment of the systems described, including their behavior. The semantics reflect that the aggregation mechanism used to build "application" schema's (OB-schemas) from general purpose object types (OT-schemas) respects information hiding. OB-schemas may be transformed losslessly into "flat" NORM schema's, thereby linking OO data models to conventional ones such as (E)ER and RM.

In ongoing work on this (meta-)model the (lossless) schema transformation of NORM into other models (such as relational, EER, ODMG-93 [1]) and the corresponding transformation of behavior are being studied. Future issues include the possibility of direct interpretation of DM specifications (as a semantically sound approach for meta-CASE tools, for instance) and the application of DM-Logic specifications e.g. to problems of interoperability of heterogeneous databases.

References and Bibliography

[1] Cattell, R.G.G. (ed), "The Object Database Standard: ODMG-93", Morgan Kaufmann Publishers, 1994, ISBN 1-55860-302-6.
[2] De Troyer O. "The OO-Binary Relationship Model: A Truly Object-Oriented Conceptual Model." In: Proceedings CAISE '91, Lecture Notes in Computer Science 498, "Advanced Information Systems Engineering", eds. R. Andersen, J.A. Bubenko jr., A. Sølvberg, Springer-Verlag 1991 (pp. 561-578).
[3] De Troyer O., "On Data Schema Transformations", Phd Thesis, ISBN 90-900591-3-X, Tilburg University, The Netherlands, 1993.
[4] De Troyer O., "A Logical Formalization of the Binary Object Role Model", in: T. Halpin and R. Meersman, eds., Proceedings of 1st Int. conference on Object Role Modelling, ORM-1 (University of Queensland, 1994).
[5] Genesereth M., Nilsson N., "Logical Foundations of Artificial Intelligence", Morgan-Kaufmann Publishers 1988. ISBN 0-934613-31-1
[6] Halpin T., "Conceptual Schema and Relational Database Design", 2nd edition, Prentice Hall, 1995. ISBN 0-13355702-2
[7] Kifer M., Lausen G., "F-logic: A Higher-Order Language for Reasoning about Objects, Inheritance, and Scheme", Proc. of ACM SIGMOD '89 (pp.134-146).
[8] Meinke K., Tucker J.V. (eds), "Many-sorted Logic and its Applications", John Wiley & Sons, 1993. ISBN 0-471-93485-2
[9] Ng P., "Further Analysis of the Entity-Relationship Approach to Database Design", Transactions on Software Engineering Vol. 7 No 1, January 1981.
[10] Reiter, R. "Towards a Logical Reconstruction of Relational Database Theory", in: On Conceptual Modelling: Perspectives from Artificial Intelligence, Databases, and Programming Languages, eds. Brodie M. L., Mylopoulos J., Schmidt J.W., Springer Verlag, New York 1984,.
[11] Sperschneider V., Antoniou G., "Logic: A Foundation for Computer Science", Addison-Wesley, 1991.
[12] Wintraecken J.J., "The NIAM Information Analysis Method; Theory and Practice", Kluwer Academic Publishers, 1990, ISBN 0-7923-0263-X.

Object-Oriented Meta Modelling

Motoshi Saeki

Dept. of Computer Science,
Tokyo Institute of Technology,
Ookayama 2-12-1, Meguro-ku, Tokyo 152, Japan

Abstract. For efficient system specification development, it is very important that the developers can compose the development methods suitable for their problem domain and environment before starting system development. Method Engineering, especially meta-modelling technique, provides us with the powerful devices to compose the methods effectively. In this framework, we develop new methods and their supporting tools easily from the data base of the existing methods and/or method fragments (meaningful constituents of methods), called *method base*. This paper discusses a meta-modelling technique based on object-oriented concept for the method base system. Information hiding and inheritance mechanism in object-oriented concept provide method fragments with high modularity and reusability. Method fragments are modelled and described in object-oriented formal description language Object Z. We also discuss how to customize method fragments and to integrate them to a new method.

1 Introduction

Many methods and their supporting tools, so called CASE tools, have been developed to support system specification and design processes, and some of them have been put into practice[7]. However, the effects of used methods greatly depend on problem domain where the system to be developed is. That is to say, some methods work well in specific problem domain and do not work well in the other domain. For example, it was pointed out that data flow diagrams (DFDs) are not suitable for developing real-time systems and incorporating state transition diagrams to DFDs is needed[14]. What method is the most suitable for specification development in every problem domain? We think that the answer is "none". It is difficult to have an universal method which works well in every domain. The best solution that we can consider is that the developers compose suitable methods for their problem domain and development environment.

Method Engineering[4], especially meta-modelling technique, provides us with the powerful devices to develop methods effectively. According to [10], we could compose new methods and their supporting tools easily from a data base of the existing methods and/or method fragments (meaningful constituents of methods), called *method base*. How to extract method fragments and to store them in a method base is closely related to the meta-modelling technique that we employ. We should construct meta models of method fragments so that we can retrieve, customize, and integrate the method fragments into a new method which we aim at.

This paper discusses object-oriented meta modelling techniques to construct a method base which holds method fragments of high reusability and customizability. The reason why we have employed object-orientation concept is that it provides high modularity and reusability resulting from information hiding and inheritance mechanism. The organization of the paper is as follows. In the next section, we introduce our meta modelling technique based on object-oriented technique. In our approach, method fragments are described in object-oriented formal description language Object Z[3]. In the sections 3 and 4, we will illustrate how to customize method fragments and how to assemble and integrate method fragments into a method. Finally, we will discuss the research directions to developing a practical method base based on our technique.

2 Meta Modelling based on Object-Oriented Concept

2.1 Meta Modelling

Meta modelling is modelling system development methods or method fragments which they have as meaningful constituents. Until now, several meta modelling techniques based on Entity Relationship Model[11, 1], Attribute Grammer[5], and Predicate Logic[1]. Entity Relationship Model has been widely used on account of its simplicity and easiness to implement in conventional CASE tools.

Meta modelling techniques for a practical method base should provide high modularity and reusability on method-fragment descriptions. High modularity provides modifiability of method fragments. If method-fragment descriptions have high modularity, the effect of modifying them is not propagated to the other fragment modules. It results in customizable method fragments. When composing the new method from method fragments, we have to specify constraints on the method fragments[8]. So the meta modelling techniques must have enough expressive power for the constraints.

Entity Relationship Model approach does not necessarily satisfy the above requirements. In particular, it cannot represent more complex constraints although it can specify the cardinality of relationships, e.g. one-to-many. Thus we need another device such as Predicate Logic so that it can specify the varieties of complex constraints on method fragments. Furthermore almost all of the existing modelling techniques did not consider the modularity and reusability of the described method fragments.

Object-oriented approach for software development provides high reusability and modularity of software components. So we adopt object-oriented approach to meta-modelling and represent meta-models, i.e. description of methods, in an object-oriented language. We call our approach *object-oriented meta modelling*. Furthermore we use more expressive and formal language such as Object Z. Object Z is an object-oriented extended version of Z[12] based on ZF set theory and Predicate Logic. Logical formulas in Predicate Logic are very powerful to express any constraints on method fragments. Similar to complex constraints on a method fragment, intra-constraints can be expressed in logical formulas of Object Z.

2.2 Object-Oriented Meta Modelling

The major aim of development methods is the navigation of the human activities to develop information systems. The methods tell the developers what artifacts such as documents and codes they should produce in a development process, and what activities and in what order the workers should perform for producing their artifacts. Thus we can consider that a method has two types of information — the structure of the artifacts to be produced and the procedures to produce them.

In our approach, we define a method or method fragment (we will use representatively the word "method fragment" below for simplicity) as a class, and its object instances denote the application instances of the method fragment. The structure of artifacts produced according to the method fragment is defined as attributes of the class corresponding the method fragment. Operations on object instances, which are encapsulated in a class definition, express method procedures for producing the artifacts. In the example of Object Diagram of Coad & Yourdon's OOA[2], the method procedure "identifying objects" is defined as an operation to the object instances whose class is Object Diagram. These operations change the attribute values of the object instance. Suppose that you develop a lift control system using an object diagram as shown in Figure 1. The information of the object diagram you are developing is stored as attribute values. When you identify an object "Emergency button", i.e. execute the operation "IdentifyObjects(Emergency Button)", the emergency button object is added to the attribute value.

Figure 2 shows a part of a meta model of Object Diagram described in Object Z, which is also represented in Entity Relationship Model approach in the figure. By using Object Z, we can specify formally method procedures as operations. Their definitions include the pre-conditions which hold before their execution, and post-conditions which hold after their execution. In the case of "IdentifyStructures", the inputs *"parent?"* and *"child?"* are included in the identified objects before its execution. It means that the method procedure "IdentifyObjects" should be performed to identify the objects ""*parent?*" and *"child?*" before the execution of "IdentifyStructures". After its execution, the relation *"parent? ↦ child?"* is added to the relationship *"aggregation"*. Pre- and post-conditions can specify the execution order of method procedures. We must note briefly the conventions on variables used in operation Z schema. The Δ notation in the signature part (variable declaration part : the upper of the Z schema) declares the variables whose values may be updated by the operation. The state variables with the prime (') decoration represent the state after the operation, while the variables which are not decorated represent the state before the operation. Inputs and outputs of the operation are denoted by the variables with "?" and "!" respectively. The symbol $\mathbb{P}$ dotes the power set.

3 Method Customization

One of the major characteristics of object-orientation is *inheritance* mechanism. The attributes and operations of a super class are inherited to its sub classes. So we do not need to re-define attributes and operations that its super class has. This mechanism allows us to define new method fragments incrementally

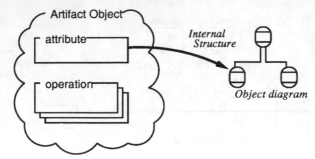

(a) Class for Method Fragments

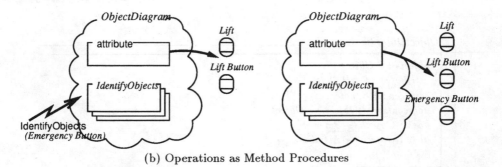

(b) Operations as Method Procedures

Fig. 1. Object-Oriented Meta-Modelling

and helps us to customize the existing method fragments to new ones[9, 6]. We select the method fragment that we will customize, and defines a new method fragment, its customized version, as its sub class. We newly describe the parts that are different from the original method fragment. Lets' consider a simple example of the customization of Entity Relationship Diagram to Object Diagram as shown in Figure 3. Object Diagram can be considered as a specialization of Entity Relationship Diagram because the constituents of Entity Relationship Diagram is a proper subset of Object Diagram's. The first line of class definition "ObjectDiagram" declares that Object Diagram class is a sub class of "Entity Relationship Diagram". Object Diagram class has two special relationships "aggregation" and "classification", and the concept "service", so all that we must do is to define them in "ObjectDiagram" class. Thus we additionally define dashed boxes and dashed arrows in the right side of diagrams in Figure 3.

4 Method Integration

The functions to assemble and integrate method fragments into a new method or new method fragment is very important. New constraints among method fragments appear in method-integration processes. Consider that we integrate the method fragment Object Diagram, shown in Figure 2, and State Transition

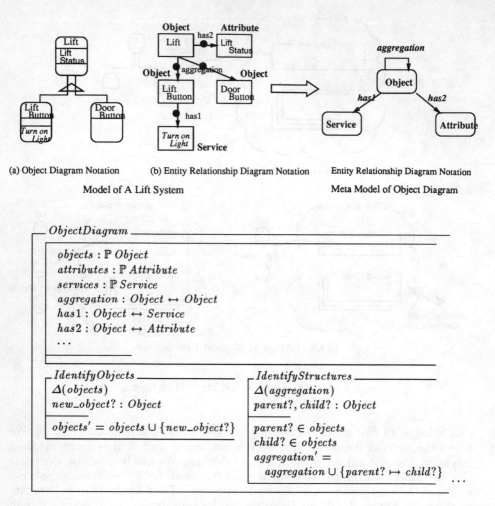

(a) Object Diagram Notation

(b) Entity Relationship Diagram Notation

Entity Relationship Diagram Notation

Model of A Lift System

Meta Model of Object Diagram

Object Z Notation
Meta Model of Object Diagram

Fig. 2. Examples of Artifacts and Meta Models

Diagram. State Transition Diagram is used to specify behavior of objects appearing in object diagram descriptions. So we must have a relationship between the attribute "Object" in the Object Diagram and the State Transition Diagram class. In addition, we have to define constraints associated with the relationship. New constraints are represented in relationships among the method fragments and logical formulas can be used to express complex constraints. To inherit the properties of the assembled method fragments to the new method, we use multiple inheritance mechanism. The new method also has the attributes and the operations of the assembled method fragments. The outlined sketch of method

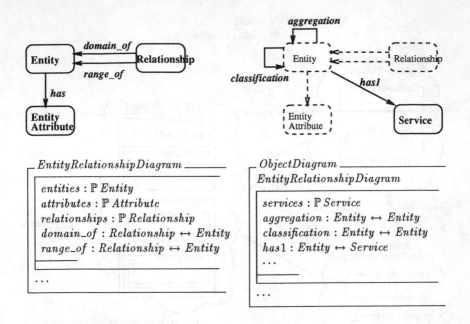

Fig. 3. Customizing ER Diagram to Object Diagram by Incremental Inheritance

integration is shown in Figure 4. In the figure, Method#1 and Method#2 are assembled and integrated into IntegratedMethod. Method#1 class, i.e. Artifact#1, and Method#2 are connected under some constraints to get the consistent integrated method. These constraints can be considered as a relationship among them. IntegratedMethod are composed with inheritance from Method#1 and Method#2. The attributes and the operations of Methods #1 and #2 are inherited to IntegratedMethod. The relationship between Methods #1 and #2 is embedded as a new attribute to IntegratedMethod.

We show the details by using the integration of Object Diagram and State Transition Diagram. Any object occurring in an object diagram has internal state and input events to the object change the state. This state-change may be specified in a state transition diagram. In this case, the constraints among Object Diagram and State Transition Diagram are

1. An object has a state transition diagram,
2. Any input event occurring in the state transition diagram is defined in a service of the object.

These constraints are defined as a relationship in the Z schema *connection_between_OBJD_and_STD* and specified in the logical formulas of the predicate part of the Z schema as shown in Figure 5.

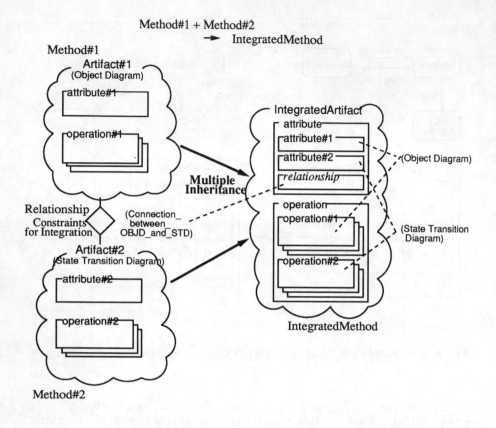

Fig. 4. Method Fragment Integration

5 Towards A Method Base System — Future Directions

A method base system provides the functions to store method fragments, to get suitable fragments, and to assemble and integrate them into a new method. It also generate a CASE tool for supporting the new method. In this section, we discuss the directions to method base development based on our meta-modelling technique.

First, we should consider the representation form of the artifacts to provide the CASE tool that supports their development. The existing practical methods have various kinds of representation form such as graphs, tables, and even structured text to enhance comprehensiveness and user-friendly interface to the workers. For example, we generally use a graph consisting of circles, rectangles, pairs of bars, and arrows to represent a data flow diagram. The workers input and edit graphs, figures, tables, and texts by the CASE tool. Therefore we need embed the information on artifact representation to the meta-model to implement a practical method base.

Second, how do we generate a new CASE tool supporting the new integrated method? One of the solutions is to hold not only method fragments but also their

```
┌─ ObjectDiagram ──────────────────        ┌─ StateTransitionDiagram ─────────
│                                          │
│  objects : ℙ Object                      │  states : ℙ State
│  attributes : ℙ Attribute                │  transitions : ℙ Transition
│  services : ℙ Service                    │  events : ℙ Event
│  aggregation : Object ↔ Object           │  previous_to : Transition ⇸ State
│  has1 : Object ↔ Service                 │  next_to : Transition ⇸ State
│  has2 : Object ↔ Attribute               │  input_event : Transition ⇸ Event
│                                          │  output_event : Transition ⇸ Event
│  ─────────────────────────────          │  ────────────────────────────────
│  . . .                                   │  . . .
└──────────────────────────────────        └──────────────────────────────────
```

```
┌─ connection_between_OBJD_and_STD ───────────────────────────────────────
│  connect : ObjectDiagram ↔ (Object ⇸ StateTransitionDiagram)
│  ──────────────────────────────────────────────────────────────────────
│  ∀ objd : dom connect • objd.objects = dom(ran connect)
│  ∀ obj : dom(ran connect); objtostd : ran connect
│       • input_event.objtostd(obj) ⊆ service.obj
└──────────────────────────────────────────────────────────────────────────
```

$$\Downarrow$$

```
┌─ IntegratedMethod ──────────────────────────────────────────────────────
│  ObjectDiagram
│  StateTransitionDiagram
│  ──────────────────────────────────────────────────────────────────────
│    connection_between_OBJD_and_STD
│
└──────────────────────────────────────────────────────────────────────────
```

Fig. 5. Method Fragment Integration Example

implementations in the method base. What is the implementation of a method
fragment? It can be considered as a part of a CASE tool, i.e. a tool fragment.
Suppose that our method base has a method fragment "Data Flow Diagram".
Its tool fragment is an editor for handling data flow diagrams. The method
base holds pairs of a method fragment and its tool fragment. Assembling and
integrating method fragments forces us to assemble their tool fragments into a
CASE tool. To maintaining consistency in artifacts on assembled CASE tool, we
should add a new function such as a consistency checker when assembling the tool
fragments as shown in Figure 6. Method engineers select method fragments from
method base and customize them by using a method editor. And they assemble
and integrate them to a method which they want. Method base holds method-
fragment implementations associated with their method-fragment specifications.
Method composer checks its consistency by performing the consistency checkers
which the implementations of the method fragments have.

The third point is concerned with how to store method fragments so that
the workers could retrieve them. Several information for the users of the method

258

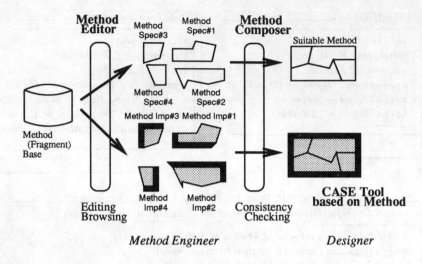

Fig. 6. Method Base System and Supporting Tools

base to retrieve the method fragments should be modelled. It may be modelled as attributes of method fragments and as relationships among them, and is related to the design of a schema of our method base. The method base schema can be sketched out as shown in Figure 7 when we use PCTE OMS[13] as a platform. The attributes of the method fragments shown in Figure 7, e.g. "difficulty", "domain", "keywords", "manual", and so on are examples of useful information for retrieval. The difficulty denotes the difficulty or simplicity of mastering the method fragment. The attribute "domain" shows the domain names, e.g. real-time system, business application, and data base system, where the application of the method fragment seems to be suitable. "Keywords" includes words which characterize the method fragments. The method engineer may use a thesaurus of keywords when retrieving method fragments by this attribute value. "Phase" denotes the phases in a system development process, e.g. requirements elicitation, data modelling, and architectural design, where the method fragment is suitably applied. These attributes and relationships for retrieval are just examples and we should explore effective attributes and relationships through many case studies.

The major hierarchy of method fragments in it results from super-sub class hierarchy. The relationship "is" between method fragments in Figure 7 stands for this hierarchy. Exploring super-sub class hierarchy is also one of the future work.

References

1. S. Brinkkemper. *Formalisation of Information Systems Modelling*. Thesis Publisher, 1990.
2. P. Coad and E. Yourdon. *Object-Oriented Analysis*. Prentice Hall, 1990.
3. R. Duke, P. King, R. Rose, and G. Smith. The Object-Z Specification Language.

259

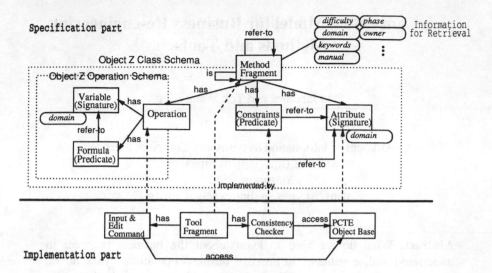

Fig. 7. Schema of A Method Base

Technical Report 91-1, Software Verification Center, University of Queensland, 1991.

4. F. Harmsen, S. Brinkkemper, and H. Oei. Situational Method Engineering for Information System Project Approaches. In *Methods and Associated Tools for the Information Systems life Cycle*, pages 169–194. North-Holland, 1994.

5. T. Katayama. A Hierarchical and Functional Software Process Description and its Enaction. In *Proc. of the 11th ICSE*, pages 343–352, 1989.

6. S. Kelly and V. Tahvanainen. Support for Incremental Method Engineering and MetaCASE. In *Proc. of the 5th Workshop on the Next Generation of CASE Tools*, pages 140–150, 1994.

7. T.G. Lewis. *CASE : Computer-Aided Software Engineering*. Van Nostrand Reinhold, 1991.

8. B. Nuseibeh, J. Kramer, and F. Finkelstein. Expressing the Relationships between Multiple Views in Requirements Specification. In *Proc. of the 15th ICSE*, pages 187–196, 1993.

9. M. Saeki and K. Wenyin. Specifying Software Specification & Design Methods. In *Lecture Notes in Computer Science (CAiSE'94)*, pages 353–366. Springer-Verlag, 1994.

10. K. Slooten and S. Brinkkemper. A Method Engineering Approach to Information Systems Development. In *Information System Development Process*, pages 167–186. North-Holland, 1993.

11. K. Smolander, K. Lyytinen, V.P. Tahvanainen, and P. Marttiin. MetaEdit — A Flexible Graphical Environment for Methodology Modelling. In *Proc. of 3rd International Conference CAiSE91, LNCS 498*, pages 168–193, 1991.

12. J.M. Spivey. *The Z Notation — A Reference Manual*. Prentice Hall, 1987.

13. L. Wakeman and J. Jowett, editors. *PCTE : The Standard for Open Repositories*. Prentice Hall, 1993.

14. P. Ward. The Transformation Schema : An Extension of the Data Flow Diagram to Represent Control and Timing. *IEEE Trans. on Soft. Eng.*, 2(12):198–210, 1986.

A Conceptual Model for Business Re-engineering Methods and Tools

Stan Jarzabek and Tok Wang Ling

Department of Information Systems and Computer Science
National University of Singapore
Singapore 0511
stan@iscs.nus.sg, lingtw@iscs.nus.sg

Abstract. What do we need to know about the business in order to understand and, eventually, to improve business operations? How do we capture the business knowledge? We feel that current business re-engineering methods do not have a precise enough model of the underlying business knowledge. A model should be comprehensive enough to allow for a systematic study and precise formulation of re-engineering methods. It should also provide a framework for designing tools to support business re-engineering projects. We identified information requirements for business re-engineering based on the commonly used business re-engineering methods and case studies published in the literature. We formalized these requirements within the business knowledge model that is described in this paper.

1. Introduction

Operational transformation of business is a hot topic on the agenda of corporate management. Trends such as business re-engineering, business process re-engineering, business redesign, process improvement and process innovation all emphasize the need for transformation of business operations in order to achieve improvements in productivity and quality. Such improvements are required for companies to remain competitive in the market. The scale of required changes varies from company to company and ranges from incremental improvement scenarios [4,8] to radical rethinking of the way business operates [6]. Operational changes are oriented on the customer and may involve, among others, simplification of the work flow, decentralization of responsibilities, standardization of procedures, reduction of redundant procedures and automation. Better use of information systems and technology often makes such changes possible [4,5,6,8,16]. In this paper, we assume an approach to business re-engineering in which the assessment of current business processes is done prior to the design of improved business processes. (Some other approaches advocate design of new business processes from scratch, based on company goals, to allow for radical changes without any limitations that may be implied by the current way of conducting business processes.)

We identified information requirements for business re-engineering based on the business re-engineering methods and case studies described in the literature. We formalized these requirements within the business knowledge model that is described in this paper. We feel that such a model is needed to allow for a systematic study and precise formulation of re-engineering methods and to facilitate demonstration of business re-engineering benefits and risks.

We model business features (such as a customer, business process or event) by frames [1]. Frames are organized into an inheritance network. Frame slots describe properties of features in the mixture of formal and informal specifications. A business knowledge model is bound to be complex. Therefore, *business analysts are not supposed to work directly with the model.* Tools are needed to provide an easy interface to the business knowledge stored according to the model, so that the model adds value to (rather than further complicates) business re-engineering projects. Our business model defines an internal mechanism for such tools [10].

The premise of our approach is that business re-engineering is a creative thinking process (like software or engineering design) and as such cannot be fully automated. But tools can assist business analysts in business re-engineering, just like CASE tools assist software engineers in software design. Many business process re-engineering planning techniques (interviews, business modeling workshops, performance analysis, etc.) can then be effectively supported by tools. Our business knowledge model is semi-formal and reflects this human-centered nature of the business re-engineering process.

In the remaining part of the paper, we describe the generic business knowledge model and explain how we use the model. In the another paper [10], we described in detail a model-based design of a tool environment for business re-engineering.

2. Relation to other work

Many sources discuss motivation for business re-engineering, describe detail business process re-engineering methods and discuss tools that can support business process re-engineering activities [4,6,7,8,15]. Some tools allow analysts to simulate and do performance analysis of business processes [7,15]. This is possible due to a well defined underlying model (usually based on a variant of Petri nets). Yu and Mylopoulos [17] show that by capturing goals, rules and methods we can formally reason about implications of proposed business process changes.

We agree with authors of simulation and reasoning tools that a possibly precise internal information model is the first necessary step towards building successful tools. We also think that to effectively support business analysts, the underlying model should comprehensively cover many aspects of business structure and dynamics. In addition to executability, the model should record the many kinds of dependencies between business entities that have to do with understanding of business operations. We hope the model described in this paper is a small step towards achieving this end.

3. A generic business knowledge model

The scope and detailed schema of a business knowledge model depend on the business re-engineering goals, on re-engineering methods to be used and on specifics of a company to be re-engineered. However, we can try to characterize a common core of business knowledge that, after customizations, can be reused across a range of companies and re-engineering projects. We build the core of a tool environment for business understanding and re-engineering around the generic business model. Tools support user-level views of the business model (such as action flowcharts of Fig. 5). The business knowledge model forms conceptual schema for the tool repository. Business re-engineering tools must be adaptable to versions of a generic business model customized to specific business re-engineering projects. To satisfy this requirement, we use a CASE generator that can construct editors from specifications of modeling methods. We derive the physical schema for the repository and generate customized tools from the customized business knowledge model specifications (Fig. 1).

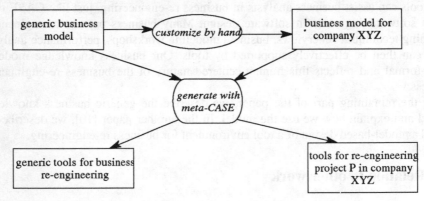

Fig. 1. Business model and tool customization

Many business modeling methods, both formal [2,12] and informal [8,15], have been described in the literature. Our approach is based on modeling concepts used by others. We model business in terms of *features*. Features are types of business entities that we want to analyze during business process re-engineering and about which we want to store information (Fig. 2-4).

Features are described by properties. For example, the feature *BusinessProcess* has properties such as process owner, cost, work flow, efficiency and many others. (For readability, in the remaining text feature and relationship names are in italic and start with a capital letter.) Features can be related one to another using inheritance, aggregation and association. Relationships may also have properties. Each feature property identifies a piece of knowledge about the business that must be collected during business re-engineering planning. A syntactic construct to describe properties of features is a *frame*, the term used in knowledge representation [1]. Frame slots contain properties of features.

3.1 Modeling features and feature relationships

We use Rumbaugh notation OMT [14] to model features. We chose OMT because it allows us to express the macro structure of the business knowledge model in a natural way. Figures 2-4 define the scope of the knowledge that we model[1] .

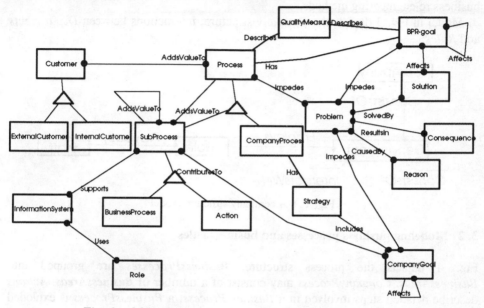

Fig. 2. Major features in a generic business knowledge model

Features are represented by rectangular boxes, triangles represent inheritance and lines between features represent binary relationships. Dots stand for 'many' connectivity in a relationship link. The meaning of a relationship link is clarified by the name attached to a link. In the inheritance link, a parent feature appears above the triangle and derived features appear below. We believe models are intuitive, so we only briefly comment on them. In Fig. 2, we see three types of processes derived from an abstract feature *Process*: a *CompanyProcess*, *BusinessProcess* and *Action*. *BusinessProcesses* represent well defined and important areas of company operations. *BusinessProcesses* are composed of *Actions*. We model company *Strategy*, *CompanyGoals* and *Problems* that impede *CompanyGoals* and *Processes*. We show how *Solutions* to *Problems* affect goals of business re-engineering (feature *BPR-goal*). Value-added impact of *Processes* on each other and on *Customers* are modeled by a family of relationships *AddsValueTo*. (Remark: A relationship defined for feature *Process* applies to all the features derived from *Process*.) The model also shows which *BusinessProcesses* and *Actions* contribute to which *CompanyGoals*. *CompanyGoals* and *BPR-goals* are organized into a hierarchy by relationship *Affects*. Based on feature *QualityMeasure*, *Process* quality can be judged. *QualityMeasure* represents performance measures (such as cost, resource consumption, duration and efficiency), effectiveness and adaptability. By examining *QualityMeasures*, we select candidates

---

[1] Business models are produced with MetaEdit, by MetaCase Consulting Oy.

for business re-engineering and evaluate the impact of business re-engineering on a company. Feature *QualityMeasure* can describe either the quality of current *Processes* or quality requirements to be met by re-engineered *Processes*. Target values for *Process* characteristics are set up based on company standards and world-class operation benchmarks [8]. Features *Solution* and *BPR-goal* reflect the application of business re-engineering methods.

Model in Fig. 3 depicts the *Company* structure, interactions between *Departments* and *Roles*.

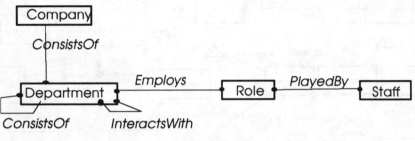

Fig. 3. A company structure model

3. 2 Modeling business processes and business rules

Fig. 4 depicts the process structure. *BusinessProcesses* are grouped into *BusinessAreas*. *CompanyProcess* may consist of a number of *BusinessAreas*. *Actions* describe detailed steps involved in a *BusinessProcess*: a *BusinessProcess* is exploded into level 1 *Actions*, each level 1 *Action* can be further exploded into more detail level 2 *Actions*, etc. One *Action* can be involved in many *BusinessProcesses*.

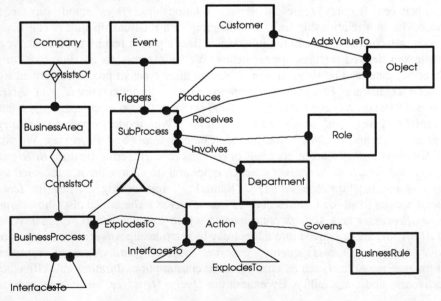

Fig. 4. A business process model

A *BusinessProcess* describes an end-to-end, usually cross-departmental, chain of business activities that deliver a product or service to a customer. *BusinessProcesses* are often triggered by external events, for example an arrival of a customer order. The *BusinessProcess* triggered by this event involves activities that start by customer order processing and end with product delivery to a customer. *BusinessProcesses* may also be initiated at fixed time intervals or when a certain condition arises. Feature *Event* models all situations that have to do with activation of a *BusinessProcess*. *Events* may also occur during *BusinessProcess* execution and influence execution of *Actions* that compose a *BusinessProcess*. *Action* execution is governed by *BusinessRules*.

The *BusinessProcess* structure can be depicted by a flow chart of *Actions* (Fig. 5). Each *Action* can be further exploded into a more detail flow chart. In Fig. 5, diamonds mark decision points at which alternative *Actions* can be taken. Issues that affect the decision are modeled as conditions. *BusinessRules* describe what happens at decision points or indicate chains of *Actions* that can be performed in parallel.

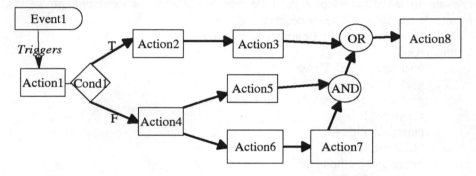

Fig. 5. A business process flow chart

In Fig. 5, Event1 triggers a business process whose first level of decomposition involves eight actions. After Action1 is completed, depending on condition 'Cond1', either Action2 or Action4 is initiated; Action3 is initiated once Action2 is completed; when Action4 is completed, Action5 may be performed in parallel with Action6 and Action7. In the diagram, small circles mark the end points of chains of alternative or concurrent *Actions*. Fat arrows depict flows of business objects (information, documents, materials, etc.) between *Actions*.

An action flow chart is an example of a *user-level view* of the business knowledge model. Many other useful views can be derived from our business knowledge model. User-level views are supported by tools that enable the staff involved in a re-engineering project to communicate with the model in an easy and intuitive way [10].

3. 3 Modeling properties of features and relationships

Features and feature relationships have properties. A *frame* [1] is a syntactical structure to define feature properties. For each feature, we have a corresponding frame (with the same name) that defines feature's properties. Each property has a name, value type and an optional value. Property values can be defined at any level of feature inheritance network and are subject to inheritance.

Property value types include usual basic types such as TEXT (free text), INTEGER, (n:m) (a range of integers between n and m), REAL, BOOL, CHAR, DATE and MONEY. Built-in types are written in capital letters. Often used property value type is an enumeration, e.g., TIME-UNIT = (minute, hour, week, month, year). Value types also include constraints and assertions expressed in a formal notation (value type FORMAL). User-defined value types include enumeration and faceted classification scheme [13]. Faceted classification consists of a set of typed keywords. Type name consists of feature name followed by keyword FACETS, such as CompanyGoal-FACETS in the example below. CompanyGoal-FACETS might specify the nature of a *CompanyGoal*. For example, *CompanyGoal* "increase revenue from sales" might be specified by types of issues involved: [Activity : Sales], [Measure : Money], [Objective : Increase], etc. If lists of keywords are used uniformly across features, faceted classification scheme enables one to selectively extract features relevant to a certain aspect. For example, one can retrieve all the *CompanyGoals* relevant to sales. Facets provide a flexible mechanism for extending pre-defined feature descriptions, whenever necessary.

Below is an example of a *CompanyGoal* frame:
CompanyGoal
      goal-name : TEXT <u>ident</u>
      goal-description : TEXT
      goal-specs : CompanyGoal-FACETS
      priority : (1:5)
      current-rating : (1:5)
      target-rating : (1:5)
      evaluation-method : TEXT
      due-date : DATE
end CompanyGoal
Explanations: Underlined <u>ident</u> indicates that a *CompanyGoal* is identified by a unique goal-name. Other properties describe *CompanyGoal's* priority on the scale between 1 and 5, assess current level of *CompanyGoal's* satisfaction, explain how to evaluate the level of *CompanyGoal's* satisfaction and provide the date by which the *CompanyGoal* should be met.

SubProcesses are related to *CompanyGoals* (Fig. 2). Properties of relationship *ContributesTo* include:
ContributesTo (SubProcess, CompanyGoal)
      description-of-contribution : TEXT
      evaluation-method : TEXT
      current-rating : (1:5)
      target-rating : (1:5)
end ContributesTo
The reader can find more examples of frames in [11].

4. Modeling objects

Often problems occur at the interface points between *Actions* or between *BusinessProcesses*. Therefore, we explicitly model process interfaces (Fig. 4). Process interfaces are described in terms of objects that are transferred among processes. An OBJECT is a family of features such as *Material, Document, Information, File, Database,* etc. OBJECTs are produced and received by processes (relationships *Receives* and *Produces* in Fig. 4). OBJECT properties include attributes, methods and constraints. Some of the *Actions* can be often mapped into OBJECT methods. For example, *Action* "print invoice" is likely to be a method "Print" of document "Invoice". We refer the reader to [11] for more details.

As during business re-engineering attention is focused on processes, some of the authors do not consider modeling of objects essential [15]. However, we feel that modeling objects offers the following three advantages to business re-engineering:

1. With objects we can better describe interfaces among processes.
2. Object analysis enables us to capture rules that characterize business operations in general rather then particular instances of business rules.
3. Object models form a natural link between business models and software systems to support business operations after re-engineering. Some of the objects correspond to entities that will be represented in future software systems. Software requirements can be formulated in terms of such objects and the first-cut software architecture can be derived from them. Some of the object methods form sound candidates for software modules. With object models, business analysis, business process re-engineering and future software development efforts can be addressed within a common modeling framework.

5. Who and how is going to use the business knowledge model?

Two different stakeholders use the business model, namely business analysts and designers of tools for business understanding and re-engineering. To *business analysts* the business knowledge model helps in planning a business re-engineering project. In particular, the model identifies types of business knowledge that must be collected during business re-engineering planning, defines parameters by which the quality of business processes and the impact of a business re-engineering project on a company can be judged, provides a reference model for business re-engineering methods and supports the many types of business analysis required in business re-engineering.

Business analysts are not supposed to work directly with the model. Tools are needed to provide an easy, intuitive and diagram-based access to the business knowledge. The business model defines an internal mechanism for such tools. To the *designers of business re-engineering tools,* the business knowledge model defines a framework for automation of some of the routine tasks involved in business process re-engineering. In particular, the model defines conceptual schema for a repository where all the business knowledge will be stored and through which various business re-engineering tools can be integrated.

6. Customization of the generic business model

A generic business knowledge model must be customized before it can be used on a specific re-engineering project. We customize the model by modifying properties of features and relationships, by modifying domains and values of properties and by defining company-specific OBJECT features. A customized business model is instantiated when we insert the actual business knowledge into the repository in the course of the business re-engineering project. As indicated in Fig. 1, a re-engineering expert must customize a generic model by hand. We customized the generic model using textbook case studies and generated tools from customized models. We have not identified essential problems with applying concepts described in this paper, but we have not done experiments in an industrial setting yet.

7. Conclusions

In this paper, we formalized information requirements for business re-engineering within a business knowledge model that:
1. Provides a reference model for business re-engineering methods. Business re-engineering methods can be related to the model and organized around it. In particular, for each business re-engineering method, the information that must be collected, the impact on business, etc. can be expressed in terms of the business knowledge model.
2. Defines the schema for a repository of the business knowledge. Tools can be implemented around the repository to provide a simple, user-friendly access to the business knowledge acquired in the course of a business re-engineering project.

The tools must be adaptable to versions of a generic business model customized to specific business re-engineering projects. To satisfy this requirement, we use a CASE generator that can construct editors from specifications of modeling methods.

We started a project with the Temasek Polytechnic in which we customize and refine our business model and tools. In this project, we shall validate the overall approach to model-based support for business re-engineering projects described in this paper. In the future, we plan to address business re-engineering methodology issues. If heuristic rules reflecting knowledge about re-engineering methods could be identified, then tools could also provide assistance for decision making and methodological guidance through out the business re-engineering project.

8. Acknowledgments

This work was supported by National University of Singapore Research Grant RP950616. Thanks are due to the students who implemented various components of tool prototypes. Seow Mui Leng refined the business model, implemented tools for graphical modeling, contributed diagrams to this paper and did a case study. Lau Ai Leng, Kuan Sook Peng and Catherine Tan implemented an interview assistant.

References

[1] Adeli, H. (editor) *Knowledge Engineering*, vol I, McGraw-Hill, 1990
[2] Berztiss, A. (1990) 'The Specification and Prototyping Language SF' Report No 78, SYSLAB, The Royal Institute of Technology, Sweden

[3] Chen, P. 'The Entity-Relationship model -- toward a unified view of data' *ACM Transactions on Database Systems*, vol. 1, no. 1, 1976, pp 9-36

[4] Davenport, T.H. *Process Innovation: Reengineering Work through Information Technology*, Harvard Business School Press, Boston, Massachusetts, 1993

[5] Dennis, A. et al "Methodology-Driven Use of Automated Support in Business Process Re-engineering," *Journal of Management of Information Systems*, vol. 10, no. 3, Winter 1993-94, pp. 117-138

[6] Hammer, M. and Champy, J. *Re-enginereing the corporation: A manifesto for business revolution*, Nicholas Brealey Publications, 1993

[7] Hansen, G. *Automating Business Process Re-engineering*, Prentice Hall, Englewood Cliffs, 1994

[8] Harrington, H. *Business Process Improvement*, McGraw-Hill, Inc., 1991

[9] Jarzabek, S. 'Life-cycle approach to Strategic Re-engineering of Software," *Journal of Software Maintenance: Research and Practice*, vol. 6, no. 6, November-December 1994, pp. 287-317

[10] Jarzabek, S. and Ling, T.W. "Model-based Design of Tools for Business Understanding and Re-engineering," *Proc. 7th Int. Workshop on CASE, CASE95*, Toronto, July 1995, pp. 328-337

[11] Jarzabek, S. and Ling, T.W. "Model-Based Support for Business Re-engineering," to appear in *Journal of Information and Software Technology*; also as *Technical Report TRC3/95,* Dept. Info. Syst. & Comp. Sc., National University of Singapore, March 1995

[12] McBrien, P. et al 'A Rule Language to Capture and Model Business Policy Specifications' *Proc. 3rd Int. Conference on Advanced Information Systems Engineering CAiSE'91,* Trondheim, May 1991, Lecture Notes in Computer Science, no. 498, Springer-Verlag, pp 307-318

[13] Prieto-Diaz, R. "Classification of reusable modules," *IEEE Software* 4(1), 1987, pp. 6-16

[14] Rumbaugh, J., Blaha, M., Premerlani, W., Eddy, F. and Lorensen, W. *Object-Oriented Modeling and Design,* Prentice-Hall, 1991

[15] Spurr, K., Layzell, P, Jennison, L. and Richards, N. *Software Assistance for Business Re-engineering,* John Wiley & Sons, 1993

[16] Strassmann, P. *The Business value of computers,* The Information Economics Press, 1990

[17] Yu, E.S.K. and Mylopoulos, J. "Using Goals, Rules and Methods to Support Reasoning in Buisness Process Reengineering," *Proc. 27th Annual Hawaii International Conference on System Sciences*, 1994, pp. 234-243

Data Model Evolution
as a Basis of
Business Process Management

Volker Gruhn[1], Claus Pahl[2], Monika Wever[1]

[1] LION Gesellschaft für Systementwicklung mbH, Universitätsstraße 140,
D–44799 Bochum
[2] Universität Dortmund, Fachbereich Informatik, Baroper Straße 301,
D–44221 Dortmund

Abstract. In this article we propose an approach to business process management which meets the demands of business process evolution. This approach allows for on–the–fly modifications of business processes. In contrast to many other approaches, we do not only concentrate on activities to be carried out in business processes, but also on the data created and manipulated by these activities. We propose to apply data model analysis and improvement strategies well–known from the information system field in the context of business process management.

Keywords
business processes, data model, data model analysis, evolution

1 Motivation

Business process (re–)engineering [10], process innovation [5] and continuous process improvement are buzzwords meaning more or less the same: to organize business processes in an efficient way. This may mean to completely redesign processes in order to achieve breakthroughs in productivity or it may mean to adapt an existing process to changing circumstances. Software processes are business processes in a software house. The question how to manage software processes has been addressed with increasing interest [17] during the last decade .

In the following we use the notion of *process* to denote general business processes as well as software processes. Process modeling, process model analysis, and the enaction of process models (i.e. to govern a real world process on the basis of an underlying model) is summed up as *process management*.

Analysis of process models turned out to be necessary in order to avoid the enaction of faulty process models. Process evolution turned out to be a central issue in order to ensure that process models can be adapted to changing circumstances. A closer look at existing process management approaches reveals that some provide analysis facilities for process models [3] while others somehow care for on–the–fly modifications of activity models [7]. Most however, do not support the analysis of data models and evolution of data which has already been produced by processes. Thus, the process management perspective could be called *process–oriented* (data models and database schemas underlying these processes are usually considered less important).

In contrast, research in the field of information systems deals with questions of what *good* data models should look like and how evolution of database schemas can be managed [1] without considering the business processes supported on top of the data stored in the database. Thus, in modeling information systems one usually starts from a *data–driven* perspective (i.e. what is the information to be administrated, how can this data be organized efficiently). Dynamic aspects of information systems are either — if at all — expressed in the form of integrity constraints or they are hard–wired in the form of application programs.

In this article we describe how the $\mathcal{L}eu$ approach [8] has been extended to cover data model analysis, improvement, and schema evolution.

In section 2, we briefly introduce our process management approach. In section 3, we discuss an example of a $\mathcal{L}eu$ process model in detail. Section 4 deals with requirements related to data model analysis and schema evolution. In section 5, we discuss the improvement mechanisms implemented in $\mathcal{L}eu$. Section 6 illustrates database evolution in relation to the example in section 3. Finally, section 7 concludes this paper with a discussion of experiences.

2 The $\mathcal{L}eu$ approach to process management

In the $\mathcal{L}eu$ approach we consider activity models, data models and organization models as constituent parts of process models [8]. In detail this means:

Data modeling: In $\mathcal{L}eu$, data models are used to describe the structure of objects which are manipulated within a process. Data models in $\mathcal{L}eu$ are described by means of extended entity–relationship diagrams [8].

Activity modeling: In $\mathcal{L}eu$, activity models are used to define activities to be executed in a process. Moreover, activity models define the order in which activities of a process have to be carried out. Activity models in $\mathcal{L}eu$ are described by means of FUNSOFT nets [6], which are high level Petri nets (compare section 3.4).

Organization modeling: Organization models in $\mathcal{L}eu$ are used to define which organizational entities are involved in a process. Organization modeling is based on a hierarchical role concept. Roles are sets of permissions for the execution of activities. Roles can be attached to organizational entities. Organization models in $\mathcal{L}eu$ are described by means of organizational diagrams which identify organizational entities and their hierarchical relationships.

Once these aspects of processes have been modeled, it is necessary to integrate them. A data model and an activity model are integrated by associating data model entities and activity parameters in a typing relation. An activity model and an organization model are integrated by associating organizational entities to those activities for which they are responsible.

3 Example of a process model

In this section we take a closer look at a data model and an activity model. This is illustrated by a simplified process model from the building construction administration area. The organizational structure is not discussed here since it is irrelevant for analysis, improvement and evolution of a data model.

3.1 Data modeling in *ℒeu*

Data modeling in *ℒeu* is based on extended entity–relationship diagrams (ER diagrams) [8]. Figure 1 shows a simplified data model for *lease management*.

Relationships can be of the cardinalities 1:1, 1:n, or n:m. This is depicted in single–ending and multi–ending edges. Furthermore, they can be mandatory or optional. This is represented by solid and dashed lines.

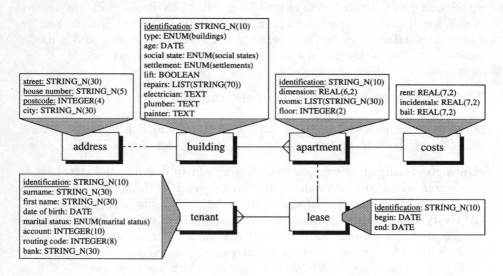

Fig. 1. Data model for lease management

Some object–oriented features have been introduced into the entity–relationship modeling as supported by *ℒeu*. First of all, we understand entity types as object types, i.e. each entity has a unique object identity. We use the term *object* to denote an entity. Objects can be of a predefined format (Postscript, WordPerfect documents, etc.) or of a complex type. Objects of these complex types are described by means of their attributes. Attributes can be mandatory or optional. Mandatory attributes can be used to compose a user–defined primary key of an object type. In figure 1 the primary keys are underlined. Non–primitive attribute types are lists that can be composed of primitive types and enumeration types which can be defined by the user.

Another object–oriented feature of *Leu* data modeling is the encapsulation of object types by means of user–defined operations. Each object can only be manipulated by means of operations attached to the corresponding object type. Moreover, we use the concept of delegation between object types [20] in order to define relationships between closely related object types. By means of delegation it is possible to enforce the execution of certain operations to be delegated to another object. Thus, the concept of delegation is applied to the type level *and* to the object level. This is the main difference to the inheritance concept. A more detailed motivation for using the delegation concept is described in [21].

3.2 Generating a database schema

A data model in *Leu* is used to describe the structure of objects which are manipulated within processes. To store these objects, a relational database schema is generated from the data model which is accessed within running processes interacting with process participants (compare figure 2).

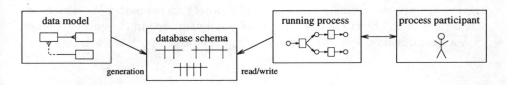

Fig. 2. Generation and use of a database schema

For each object type at least one table is generated. This table contains one column for each attribute and one additional column for a primary key called *surrogate*. A surrogate is an automatically generated identifier for an object. Several types of attributes offered by *Leu* are not supported by a relational database. For example, attributes like a list cannot be stored in one column of a flat relational table. Therefore, only the first element of a list is stored in the column of the list attribute. Additionally, a further table is generated to store the whole list. Attributes of enumeration or text types are treated similarly. For each n:m relationship one table is generated. It contains two columns for the surrogates of the two related object types. For other relationships the table of one object type contains an additional column to store the surrogates of the other object type as foreign keys. Figure 3 shows some of the tables generated for the *lease management*.

Basic operations for creation, update and deletion of objects are also generated out of the data model. Thus, the internal representation of objects in the database does not have to be known in order to store and retrieve objects. These operations (and some more sophisticated operations like *get–all–objects–of–type*) build a programming interface up to the generated database schema.

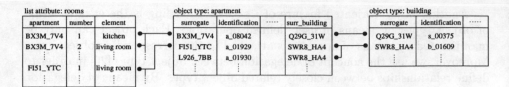

Fig. 3. Database schema for lease management

3.3 Access paths

To manipulate the objects stored in the generated database the activities carried out in the processes either use operations of the database programming interface or they use database queries. While the operations are sufficient for simple retrievals, individual queries covering objects of several types are needed for more complicated retrievals. They are formulated on the abstraction level of data models. Details of the internal database schema do not have to be known. In order to avoid potential performance problems caused by too complicated queries, the process modeler should describe object access paths. We define the access path of an object query as the set of attributes used in the query together with a quantification specifying how frequent the access path is used.

3.4 Activity modeling in $\mathcal{L}eu$

In $\mathcal{L}eu$, FUNSOFT nets are used to specify activities to be carried out and their order. FUNSOFT nets are high level Petri nets, of which semantics is defined in terms of Predicate/Transition nets [9]. In FUNSOFT nets, the T–elements (represented as rectangles) are called agencies. Agencies represent activities. S–elements (represented as circles) are called channels. They are used to store objects. FUNSOFT nets are hierarchically structured by means of T–element refinement [11]. FUNSOFT nets do not only contain a definition of activities and their parameterization, but also an order of activities. They allow to define that activities have to be carried out sequentially, concurrently or alternatively. For more details about FUNSOFT nets we refer to [6].

Figure 4 shows a FUNSOFT net which describes the activity model of agreeing on leases. In the upper branch of the net an apartment is selected. In the lower branch a potential tenant is selected. If an object of type *apartment* is available in channel *Apartment*[3] and if an object of type *tenant* is available in channel *Cleared tenant*, then agency *Write lease* can be started. The result is a lease which is then subject to the legal check.

---

[3] The annotation above a channel symbol displays the type of objects to be stored in this channel, the annotation below a channel symbol is the channel name.

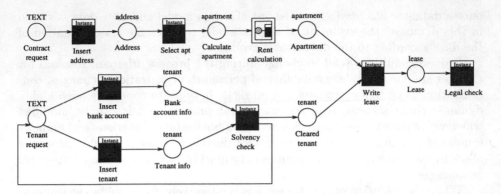

Fig. 4. Activity model for agreeing on leases

4 Related work

Process models used for governing real world processes are crucial for the efficiency of any business operation. Thus, process model analysis is necessary in order to avoid the enaction of inefficient and/or inconsistent process models. The analysis of activity models and organization models has been discussed intensively in the process management literature [13, 16]. In the following we will discuss some approaches which focus on data model analysis.

In principle, we can distinguish between data model analysis that is independent from an individual customer and customer–specific data model analysis. While the first kind of analysis can be realized without considering any details of customer circumstances, the latter requires detailed knowledge of the customer situation.

In [14] efficiency of data models is identified as one of the key success factors of any information system. Abstract properties of data models such as completeness, comprehensibility, simplicity, flexibility and others are considered as substantial properties of data models. The necessity to measure these properties on the basis of metrics and to develop improvement strategies is illustrated.

Unfortunately, properties like efficiency and completeness can only be checked with respect to individual customer situations. A data model consisting of a set of object types may, for example, be an efficient basis for processes being carried out at one company, while it can be awfully inefficient as a basis of the same processes carried out at another company. This may be due to differences in execution frequencies of processes or it may be due to different arrival frequencies of objects to be processed. Thus, information about the customer specific situation is needed in order to detect such data model shortcomings.

Once process models have been customized, the customer situation does not remain completely stable. Internal organization as well as legal changes and modified business targets demand process model flexibility. This flexibility concerns activity models, organization models, and data models as well as their integration. We realize an additional problem regarding the evolution of data models:

once a database has been generated out of a data model and once data is stored in this database, the evolution of a data model requires the transformation of the data according to the data model evolution.

Process conditions tend to change during the process' lifespan. Reasons for changes are, for example, availability of personnel, organizational changes, concentration on certain customers and markets. In order to cope with such highly dynamic circumstances, it is necessary that process models can be modified whenever required. General tendencies like globalization of markets and empowerment of people reinforce the demand for flexible processes. Flexible processes allow to react to market opportunities very quickly and thus obtain competitive advantages.

While the evolution of activity models is intensively discussed in the software process literature, the question how data models evolve is hardly considered in this context. In contrast, the question of schema evolution is discussed with respect to information system design and maintenance [12, 1]. Some approaches relevant to the work proposed in this article are discussed in the following.

In [15] different types of database schema evolutions for object–oriented database schemas are distinguished. Evolution of class definitions, evolution of relationships between class definitions and evolution of the set of class definition (add a class, delete a class, change name of a class) are identified as typical kinds of schema evolution. In [15] it is pointed out that most object–oriented database systems do not support the complete propagation of schema modifications to the object level. Mechanisms to manage this propagation are

- the use of an explicit *convert* operator which can be used to convert objects concerned when modifying a data model [19],
- an automatic start of propagation after each data model modification [2], or
- a propagation to an object as soon as this object is accessed [4].

The advantage of the manually started propagation is its efficiency because only objects actually needed in the future are converted. Its disadvantage is the danger of inconsistencies because old and not converted objects may exist at any time. The advantage of automatic propagation to all objects is its consistency, its disadvantage is its bad performance. In the ℒeu approach some object–oriented features like delegation between classes and objects (compare [20]) and association of object types and operations have been introduced into an entity-relationship oriented modeling. Thus, the types of modifications are obviously the same as discussed in [15]. Our conversion strategy is to convert all objects interactively in cooperation with the data modeler to ensure that information loss and inconsistencies can be minimized (compare section 6).

5 Analysis and improvement of data models

In this section we describe what kinds of data model analysis facilities are available in the ℒeu approach and which improvements of data models turned out to be typical in order to remove certain data model weaknesses. The work presented in this section is described in more detail in [18][4].

The data model improvement consists of two steps. First, the syntactical completeness of the data model is analyzed. It is examined whether all object types have attributes, relationships and primary keys and whether they are used by at least one access path. If all object types satisfy these demands, the data model is syntactically complete and its analysis will be continued. Then, four kinds of improvement are applied:

Removal of certain types of attributes: The representation of attributes of list, text and enumeration types in the database demands the generation of additional tables, as mentioned in section 3.2. Queries refering to attributes of such types have to access more than one table. The more tables a query accesses, the longer its execution will take. Therefore, the user should consider whether some lists, texts, or enumerations can be replaced by other types.

New relationships to avoid long access paths: The more object types a query uses, the more time takes its execution, because at least one additional table has to be accessed for each further object type. Hence, an access path should be as short as possible. In order to cut a long access path short, new relationships have to be added to the data model.

Merge of object types: Object types with a 1:1/mandatory:mandatory relationship are similar to one object type. Just looking at the syntax, they could be combined. However, this may not be appropriate looking at the object types' semantics. Hence, the mergence of object types can be proposed but the modeler must decide whether it is reasonable.

Split of object types: There are two reasons to split an object type. First, the attributes of the object type may be divided into two groups. Each of these groups of attributes is used by a group of access paths. There is no access path using attributes of both groups. In this case the unused attributes only enlarge the object type and slow down the execution time. Consequently, the object type should be split into two disjoined object types with one group of attributes belonging to each of them. Secondly, the attributes of the object type may also be divided into two groups but in a different way. One of these groups consists of very frequently used attributes. The attributes of the second group are used very rarely. In this case, the rarely used attributes enlarge the object type for access paths using only the frequently used attributes. Therefore, the object type should be split, too.

The user will be informed of all defects found by the analysis. The improvement only recommends certain data model changes to the modeler. He has to decide whether the proposed changes should be applied.

In the data model for *lease management* (figure 1) all four types of improvement can be applied. First, the building has one list attribute, three enumeration attributes and three text attributes. According to the first type of data model improvement (removal of certain types of attributes), some of these attribute

---

[4] Schneider Monika Wever's maiden name.

types should be changed. Assume the type *STRING_N(70)* is long enough to store the names of the craftsmen. Then the text attributes can be changed into strings. Secondly, the access path leading from *tenant* to *address* across *lease*, *apartment* and *building* is too long. Therefore a new n:1/mandatory:optional relationship between *tenant* and *address* will be added. Thirdly, *apartment* and *costs* will be merged by adding the attributes of *costs* to *apartment*. This way the 1:1/mandatory:mandatory relationship between them is dropped. Finally, the *tenant* will be split into *tenant* and *bank account*. This is based on an analysis of access paths implemented by the agencies of the activity model for *agreeing on leases* (figure 4).

All changes discussed above are only performed on the data model in the first instance. They also have to be propagated to the database schema. This means the generation has to be started again to change the tables of the schema according to the changes of the model. It would also be possible to delete the whole database schema and generate it again. But in most cases only a part of the data model is changed so that it takes less time to change the existing database schema.

6 Evolution

Business process models are subject to modifications because of changing circumstances. Sometimes, only activity models have to be changed. In other situations data models are concerned. Since modifications of the first kind have been addressed in the process literature, we will restrict to modifications that cause changes of data models.

Potential changes of a data model are: adding new object types or relationships, deleting object types or relationships, adding new attributes to object types, removing attributes and changing the types of attributes.

As an example four customer–specific changes are performed on the data model for *lease management*. A new text attribute called *form* is added to the object type *lease*. The attribute *lift* is removed from the object type *building*. The *postcode* is extended from a four–digit to a five–digit format. And finally, the type of *first name* is changed from string into a list of strings.

Further changes of data models can be due to additional or modified process models. If, for example, a new process has to be established, requirements for efficient access to certain data may change substantially.

When changes are performed on the data model, the generation procedure has to be started again to propagate them to the object level. This implements an immediate coercion strategy.

Whenever an attribute type is changed, the generation tries to minimize the loss of information. Loss of information can be avoided in the following cases:

– the length of an attribute type is extended
– an attribute type is changed from boolean, integer, real, time, or date to string,
– an attribute type is changed from single–valued to multi–valued, or

– an attribute type is changed from multi–valued to single–valued (only the first element of the list is kept).

In these cases the generation converts the values of the changed attributes automatically according to the new type. In all other cases an automatic conversion is impossible and the values are lost.

Besides the loss of information, the evolution of a data model causes other problems. Some of them are solved during the generation:

– Objects of optional attributes may contain null–values. If such an attribute is changed to mandatory, the generation will replace the null–values with dummy values.
– If a new attribute is added to an object type, all existing objects will have null–values in the column of this attribute. If the new attribute is mandatory, the generation will also replace the null–values with dummy values.

Other changes of data models are not automatically propagated to the object level in order to avoid inconsistencies in the database. Examples of such changes are given in the following. They all focus on the primary key of an object type:

– A new attribute is added to an object type without primary key. This new attribute must not be a primary key itself because its values are either null–values or dummy values and neither of them is unique.
– An existing attribute of an object type without primary key must not become a primary key because its values may not be unique.
– The number of attributes building the primary key of an object type must not become smaller because the values of the remaining primary key attributes may not be unique.
– The attribute type of a primary key must not be changed with loss of values because after the generation the lost values are replaced with dummy values that are not unique.

It is impossible to perform these changes on the database during the generation because reasonable unique values can not be created automatically. When some of these changes are necessary, the data modeler has to perform them "by hand" directly on the database.

To sum up, the generation of database schemas out of modified data models tries to minimize the loss of information. Whenever it cannot be avoided, the data modeler has to give his explicit agreement in order to avoid unexpected loss of information.

7 Conclusions

In our approach we deal with processes based on information systems. One of our main goals is a high degree of performance enacting these processes on information systems. Efficient storage and retrieval of data used by processes is crucial for achieving this goal. Therefore we presented methods for analysis and improvement of data models.

In this article we have motivated why evolution of data models is a prerequisite for flexible processes. Coping with evolution means being concerned with the problems of data integrity and loss of data. We have analysed possible changes in activity and data models and their effects on data. Our experience is that the benefits of graphical modeling of processes and the entailed easy modification of processes can only be fully exploited when data building the basis of processes can evolve according to changing circumstances and modified business goals.

Acknowledgements: We would like to thank all members of the $\mathcal{L}eu$ team for their cooperation in implementing these strategies. Moreover, we would like to thank Ernst–Erich Doberkat for fruitful discussions about focus and contents of the diploma thesis which contributed to this article.

References

1. J. Andany, M. Leonard, and C. Palissier. *Management of Schema Evolution in Databases*. In *Proceedings of the 17th Conference on Very Large Databases*, pages 161–170. Morgan-Kaufmann, 1991.

2. F. Bancilhon. *Object-oriented Database Systems*. In *Proceedings of the 7th ACM Symposium on Principles of Database Systems*, Austin, Texas, US, March 1987.

3. S. Bandinelli, A. Fugetta, and S. Grigolli. *Process Modelling In-the-Large with SLANG*. In *Proceedings of the 2nd International Conference on the Software Process - Continuous Software Process Improvement*, pages 75–83, Berlin, Germany, February 1993.

4. J. Banerjee, W. Kim, H.J. Kim, and H.F. Korth. *Semantics and Implementation of Schema Evolution in Object-Oriented Databases*. In *Proceedings of the Conference on Management of Data 1987*, 1987.

5. T. Davenport. *Process Innovation - Reengineering Work through Information Technology*. Harvard Business School Press, Boston, US, 1993.

6. W. Deiters and V. Gruhn. *Managing Software Processes in MELMAC*. In *Proceedings of the Fourth ACM SIGSOFT Symposium on Software Development Environments*, pages 193–205, Irvine, California, USA, December 1990.

7. W. Deiters, V. Gruhn, and H. Weber. *Software Process Evolution in MELMAC*. In Daniel E. Cooke, editor, *The Impact of CASE on the Software Development Life Cycle*. World Scientific, Series on Software Engineering and Knowledge Engineering, 1994.

8. G. Dinkhoff, V. Gruhn, A. Saalmann, and M. Zielonka. *Business Process Modeling in the Workflow Management Environment LEU*. In P. Loucopoulos, editor, *Proceedings of the 13th International Conference on the Entity-Relationship Approach*, pages 46–63, Manchester, UK, December 1994. Springer. Appeared as Lecture Notes in Computer Science no. 881.

9. H.J. Genrich. *Predicate/Transition Nets*. In W. Brauer, W. Reisig, and G. Rozenberg, editors, *Petri Nets: Central Models and Their Properties*, pages 208–247, Berlin, FRG, 1987. Springer. Appeared in Lecture Notes on Computer Science 254.

10. M. Hammer and J. Champy. *Reengineering the Corporation*. Harper Business, New York, US, 1993.

11. P. Huber, K. Jensen, and R.M. Shapiro. *Hierarchies in Coloured Petri Nets*. In *Proc. of the 10th Int. Conf. on Application and Theory of Petri Nets*, pages 192–209, Bonn, FRG, 1989.

12. M. Jarke, J. Mylopoulus, J.W. Schmidt, and Y. Vassiliou. *DAIDA - An Environment for Evolving Information Systems*. ACM Transactions on Information Systems, 10(1):1–50, January 1992.

13. M.I. Kellner and G.A. Hansen. *Software Engineering Processes: Models and Analysis*. In B.D. Shriver, editor, *Proceedings of the 22nd Annual Hawaii International Conference on System Sciences, Vol. II*, 1989.

14. D.L. Moody and G.G. Shanks. *What Makes a Good Data Model? Evaluating the Quality of Entity Relationship Models*. In P. Loucopoulos, editor, *Proceedings of the 13th International Conference on the Entity-Relationship Approach*, pages 94–111, Manchester, UK, December 1994. Springer. Appeared as Lecture Notes in Computer Science no. 881.

15. G. Nguyen and D. Rieu. *Schema Change Propagation in Object-Oriented Databases*. In G.X. Ritter, editor, *Information Processing 89*, pages 815–820. Elsevier, 1989.

16. A. Oberweis, P. Sander, and W. Stucky. *Petri net based modelling of procedures in complex object database applications*. In D. Cooke, editor, *Proceedings of the COMPSAC 1993*, Phoenix, Arizona, US, 1993.

17. W. Schäfer, editor. *Software Process Technology - Proceedings of the 4th European Workshop on Software Process Modelling*, Noordwijkerhout, The Netherlands, April 1995. Springer. Appeared as Lecture Notes in Computer Science 913.

18. M. Schneider. *Werkzeuge zur Optimierung erweiterter Entity–Relationship Modelle und deren Abbildung in ein relationales Datenbankschema (in German)*. August 1994. Diplomarbeit, University of Dortmund.

19. A. Skarra and S. Zdonik. *The Management of Changing Types in an Object-Oriented Database*. In N. Meyrowitz, editor, *Object-Oriented Programming Systems, Languages and Applications (OOPSLA) 1986 - Conference Proceedings*, pages 483–495, Portland, Oregon, USA, October 1986. ACM Press.

20. R. Wieringa, W. de Jonge, and P. Spruit. *Roles and dynamic subclasses: a modal logic approach*. In M. Tokoro and R. Pareschi, editors, *Proceedings of the European Conference on Object-Oriented Programming, Bologna*, pages 32–59, Berlin, 1994. Springer. Appeared as Lecture Notes in Computer Science no. 821.

21. W. Wilkes. *Instance Inheritance Mechanisms for Object Oriented Databases*. In K. Dittrich, editor, *Advances in Object-Oriented Database Systems*, pages 274–279, Berlin, 1988. Springer. Appeared as Lecture Notes in Computer Science no. 334.

Reengineering Processes
in Public Administrations

Silvana Castano[1] and Valeria De Antonellis[2]

[1] University of Milano, ITALY
e-mail: castano@dsi.unimi.it
[2] University of Ancona and Politecnico di Milano, ITALY
e-mail: deantone@elet.polimi.it

Abstract. The paper presents a methodological approach to the reengineering of work processes. Reengineering in the Public Administration domain is considered, and tools to support the analysis, classification and composition of processes are presented. In particular, the organization of a library of process specifications is described.

1 Introduction

Process reengineering is generally considered a challenging and critical issue for organizations, since it has the objective of optimizing work processes (information processes and material processes) with respect to business aspects, such as, efficiency of business operations, customer satisfaction, improvement of product quality [7]. The premise to perform process reengineering is to correctly understand and capture the processes themselves. For this purpose, models and methodologies for workflow specification are currently under study in literature, to describe, possibly formally, the constituents of a process, that is, tasks (a piece of work to be done), roles or executing entities (one or more people, or a software system), and relationships among tasks (dependency rules, constraints) [9].

The need of methods and techniques to support process reengineering is more and more relevant in the Public Administration (PA) domain. In fact, over the years, continuous modifications of Information Systems to cope with changing requirements and business rules has lead to a proliferation of partially overlapping data and processes, which are source of potential inconsistencies [1]. The lack of standardized data and process structures across Information Systems makes process reengineering a crucial activity for PA, and methodological support is required. In particular, when only few processes are automatically performed, the level of computerization must be determined during reengineering, in order to plan automation interventions. When downsizing strategies are adopted, guidelines for the migration towards new architectures have to be provided.

In this paper we provide modeling techniques and tools to support these activities. In particular, we propose the organization of a library containing process specifications accessible through similarity-based retrieval tools. For process specifications we refer to our experience with the Italian Information System Authority for Public Administration (AIPA), that is pursuing a deep revision and redesign of work processes in the Public Sector, to meet growing and changing needs of clients and the general public.

The paper is organized as follows. In Sect.2, basic definitions and modeling concepts are described. Sect.3 introduces the structure of the process specifications library. In Sect.4, criteria and techniques for building the library are provided. Sect.5 illustrates possible uses of the library. Finally, in Sect.6, concluding remarks are stated.

2 Basic definitions and reference concepts

PA processes are work processes with the following characterisics. They are performed either manually by humans, or automatically by a program or a computer system, or by both. They create, destroy, transfer and manipulate information. For example, the process "Employee Engagement" receives information on curriculum of people and on the results of a public competition, and produces the dossiers for the selected people, which are engaged as employees of PA departments. PA processes are classified into *service processes*, whose objective is to provide a service to a user external to the PA (e.g., releasing a document), and *autoadministration processes*, which provide a service for users internal to the PA. Service processes are organized at a higher-level of abstraction into *macroprocesses*, that is, complex activities with a well defined objective, pursued by means of the coordinated execution of the constituent processes. For example, the "Engagement Management" is composed of the processes to be performed to take on a new staff, such as "Employee Selection", "Employee Engagement", "Job Assignment". Processes communicate through data bases and information. Executing entities are the Organizational Units (OU), which can be client or supplier of a process, as well as software applications.

Actually, we are working on process descriptions provided by AIPA, in form of questionnaires, natural language texts, and conceptual schemas. According to the characteristics and the abstraction level of the analyzed descriptions, we describe macroprocesses with workflows, and PA processes with tasks; OUs correspond to executing entities of a workflow specification.

AIPA collected information about PA processes through a set of properly defined questionnaires, released to experts and users of various OUs, in order to acquire as much information as possible on processes and data circulating among them. On the basis of the collected information, process specifications have been defined for PA processes. A process specification is composed of:

- The name of the process, univocally identifying the process within the OU to which it pertains. The name is composed of an *identifier* $\langle P\_ID, OU\_ID \rangle$ (where P_ID is the process identifier, and OU_ID is the OU identifier), and of a *title*, which is a string.
- A textual information, which provides general description of the process and its functionality. It is a natural language description of input/output data,

starting/ending events, possible supporting application program(s), type of the process (e.g., management, administration).

- An Entity-Relationship (ER) conceptual schema, which describes the data used by the process, in form of entities and relationships among entities. The ER model has been chosen to provide a conceptual level of description, independent of the support on which data are stored, to facilitate data analysis during reengineering.

Currently, we are analyzing about 150 process specifications to be used for reconstructing information flows and workflows between processes, possibly crossing different functional areas.

3 Library of process specifications

Libraries capable of supporting systematic organization and classification of data and process specifications are essential for reengineering, to facilitate systematic analysis, retrieval, and integrated reconstruction of data and processes [1,4].

A fundamental problem in organizing a library is to define proper classification models to store elements in an organized way, for effective search and retrieval. Classification models have been proposed in the domain of reuse to build and use libraries of software components [11,8,10]. Affinity criteria based on the structure of components in a conceptual schema have been proposed by the authors, to construct a library of conceptual components to be used as the starting point in designing Information System conceptual schemas [2,3].

In this paper we propose a classification model based on the use of *descriptors*, to organize process specifications in a library, and a set of *similarity criteria*, to support flexible retrieval of process specifications from the library (that is, retrieval of specifications of similar processes, as well as of processes operating on similar data). The classification model is described in Sect. 3.1, while similarity criteria are illustrated in Sect. 3.2.

3.1 Classification model

Our model for classifying and computing similarity between processes is based on having a library of process specifications. The specifications are described by means of *descriptors* which allow the computation of similarity coefficients between corresponding processes.

A process descriptor is a 6-tuple:

$$\langle \textit{F-Area, I-Object, O-Object, Operation, Const-Object, Circ-Object} \rangle$$

where:

- *F-Area* is a feature characterizing a process with respect to the functional area to which it pertains within the organization. In our case, a functional area corresponds to an OU within a PA department.

- *I-Object* is a feature characterizing a process with respect to its input data. One or more entities can be specified, that represent the entities required by the process to be executed.
- *O-Object* is a feature characterizing a process with respect to its output data. One or more entities can be specified, that are the entities produced/modified as a result of process execution.
- *Operation* is a feature characterizing a process with respect to its performed operation.
- *Cons-Object* is a feature characterizing a process with respect to the mandatory constitutive entities required by its operation. One or more entities/roles can be specified in this feature.
- *Circ-Object* is a feature characterizing a process with respect to the optional circumstantial data involved in its operation. One or more entities/roles can be specified in this feature.

Features *I-Object* and *O-Object* describe the data manipulated by a process. Features *Operation, Const-Object,* and *Circ-Object* describe process functionality in a disciplined way, following the approach for process requirement analysis presented in [6].

A feature f has a set of related *terms*. Each process specification defines a mapping between each feature f and one term t (or a set of terms $t_1, \ldots, t_n$), which is (are) the terms describing the process with respect to f.

For example, let us consider the process "Employee Engagement", hiring new people, on the basis of the results of a public competition. People are allocated on the basis of their preferences and of their professional skills specified in the curriculum. The process produces a contract for each new engaged employee, and assigns an employee to a given PA department. Specification of process "Employee Engagement" could be described by means of the descriptor shown in Fig. 1.

Employee Engagement

```
⟨F-Area⟩:        General Management of General Affairs and Personnel
⟨I-Object⟩:      { Curriculum, Employee, Organization, Professional role }
⟨O-Object⟩:      { Contract, Employee, Department }
⟨Operation⟩:     Engage
⟨Cons-Object ⟩:  Employee
```

Fig. 1. An example of process descriptor

We state that two features f and f' are *comparable* if they both refer to the same set of terms (i.e., entity names or operation names). Pairs of corresponding features in different process descriptors are comparable by definition (in the following, we will refer to these features as comparable and equal features). In addition, features *I-Object*, *O-Object*, *Cons-Object*, and *Circ-Object* are comparable too (they refer to the set of terms that are entity names).

Features of descriptors are filled in with terms extracted from process specifications, selected for their capability of providing a suitable characterization of a process with respect to each feature. Terms are extracted according to the following extraction method:

- Terms of features *I-Object*, *O-Object*, *Cons-Object*, and *Circ-Object* are extracted from conceptual schemas and textual documentation of process specifications, by examining entity names therein contained.
- Terms of feature *Operation* are extracted from textual documentation in process specifications, according to the categories of operations presented in [6], which are: exchange of objects with outside; creation of objects; transformation of objects; modification/observation of the status of input objects; deletion or removal of objects; actions on roles.

3.2 Criteria for process specification comparison

Criteria for comparing process specifications are defined, allowing flexible retrieval of specifications from the library. Process specifications are compared on the basis of the information contained in the descriptors associated with them. Let P_i and P_j be two process specifications, and $D(P_i)$, $D(P_j)$ their corresponding descriptors. Basic criteria for process specification retrieval are the *similarity* criterion and the *closeness* criterion.

Similarity

Two process specifications P_i and P_j are said to have similarity if they perform the same or similar operations, on the same or similar entities. To evaluate process similarity, the terms specified in the features of their associated descriptors are compared. Depending on the features considered, the following types of similarity are defined.

- **Functionality similarity.** This criterion captures the similarity of P_i and P_j with respect to their performed operations. Terms specified in features *Operation*, *Cons-Object*, and *Circ-Object* of $D(P_i)$ are compared with the terms of each corresponding feature of $D(P_j)$, to establish their level of similarity.
- **Entity similarity.** This criterion captures the similarity of P_i and P_j with respect to their input entities, or to their output entities, or to both. Terms specified in feature *I-Object* (respectively, *O-Object*) of $D(P_i)$ are compared with the terms specified in the feature *I-Object* (respectively, *O-Object*) of $D(P_j)$, to establish their level of similarity.

Note that a similarity criterion involving feature *F-Area* is not useful, because the user generally looks for process specifications of a certain functional area, that is, the extact matching criterion is used.

Closeness

Two process specifications P_i and P_j are said to have closeness if they are related by means of an information flow. An information flow exists between P_i and P_j if at least one output entity of P_i is equal or similar to an input entity of P_j, or vice versa. To evaluate process closeness, features *I-Object* and *O-Object* of process descriptors are compared. The more the common entities, the higher the process closeness. Precisely, the following closeness criteria are defined.

- **Pre-closeness.** This criterion captures the closeness of two processes P_i and P_j with respect to the information flow from P_j to P_i. In particular, P_i has pre-closeness with P_j if one or more input entities of P_i have similarity with one or more output entities of P_j. Each entity name specified in feature *I-Object* of $D(P_i)$ is compared with all entity name(s) of feature *O-Object* of $D(P_j)$, to find the pair(s) of entities that are similar.
- **Post-closeness.** This criterion captures the closeness of P_i and P_j with respect to the information flow from P_i to P_j. In particular, P_i has post-closeness with P_j if one or more output entities of P_i have similarity with one or more input entities of P_j. Each entity name specified in feature *O-Object* of $D(P_i)$ is compared with all entity name(s) of feature *I-Object* of $D(P_j)$, to find the pair(s) of entities that are similar.

To measure the level of similarity and closeness between process specifications, we need to know the similarity between terms used in features of their descriptors. For this purpose, we maintain a Thesaurus of terms, which is an essential tool when adopting descriptor-based approaches for classification of objects, such as documents [12], software components [10], or conceptual components [2]. Thesaurus introduces vocabulary control, by providing capabilities to manage duplicate and ambiguous descriptors for the same process, resulting from use of synonym terms for expressing the same concept. Extracted terms for each feature are stored in the Thesaurus, together with relevant synonyms. In the Thesaurus, terms are organized into hierarchical structures, called *affinity trees*, capable of capturing the different levels of similarity existing between terms, as will be illustrated in the next section.

4   Features comparison

In order to determine process similarity, it is necessary to know the degree of similarity between the terms in process descriptor features. We call *affinity* the degree of similarity between terms. To relate terms according to their affinity, we arrange them into *affinity trees*, playing the role of the weighted conceptual graphs usually employed in reuse libraries [10,11]. Two affinity trees are defined, one for terms that are entity names (considering features *I-Object*, *O-Object*, *Cons-Object*, and *Circ-Object*), and the other for terms that are operation names

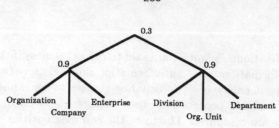

Fig. 2. An example of affinity tree

(for feature *Operation*). An example of affinity tree for entity names is shown in Fig. 2.

In an affinity tree, leaves are the terms characterizing processes with respect to one or more features f, and intermediate nodes are weights. A weight $w_k \in [0, 1]$, is a numerical value expressing the affinity of all terms contained in the sub-tree having w_k as root (this sub-tree is called cluster in the Information Retrieval terminology [12]).

Given a pair of terms t_i and t_j, the affinity weight of t_i and t_j is their first common ancestor weight $\overline{w}$ in the affinity tree to which they belong. If their first common ancestor is the root of the tree, affinity weight of t_i and t_j is the minimum affinity value in the tree (possibly 0). If t_i and t_j are the same, their affinity weight is equal to 1. For example, with reference to Fig. 2, the affinity weight for the pair of terms "Organization" and "Company" is 0.9, while the affinity weight for the pair of terms "Organization" and "Division" is 0.3. Terms are considered to have affinity if their affinity weight exceeds a given threshold, as stated in the following definition.

Definition 1 Term affinity. Two terms t_i and t_j have *affinity*, denoted as $t_i \sim t_j$, if their affinity weight $\overline{w}$ in the affinity tree is greater than or equal to an established threshold α.

$$t_i \sim t_j \leftrightarrow \overline{w} \geq \alpha$$

4.1 Construction of affinity trees

To construct affinity trees from the terms appearing in features of process descriptors we use the "complete-link" clustering technique used in Information Retrieval for document classification [12]. Following this technique, the affinity tree construction is articulated in the following steps:

1. Extraction from descriptors of the terms of interest for the tree to be constructed (i.e., entity names, operation names).
2. Terms are submitted to pairwise comparisons, and a weight is defined for each pair, which express the level of confidence of a domain expert about the fact that t_i and t_j describe the same or similar concepts/objects in the domain. For n terms to be compared, $n \cdot (n - 1)/2$ term comparisons are

performed. In our approach, for entity names and operation names, weights are semi-automatically computed, with the support of the EXTRACT tool [3], and by exploiting the information expressed in PA process specifications.

3. Construction of the affinity tree, following the "complete-link" technique. As output of this technique, terms are partitioned into clusters on the basis of their mutual affinity, and the affinity weight associated with a cluster holds for all possible pairs of terms belonging to the cluster.

4.2 Computing similarity between processes

Affinity trees constitute the basis for similarity computation. Before illustrating how to measure process similarity, let us describe how feature similarity is determined.

The similarity between a pair of comparable features in different process descriptors is a function computed on the terms associated with them. Let P_i be a process specification, and $D(P_i)$ the descriptor associated with it in the library. The notation $D(P_i).f$ represents the term t or the set of terms $t_1, \ldots, t_n$ associated with the feature f in descriptor $D(P_i)$.

Definition 2 Feature similarity. The *feature similarity* of a pair of comparable features f and f' of process descriptors $D(P_i)$ and $D(P_j)$, denoted by $Sim(D(P_i).f, D(P_j).f')$, is the measure of the affinity between their terms, computed as follows.

$$Sim(D(P_i).f, D(P_j).f') = \begin{cases} \overline{w} & \text{if } f, f' \text{ are single-term and } t \sim t' \\ \frac{2 \cdot |F|}{|D(P_i).f| + |D(P_j).f'|} & \text{if } f, f' \text{ are multiple-term and } F \neq \emptyset \\ 0 & \text{otherwise} \end{cases}$$

where $\overline{w}$ is the affinity weight of terms t and t' of $D(P_i).f$ and $D(P_j).f'$ respectively, $F = \{\langle t, t' \rangle \mid t \in D(P_i).f, t' \in D(P_j).f', t \sim t'\}$ is the set composed of the pairs of terms of $D(P_i).f$ and $D(P_j).f'$ that have affinity, and notation $\mid X \mid$ indicates the cardinality of set X.

Definition 2 states that the similarity of two comparable features is the affinity weight of their terms in the corresponding affinity tree, if features are single-term, is the number of their terms that have affinity over the total number of their terms (Dice's metric [2]), if features are multiple-term, and is 0 otherwise. For multiple-term features, the greater the number of terms that have affinity, the higher the feature similarity. Note that each term of $D(P_i).f$ and $D(P_j).f'$ can participate at most in one pair.

The similarity between two process specifications is computed by means of *similarity coefficients* defined as follows.

Definition 3 Entity similarity coefficient. The *Entity similarity coefficient* of two process specifications P_i and P_j, denoted by $ESim(P_i, P_j)$, is the measure of the similarity of their comparable and equal features related to input and output entities in their respective descriptors $D(P_i)$ and $D(P_j)$, computed as follows.

$$ESim(P_i, P_j) = \sum_{f \in \Im} Sim(D(P_i).f, D(P_j).f)$$

where $\Im$ is a set of features.

Definition 3 states that the entity similarity of two process specifications is the sum of the similarity of their comparable and equal features specified in the set $\Im$. Depending on the features specified in this set, this coefficient can be used to compute the different types of similarities according to the entity similarity criteria illustrated in Sect.3.2. In particular, similarity on input entities (respectively, output entities) is computed by specifying only the feature *I-Object* (respectively, *O-Object*) in the set $\Im$. Similarity on input and output entities together is computed by specifying both features *I-Object* and *O-Object* in the set $\Im$. According to what stated for affinity weights, coefficient $ESim(P_i, P_j)$ can assume values in the range $[0, 2]$. It has value 0 when all features $f \in \Im$ have similarity equal to 0. It has value 2 when both features *I-Object* and *O-Object* are specified in the set $\Im$, and feature similarity is 1 for both.

Definition 4 Functionality similarity coefficient. The *Functionality similarity coefficient* of two process specifications P_i and P_j, denoted by $FSim(P_i, P_j)$, is the measure of the similarity of their comparable and equal features related to functionality in their respective descriptors $D(P_i)$ and $D(P_j)$, computed as follows.

$$FSim(P_i, P_j) = \sum_{f \in \Im} Sim(D(P_i).f, D(P_j).f)$$

where $\Im = \{$Operation, Cons-Object, Circ-Object$\}$.

Definition 4 states that the functionality similarity of two process specifications is the sum of the similarity of their comparable and equal features used to describe process functionality. This coefficient returns a similarity value in the range $[0, 3]$, depending on the number of features that have similarity, and on their level of similarity. For values 0 and 3 hold the same considerations previously done for the Entity similarity coefficient.

As an example, let us consider the process "Hiring" (which will be referred to as P_2), whose descriptor is shown in Fig.3.

The entity similarity coefficient between process "Employee Engagement" described in Fig.1 (which will be referred to as P_1) and process P_2 with respect to both input and output entities is computed as follows:

$$ESim(P_1, P_2) = (\frac{2 \cdot 2}{4 + 3}) + (\frac{2 \cdot 3}{3 + 3}) = 1.57$$

Hiring

⟨F-Area⟩:	General Management of Labour
⟨I-Object⟩:	{ Enterprise, Employee, Business area }
⟨O-Object⟩:	{ Division, Employee, Contract }
⟨Operation⟩:	Hire
⟨Cons-Object ⟩:	Employee

Fig. 3. Second example of process descriptor

taking into account that terms "Organization" and "Enterprise" have affinity in the Thesaurus, as well as "Department" and "Division" (here we assume an affinity threshold $\alpha = 0.5$).

The functionality similarity coefficient between the same process descriptors is computed as follows:

$$FSim(P_1, P_2) = 0.9 + 1 = 1.9$$

where 0.9 is the affinity weight assigned to operation names "engage" and "hire" in the operation names affinity tree in the Thesaurus (they both belong to the "operation on roles" category), and 1 is the affinity weight of "Employee" with itself.

The closeness between two process specifications is computed by means of a set of *closeness coefficient*, which are based on the similarity between their comparable features *I-Object* and *O-Object*. In particular, the *Pre-closeness* and the *Post-closeness* coefficients are defined as follows.

Definition 5 Pre-closeness coefficient. The *pre-closeness coefficient* of two process specifications P_i and P_j, denoted by $PrC(P_i, P_j)$, is the measure of their closeness with respect to the incoming information flow from P_j to P_i, computed as follows.

$$PrC(P_i, P_j) = Sim(D(P_i).I - Object, D(P_j).O - Object)$$

Definition 5 states that the pre-closeness of two process specifications is the measure of the similarity between the output entities of the first process and the input entities of the second one.

Definition 6 Post-closeness coefficient. The *post-closeness coefficient* of a pair of process specifications P_i and P_j, denoted by $PoC(P_i, P_j)$, is the measure of their closeness with respect to the outgoing information flow from P_i to P_j, computed as follows.

$$PoC(P_i, P_j) = Sim(D(P_i).O - Object, D(P_j).I - Object)$$

Definition 6 states that the post-closeness of two process specifications is the measure of the similarity of the output entities of the first process and the input entities of the second one.

As an example, let us consider the process "Employee Selection" (which will be referred to as P_3), whose descriptor is shown in Fig.4. The pre-closeness coefficient between P_1 and P_3 is computed as follows:

$$PrC(P_3, P_1) = (\frac{2 \cdot 4}{4 + 4}) = 1$$

because all the output entities of P_3 are the same as the input entities of P_1.

Employee Selection

⟨F-Area⟩:   General Management of General Affairs and Personnel
⟨I-Object⟩:   { Candidate, Curriculum, Organization, Professional role}
⟨O-Object⟩:   { Employee, Professional role, Curriculum, Organization}
⟨Operation⟩:   Select
⟨Cons-Object ⟩: Employee

Fig. 4. Third example of process descriptor

5 Use of the library for reengineering processes

Several activities can be performed in process reengineering in general, and in PA process reengineering in particular, such as (i) discovering possible replications and inconsistencies of data used by different processes, with the aim of defining reference conceptual architectures describing, in an integrated and normalized way, the data used by different processes [5]; (ii) identifying information flows among processes pertaining to different functional areas and, possibly, referring to heterogeneous data descriptions; (iii) reconstructing complex activities, or macroprocesses, on the basis of discovered information flows and available process descriptions.

In this section we describe how to use the library for retrieval and composition of process specifications, according to the similarity and closeness criteria and coefficients previously illustrated. In particualr, the library can be used to support the following activities:

– *Retrieval of similar process specifications.*
  The capability of discovering similar processes repeated in different functional areas is a basic requirements for reengineering, to define normalized, integrated reference specifications, for both data and processes, which is a generally recognized need for legacy systems [1]. Due to possible lack of integration over the years, processes pertaining to different functional areas

can have been implemented separately, pursuing local objectives, without a global vision of the organization. Consequently, different functional areas result often characterized by similar/overlapping requirements and, consequently, by the same/similar processes. To identify and retrieve such process specifications among those stored in the library, we use the similarity coefficients, as described in Sect.5.1.

- *Reconstruction of workflows.*

A basic requirement for reengineering macroprocesses is to understand and capture them, and this is possible by reconstructing their workflows. Starting from stored process specifications, workflows for macroprocesses can be derived, by proper selecting and composing specifications of processes communicating through information flows. For the purpose of reconstructing workflows, we use the closeness coefficients, as discussed in Sect.5.2.

5.1 Retrieval of similar process specifications

Retrieval of similar process specifications, possibly pertaining to different functional areas, is performed using the similarity coefficients illustrated in Sect.4.2. The user defines a *reference* process specification P_i, selected among those stored in the library, or specified by means of a "query", and uses the similarity coefficients to retrieve other processes similar to it.

The selection of the reference specification directly from the library is suggested when the user has knowledge about the type of processes performed within functional areas, and about the relevance of a process within a functional area. Selection can be done by specifying the name of a process considered relevant, or by selecting it among the processes pertaining to a certain functional area.

The query-based mechanism is suggested when the user has in mind a target process, not necessarily corresponding to any processes stored in the library. With this mechanism, the user fills in a query having the same format of a process descriptor, with terms apt to describe the target specification according to the features of the classification model.

Once the reference specification P_i has been defined, the user selects the type of similarity to be computed on the library, and specifies the features to be included in the set $\Im$. The selected similarity coefficient is automatically computed between P_i and process specifications stored in the library. As a result, a set of process specifications, $ESIM(P_i)$ or $FSIM(P_i)$, is retrieved from the library and proposed to the user, where selected specifications are listed in decreasing order of similarity. $ESIM(P_i)$ is the set composed of the process specifications P_j whose entity similarity coefficient with P_i is greater than or equal to a defined threshold t_0, $ESIM(P_i) = \{P_j \mid ESim(P_i, P_j) \geq t_0\}$. $FSIM(P_i)$ is the set composed of the process specifications P_k whose functionality similarity coefficient with P_i is greater than or equal to a defined threshold t_1, $FSIM(P_i) = \{P_k \mid FSim(P_i, P_k) \geq t_1\}$.

The user can separately retrieve the sets $ESIM(P_i)$ and $FSIM(P_i)$ for the reference specification P_i, and compare their contents, to find the process specifications that are similar with respect to both entities and functionality. For example, assuming "Employee Engagement" as reference process specification (see Fig.1), a possible similar process retrieved from the library is "Hiring" (see Fig.3).

5.2 Reconstruction of workflows

Composition of process specifications is useful for reconstruction of workflows. The closeness coefficients illustrated in Sect.4.2 are used to retrieve from the library the specifications connected by information flows. Also in this case, the user selects a reference process specification P_i, which is used as the starting point for the reconstruction activity.

The pre-closeness and the post-closeness coefficients are computed between P_i and the process specifications stored in the library. Two sets of process specifications, $PRE(P_i)$ and $POST(P_i)$, are retrieved from the library and presented to the user. $PRE(P_i)$ is the set composed of the process specifications P_j whose pre-closeness coefficient with P_i is greater than or equal to a defined closeness threshold t_2, $PRE(P_i) = \{P_j \mid PrC(P_i, P_j) \geq t_2\}$. $POST(P_i)$ is the set composed of the process specifications P_k whose post-closeness coefficient with P_i is greater than or equal to a defined closeness threshold t_3, $POST(P_i) = \{P_k \mid PoC(P_i, P_j) \geq t_3\}$.

The user can examine retrieved sets, and select, among retrieved processes, those the can precede and follow P_i, on the basis of his own knowledge, and on the basis of the computed closeness coefficients. For example, given the reference specification "Employee Engagement" shown in Fig.1, a possible process preceding it retrieved from the library is "Employee Selection" shown in Fig.4. By repeating the closeness computation on the newly selected processes, workflows can be incrementally constructed. Different workflows can be constructed for the same reference specification P_i, by evaluating different combinations on the basis of the level of closeness of retrieved process specifications, and on the basis of the user's process knowledge.

6 Concluding remarks

Reengineering in the Public Administration domain has been discussed in this paper. The presented approach proposes a classification model for work processes, and criteria and methods for their analysis. In particular, similarity-based techniques are defined for discovering similar processes in a structured library, and for supporting macroprocess reconstruction. The proposed approach is being experimented in the framework of a project with AIPA.

A computer-based support tool is under development. The tool is being implemented on the top of the existing tool EXTRACT [3], which provides the basic functionalities for affinity computation and affinity tree construction. Up to now, the classification functionalities of the tool are implemented, and process specifications are stored in the library, with their associated descriptors. EXTRACT functionalities are used to determine affinity weights for entity and operation names, and to construct the corresponding affinity trees. Similarity-based and closeness-based retrieval functionalities are under development, and constitute the objective of ongoing research.

Acknowledgements

This work is part of a project supported by the Information System Authority for Public Administration (AIPA).

References

1. P. Aiken, A. Muntz, R. Richards, "DoD Legacy Systems - Reverse Engineering Data Requirements", *Communications of the ACM*, Vol.37, No.5, May 1994.
2. S.Castano, V. De Antonellis, B. Zonta, "Classifying and Reusing Conceptual Schemas", in *Proc. of ER'92, Int. Conf. on the Entity-Relationship Approach*, Karlsruhe, LNCS, n.645, Springer Verlag, October 1992.
3. S. Castano, V. De Antonellis, "The F^3 Reuse Environment for Requirements Engineering", *ACM SIGSOFT Software Engineering Notes*, Vol.19, No.3, July 1994.
4. S. Castano, V. De Antonellis, B. Pernici, "Building Reusable Conceptual Components in the Public Administration Domain", in Proc. of *SSR'95, ACM SIGSOFT Conference on Software Reuse*, Seattle, USA, April 1995.
5. S. Castano, V. De Antonellis, "Reference Conceptual Architectures for Reengineering Information Systems", accepted for publication on *IJICIS, Int. Journal of Intelligent and Cooperative Information Systems*, 1995.
6. V. De Antonellis, B. Zonta, "A disciplined Approach to Office Analysis", *IEEE Transactions on Software Engineering*, Vol.16, No.8, 1990.
7. D. Georgakopoulos, M. Hornik, A. Sheth, "An Overview of Workflow Management: From Process Modeling to Workflow Automation Infrastructure", *Distributed and Parallel Databases*,, Kluwer Academic Publishers, Vol.3, 1995.
8. Y.S. Maarek, D.M. Berry, G.E. Kaiser, "An Information Retrieval Approach For Automatically Constructing Software Libraries", *IEEE Transactions on Software Engineering*, Vol.17, No.8, August 1991.
9. R. Medina-Mora, H. Wong, P. Flores, "The ActionWorkflow Approach to Workflow Management", *Proc. of the 4th Conference on Computer-Supported Cooperative Work*, June 1992.
10. E. Ostertag, J. Hendler, R. Prieto-Diaz, C. Braun, "Computing Similarity in a Reuse Library System: An AI-Based Approach", *ACM Transactions on Software Engineering and Methodology*,, Vol.1, No.3, July 1992.
11. R. Prieto-Diaz, P. Freeman, "Classifying Software for Reusability", *IEEE Software*, Vol. 4, No. 1, January 1987.
12. G. Salton, *Automatic Text Processing - The Transformation, Analysis and Retrieval of Information by Computer*, Addison-Wesley, 1989.

Uniqueness Conditions for ER Representations

John L. Knapp

Texas Instruments Canada Ltd.,
5160 Yonge St. Ste. 1315,
North York, Ontario,
Canada, M2N 6L9

Abstract. Given a collection of entity types (database tables) there is usually more than one way to model their associations. Consequently two data models may appear different while essentially they are the same. To simplify the task of comparing data models, necessary and sufficient conditions are defined for a collection of entity types to have a unique Entity Relationship Diagram. The sufficient conditions for uniqueness are translated into modeling constraints that can be easily used to build an Entity-Relationship model. It is shown that the constraints do not prevent the representation of information requirements except for rare types of involuted relationships that seldom appear in the real world. All of this is done under the assumption that relationships are degree 2 or less. The results are extended to models containing relationships of higher degree.

1. Introduction

1.1 The Problem of Nonunique ER Representations

The development of an information system often requires the comparison of data models from old and new systems to ensure the completeness of analysis and to test the feasibility of migrating data to a new system. One of the strengths of the Entity-Relationship (ER) model is its ability to represent information objects and their associations graphically through an Entity Relationship Diagram (ERD).[1] At the same time the ERD is limited as a tool for data model comparison. Given a collection of entity types there is usually more than one way to represent their associations. Consequently two data models may appear different through their ERD when in fact they are equivalent.

The problem of data model equivalence has been studied extensively, both for relational and Entity-Relationship models [2]-[8]. However little has been done to define the conditions for a unique ER representations. The purpose of this paper is to define the necessary and sufficient conditions for a collection of entity types to have a unique ERD. The sufficient conditions are translated into modeling constraints that can be easily applied in the construction of any ER model. It is shown that the modeling constraints do not prevent the representation of information requirements except for rare types of involuted relationships that seldom appear in the real world.

1.2 A Simplified Version of Chen's ER Model

In Chen's Entity-Relationship model real world objects (entities) are classified into sets called entity types (entity sets). An *entity e* is an identifiable object for which there is persistent information. An *entity type E* is defined as $E=\{e|p(e)\}$, where p is the set qualifier expressed as a predicate. Entity types such as STUDENT, COURSE and INSTRUCTOR are represented graphically in an ERD as rectangles (see Figure 1). Associations between entities are grouped together into sets called relationships (relationship sets). Let $E=\{E_i|1\leq i\leq n\}$ be a collection of entity types (not necessarily distinct). A *relationship R over E* is defined as $R=\{<e_1,e_2,...,e_n>|e_i$ is in $E_i, 1\leq i\leq n\}$ where n is the *degree* of the relationship. Each tuple of entities $<e_1,e_2,...,e_n>$ is an *occurrence of the relationship*. Assuming that the role played by each entity is taken from its entity type, then the sequence of the e_i is unimportant and R can be thought of as a subset of the Cartesian product of entity types $E_i, (1\leq i\leq n)$.

In a simplified version of Chen's model relationships are of degree two or less[1] and can be represented graphically as straight lines e.g. INSTRUCTOR *teaches* CLASS in Figure 1. The relationship $A--B$ (where A and B are entity types) can be broken down

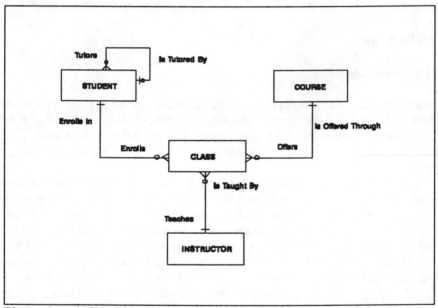

Figure 1:   A Simplified Version of Chen's ERD

into two *relationship memberships*: $A-->B$, describing the role of A with respect to B and $B-->A$, describing the role of B with respect to A. The *cardinality of a relationship membership* $A-->B$ is the maximum number of B occurrences associated with each occurrence of A under the relationship $A--B$. The cardinality values for $A-->B$ are *one* (1) and *many* (M), and can be represented as $A--|B$ and $A--<B$ respectively. In Figure 1 each INSTRUCTOR teaches 0, or many CLASSes and each CLASS is taught by

---

[1] It will be explained later in this section why this simplification is not a limitation.

exactly one INSTRUCTOR. *Many* CLASSes is represented as a crows foot beside CLASS and *one* INSTRUCTOR is represented as a bar beside INSTRUCTOR. The *optionality for a relationship membership A-->B* is the minimum number of *B* occurrences associated with each occurrence of *A*. The optionality values for *A-->B* are *zero* and *at least one*, and can be represented as *A--0B* and *A--*B* respectively. *Zero* is represented graphically as 0 beside CLASS and *at least one* it is represented by the absence of 0 beside INSTRUCTOR.

The cardinalities for the relationship memberships *A-->B* and *B-->A* can be combined to define the *cardinality for the relationship A--B* as 1-1 (A|--|B), 1-M (A|--<B, A>--|B) or M-M (A>--<B). Similarly the *optionality for a relationship A--B* is defined as *fully optional* (A0--0B), *partially optional* (A0--*B, A*--0B) or *fully mandatory* (A*--*B), depending on the optionality of its relationship memberships. Relationships of degree 1, such as STUDENT *tutors* STUDENT, are called *involuted*.

This paper assumes a simplified version of Chen's model where relationships are degree two or less. Its theorems can be extended to models containing relationships of higher degree by the fact that every ER model is equivalent to a model of this type. [2]

2. Definitions

2.1 ERD Equivalence

When two sets of relationships represent the same associations it makes sense to think of them as equivalent. For example, the sets {A|*--*|B,A|*--0<C} and {A|*--*|B,B|*--0<C} clearly represent the same associations for entity types *A*, *B* and C^2. A mathematical definition of equivalence for sets of relationships involves the following concepts.

A *path P between two entity types A and B* is a finite sequence of contiguous relationships {E_i--E_{i+1}} ($i=1,...,n-1$) such that $E_1=A$ and $E_n=B$. It should be noted that the E_i may not be distinct and that {E_i--E_{i-1}} ($i=n,...,2$) and {E_i--E_{i+1}} ($i=1,...,n-1$) define the same path. A *path P is cyclic for an entity type A* if it begins and ends with *A*. A *path P joining A and B is directed* if it is equivalent to a relationship between *A* and *B* with cardinality 1-1 or 1-M. For example, {A>0--*|B,B>0--*|C,C>0--0|A} is a directed cyclic path on *A* where as {A>0--*|B,B>0--*|C,C|0--0<A} is only cyclic on *A*. The *optionality of a path* is the optionality of its equivalent relationship. The paths {A>0--*|B,B>0--*|C,C>0--*|A} and {A>0--*|B,B>*--0|C,C>0--*|A} are partially mandatory and fully optional respectively.

Let *P* be a path between the entity types *A* and *B*. Let $B_P[a]$ represent all of the instances of *B* associated with the entity *a* from *A* as determined by the path *P*. The relationship *R* between *A* and *B* is *redundant with respect to P* if *R* is not in *P* and if for every instantiation of *A* and *B*:

· $A_P[b]=A_R[b]$ for all *b* in *B*
· $B_P[a]=B_R[a]$ for all *a* in *A*.

When there is only one relationship between the entity types *A* and *B* the notation $B_R[a]$

---

[2] We can confirm this intuitively by substituting *B* for *A*.

is simplified to $B[a]$. A relationship is *redundant in a set of relationships* R if it is redundant with respect to some path P in R.

The *closure* R^+ of a set of relationships R is the set of all nontrivial relationships that can be generated from R by adding redundant relationships to R or any of its iterations in the creation of R^+. For example, $\{A|*-0<B\}^+ = \{A|*-0<B, B>*-*<B, A|0-0|A\}$. A relationship A--B is *trivial* if it is the Cartesian product of the entity types A and B. A relationship A--A is also *trivial* if it maps each instance of A to itself. It can be shown that R^+ is unique by noting that $R^+ \supseteq R$, and hence the closure of R under any sequence of steps is contained in R^+. Two sets of relationships R_1 and R_2 are defined to be *equivalent* if $R_1^+ = R_2^+$. R_1 is a *basis* for R if $R_1^+ = R^+$ and no proper subset of R_1 has this property.

2.2 Relationship Redundancy

The closure for a set of relationships can be used to define redundant relationships. A relationship S is *C-redundant (closure redundant) with respect to* R if $(R-S)^+ = R^+$. If a set of relationships R has no C-redundant relationships it is said to be *C-nonredundant*. Lemma 1 shows that C-redundancy is equivalent to redundancy within a set of relationships.

Lemma 1: A relationship S is C-redundant in a set of relationships T if, and only if, S is redundant in T.

Proof: If S is redundant in T, then it is redundant with respect to some path in T-S. Hence $T^+ = (T-S)^+$.

To prove the converse let S be a relationship in T such that $T^+ = (T-S)^+$. Then S is in $(T-S)^+$. Let $\{T_i\}$ $(i=1,...,m)$ be a sequence of relationship sets that converges to $(T-S)^+$. Because S is in $(T-S)^+$, S is in T_i for some i. We will prove by induction on i that if S is added to T_i, then it is redundant with respect to some path in T-S and hence redundant in T.

Let $i=1$. Then $T_1 = T-S$, and S is redundant with respect to some path in T-S.

Assume for $1 < i \leq n$, that any redundant relationship added to T_i is redundant with respect to some path in T-S. Suppose S is added to T_{n+1}. Then S is redundant with respect to some path $P = \{P_1, C--D, P_2\}$ in T_{n+1} as shown in Figure 2. If P is contained entirely in T-S, then S is redundant with respect a path in T-S. Otherwise C--D is some relationship not in T-S. Therefore C--D was added to some T_i $(1 < i \leq n)$, and by our induction assumption is redundant with respect to some path Q_1 in T-S. If S is redundant with respect to P, then it can be shown that S is redundant with respect to $Q = \{P_1, Q_1, P_2\}$ since S is not in Q_1 and C--D is redundant with respect to Q_1. Without loss of generality we can assume that P_1 and P_2 are in T-S. Otherwise they too could be replaced by paths in T-S. Therefore S is redundant with respect to a path in T-S. This completes the proof.[3]

---

[3] It should be noted that this proof only requires A--B and C--D to be distinct relationships. The entity types A, B, C and D may be the same.

300

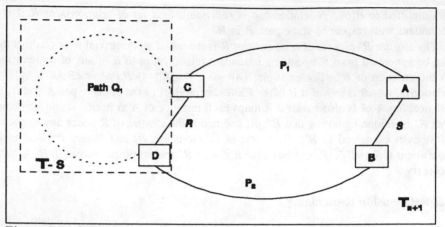

Figure 2: C-Redundancy Equivalent to Redundancy With Respect to a Set of Relationships

3. Uniqueness Conditions

3.1 Necessary and Sufficient Conditions

A set of relationships R is a *unique representation* if whenever $R^+ = R'^+$, then $R = R'$. The necessary and sufficient conditions for uniqueness follow naturally from the definition of closure on a set of relationships.

Theorem 1: A nonredundant set of relationships R is a unique representation if, and only if, R is nonredundant in R^+.

Proof: Suppose R is nonredundant in R^+. If R' is another basis for R, then R' must be derivable from R^+ by removing redundant relationships. R is nonredundant in R^+. Therefore $R' \supseteq R$. However R' is nonredundant. Therefore $R' = R$.

On the other hand if S is a relationship in R that is redundant in R^+, then it is possible to remove S from R^+ in the derivation of a basis R'. Hence $R' \neq R$.

3.2 Examples of Relationship Types Generating More Than One ERD

Although Theorem 1 is definitive, it does not provide practical guidelines for building a unique ERD. Ideally the sufficient conditions for uniqueness can be translated into restrictions on the types of relationships used to model associations. We have already seen how the use of 1-1 relationships can generate two representations for the set {A|*-- *|B, A|*--0<C}, namely {A|*--*|B, A|*--0<C} and {B|*--*|A, B|*--0<C}. Proposition 1 shows how M-M relationships have a similar potential to generate nonunique representations. Proposition 2 defines conditions where the existence of more than one directed cyclic path on an entity type can produce several representations.

Proposition 1: If B>--0<C is redundant with respect to B>*--*|A and A>*--0<C, then*

$A>*--0C$ is redundant with respect to $A|*--*<B$ and $B>*--0<C$.

Proof: Let $B>*--0<C$ be redundant with respect to $B>*--*|A$ and $A>*--0<C$. Then,

1) $B[c] = B[A[c]]$ for all c in C and
2) $C[b] = C[A[b]]$ for all b in B.

By the properties of $A|*--*<B$

3) $A[B[a]] = a$ for all a in A.

Combining 2) and 3) we get

4) $C[a] = C[A[B[a]]] = C[B[a]]$ for all a in A.

Combining 1) and 3) we get

5) $A[c] = A[B[A[c]]] = A[B[c]]$ for all c in C.

Together 4) and 5) prove that $A>*--0<C$ is redundant with respect to the path $\{A|*--*<B, B>*--0<C\}$.

Hence there are two bases for the set $\{A|*--*<B, B>*--0<C, A>*--0<C\}$.

Proposition 2: Let $A/0--0/B$, $A/0--0<A$ and $B/0--0<B$ be relationships on entity types A and B such that the relationship $B/0--0<B$ is redundant with respect to the path $\{B/0--0/A, A/0--0<A, A/0--0/B\}$. Assume that a in A is related to an instance of B if it is related to an instance of A. Then $A/0--0<A$ is redundant with respect to the path $\{A/0--0/B, B/0--0<B, B/0--0/A\}$.

Proof: Let $A_c[a]$ represent all of the instances of A associated with a in the clockwise direction under the relationship $A|0--0<A$. It suffices to show that,

$A_c[a] = A[B_c[B[a]]]$ for all a in A

Because $B|0--0<B$ is redundant with respect to the path $\{B|0--0|A, A|0--0<A, A|0--0|B\}$ it follows that,

1) $B_c[b] = B[A_c[A[b]]]$ for all b in B

The 1-1 relationship between A and B implies,

2) $A[B[a]] = a$ for all a in A that are related to instances of B.

From the given, a in A is related to some instance of B if it is related to an instance of A under the relationship $A|0--0<A$. Hence,

3) $A_c[a] = A_c[A[B[a]]]$ for all a in A.
4) $A_c[a] = A[B[A_c[a]]]$ for all a in A.

Substituting $B[a]$ for b in 1) we get,

5) $B_c[B[a]] = B[A_c[A[B[a]]]]$ for all a in A

Applying 3) and 4) to 5) we get,

6) $A[B_c[B[a]]] = A[B[A_c[A[B[a]]]]] = A_c[A[B[a]]] = A_c[a]$ for all a in A,

which is the desired result.

3.3 Modeling Constraints Based on Relationship Types

Let R_1 and R_2 be two different nonredundant sets of relationships where $R_1^+ = R_2^+$. Let $R_1 + R_2$ represent the set union of R_1 and R_2. By Lemma 1, relationships in $R_1 - R_2$ are redundant in $R_1 + R_2$. However they are nonredundant in R_1. Therefore as relationships in $R_2 - R_1$ are removed from $R_1 + R_2$ to derive R_1, they force relationships in $R_1 - R_2$ to be nonredundant. The following lemma suggest a natural mapping between the redundant relationships in $R_1 - R_2$ and $R_2 - R_1$.

Lemma 2: If S and T are two redundant relationships in a set R such that the removal of S forces T to be nonredundant, then the removal of T forces S to be nonredundant.
  Proof: Let *S* and *T* be the relationships *A--B* and *C--D* respectively as shown in

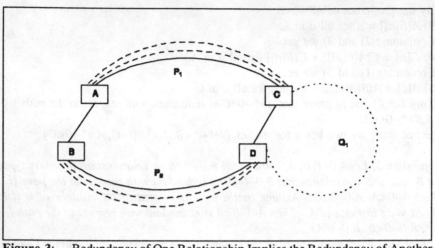

Figure 3:   Redundancy of One Relationship Implies the Redundancy of Another

Figure 3. Assume that the removal of *C--D* forces *A--B* to be nonredundant in *R-T*. Then *C--D* is on every path in *R* where *A--B* is redundant. To complete the proof we need to show that *A--B* is on every path in *R* where *C--D* is redundant.

Assume the converse. Let *C--D* be redundant with respect to some path Q_1 in *R* that does not contain *A--B*. *A--B* is redundant with respect to some path $P=\{P_1,C--D,P_2\}$. Because Q_1 does not contain *A--B*, it can be shown that *A--B* is also redundant with respect to $Q=\{P_1,Q_1,P_2\}$. However *C--D* is not on *Q*. This is the desired contradiction.

A *path P is fully disclosed* if the cardinality and optionality of every relationship redundant with respect to *P* can be deduced from the cardinalities and optionalities of the relationships in *P*. An example of a path that is not fully disclosed is *P*={*C*>0--|*B*,*B*>0--0|*A*} where *C*>0--*|A* is redundant with respect to *P* under the rule that an instance of *B* is associated with *C* if, and only if, it is associated with *A*. The optionality of *C*>0--*|A* cannot be deduced from the optionality of the relationships in *P*. A *set of relationships R is fully disclosed* if every path in *R* is fully disclosed. That is, the cardinality and optionality constraints for relationships in *R* are shown in the ERD.

Lemma 3: Let R_1 and R_2 be two nonredundant fully disclosed sets of relationships where $R_1^+=R_2^+$. Let C--D be in R_2-R_1 and let A--B be in R_1-R_2. If the removal of C--D from some subset S $(R_1+R_2 \supseteq S \supset R_1)$)forces A--B to be nonredundant, then A--B and C--D have the same cardinality and optionality. If A--B is not M-M, then there is directed cyclic path on A in R_1 or a path of 1-1 relationships joining A and C in R_1. If A--B is partially mandatory, then there is a partially mandatory cyclic path on A in R_1 or a path of fully mandatory relationships joining A and C in R_1.

Proof: Without loss of generality we can assume that *A--B* is a 1-M, partially

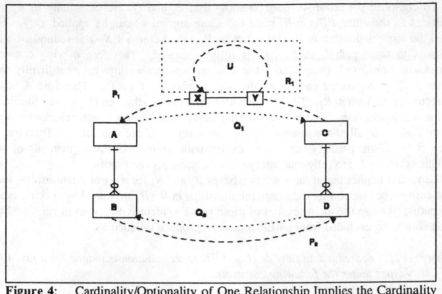

Figure 4: Cardinality/Optionality of One Relationship Implies the Cardinality /Optionality of Another.

optional relationship as shown in Figure 4. By Lemma 1 *C--D* is redundant in *S*. If the removal of *C--D* from *S* forces *A--B* to be nonredundant, then by Lemma 2 the removal of *A--B* from *S* forces *C--D* to be nonredundant. Therefore *A--B* is redundant with respect to some path $P=\{P_1,C\text{--}D,P_2\}$ in *S* and *C--D* is redundant with respect to some path $Q=\{Q_1,A\text{--}B,Q_2\}$ in *S*. Looking at the cardinality of the relationship *A--B*, for every *b* in *B* there is at most one *a* in *A*. Therefore moving counter-clockwise from *B* to *A* along *P*, all of the relationship memberships in *P* have cardinality one, since *P* is fully disclosed. Therefore for every *d* in *D* there is at most one *c* in *C*. If for every *a* in *A* there are possibly many *b* in *B*, then for every *c* in *C* there are possibly many *d* in *D*, since *Q* is fully disclosed. Therefore *C--D* and *A--B* have the same cardinality.

By the above argument *P* is a directed path (as shown by the arrows). Similarly it can be shown that *Q* is a directed path. Therefore $N=\{Q_1,P_1\}$ is a directed cyclic path on *A*. If $P_1=Q_1$ then *A* and *C* are joined by a path containing only 1-1 relationships.

Looking at the optionality of *A--B*, for every *b* in *B* there is at least one *a* in *A*. Therefore moving counter-clockwise from *B* to *A* along *P*, all of the relationship memberships in *P* are mandatory, since *P* is fully disclosed. Therefore for every *d* in *D* there is at least one *c* in *C*. If for every *a* in *A* there are possibly no *b* in *B*, then for every *c* in *C* there are possibly no *d* in *D*, since *Q* is fully disclosed. Therefore *C--D* and *A--B* have the same optionality.

P is a mandatory path in the counter-clockwise direction. Using a similar argument it can be shown that *Q* is a mandatory path in the clockwise direction. Therefore

$N=\{Q_1,P_1\}$ is at least a partially mandatory cyclic path on A. If $P_1=Q_1$ then A and C are joined by a path of fully mandatory relationships.

To complete the proof we need to show that P_1 and Q_1 are essentially in R_1. It suffices to show that P_1 is in R_1 since the same arguments can be applied to Q_1. Let X--Y be any relationship in P_1 that is not in R_1. By Lemma 1 X--Y is redundant with respect to some path U in R_1. R_1 is fully disclosed. Therefore moving counter-clockwise from Y to X along U all of the relationship memberships have cardinality one. That is, U is a directed path in R_1 that can replace X--Y on P_1. Therefore A has a directed cyclic path in R_1. If $P_1=Q_1$ then all of the relationships in U are 1-1. Similarly if the relationship membership Y-->X is mandatory, then moving counter clockwise from Y to X along U, all of the relationship memberships in U are mandatory. Therefore A has at least one partially mandatory cyclic path in R_1. If $P_1=Q_1$ then all of the relationships in U are fully mandatory. This completes the proof.

Lemma 3 implies that if there are two bases R_1 and R_2 for a set of relationships, then the entity types supporting redundant relationships in R_1+R_2 are joined by specific types of paths. We can use the properties of these paths to identify the types of relationships that should be excluded from an ER model to produce uniqueness.

Theorem 2: A nonredundant fully disclosed ER representation is unique for a given set of entity types under the following constraints:
- *No M-M relationships*
- *No fully optional degree 2 relationships*
- *No fully mandatory 1-1 relationships*
- *All directed cyclic paths are fully optional*
- *An entity type can have at most one directed cyclic path.*

Proof: Let R be a set of relationships with two different bases R_1 and R_2 that satisfy the constraints of the theorem. By Lemma 1 there is a relationship A--B in R_1-R_2 that is redundant in R_1+R_2. Let C--D be a relationship in R_2-R_1 whose removal from S $(R_1 \subset S \subseteq R_1+R_2)$ forces A--B to be nonredundant. Then A--B, C--D, R_1 and R_2 satisfy the conditions of Lemma 3. It can be shown that the existence of A--B and C--D implies a violation of at least one of the constraints on relationship types as defined above.

Let A--B be degree 2 as shown in Figure 4. From the constraints of the theorem A--B is partially mandatory and either 1-1 or 1-M. Without loss of generality we can assume $A1^*$--$0<B$. Therefore there is a cyclic path on A in R_1 that is not fully optional or there are fully mandatory 1-1 relationships in R_1 (Lemma 3). This is the desired contradiction.

Let A--B be degree 1. That is, A and B are the same entity type. From the given constraints of the theorem, A--B is fully optional. Therefore C--D is fully optional (Lemma 3). From the constraints we are given for relationships only involuted relationships are fully optional. Therefore C--D is involuted and A has more than one directed cyclic path in R_1. This is the desired result and completes the proof.

3.4 Limitations for Representing Information Requirements

Information requirements are represented by an ER model if all information objects in the problem domain can be classified by entity types and all associations can be

classified by relationships. The following constraints implied by the uniqueness conditions do not prevent the representation of information requirements:
- No M-M relationships
- No fully optional degree 2 relationships
- No fully mandatory 1-1 relationships

M-M Relationships: A common method of representing M-M relationships for relational tables is to introduce an associative table (entity type). Using this technique $A>0--0<B$ becomes $A|*--0<AB>0--*|B$, where AB is an entity type whose identifier is the concatenation of the identifiers of A and B.

Fully Optional Relationships of Degree 2: Fully optional relationships, such as $A|0--0<B$, often hide business rules because their graphic representation does not define the conditions under which A is associated with B and vice versa? A more specific representation is $A|*--0<B'|0--*|B$, where B' is the qualified subset of B always related to A.

Fully Mandatory 1-1 Relationships: Entity types related by fully mandatory 1-1 relationships can be easily merged into a single entity type. The only loss is semantic content.

The constraints on directed cyclic paths and degree one relationships prevents the representation of information requirements, but only in rare situations.

At Most One Directed Cyclic Path: If there is a cyclic path of the form $\{A>0--*|B,B>*--0|A\}$ then the level of abstraction for A or B may be too high and one of them should be redefined. An alternative representation may be $B'>*--*|A>0--*|B$ where B' is the subset of B always related to A by the second relationship $B>*--0|A$. If there are several involuted relationships on an entity type A, they can be generalized into a single relationship or A can be split into several entity types such that each entity type has at most one involuted relationship. Sometimes involuted relationships are generalizations of entity type hierarchies built from degree 2 relationships.

Fully Optional Directed Cyclic Paths: Cyclic paths that are not fully optional imply continuous chains of associated entities[4]. For example, an instantiation of the relationship $A|*--0<A$ is $\{(a_2,a_1),(a_3,a_1),(a_4,a_3),(a_1,a_4)\}$. Here a_1 is the parent of a_2 and a_3, a_3 is the parent of a_4 and a_4 is the parent of a_1.

4. Conclusion

4.1 Applications

When there are no restrictions on the types of relationships that may appear in an ER model, there is the possibility of more than one ERD for the same associations. The models shown in Figure 5 appear different but can be shown to be equivalent using Propositions 1 and 2. Their apparent difference stems from 1-1 fully mandatory relationships, M-M relationships and more than one directed cyclic path on an entity type.

In Figure 5 $A|*--0|E$ holds for an entity a in A if $A|0--0<A$ holds for the same entity.

---

[4] Otherwise an entity type has an infinite number of occurrences.

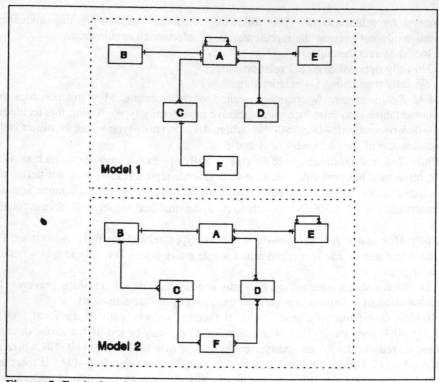

Figure 5: Equivalent Models with Different ERDS.

Under this assumption the involuted relationship on A in Models 1 can be replaced by an involuted relationship on E (Proposition 2). The relationship $A|*--*<C$ in Model 1 can be replaced by $B|*--*<C$ in Model 2 because of $A|*--*|B$. By Proposition 1, $A>*--0<D$ can be replaced by $C>*--0<D$ which can be replaced by $F>*--0<D$.

4.2 Further Research

One of the applications of Theorem 2 is the automation of data model comparison at the entity-relationship level. The enforcement of the uniqueness conditions can also be automated because the types of relationships that generate nonunique representations are easily identified. Computerized algorithms need to be defined for these purposes.

For equivalent models with different ERDs procedures need to be developed to show how one model can be transformed into another. The transformation of the models in Figure 5 is a simplified example of how this might be done.

The problem of uniqueness can be addressed in a broader sense to include the representation of entity types as well as relationships. One of the challenges is to define a common starting point for the definition of each. Within the context of the relational model Philip Bernstein used attributes and functional dependencies as a starting point for the definition tables and their associations. He showed there is a 1-1 mapping between tables contained in two different 3NF, dependency preserving, nonredundant, minimal representations for a given set of attributes and the functional dependencies defined over them. [5]

Acknowledgements

I would like to thank Dr. A.O. Mendelzon, University of Toronto, Computer Systems Research Group, Toronto, Canada, for helping to review this paper.

References

[1] Chen, Peter P., "The Entity-Relationship Model - Toward a Unified View of Data", ACM Transactions on Database Systems, Vol 1, No. 1, Mar. 1976, pp. 9-36.

[2] Ng, Peter A., "Further Analysis of the Entity-Relationship Approach to Database Design", IEEE Transactions on Software Engineering, Vol. se-7, No. 1, Jan. 1981, pp. 85-99.

[3] Hull, R., "Relative Information Capacity of Simple Relational Database Schema", Proc of the Third ACM Symposium on Principles of Database Systems, 1984 pp. 97-109.

[4] Japoda, S, Ng, P.A., Springnoel, F.N. "The problem of Equivalence for the Entity Relationship Diagrams", IEEE Trans. on Software Engineering SE-9.5 Sept. 1983, pp. 617-630

[5] Bernstein, P., "Synthesizing Third Normal Relations from Functional Dependencies", ACM Transactions on Database Systems, Vol. No. 4 Dec. 1976, pp. 277-298.

[6] Beeri, C., Mendelzon, A.O., Sagiv, Y., Ullman, J.D., "Equivalence of Relational Database Schemes, SIAM Journal on Computing 10:2, May 1981, pp. 352-370.

[7] Graham, M.H., "Functions in Databases", Computer Systems Research Group Report, University of Toronto, Canada, June 1981.

[8] Beeri, C. and Rissanen, J., "Faithful Representations of Relational Database Schemes", IBM Report RJ2722, San Jose, CA, January 1981.

Rapid Prototyping : An Integrated CASE Based Approach

Ian Mitchell, Ian Ferguson, Norman Parrington
Ian.Mitchell@sunderland.ac.uk

School of Computing & Information Systems,
University of Sunderland, Sunderland, United Kingdom

Abstract: Seamless methodology integration covering the entire lifecycle has proven to be an elusive Grail for software engineers. Mix-and-match approaches (where the best elements of various methodologies are "cut and pasted" together into an ad-hoc solution) have proven to be unsatisfactory since the parts rarely interface cleanly, a problem that is compounded in CASE support where dissimilar notational techniques and views may be used that reflect differing approaches to orthogonality. The authors take the opinion that the success of an integrated methodology depends upon the interoperability of the tools that support it, and to this end the topic of synergistic primitives and models has been subjected to much investigation. This paper proposes an object-oriented approach to rapid prototyping, analysis and design using the same object toolset and procedural view in each phase.

1.　　Introduction

In this paper we use rapid prototyping as a vehicle for requirements analysis and elicitation. We implement this within a fully integrated, tool supported environment covering each phase of the software development process using a "loosely orthogonal" approach to the O-O paradigm. The strictly orthogonal approach used in other models is rejected as an overly Romanesque interpretation of the Olduvai Imperative [Degrace93] and a "Greek" solution, which allows the analyst to concentrate upon modelling the problem rather than upon how to reconcile different modelling paradigms, is implemented.

2.　　Primitives for the Object Toolset

2.1　　Some Notational Models compared

Three popular models have been deconstructed in the development of the notation used in our integrated methodology - the generic E-R model, the Object Model used in the Object Modelling Technique [Rumbaugh91], and the Information Model used in Object-Oriented Analysis [Shlaer92]. The results of this investigation were presented at the 1995 International Congress on MetaCASE [Mitchell95], where we argued that a modelling technique should be both syntactically rich and semantically potent. Such a notation will use fewer primitives to express a concept, and should therefore be easier to learn....and yet these primitives should still be powerful enough to represent *all* the semantics the modeller wishes to utilise in a schema.

2.2   Mapping out a strategy for an object model

We do not attempt to represent methods in our object schema, since they are best represented using an orthogonal functional model designed for that purpose (see 3). The ramifications of this decision are considerable. Firstly, since we are modelling static data structure rather than dynamics, we avoid the need to model instances on the schema as instantiation occurs dynamically over time (i.e. on a time-line). Secondly, although the exact cardinality of a relationship refers to the number of instances being associated - which may vary over time - this does not mean we can simplify the notation for associations by using the crow's foot notation [Martin92] to represent any plurality, since not all associations are intrinsically dynamic. For example, if an association is expressing the notion *is a part of*, this relationship could be static. The cardinality may be set to either an exact quantity or **many** if the cardinality of the aggregated object varies from subtype to subtype or instance to instance.

The E-R model can be used as a basis for an object model [Martin92]. However, the associations of the E-R model, whilst syntactically rich, are not semantically potent i.e. they cannot truly represent the semantics of an aggregative relationship which exhibits transitivity, antisymmetricity, and propagation. Therefore, aggregation must be included in our dictionary of primitives.One area in which the associations of the E-R model *do* exhibit potency - and without any loss of syntactical richness - is in their use of intersection entities. These are entities like any other, and therefore a separate primitive for modelling associations as classes is unnecessary.

2.3   Entropy and Analysis

The set of primitives in the dictionary (entity, generalisation, association, attribute, and aggregation) have one key characteristic - they are all highly entropic. This contrasts with some object models (e.g. OMT, Shlaer-Mellor) where it is possible to express some concepts (e.g. grouped attributes, subtyping, intersection entities) using redundant analogues (e.g. composite attributes, associations as classes).

This leaves the analyst with fewer shades on the palette, but it does supply all of the primary hues. These primitives can be mixed and blended to develop an object model with no loss in semantic potency. The syntactical richness, meanwhile, ensures that the analyst concentrates upon *modelling the problem* rather than upon making artificial choices about which primitive to use in a certain situation.

3.   A procedural model for the toolset

Our next task is to find the best way to model the dynamics of the system. We cannot contemplate a strictly orthogonal solution (employing an object model, Data Flow Diagram, and Finite State Machine) since this is too rigorous at the analysis stage. The concern we have with conventional orthogonal models featuring DFD's is that a functional object may or may not correspond to an object in the object model, and the abstractions may overlap in some areas. This is because DFD actors and data stores are the product of an investigation that has concentrated on *what goes on* in a system, rather than an investigation of the entities or objects that reside there [Birchenough89]. An additional complication with these tools is that the thread of control, being defined in the dynamic model (such as a finite state machine), must also be mapped onto the other models. This approach means that the data and functional aspects of the system often need to be rigorously defined before any prototyping and experimentation can begin. This effectively limits the use of the tools to the design phase of the software engineering process. The inherent difficulty of mapping orthogonal models onto each other renders them less suitable for use in the analysis phase, where the key objects and procedures are still in the process of being abstracted and where a developer should not bog down building unnecessarily elaborate "correct" class hierarchies [Colbert94].

Masiero [Masiero88] has proposed Jackson Structured Design as a possible Object-Oriented solution for systems engineering. This approach has been subject to detailed investigation by Lewis [Lewis91], who observes that "traditionally, JSD has been associated with the operational rather than the Object-Oriented paradigm owing to the fact that JSD specifications are (at least in principle) executable". Lewis extends the *implementation capability* of JSD into O-O by constructing a set of general transformations for mapping JSD specifications into a non-specific Object-Oriented (O-O) language. Whilst we acknowledge that SD's can be instrumental in providing an executable systems specification, and as such are ideally suited to the purposes of rapid prototyping, we seek to exploit this by using an object model for mapping the problem space rather than by using transformations. We feel this is necessary in order to retain the benefits of the O-O approach. Whereas the identification of actions is the first task of the analyst when developing a JSD specification, the development of an O-O specification requires the reverse - objects themselves are first identified and their behaviour is then mapped on to this [Shlaer89]. Specifically, we seek to make an SD decomposition of "objects" in the system, thereby effectively representing control flow.

4.   Natural Language Processing

The first step in our integrated lifecycle approach is to identify the entities that make up a system and the relationships between them. The relationships are then categorised and refined. The data necessary to represent those entities are then added followed by the operations that can be performed on them. Each identified entity is then refined recursively. Ultimately, each entity is implemented as an Object-Oriented "class". The terms "entity", "module" and "class" are considered to be synonymous here. Analysis uses a natural language description of the problem as its starting point. The entities identified from this description are then shown on a form of modified Entity-Relationship diagram [Chen76] known as the analysis diagram.

"Entity/Object spotting" is one of the unsolved problems of Object Orientation [Stroustrup91]. To assist in the process, an AI based approach is being investigated. There are two thrusts to this approach. One is natural language processing (NLP), the idea being that nouns form the objects and verbs the operations. The second is the capturing of the knowledge of an experienced OO software engineer in an expert system.

The relationships between the objects that have been identified are then examined. Relationships fall into four significant categories based on those used by Booch [Booch94]: "has_a", "is_a_kind_of", "contains" and "uses". A hierarchy of classes is associated with each category. The cardinality of each relationship (1:1, 1:M, M:M) is identified. This information is used to infer requirements for container classes during design.

Once this diagram is complete, the analysis process begins again, this time taking each identified entity as a starting point and treating it as a separate system. The process is iterative, refining until a sufficient understanding of the system has been gained to permit design to commence.

5.   Analysis

5.1   Rapid Prototyping and software costs

Software costs often exceed predicted values because of the rework done on applications that have been found to be inadequate too late in the development lifecycle. Requirements errors are the most expensive to repair because of the redesign which is usually involved [Sommerville92]. This problem can manifest itself in projects that are technically well controlled at a coding level; i.e. they may overrun budget not because of poor programming skills but because the requirements analysis did not reveal the *intended* properties of the system.

Rapid Prototyping can help here. Instead of attempting to perform a perfect requirements analysis first time, an initial "throwaway" system is developed which can be criticised and used for bringing the true requirements into perspective. Several such prototypes may be redeveloped iteratively before formal analysis begins, a process which is similar to (though not identical with) *Evolutionary Prototyping* where only those parts of the system that are well understood are developed at first, and the prototype then evolves as the understanding of the whole system becomes clearer [Zhou94]. In the context of rapid prototyping however, we have the goal of terminating this evolutionary process once the requirements have been elicited. These prototypes can also assist domain analysis by permitting the analysts to experiment with different abstractions.

Although the end product of rapid prototyping is a disposable prototype solution, the *information models* used in developing the prototype are extremely valuable. They may serve the purpose of *requirements elicitation and specification* and can be directly introduced into formal analysis, or, if this is thought to be unnecessary, the design phase.

5.2   Key features of our supporting toolset

We have developed two complementary CASE tools that implement the loosely orthogonal modelling concepts described over the previous sections (i.e. they provide support for the 5 basic primitives for the object model and SD's) . The first tool is used for rapid prototyping during analysis in order to elicit requirements, the second is a tool for formal system development that uses the products of rapid prototyping as an input. Each tool supports following broad operations :
   1) Abstract the PD classes, relationships, attributes, & required services
   2) Abstract application classes & how they pass messages with the PD
   3) Add implementation specific features to the application space to test the integrity
   4) Add implementation specific features to the PD model to shadow run the blueprint
The analyst should initially construct an object schema using the primitives described earlier. Methods can then be added to the objects in the schema. Initially the granularity of the processes may be very high, although the ability to paste in detailed methods - including C code from a variety of sources - is also supported.

5.3   Making the tool fit the hand

Tools are used in order to make working practices easier. Human beings are tool inventors as well as tool users, and CASE is one of the more recent manifestations of the human need to make and use tools in order to gain an advantage. This need is discussed extensively by Degrace and Stahl in their book *The Olduvai Imperative* [Degrace93].

Degrace and Stahl draw analogies between contemporary CASE practice and the approaches taken by the early civilisations of Greece and Rome in the field of technology management. They observe that the Greek approach - which focuses upon individuals acting on their own behalf, spontaneously and creatively, choosing and using their own tools, only forming groups on an informal ad-hoc basis - has parallels with the way many programmers work. The Roman approach, meanwhile - where individuality is sacrificed for the good of the organisation under a clearly defined hierarchy, and the only tools that can be used are those supplied by the organisation itself - has much in common with the way managers work.

They observe that some organisations are predominantly Greek or Roman in nature, and that a balance between the two should ideally be achieved. We should be aware of the fact that "there are some overly Romans in the CASE field who select tools based not on what the programmers actually need, but on what they *think* the programmers need....so [in response the programmers] simply did double duty. They did what had to be done to get the software built, and they also fulfilled the requirements of the method that was being enforced by the tool"

Human understanding of a problem is non-linear and evolves in a piecemeal fashion; it is incontrovertibly Greek. It is our opinion that contemporary CASE tools tend to enforce Roman working practices upon programmers. Degrace and Stahl concur that "we don't acquire knowledge about problems smoothly....rather, we seem to take in information in chunks and then process them to one level or another....in any case, we apparently fit new stuff into old patterns". This "interleaving" of problem space with solution space is, we feel, essentially Greek and a rapid prototyping CASE tool, which assists in the identification of requirements, must fit these Greek working practices.

6.   Formal Analysis & Design

Although our rapid prototyping/requirements elicitation approach is central to the analysis phase, the products of this early analysis must be formalised before a migration into design can commence. In the design activity, each module identified on a formalised analysis diagram is converted to an individual design diagram. Modelling of things "systemic" [Checkland81] to this level then commences; i.e things relevant to this level of abstraction. This modelling includes :

i) - remodelling of data members where necessary (the data necessary to describe an instance of that class). This would typically include activities such as normalisation.
ii) - reallocation of function members. (operations that can be carried out on or by an instance of a class)
iii) -derivation of a formal (Z or VDM based) specification.[Abrial80]
iv) -algorithm design using pseudocode or JSP[Jackson75]
v) - checking of parameter passing information

7.   Coding

If a "top-down" approach has been used exclusively, a complete set of design diagrams will exist following completion of the design activity. The diagramming notation has been so designed as to reduce coding to a mechanical process. Although it is not yet implemented we expect that to a large extent, code generation can be automated.

Conversely, if an exclusively experimental-programming approach has been taken, coding may well be the first activity undertaken. (Conversations with practising software engineers suggest that this may well be the case.) By using built in editors the code is entered directly into the system database. From there, it can be reverse engineered into diagrammatic form, in real time thus providing design documentation `on-the-fly'.

8. Notation of the formal development phase

8.1 Formal Analysis diagrams

Formal Analysis diagrams are closely related to the diagrams used in the rapid prototyping phase which occurred earlier in analysis. Their main features are as follows:-

Modules : The presence of a module simply indicates the existence of an entity in the real-world system being modelled. These are designed to look like the "class" of the design notation. Each module must have a unique name; using the design tool, they can be expanded to their corresponding "class" diagram at the click of a button.

Relationships : Relationships indicate a link of some sort between two entities. Each relationship must have a name and cardinality.

Categories : Relationships fall into 4 categories, each of which is implemented in a different way. An "is_a_kind_of" relationship indicates inheritance of some kind is required. A "contains" relationship is implemented using a container class. "Has_a" relationships indicate participation in a whole/part hierarchy and usually means the source entity will have a variable of the type of the destination entity. The "uses" type of relationship implies the use of pointers to maintain links between instances of two classes.

From the identification of these relationships part of the design can be inferred automatically. The identification of "is_a_kind_of" and "has_a" relationships leads to the construction of hierarchies of entities. It can be useful to identify the existence of such structures on separate analysis diagrams.

8.2 Design diagrams

A single design can be made up of a series of design diagrams. For every entity identified on an analysis diagram, a corresponding diagram should exist. Navigation between the two is possible using "hypercase" links between diagrams, subsections of diagrams and other parts of the database. It is almost impossible to draw them by hand and to do so would produce diagrams so cluttered with lines as to be indecipherable. The design tool is essential for this activity as it attempts to achieve clarity via the layering of information [Tufte] using visibility controls. The design diagrams include notation for the following features:-

Data members : Data members can be added to a class by placing them on the right hand side of the owning classes' bounding box. The member may be of either object or non-object type. The visibility of a member is indicated by its position: inside the class - private, touching the edge of the class - public.

Function members : Function members are added on the left hand side. Implementation functions appear entirely within the bounding rectangle of the owning class. "Policy" methods are shown partially protruding from the bounding box.

Function icon : The function member "icon" has several parts.

i) - The name of the function (or method).

ii) -A local variable area/ "landing area" for formal parameters.(See "function calls" below). Local variables and parameters have the same scope and are thus are represented in the same area.

iii) -A code icon. Code representations are accessed via "clicking" on this icon. The impossibility of having the code represented directly in this space is a consequence of designing the notation with tool support in mind.

Parameters : Three types of formal parameter are supported, based on the Ada standard parameter declarations (in, out, in/out)

Procedural logic : Procedural logic can be represented in three ways (pseudocode, JSP, or directly in target language code). The design phase is language independent.

Figure 1 : Procedural Logic

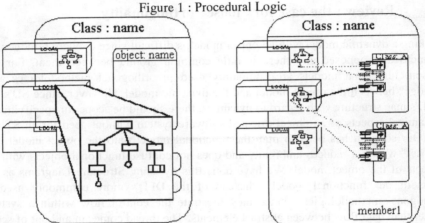

The code icon is shown here as exploding to a JSP diagram editor. This could alternatively be a structured text editor or even both with simultaneous translation between the two formats.

Function calls (message passing) : Function calls ("message passing" is the OO term) take place between methods. They originate with the methods of the class being designed and are targeted on methods of member data and are simply shown as un-annotated lines. If every possible function call were shown simultaneously on a design diagram the result would be an extremely cluttered diagram. To avoid this, the number of links shown at any one time are limited by visibility controls. The following options are possible : (i) - all calls. (ii) -all calls to given object (iii) -all calls to one particular method (iv) -all calls from one method (v) -individual calls

Call editor : A fundamental part of function calls are the data required and produced by the call. Again, clutter prevents this information being shown directly on the design diagram. "Clicking" on any call will execute an editor tool to show the source and destination of all parameters in a given call. This editor allows the drawing of lines representing data transfer between destination and source on the design diagram.

Inheritance : On a class's defining design diagram, any members which are defined as "protected" (accessible only to the methods of descendant inheriting classes) are shown in a different colour to "private" or "protected" members. In any descendant class, only the public members inherited will be displayed. Inheritance is shown in the following fashion. The idea being that descendants appear to be "built upon" their ancestors.

Genericity : No special graphic notation is required to define a generic (template) class. Any variables (usually parameters of the classes method) that are of unknown type at design time are represented on the diagram prefixed with a designatory identifier surrounded by "<" and ">" characters in much the same manner as they are treated in C++. e.g. <T> my_variable.

9 Review : the case for "loose" orthogonality

Linking a dynamic model with an object model is difficult since they are orthogonally diametrically opposed and there is little common ground between them. For this reason, functional models are commonly used in orthogonal methodologies as a "bridge" between the object model and the dynamic model. However, since SD's and DFD's map structure with regard to dynamics, there should be scope for specifying the dynamical aspects of an object-oriented software system without need for an STD at all. Our solution has been to map the functional model onto the object model in a "looser" way that reduces ambiguity and does not confuse functional objects with the objects of the object model. We have done this by using Structure Diagrams as the basis of our functional model - instead of the DFD's more commonly used in orthogonal methodologies - since they illustrate the control flow within a system, rather than data flow between abstract elements. The thread comes in and out of scope for each method as other methods are invoked. Note also that aspects of data structure which conceptually belong to a method, rather than the object schema, can be allocated to the functional model by instantiating the structure during the flow of control. A typical example would be an attribute, such as a loop variable, that is only used within a method of an object.

Although Meyer [Meyer88] has claimed that the sequencing of actions is an aspect of systems architecture that tends to change often during development and evolution, Lewis [Lewis91] challenges this. "The ordering of these actions does *not* change very often.....the whole point of the modelling phase of JSD [is] to capture, as accurately as possible, the stable features of the problem domain". In practice, we have found that Lewis's assertion is broadly correct - the sequencing of actions rarely changes although they may be placed in different behavioural contexts belonging to the object exhibiting the actions.

10 Conclusion

A unified CASE supported lifecycle methodology has been presented. The tools embrace the same "loosely orthogonal" approach to modelling. Their toolsets are based upon the same object-oriented primitives, and they employ the same "loosely orthogonal" views. This facilitates the seamless integration of phases.

The use of rapid prototypes in the analysis phase of software engineering can greatly assist requirements elicitation, and this would ultimately translate into less rework and lower costs. Contemporary orthogonal O-O CASE tools are not suited for this purpose; whilst many can produce an executable specification they are too rigorous for use in requirements identification and are best used as design tools. A tool for rapid prototyping has been presented in this paper as a "loosely orthogonal" solution that fits the hand of "Greek" analysts and integrates seamlessly with design tools.

References

[Abrial80] J.R. Abrial, S.A. Schuman, B. Meyer, "Specification Language", On the Construction of Programs : An Advanced Course, Cambridge University Press 1980.
[Birchenough89] A. Birchenough, J.R. Cameron The Implementation of LSD Specifications via JSD, ARE(MOD) 12/1989.
[Booch94] G. Booch, "Object-Oriented Analysis and Design", Benjamin-Cummings 1994.
[Checkland81] P. Checkland, "Systems Thinking, Systems Practice", Welly 1981.
[Chen76] P. Chen. The Entity-Relationship Model - Toward a unified view of data. ACM Transactions on Database Systems. pp 9-36, March 1976.
[Colbert94] E. Colbert, Abstract better and enjoy life, Journal of Object-Oriented Programming March/April 1994 Vol. 7 No. 1.
[Degrace93] P. Degrace & L.H. Stahl, "The Olduvai Imperative : CASE and the State of Software Engineering Practice", Prentice-Hall 1993.
[Jackson75] M.A. Jackson. Principles of Program Design. Academic Press, 1975.
[Lewis91] C.T. Lewis, The Realisation of JSD Specifications in Object-Oriented Languages, Aston PhD 1991.
[Martin92] J. Martin, J.J. Odell, "Object-Oriented Analysis and Design", Prentice-Hall 1992.
[Masiero88] P.C. Masiero, F.S.R. Germano, JSD as an Object-Oriented Design Method, ACM SIGSOFT Software Engineering Notes (USA) July 1988.
[Meyer88] B. Meyer, "Object-Oriented Software Construction", Prentice-Hall 1988.
[Mitchell95] I. Mitchell, P.Dunne, J. Moses, N. Parrington, "An Object-Oriented CASE Tool for Analysis", 1995 International Congress on MetaCASE (proceedings).
[Rumbaugh91] J. Rumbaugh, M. Blaha, W. Premerlani, F. Eddy, W. Lorensen. Object-Oriented Modelling and Design. Prentice Hall, Englewood Cliffs, NJ, 1991.
[Shlaer89] S. Shlaer, An Object-Oriented Approach to Domain Analysis, ACM SIGSOFT Software Engineering Notes (USA) July 1989.
[Shlaer92] S. Shlaer, S.J. Mellor. Object-Oriented Systems Analysis: Modeling the World in Data. Yourdon Press, Englewood Cliffs, NJ, 1992.
[Sommerville92] I. Sommerville, Software Engineering, Addison-Wesley 1992.
[Stroustrup91] B. Stroustrup, "The C++ Programming Language", Addison-Wesley 1991.
[Tufte] E. Tufte, "Envisioning Information", Graphics Press, Connecticut.
[Zhou94] W. Zhou, A Rapid Prototyping System for Distributed Information System Applications, Journal of Systems and Software Jan 94 Vol. 24 No. 1.

Integrating and Supporting Entity Relationship and Object Role Models

John R. Venable and John C. Grundy

Department of Computer Science, University of Waikato
Private Bag 3105, Hamilton, New Zealand
email: jvenable@cs.waikato.ac.nz or jgrundy@cs.waikato.ac.nz

Abstract. This paper describes the conceptual integration and computer-based support of two important groups of conceptual data models, Entity Relationship Models and Object Role Models (e.g. NIAM). We perform conceptual integration using the conceptual data modelling language CoCoA to specify separate data models of individual notations. We then merge these into an integrated conceptual data model for both notations. These data models form the basis of the repository for an I-CASE tool supporting modelling with both notations, with full consistency management between the two notation data models.

1 Introduction

1.1 ER and NIAM Models

Conceptual data modelling is an important perspective used in describing information systems during requirements analysis and specification. Conceptual data models are information systems modelling languages (ISMLs) that are used to describe, reason about, or document the logical structure and meaning of data and the concepts they represent. They are not concerned with what the data is used for or how. They are also unconcerned with how data is represented within a computer-based information system.

Two important groups or classes of conceptual data models are Entity Relationship (ER) Models and Object Role Models (ORM). Each group has its advantages and disadvantages as well as its adherents and critics. The ER model group follows from the work of Chen [2], and ER models have become very popular for Information Systems development. ER models utilise attributed entities and relationships to describe information structure. Fig. 1 shows an example of an ER data model for a simple invoicing system.

ORM models follow from the work of Nijssen and others at Control Data in the Netherlands. The most well known ORM is NIAM, as described in [15] and refined in [9]. ORM offer a well-thought-out system of constraints, rigorous means of dealing with higher arity relationships (i.e., n-ary with n>2), and an effective means of communicating with users via examples of data. Fig. 1 also shows an example of a NIAM data model for a simple invoicing system.

Some problems suit ER modelling while others suit ORM modelling, and developers have a preference to which notation they use. In order to facilitate system development using both of these modelling techniques simultaneously, an I-CASE tool is required which supports integrated modelling with both notations. Consistency management between ER and NIAM models must be supported in order to effectively use both notations on the same problem domain. Without such tool support, effective utilisation of both models is difficult, as inconsistencies are difficult to manually detect and correct.

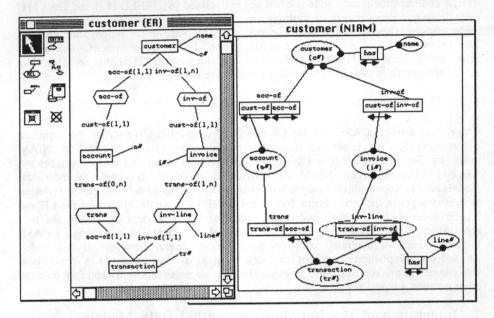

Fig. 1. ER and NIAM data models for an invoicing Information System.

1.2 Related Research

Integrated ISEEs (or Integrated CASE tools and programming environments) allow designers to analyse, design, and implement Information Systems from within one environment, providing a consistent user interface and consistent repository (data dictionary). They help to minimise inconsistencies that can arise when using several separate tools for information systems development [16, 12].

Some work has been done on the static integration of notations. We base this work on Venable [14] who has performed detailed analyses and integrations of both data flow models and conceptual data models. Campbell and Halpin [1] have also analysed abstraction techniques for conceptual schemas, including those in the ER and NIAM models. Falkenberg and Oei [3] have proposed a metamodel hierarchy but it has not yet been applied to the ER and ORM areas. Data modelling has been used to compare different notations [10] and support methodology engineering [7]. Process-modelling has also been applied to compare and integrate notations [13]. Little has been done to translate conceptually integrated notations into tool-based implementations.

Limited dynamic notation integration is supported by many CASE tools, such as Software thru Pictures™ [16]. These ICASE environments allow developers to analyse and design software using a variety of different notations, with limited inter-notation consistency. Such tools do not generally support complex mappings between the design notations, such as propagating an ER relationship addition to a corresponding OOA/D or NIAM diagram. The implementation of these environments is generally not sufficient to allow different design notations to be effectively integrated, and consistency between design and implementation code is often not maintained [8]. FIELD [12] and Dora [11] provide abstractions for keeping multiple tools and textual and graphical views consistent under change. They do not, however, provide any mechanism for propagating changes between views which can not be directly applied by the environment, such as ER relationship changes to NIAM or OOA/D relationship changes. Thus changes which can not be automatically translated to another notation are not supported.

1.3 Our Approach

To produce a true I-CASE tool for ER and NIAM modelling, we utilise the approach described in [5]. First, conceptual data models are developed for both the ER and NIAM notations. Second, an integrated conceptual data model is derived which captures the concepts of both the ER and NIAM. Third, dynamic data mappings between the individual models are developed which describe how changes to data in one notation can be reflected as data changes in the other. Forth, individual CASE tools are developed for the ER and NIAM notations, using their individual conceptual data models to specify the tool repositories. Finally, these individual modelling tools are integrated into a single I-CASE tool by defining an integrated repository based on the integrated conceptual data model. The individual repositories are kept consistent by using the data mappings to specify how data changes in one repository are propagated to the integrated repository and then onto the other notation's repository.

2 Integration of the Notation Conceptual Data Models

2.1 CoCoA

We use the CoCoA conceptual data modelling language [14] as a meta-model for modelling Information System Modelling Languages (ISMLs) and their concepts. CoCoA is designed to support modelling of complex problem domains and extends existing Entity Relationship (ER) models. Fig. 2 depicts the seven main CoCoA abstractions. Entities are the things in a problem domain and attributes describe and/or identify them (Fig. 2 (a)). Named relationships have the semantics of ER relationships, and are composed of named roles, played by entities. Cardinalities are indicated with each role (Fig. 2 (b)).

CoCoA supports generalization and specialization, and where specialization is based on a partitioning attribute, that attribute is shown (Fig. 2 (c)). CoCoA extends other ER models by the implicit use of categories, allowing more than one entity (type) to play the same role in the same named relationship (Fig. 2 (d)). CoCoA derives its name from a fifth data modelling concept, that of Complex Covering Aggregation. Covering aggregation distinguishes the aggregation of entities into composite entities from the aggregation of attributes into entities. Complex covering aggregation is distinguished from simple covering aggregation in that aggregation of named relationships into the composite entity is allowed (Fig. 2 (e)). CoCoA supports aliases, which are useful for model integration, showing old local names together with standardized names for synonyms (Fig. 2 (f)). Derived concepts (attributes, entities, named relationships, or covering aggregation relationships) are annotated with a '*' (Fig. 2 (g)).

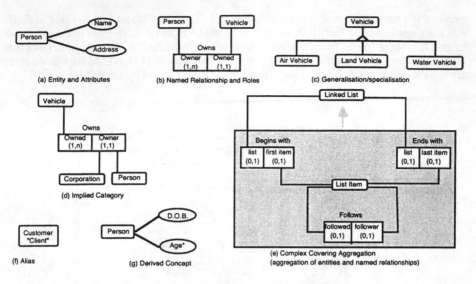

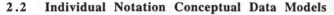

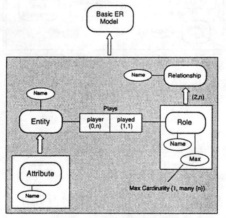

Fig. 2. The CoCoA model notation

2.2 Individual Notation Conceptual Data Models

Fig. 3. ER conceptual data model.

We have used CoCoA to derive conceptual data models for ER and NIAM. The data model describing the fundamental abstractions of ER models is shown in Fig. 3. Entities are named and have zero or more named attributes. Relationships are named and have two or more named roles. Roles link entities and relationships and may include a maximum cardinality. Extensions to this basic ER schema include provision for entity subtyping, optional and mandatory roles, and distinguished key attributes of entities [14].

Fig. 4 shows NIAM's main abstractions. A NIAM entity is named and may have a reference, made by one or more named labels. Fact types are named and have one or more roles. The "derived" attribute of the fact type entity is marked as derived (by the asterisk)

322

because it's value is true if it is related to a derivation rule. Roles link entities to facts, and are named. Nested fact types are both entities and facts i.e. have roles but also behave as entities, being linked to zero or more facts via further roles. A CoCoA model of other NIAM constraints is omitted for brevity, but can be found in [14]. NIAM derivation rules are not specified further because they are not fully specified by Nijssen and Halpin [9].

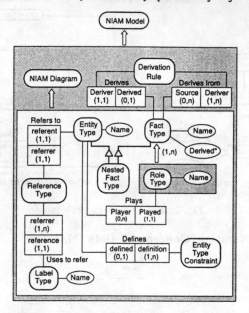

Fig. 4. NIAM entities conceptual data model.

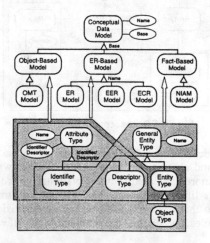

Fig. 5. An integrated conceptual data model.

2.3 An Integrated Conceptual Data Model

We have developed an integrated data model which captures the overlaps between ER and NIAM. We have included in this data model the OMT notation, an object-oriented modelling approach, as shown in Fig. 5. The ER and OMT models differentiate between entities and attributes, whereas NIAM integrates these concepts into a general entity type. The main difference between the OMT and ER conceptual data models is OMT's support for class methods. The overlaps between the notations are indicated by covering aggregation showing the composition of each data model from the integrated data model entities and relationships. Further discussion of relationship type classifications is in [14].

3 Internotation Mappings

Our integrated conceptual data model specifies the *static* integration of the two notations i.e. which ER concepts correspond to which NIAM concepts and vice-versa. This integrated data model can form the specification for an integrated tool repository for ER and NIAM notations. It does not, however, specify *dynamic* mappings between the two notations i.e. when an ER model is changed, what is the affect on the NIAM model for the same problem? It is straightforward to translate an ER change into the integrated repository change, as the integrated model fully describes the ER data model. It is often more difficult to translate a change to the integrated data model into a change in the NIAM model, as some of the concepts modified may not directly correspond. This is also true in the reverse direction (NIAM to integrated model to ER model).

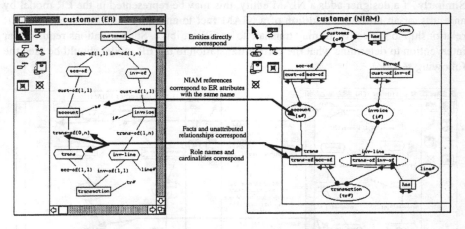

Fig. 6. Direct mappings between ER and NIAM models.

Some dynamic mappings are quite straightforward, and we term them *direct* mappings. For example, ER entities map directly to NIAM entities, so adding, updating or deleting an ER entity can be automatically reflected as appropriate changes on the corresponding NIAM entity. Unattributed ER relationships correspond to NIAM facts, and thus adding an ER relationship and roles can be directly propagated to the addition of a NIAM relationship and roles. Renaming ER roles and relationships can be translated into renaming NIAM roles and facts. NIAM entity references, which are used to refer to an entity, correspond to ER attributes of the same name. Direct mappings between the two models are shown in Fig. 6.

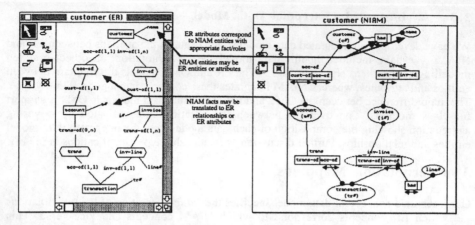

Fig. 7. Indirect mappings between ER and NIAM models.

Some concepts do not directly map to concepts in the other notation, and we term these *indirect* mappings. See Fig. 7. For example, ER attributes must be mapped to NIAM entities, with appropriate NIAM roles and a fact to link the "attribute" entity to its owner. In Fig. x, a designer adding a "name" attribute to the ER model results in a corresponding "name" entity and binary fact ("has") being added to the corresponding NIAM model. Similarly, if a designer adds a NIAM entity, this may be represented in the ER model by an entity or an attribute. Addition of a NIAM fact to an entity may translate to an ER relationship to the entity, or may translate to an ER attribute. Such situations require user intervention to determine what the correct translation to the ER model should be (see the following section).

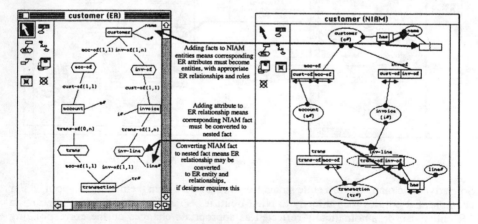

Fig. 8. Further indirect mappings between ER and NIAM models.

NIAM supports many constraints between facts, such as uniqueness values for single or composite roles. Subtyping and mandatory/optional roles correspond to the same concepts in most ER models. The other constraints do not have similar concepts in ER models, and can not be translated into ER changes. However, designers should be informed when using ER diagrams that such untranslatable constraints have been added to the corresponding NIAM model.

Some mappings between the notations can be translated initially, but may need to be modified depending on further development of the system being designed. For example, if the customer name attribute was added to the ER model, a corresponding NIAM entity and fact would be added. If the designer subsequently added further facts about this entity to the NIAM view, such as first name and last name, the ER customer name attribute would need to be converted to an ER entity, with appropriate relationship and roles to the customer entity. Similarly, if attributes are added to an ER relationship, the corresponding NIAM fact must be converted to a nested fact type, which can have facts of its own. Thus some modifications to one notation result in many modifications to the other model. Some may be defaulted by an I-CASE tool, but some user intervention may be required. Fig. 8 illustrates complex indirect mappings.

4 An Integrated CASE Tool for NIAM/ER Modelling

4.1 MViews

NIAMER is implemented as a collection of classes, specialised from the MViews framework [4, 6]. MViews supports the construction of Integrated Software Development Environments (ISDEs) by providing a general model for defining software system data structures and tool views, with a flexible mechanism for propagating changes between software components, views and distinct software development tools.

MViews describes ISDE data as *components* with *attributes*, linked by a variety of *relationships*. Multiple views are supported by representing each view as a graph linked to the base software system graph structure. Each view is rendered and edited in either a graphical or textual form. Distinct environment tools can be interfaced at the view level (as editors), via external view translators, or multiple base layers may be connected via inter-view relationships.

When a software or view component is updated, a change description is generated. This is of the form UpdateKind(UpdatedComponent, ...UpdateKind-specific Values...). For example, an attribute update on Comp1 of attribute Name is represented as: update(Comp1, Name, OldValue, NewValue). All basic graph editing operations generate change descriptions and pass them to the propagation system. Change descriptions are propagated to all related components that are dependent upon the updated component's state. Dependents interpret these change descriptions and possibly modify their own state, producing further change descriptions. This change description mechanism supports a diverse range of software development environment facilities, including semantic attribute recalculation, multiple views of a component, flexible, bi-directional textual and graphical view consistency management, a generic undo/redo mechanism, and component "modification history" information.

New software components and editing tools are constructed by reusing abstractions provided by an object-oriented framework. ISDE developers specialise MViews classes to define software components, views and editing tools to produce the new environment. A persistent object store is used to store component and view data.

4.2 NIAMER Architecture

NIAMER was built by integrating two independently developed CASE tools. MViewsER [5] provides multiple graphical ER views and textual relational schema views. MViewsNIAM provides multiple NIAM modelling views. These two tools were integrated by developing an integrated repository, based on the integrated conceptual data model from section 2. The items in this integrated repository are linked to items in the individual tool repositories. Changes to ER tool data are translated into changes to the integrated repository data and then into changes on NIAM tool data (and vice-versa), by the inter-repository relationships.

An advantage of using an integrated repository to maintain inter-notation consistency is when extending the environment. For example, the authors have developer another environment supporting integrated EER and OOA/D modelling, called OOEER [5], with many of the NIAM and ER mappings used in OOEER. Thus it is far easier to integrate OOEER and NIAMER by using the integrated repository, to produce an environment supporting EER, OOA/D and NIAM modelling, than by respecifying many of the mappings already implemented in each environment. In fact, a third integrated repository could be used to link the integrated NIAMER and OOEER repositories.

4.3 Examples of NIAMER Consistency Management

Some translations between NIAM and ER diagrams can be fully automated by NIAMER. In this case, when a designer selects a view from the other notation from which they have been working in, it is updated to reflect any changes which can be automatically carried out. Some updates can not be automatically carried out. In this case, NIAMER allows designers to browse a "modification history" for the view or the components rendered in the view, to determine if manual updates are needed to complete a translation.

Fig. 9 shows the modification history for the NIAM transaction entity. This contains a list of human-readable change descriptions which inform the designer of changes which have affected the transaction entity. The lines prefixed by 'ER:' have been carried on ER model diagrams, affecting the ER transaction entity. These have been sent to the NIAM transaction entity and are stored to document ER changes affecting this entity. NIAMER has also translated some of these updates into NIAM model updates, indicated by the following lines prefixed by a '→'. Changes not prefixed by a '→' have been manually carried out by the designer to maintain full internotation consistency.

NIAMER supports textual views showing relational database tables for entities and facts/relationships. This facility is provided by MViewsER, but as the NIAM model is kept consistent with the ER model, relational tables can be produced for the NIAM model as well. These textual views can be kept consistent with the graphical views by expanding change descriptions into the view's text. Some expanded changes can be automatically applied to the textual view on programmer request. For example, update 12 in Fig.9 can be automatically applied by NIAMER, resulting in the acc-of table field being renamed.

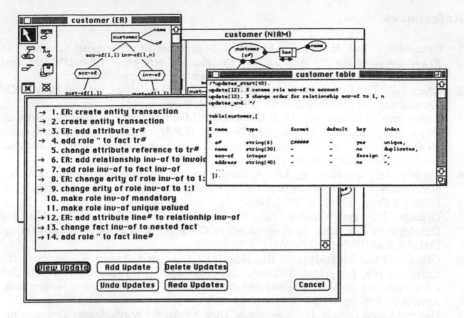

Fig. 9. Examples of translation of ER updates to NIAM updates.

5 Summary

We have integrated the conceptual data models for two common conceptual data modelling notions, ER and NIAM. This integrated model facilitates mapping dynamic data changes between the individual data models for each notation. These conceptual data models can form the basis for integrated CASE tool repositories, and we have implemented an I-CASE tool, NIAMER, which supports fully integrated NIAM and ER data modelling. Unlike other CASE tools, our data models are kept fully consistent, with any change to data in one model being translated into appropriate changes in the other model. Some changes can be automatically translated, while others require some degree of designer assistance. NIAMER always highlights such updates, and its default attempt at a translation, to assist designers in keeping their designs in each notation consistent.

We are currently integrating NIAMER and OOEER, to produce an I-CASE tool which supports EER, OOA/D and NIAM modelling, and relational schema and OO program construction. We are extending OOEER to support DFD and object-oriented functional diagram consistency. Keeping the data modelling parts of such diagrams consistent with ER and NIAM models is also being investigated. We are producing a metaCASE tool, incorporating our CoCoA modelling language and MViews framework. This will allow I-CASE tools such as NIAMER to be more easily specified, generated and integrated.

References

1. Campbell, L. and Halpin, T. Abstraction Techniques for Conceptual Schemas. In *Proceedings of the 5th Australasian Database Conference*, GlobalPublications Services, Christchurch, New Zealand, 17-18 January 1994, pp. 374-388.
2. Chen, P.P. The Entity-Relationship Model - Toward a Unified View of Data. *ACM Transactions on Database Systems 1*, 1 (1976), 9-36.
3. Falkenberg, E.D. and Oei, J.L.H.D.F.I.C.O.R.M. Meta Model Hierarchies from an Object-Role Modelling Perspective. In *F.I.C.O.R.M.irst International Conference on Object-Role Modelling*, Halpin, T. and Meersman, R., University of Queensland, Brisbane, Australia, 4-6 July 1994, pp. 310-323.
4. Grundy, J.C. and Hosking, J.G. A framework for building visual programming environments. In *Proceedings of the1993 IEEE Symposium on Visual Languages*, IEEE CS Press, 1993, pp. 220-224.
5. Grundy, J.C. and Venable, J.R. Providing Integrated Support for Multiple Development Notations. In *Proceedings of CAiSE'95*, LNCS 932, Springer-Verlag, Finland, June 1995, pp. 255-268.
6. Grundy, J.C., Mugridge, W.B., Hosking, J.G., and Amor, R. Support for Collaborative, Integrated Software Development. In *Proceeding of the 7th Conference on Software Engineering Environments*, IEEE CS Press, Netherlands, April 5-7 1995, pp. 84-94.
7. Heym, M. and Österle, H. A Semantic Data Model for Methodology Engineering. In *Proceedings of the Fifth International Workshop on Computer-Aided Software Engineering*, IEEE CS Press, Washington, D.C., 1992, pp. 142-155.
8. Meyers, S. Difficulties in Integrating Multiview Editing Environments. *IEEE Software 8*, 1 (January 1991), 49-57.
9. Nijssen, G.M. and Halpin, T.A. *Conceptual Schema and Relational Database Design: A Fact Oriented Approach*, Prentice-Hall, Englewood Cliffs, NJ (1989).
10. Nuseibeh, B. and Finkelstein, A. ViewPoints: A Vehicle for Method and Tool Integration. In *Proceedings of the Fifth International Workshop on Computer-Aided Software Engineering*, IEEE CS Press, Washington, D.C., 1992, pp. 50-61.
11. Ratcliffe, M., Wang, C., Gautier, R.J., and Whittle, B.R. Dora - a structure oriented environment generator. *IEE Software Engineering Journal 7*, 3 (1992), 184-190.
12. Reiss, S.P. Connecting Tools Using Message Passing in the Field Environment. *IEEE Software 7*, 7 (July 1990), 57-66.
13. Song, X. and Osterweil, L.J. A Process-Modeling Based Approach to Comparing and Integrating Software Design Methodologies. In *Proceedings of the Fifth International Workshop on Computer-Aided Software Engineering*, IEEE CS Press, Washingon, D.C., 1992, pp. 225-229.
14. Venable, J.R. *CoCoA: A Conceptual Data Modelling Approach for Complex Problem Domains*, Ph.D. dissertation, Thomas J. Watson School of Engineering and Applied Science, State University of New York at Binghamton, 1993.
15. Verhijen, G.M.A. and van Bekkum, J. NIAM: An Information Analysis Method. In *Proceedings of the IFFIP WG 8.2. Working Conference on Comparative Review of Information Systems Design Methodologies*, North-Holland, New York, NY, 1982.
16. Wasserman, A.I. and Pircher, P.A. A Graphical, Extensible, Integrated Environment for Software Development. *SIGPLAN Notices 22*, 1 (January 1987), 131-142.

From Object Specification towards Agent Design*

Gunter Saake   Stefan Conrad   Can Türker

Otto-von-Guericke-Universität Magdeburg
Institut für Technische Informationssysteme
Postfach 4120, D–39016 Magdeburg, Germany
E-mail: {saake|conrad|tuerker}@iti.cs.uni-magdeburg.de
Phone: ++49-391-67-18665   Fax: ++49-391-67-12020

Abstract. Nowadays, object specification technology is successfully used for modelling information systems. However, object-oriented modelling cannot cover all aspects (e.g. dynamic behaviour evolution) of such systems. A promising approach to get a grasp of these additional requirements for modelling information systems is the specification of systems as communicating, cooperating and autonomous agents. In the present paper we sketch an evolutionary extension of object specification towards agent modelling. Here, we have to emphasize that this paper is not intended to offer perfect solutions. Our aim is to discuss and fix a research agenda for a formal agent approach which promises to provide a semantically richer framework for the specification of information systems.

1   Motivation

Object-oriented modelling of information systems has become a widely accepted approach. Object-oriented data models allow to describe the structure of application domains in an adequate way. In addition, several approaches make it possible to specify the dynamic behaviour of objects and object systems. In general, versions of temporal and dynamic logic are used for this purpose. However, it seems that the concept of "object" (at least in its current understanding) cannot cover all aspects of information systems. A new concept, the concept of *agent* which can be seen as a further development of "object" is currently emerging as an important concept in many fields of Information Technology. The key facets of the concept *agent* appear to be *goal, state, behaviour,* and *heterogeneity.*

Considering the modelling of heterogeneous information systems (e.g. [Buc91, Bro92]) motivates the identification of "objects", each of them incorporating some knowledge about an application domain (like facts, rules, strategies, etc.) and being a unit of design that can be composed with other objects via aggregation and specialization hierarchies (cf. [HJS92, SJH93]). Whereas structural aspects of such systems can easily be dealt with by current object-oriented approaches, these approaches succeed to cope with dynamic behaviour only up to a certain degree.

---

* This research was partially supported by the ESPRIT Basic Research Working Group No. 8319 ModelAge (A Common Formal **Model** of Cooperating Intelligent **Agents**).

The concept of "agent" is intended to deal with such aspects. In particular, an agent (as a software unit) is assumed to have an internal state which reflects its knowledge (facts, rules, etc.). In order to use its knowledge an agent needs some reasoning capabilities. Furthermore, it must be able to update or revise its knowledge. An agent has goals, i.e. its behaviour is goal-driven. The satisfaction of goals must be achieved by performing (sequences of) actions. Agents may have conflicting goals. In consequence, goal revision must be possible or there must exist a preference order on goals. In composed systems several agents cooperate. For that, some kind of cooperation and communication structure is needed. Agents are assumed to have (incomplete) knowledge about other agents and their goals. In order to satisfy a goal agents may play different roles and can delegate tasks. The concept of agent presents a unique opportunity to integrate many significant results from many different research areas, like Database Systems, Software Engineering, or Artificial Intelligence to name a few. For example, federated information systems may be built up by cooperating (autonomous) agents which are integrated in a flexible framework.

In the remainder of this paper we first discuss requirements for agent modelling (Section 2) and then the current state of object specification technology. In Section 4 we compare the concepts and modelling constructs for objects and agents. Afterwards we present a first way of extending object specification towards agent specification. Finally, we conclude by pointing out future work. It should be clear that in this paper we mainly fix the starting point for a promising research area and present already first ideas.

2 Requirements for Agent Modelling

The concept of *agent* is proposed as a generalization of the object concept to provide a more flexible and semantically richer framework for modelling heterogeneous information systems. Agents can be interpreted as *autonomous* and *intelligent* objects, which are equipped with knowledge and reasoning capabilities to satisfy various goals (cf. [BG88, GK94]). In this section we briefly characterize some important requirements for agent modelling.

Internal State. Agents have an internal *state* which includes an internal, imperfect representation of the world. The internal state of an agent reflects the knowledge of that agent at a given time. But, this knowledge is not fixed at specification time, it is changing throughout the lifetime of an agent. Therefore, agents require knowledge acquisition and revision capabilities to be able to adapt their knowledge or to react to changing environments [DT91]. Furthermore, agents need reasoning capabilities to make use of their knowledge. In addition to state information which is coded in attribute values, the concept of agent requires disjunctive knowledge as well as handling of default knowledge [BLR93].

Goals. Agents have *goals* which they try to achieve (by cooperation) under given constraints. Each agent is obliged to satisfy its goals. In general, this is done by executing a *sequence of actions*. Goals may be changed during the lifetime of an agent. They can be extended, revised or replaced through other (more important) goals. Agents may also have conflicting goals. Hence, agents must be able to resolve conflict situation in which not all goals may be achieved. In such cases agents must be able either to revise some of its goals or to satisfy only a few of its goals which are not conflicting.

Actions. Agents are able to act and communicate. Thus, they show an external *behaviour* that obeys the given constraints and results in life cycles like for objects [DDP93]. The internal state of an agent is determined by its history which is represented by its life cycle. The revision or modification of a state is the result of the execution of a *permitted* action. As already mentioned, agents are autonomous. Therefore, agents can decide independently whether to fulfill a request or not. Thus, they may show a non-normative behaviour.

Cooperating Agents. In most cases agents have to cooperate to achieve their goals. Especially in federated information systems, where agents have to interoperate in order to provide a powerful interface for application programs, appropriate structures and protocols for agent communication and cooperation are required [GK94]. Because of the fact that agents may change their behaviour and/or may even change their signature, there must exist varying communication structures. Agents are assumed to have (incomplete) knowledge about the internal state of other agents and their goals. In order to satisfy a goal, an agent may play different roles, authorize or delegate some tasks to other agents. Hence, an agent must be able to decompose a given goal into subgoals and to assign this subgoals to the various other agents [RK91].

3 Object Specification

We base our presentation on the concept of object as introduced in [SSE87]. An object is an observable process. The dynamic behaviour of objects is described by life cycles built from basic events which may modify the object state. These events can be seen as an abstraction from implemented methods. Attributes can be defined to observe the internal state of an object. An object template serves as pattern for instances of an object class. As a logical framework, we use temporal logic specification of objects using a variant of the object specification logic OSL [SSC92]. Basically, the temporal logic used is a variant of linear temporal logic as used successfully in system specification [FM91, MP92]. For textual presentation of object specifications, we use a notation close to the syntactical conventions of the languages TROLL [SJH93, JSHS95, HSJ+94] and Oblog [SSE87]. Here, we focus on a few basic concepts and omit all language features not relevant for the problem handled in this paper.

3.1 Specification In TROLL-like languages, an object template specification mainly consists out of two parts: a *signature* section which lists object events and attributes together with parameter and co-domain types, and a behaviour section containing the axioms. As axioms we do not have general temporal logic formulas but special syntactic notations for typical specification patterns. For our discussion, we restrict the language features to the following list of specification patterns:

- Attribute valuation:
  valuation {Counter > 0} ==> [Decrease] Counter = Counter - 1;
  Attribute valuation rules expresses which effect events have on attribute values. These rules can be restricted using conditions on state attributes.
- Birth and death events:
  In the declaration section for events, we mark some events as birth events or as death events corresponding to creation and destruction of objects.
- Event permission: permissions { Counter > 0 } Decrease;
  In contrast to the conditional attribute valuation rule above, a permission restricts the occurrences of events.
- Event obligations: obligation DestroyCounter;
  Event obligations can be understood as liveness conditions, i.e. the given event must occur in the life cycle of the object. In this example the death event DestroyCounter has to occur. This means that we do not allow that the specified object can live forever.
- Event calling: interaction Withdraw(m) >> IncreaseBookingCounter;
  Event calling is used to model interaction inside (composite) objects. Similar to valuations, we may have conditional event calling, too. In our example, the withdrawal of money of an account object enforces the event IncreaseBookingCounter to occur simultaneously.

Each of the mentioned languages supports additional language features for template description, for example attribute constraints and operational process declaration. Moreover, several abstraction concepts and associations between objects like classification, relationships, specialization, aggregation are supported in these languages, too, which we will ignore in this presentation.

3.2 Models In order to interpret object specifications object models are needed. Here, we briefly sketch the ingrediences of such an object model.

Life cycles: Object behaviour is described by life cycles. A life cycle (or trace) is a sequence of (sets of simultaneously occurring) events:

$$
\langle b \rangle \longrightarrow \left\langle \begin{matrix} e_1 \\ e_2 \\ e_3 \end{matrix} \right\rangle \longrightarrow \cdots \longrightarrow \langle e_k \rangle \longrightarrow \langle d \rangle
$$

An event snapshot is a set of simultaneous occurrences of events. Thereby, this way of describing object behaviour can be applied to single objects as well as to composed (aggregated) objects.

Time-varying states: Due to the temporal evolution of an object its attributes values are evolving as well. This can be described by a sequence of states corresponding to the life cycle:

$$
\overset{birth}{\longrightarrow} [S_1] \overset{events}{\longrightarrow} [S_2] \overset{events}{\longrightarrow} \cdots \overset{events}{\longrightarrow} [S_n] \overset{death}{\longrightarrow}
$$

Observation structure: An observation structure is a mapping from states to attribute-value-pairs.

Object embedding: In order to build large systems, objects must be composed forming larger objects. This aggregation of communicating objects can be formally understood as object embedding.

Now, we can formally describe an object model as follows:

An *Object Model* **ob** $= (ACT, B, ATT, obs)$ consists of a set of actions ACT, an object behavior B over ACT, a set of attributes ATT, and an observation structure obs.

It is necessary to make some general assumptions about objects (i.e., to state some frame rules). For instance, only the occurrence of events may alter an observation. This appears to be reasonable because we expect attribute values to be changed only by explicit manipulation.

3.3 Logics As already indicated before, temporal logic is an adequate means for logical specification of object behaviour. Here, we present the use of first-order temporal logic by giving typical examples.

Temporal integrity constraints: The integrity constraint *"Value of* Counter *never decreases."* could be expressed in temporal logic as follows:
$$\forall x (\textbf{always}(\ (\texttt{Counter} = x) \Rightarrow (\textbf{next}(\texttt{Counter} \geq x)) \ ))$$

Effect of events: The effect of event Increase(n) on an attribute Counter can be described by the following temporal logic formula:
$$\forall x \forall n (\textbf{always}(\ ((\texttt{Counter} = x) \wedge \textbf{occurs}(\texttt{Increase}(n))) \Rightarrow$$
$$(\textbf{next}(\texttt{Counter} = x + n)) \ ))$$

Permission conditions for events: Assuming that Decrease(n) is only permitted to occur if the value of Counter is greater than n:
$$\forall n (\textbf{always}(\textbf{occurs}(\texttt{Decrease}(n)) \Rightarrow (\texttt{Counter} \geq n)))$$

Event synchronization ('event calling'): Expressing the event calling $a_1 \gg a_2$ (the occurrence of a_1 causes the simultaneous occurrence of a_2) in temporal logic yields the following formula:
$$\textbf{always}(\textbf{occurs}(a_1) \Rightarrow \textbf{occurs}(a_2))$$

Of course, we can not give a complete presentation of temporal logic used for object specification at this place. More detailed presentations and discussions can be found for instance in [FM91].

3.4 Limitations of Object Specification The object specification concepts presented so far lead to certain limitations in the presence of object evolution. All specification parts restrict the object behaviour for the complete life span of an object. Conditional rules can be used, however, to model changing object behaviour. This shows us the following observation: languages like TROLL or Oblog are expressive enough to model even changing object behaviour depending on state changes, *but these modifications have to be fixed during specification time, e.g. before object creation.* As argued before, this is too restrictive for handling object evolution in information systems. Therefore, an extension of the framework underlying such object specification languages is needed to support the aspect of evolution in an adequate way.

4 Comparison of Object and Agent Approach

Up to now, we have looked at the state of the art in object specification and have listed on the other hand some requirements for designing artificial agents as software units. In the sequel we compare these two design paradigms and identify similarities as well as principal differences. This comparison will enable us to sketch the research road towards an evolutionary extension of object technology towards agent modelling. The comparison is divided into two main sections, a first to compare fundamentals concepts and design principles, and a second one for higher modelling principles. Both parts are summarized in a table. We will present the comparison following the order given by the table.

4.1 Basic Concepts

A summary of the concepts discussed in this subsection is shown in Table 1.

- Both objects and agents have an *internal state* based on their history and influencing their behaviour. For objects, this state is determined by the values of attributes. Agents on the other hand have a more general notion of state: it may contain disjunctive information, partial knowledge, default assumptions etc. Besides these extensions of the determined state concept of agents, an agent state may contain explicit reasoning rules.
- The *constraints* for object states and behaviour are fixed at specification time. For agents, the constraints may vary from time to time, and may be violated as result of non-normative behaviour.
- For *behaviour* description, we have a similar situation as for constraints.
- An *action* (or method) of an object corresponds to a fixed computed function whereas an agent's action may be more general, for example a problem solving step using heuristics, default knowledge, etc.
- *Goals* to be satisfied by an object are fixed at specification time, and may serve as formal requirements for implementing behaviour. Therefore they have to be logically consistent. The goals of agents may vary during an agent's lifetime, they may be conflicting or may not at all unsatisfiable.
- The *communication structure* for objects is fixed at specification time; for agents it may vary and can be influenced by actions.
- *Identity* and *encapsulation* are important concepts for both objects and agents.
- As *quality criterion* for object implementation we have correctness w.r.t. the specification. For agents, we have to look at a much broader spectrum of properties: a preference ordering of alternative "correct" behaviours, normative versus non-normative behaviours, minimization of the number of goal conflicts, maximal number of satisfied goals, etc.

Basic Concepts		
	Object Design	Agent Design
Internal State	determined by history, value-based	... + disjunctive information + partial + default + ...
Constraints	fixed	varying
Behaviour	fixed	varying
Actions	computed function	problem solving step
Goals	fixed	varying, conflicting
Communication Channels	fixed	varying
Identity	√	√
Encapsulation	√	√
Quality criterion	Correctness	Preferred Behaviour, Normative B., Minimal Number of Conflicts

Table 1. Object versus Agent Design: Basic Concepts

4.2 Modelling Constructs

In general, most of the modelling constructs known for objects are useful for agents, too (see Table 2). We will not go through the list in detail, but state some interesting differences only:

- In general, the agent framework sees all modelling constructs as something which is varying in time and may be modified by agents actions. Not all object design frameworks emphasize such dynamics.
- *Type systems* are seen as very important for object design formalizing for example inheritance. Agents may have different interfaces to different agents and they even may change their interfaces during their existence. Usual static type systems are in conflict with these requirements. Moreover, *inheritance* between agents is discussed on the level of knowledge rather than on the formal interface level.
- The concept of *role* seems to be very basic for agent design. It is connected with such concepts like authority, delegation, power to do something, etc. Even if roles were proposed for objects, too [WD92], it seems to us that the support of roles played by agents is a fundamental new modelling concept for agent design.
- *Aggregation* and *composition* are very fundamental concepts of object frameworks. For agents we may need other types of aggregation: Can a group of agents itself being considered as an (composed) agent? If so, what are the basic composition principles? For object design, we use the basic data structure ideas of lists, tuples, etc. for composition, and it is questionable whether this may be appropriate for agents, too.
- With regard to *modularization* it is not clear whether the object-oriented concepts (classes and class hierarchies) are sufficient in the context of agents. Here, more work has to be done to clarify this item.
- In object-oriented approaches *relationships* are fixed by explicitly naming classes such that only objects of these classes may participate. If we use re-

lationships for modelling communication structures between agents, we need a more flexible concept of relationships because communication structures may vary for agents.

Modelling Constructs		
	Object Design	Agent Design
Classification	√	√
Specialization & Inheritance	√	√
Type System	√	???
Roles	(√) ?	√ !
Aggregation / Composition	√	(√) ?
Local versus Global / Modularization	√	?
Explicit Relationships	fixed	varying

Table 2. Object versus Agent Design: Modelling Constructs

5 Towards Agent Specification

In this section we propose an extension of current object specification technology in such a way that concepts which have been identified as indispensable for agents can be integrated. Instead of inventing a new specification language, we aim at a sound extension of existing object-oriented specification languages like TROLL (cf. Section 3).

In current object specification approaches object states are given by a mapping from attributes to values. From our point of view, such value maps are not flexible enough for capturing further requirements of agents. Instead of a value map it seems to be more adequate to describe the state of an agent by a set of formulas, i.e. a state is given by a logical theory (this point of view has already been used in e.g. [Rei84]). In addition, state changes have to be considered as theory revision, i.e. adding or removing of formulas.

Taking logical theories for states we do not loose any possibility of current object specification. This is due to the fact that value maps for attributes can easily be expressed in terms of standard logic.

Moreover the theory approach to states allows us to introduce new agent-specific concepts in a rather straightforward way. Beside the current values of attributes it is now possible to explicitly describe the agent's current knowledge (as logical rules). Furthermore we may now change the behaviour of an agent during its lifetime by adding or removing formulas from its current "state".

Example: A possible specification of an `Account` agent class is depicted in Fig. 1. The specification language used in this example can be considered as an extension of the object-oriented language TROLL sketched in Section 3. Similar to objects, agents have attributes (here: `Balance`) and events (e.g. `Withdraw`). The part of the behaviour specification which must not be changed is specified in the **rigid axioms** section. In our example the effect of the events `Withdraw` and `Deposit` on the attribute `Balance` is fixed.

agent class Account
   identification   ByAccNo: AccNo;
   attributes   AccNo: nat **constant**;
                       Balance: money **initialized** 0.00;
   events   Open(H:|Holder|, AN: nat) **birth**;
                       Withdraw(W:money);
                       Deposit(D:money);
                       Alarm(S:string);
   mutators   AddAxioms(P:setOfAxioms);
                       ResetAxioms;
   rigid axioms   [Withdraw(W)] Balance := Balance - W;
                       [Deposit(D)]   Balance := Balance + D;
   axiom attributes ControlAxioms **initialized** {**true**};
   dynamic specification
                       [AddAxioms(P)] ControlAxioms := ControlAxioms ∪ P;
                       [ResetAxioms]   ControlAxioms := {**true**};
end agent class Account;

Fig. 1. Specification of an Account agent class.

In addition to the concepts used for objects, agents may have **axiom attributes**, i.e., attributes that have sets of axioms as values. For instance, Account agents have an axiom attribute ControlAxioms which is initialized by the set containing the formula **true**. Because there is only one axiom attribute specified, this contains the set of currently valid axioms for the agent. In case we specify several axiom attributes we have to explicitly mark one of them for that purpose. Each formula which is included in the value of this special axiom attribute at a certain state must be fulfilled in that state.

The values of axiom attributes may be manipulated by a special kind of events, called **mutators**. For our Account agents we have introduced two mutators: AddAxioms and ResetAxioms. The effect of mutators is described in the **dynamic specification** section. Here, we restrict the manipulation of the axiom attribute ControlAxioms to adding of further axioms and to resetting to the initial state. Please note that adding axioms means to restrict the possible behaviour of the specified agent. The mutator ResetAxioms removes all these additional restrictions.

In Fig. 2 some possible values for the parameter P of the mutator AddAxioms are listed. These values are sets of formulas written in the syntax of our specification language. The first value contains a formula which requires to trigger an alarm if the amount of a withdrawal is larger than 300. In the next value there is an additional restriction saying that a Withdraw event may only occur with an amount smaller than the current value of the attribute Balance. Thereby, overdrawing of an account is ruled out. The third listed value contains a formula which specifies the following behaviour: in case that a second withdrawal is tried within one day an alarm must be triggered (in this formula we refer to a Clock assuming that it is specified elsewhere as a part of same system).

```
{ interaction
    { W > 300 } Withdraw(W) >> Alarm("Withdrawal limit exceeded!"); }

{ permission    { W ≤ Balance } Withdraw(W); }

{ interaction
    { not(occurs(Clock.NextDay)) since last occurs(Withdraw(W)) }
    Withdraw(W) >> Alarm("Two withdrawals within one day!");        }
```

Fig. 2. Examples for possible values for P in `AddAxioms(P)`.

In the classical object-oriented view temporal evolution is only seen as value changes of attributes. In this way we can only manipulate attribute values. The behaviour of an object is fixed (*at specification time*). For systems which are intended to run over a long time this does not seem to be adequate.

In addition to the change of attribute values the theory approach to states facilitates another view to temporal evolution of a system. The change of theories (instead of attribute values) can be seen as knowledge revision and knowledge acquisition. Default knowledge may be overwritten (*at run-time*) by more specific knowledge, partial knowledge may be completed.

The idea of "states as theories" for object specification with evolving behaviour is described in more detail in [SSS95] where other aspects like evolving knowledge of an object or agent are not considered.

In order to support this more powerful approach of states as theories, we need adequate logics for dealing with the new possibilities. Obviously, classical temporal logic used in current object specification approaches is not sufficient.

Logics are needed which cope with belief revision, knowledge evolution and revision, change of defaults (default knowledge), and normative behaviour.

A large number of non-standard logics already exists which are tailored for these purposes, e.g. [Mey92, Rya93, JS93]. Here, we can choose logics having those properties we are interested in. To come as close as possible to the idea of "agent" presented before, choosing one or two logics is not enough. They must be integrated into one logical framework, into a logic of agents.

Especially, we think that a temporal logic for specifying temporal evolution, a logic of belief or knowledge, a default logic, and a deontic logic for specifying normative and non-normative behaviour could be a useful combination. First results already show that the composition of different logics can really work [FM91]. However the work in this area is still at the beginning.

6 Conclusions and Outlook

In this paper we have presented a framework for agent design. After describing some important requirements for modelling of agents, we took a brief look at the current state of object specification technology. For that, we reviewed the basics of object specification (in the context of the object-oriented specification language TROLL), models, and logics. Then we compared the two approaches object specification and agent design. We pointed out that on the one hand both approaches have many similarities, but on the other hand there also exist some serious differences between these two approaches. Especially, we show that the concept of agent overcome the limitations of current object models to describe object behaviour evolution. The main reason for that is due to the fact that the agent paradigm allows agents to have changing goals, behaviour, constraints and communication structures.

Further, we present first ideas of extending current object specification framework towards agent specification. We think that this extension can be done in several smaller steps, integrating one agent-specific concept after the other. In fact, a first step of extending an object specification approach to capture temporal evolution of object behaviour is described in [SSS95]. In this approach the idea of *states as theories* is used. The next steps will be the integration of concepts like normative behaviour specification (i.e. some kind of deontic logic) and knowledge and goal reasoning capabilities.

We do not want to conceal that there are several properties of agents for which we do not know at the moment how to put them into an adequate logic. For instance, current object-oriented approaches in general use a fixed communication structure between objects which can easily be represented in a logic. But we want to allow a more flexible communication between agents. Furthermore, we would like to distinguish different states of activities for agents. For that we have to express that an agent reacts only on demand or is active in a sense that it initiates actions in order to fulfill its goals.

Although there are many open question, it is obvious that the concept of *agent* may be useful for modelling federated information systems in which the single components are assumed to be autonomous. In order to describe such components in an adequate way the concepts of current object-oriented approaches are often not sufficient. We are aware of the fact that the ideas presented in this paper are in a preliminary state. The presentation aims at showing current research efforts rather than stable results.

References

[BG88]   A. H. Bond, L. Gasser, eds. *Readings in Distributed Artificial Intelligence.* Morgan Kaufmann, 1988.

[BLR93] S. Brass, U. W. Lipeck, P. Resende. Specification of Object Behaviour with Defaults. In U. W. Lipeck, G. Koschorreck, eds., *Proc. Int. Workshop on Information Systems – Correctness and Reusability (IS-CORE'93), Tech. Rep. 01/93, University of Hanover*, pp. 155–177, 1993.

[Bro92] M. L. Brodie. The Promise of Distributed Computing and the Challenges of Legacy Systems. In P. M. Gray, R. J. Lucas, eds., *Advanced Database Systems (Proc. BNCOD-10)*, pp. 1–28. Springer LNCS 618, 1992.

[Buc91] A. P. Buchmann. Modeling Heterogeneous Systems as an Active Object Space. In A. Dearle, G. M. Shaw, S. B. Zdonik, eds., *Proc. 4th Int. Workshop on Persistent Object Systems*, pp. 279–290. Morgan Kaufmann, 1991.

[DDP93]   E. Dubois, P. Du Bois, M. Petit. O-O Requirements Analysis: An Agent Perspective. In O. Nierstrasz, ed., *ECOOP'93 – Object-Oriented Programming*, pp. 458–481. Springer LNCS 707, 1993.

[DT91]   R. Dieng, P. A. Tourtier. A Composite System for Knowledge Acquisition and User Assistance. In *Proc. AAAI Spring Symp. Design of Composite Systems*, 1991.

[FM91]   J. Fiadeiro, T. Maibaum. Temporal Reasoning over Deontic Specifications. *Journal of Logic and Computation*, 1(3):357–395, 1991.

[GK94]   M. R. Genesereth, S. P. Ketchpel. Software Agents. *Communications of the ACM*, 37(7):48–53, 1994.

[HJS92]   T. Hartmann, R. Jungclaus, and G. Saake. Aggregation in a Behavior Oriented Object Model. In O. Lehrmann Madsen, editor, *Proc. of the European Conf. on Object-Oriented Programming (ECOOP'92)*, pages 57–77. Springer-Verlag, LNCS 615, Berlin, 1992.

[HSJ+94] T. Hartmann, G. Saake, R. Jungclaus, P. Hartel, J. Kusch. Revised Version of the Modelling Language TROLL (Version 2.0). Report 94–03, TU Braunschweig, 1994.

[JS93]   A. Jones, M. Sergot. On the Characterisation of Law and Computer Systems: The Normative System Perspective. In J.-J. Ch. Meyer, R. J. Wieringa, eds., *Deontic Logic in Computer Science: Normative System Specification*, chapter 12. Wiley, 1993.

[JSHS95] R. Jungclaus, G. Saake, T. Hartmann, C. Sernadas. TROLL – A Language for Object-Oriented Specification of Information Systems. *ACM Transactions on Information Systems*, 1995. *To appear*.

[Mey92]   J.-J. Ch. Meyer. Modal Logics for Knowledge Representation. In R. P. van de Riet, R. A. Meersman, eds., *Linguistic Instruments in Knowledge Engineering*, pp. 251–275. North-Holland, 1992.

[MP92]   Z. Manna, A. Pnueli. *The Temporal Logic of Reactive and Concurrent Systems. Vol. 1: Specification*. Springer, 1992.

[Rei84]   R. Reiter. Towards a Logical Reconstruction of Relational Database Theory. In M. L. Brodie, J. Mylopoulos, J. W. Schmidt, eds., *On Conceptual Modeling*, pp. 191–239. Springer, 1984.

[RK91]   E. Rich, K. Knight. *Artificial Intelligence*. McGraw-Hill, 1991.

[Rya93]   M. Ryan. Defaults in Specifications. In A. Finkelstein, ed., *Proc. of the IEEE Conf. on Requirements Engineering (San Diego)*, 1993.

[SJH93]   G. Saake, R. Jungclaus, T. Hartmann. Application Modelling in Heterogeneous Environments Using an Object Specification Language. *Int. Journal of Intelligent and Cooperative Information Systems*, 2(4):425–449, 1993.

[SSC92]   A. Sernadas, C. Sernadas, J. F. Costa. Object Specification Logic. Internal Report, INESC, University of Lisbon, 1992.

[SSE87]   A. Sernadas, C. Sernadas, H.-D. Ehrich. Object-Oriented Specification of Databases: An Algebraic Approach. In P. M. Stocker, W. Kent, eds., *Proc. VLDB'87*, pp. 107–116. Morgan Kaufmann, 1987.

[SSS95]   G. Saake, A. Sernadas, C. Sernadas. Evolving Object Specifications. In R. Wieringa, R. Feenstra, eds., *Information Systems - Correctness and Reusability. Selected Papers*. World Scientific Publishing, 1995.

[WD92]   R. Wieringa, W. De Jonge. The Identification of Objects and Roles – Object Identifiers Revisited. Report IR–267 (Vers. 2), VU Amsterdam, 1992.

Conceptual Modeling of WorkFlows

F. Casati, S. Ceri, B. Pernici, G. Pozzi

Dipartimento di Elettronica e Informazione - Politecnico di Milano
Piazza L. Da Vinci, 32 - I20133 Milano, Italy
ceri/pernici/pozzi@elet.polimi.it

Abstract. Workflow management is emerging as a challenging area for databases, stressing database technology beyond its current capabilities. Workflow management systems need to be more integrated with data management technology, in particular as it concerns the access to external databases. Thus, a convergence between workflow management and databases is occurring.

In order to make such convergence effective, however, it is required to improve and strengthen the specification of workflows at the conceptual level, by formalizing within a unique model their "internal behavior" (e.g. interaction and cooperation between tasks), their relationship to the environment (e.g. the assignment of work task to agents) and the access to external databases.

The conceptual model presented in this paper is a basis for achieving convergence of workflows and databases; the workflow description language being used combines the specification of workflows with accesses to external databases. We briefly indicate how the conceptual model presented in this paper is suitable for being supported by means of active rules on workflow-specific data structures. We foresee an immediate application of this conceptual model to workflow interoperability.

1 Introduction

Workflows are activities involving the coordinated execution of multiple tasks performed by different processing entities. A task defines some work to be done by a person, by a software system or by both of them. Specification of a workflow (**WF**) involves describing those aspects of its component tasks (and the processing entities that execute them) that are relevant to control and coordinate their execution, as well as the relations between the tasks themselves.

Information in a WF mainly concerns when a certain work task (**WT**) has to start, the criteria for assigning the WT to agents and which WTs it activates after its end; therefore, less emphasis is placed on the specification of the WT itself (which may be unformally described and only partially automated), while the focus is on the WTs' coordination. Connections among WTs can be rather complex, and some of them may be run-time dependent. A workflow management system (**WFMS**) permits both to specify WFs and to control their execution. During a WF execution, a WFMS has to schedule WTs (including their assignment to users) on the basis of the (static) WF specifications and of the (dynamic) sequence of events signaling the completion of WTs and of generic events produced within the execution environment (including exceptions).

The first descriptions of WFs have been proposed by *office modeling*, as a way of describing office procedures [4]. Such descriptions were based on extensions of classical formal models (such as Petri Nets, production rules and flowcharts); a number of modeling support tools were proposed. The need of a closer relationship between modeling techniques and enactment of processes has been particularly developed within the *process modeling* area in software engineering. This research has produced several methodological contributions and WF specification languages [11, 8]. Several tools for process modeling, generally based on Petri Nets, are focused on the ability of "animating" WFs, thereby understanding their dynamic behavior [3].

Recently, a growing interest has concentrated on connecting WF systems to existing information systems. In particular, the desire of interconnecting to existing data and of coping with large volumes of WF information has provided impetus to the bridging of WF and database technologies. The challenge posed by WF management pushes towards removing some of the classical limitations of databases in the context of concurrency and transactional models [14]. Novel features of databases, such as active rules, are seen as particularly promising in the context of WFs [7, 19]. In this context, we are proposing a new conceptual model and language specifically focused on modeling WF interaction with external sources of information. The conceptual model and languages described in this paper are the starting point of a wider research project aiming at the integrated management of different WFs (*workflow interoperability*) and at the implementation of a WFMS on the basis of an active DBMS.

The purpose of the paper is to propose an innovative approach to WF modeling. In the literature [2, 7, 8, 10, 11, 14, 16, 17] the proposed models lack expressive power concerning the possibility of specifying WT interactions and the mapping from the WF specification to WF execution, in particular concerning exception handling. The model we propose in this paper is the basis for overcoming this "semantic gap" [1].

The paper is structured as follows: Section 2 presents the main concepts of the proposed WF model and language; we illustrate the graphical symbols used for describing WFs. Section 3 describes the architecture of the proposed WFMS and informally illustrates the operational semantics of WT executions and of WF execution. We also briefly indicate how active rules may be used to implement and support such operational semantics; a full description of the semantics, however, falls outside the scope of this paper. Section 4 presents a classical WF example by giving both its linguistic and its graphical description.

---

[1] The proposed conceptual model allows us to describe WF structures of Foro-10 [12] and of a Workflow Manager developed at HP [13], which are the target of two separate, ongoing research projects with SEMA Spain (Madrid) and with the HP Laboratories of Palo Alto.

2 WorkFlow Concepts

We define a *WF schema* as a structure describing relations among the WTs that are part of a WF. In the schema, we describe which WTs should be executed, in which order, who may be in charge of them, which operations should be performed on tables of external databases. WF schemas are described by means of *WF Description Languages* (**WFDL**).

A *WF instance* (or *case*) is a particular execution of a schema. For example, a WF schema may describe the process of reviewing submitted papers; a WF instance of that schema is created whenever an editor receives a new paper. Thus, normally, several WF instances of the same WF schema may be active at the same time.

2.1 Workflow Description Language

A Workflow Description Language describes WTs to be performed during the WF executions and the mechanisms which are used for their activation and termination, both in normal and in exceptional situations. WT coordination is supported in a restricted number of alternative ways, thereby providing classical constructs for parallelism, such as *fork* and *join* [3, 7, 16]. In addition, the behavior of WTs is formally described by listing their preconditions, their actions, and their exceptional conditions during their execution. The peculiar feature of the proposed WFDL is to enable, within WTs' conditions, actions, and exception sections, the manipulation of external databases (by means of standard SQL2 statements). This section presents a "bird eye's view" on WFDL features; the full syntax of the WF description language can be retrieved from *ftp://xerox.elet.polimi.it/pub/papers/WF/InternalReport95_018.ps*.

Definition Sections A WF schema is composed of descriptions of flows, supertasks, and tasks; each of the above sections starts with definitions of constants, types, variables, and functions. Definitions in the context of flow descriptions are global (visible to every WT in the WF); definitions in the context of supertasks or WTs are local (visible in a supertask or WT). In both cases, variables are not persistent: thei exist only during an execution of the WF or WT instance. Therefore, variables cannot be used within WF instances in order to link to other WF instances.

The flow declaration may also include the definition of persistent data (**DB**) which are shared by all WF agents and possibly by agents of other WFs. These data can normally be externally defined (i.e. their existence can be independent of the particular WF application being modeled); for simplicity, we use the relational data model to denote persistent data. In our approach, data manipulation and retrieval is the only way of exchanging structured data with other WFs, thus following a blackboard approach. Other external databases which are independently accessed by agents during the execution of their WTs do not need to be explicitly defined.

Tasks WTs are the elementary work units that collectively achieve the WF goal. The WFMS takes care of determining when a certain WT must start being executed and of assigning it to an executing agent, according to some assignment polices.

Each WT has five major characteristics:

- *Name*: a mandatory string identifying the WT.
- *Description*: few lines in natural language, describing the WT.
- *Preconditions*: a boolean expression of simple conditions which must yield a truth value before the action can be executed. Simple conditions may either contain (conventional) boolean expressions in WFDL, or be based on the (boolean) query **exists** on an SQL2 statement.
- *Actions*: an action is a sequence of statements in WFDL which define how both temporary and persistent WF data are manipulated by the WT. Inputs from the agent who executes the WT are collected by the **get** statement; the **select-one** query extracts one tuple randomly selected from the query result; database actions are performed by means of SQL2 **update queries**. Note that the specification of actions in the WT is concerned with a fraction of the WT's semantics; in general, the user executing the WT has full freedom on the way the WT itself should be executed, provided that eventually the actions which are listed in its action part are performed. Therefore, the action specification is somehow equivalent to giving the WTs' postcondition, however with a procedural description.
- *Exceptions*: in every WT it is possible to specify a set of pairs <**Exception, Reaction**> to handle abnormal events: every time an exception is raised, the corresponding reaction is performed. An exception is a WFDL predicate, which may include time-related and query predicates. All exceptions are monitored by the WFMS; when they become true (possibly at the start of the WT), the exception is raised. A reaction is next performed by the WFMS to handle the exception. Reactions can be selected among a restricted set of options that includes **END** (imposes the termination of the WT), **CANCEL** (the WT is canceled), **NOTIFY** (a message is escalated to the person responsible for the WT) and a few others; a brief description of available reactions can be found in [5]. A typical exception is raised when a WT is not completed within a specified deadline.

Connections among Tasks Connections describe interactions among WTs; connections have both a linguistic description (in WFDL) and a graphical description. A WT can have only one input connection and only one output connection. Two WTs **A** and **B** can be directly connected, in which case they are linked by an edge; the intuitive meaning is that, as soon as **A** ends, **B** is ready for execution. In all other cases, connections among WTs are performed by *routing tasks* (**RT**). Each RT can be a *fork task* (**FT**), for initiating concurrent WT executions, or a *join task* (**JT**), for synchronizing WTs after concurrent execution.

FTs are preceded by one WT, called its *predecessor*, and followed by many WTs, called *successors*. They are classified as:

- *Total*: after the predecessor ends, all successors are ready for execution.
- *Non deterministic*: the fork is associated with a value k; after the predecessor ends, k successors nondeterministically selected are ready for execution.
- *Conditional*: each successor is associated with a condition; after the predecessor ends, conditions are instantaneously evaluated and only successor WTs with a **true** condition are ready for execution.
- *Conditional with mutual exclusion*: it adds to the previous case the constraint that only one condition can be **true**; thus, after the predecessor ends, if no condition or more than one conditions are **true** an exception is risen, otherwise one of the successors is ready for execution.

JTs are preceded by many WTs, called its *predecessors*, and followed by one WT, called *successor*. They are classified as:

- *Total*: the successor becomes ready only after the end of all predecessors.
- *Partial*: the JT is associated with a value k; the successor becomes ready after the end of k predecessor WTs. Subsequent ends of predecessor WTs have no effect.
- *Iterative*: the JT is associated with a value k; the successor becomes ready whenever k predecessor WTs end. Iterative JTs are implemented by counting terminated WTs and resetting the counters to zero whenever a successor becomes ready. Iterative join with two predecessors and $k = 1$ is used to describe cycles.

The above values k may be associated with constants, variables, or functions expressed in WFDL; in the last two cases, their value becomes known at execution time.

Start and Stop Symbols Start and stop symbols enable the creation and completion of WF instances (cases). Each WF schema has one start symbol and several stop symbols; the start symbol has one successor WT (possibly a connection WT) and each stop symbol has several predecessor symbols. After the WF instance creation, the successor of the start symbol becomes ready for execution; when any stop symbol becomes ready, the WF is completed. WTs which are still active are canceled.

Supertasks It is often useful to group several related WTs, so as to introduce a notion of modularization and to define common preconditions and exceptions for a set of WTs. This is possible by a particular type of WT, called *supertask* (**ST**).

STs have features of both WFs and WTs. Like WFs, they are internally decomposed into WTs (and possibly other STs); each ST has one start symbol and several stop symbols. Like WTs, STs have name, description, preconditions and exceptions. The action part of a ST is instead missing, as the job the ST performs is in effect decomposed into smaller jobs performed by the component

WTs. STs have constant, types, variables and functions definitions, whose scope is restricted to the component WTs.

When a ST is ready, the successors of its start symbol becomes ready; when any stop symbol becomes ready, the ST is completed. The meanings of preconditions and exceptions in a ST are as follows:

– When a ST is ready, its precondition is evaluated; if it is `false`, then the successors of its start symbol become *inhibited* (see Section 3.3).
– Reactions to exceptions specified for a ST are propagated to the component WTs which are active at the time the exception is raised. For example, if the reaction is SUSPEND, all component WTs are suspended; only a RESUME at the ST level will enable the continuation of the WTs.

Figure 1 represents the adopted graphical symbology for WTs and RTs.

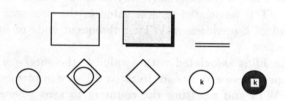

Fig. 1. Graphical symbology for WTs and RTs. WTs (left to right, first line): WT, ST, start/stop symbols; RTs (second line): total fork, conditional fork, conditional fork with mutual exclusion, non deterministic fork, iterative join. A total join has the same symbol as a total fork; a partial join has the same symbol as a non deterministic fork.

Multitasks In many WFs it is necessary to define a set of WTs that perform exactly the same job in parallel, but are assigned to different agents. In order to do so, we introduce a *multitask* (**MT**); each MT has a *component* which can be either a WT or a ST; the MT acts as a "multiplier" that generates several instances of its component, and assigns them for execution to several agents.

Each MT is associated with a value j indicating the number of WT instances that becomes ready when the MT's predecessor ends. It is also possible to specify when a MT must be considered finished, by associating it to a threshold value called *quorum*. When the number of components which have ended reaches the quorum, the MT is also ended, and the MT's successor becomes ready. Subsequent ending of components has no effects.

Note that the semantics of MTs can be expressed by means of nondeterministic forks and partial joins. For example, consider a WF with WTs A, B, and C, where j instances of B become ready at the end of A and C becomes ready after the end of k instances of B. Two equivalent representations of this WF are given in Figure 2: on the left, the WF is represented by using a non deterministic fork and a partial join with multiple copies of WT B, while on the right a MT is used.

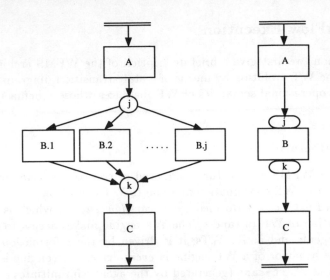

Fig. 2. Two equivalent WF representations by means of non deterministic fork and partial join (on the left) and by means of a MT (on the right).

2.2 Agents

A WF is populated by WTs, types, variables, and also by persons. These are called the *workflow agents*.

Each WF is defined by a "workflow administrator" (**WFA**) who is responsible of generating and compiling the WF schema. The WFA is notified of certain exceptions that may occur in the WF execution. Then, WF execution is performed by assigning WTs to agents. In general, agents have also the privilege of initiating the execution of a WF (in the terminology of [12], they create a new "WF case"). This agent is known to the WFMS, and is normally notified of exceptional behaviors; the WF creator is also informed when the WF is terminated.

Each WT may be fully automated or be assigned to one agent. If the WT is fully automated, i.e. an external system like a software program or a machine can perform the WT, then this feature must be specified adding the qualification **auto** to the WT name. If instead the WT is manual, then it has to be assigned to an agent. Note that we required each WT execution to be under control of one specific agent; this is a requirement that should be taken into account in designing WT granularity.

The assignment of a WT to an agent can be predefined in the WF description, or can be selected by the WFMS. In this latter case, which is most interesting and also most frequent in practice, the WFMS performs the selection by means of application-specific rules (such as: equalization of load, use of "experienced" agents for "critical tasks", and so on). Agents are in this case described by suitable dictionary information in the WFMS.

A ST is not assigned to any agent; however, some agents (or the WFA) may be in charge of managing the ST's exceptions.

3 WorkFlow Execution

In this section, we first give a brief description of the WFMS architecture, and then describe WT evolution by means of a state-transition diagram. Finally, we explain the operational semantics of WF instances whose schema is written in WFDL.

3.1 Architecture

We assume a WFMS architecture composed of two cooperative environments, one dedicated to WF coordination and one to WT execution.

WF coordination is performed by a *workflow engine*, which is responsible of the execution of WF instances. The WF engine makes access to stored data describing agents and active WTs; it is driven by the information in the WF schema. The behavior of a WF engine is *event-driven*: the engine is sensible to events, such as **start-case** (generated by the agent who initiates a case), **end, cancel, suspend, refuse** (generated by WTs at the end of their execution; see the next section), time-related events (generated by a clock), and manipulation of shared databases (insert, delete, or update operations on specific tables). The WF engine reacts to events by activating WTs, assigning them to agents, compiling historical information, and sending warning messages to agents. The WF management environment supports also tools for editing and compiling WF schemas (specified in WFDL) and administration tools (for agent management and for reporting the WF history).

The WT management environment is organized with a client-server architecture, where the client environment of an agent is application-specific; the WT server is created by the WF engine and is responsible of managing WT evolution, according to the schema that will be presented in the next section. In particular, a WT server communicates WT termination to the WF engine (through the **end, cancel, suspend,** and **refuse** events) and can update shared databases, thereby generating events for WTs of other WFs.

Figure 3 shows the WFMS architecture.

3.2 Task Execution

The execution of a WT is initiated by the WF engine and next controlled by the agent in the context of the WT management environment. Two state diagrams, represented in Figure 4, define WT execution in the two environments.

In the engine environment, a WT becomes *ready* for execution only due to the completion of some predecessors. If the WT has no precondition or if the preconditions are **true**, then the WT becomes *active* on the agent's environment by creating a unit of execution within the agent's WT server. If instead the WT's precondition is **false**, then the WT's state becomes *inhibited* and

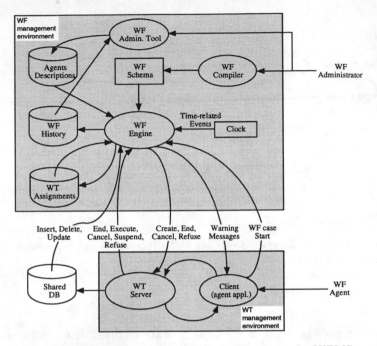

Fig. 3. Schematic description of the architecture of a WFMS.

the WF engine waits for some external event which changes the truth value of the precondition; after such an event occurs, the WT becomes *active*. However, exceptional conditions may cause the WT termination from the *inhibited* state. WT termination is represented by two exclusive states: a WT can be *done*, in which case the WF continues with the WT's successors selected according to the WF schema; or it can be *re-assign*, in which case the WT's execution must be repeated by re-assigning it to a different agent.

When a WT is activated, its execution state is decided by the agent. Initially, a created WT is in the *waiting* state, and the agent changes the WT's state to *executing* as soon as it starts operating on the WT (for instance, by opening a window on his screen which corresponds to the WT). He can suspend execution, by entering a *suspended* state, and then resume execution. Eventually, the agent indicates that the WT is *ended, canceled,* or *refused*; in all these cases, the control returns to the WF engine. The first case corresponds to a normal termination; the second case corresponds to an abnormal termination which, however, does not suspend the WF execution. Thus, in both cases the WT enters the *done* state; the two cases, however, are distinguished in the WF history. Finally, the *refused* state on the WT environment corresponds to the *re-assign* state on the WF engine. When a WT is *waiting, executing,* or *suspended*, it can be forced into a final state by exceptions which are generated by the WF engine.

STs have three associated states: they are *active* due to the completion of their predecessors, *suspended* due to an exception raised at the ST level, and

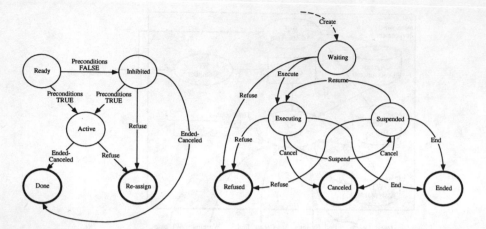

Fig. 4. Left side: State diagram describing WT execution in the WF engine. Done and Reassign are final states.
Right side: State diagram describing WT execution in the WT server. Refused, Canceled, Ended are final states.

done when their execution is completed. State changes of the STs may cause state changes of the component WTs; for instance, ST suspension causes the suspension of all component WTs, and ST termination causes the completion (in the *canceled* state) of components' active WTs.

3.3 Flow Execution

The WFDL schema expresses the interaction and cooperation among WTs. In particular, fork and join tasks enable some controlled forms of parallelism among WTs. Thus, based on the termination events from WTs (**end, cancel, refuse**), the WF engine is capable of deciding which WTs become *ready*. When a WT or a ST is ready, the WF engine becomes also sensible to the (asynchronous) exceptions which are associated with the WT, until the WT is *done*. Exceptions normally correspond to actions that must be performed upon active WTs (thus, also the WT server must be able of accepting asynchronous commands) and to messages that should be sent to agents.

Finally, the WF engine is responsible of performing several actions when a WF is completed, so that the current WF instance is eliminated from structures defining active flows and summary information is entered into the WF history.

3.4 Operational Semantics for WorkFlows and WorkTasks

The above execution models, so far expressed by means of state-transition diagrams, can be conveniently expressed by means of active rules. We briefly classify the active rules which should be provided for the WF engine (the specification of WT execution is much simpler). Active rules are classified as follows:

- *Schema Interpretation Rules*: these rules implement the flow description part of a WFDL specification. When a WT enters the *ended, canceled* or *refused* state, these rules determine which WTs must be prepared for execution, or if the WF case must be considered finished;
- *Task Assignment Rules*: these rules describe the privileges of agents upon WTs and express the application-specific policies for WT assignment to agents. We expect these rules to be easily customizable.
- *Exception Management Rules*: on the basis of WT state transitions, DB modifications and time events, these rules determine if an exception was raised and perform the corresponding reactions; these rules are also responsible of recognizing that preconditions of inhibited WTs are satisfied.
- *Administration Rules*: these rules react to the completion of WF instances and transform its associated information into historical data.

A summary of these 4 classes of rules is illustrated in Figure 5. Note that schema interpretation rules and exception rules react to external events, while WT assignment and administration rules react to internal events (WT ready, WF completed).

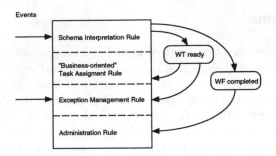

Fig. 5. Schematic description of WF engine functionalities.

4 Example of WFDL

Consider the process of refereeing a paper. A WF instance is created by the editor when he receives a new submission. As the editor receives the envelope (`exists(select * from Incomingpapers`) with the paper (WT `get Paper` in Figure 6), a new tuple with data about that paper is inserted into the *Submissions* table. The editor indicates the *NumberOfReferees* for the specific paper (by means of the `get NumberOfReferees` statement).

Then, one *Dispatch* WT is created for each referee; a variable number of copies of the WT is achieved by means of a MT. The WT consists of assigning a specific referee (by means of the `get Referee` statement) and dispatching her the manuscript. The editor traces the referee assignment by means of persistent data, by inserting tuples into the table *UnderRevision*.

After dispatching, referees are at work. We assume that each referee express a binary vote (accept or reject) and that the editor makes a decision on accepting or rejecting the paper based on the majority of votes. Such a simplified decision process is postulated so as to enable an automatic decision making process, which can be coded in WFDL; a MT `Report Collection` is activated which traces all decisions made by referees and enters the referee's *Vote* into the *UnderRevision* table. A more realistic situation where the editor's decision is not automatic corresponds to a simpler WF, where the decision process would be hidden inside the `Report Collection` WT.

The termination condition for the MT is that a *RefereeQuorum* be reached, i.e. that enough responses are collected from referees to guarantee a majority of votes. If the quorum is reached, the paper is accepted or rejected; further referee reports do not change the decision. The functions *RefereeQuorum* and *Approved*, specified in WFDL, evaluate whether enough reports are collected and what is the final decision. Finally, the WTs *Accept* and *Reject* complete the WF; the editor communicates with the authors and updates its persistent information on tables *Submissions* and *UnderRevision*. A graphical description of the WF is given in Figure 6.

5 Conclusions

This paper has presented a conceptual model and language for the specification of WF applications. Although this model reuses several concepts from several existing models, it contributes to the clarification of both the behavior of WFs and their relationship to the environment and to external databases. This specification is sufficiently rich and formal to enable a syntax-directed translation of WFDL definition into active rules, thereby providing an operational semantics and an implementation scheme for many components of a WFMS.

Our future research agenda includes completing such a syntax-directed translation and adding to the WFDL a separate section for describing WT assignment policies; this will enable the development of a prototype implementation, based on relational products and their trigger subsystems. We further anticipate the use of this conceptual model for attaching another critical problem of WF applications, namely the integration of distinct WFs. In particular, the use of external databases by WFs constitutes a simple yet practical and efficient solution to WF interoperability. At the conceptual level, we plan to study the interaction between distinct WFs, developing a methodological background as well as some concrete techniques for checking that distinct WFs can correctly interact and cooperate.

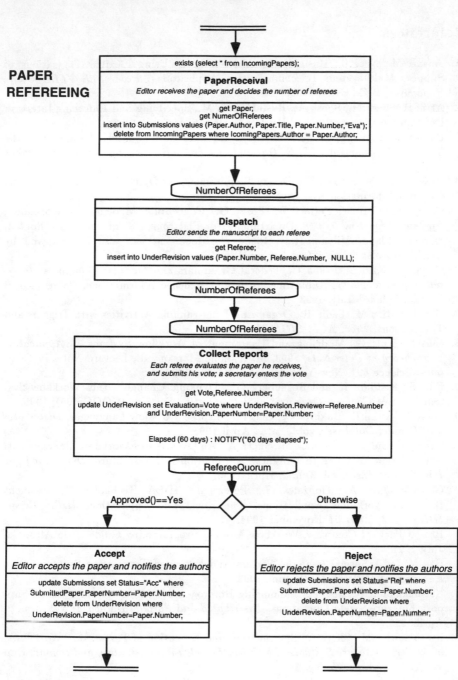

PAPER REFEREEING

exists (select * from IncomingPapers);

PaperReceival
Editor receives the paper and decides the number of referees

get Paper;
get NumerOfReferees
insert into Submissions values (Paper.Author, Paper.Title, Paper.Number,"Eva");
delete from IncomingPapers where IcomingPapers.Author = Paper.Author;

NumberOfReferees

Dispatch
Editor sends the manuscript to each referee

get Referee;
insert into UnderRevision values (Paper.Number, Referee.Number, NULL);

NumberOfReferees

NumberOfReferees

Collect Reports
*Each referee evaluates the paper he receives,
and submits his vote; a secretary enters the vote*

get Vote,Referee.Number;
update UnderRevision set Evaluation=Vote where UnderRevision.Reviewer=Referee.Number
and UnderRevision.PaperNumber=Paper.Number;

Elapsed (60 days) : NOTIFY("60 days elapsed");

RefereeQuorum

Approved()==Yes   Otherwise

Accept
Editor accepts the paper and notifies the authors

update Submissions set Status="Acc" where
SubmittedPaper.PaperNumber=Paper.Number;
delete from UnderRevision where
UnderRevision.PaperNumber=Paper.Number;

Reject
Editor rejects the paper and notifies the authors

update Submissions set Status="Rej" where
SubmittedPaper.PaperNumber=Paper.Number;
delete from UnderRevision where
UnderRevision.PaperNumber=Paper.Number;

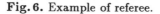

Fig. 6. Example of referee.

References

1. Ansari M., Ness L., Rusinkiewicz M., Sheth A., Using Flexible Transations to Support Multi-system Telecomunication Applications, *Proc. 18th VLDB Conf.*, Vancouver, B.C., CAN, 1992.

2. Attie P., Singh M., Sheth A., Rusinkiewicz M., Specifying and Enforcing Intertask Dependencies, *Proc. 19th VLDB Conf.*, Dublin, Ireland, 1993.

3. Bandinelli S., Fuggetta A., Ghezzi C., Software Process Model Evolution in the SPADE Environment, *IEEE Transactions on Software Engineering*, December 1993.

4. Bracchi G., Pernici B., The Design Requirements of Office Systems, ACM Trans. on Office Information Systems, 2(2), April 1984.

5. Casati F., Ceri S., Pernici B., Pozzi G., Conceptual Modeling of Workflows, *Internal Report n. 95.018*, Dipartimento di Elettronica e Informazione, Politecnico di Milano, Milano, Italy, 1995. The document can also be retrieved by *ftp://xerox.elet.polimi.it/pub/papers/WF/InternalReport95_018.ps.*

6. Crespi-Reghizzi S., Psaila G., Federal Grammars and Modular Compilers, *Internal Report n. 93.054*, Dipartimento di Elettronica e Informazione, Politecnico di Milano, Milano, Italy, 1993.

7. Dayal U., Hsu M., Ladin R., Organizing Long-running Activities with Triggers and Transactions, *Proc. ACM SIGMOD*, 1990.

8. Ellis C., Nutt G., Modeling and Enactment of Workflow Systems, in *Application and Theory of Petri Nets*, 1993, M. Ajmone Marsan Ed., Lecture Notes in Computer Science 691, New York: Springer Verlag, 1993.

9. Ellis S., Keddara K. and Rozenberg G., "Dynamic Change within Workflow Systems", *ACM Conf. on Organizational Computing Systems* (COOCS 95), 1995.

10. Forst A., Kuhn E., Bukhres O., General Purpose Workflow Languages, *Distributed and Parallel Databases*, vol. 3, n. 2, April 1995.

11. Georgakopoulos D., Hornick M., Sheth A., An Overview of Workflow Management: from Process Modeling to Workflow Automation Infrasctructure, *Distributed and Parallel Databases*, vol. 3, n. 2, April 1995.

12. Gonzales-Quel A., Gonzales S., Perez M., IDEA Technology Assessment Based on WorkFlow Applications. The Royal Life Application, *IDEA Report IDEA.DE.21S.001.01*, November 1994.

13. Hewlet Packard Company, Workflow Module Programming Guide, Palo Alto, Ca, July 1994.

14. Hsu M. (ed.), Special Issue on Worflow and Extended Transaction Systems, *Data Engineering Bulletin*, 16(2), June 1993.

15. Krishnakumar N., Sheth A., Managing Heterogeneous Multi-system Tasks to Support Enterprise-wide Operations, *Distributed and Parallel Databases*, vol. 3, n. 2, April 1995.

16. Rusinkiewicz M., Sheth A., Specification and Execution of Transaction Workflows, in *Modern Database Systems: the Object Model, Interoperability, and beyond*, Kim W. (ed.), Addison-Wesley, 1994.

17. Sheth A., Rusinkiewicz M., On Transactional Workflows, *Data Engineering Bulletin*, 16(2), June 1993.

18. Stonebraker M., The Integration of Rule Systems and Database Systems, *IEEE TKDE*, 4(5), October 1992.

19. Widom J., Ceri S., *Active Database Systems*, Morgan-Kaufmann, San Mateo, Ca, May 1995.

An Object Oriented Approach for CSCW System Design

Igor T. Hawryszkiewycz

School of Computing Sciences
University of Technology, Sydney
e-mail: igorh@socs.uts.edu.au

Abstract. This paper describes an object oriented design approach that uses classification mappings rather than conventional structured mappings in design. It argues that design in environments where a large number of choices can be used to create designs proceeds in an unstructured manner. The design process can be structured by providing support for mappings between analysis and design objects using different classification schemes. The paper illustrates this approach in the CSCW domain .

1. Introduction

One distinction between the Entity-Relationship (E-R) and object oriented (O-O) design approaches is in the way design decisions are made. Design decisions are here seen as the mapping of analysis objects to design objects. In E-R design, design often follows a structured process where design choices are based on well-defined mappings. Mappings in this case are often deterministic (Hawryszkiewycz, 1994) in the sense that they follow a predetermined set of rules to create the design objects. Thus entities and relationships, which are the analysis objects, are mapped to relations and then to databases. These structured design methods have been found suitable for transaction based systems, whose processes can often be prespecified. However, more and more often, designers are called to build more open systems, giving designers more choices and calling for systems that can easily adapt to new working methods.

The object oriented approach is more suitable in these latter cases. It provides the ability to select components using behaviour and structure criteria concurrently, and to synthesize systems from components that can be readily changed to meet evolving system needs. It thus lends itself to designing the more open systems that must often be synthesized from available design objects and which must be adaptable to emerging processes.

What is needed to design such systems are methodologies that simplify mappings from requirements expressed in terms of semantic concepts to design objects. Design objects can be selected from a class of design objects to match an analysis object using rationale based on application semantics and assisted by classification schemes. This paper examines this approach to designing systems generally known as CSCW (Computer Supported Collaborative Work) (Schmidt and Bannon, 1992) systems and describes object classes that can be used to synthesize these systems. The paper proposes a classification scheme for analysis objects and design objects in the CSCW domain and illustrates how they are used in a design methodology.

2. Methodology

The methodology described here follows the traditional sequence of physical analysis, logical analysis, logical design and physical design. In summary the goals of each of these phases is as follows.

Physical analysis - to develop an understanding of system requirements, through interviews, observations, rich pictures and other tools. This phase determines how the system works now and identifies physical objects in the system.

Logical analysis - to describe the system in using object classes generic to the collaborative process. The goal is to determine what is being done.

Logical design - to develop a set of logical requirements, by specifying what the new system should look like in terms of logical object classes,

Physical design - to propose how the logical requirements will be satisfied by choosing collaborative software services, or groupware, needed to realize the logical objects.

The first two phases develop an understanding of the system, initially using rich pictures to identify objects within the problem domain and then classifying these objects using a semantic classification scheme. The next two phases, logical and physical design, start by identifying logical objects and then proposing physical groupware services to realize these logical objects.

3. Analysis Classification

The paper focuses on object classification schemes for CSCW applications and describes ways to make design choices. Analysis begins with a rich picture, such as that shown in Figure 1. Rich pictures are an important part of open systems design methodologies and are used to identify the major physical components, which are described using logical concepts appropriate to the problem domain. n CSCW design these major components are roles, their interactions and artifacts used in the interactions. As an example, Figure 1 describes a system where a designer produces artifacts for sale to the general public. The designer uses a market research service to identify the kinds of products likely to be accepted in the market. In addition, the designer has an assistant, who is required to coordinate production and distribution to assist the designer to produce designs.

Arranging production involves negotiating a contract with potential producers. Such contracts are generally arranged by the designer because they have the specialist knowledge about the proposed product. The assistant usually arranges transfers of the product to distributors or direct sales. Such transfers can often involve third parties, such as transport of delivery firms.

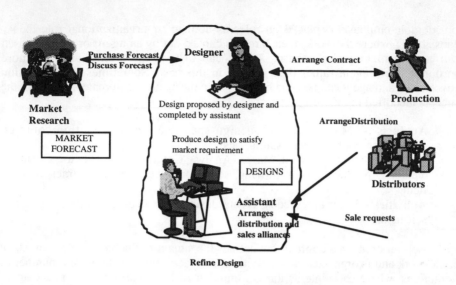

Figure 1 - The Independent Designer

3.1   Semantically   Classifying   Analysis   Objects

Logical analysis formalizes the rich picture by classifying objects in terms of concepts specialized to the CSCW problem domain. These concepts been described earlier (Hawryszkiewycz, 1993, 1994) and are summarized in Figure 2. The central semantic here is that **roles** carry out **tasks** that change **artifacts**, be they documents or other physical elements. Thus in Figure 2, two roles, (designer and tester) carry out the task (testing) on an artifact (program). Other roles in software engineering include designer, or programmer or project manager. Other tasks are to assure quality of a program, or develop a program, or validate the program against requirement. Artifacts can be specifications, design documents or programs themselves.

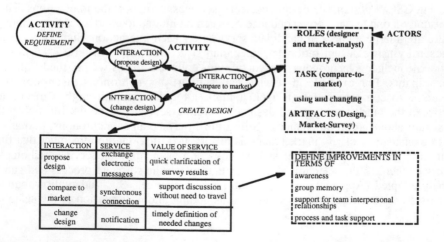

Figure 2 - Concepts for Collaborative Work

Considerable emphasis is placed on roles as defined by organizational role theory (Roos, 1981), where the work of each role is carried out by an **agent** or **actor**, chosen from an organizational database. Actors can also be programs, and the more appropriate term agent rather than is used in this case. Sometimes the distinction between role and agent can become blurred when the agent is automated. Some of the concepts identified in Figure 2 are:

- **Artifacts** - Market-survey, design-specification, production-contract, distribution-contract, sales-summaries.
- **Roles** - Designer, Assistant, Market-Analyst, Contractor, Distributor, Client.
- **Tasks** - produce-design-drawing, select-producer, create-contract, deliver-item.
- **Activities** - Determine-needs, create-design, produce-item, distribute-items, sell-items.

Work itself proceeds in a **context** that defines the situation (Suchman, 1987) in which people work and is organized into activities. Each activity is made up of a number of interactions, where each interaction is a number of roles carrying out a task on an artifact. Two activities shown in Figure 2 are to "define requirement" from the market analysis and to "create a design". In Figure 2, the "create a design" activity is made up of three interactions - "propose design", "compare to market" and "change design". Each interaction can itself be specified in terms of a number of parameters, in particular, interaction roles, artifacts and a general interaction script. At more detailed levels, interactions themselves can be classified in terms of speech acts or conversations (Winograd, 1986). For the compare-to-market interaction these may be:

- **interaction roles** - designer, market-analyst;
- **artifacts** used in the interaction - design, market-survey;
- **interaction script** that describes the actions taken during the interaction - {a general explanation of the design by the designer followed by a joint comparison of design features against market needs}.

3.2   Extending to Design

During CSCW design, the designer selects services to support the interactions. There is usually a one to one correspondence between an interaction and a service, although there are a large number of candidate services for each interaction. Such services are chosen by using design rationale rather than structured rules. Criteria used in such rationale include synchronous or asynchronous collaboration as well as the location of participants. For example, a service can support a synchronous discussion over distance to compare a design against market requirements through a discussion between the market analyst and designer. Another service can be used to notify the assistant about proposed changes. Still a third may be an asynchronous, perhaps e-mail exchange, to clarify market analysis results. It is important to remember that final outcome will be a platform of synchronous and asynchronous services. Choice of services requires the selection of services that match the software process and can be easily adapted (Applegate, 1991) as the process changes. Such adaptation requires seamlessness between process services thus adding another criterion to the selection process.

4. Logical Design

Logical design chooses logical objects to match the objects identified during analysis. The design classification is made up of three major object classes - repository services, communication services and process services. The classification has been chosen to provide a bridge between the abstract analysis concepts and concrete physical implementation objects. The classification sees repositories as active components that contain data as well as providing services, in terms of methods. Communication services are seen more as system components used to bring people together. For example, suppose one looks at negotiation as one of the processes often quoted in CSCW literature. The repository contains the negotiation issues and methods to manipulate them. The communication services allow people to access these methods, whereas process services contain the protocol to be used in negotiation.

4.1   Repository Services

Repository services store information and provide the methods to process it. Such repositories not only contain data but also the methods used to manipulate this data. They closely correspond to objects and can be specialized to particular applications. A pictorial representation of a repository is shown in Figure 3. This describes an idea repository that records and displays ideas as well as collecting comments on ideas.

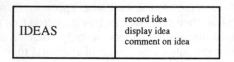

IDEAS   record idea
             display idea
             comment on idea

Figure 3 - A Representation of a Repository Service

Other typical repositories may be:

NEWS-ITEMS (<news-item-structure>, <user-registration, news-distribution, access-methods, news-collection>);

VOTE-REPOSITORY (<vote-structure>, <vote-collection, vote-counting, voting-rules>)

DISCUSSION (<discussion-structure>, <organize-statements, access-rules, summarize>)

DOCUMENT (<document-structure>, <version-control, distribution-rules, access-methods>)

For example, a document repository stores documents and methods of accessing and distributing them, as well as methods to create and store versions of the documents. A vote repository, will collect and count votes and manage lists of people eligible to vote. A news repository will store news items and contain methods to collect and distribute the news items as well as registering readers of the news messages. People gain access to the repositories through communication services. Repositories can be specialized for particular applications. For example, a vote repository can be specialized for different ways of counting votes.

A platform can contain any number of repositories and information can be moved between the repositories. Some repositories may be connected to communication services while others may not. It is thus common to move information from a repository with no communication services to one that has such a services to send information.

4.2. Communication Services

Communication services primarily distribute information but do not process it. The following set of generic communication services are considered complete for this purpose:

- Distribution - directs information asynchronously to different locations,
- Collection - collects information asynchronously from different locations,
- Interaction - supports synchronous interaction by one user, and
- Joint Interaction - supports synchronous interaction by a number of users.

This paper uses a notation shown in Figure 4 to describe communication services. Each arrow identifies one communication path, which is between a repository and a role. The arrow shows the direction of information flow in a communication path. The circles at the ends of the arrow illustrate the connections, here called *ports*, to repositories or roles. Such ports themselves can be specialized. Where the port connected to a repository is filled in, then access is real time, otherwise it is non-real time. Similarly ports connected to roles are also specialized into two major classes. Where the port is filled in, then one role can be connected to a port at the same time. This allows synchronous discussion. Otherwise only one role can communicate with the repository at a given instant of time. Each of the ports may themselves be further specialized to a particular application. Thus for example, a port that has more than one role connected at the same time can also include the rules that specify the protocols to be used by the roles.

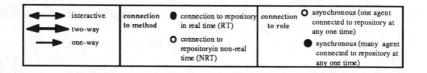

Figure 4 - Notation for Communication Services

4.3 Combining Repository and Communication Services

This notation together with the kind of diagrams shown in Figure 3 for repository services can be used to logically describe collaborative systems. Figure 5 illustrates how applications can be put together using the services described in the last section. It includes two repositories, ARGUMENT that knows how to manage arguments, and VOTE that knows how to count votes.

Both of the repositories are connected to roles using communication services. The ARGUMENTS repository is connected to collect arguments. The VOTE repository collects votes. Furthermore, the two repositories are linked with special ports to move arguments to the VOTE service to collect peoples votes on particular proposals.

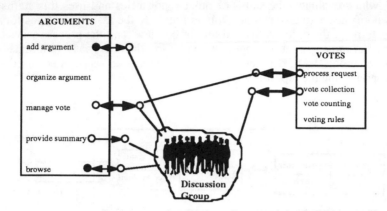

Figure 5 - An Example

It is possible to connect many communication services to one repository. Thus for example, the ARGUMENTS repository could be surrounded by a distribution notification communication service. To do this additional ports would be added to the repository and activated by defined argument states. One such state would be to detect whenever a new argument appears for a selected issue and selected roles could then be notified of the new argument.

4.4   Extending to Process Services

The combination of communication services and repository allows many users to exchange information through the repositories. The process used to exchange the information is determined by the users. Process services provide assistance to support standard processes.

- defining flows and conversation rules, and
- assigning roles and responsibilities.

Some examples of process support can include:

- Negotiation processes, where agreement is reached on arrangements made between a group of people,
- Notification processes, where people are informed of activities and changes taking place within their context,
- Client-server processes, where one person, the server, agrees to provide a service to another person, the client, and
- Decision processes, where a group of people agree on a course of action.

One example of extension to include process services is shown in Figure 6. Here ORDERING RULES is the process service that specifies the process to be followed in filling an order.

The process service is similar to a repository and stores the rules to be followed by the process. Thus in Figure 8, the process service stores ordering rules whereas the repository contains the orders. Communication services can go through the process service, which evaluates the status of other repositories and uses this status and its rules to notify users to take action. Thus in Figure 8, the associated repository can be an order form. If the order status is found to be 'new' and the process service knows that the order must be sent for approval. On return, the order has a new state which is used to determine the next process step. Communication services are used both the process service and the repository.

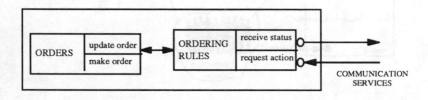

Figure 6 - Including a Process Service

5. Logical and Physical Design

The main purpose of logical design is to select services to realize the interactions. Selection can start with the following mappings:

Artifact	-->	Repository Service sometimes requiring detailed E-R analysis
Role	-->	Actor or Agent
Interaction	-->	Communication Service specifying synchronous or asynchronous work
Process	-->	Process Service
Context	-->	Platform seamlessly combining services
Task	-->	Tools

Such conversions can be guided by more detailed interaction classifications. The idea is that each interaction can be implemented using a variety of services. Each interaction is examined and its broad implementation compared against these services. Structured rationale can be used to choose the most appropriate of the candidate services to satisfy the interaction needs.

The initial choice of services is entered in a selection table like that shown in Figure 7. Here the rows correspond to interactions identified during analysis together with identified issues. The columns describe the selected service. Each entry then describe the way the service will be used.

SERVICE / ACTIVITY	WWW (or Internet) Retrieval	E-mail Distribution	Document Management	Sketchpad	Teleconfencing or Face to Face
ANALYSIS A.Propose Design				X2	X1
B. Compare to Market	X4				X3
C. Propose Change				X5	X6
D. Make Change				X7	
E. Arrange Production		X8	X11		
F. Arrange Diustribution		X9	X12		
G. Market Analysis	X10				

Figure 7 - Summarizing Potential Services

5.1 Evaluating Services

Proposed services are then evaluated against a chart of process gains and losses. Generic guidelines for specifying such gains and losses must be converted to concrete terms of the application. One example of structuring evaluation is to use a table like that shown in Figure 8. In the table, the services are listed against the interactions. Each interaction is examined to choose the best service to support that interaction. Social issues can come into play by providing guidelines or checks and the table entry specifies the benefits or losses of each service for the interaction using selected evaluation criteria.

SERVICE	INTERACTION	PROCESS STRUCTURE	PROCESS SUPPORT	TASK STRUCTURE	TASK SUPPORT
Internet or WWW	Compare to Market		Easier to maintain contact		Easier access to survey results
	Market Analysis				Better way to distribute survey results
E-mail distribution	Arrange Production Arrange Distribution		Faster resolution of problems		
Document Management	Arrange Production Arrange Distribution		Easier to keep track of contracts		
Sketchpad	Propose Design Propose Change Make Change			Improved ability to keep track of alternatives	
Teleconference	Compare to Market				Improved method of clarifying results
	Propose Design Propose Change				Improved ability to discuss detailed design aspects

Figure 8 - An Evaluation Table

5.1.1 Guidelines for Evaluation

The evaluation takes each selected service in turn and evaluate it to see whether it improves the process structure or support, or task structure and support. The evaluation arguments should be directly related to the process gains and losses with a service justified only if it contributes substantially to the process. The arguments must also satisfy specific evaluations as for example **improves** awareness of latest customer status. or provides **better coordination** between client and salesperson. The general guidelines here are:

Improve the process structure - this defines changes to the steps to be followed by a process and how they can be improved. It can include adding new roles like a facilitator to smooth workflows or simply removing unnecessary steps.

Provide better process support - this provides better support for a process. Examples may be quicker transfer of information or ability to communicate better across distance. It may also include better scheduling of process tasks by using an appointments system. Improvements to awareness of the process may also come under this heading.

Provide support for task structure - this is to help structure the information in a task. Examples are the IBIS structure for arguments in decision support, keeping track of documents and so on.

Provide better task support - this actually makes it easier to carry out a task as for example better access to information, recording of results and so on.

In general, task support and structure apply to the interactions, whereas process support and structure apply to activities. Process evaluations must also consider the general social effect of computer supported collaboration. Important question are effects on the level of satisfaction and consequently contribution to the group. The acceptance of such work in organizations is also important. Possible outcomes to measure are:

- direct measures such as travel time, time to do a task,
- improvements to output quality,
- reduction in internal tasks such as making copies, sending FAXes and other minor jobs,
- reduction in the number of meetings
- the degree of satisfaction.

5.2   Verification

A structured design approach also provides the ability to verify the design by ensuring that no object is lost during the design process. Some verification checks are:

- each artifact must be converted to a repository service,
- each interaction must result in at least one communication service,
- each interaction must appear in the selection table,
- each interaction must appear in the evaluation table.

These checks can be used as one proceeds from analysis through logical and physical design.

5.3 Combining into a Platform

As a final step selected services are integrated into a platform (Schmidt and Rodden, 1992). This requires the creation of menus that allow users to easily select services and move easily between them. Platforms themselves are constructed in layered form, stating with the generic collaborative services such as e-mail, or bulletin boards and integrating them into collaborative business applications.

6. Conclusion

This paper described an object oriented design approach based on classifications rather that deterministic mappings as used commonly in E-R design. It argued that design in this environment proceeds as non-deterministic mappings between objects in different classification schemes and illustrated this approach in the CSCW domain. The paper then described some classifications used in analysis and design and a process used to choose design objects for given requirements.

7. References

Applegate, L.M. (1991): "Technology Support for Cooperative Work: A Framework for Studying Introduction and Assimilation in Organizations" *Journal of Organizational Computing*, Vol. 1, pp. 11-39.

Hawryszkiewycz, I.T. (June, 1993): "A CSCW Design Tool based on Semantic Concepts" *12th International Conference on the Design of CSCW and Groupware Systems*, Schaerding, Austria.

Hawryszkiewycz, I.T. (September, 1994): "A Generalized Semantic Model for CSCW Systems" *Proceedings of the 5th International Conference on Database and Expert Systems*, Athens, Greece, published by Springer-Verlag, pp. 93-102..

Hawryszkiewycz, I.T. (1994): *"Database Analysis and Design"* Prentice-Hall, New York, Second edn.

Roos, L.L., and Starke, F.A. (1981): "Organizational Roles" in Nystrom, P.C. and Sturbuck, W.H. (eds), Handbook of Organizational Design, Vol. 1: Adapting organizations to their Environments, pp. 290-308, Oxford University Press.

Schmidt, K., Bannon, L. (1992): "Taking CSCW Seriously" *Computer Supported Cooperative Work*, Kluwer Publications, Vol.1., No.1, 1992.

Schmidt, K., Rodden, T. (1992): "Putting it Together: Requirements of a CSCW Platform", *Proceedings of 12th. Interdisciplinary Workshop on Informatics and Psychology, Shaerding, Austria*, June, North-Holland.

Suchman, L. (1987): *Plans and Situated Action: The Problem of Human-Machine Communication* Cambridge University Press, Cambridge.

Winograd, T., Flores, F. (1986): *Understanding Computers and Cognition: A New Foundation for Design*, Ablex Publishing Corporation, Norwood, New Jersey, 1986.

Semantics of Time-Varying Attributes and Their Use for Temporal Database Design

Christian S. Jensen[1]   Richard T. Snodgrass[2]

[1] Department of Mathematics and Computer Science, Aalborg University, Fredrik Bajers Vej 7E, DK–9220 Aalborg Ø, DENMARK, csj@iesd.auc.dk
[2] Department of Computer Science, University of Arizona, Tucson, AZ 85721, USA, rts@cs.arizona.edu

Abstract. Based on a systematic study of the semantics of temporal attributes of entities, this paper provides new guidelines for the design of temporal relational databases. The notions of observation and update patterns of an attribute capture when the attribute changes value and when the changes are recorded in the database. A lifespan describes when an attribute has a value. And derivation functions describe how the values of an attribute for all times within its lifespan are computed from stored values. The implications for temporal database design of the semantics that may be captured using these concepts are formulated as schema decomposition rules.

1 Introduction

Designing appropriate database schemas is crucial to the effective use of relational database technology, and an extensive theory has been developed that specifies what is a good database schema and how to go about designing such a schema. The relation structures provided by temporal data models, e.g., the recent TSQL2 model [13], provide built-in support for representing the temporal aspects of data. With such new relation structures, the existing theory for relational database design no longer applies. Thus, to make effective use of temporal database technology, a new theory for temporal database design must be developed.

We have previously extended and generalized conventional normalization concepts to temporal databases [7, 8]. But the resulting concepts are still limited in scope and do not fully account for the time-varying nature of data. Thus, additional concepts are needed in order to fully capture and exploit the time-varying nature of data during database design. This paper proposes concepts that capture the time-related semantics of attributes and uses these as a foundation for developing guidelines for the design of temporal databases. The properties of time-varying attributes are captured by describing their lifespans, their time patterns, and their derivation functions. Design rules subsequently allow the database designer to use the properties for (view, logical, and physical) schema design.

The paper is structured as follows. Section 2 first reviews the temporal data model used in the paper. It then argues that the properties of attributes are relative to the objects they describe and then introduces surrogates for representing real-world objects in the model. The following subsections address in turn different aspects of time-varying attributes, namely lifespans, time patterns, and derivation functions. Section 3 is devoted to the implications of the attribute semantics for logical schema, physical schema, and view design. The final section summarizes and points to opportunities for further research.

2 Capturing the Semantics of Time-Varying Attributes

This section provides concepts that allow the database designer to capture more precisely and concisely than hitherto the time-varying nature of attributes in temporal relations. The temporal data model employed in the paper is first described. Then a suite of concepts for capturing the temporal semantics of attributes are introduced.

2.1 A Conceptual Data Model

We describe briefly the relation structures of the Bitemporal Conceptual Data Model (BCDM) (see [9] for a more complete description) that is the data model of TSQL2 and which is used in this paper.

We adopt a linear, discrete, bounded model of time, with a time line composed of chronons. The schema of a bitemporal conceptual relation, R, consists of an arbitrary number, e.g., n, of explicit attributes and an implicit timestamp attribute, T, defined on the domain of sets of bitemporal chronons. A bitemporal chronon $c^b = (c^t, c^v)$ is an ordered pair of a transaction-time chronon c^t and a valid-time chronon c^v. A tuple $x = (a_1, a_2, \ldots, a_n | t^b)$, in a relation instance r of schema R thus consists of n attribute values associated with a bitemporal timestamp value. An arbitrary subset of the domain of valid times is associated with each tuple, meaning that the information recorded by the tuple is *true in the modeled reality* during each valid-time chronon in the subset. Each individual valid-time chronon of a single tuple has associated a subset of the domain of transaction times, meaning that the information, valid during the particular chronon, is *current in the relation* during each of the transaction-time chronons in the subset. Any subset of transaction times less than the current time may be associated with a valid time. Notice that while the definition of a bitemporal chronon is symmetric, this explanation is asymmetric, reflecting the different semantics of transaction and valid time.

We have thus seen that a tuple has associated a set of so-called *bitemporal chronons* in the two-dimensional space spanned by transaction time and valid time. Such a set is termed a *bitemporal element* [4, 6]. We assume that a domain of surrogate values is available for representing real-world objects in the database.

Example 1. Consider the relation instance, `empDep`, shown next.

EName	Dept	T
Bob	Ship	$\{(5,10), \ldots, (5,15), \ldots, (9,10), \ldots, (9,15), (10,5), \ldots, (10,20), \ldots,$ $(14,5), \ldots, (14,20), (15,10), \ldots, (15,15) \ldots, (19,10), \ldots, (19,15)\}$
Bob	Load	$\{(20,10), \ldots, (20,15), (21,10), \ldots, (21,15)\}$

The relation shows the employment information for an employee, Bob, and two departments, Ship and Load, contained in two tuples. In the timestamps, we assume that the chronons correspond to days and that the period of interest is some given month in a given year, e.g., July 1995. Throughout, we use integers as timestamp components. The reader may informally think of these integers as dates, e.g., the integer 15 in a timestamp represents the date July 15, 1995. The current time is assumed to be 21.

Valid-time relations and transaction-time relations are special cases of bitemporal relations that support only valid time and transaction time, respectively. For clarity, we use the term snapshot relation for a conventional relation, which supports neither valid time nor transaction time.

This completes the description of the objects in the bitemporal conceptual data model—relations of tuples timestamped with temporal elements. An associated algebra and user-level query language are defined elsewhere [13, 14].

2.2 Using Surrogates

An attribute is seen in the context of a particular real-world entity. Thus, when we talk about a property, e.g., the frequency of change, of an attribute, that property is only meaningful when the attribute is associated with a particular entity. As an example, the frequency of change of a salary attribute with respect to a specific employee in a company may reasonably be expected to be relatively regular, and there will only be at most one salary for the employee at each point in time. In contrast, if the salary is with respect to a department, a significantly different pattern of change may be expected. There will generally be many salaries associated with a department at a single point in time. Hence, it is essential to identify the reference object when discussing the semantics of an attribute.

We employ surrogates for representing real-world entities in the database. In this regard, we follow the approach adopted in, e.g., the TEER model by Elmasri [3]. Surrogates do not vary over time in the sense that two entities identified by identical surrogates are the same entity, and two entities identified by different surrogates are different entities. We assume the presence of surrogate attributes throughout logical design. At the conclusion of logical design, surrogate attributes may be either retained, replaced by regular (key) attributes, or eliminated.

2.3 Lifespans of Individual Time-Varying Attributes

In database design, one is interested in the interactions among the attributes of the relation schemas that make up the database.

Here, we provide a basis for relating the lifespans of attributes. Intuitively, the lifespan of an attribute for a specific object is all the times when the object has a value, distinct from $\perp_i$, inapplicable null, for the attribute. Note that lifespans concern valid time, i.e., are about the times when there exist some valid values.

To more precisely define lifespans, we first define an algebraic selection operator on a temporal relation. Define a relation schema $R = (A_1, \ldots, A_n | \mathrm{T})$, and let r be an instance of this schema. Let P be a predicate defined on the A_i. The selection P on r, $\sigma_P^{\mathrm{B}}(r)$, is defined by $\sigma_P^{\mathrm{B}}(r) = \{z \mid z \in r \wedge P(z[A_1, \ldots, A_n])\}$. It follows that $\sigma_P^{\mathrm{B}}(r)$ simply performs the familiar snapshot selection, with the addition that each selected tuple carries along its timestamp, T. Next, we define an auxiliary function **vte** that takes as argument a valid-time relation r and returns the valid-time element defined by $\mathbf{vte}(r) = \{c^v \mid \exists s \, (s \in r \wedge c^v \in s[\mathrm{T}])\}$. The result valid-time element is thus the union of all valid timestamps of the tuples in an argument valid-time relation.

Definition 1. Let a relation schema $R = (S, A_1, \ldots, A_n \mid \mathrm{T})$ be given, where S is surrogate valued, and let r be an instance of R. The *lifespan* for an attribute A_i, $i = 1, \ldots, n$, with respect to a value s of S in r is denoted $\mathbf{ls}(r, A_i, s)$ and is defined by $\mathbf{ls}(r, A_i, s) = \mathbf{vte}(\sigma_{S=s \wedge A \neq \perp_i}^{\mathrm{B}}(r))$.

Lifespans are important because attributes are guaranteed to not have any inapplicable null value during their lifespans. Assume that we are given a relation schema empDep = (EmpS, EName, Dept) that records the names and departments of employees (represented by the surrogate attribute EmpS). If employees always have a name when they have a department, and vice versa, this means that inapplicable nulls are not present in instances of the schema. With lifespans, this property may be stated by saying that for all meaningful instances of EmpSal and for all EmpS surrogates, attributes EName and Dept have the same lifespans.

The importance of lifespans in temporal databases has been recognized in the context of data models in the past (c.f. [1, 2, 3]). Our use of lifespans for database design differs from the use of lifespans in database instances. In particular, using lifespans during database design does not imply any need for storing lifespans in the database.

2.4 Time Patterns of Individual Time-Varying Attributes

In order to capture how an attribute varies over time, we introduce the concept of a *time pattern*. Informally, a time pattern is simply a sequence of times.

Definition 2. The *time pattern* T is a partial function from the natural numbers $\mathcal{N}$ to a domain $\mathcal{D}_T$ of times: $T : \mathcal{N} \hookrightarrow \mathcal{D}_T$. If $T(i)$ is defined, so is $T(j)$ for all $j < i$. We term $T(i)$ the i'th time point.

In the context of databases, two distinct types of time patterns are of particular interest, namely observation patterns and update patterns. The *observation pattern* O_A^s, for an attribute A relative to a particular surrogate s, is the times when the attribute is given a particular value, perhaps as a result of an observation (e.g., if the attribute is sampled), a prediction, or an estimation. We adopt the convention that $O_A^s(0)$ is the time when it was first meaningful for attribute A to have a value for the surrogate s. Observation patterns concern valid time. The observation pattern may be expected to be closely related to, but distinct from, the actual (possibly unknown) pattern of change of the attribute in the modeled reality. The *update pattern* U_A^s is the times when the value of the attribute is updated in the database. Thus, update patterns concern transaction time.

Note that an attribute may not actually change value at a time point because it may be the case that the existing and new values are the same. The times when changes take place and the resulting values are orthogonal aspects. In the latter half of Section 3.1, we will return to this distinction.

2.5   The Values of Individual Time-Varying Attributes

We proceed by considering how attributes may encode information about the objects they describe. As the encoding of the transaction time of attributes is typically built into the data model, we consider only valid-time relations.

A relation may record directly when a particular attribute value is valid. Alternatively, what value is true at a certain point in time may be computed from the recorded values. In either case, the relation is considered a valid-time relation. An example clarifies the distinction between the two cases.

Example 2. Consider the two relations shown below. The first, empSal, records names and salaries of employees, and the second, expTemp, records names and temperature measurements for experiments. Attributes EmpS and ExpS record surrogates representing employees and experiments, respectively.

EmpS	EName	Sal	T
e1	Bob	30k	$\{1, \dots, 9\}$
e1	Bob	32k	$\{10, \dots, 19\}$
e1	Bob	36k	$\{30, \dots, 39\}$
e1	Bob	40k	$\{40, \dots, 49\}$
e2	Sam	25k	$\{1, \dots, 19\}$
e2	Sam	30k	$\{20, \dots, 49\}$

empSal

ExpS	Exp	Temp	T
x1	Exp1	75	$\{5, 65\}$
x1	Exp1	89	$\{15\}$
x1	Exp1	98	$\{25\}$
x1	Exp1	90	$\{35\}$
x1	Exp1	84	$\{45\}$
x1	Exp1	79	$\{55\}$

expTemp

Relation empSal records Bob's and Sam's salaries at all the times they have salaries. This is clearly consistent with what a valid-time relation is. At first sight, relation expTemp is more problematic. It does not appear to record temperatures for all the times when there exists a temperature for experiment x1. Specifically, we may envision that the temperature of x1 is sampled regularly and that we may later want to compute x1 temperature values for times with no explicitly recorded value.

Traditionally, empSal has been considered a state relation and expTemp has been considered an event relation; most data model proposals (with notable exceptions, e.g., [13, 15, 16]) have considered only the first type of relation. However, note that the relations are similar in the sense that they both record when information is true. Due to this observation, we make no fundamental distinction between the two types of relations, but instead treat them quite similarly.

The difference between relations such as empSal and expTemp in the example above is solely in what additional, or even different, information is implied by each of the relations. At the one extreme, relation empSal does not imply any additional information at all. No salary is recorded for Bob from time 20 to time 29, and the existing tuples do not imply any salary for Bob in that time interval. The other sample relation is different. For example, while no temperature for Exp1 at time 40 is recorded, clearly such a temperature exists. Further, we may even have a good idea what the temperature may be (i.e., close to 87).

Thus, the difference is that different *derivation functions* apply to the salary and temperature attributes of the two relations. A derivation function f_A for a specific attribute A of a relation schema R takes as arguments a valid-time chronon c^v and a relation instance r and returns a value in the domain of attribute A. For the salary attribute, a discrete derivation function applies; and for the temperature, a nearest-neighbor derivation function may satisfy some users while other users may need a more sophisticated function.

Definition 3. A *derivation function* f is a partial function from the domains of valid times $\mathcal{D}_{VT}$ and relation instances r with schema R to a value domain D in the universal set of domains $\mathcal{D}_D$, i.e., $f : \mathcal{D}_{VT} \times r(R) \hookrightarrow D$.

The importance of derivation functions in data models has previously been argued convincingly by, e.g., Klopprogge [10], Clifford [1] and Segev [16]. They should thus also be part of a design methodology.

2.6 Summary of Attribute Semantics

In summary, the database designer is expected to initially identify and model entity types using surrogates. Then, the notions of lifespans, time patterns, and derivation functions are used for capturing the semantics of attributes.

Elsewhere, we have generalized conventional functional dependencies to temporal databases [7]. Essentially, a *temporal dependency* holds on a temporal relation if the corresponding snapshot dependency holds on each snapshot relation contained in the temporal relation. With this generalization, conventional relational dependency theory applies wholesale to temporal databases. For example, *temporal keys* may be defined. Such keys are generally time-varying. As a basis for defining time-invariant attributes and keys, we have also defined so-called *strong temporal functional dependencies* and *strong temporal keys* [8]. While not discussed here, the designer is also expected to identify temporal and strong temporal functional dependencies.

3 Temporal Relational Database Design Guidelines

In this section, we discuss how the properties of schemas with time-varying attributes as captured in the previous section are used during database design. Emphasis is on the implications of the properties for design of the logical schema, but implications for view design and physical design are touched upon as well.

3.1 Logical-Design Guidelines

Two important goals of logical database design are to design a database schema that does not require the use of inapplicable nulls and avoids representation of the same information. We define two properties that illuminate these aspects of relation schemas and guide the database designer.

Database designers are faced with a number of design criteria which are sometimes conflicting, making database design a challenging task. So, while we discuss certain design criteria in isolation, it is understood that there may be other criteria that should be taken into consideration during database design, such as minimizing the impact of joins required on relations that have been decomposed.

Lifespan Decomposition Rule One important design criterion in conventional relational design is to eliminate the need for inapplicable nulls in tuples of database instances. In the context of temporal databases, we use the notion of lifespans to capture when attributes are defined for the objects they are introduced in order to describe. Briefly, the lifespan for an attribute—with respect to a particular surrogate representing the object described by the attribute—is all the times when a meaningful attribute value, known or unknown, exists for the object.

Inapplicable nulls may occur in a relation schema when two attributes have different lifespans for the same object/surrogate. To identify this type of situation, we introduce the notion of lifespan equal attributes. Examples follow the the definition.

Definition 4. Let a relation schema $R = (S, A_1, \ldots, A_n \mid T)$ be given where S is surrogate valued. Two attributes A_i and A_j in R are termed *lifespan equal* with respect to surrogate S, denoted $A_i \overset{\text{LS}}{=}_S A_j$, if for all meaningful instances r of R, $\forall s \in \text{dom}(S)\ (\text{ls}(r, A_i, s) = \text{ls}(r, A_j, s))$.

To exemplify this definition, consider a relation schema Emp with attributes EmpS (employee surrogates), Dept, Salary, and MgrSince. The schema is used by a company where each employee is always assigned to some department and has a salary. In addition, the relation records when an employee in a department first became a manager in that department.

For this schema, we have Dept $\overset{\text{LS}}{=}_{\text{EmpS}}$ Salary because an employee has a salary (it might be unknown or zero) exactly when associated with a department. Thus, no instances of Emp will have tuples with an inapplicable-null value for one of Dept and Salary and not for the other. Next, it is not the case that Dept $\overset{\text{LS}}{=}_{\text{EmpS}}$ MgrSince and (by inference) not the case that Salary $\overset{\text{LS}}{=}_{\text{EmpS}}$ MgrSince. This is so because employees often are associated with a department where they have never been a manager. Thus, instances of Emp may contain inapplicable nulls. Specifically, the nulls are associated with attribute MgrSince as the lifespan of this attribute is shorter than that of Dept and Salary.

Next, observe that Dept and Salary being lifespan equal with respect to EmpS does not mean that all employees have the same lifespan for their department (or salary) attribute. Employees may have been hired at different times, and the lifespans are thus generally different for different employees. Rather, the equality is between the department and the salary lifespan for individual employees.

The following definition then characterizes temporal database schemas with instances that do not contain inapplicable nulls.

Definition 5. A relation schema $R = (S, A_1, \ldots, A_n \mid T)$ where S is surrogate valued is *lifespan homogeneous* if $\forall A, B \in R \, (A \stackrel{\text{LS}}{=}_S B)$.

These concepts formally tie the connection between the notion of lifespans of attributes with the occurrence of inapplicable nulls in instances. With them, we are in a position to formulate the Lifespan Decomposition Rule.

Definition 6. *Lifespan Decomposition Rule.* To avoid inapplicable nulls in temporal database instances, decompose temporal relation schemas to ensure lifespan homogeneity.

It is appropriate to briefly consider the interaction of this rule with the the existing temporal normal forms that also prescribe decomposition of relation schemas. Specifically, while the decomposition that occurs during normalization does, as a side effect, aid in eliminating the need for inapplicable nulls, a database schema that obeys the temporal normal forms may still require inapplicable nulls in its instances. To exemplify, consider again the Emp schema (and think of the temporal dependencies on temporal relations as regular dependencies on the corresponding snapshot tables). Here, EmpS is a temporal key, and there are no other non-trivial dependencies. Thus, the schema is in temporal BCNF. It is also the case that Emp has no non-trivial temporal multi-valued dependencies, and it is thus also in temporal fourth normal form. In spite of this, we saw that there are inapplicable nulls. The solution is to decompose Emp = (EmpS, Dept, Salary, MgrSince) into Emp1 = (EmpS, Dept, Salary) and Emp2 = (EmpS, MgrSince). Both resulting relations are lifespan homogeneous.

Synchronous Decomposition Rule The synchronous decomposition rule is based on the notion of observation pattern, and its objective is to eliminate a particular kind of redundancy. We initially exemplify this type of redundancy. Then we define the notion of synchronous attributes, which leads to a definition of synchronous schemas and an accompanying decomposition rule that are aimed at avoiding this redundancy. Finally, we view synchronism in a larger context, by relating it to existing concepts, and discuss the decomposition rule's positioning with respect to logical versus physical design.

Example 3. Consider the relation instance, empDepSal, that follows next, recording departments and salaries for employees. The schema for the relation is in temporal BCNF, with the surrogate-valued attribute EmpS being the only minimal key and no other non-trivial dependencies. Yet, it may be observed that the salary 30k and the departments A and B are repeated once, once, and four times in the instance, respectively. These repetitions are due to attributes `Dept` and `Salary` having different observation patterns. Specifically, the instance is consistent with the patterns shown to the right of the instance.

EmpS	Dept	Salary	T
e1	A	30k	$\{1,\dots,5\}$
e1	B	30k	$\{6,\dots,9\}$
e1	B	32k	$\{10,\dots,14\}$
e1	B	36k	$\{15,\dots,27\}$
e1	B	40k	$\{28,\dots,42\}$
e1	A	50k	$\{43,\dots,49\}$

$$O_{\texttt{Dept}}^{\texttt{e1}} = <[0 \mapsto 1], [1 \mapsto 6], [2 \mapsto 43], [3 \mapsto 50]>$$

$$O_{\texttt{Salary}}^{\texttt{e1}} = <[0 \mapsto 1], [1 \mapsto 10], [2 \mapsto 15], [3 \mapsto 28],$$
$$[4 \mapsto 43], [5 \mapsto 50]>$$

In combination, these observation patterns imply the redundancy that may be observed in the sample instance. Thus, capturing during database design which attributes of the same relation schema have different observation patterns is a means of identifying this type of redundancy.

To capture precisely the synchronism of attributes, define $T|_t$ to be the restriction of time pattern T to the valid-time element t, that is, to include only those times also contained in t.

Definition 7. Define relation schema $R = (S, A_1, \dots, A_n \mid T)$ where S is surrogate valued. Two attributes A_i and A_j in R, with observation patterns $O_{A_i}^S$ and $O_{A_j}^S$, are *synchronous* with respect to S, denoted $A_i \overset{\text{s}}{=}_S A_j$, if for all meaningful instances r of R and for all surrogates s,

$$O_{A_i}^S |_{\mathbf{ls}(r,A_i,s) \cap \mathbf{ls}(r,A_j,s)} = O_{A_j}^S |_{\mathbf{ls}(r,A_i,s) \cap \mathbf{ls}(r,A_j,s)} .$$

Thus, attributes are synchronous if their lifespans are identical when restricted to the intersection of their lifespans. With this definition, we can characterize relations that avoid the redundancy caused by a lack of synchronism and then state the Synchronous Decomposition Rule.

Definition 8. Define relation schema $R = (S, A_1, \dots, A_n \mid T)$ where S is surrogate valued. Relation R is *synchronous* if $\forall A_i, A_j \in R \; (A_i \overset{\text{s}}{=}_S A_j)$.

Definition 9. *Synchronous Decomposition Rule.* To avoid repetition of attribute values in temporal relations, decompose relation schemas until they are synchronous.

Alternative notions of synchronism have previously been proposed for database design by Navathe and Ahmed [12], Lorentzos [11], and Wijsen [18]. While these notions are stated with varying degrees of clarity and precision and are defined in different data-model contexts, they all seem to capture the same basic idea, namely that of *value-based synchronism* which is different from the synchronism proposed in this paper.

To explain the difference, consider the relation instance shown next.

S	A_i	A_j	T
s	a_1	a_2	$\{1, \ldots, 5\}$
s	a_1	a_3	$\{6, \ldots, 10\}$

In value-based synchronism, value-changes of attributes must occur synchronously for attributes to be synchronous. Consequently, the relation instance implies that the attributes A_i and A_j in its schema are not value synchronous, and (value-based) decomposition is thus prescribed. Next, it may be that the attributes in the relation have identical observation patters and that it just (accidentally!) happened that the new value of A_i when both attributes were observed at time 6 was the same as its old value. This means that the relation is consistent with attributes A_i and A_j being (observation-pattern based) synchronous, and the synchronous decomposition rule does then *not* apply. To conclude, the value-based and pattern-based synchronisms are quite unrelated.

Further, it is our contention that using the concept of value-based synchronism during database design is problematic. Specifically, it seems quite rare that the database designer can guarantee that, at *all* times in the future, when two attributes in a tuple of relation are updated, one of them does not get a new value that is identical to its old value. Thus, it appears that decomposition based on value-based synchronism effectively (and unnecessarily) leads to a binary data model, in which all relations have just two attributes, a time invariant attribute and a single time-varying attribute. This is in contrast to the pattern-based decomposition prescribed in this paper.

This study is carried out in the context of TSQL2. It is our contention that in this context, the synchronous decomposition rule is relevant only to physical database design. Surely, the redundancy that may be detected using the synchronism concept is important when *storing* temporal relations. At the same time, this type of redundancy is of little consequence for the querying of logical-level relations using the TSQL2 query language [8, 13]. Indeed, it will often adversely affect the ease of formulating queries if logical-level relations are decomposed solely based on a lack of synchronism. In conclusion, the presence of synchronous attributes in a relation may affect performance (positively or negatively), but it does not negatively affect correctness or the ease of formulating queries, and it is thus a non-issue at the logical level.

The widespread presence of asynchronous attributes in relation schemas has been used for motivating various attribute-value timestamped data models where in relations, time is associated with attribute values rather than with tuples, because these models avoids the redundancy (see, e.g., [2, 4, 5]). Since this redundancy is not a problem in TSQL2, which employs tuple-timestamped relations, asynchronous attributes is not strictly an argument for attribute-value timestamped models.

Finally, the need for synchronism at the logical level has previously been claimed to make normal forms and dependency theory inapplicable (e.g., [5]). The argument is that few attributes are synchronous, meaning that relation schemas must be maximally decomposed, which leaves other normalization concepts irrelevant. This claim does not apply to our data model.

For completeness, it should be mentioned that while the synchronism concepts presented in this section have concerned valid time, similar concepts that concern transaction time and employ update patterns rather than observation patterns, may also be defined.

3.2 Implications for View Design

The only concept from Section 2 not covered so far is derivation functions. These relate to view design, as outlined next.

For each time-varying attribute, we have captured a set of one or more derivation functions that apply to it. It is often the case that exactly one derivation function applies to an attribute, namely the discrete interpolation function [8] that is a kind of identity function. However, it may also be the case that several nontrivial derivation functions apply to a single attribute.

The problem is then how to apply several derivation functions to the base data. We feel that there should be a clear separation between recorded data and data derived from the stored data via some function. Maintaining this separation makes it possible to later modify existing interpolation functions.

The view mechanism provides an ideal solution that maintains this separation. Thus, the database designer first identifies which sets of derivation functions that should be applied simultaneously to the attributes of a logical relation instance and then, subsequently, defines a view for each such set. Although interpolation functions have previously been studied, we believe they have never before been associated with the view mechanism.

4 Summary and Research Directions

In order to exploit the full potential of temporal relational database technology, guidelines for the design of temporal relational databases should be provided.

This paper has presented concepts for capturing the properties of time-varying attributes in temporal databases. These concepts include surrogates that represent the real-world objects described by the attributes, lifespans of attributes, observation and update patterns for time-varying attributes, and derivation functions that compute new attribute values from stored ones. It was subsequently shown how surrogates and lifespans play an role during design of the logical database schema. In particular, the notion of lifespans led to the formulation of a lifespan decomposition rule. The notion of observation (and update) patterns led to a synchronous decomposition rule; it was argued that this rule should ideally apply to physical database design. Finally, it was shown how derivation functions are relevant for view design.

We feel that several aspects merit further study. An integration of the various existing contributions to temporal relational database design into a coherent framework has yet to be attempted. Likewise, a complete design methodology, including conceptual (implementation-data-model independent) design and logical design, for temporal databases is warranted. Finally, a next step is to adopt the concepts provided in this paper in richer, entity-based (or semantic or object-based) data models.

Acknowledgements

This work was supported in part by NSF grant ISI-9202244. In addition, the first author was supported in part by the Danish Natural Science Research Council, grants 11-1089-1, 11-0061-1, and 9400911.

References

1. J. Clifford and A. Croker. The Historical Relational Data Model (HRDM) and Algebra Based on Lifespans. In *Proceedings of ICDE*, pp. 528–537, February 1987.

2. J. Clifford and A. U. Tansel. On an Algebra for Historical Relational Databases: Two Views. In *Proceedings of ACM SIGMOD*, pp. 247–265, May 1985.

3. R. Elmasri, G. Wuu, and V. Kouramajian. A Temporal Model and Query Language for EER Databases. In [17], pp. 212–229.

4. S. K. Gadia. A Homogeneous Relational Model and Query Languages for Temporal Databases. *ACM TODS*, 13(4):418–448, December 1988.

5. S. K. Gadia and J. H. Vaishnav. A Query Language for a Homogeneous Temporal Database. In *Proceedings of ACM PODS*, pp. 51–56, March 1985.

6. C. S. Jensen, J. Clifford, R. Elmasri, S. K. Gadia, P. Hayes, and S. Jajodia (eds). A Glossary of Temporal Database Concepts. *SIGMOD Record*, 23(1):52–64, March 1994.

7. C. S. Jensen, R. T. Snodgrass, and M. D. Soo. Extending Normal Forms to Temporal Relations. Technical Report TR-92-17, Department of Computer Science, University of Arizona, Tucson, AZ, July 1992.

8. C. S. Jensen and R. T. Snodgrass. Semantics of Time-Varying Attributes and Their Use for Temporal Database Design. Technical Report R-95-2012, Department of Math. and Computer Science, Aalborg University, Denmark, May 1995.

9. C. S. Jensen, M. D. Soo, and R. T. Snodgrass. Unifying Temporal Models via a Conceptual Model. *Information Systems*, 19(7):513–547, 1994.

10. M. R. Klopprogge and P. C. Lockemann. Modelling Information Preserving Databases: Consequences of the Concept of Time. In *Proceedings of VLDB*, pp. 399–416, 1983.

11. N. A. Lorentzos. Management of Intervals and Temporal Data in the Relational Model. Technical Report 49, Agricultural University of Athens, 1991.

12. S. B. Navathe and R. Ahmed. A Temporal Relational Model and a Query Language. *Information Sciences*, 49:147–175, 1989.

13. R. T. Snodgrass (ed). The TSQL2 Temporal Query Language. Kluwer Academic Publishers, 1995, 674+xxiv pages.

14. M. D. Soo, C. S. Jensen, and R. T. Snodgrass. An Algebra for TSQL2. In [13], chapter 27, pp. 505–546.

15. R. T. Snodgrass. The Temporal Query Language TQuel. *ACM TODS*, 12(2):247–298, June 1987.

16. A. Segev and A. Shoshani. A Temporal Data Model based on Time Sequences. In [17], pp. 248–270.

17. A.U. Tansel, J. Clifford, S.K. Gadia, A. Segev, and R.T. Snodgrass (eds). Temporal Databases: Theory, Design, and Implementation. Benjamin/Cummings, 1993.

18. J. Wijsen. Extending Dependency Theory for Temporal Databases. Ph.D. Thesis. Department Computerwetenschappen, Katholieke Universiteit Leuven, 1995.

Handling Change Management using Temporal Active Repositories

Avigdor Gal and Opher Etzion

Information Systems Engineering Department
Faculty of Industrial Engineering and Management
Technion - Israel Institute of Technology
Haifa, Israel, 32000
Email: [avigal, ieretzn]@ie.technion.ac.il

Abstract. Business Re-engineering requires frequent changes in the enterprises' information systems, however the current technology of data dictionaries is not effective for the tracing of required changes and their management. In this paper we introduce an architecture of change management using active temporal repositories. Flexible change management allows the support of information about past or future versions of information systems, as well as the capability to retrieve and update temporal information. The implementation of change management in a temporal environment is carried out by the partition of the temporal universe among temporal agents, each of them handles a single version of an application with a required collaboration among them. The change management process, and the inter and intra agent processing are described in this paper.

keywords: change management, information agents, cooperative databases, temporal databases, active databases

1 Introduction and Motivation

1.1 Background

In today's business environment, re-engineering has become a vital process in many enterprises [11]. The process of re-engineering involves changes in the enterprise's structure and processes to meet its evolving goals in a constantly changing environment. Alas, current information technologies, using abstractions such as data dictionaries, form an obstacle to the implementation of re-engineering due to difficulties in tracing the consequences of such changes on the information systems and on the application programs.

Data dictionaries [1] have been proposed as abstractions of concepts that are vital to model information systems. However, the contribution of data dictionaries to change management has been marginal due to the following three major problems:

- Data dictionaries are loosely coupled with the actual applications. Consequently, there is no automatic way to infer the implication of a change in an application. Modelling such an implication requires manual intervention; thus, the reliability of such information is left to the user discretion, resulting in frequent inconsistencies.

- Data dictionaries are passive in the sense that they only document information about the application but do not include automatic tools to initiate actions in the wake of a change in any of the application's components.

- Many application systems maintain concurrently active versions. Changes in the applications may refer to various versions or create a new one. Data dictionaries are unable to assist in change management over versioned systems, since they do not have temporal capabilities.

In this paper we propose an architecture for a *change management* based on a combination of several technologies:

- The *information repository technology* which controls the application behavior in a tightly-coupled manner [12].
- The *object oriented technology* that enables flexible structuring.
- The *active technology* that supports automatic activation of derived changes [7].
- The *temporal technology* which supports several versions of the information repository entities and sustain the modelling of time characteristics for any information about the application [15].

1.2 A Motivating Example

Throughout this paper we use the following example as both a motivating example and a demonstration of the change management architecture capabilities.

A distributed information system consists of a global information repository and local information repositories with local agents. The global repository includes information about globally compatible data-items. Globally compatible data-items are data-items whose type is enforced to be the type defined in the global repository. We assume a shared naming conventions to avoid semantic conflicts such as synonyms and homonyms.

Each data-item has an accessibility indication that states whether it is shared with other repositories or it is a private data-item. For simplicity, we assume that if a data-item is shared, it is accessible to all repositories. Unlike shared data-items, private data-items do not have to be globally compatible, even if they have the same name. Both the type and the accessibility indication of each data-item may change over time, e.g., a data-item may be accessible during certain temporal element and inaccessible during other temporal element.

The rest of the paper is organized as follows. Section 2 describes the data model of a temporal active database, based on [4]. Section 3 discusses the change management process. Section 4 concludes the paper.

2 The Temporal Active Repository

In recent papers ([4], [9]) we investigated the combination of temporal database technology and active database technology as a key combination for supporting complex applications. We use this combination as an information model for the repository. A full description of the temporal active database model can be found in [4]. Section 2.1 describes the temporal data model, section 2.2 describes the dependency language, section 2.3. describes the temporal dependency graph.

2.1 The Temporal Data Model

The temporal database infrastructure [13] advocates a bi-temporal database that contain the two temporal characteristics of each data element.

Transaction Time (t_x) - The commit time of the transaction which updated the data-item.

Valid Time (t_v) - The time points in which the decision maker believes that this value reflects the data-item's value in the "real world". t_v is expressed using a temporal element.

For the change management application we add a third type of time:

Decision Time (t_d) - The time at which the data-item's value was decided in the database's domain of discourse [4]. For example, if a decision about the type of a product price was decided in November 11 1991, and inserted to the database in November 12 1991, t_d would be November 11 1991, and t_x would be November 12 1991. The decision time is employed to maintain the correct order of occurrences in the real world, which becomes extremely important in databases with time constraints relative to the real world occurrences.

For example, Figure 1 presents a partial schema of the example presented in Section 1. The class *Globally-Defined-Data-Item* represents information about data-items that are shared among the repositories. This information resides in the global repository that contains only the meta-data entities. The values of the data itself reside in local repositories and may vary from one repository to another. The class *Local-Data-Item* represents information about data-items in the various repositories, their location, their accessibility and their type. Each object is identified by the data-item's name and the repository id. It is worth noting, that a data-item with the same name may have different properties in different repositories. The class *Local-Repository* designates information about a repository and about grouping of data-items for default obtaining purposes. It should be noted that we use repository in the broad sense as a unified name for database, knowledge-base and the set of variables known to an information agent.

We use the time types to characterize the temporal properties of each variable value in the following way:

VS(α) (**variable state of a variable** α) is a sequence of tuples representing the history of the variable's values. The symbol α designates a variable of a given

class=	*Globally-Defined-Data-Item*
properties=	*Globally-Defined-Data-Item-Name*
	Global-Type
	Global-Range

class=	*Local-Data-Item*
properties=	*Local-Data-Item-Name*
	Local-Repository
	Accessibility-Indicator
	Given-Type
	Group-Name
	Local-Type (derived)
	Given-Local-Range
	Local-Range (derived)

class=	*Local-Repository*
properties=	*Local-Repository-Name*
	Data-Groups: set-of:
	Group-Name
	Default-Type

Fig. 1. A partial schema of the global repository

object. Each tuple in the sequence is a *state-element*.

A **state-element** is a tuple constructed of two parts: a value and a *temporal extension*.

The value can be an atom, a set, a sequence, a tuple or a reference to another object.

A **temporal extension** consists of time values of the different time types (t_x, t_d, t_v).

2.2 The Active Dimension in a Temporal Database

For the active dimension we use the invariant language as introduced in the PARDES model [5]. An *invariant* is a declarative definition of a value dependency that should be satisfied for any instance in a defined temporal-element in the database. There are two types of invariants, derivations and constraints. A *derivation* states the dependency between a derived data-item and other data-items in the database. A *constraint* is an assertion about the relationship among different data-items in the database. Figure 2 presents examples of invariants with respect to the case-study described in Section 1.

(i1) Local-Type	:= Global-Type when Accessibility-Indicator=Shared
	Given-Type when Given-Type $\neq$ nil
	Default-Type otherwise

(i2) <Local-Range, $t_v=[t_s+7, t_e]$> := < Global-Range, $t_v=[t_s, t_e]$>
(i3) Local-Range := Given-Local-Range
(i4) Local-Range $\subseteq$ Global-Range

Fig. 2. Invariants Definitions

2.3 The Dependency Graph Data Model

The data model is augmented by a *dependency graph*. As proposed in [7], the nodes of the dependency graph designate the application's elements (data-items, invariants, and events). The edges of the dependency graph designate a relationship between two elements and the role of this relationship, i.e., whether a change in the source element entails a possible change in the target element or the target element requires information from the source element.

The addition of the temporal dimension induces an extended version of this graph, a *temporal dependency graph* (TDG) which is an executable data structure used to determine the logic of the update process in a temporal environment. The temporal extension of the dependency graph is formally presented as follows:
Let **TDG** be a directed graph (V,E) where: V=PR ∪ INV ∪ EV ∪ CON.

PR is a set of hyper-nodes, where each hyper-node represents a property *pr*. A hyper-node consists of a set of sub-nodes in the form $\{(pr, \tau_{pr})\}$ where τ_{pr} is a temporal element. Each ingoing or outgoing edge may refer either to the hyper-node or to a specific sub-node. If the target node of an edge is the hyper-node itself, then this property is referred within the entire time-domain of the application.

INV is the set of all the invariants in the database.

EV is the set of all the events defined in the database. Each event detection results in the insertion of an event instance to the database.

CON is the set of connectors. A *connector* is a node that initiate message passing among agents. A connector node is created at the time of schema modification. Connectors are created in groups of *sending connectors* and *receiving connectors*.

Since the repository is tightly coupled and controlling, the dependency graph is automatically created and modified by the repository upon any relevant change. The dependency graph is transparent to the user but can be used by system administrators to reason about the system behavior and the implication of any proposed change. The dependency graph is created at the time of the definition or re-definition of the schema and is maintained as an integral part of the repository.

3 The Change Management Process

3.1 An Overview

The change management is carried out by an update transaction that receives as an input a set of update operations $u_1, \ldots, u_n$, given by the user. The change management process uses the invariants defined in the application, to create additional update operations that are required to maintain the database consistency. The change management process creates derived update operations, executes them and evaluates relevant constraints.

An update process for a non-temporal active database is presented in the PARDES project framework [5]. We extend the PARDES approach to support the following operations:

1. Schema evolution, i.e., the ability to change any component in the information system and trace changes that have been performed over time.
2. Temporal operations, that allow retroactive or proactive update operations, i.e., update operations that result in new state-elements whose t_v is either past or future. This is an important feature in modelling information about information systems. In many cases, several versions of the same system are used at the same time by different users. The ability to maintain information about all the versions and to update information that concern present, past and future (planned) versions of the system is vital to construct change management process.

These two extensions require the use of temporal agents and the consideration of the following issues:

1. Devising decision mechanism to associate an update operation with a temporal agent.
2. Devising a communication protocol among temporal agents, in the case that an update operation cannot be handled by a single temporal agent.
3. Devising a flexible modes of atomicity requirements that optionally enable to commit transactions by some temporal agents and abort by others.

Section 3.2. discusses the implications of schema evolution, Section 3.3. describes the communication protocol among temporal agents. Section 3.4. briefly describes the update process, emphasizing the decision process about partitioning update operations and allocating them to other agents. Section 3.5 highlights the main features of the change management process.

3.2 The Implications of Schema Evolution

Schema evolution results in modifications of meta-data entities. For example, some local repository administrators complained that a week period is not sufficient to override a change in the global range. As a result, the invariant (i2) was modified in July 1, 1993, to allow a delay of 14 days instead of the previous delay of 7 days until enforcing the global range. The invariant (i2) was replaced with the invariant (i'2) as follows.

(i'2) $<$Local-Range, $t_v=[t_s+14, t_e]> := <$ Global-Range, $t_v=[t_s, t_e]>$

The introduction of several schema definitions induce a partition on the application's time domain to time regions. A unique TDG is valid in each element of the partition set. Each time region is associated with a *temporal agent*.

In most cases, a transaction is handled by a single temporal agent. However, transactions may generate update operations with temporal validity that exceeds the limits of a single time region. Hence, cooperation among temporal agents is required. For example, a modification of *Global-Range* for a certain instance is issued in August 1, 1993, for the interval [June 25 1993, ∞]. This retroactive modification activates (i2), in the old TDG. However, since a *Global-Range* is enforced only 7 days after the change, the consequences of the activation of (i2) is in the interval [July 2 1993, ∞]. This time interval belongs to a new temporal agent with a new TDG. Thus, a message regarding this activation should pass between the agents.

A change in the schema level results in the following activities:

Re-partition of the application time domain: A new temporal agent is created and the application time domain is re-partitioned among the temporal agents. Thus, the validity time for existing TDG's may change. For example, the application time domain $[t_1, t_5]$ before a schema change is partitioned as follows $(t_1 < t_3 < t_5)$:

$[t_1, t_3)$ is the time region of agent #1.
$[t_3, t_5)$ is the time region of agent #2.
A new schema is introduced in $[t_2, t_4)$ where $t_1 < t_2 < t_3 < t_4 < t_5$. The new temporal agent is named "agent #3". The re-partition of the application time domain is:

$[t_1, t_2)$ is the time region of agent #1.
$[t_2, t_4)$ is the time region of agent #3.
$[t_4, t_5]$ is the time region of agent #2.

Creation of the TDG in the new time region: A new TDG is created as a result of the schema change. This new TDG is valid in the time region of the newly created temporal agent. In the example shown above, a new TDG is created for the interval $[t_2, t_4)$.

Re-evaluation of the inter-TDGs connections: The inter-TDGs connections are represented as connectors in the TDG. Re-partitioning of the application temporal domain may generate new connectors, while old connectors may be deleted. Each existing connector in the time region of the newly created temporal agent is re-evaluated. In addition, an evaluation of the connections among the new temporal agent and those temporal agents that once controlled its time region is performed.

3.3   The Communication Protocol

A communication protocol among temporal agents is required to establish the collaboration when an operation exceeds the boundaries of a single time region. The communication protocol consists of the following primitives:

Expand-Transitive-Closure(ag, x): The change management process involves the creation of the transitive closure, to guarantee update minimality. In the case that a transitive closure of a temporal agent x includes a connector node, the message *Expand-Transitive-Closure* is sent from x to each agent ag that controls a TDG with a matching connector. The receiving agent ag adds the transitive closure of the connector to the sub-graph of the transaction.

Activate-Connector (ag, operation, variable-name, value, temp, t_d): An activation of a derivation might result in updating values out of the temporal agent's time region. If during the update execution, agent x activates a connector, then a message is sent to an agent ag, which has a matching connector with the data regarding the required atomic operation.

Send-Update-Message (ag, operation, variable-name, value, temp, t_d): A temporal agent x is able to decide on temporal intervals that cannot be modified by it. This is the case when a temporal element to be updated is out of the time region of x, and x cannot reason about the transitive closure of this update, since the modification of the schema effected the target property. x selects a temporal agent ag which x believes that is capable to execute the update operation, and sends to ag an atomic operation with the relevant data, including the temporal element that is out of x's control.

3.4   A Description of The Update Process

Each update transaction contains a sequence of update operations that are given by the user. Each update operation is decomposed by the transaction manager to atomic operations, where each atomic operation is intended to update a single variable. Each atomic operation is a sequence $<$operation, variable-name, value, t_v, $t_d >$, where the last three components are the values that are used in the creation of a new state-element.

The transaction manager assigns each atomic operation to a temporal agent x if $t_s(t_v) \in \tau_{rg}(x)$. This criterion states that an atomic operation is assigned to the temporal agent that its time region includes the starting point of the operation's t_v. Since the application time domain is fully partitioned to the time regions, this criterion creates a unique assignment.

A temporal agent collects all the atomic operations that are assigned to it and that belong to the same transaction, and marks the subgraph of its TDG which contains the transitive closures of all the variables that are referred in the atomic update operations. This transitive closure is required to avoid update redundancy [10]. If a connector has been marked in this process, a message is passed to the appropriate agent, to expand its subgraph to include the transitive closure of the matching connector as well.

Each temporal agent executes independently the atomic operations that were assigned to it. Each atomic operation is analyzed and executed in the following way:

An agent receives an atomic operation. At this stage there are two possible scenarios:

1. The valid time argument is totally included in the agent's time region. In this case, the t_{up}, the actual valid time, is set to the original t_v.
2. Some of the valid time is not included in the agent's time region. The agent uses the function *retrieve-state-elements* to receive all the variables that were effected by the schema evolution in the interval starting at the end of its time region and ending at the end of the t_v of the operation.
   (a) In case that there was no change in the schema that involved the variable given as a parameter to the *Analyze-Operation* procedure, the agent is capable of handling the full t_v of the operation. In this case, the t_{up} is set to the original t_v.
   (b) If the variable was involved in one of the schema changes, the agent excludes the time as of the time of the change from t_v , search for the agent in charge for that time and sends an update message with the appropriate arguments.

4 Conclusion

This paper introduced an architecture for change management in a multi-version environment. The architecture is based upon a temporal active repository and the notion of temporal agents. This architecture issues an infrastructure for the implementation of cooperative work to support performance and functionality issues of change management.

This approach enables the high-level support of automatic change management in the schema evolution domain and support the following novel features:

- High level support of version management. This architecture supports different versions of the schema concurrently and allows high level abstractions to change several schemata in one operation. This is important in cooperative systems in which different users possess different versions of the schema. The alternative employed in current systems is to perform manually all the implications upon the distinct versions.
- The dependency graph executable data structure enable reasoning about all the consequences of any schema or invariant change in all the cooperating systems. This feature is vital for the implementation of rapid schema generation, which is an important step in the support of re-engineering.
- The view of schema history as a collection of temporal regions, each of them is controlled by a temporal agent, applies the concepts of cooperative work and parallelism to change management

A prototype of this system is currently being developed. Further research will deal with various issues, including exception-handling in the proposed environment, hypothetical change management to support possible worlds and aid in the planning of schema evolution, extend the model to a distributed environment with no global control and test the change management model on real-life case studies

Acknowledgements

The basic work of combining the active and temporal technologies has been done in collaboration with Arie Segev.

References

1. F. Allen, M. Loomis, M. Mannino - The integrated Dictionary/Directory System. *ACM Computing Surveys, 14(2), June 1982, pp 245-286.*
2. U. Dayal, M. Hsu, R. Ladin - A Transactional Model for Long-Running Activities. Proc VLDB 1991, pp 113-122
3. S. Chakravarthy S. - HiPAC: A research Project in Active, Time-Constrained Database Management, *Final Technical Report, XAIT-89-02,* July 1989.
4. O. Etzion, A. Gal, A. Segev - Temporal Active Databases, *Proceedings of the International Workshop on an Infrastructure for Temporal Database,* June 1993.
5. O. Etzion - PARDES-A Data-Driven Oriented Active Database Model, *SIGMOD RECORD, 22(1),*pp. 7-14, Mar 1993.
6. O. Etzion- Flexible Consistency Modes for Active Database Applications. *Information Systems, 18(6), 1993, pp 391-404.*
7. O. Etzion - The reflective Approach for Data-Driven Rules. *International Journal of Intelligent and cooperative Information Systems, 2(4), pp. 399-424, Dec 1993.*
8. S.K. Gadia - The Role of Temporal Elements in Temporal Databases, *Data Engineering Bulletin, 7,* pp. 197-203, 1988.
9. A. Gal, E. Etzion, A. Segev - Representation of Highly-Complex Knowledge in a Database, *Journal of Intelligent Information Systems, 3(2), pp 185-203,* Mar. 1994.
10. S. Hudson, R. King - CACTIS: A Database System for Specification Functionally Defined Data, *proc. IEEE OOBDS Workshop,* 1986.
11. S.E. Madnick - Integration Technology: The reinvention of the Linkage Between Information Systems and Computer Science. *To appear in Decision Support Systems*
12. J. Mylopoulos, E. Yu - Aligning Information System Strategy with Business Strategy: A Technical Perspective, *A keynote address in the International Workshop on Next Generation Technologies and Systems, Haifa, Israel,* June 1993.
13. N. Pissinou, et al - Towards an Infrastructure for Temporal Databases, *Sigmod Record, 23(1), pp 35-51,* Mar 1994.
14. R. Snodgrass, I. Ahn - Temporal Databases, *IEEE Computer 19,* pp. 35-42, Sep 1986.
15. A.U. Tansel, Clifford J., Gadia S., Jajodia S., Segev A., Snodgrass R. - Temporal Databases, *The Benjamin/Commings Publishing Company, Inc., Redwood City, CA.,* 1993.

A Graphical Query Language for Temporal Databases

Vram Kouramajian[1] and Michael Gertz[2]

[1] Knight-Ridder Information, Inc., 2440 El Camino Real,
Mountain View, CA 94040, vram@dnt.dialog.com
[2] Universität Hannover, Institut für Informatik,
D-30159 Hannover, Germany, mg@informatik.uni-hannover.de

Abstract. This paper addresses the issue of visual query formulation for temporal databases. We introduce a number of visual constructs that allow users to build queries in a modular fashion based on a temporal Extended Entity–Relationship Model. These constructs are: Temporal projection, temporal selection, time links, filtering and set operators, and temporal aggregates.

1 Introduction

Temporal databases preserve the complete history of the Universe of Discourse; that is, they follow the *non deletion* rule of data [16, 11, 13, 15, 17, 10]. They create a new version for each object modification without destroying or overwriting existing versions of objects. This permits users to query the current state of the database, as well as past states, and even states that are planned for the future.

Recent years have witnessed an increase in research on several aspects of temporal databases (see, e.g., [3] for an overview). These include research on temporal algebras, calculus–based query languages, valid time and transaction time databases, conceptual and physical temporal database modeling, temporal query languages, temporal active models, and access structures for temporal data. Unfortunately, not much attention has been paid to the important area of visual interfaces to temporal databases.

Most temporal query languages are extension to textual query languages such as SQL [8] or GORDAS [9]. They are aimed at users with high degree of sophistication and good knowledge of temporal constructs. What is missing in temporal databases are *human–centered* user interfaces for database design and manipulation. A human–centered visual environment should include tools for temporal database modeling, query formulation, different display metaphors, and temporal data insertion and update.

In this work, we address the problem of graphical query formulation for temporal databases. Several prototypes that provide graphical interfaces for non–temporal databases have been developed [7, 6, 5, 1]. Some prototypes use Entity–Relationship (ER) diagrams for data modeling but they offer manipulation facilities close to relational models [6]. More advanced prototypes provide a consistent view by using the same schema representation for the schema editor and query editor [1]. Successful prototypes are based on the principle of direct manipulation of objects and functions, supporting unconstrained user behavior during schema definition as well as query formulation. Our visual query language provides users with a number of simple, consistent graphical representations for temporal selection, temporal projection, temporal aggregate functions, and arbitrary, complex temporal operations over a single or multiple database states.

Our graphical query language is built on top of TEER [10], a temporal extension to the Extended Entity-Relationship (EER) Model [8]. A related work by Oberweis and Sänger describes a graphical query language (GTL) for temporal relational models [14]. GTL introduces a number of new, non-standard patterns for describing temporal queries, which may confuse database users familiar with and accustomed to EER diagrammatic notations. We believe that it is more natural to specify temporal data and queries in a conceptual, entity-oriented data model than in a tuple-oriented relational data model. The TEER model incorporates the concept of lifespan for entities and relationships into the EER model. It also extends the GORDAS ER query language [9] to handle temporal queries by introducing the concepts of temporal boolean expressions, temporal selection, and temporal projection.

The paper is organized as follows. Section 2 reviews the TEER model. Sections 3 and 4 present the basic and advanced constructs of our visual query language. A detailed presentation of our query language as well as challenges posed by visual interface design for temporal databases is given in [12].

2 Review of the TEER Model

The Temporal Extended Entity-Relationship (TEER) model adapts the EER model [8] to include the temporal dimension. Section 2.1 reviews the representation of time used in this work. Section 2.2 and Section 2.3 shortly review the TEER model and query constructs, which are discussed in more detail in [10].

2.1 Representing Time

Let T be a countably infinite set of totally ordered discrete points in time. A *time interval* $[t_s, t_e]$ is defined to be a set of consecutive time points; that is, the totally ordered set $\{t_s, t_{s+1}, \ldots, t_e\} \subset T$. We call t_s the *start time* and t_e the *end time* of the time interval. A single discrete time pont t is represented as a closed interval $[t, t]$, or simply $[t]$.

A *temporal element*, denoted as TE, is a finite union of maximal time intervals, denoted by $\{I_1, I_2, \ldots, I_n\}$, where I_i is an interval in T [11]. Union, intersection, and difference operations as well as comparison predicates on temporal elements are easily defined.

Two of the most common time dimensions in temporal databases are the *valid time* and the *transaction time* [16]. The valid time represents the actual time in the mini-world that a particular event or change occurred, or the actual time intervals during which a particular fact was true. For historical databases, the domain of a valid time attribute is the time interval $[0, now]$, where zero (0) represents the starting time of the database mini-world application, and *now* is the current time, which is continuously expanding. The transaction time represents the time that facts or events were recorded in the database. Due to space limitations, we will consider only valid time in this work.

2.2 The TEER Data Model

The *Temporal EER (TEER)* model extends the EER model [8] to include temporal information on entities, relationships, etc. We will assume that the reader is familiar with the basic concepts of the ER model and ER diagrams, and directly specify the concepts of the TEER model.

Entities and Entity Types In the TEER model, each entity e of entity type E is associated with a temporal element $TE(e)$ that gives the *lifespan* of the entity. The lifespan $TE(e)$ could be a continuous time interval, or it could be the union of a number of disjoint time intervals. The temporal value of each attribute A_i of e, which we refer to as $A_i(e)$, is a partial function $A_i(e) : TE(e) \rightarrow dom(A_i)$. This is also called a *temporal assignment* [11]. It is assumed that A_i has a *UNKNOWN* value during the intervals $TE(e) - TE(A_i(e))$.

Additionally, in the TEER model, each entity has a system-defined SURROGATE attribute whose value is unique for every entity in the database, and does not change throughout the lifespan of the entity.

Relationship Types and Relationship Instances A *relationship type R* of degree n has n participating entity types $E_1, ..., E_n$. Each *relationship instance r* in R is an n-tuple $r = \langle e_1, ..., e_n \rangle$ where each $e_i \in E_i$. In the TEER model, each relationship instance r is associated with a temporal element $TE(r)$ which gives the *lifespan* of the relationship instance. The constraint is that $TE(r)$ must be a subset of the intersection of the temporal elements of the entities $e_1, ..., e_n$ that participate in r. That is, $TE(r) \subseteq (TE(e_1) \cap ... \cap TE(e_n))$. This is because for the relationship instance to exist at some point t, all the entities participating in that relationship instance must also exist at t.

Relationship attributes are treated similarly to entity attributes; the temporal value $A_i(r)$ of each attribute A_i of r is a partial function (temporal assignment) $A_i(r) : TE(r) \rightarrow dom(A_i)$, and its temporal element $TE(A_i(r)) \subseteq TE(r)$.

2.3 TEER Query Language Constructs

To allow for temporal constructs in queries, the TEER model defines the following query language constructs:

1. **Temporal Boolean Expression:** A (temporal) boolean expression is a conditional expression on the attributes and relationships of an entity. The boolean condition, when applied to one entity e, evaluates to a function (temporal assignment) from $TE(e)$ to $\{TRUE, FALSE, UNKNOWN\}$.

2. **True Time:** The true time of a boolean expression c, denoted by $[\![c]\!]$, evaluates to a temporal element for each entity e. The temporal element is the time for which the condition c is *TRUE* for e.

3. **Temporal Selection Condition:** A (temporal) selection condition compares two true times using the set comparison operators $=$, $\neq$, $\supseteq$, and $\subseteq$. When applied to an entity type, it evaluates to those entities that satisfy the temporal selection condition.

4. **Temporal Projection:** A temporal projection, when applied to a temporal entity, restricts all temporal assignments (attributes and relationships) for that entity to a specific time period specified by a temporal element.

Temporal selection conditions are used to select particular entities based on temporal conditions, whereas temporal projections are used to limit the data displayed for the selected entities to specific time periods. Temporal boolean conditions may be used as components in the expressions for both temporal selections and temporal projections.

3 Basic Graphical Query Language Constructs

For our graphical query language we do not pre-suppose any particular visual environment but we assume a kernel architecture that provides a basic set of functionality and layouts similar to those available in SUPER [1]. Section 3.1 presents essential non-temporal query operators. Sections 3.2 and 3.3 introduce graphical query constructs for temporal projection and temporal selection.

3.1 Essential Non-temporal Operators

An EER diagrammatic model builds the starting point for query formulation in our visual environment. In the sequel, we will use the following simplified university database schema to introduce our graphical query language constructs.

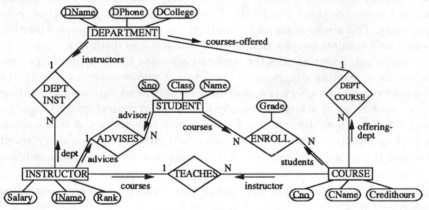

Fig. 1. University Database

The Remove Operator During query formulation, a user may apply the *remove* operator which drops one or more attributes, entities, and relationships with their attributes from the displayed database schema (and respectively from the query). Deletions are propagated to participating relationships. Applying the remove operator iteratively on the schema results in a *working diagram*.

The Restrict Operator After having selected the relevant part of the schema, a user may wish to allow for selection of data that satisfy certain criteria. The *restrict* operator is used to impose boolean conditions on attributes of entities and relationships [5, 1]. In the case of complex conditions involving attributes of multiple entities, users may place boolean conditions in a *condition box* linked to the respective attributes. All attributes that are displayed in the query result must be marked explicitly by an asterisk (*).

Example 1. *"Retrieve the name, rank, and courses of all instructors of the computer science department who teach a compiler or a programming course".*

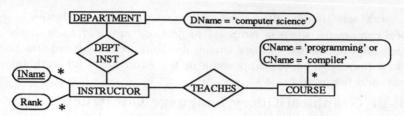

Fig. 2. Restrict Operator

This graphical query is built from Figure 1 through a number of operations, including the remove and restrict operator. The attributes DName and CName are used in restrict operators. The current values of attributes IName, Rank, and CName are displayed since they are marked by an asterisk (*). Figure 2 does not include any temporal constructs. In the context of an underlying temporal data model, restrictions and display operators are applied at the time instant *now*.

Construction of Queries During the query formulation process, a user is allowed to specify the different components of a query independently in a working diagram and to modify them separately. These sub–queries may be part of more than one query. This allows reuse and a modular way of building complex queries.

In order to formulate queries that involve multiple and distinct references to the same entity set, a user applies the *duplicate* operator which copies respective entities within a working diagram. This operation allows users to specify the different components of a query (i.e., sub–queries) independently and to combine them into expressions of arbitrary complexity. In our graphical query language, the *query result link* operator combines a query with sub–queries. A query result link is used to pass the result of a sub–query to another query. A query result link restricts the selection of entities in a query based on a boolean condition whose evaluation depends on the result of another sub–query.

Example 2. *"Retrieve the salary and rank of all instructors who earn more than the instructor Smith"*.

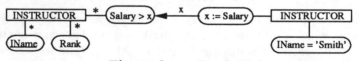

Fig. 3. Query Result Link

The right part of the Figure 3 (obtained by applying the duplicate operator) represents a sub–query determining the salary of instructor Smith. The result of the query is bounded to the variable x. The left part of the diagram represents the *root query*, which is related to the sub–query via a query result link. The evaluation of the boolean condition on the attribute Salary in the root query depends on the evaluation of Smith's salary (as indicated by the directed edge).

A query result link is bounded to a typed variable. This variable may correspond to a tuple or to a set of tuples; that is, a query result link may pass either a single tuple or a set of tuples. This implies that users must choose carefully the predicate used in the link condition. For example, in Figure 3, if the sub–query evaluates to a set of salaries (i.e., x is a set instead of single value), the condition "Salary $> x$" must be replaced with the predicate "Salary $>$**all** x".

At the end of the query formulation process, a *display* operator is applied to the completed working diagram. This operator transforms the specified query into operations that are executed on the underlying database management system. This of course requires that all sub–queries formulated in the working diagram are related to a root query via query result links or via time links which we will discuss in Section 4. Due to space limitations we will not discuss the functionality of the *display* operator in this paper.

3.2 Temporal Projection

In temporal databases, a temporal projection is used to limit the data displayed for selected entities to a specific temporal element. In our graphical query language, the *temporal projection* operator is applied to a completed schema diagram by surrounding the diagram with a dashed box and providing a temporal element at the end of an edge labeled with qualification predicates like, e.g., **before, after, during, include, start, end**, etc. [2].

Example 3. *"Retrieve the name, salary, and rank of each current computer science instructor during the time period 1985 to 1988"*.

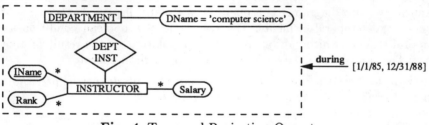

Fig. 4. Temporal Projection Operator

In Figure 4, the (non–temporal) restrict operator is applied, which selects the history of all instructors currently in computer science department. Afterwards, the temporal projection operator [1/1/85, 12/31/88] retrieves the name, salary, and rank of selected instructors during the time period 1985 to 1988. If a user wishes to retrieve the complete history of selected instructors, the temporal element [0,*now*] has to be specified at the end of the edge.

As part of temporal projection, we do not allow the assignment of a time element to a sub–part of a schema (i.e., sub–query) since this operation has no semantic meaning. It makes only sense to apply a temporal projection operator after selecting the entities (i.e., on the entire schema) instead of applying it before selecting entities (only on some part of the schema).

In our visual environment, a temporal element used in temporal projection may itself be derived from the database as the result of another query formulated separately in the working diagram. Instead of assigning a temporal element to a diagram explicitly (e.g., by means of a date), users may specify a time restriction using true times computed from a boolean condition correlated to the attributes of the diagram. The boolean condition used in the computation of a true time is represented graphically in a double box, linked to an edge associated with the diagram as shown in the following modification (Fig. 5) of Figure 4.

Example 4. *"Retrieve the history of each computer science instructor during the time period s/he was an assistant or associate professor".*

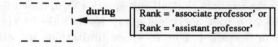

Fig. 5. Condition Based Temporal Projection

In Figure 5, a different temporal projection is applied to each selected entity based on the time that entity was assistant or associate professor. The time restriction is correlated to each individual entity, yielding a different temporal element for different instructors.

3.3 Temporal Selection

A temporal selection is used to retrieve entities based on temporal conditions over attributes. These conditions involve the comparison of two temporal elements using the set–comparison operators $=$, $\neq$, $\subseteq$, and $\supseteq$. In our graphical query language, the *temporal selection* operator is linked directly to a sub–part of a working diagram. (This is in contrast to temporal projection which is attached to the entire working diagram.) This operator is visually displayed as an association between two temporal elements: The true time of a boolean condition and a temporal element which can be either a constant time or the result of another query. The association is labeled with a set–comparison operator.

Example 5. *"Retrieve the current name and rank of all instructors who were assistant professor during the time period 1987 to 1990".*

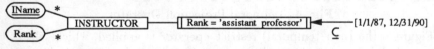

Fig. 6. Temporal Selection

This query has a temporal selection condition over the attribute Rank. For each faculty, the temporal selection condition is applied as follows: First the true time $[\![c \equiv (\text{Rank} = \text{'assistant professor'})]\!]$ is computed and then $[\![c]\!] \subseteq [1/1/87, 12/31/90]$ is evaluated. If the evaluation of the temporal selection condition returns *TRUE*, the current name and rank of the faculty is displayed since no temporal projection is specified.

Example 6. *"Retrieve for the period of 1987 to 1990, the name and rank of all instructors who were assistant professor during the time period 1987 to 1990".*

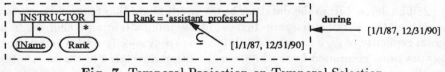

Fig. 7. Temporal Projection on Temporal Selection

Figure 7 can be built in an iterative fashion. First, a user may specify the temporal selection condition as indicated in Figure 6. Afterwards a temporal projection condition on the entire working schema diagram is added by surrounding the diagram with a dashed box and providing a temporal element [1/1/87, 12/31/90] at the end of an edge labeled with **during**.

The above example nicely illustrates how temporal projection and temporal selection operators can be easily combined. It also demonstrates how graphical queries can be constructed in a stepwise fashion by gluing together various temporal operators. These temporal operators can be easily modified, thus providing the flexibility to examine different formulations and conditions for selections and projections in a query diagram.

4 Advanced Graphical Query Language Constructs

In this section, we introduce a number of advanced features of our graphical query language. Section 4.1 presents the time link operator which is similar to a pipe operation. Section 4.2 introduces the concepts of filtering and set operators on time links. Finally, Section 4.3 describes how users graphically specify temporal aggregate functions.

4.1 The Time Link Operator

Temporal elements used during query formulation may either be assigned constant values by users or be computed from sub–query results. In order to formalize the concept of temporal elements derived from sub–queries, we introduce the *time link* operator which retrieves the temporal elements of entities selected as a result of query computation. The time link operator is similar to a *pipe* operation, which takes input from one function (in this case a temporal element), and either sends the input to another function (in this case the root query) or directly displays the temporal elements. The time link operator is a one–directional association labeled on one side with the mandatory **get time** words and the other side with either a temporal comparison operator [2] or an empty label. In the next two examples, we illustrate the two variations of the time link operator.

Example 7. *"Retrieve the time period(s) when Smith taught a compiler course"*.

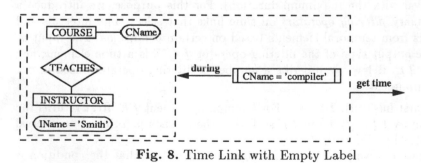

Fig. 8. Time Link with Empty Label

Figure 8 shows how a time link operator with an empty label is used. The entire schema is enclosed in a dashed box, which is associated with a time link operator.

Inside the first dashed box, a non–temporal selection condition is applied to the attribute IName. Inside the second dashed box, a temporal projection operation is applied to limit the teaching history of Smith to compiler course. At the end, a time link operator is applied to display the time period(s) that Smith taught a compiler course.

Example 8. *"Retrieve the name and rank of all instructors with their courses when Smith taught a compiler course"*.

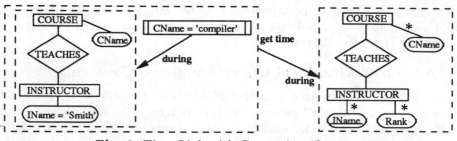

Fig. 9. Time Link with Comparison Operator

The time link operator used in Figure 9 shows how the pipe operation works: Instead of displaying the input of the time link operator, the user sends it to another query. The **get time** words indicate that the schema diagram on the left is used to compute temporal elements. These temporal elements are used in the temporal projection operator applied to the schema diagram on the right.

The time link operator is very flexible: (1) Any of its subparts can be modified, thus allowing users to experiment with different queries and (2) any of its subparts can be tested separately, thus allowing users to localize errors easily. In addition, the label of the time link operator can be replaced with another temporal comparison predicate without modifying the associated sub–queries.

4.2 Temporal Functions

Filtering Operators In general the time link operator may yield a temporal element that contains more than one time interval. However, during query formulation a certain time interval of a temporal element may be needed (e.g., the time interval with the maximum duration). For this purpose, we introduce a set $\mathcal{F}$ of unary *filtering operators* on time links that select time intervals and time points from temporal elements based on certain conditions. The input as well as the output type of the filtering operator $f \in \mathcal{F}$ is a time element; i.e., $f : TE \to TE$. Below, we describe a number of filtering operators used in our visual environment.

- **first** (first interval): $TE \to I$. For a temporal element TE, **first** returns the time interval $I = [t_s, t_e]$ in TE such that there exists no other time interval $I' = [t'_s, t'_e]$ in TE with $t'_s < t_s$.
- **last** (last interval): $TE \to I$. Similar to **first** except that the condition is replaced with $t'_s > t_s$.
- **min_duration** (minimal duration): $TE \to I$. For a temporal element TE,

min_duration returns the time interval $I = [t_s, t_e]$ in TE such that there exists no other time interval $I' = [t'_s, t'_e]$ in TE with $(t'_e - t'_s) < (t_e - t_s)$.

– **max_duration** (maximal duration): $TE \rightarrow I$. Similar to **min_duration** except that the condition is replaced with $(t'_e - t'_s) > (t_e - t_s)$.

Note that in the case of **min_duration** and **max_duration**, there may be more than one time interval that satisfies the condition. In that case, the result will be a set of time intervals all with the same length

In a working diagram, a filtering operator on a time link is represented as a triangle with the operator name inside. For instance, a user may wish to modify Example 8 to retrieve the name and rank of instructors with their courses during the first time period Smith taught the compiler course. In that case, the time link operator of Figure 9 is replaced with that of Figure 10.

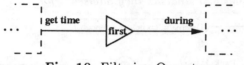

Fig. 10. Filtering Operator

Set-Operators on Time Links In our visual environment, we allow temporal elements (computed from sub–queries and time links) to be combined through set-oriented operators. These set operators are:

1. An n–ary set operator $\cup : TE_1 \times \ldots \times TE_n \rightarrow TE$. This operator returns the union of the temporal elements $TE_1, \ldots, TE_n$.
2. An n–ary set operator $\cap : TE_1 \times \ldots \times TE_n \rightarrow TE$. This operator returns the intersection of the temporal elements $TE_1, \ldots, TE_n$.
3. A binary operator $- : TE_1 \times TE_2$. This operator returns the difference of TE_1 and TE_2.

Fig. 11. Set Operators on Time Links

Both operators, $\cup$ and $\cap$, have two or more incoming edges and exactly one outgoing edge. The incoming edges represent the input temporal elements and the outgoing edge represents the resulting temporal element. In the case of the difference operator $-$, the temporal element marked with a "o" is subtracted from the other incoming temporal element.[3]

4.3 Temporal and Non-Temporal Aggregation

In non-temporal databases, aggregate functions such as **count**, **sum**, **avg**, **min**, and **max** are applied either to sets of entities or to attribute values of sets of entities. In a temporal database, whenever an aggregate function is applied to a set of temporal entities, it is conceptually applied for each time granularity

---

[3] The idea of set operators can also be extended to combine query result links.

separately. Thus, the result of an aggregate function is a temporal assignment from a temporal element to a range of non–temporal aggregate functions.

In our graphical query language, we allow temporal aggregate operators to be applied directly to a schema diagram (inside dashed boxes used for temporal projections if any temporal projection is specified). We also allow temporal selections on temporal attributes together with temporal aggregates.[4]

In a temporal aggregation, a user marks an attribute as the grouping attribute by associating it with an oval labeled with **G**. All other non-restricted attributes are linked with aggregate functions by associating them with ovals labeled with function names. Useful aggregate functions are: $\oplus$ (**count**), Σ (**sum**), ϕ (**avg**), $\perp$ (**min**), and $\top$ (**max**).

Example 9. *"For each rank of instructors in the computer science department, retrieve the total number of students they advised before 1/1/88".*

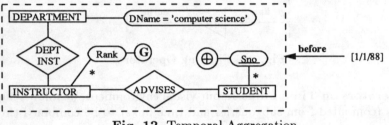

Fig. 12. Temporal Aggregation

In Figure 12, the attribute Rank is marked as the grouping attribute and the attribute Sno is associated with the function $\oplus$ (**count**). In this example, the query returns the number of students advised for each granularity. However, if a user wishes to modify the granularity of the temporal aggregate function, s/he may refine the grouping operator to a coarser granularity. For instance, if in Figure 12 the oval containing the label **G** is replaced with **G←month**, the total number of students advised per month is computed.

5 Conclusions

In this paper, we addressed the issue of graphical query formulation for temporal databases. We introduced a number of visual temporal constructs that allow users to build queries in a modular fashion. These constructs are: Temporal projection, temporal selection, time links, filtering and set operators, and temporal aggregates. This work will be extended in a number of ways: Firstly, we will formalize our graphical query language and provide formal mapping algorithms of temporal graphical queries to temporal GORDAS queries [10]. Secondly, we will incorporate the TIME-SLICE and MOVING WINDOW operators [13] in our query language. Finally, we intend to extend our work and provide a visual environment (on top of existing database management systems) for the entire life cycle of temporal database development. Possible extensions include a design editor, an update editor, and a display editor [12].

---

[4] The aggregate operators presented in this section correspond to a preliminary proposal and we plan to extend them in a number of ways.

References

1. A. Auddino, E. Amiel, Y. Dennebouy, Y. Dupont, E. Fontana, S. Spaccapietra, Z. Tari: SUPER – Visual Interaction with an Object-based ER Model. In G. Pernul, A.M. Tjoa (Eds.), *Eleventh International Conference on the Entity-Relationship Approach*, LNCS 645, Springer-Verlag, Berlin, 1992, pp.340-356.
2. J. F. Allen: Maintaining Knowledge about Temporal Intervals. *Communications of the ACM 26:11 (1983)*, 832–843.
3. K. K. Al-Taha, R. T. Snodgrass, M. D. Soo: Bibliography on Spatiotemporal Databases. *SIGMOD Record 22:1 (1993)*, 59–67.
4. C. Batini, T. Catarci, M. F. Costabile, S. Levialdi: On Visual Representations for Database Query Systems In *Proceedings of the Interface to Real and Virtual Worlds Conference*, Montpellier, France, 1993, pp273-283.
5. B. Czejdo, R. Elmasri, M. Rusinkiewicz, D. W. Embley: A Graphical Data Manipulation Language for an Extended Entity-Relationship Model. *IEEE Computer 23:3 (1990)*, 26–36.
6. T. Catarci, G. Santucci: Query by Diagram: A Graphic Query System. In F. Lochovsky (ed.), *Eight International Conference on the Entity-Relationship Approach*, North-Holland, Amsterdam, 1989, 291–308.
7. R. Elmasri, J. Larson: A Graphical Query facility for ER Databases. In J. Liu (ed.), *Proc. 4th International Conference on the Entity-Relationship Approach*, 1985, 236–245.
8. R. Elmasri, S. B. Navathe: *Fundamentals of Database Systems (Second Edition)*. Addison-Wesley, Amsterdam, 1994.
9. R. Elmasri, G. Wiederhold: GORDAS: A Formal High-Level Query Language for the ER Model. In P. Chen (ed.), *Entity-Relationship Approach to Information Modeling and Analysis*, Elsevier Science, 1981.
10. R. Elmasri, G. T. Wuu, V. Kouramajian: A Temporal Model and Query Language for EER Databases. In A. Tansel, J. Clifford, S. Gadia, S. Jajodia, A. Segev, R. Snodgrass (eds.): *Temporal Databases: Theory, Design, and Implementation*, Database Systems and Applications Series, Benjamin/Cummings, 1993, 212–229.
11. S. K. Gadia, C.-S. Yeung: A Generalized Model for a Relational Temporal Database. In H. Boral, P.-A. Larson (eds.), *Proc. ACM SIGMOD Int. Conf. on Management of Data 1988, Chicago*, ACM Press, New York, 1988, 251–259.
12. V. Kouramajian, M. Gertz: A Visual Query Language for Temporal Databases. Informatik-Berichte 02/95, Institut für Informatik, Universität Hannover, 1995.
13. S. B. Navathe, R. Ahmed: A Temporal Relational Model and a Query Language. *Information Sciences 49:2 (1989)*, 147–175.
14. A. Oberweis, V. Sänger: GTL – A Graphical Language for Temporal Data. In H. Hinterberger, J. French (eds.), *Proc. of the Seventh Int. Working Conf. on Scientific and Statistical Database Management*, IEEE Computer Press, 1994.
15. E. Rose, A. Segev: TOODM – A Temporal Object-Oriented Data Model with Temporal Constraints. In T. Teorey (ed.), *Entity-Relationship Approach: The Core of Conceptual Modelling*, Elsevier Science, Amsterdam, 1991, 205–229.
16. R. Snodgrass: The Temporal Query Language TQuel. *ACM Transactions on Database Systems 12:2 (1987)*, 247–298.
17. G. Wuu, U. Dayal: A Uniform Model for Temporal Object-Oriented Databases. In F. Golshani (ed.), *Eighth International Conference on Data Engineering*, IEEE Computer Society Press, 1992, 584–593.

Managing Object Identity in Federated Database Systems

Ingo Schmitt and Gunter Saake

Otto-von-Guericke-Universität Magdeburg
Institut für Technische Informationssysteme
Universitätsplatz 2, D-39106 Magdeburg, Germany
E-mail: {schmitt|saake}@iti.cs.uni-magdeburg.de
Phone: ++49-391-67-12994   Fax: ++49-391-67-12020

Abstract. The federation of heterogeneous data management systems is still a challenge for the database system research. A main topic in federated system environments is the global identification of objects. On the federation level, a framework for object identification is needed that meets the demand for global uniqueness and allows to access the objects in the local systems. Furthermore, we suggest an identification module in this paper which satisfies these requirements and supports the handling of proxy-objects representing the same real-world entity as well as restructuring objects during the federation process. After describing this module we shall examine some aspects of implementation.

1   Introduction

In many large organizations, different legacy data management systems are maintained and operated. These data management systems and the data managed by them have developed independently from each other. The data management systems are often database management systems or merely file-based systems differing in several aspects such as data model, query language, system architecture, etc. as well as the structure and semantics of the data managed. In this context the term 'heterogeneity of the data management systems' is commonly used. As a rule, applications for specific needs continue to be based on such systems. More recent applications often require access to the distributed databases but their implementation fails due to heterogeneity. *Federated database management systems* (FDBMS) are designed to overcome this problem. The need for FDBMS is explained in greater detail in [McL93]. In this paper we concentrate on the requirements to be attributed to FDBMS:

1. A virtual, homogeneous interface (federated schema) has to be provided that supersedes this heterogeneity;
2. The autonomy of the local data management systems (*component database system* CDBS) has to be maintained in order to guarantee that the local legacy applications can continue to be used without any changes;
3. The federated schema is to facilitate the definition of an external schema, which can either be a view or the same schema with some other underlying data model;

4. The support of mechanisms to guarantee consistency (e.g. the transaction mechanism).

In many papers such as in [SL90], architectures of FDBS's have been suggested. But the requirements mentioned above have not yet been met. Especially the process of reconciling the heterogeneous component schemata with a federated schema raises various questions, among which is the problem of how to handle properly the identity of the objects provided in a federated schema. Schema mappings, transactions and other mechanisms are only possible if intelligent techniques are used to identify the objects in heterogeneous databases [Bee93]. The issue of *identifying objects* in a federated environment was discussed in [EK91, NKS91, Mar91, HD93]. [BEK+94, Kac94] and [Rad94] describe a prototype architecture including a data identification module that serves to manage identity.

The papers mentioned describe ways to globalize local object identifiers for federation purposes. Apart from generating global identifiers this paper also analyzes some additional aspects of the object identification in a federated environment, formulates requirements and suitable operations of an identification module. Only then implementation aspects will be considered.

2   Managing Global Object Identity in a Federated Environment

The *object identity* (OID) is a property of an object that provides a means to uniquely denote or refer to the object irrespective of its state or behavior [KC86]. The object identity has two dimensions which influence the degree of support of identity. The scope dimension refers to the scope within which uniqueness can be guaranteed. The temporal dimension expresses the duration, in which the OID of an object remains unchanged. In an FDBMS the scope of the OID is represented by the federated database. The duration, however, is represented by the availability of the federated database.

The data objects available within the federation schema are stored in the local data management systems and can be accessed by means of local identifiers. [EK91] distinguishes three kinds of local support levels of object identities: *value based identity, session* and *immutable object identifiers*. Another classification was made by [HD93].

Objects (tuples) in relational database management systems (RDBMS) are unique due to the user-defined primary key within the scope of their relation. Any local application can change the key value of a tuple if required. Its visibility is necessary as it serves to carry additional user-defined information.

Each object in object-oriented database systems (OODBMS) is identified by an invisible and unchangeable object identifier generated by the system itself and is unique within the scope of the database. The invisible object identifiers are handled by techniques of storing object identifiers as references and comparing them with each other.

In file-based data management systems, statements about object identifiers are not predictable.

Thus an FDBMS requires a module to handle OIDs, so that it

1. possesses the property of uniqueness as mentioned above;
2. maintains the autonomy of the CDBS;
3. enables access to the objects in the CDBS via local object identifiers;
4. allows for an efficient navigation;
5. supports object migration (see also [Kac94, RS94]).

Consequently, an object identification module has to deal with system-generated *global object identifiers* (GOID), with *local object identifiers* (LOID) and with a dynamic assignment between them (see also [Mar91, NKS91, HD93]). In addition to LOID and GOID mapping, a management of information about the location of the object is needed in order to support object migration and to bridge the different scope sizes of the object identifiers.

The uniqueness scopes [Ken91] of the different object identifiers can be visualized in a scope model. In this model, tuples, objects, relations, database systems, and also the FDBS are considered as objects with a specific ID. [Bee93] strongly recommends to regard meta-constructs as objects. The identifier of each object is only unique within the scope defined by the meta-object enclosing it. From now on we shall refer to an enclosing meta-object as a *container object* and to an enclosed object as an *element object*. Each object can only be a direct element object of no more than one container object.

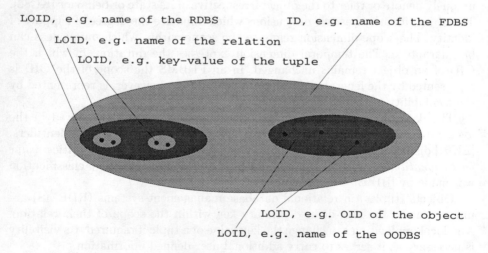

Fig. 1. Scope model

According to the model depicted in figure 1, the following identification module satisfies the requirements described above.

The OID module encompasses the operations *null, next, get, combine, re-name, migrate* and *delete* and a data structure that stores the current assignments. Before a GOID can be assigned to an object which does not yet have a GOID of its own, a new GOID has to be generated. The operation *get(next)* produces unique OIDs in succession. The *combine* operation relates the LOID of a local object to a generated GOID and to the GOID of its container object. It is obvious that the GOID of the container object has to exist before the *combine* operation can be carried out. Thus we assign the default GOID *get(null)* to the FDBMS. *Get(null)* is the first possible GOID of the GOID generator. To ensure the uniqueness of the identification, each GOID has to be assigned to only one federated object at most. Furthermore, the GOID of any element object has to be different from the GOID of its container object.

As local applications are capable of changing the LOIDs of objects, any change of this kind must be announced to the OID module by means of the *rename* operation. The *rename* operation changes the LOID of an object. Thus the OID module satisfies the requirements for stable GOIDs.

Any object can migrate to another container object without changing its GOID. This procedure can be performed with the help of the *migrate* operation which only changes the assignment of the GOID of the migrated object to the GOID of its changed container object. If the migrated object is a container object then all its element objects assigned have virtually migrated accordingly.

The deletion of an object in a local application must be propagated to the OID module by means of the *delete* operation.

The effect of each operation has to be stored in a suitable data structure. The implementation of this data structure will be discussed in section 5. Operations changing the assignments have to be accompanied by query operations. The latter are not considered here. The following figure exemplifies the assignments related to the OID structure.

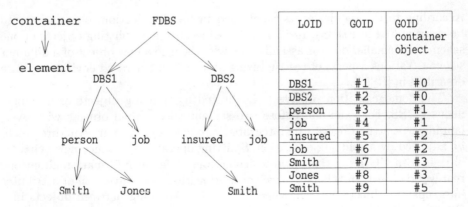

Fig. 2. Sample scope and corresponding *is-combined* relation

3 Managing Proxy-Objects of same Real-World Entities

As the component databases are developed independently from each other, objects representing one real-world entity can be stored as local objects in more than one CDBS. These local objects have varying LOIDs and are often structured differently [RS94]. Such objects are called *proxy-objects of same real-world entities* [KAA+93, TS93, Tre95]. For example, data about the same person can be stored both in the database of a university and that of an insurance company.

The management of such proxy-objects is inevitable for homogenizing heterogeneous databases properly. The GOIDs of objects that refer to the same real entity must be related to each other. This relation can be the basis of a controlled redundancy. The problem of how to guarantee value equality between such redundancy objects might be an interesting subject, which, however, shall not be discussed here. In [TS93, Tre95] the relation between the GOIDs of such proxy-objects is called *same-relation*. The same-relation is an equivalence relation in a mathematical sense. Consequently, it has the properties of reflexivity, symmetry and transitivity. If such an equivalence relation were simply stored it would cause redundancy that may imply incorrect entries and inefficient handling. For instance, the property of symmetry would necessitate to store the tuples $(GOID_1, GOID_2)$ and $(GOID_2, GOID_1)$ explicitly.

The OID module proposed here contains the *is-same* relation and a derived *is-equivalent* relation that corresponds to the properties of an equivalence relation. The *same* operation establishes the relation of the GOIDs of two proxy-objects representing one same real-world entity provided that the GOIDs of these objects are not in an *is-combined* relation to each other. This handling of such proxy-object is illustrated in the next section.

4 Restructuring Objects

According to the requirements mentioned in the first section, objects have to be restructured in FDBSs. Restructuring objects means splitting objects of one schema into smaller ones or assemble a few of them to a new object of a different schema. Various aspects of restructuring objects in a federated environment are described in [RS94].

The homogenization process is facilitated by splitting objects of heterogeneous CDBS. For example, before two semantically related objects with overlapping type structures can be integrated into one object, their structure has to be adjusted by a splitting operation. Splitting operations produce new (virtual) objects with GOIDs of their own which contain different information about one real-world object. In this paper we consider neither the conversion of attributes into separate objects nor vice versa [KAA+93]. Mapping between objects in a federated schema and objects in a component schema requires the management of *is-composed* relations between the objects involved in the splitting operation.

An FDBS has to support the generation of views and schemata with other underlying data models form an external schema [Bee93, SCG91]. This can be achieved by assembling new (virtual) objects with their own GOIDs from other existing objects which may have been split up before. Managing the *is-composed* relation is also essential in this context in order to map external and federated schemata.

The *is-composed* relation always relates objects from different schemata. As regards the *is-composed* relation, the terms *aggregate object* and *component object* shall be used here henceforth. The relation between aggregate objects and their component objects can only be established properly by using their GOIDs. Managing the *is-composed* relation within the OID module proposed makes sense as it is dependent on the *is-equivalent* relation.

- During the homogenizing process each aggregate object of the component schema level can be split into component objects of the federated schema level. These component objects represent proxy-objects of the same real-world entity. Therefore, the derivation of the *is-equivalent* relation from the *is-same* relation includes such proxy-objects.

- *Is-same* relations between objects of the component schema level survive any splitting operations. So if two objects of the component schema level related by the *is-same* relation are decomposed into component objects of the federated schema level then these component objects are related by the *is-equivalent* relation too.

- Only component objects of the federated schema level related by the *is-equivalent* relation are allowed to be component objects of an aggregate object of the external schema level.

The OID mechanism provides the operation *decompose(component,aggregate)* to relate a new component object to its aggregate object, the operation *compose(component,aggregate)* to relate a new aggregate object to a component object and the operation *revoke-compose-decompose(component,aggregate)* to undo the *compose* and the *decompose* operations. As the transitive *is-composed* relation is hierarchic, cycles are not permitted.

Note: The *is-composed* relation must not be confused with the customary part-of relation between objects within the same schema.

The figure 3 and the table 1 below show an example of interrelations between the *is-same*, *is-combined*, *is-composed* and *is-equivalent* relations.

One object from a relational database and one from an object-oriented database are exported for federation purposes. The LOIDs of these objects ("Smith" and #5) are globalized by the *is-combined* relation to the GOIDs #8 and #9. Since the object #8 and #9 represent the same real-world entity, they are related by the *is-same* relation. The following splitting process of both objects generates the component objects #10, #11, #12 and #13 of the federated schema level which are mutually related by the *is-equivalent* relation. Therefore, the object #14 of the external schema level can be composed of the component objects #10, #11 and #13.

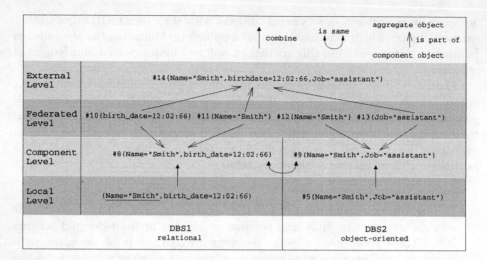

Fig. 3. Example of restructuring objects

is-same		is-combined			is-composed		is-equivalent	
GOID	GOID	LOID	GOID	GOID	component	aggregate	GOID	GOID
#8	#9			container object	#10	#8	#8	#9
					#11	#8	#10	#11
		DBS1	#6	#0	#12	#9	#12	#13
		DBS2	#7	#0	#13	#9	#11	#12
		Smith	#8	#6	#10	#14	#9	#8
		#5	#9	#7	#11	#14	#8	#8
					#13	#14	#10	#13
							#13	#10
							...	...

Table 1. OID relations

5 Aspects of Implementation

The most obvious implementation of the OID module presented here utilizes an
RDBMS. The OID module is characterized by a state-dependent semantics[1]. The
state has to be structured and maintained by the DBMS. It can be expressed
by the *is-combined*, *is-same*, *is-composed* relations and the single column and
single row relation termed *counter* relation that represents the current counter
value of the GOID generator. The data type of a GOID can be the SQL data
type *integer*.

---

[1] A formal algebraic specification of the OID module can be obtained from ftp
anonymous on otto.cs.uni-magdeburg.de in /pub/identity/Spec.ps or from www on
http://max.cs.uni-magdeburg.de/institut/staff/schmitt.html.

Due to the different data types of the given LOIDs, the data type *char(n)* as a sequence of bytes and suitable (bijective) converters can be employed to represent the LOID's [Mar91].

The operation

- *null* initializes the state. The relations have to be empty but the *counter* value has to be set to 0;
- *next* increases the *counter* value;
- *get* only reads the current *counter* value;
- *combine, same, compose* and *decompose* are expressed by the SQL *Insert* commands which insert new tuples into the *is-combined, is-same* and *is-composed* relations;
- *rename* and *migrate* update a tuple of the *is-combined* relation;
- *delete* removes tuples from the *is-combined, is-same* and *is-composed* relations;
- *revoke-compose-decompose* merely removes tuples from the *is-composed* relation.

Most operations have to check some integrity conditions before they can be carried out. During this check the current state has to be read. Queries about the state of the OID module can be performed by the *Select* command of SQL.

The derivation of the *is-combined-trans* (transitivity), *is-equivalent* (reflexivity, symmetry, transitivity) and *is-composed-trans* relations from the *is-combined, is-same* and *is-composed* relations requires the transitive closure to be computed. This computation cannot be achieved by standard SQL commands. But some RDBMSs offer additional functions to solve this problem. In this case the relations derived can be handled as views. Otherwise the computation has to be done operationally.

In the following we shall discuss some problems with respect to the implementation of our OID module. We shall try to outline some improvements.

1. *Problem*: The *counter* relation and some update (*next*) and select (*get*) commands are too awkward for generating GOIDs.
   Solution: Most commercial RDBMS offer sequence generators which can be used instead.
2. *Problem*: Applications operating on the federated level require efficient techniques for handling objects. This handling is influenced by the OID module. The efficiency (access time) of the OID module is to be improved.
   Solution: Suitable cache algorithms are able to decrease the access time to complex objects using GOIDs [KM92].
3. *Problem*: LOIDs can be changed by local applications. These local changes have to be propagated to the global GOID module by the *rename* operation. Since the GOID module is located on the global level, the above mentioned propagation goes beyond the boundaries of the local data management systems. Therefore, it is often impossible to use system based propagation techniques. Other techniques can be inefficient.

Solution: The *is-combined*(LOID,GOID$_1$,container object GOID$_2$) relation is split up vertically into the r1(LOID,GOID$_1$) relation and the r2(GOID$_1$, container object GOID$_2$) relation. r1 can then be subdivided horizontally into further relations. Each of them only contains GOID's of objects of the same data management system and can therefore reside in the local data management systems. Now, local changes of OIDs will influence the local mapping table only. The splitting process can be continued into smaller relations that contain only element objects of the same container object, e.g. relation or class.

A *migration* operation would then require to move both the objects and their respective r1(LOID, GOID$_1$) tuples to another container object. The r2 relation cannot be moved from the global level to the local level, because any access to an object via GOID from global level account is not feasible without any navigation information, i.e. the information, in which CDBS the required object is stored.

4. *Problem*: Local applications have to announce the creation and deletion of any object as well as changes of LOIDs to our GOID module. But local applications have to be considered as autonomous systems. The problem is here, how to detect an occurrence of such an operation without violating the autonomy of the local applications [EK91].

Possible solutions: Up to now no general solution has been known which enables stable OID's and likewise guarantees the autonomy of local applications. But considering the given local situations some of the following methods can be applied.

- A number of data management systems offer methods to detect these critical operations. Such methods can be trigger techniques or ways of generic operations with cascading effects [Mar91]. Using these methods local applications do not have to be changed.

- If a data management system does not support such detecting techniques, the evaluation of system data can be used to detect the specific operations. For instance, the transactions log file can be monitored [EK91].

- If updates on LOIDs are not allowed, the mapping table remains correct. Some applications satisfy this requirement. Modifying other local applications is acceptable. But there may be local applications for which such modifications are unacceptable because their autonomy should not be violated.

- If the creation and deletion of objects and the change of LOIDs are not detectable, a polling technique, that periodically scans the data managed can detect the effects of critical operations. But it is often impossible to conclude the operation that has caused that effect. This method is only useful to detect problems and to announce them to the administrator.

- If the data management system is an OODBMS, the stored objects can be modified by an overriding technique. Any critical method will have to be refined adding operations that announce changes to the GOID module. Using this method will violate the autonomy of the local applications. The refined classes will have to be relinked to the applications.

Note: The demand for autonomy of local applications is contradictory to the requirement to stable GOIDs. Therefore, [HD93] advises to refrain from the requirements to stable GOIDs. In our opinion, reliable GOIDs are more important than maintaining strict autonomy.

5. *Problem*: The LOID-GOID$_1$ mapping table is an additionally managed data object. Managing additional data objects can be inefficient.

   Solution: The GOID of an object is appended to the local object data structures. Relations are extended by a new column using the *Alter Table ... Add Column ...* commands and the type of classes are extended by using the inheritance technique. This method also violates the autonomy of local applications.

6. *Problem*: How can the *is-combined*, *is-same* and *is-composed* relations be built?

   The process of building these relations can be subdivided into two phases, the preparation and the online phase. During the preparation phase both the existing exported schemata and the local legacy data have to be integrated with no user application running. But user applications can create, update and delete local objects that have to be exported during the online phase. Such operations have to be propagated to the federated database system as soon as possible by one of the technique described above.

   Building the

   - *is-combined* relation during the preparation phase simply means scanning the extensions of the exported meta-objects, generating new GOID's and storing them as *is-combined* tuples.
   - *is-same* relation appears more difficult than building the *is-combined* relation. The problem is how to recognize proxy-objects related to same entities which are based on local data. [LSPR93] describe various aspects of this process.
   - *is-composed* relation depends on the homogenizing process. Due to the limitation of this paper, this aspect is not detailed here. Future work on homogenizing heterogeneous schemata by means of the OID module are to follow soon.

We believe that these suggestions can contribute to improving real OID techniques in specific situations. Some methods, however, will violate the autonomy of local applications. Other methods are inefficient, but preserve this autonomy. Therefore, both the specific situation of the federation and the applications have to be taken into account when using any of the methods described above.

6 Conclusions

The first part of this paper described requirements attributed to the OID module in a federated environment. Then the OID module proposed was developed in order to obtain unique global object identifiers on the federation level. Due to the dynamic assignment of LOID's to GOID's in federated objects, local changes of the LOID's of objects will not affect their GOID's. The OID module suggested also supports the management of location information about the objects referred to by the GOID's. A migration operation on objects will change their locations, that is why it has to be announced to the module. This module is able to guarantee stable GOID's after such migration operations have taken place.

During the homogenization process proxy-objects of same real-world entities are likely to appear. There are specific integrity conditions, e.g. the semantic equivalence of the values of the same attributes that have to be considered. In order to monitor such conditions, the relations between the GOID's of such proxy-objects managed by the OID module have to be known.

In order to homogenize CDBSs and to establish external levels, objects will have to be restructured. New, smaller objects arise from splitting operations and bigger objects from merging operations. The new (virtual) objects are existentially dependent on the old (real or virtual) objects. In order to enable consistency techniques their connections have to be known. Our OID module allows for the handling of object relations involved in a restructuring process.

The previous section demonstrated that the demand of autonomy for local applications is contradictory to the requirement to stable GOIDs. Compromises between them are listed. The choice of the proper compromise is dependent on local and current situations.

Improvements in terms of aspects of implementation are open for further investigation. Moreover, the feasibility of the OID module suggested in the present paper is still to be explored in the practical field.

Acknowledgements

Thanks to Can Türker for many creative discussions. We also have benefited from linguistic advice provided by Mark Krogel and Dietmar Schmitt.

References

[Bee93]   C. Beeri. Some Thoughts on the Future Evolution for Object-Oriented Databases Concepts. In W. Stucky and A. Oberweis, editors, *Proc. GI-Fachtagung "Datenbanksysteme in Büro, Technik und Wissenschaft" (BTW'93), Braunschweig*, pages 18–32. Springer-Verlag, Informatik aktuell, May 1993.

[BEK+94] R. Böttger, Y. Engel, G. Kachel, S. Kolmschlag, D. Nolte, and E. Radeke. Enhancing the Data Openness of Framworks by Database Federation Services. Technical Report, Cadlab Paderborn, 1994.

[EK91]   F. Eliassen and R. Karlsen. Interoperability and Object Identity. *ACM SIGMOD RECORD*, 20(4):25–29, December 1991.

[HD93]   M. Härtig and K. Dittrich. Objektidentifikation in Heterogenen Datenbanksystemen. In W. Stucky and A Oberweis, editors, *Proc. of GI-Conf.*

Datenbanksysteme in Büro, Technik und Wissenschaft (BTW'93), pages 296–305. Springer-Verlag, Informatik aktuell, May 1993 (in german).

[KAA+93] W. Kent, R. Ahmed, J. Albert, M. Ketabchi, and M. Shan. Object identification in multidatabase systems. In *Proc. of IFID DS-5 Working Conference on the Semantics on Interoperable Systems*, Elsevier, 1993.

[Kac94] Gerd Kachel. Coupling of Heterogeneous Databases by Federation Services. Technical Report, Cadlab Paderborn, September 1994.

[KC86] S. N. Khoshafian and G. P. Copeland. Object Identity. In N. Meyrowitz, editor, *Proc. of the 1st Int. Conf. on Object Oriented Programming Systems, Languages and Applications, Portland, Oregon*, pages 406–416. ACM Press, SIGPLAN Notices 21(11), November 1986.

[Ken91] W. Kent. A Rigorous Model of Object Reference, Identity, and Existence. *Journal of Object-Oriented Programming*, 1991.

[KM92] K. Kato and T. Masuda. Persistent Caching: An Implementation Technique for Complex Objects with Object Identity. *IEEE Transaction on Software Engineering*, July 1992.

[LSPR93] E.-P. Lim, J. Srivastava, S. Prabhakar, and J. Richardson. Entity identification in database integration. In *Proc. 9th Intern. Conf. on Data Engineering Conference*, pages 294–301, Vienna, Austria, April 1993.

[Mar91] V. Markowitz. An Architecture for Identifying Objects in Multidatabases. In *Proc. of the First Int. Workshop on Interoperability in Multidatabase Systems*, pages 294–301. IEEE Computer Society and the Information Processing Society of Japan, April 1991.

[McL93] D. McLeod. Beyond Object Databases. In W. Stucky and A. Oberweis, editors, *Proc. of GI-Conf. Datenbanksysteme in Büro, Technik und Wissenschaft (BTW'93)*, pages 1–17. Springer-Verlag, Informatik aktuell, May 1993.

[NKS91] E. Neuhold, W. Kent, and M. Shan. Object Identification in Interoperable Database Systems. In *Proc. of the First Int. Workshop on Interoperability in Multidatabase Systems, Kyoto, Japan*, pages 302–305. IEEE Computer Society, April 1991.

[Rad94] E. Radeke. Efendi: Federated Database System of Cadlab. Technical Report, University of Paderborn & Siemens Nixdorf, 1994.

[RS94] E. Radeke and M. H. Scholl. Federation and Stepwise Reduction of Database Systems. In W. Litwin and T. Risch, editors, *Proc. of the 1st Int. Conf. on Applications of Databases, Sweden*, pages 381–399. Springer-Verlag, LNCS 819, June 1994.

[SCG91] F. Saltor, Castellanos, and M. Garcia-Solaco. Suitability of Data Models as Canonical Models for Federated Databases. In *Proc. of the ACM Conf. on Management of Data (SIGMOD'91)*, pages 44–48. ACM Press, 1991.

[SL90] A. P. Sheth and J. A. Larson. Federated Database Systems for Managing Distributed, Heterogenous, and Autonomous Databases. *ACM Computing Surveys*, 22(3):183–236, September 1990.

[Tre95] M. Tresch. *Evolution in Objekt-Datenbanken*. Teubner Verlag Stuttgart, Leipzig, 1995 (in german).

[TS93] M. Tresch and M. Scholl. Schema Transformation Processors for Federated Objectbases. In *Proc. of the 3rd Int. Symposium on Database Systems for Advanced Applications (DADFAA'93), Daejon, Korea*, April 1993.

Management of Inconsistent Information in Federated Systems

Janusz R. Getta[1] and Leszek A. Maciaszek[2]

[1] University of Wollongong, Department of Computer Science, Wollongong, Australia
[2] Macquarie University, Department of Computing, Sydney, Australia

Abstract. Lack of global consistency control mechanisms, replication of data and uncontrolled transfer of information among the database servers of a federated database system are the main reasons for information inconsistencies in such systems. Database models are largely incapable of handling *inconsistent information* and the responsibility for managing inconsistencies is transferred to the application or "middleware" software. The paper introduces an *object database model* that provides for the flexible representation of a variety of inconsistent information. The model can be considered as a middleware solution to the problem. The model includes the definition of a declarative query language and the evaluation of its formulas in a database with inconsistently specified objects. Furthermore, the problems related to the elimination of redundancies and the nonloss decomposition of the inconsistent information are discussed. The decomposition reduces the complexity of inconsistently specified objects. The decomposed objects can be reconstructed and, therefore, the inconsistent information coming from a number of different sources can be consistently merged. Basic operators for the manipulation of inconsistently specified properties of objects are defined.

1 Introduction

The growing number of independently developed and fully autonomous information systems integrated within the global information networks requires more sophisticated solutions to the problem of information management in such systems. Numerous examples exist where exchange of information is extremely valuable for individuals and organizations working from their desktop workstations on the common problems in the same areas. It is inevitable that because of the benefits from information transfer the number of nodes and the traffic in global information networks will significantly increase in the nearest future. The experiments show that integration and management of extremely large number of information sources within a single global system is not a realistic solution (Jakobson et al. 1988; Landers 1982, Siegel 1991). Modern approaches to this problem are based on decentralized architectures such as loosely coupled information systems, or federated information systems (Sheth 1990). An ultimate idea is an interoperable federation of loosely coupled information systems (Heimbinger 1985, Johanesson 1989, Ahlsen 1990), where each site within the system has its own local database, each site preserves its full autonomy (i.e. it is in control of its own data), but it is always allowed to exchange information with other sites within the federation. A federation does not impose any global control over transfer and modification of local information resources. The sites are allowed to request information from other sites in the federation and to keep information obtained from them, but none of the sites has a global knowledge of information kept in the system. Moreover, each site is allowed to take necessary actions to synchronize data replicated with other sites, after a replica has been modified.

Such a model of interoperable federated information system has several desirable properties:

(i) Lack of global co-ordination mechanisms considerably improves performance of the system. For instance, there is no need to prohibit access to any data resources while updates are distributed all over the network.

(ii) It is far easier to design, to implement and to modify the structures of the local sites.

(iii) New sites can be easily appended to a system, because a link to at most one site which already is a member of a federation is sufficient to access any information within a system.

(iv) Lack of a global view reduces the number of structural and semantic translations that have to be implemented in the case of heterogeneous systems.

Together with the experimental implementations of the large interoperable federated information systems (Lenat 1990, Ahrens 1992), some work has been done on the formal underpinnings of such systems. A theoretical model of interoperable information system based on epistemic logic has been proposed by Bowan 1990. Farquhar 1995 used the context logic for formalization of integrated information systems. In our previous work (Getta 1993), we have proposed a centralized object database model for representing imprecise information.

Unfortunately the decentralized architecture of interoperable federated information systems raises new problems. One of them is the structural and semantic heterogeneity of the local information sources. Another one, is the preservation of the global logical consistency of the system. Here, the full autonomy of local systems is a disadvantage. It is simply impossible to enforce full logical consistency of all information sources within the federated system when there is no global control over distribution of updates. The logical consistency of local systems does not guarantee the consistency of the entire federation. The main source of inconsistent information in federated systems are overlapped conceptual domains and discrepancies between the replicated contents of the local databases. We frequently obtain variant contents of the objects such that one of the variants is definitely true but at a particular moment of time we do not have enough information to sort out which one it is.

In this paper we focus our attention on management of inconsistent information in interoperable federated information systems based on object database model. The aspects of structural and semantic heterogeneity of the local information systems are not discussed here. The object model used in this paper is generally compliant with the ODMG'93 standard (ODMG-93) and it is consistent with the main principles of the database object-orientedness enlisted in Atkinson 1989. More detailed description of the basic model briefly defined below can be found in Maciaszek 1992. However, this paper extends the basic model so that the representation and manipulation of inconsistent descriptions of objects is possible. The model supports the representation of inconsistent information such as for instance:

(i) for a given object kept in the database b_i, the value of an attribute a has been set to v_i at time t_i and the database b_i obtained information from the database b_j in a moment $t_{i'}$ that a value of the same attribute in the database b_j has been set to v_j at time t_j, i.e. the database b_i since $t_{i'}$ "knows" the value of an attribute a in the database b_j and when it has been set.

(ii) in the database b_i, the value of a reference attribute r has been set to $\{oid_1, oid_2, \ldots, oid_k\}$ at time t_i, and since $t_{i'}$ the database b_i knows that since t_j the database b_j knows that at time t_k the value of the same reference attribute has been set in b_k to $\{oid_k, oid_{k+1}, \ldots, oid_n\}$

(iii) and so on.

The properties of an object are literal and collection attributes as well as reference attributes - called *relationships* in the ODMG model. *Literal attributes* accept only simple system-defined values, such as integers, character strings or dates. Attributes that are *collections* (lists, sets, arrays, etc.) express *repeating* literal or reference attributes. *References* represent semantic relationships between objects, such as aggregation, membership, and more conventional relationships. *Generalization* relationships are implemented by inheritance and specified by the *subtype statement* . Values of references are object identifiers (OID-s) to other objects. Collections of references (called also *OID-multivalued* or *reference-set* attributes) are implemented as *parameterized types* and indicate multiple connectivity of relationships. The consistency of relationships is maintained by means of *reference inverses* .

A *variant* of selected values of object attributes associates with each attribute name the respective attribute value. Description of each object may consist of more then one variant defined on the same or different subsets of its attributes. A set of variants associated with an object and defined over the same set of attributes represents inconsistent description of such object where different variants represent different attribute values for the same object in different databases. Each variant has a set of *information transfer paths* , or simply *t_paths* , associated with it. An information transfer path determines the source of information, its "timestamp" and all sites that information travelled through to reach a given site. Formally, a t_path is the sequence of pairs $b : t$ where b is an identifier of the database site from where information has been received and t is a time-stamp that determines a moment of local time since that information is "known" to the database b. For instance, a t_path $b_1 : t_1 \rightarrow b_2 : t_2 \rightarrow b_3 : t_3$ associated with a variant v means that information represented by v has been entered to b_1 at time t_1 of its local time and then it has been transferred to b_2 at local time t_2 and finally it appeared in b_3 at t_3 of b_3's local time. The concept of information transfer paths unifies two kinds of information that may appear in a database, i.e. information set by a database user, and information transferred from another database. If in the database b_i a variant c has been set by a database user at time t_i then its t_path is equal to $b_i : t_i$.

Our model does not impose any limitations on the total number of variants that represent inconsistent description of an object. On the other hand, a large number of variants may significantly reduce readability and processing of object states. Moreover, as flow of information among the database continues certain variants may no longer be up to date and should be removed. For instance, a variant associated with a t_path $b_1 : t_1 \rightarrow b_2 : t_2$ is no longer valid if after t_2 a database b_2 obtains a variant describing the same object properties but associated with a t_path $b_1 : t_{1'} \rightarrow b_3 : t_3 \rightarrow b_2 : t_{2'}$ and such that $t_{1'} > t_1$. Uncontrolled additions and modifications of inconsistent properties may introduce redundancies into the database. In order to detect and remove such anomalies, we provide the tools for the manipulation of inconsistent description of objects formalized as an algebra of the *inconsistent properties* .

The paper is organized as follows. Section 2 introduces the extension of the ODMG model to handle the inconsistent specification of objects. In Section 3, the algebra of inconsistent properties is defined. Section 4 discusses elimination of variants in order to minimize the redundant specification of inconsistent object states. Section 5 contains the definition of a formal query language and the evaluation of the language formulas in the database of the inconsistently specified objects. We then conclude the paper and provide some directions for future work.

2 Representation of inconsistent information

We start by defining an elementary unit of inconsistent information. An *inconsistent set of property values* (or just *i-property*) is defined as a pair (P, V) where P is a set of property names (i.e. literal attribute names, collection attribute names and reference attribute names) and V is a set of mappings (i.e. variants) from P into union of their domains such that property names are only mapped into the values of their domains. More formally:

$V = \{v | v : P \rightarrow \cup_{p \in P} dom(p)\}$

such that $\forall v \in V, \forall p \in P \ v(p) \in dom(p)$.

We define an *information transfer path* (or just *t_path)* as a sequence $b_1 : t_1 \rightarrow \ldots \rightarrow b_k : t_k$ where each $b_i, i = 1, \ldots, k$ is an identifier of a database site in the federation and $t_i s$ are the active local timestamps determining when a site b_i obtained information about variant associated with a given t_path. Each variant in V has a set of t_paths associated with it.

A set of t_paths represents the transfer of information from other database sites. In special case when a database b_i receives at time t_i information about variant v from its user the respective set of transfer paths is equal to $\{b_i : t_i\}$. Then, if b_i learns from b_j about the same variant at time $t_{i'}$ we add $b_j : t_j \rightarrow b_i : t_{i'}$ to its set of transfer paths. Consider the following definition for the class $MANAGER$, where the value of *supplement* is related to the value of

date_appointed.
interface MANAGER :EMPLOYEE
  (*extent MANAGERS*)
  {
      attribute DATE date_appointed;
      attribute MONEY supplement;
      relationship set < *COMMITTEE* > *is_member_of*
          inverse COMMITTEE :: *manager_member*
      float compute_salary(. . .)
  };

Now, let us assume that a database b_1 contains information that a particular manager (i.e. an instance object of class $MANAGER$) was appointed on 10_SEP_90 with the *supplement* of \$1000, and the same database received information from the database site b_2 that the same manager was appointed on 11_SEP_91 with the same supplement. Later on the database b_3 provided information that the same manager was appointed on 10_SEP_90 but with different *supplement*. Moreover, the database b_4 confirmed the original values set in b_1. Then, we represent such an inconsistent information as shown below.

attribute	$\{b_1 : t_1, b_4 : t_4 \rightarrow b_1 : t_{1'''}\}$	$\{b_2 : t_2 \rightarrow b_1 : t_{1'}\}$	$\{b_3 : t_3 \rightarrow b_1 : t_{1''}\}$
date_appointed	10_SEP_90	11_SEP_91	10_SEP_90
supplement	\$1000	\$1000	\$1200

Figure 1. Example of imprecisely specified set of property values (i-property)

A mapping $v \in V$ represents one of our believes about the possible values of the properties in P. When it is not precisely known what are the values of certain properties and more than one case is possible, then each one of these cases is represented by a single variant. The set V represents all possible variants that have some chance to be true and we are willing to believe that one of them can be true. Moreover, we assume that if a particular variant is true then each property value represented by such variant is true. Therefore, a set of properties P determines in some sense granulation of inconsistent information. If description of an object requires another granulation of inconsistent information then such object may be associated with another i-property. For instance an i-property given in Fig. 2(a) is not equivalent to two i-properties given in Fig. 2(b).

attribute	$\{b_1 : t_1\}$	$\{b_2 : t_2 \rightarrow b_1 : t_{1'}\}$
A	a_1	a_2
B	b_1	b_2

(a)

attribute	$\{b_1 : t_1\}$	$\{b_2 : t_2 \rightarrow b_1 : t_{1'}\}$
A	a_1	a_2

attribute	$\{b_1 : t_1\}$	$\{b_2 : t_2 \rightarrow b_1 : t_{1'}\}$
B	b_1	b_2

(b)

Figure 2. Different granulation of inconsistent information

The first one represents the case where the values of attributes A, B are either $< a_1, b_1 >$ or $< a_2, b_2 >$. In the second case all four combinations $< a_1, b_1 >$,

$< a_1, b_2 >$, $< a_2, b_1 >$, $< a_2, b_2 >$ are possible. The number of i-properties that can be defined for an object is unlimited in our model.

Object databases allow direct storage and manipulation of properties, literal or reference attributes. In our approach, the repeating properties can also be imprecisely specified. In our example, the class $MANAGER$ inherits properties and methods from its superclass $EMPLOYEE$. Let us assume that $MANAGER$ inherited the repeating literal attribute $phone\_number$ from $EMPLOYEE$, defined as follows:

$phone\_number : set[VARCHAR(12)]$

The definition of the class $MANAGER$ contains also the repeating reference attribute is_member_of. Let us assume that in database b_1 there exists an instance object of $MANAGER$ such that $phone\_number =' 8058924'$ and that object is_member_of $staff\_selection$ committee. Let us also assume that database b_1 received at time $t_{1'}$ from database b_4 through databases b_2, b_3 information that in b_4 the same object has $phone\_numbers$ (042)214339, (042)214859 and it is_member_of $equipment$ committee. Then the tabular representation of such information is visualized as an i-property given in Figure 3. For clarity, we use descriptive names for values of the reference attribute is_member_of, rather than values of object identifiers.

attribute	$\{b_1 : t_1\}$	$\{b_4 : t_4 \rightarrow b_2 : t_2 \rightarrow b_3 : t_3 \rightarrow b_1 : t_{1'}\}$
$phone\_number$	8058924	(042)214339, (042)214859
is_member_of	$staff\_selection$	$equipment$

Figure 3. Example of inconsistently specified set of property values (i-property)

We say that value α' obtained in a database b_k from a database b_1 through a certain t_path $b_1 : t_1 \rightarrow \ldots \rightarrow b_k : t_k(\alpha')$ is *more up-to-date* than value a obtained by b_k from b_1 through another t_path $b_1 : t_1 \rightarrow b_m : t_m \rightarrow \ldots \rightarrow b_n : t_n \rightarrow b_k : t_{k'}(\alpha')$ if $t_{k'} > t_k$.

A variant v *subsumes* variant w in the same i-property if a set of t_paths associated with v contains a t_path that is more up-to-date than a t_path included in a set of t_paths associated with w.

Informally, a variant w may be replaced with variant v if v determines the values of at least the same attributes as w and information represented by w is "older" than information represented by v.

We say that i-property j is specified *more precisely* than i-property k and we denote it with $j \geq k$ if and only if the representation of j is properly included within the representation of k.

An instance of the *inconsistently specified object* of the class C is a pair: (OID, I) where OID is a unique object identifier and I is a set of i-properties defined over properties of class C and inherited by C. Sample graphical representation of the inconsistently specified object with three i-properties is shown in Figure 4.

In general, inconsistent properties can be acquired from different sources of information and an inconsistently specified object can contain overlapping i-properties. In Section 4, we show how to decompose i-properties and control the redundant specification of inconsistent object states.

oid		

attribute	$\{b_1 : t_1\}$	$\{b_3 : t_3, b_1 : t_{1''}\}$
date_appointed	10_SEP_90	11_SEP_90
supplement	1000	1000

attribute	$\{b_1 : t_1\}$
is_member_of	staff_selection

attribute	$\{b_1 : t_1\}$	$\{b_4 : t_4 \to b_2 : t_2 \to b_3 : t_3 \to b_1 : t_{1'}\}$
phone_number	8058924	(042)214339, (042)214859

Figure 4. Instance of inconsistently specified object

3 Algebra of imprecisely specified properties

The problems related to the maintenance of inconsistent information such as finding nonredundant inconsistent description of an object, updating object specification by adding new variants to i-properties and confronting them with already existing information need appropriate tools for manipulation of inconsistently specified properties. A similarity between the structure of i-properties and the relational tables suggests a solution close to the concepts of the relational algebra. In this Section, we propose a set of basic operations for i-properties.

Let c be an i-property, $c = (P, V)$. *Projection of i-property* c onto a set of attributes X is denoted by $\Pi_X(c)$ and it is computed by taking all rows indexed by the attributes in X and removing the others. Moreover, any two identical variants v, w obtained after projection are merged into a single variant v' such that $t\_paths(v') = t\_paths(v) \cup t\_paths(w)$. More formal definition follows.
$\Pi_X(c) = (X, V')$ such that
$V' = \{v' | \exists v \in V, \forall x \in X \; v'(x) = v(x) \; and$
$\qquad\qquad t\_paths(v') = t\_paths(v') \cup t\_paths(v)\}.$
An example of projection onto attribute *date_appointed* of an i-property given in Figure 1 is included below.

attribute	$\{b_1 : t_1, b_4 : t_4 \to b_1 : t_{1'''}, b_3 : t_3 \to b_1 : t_{1''}\}$	$\{b_2 : t_2 \to b_1 : t_{1'}\}$
date_appointed	10_SEP_90	11_SEP_91

Figure 5. Sample projection of i-property

Let $\Phi(X)$ be a selection condition defined as an expression of the prepositional calculus over an alphabet of attributes X, relational operators and constants. *Selection* over i-property $c = (P, V)$ is denoted by $\Sigma_{\Phi(X)}(c)$ and it is computed by removing all variants from V that fail evaluation of Φ.

For instance, only the first variant of i-property given in Figure 5 will be selected as the result of $\Sigma_{date\_appointed='10\_SEP\_90'}(c)$.

Cartesian product of the i-properties $c = (P, U)$ and $d = (R, V)$ is denoted by $c \times d$ and it is defined as an i-property (S, W) such that $S = P \cup R$ and $W = \{w | \exists u \in U, \exists v \in V \ t\_paths(w) = t\_paths(u) \cup t\_paths(v) \ and \ w = u \cup v\}$

An example of Cartesian product of i-properties given in Figure 2(b) is presented below.

attribute	$\{b_1 : t_1\}$	$\{b_2 : t_2 \rightarrow b_1 : t_{1'}\}$	$\{b_1 : t_1,$ $b_2 : t_2 \rightarrow b_1 : t_{1'}\}$	$\{b_1 : t_1$ $b_2 : t2 \rightarrow b_1 : t_{1'}\}$
A	a_1	a_2	a_1	a_2
B	b_1	b_2	b_2	b_1

Figure 6. Sample product of i-properties

Set operations on i-properties are denoted in the usual way. For example, if $c = (P, U)$ and $d = (P, V)$, then union of i-properties c and d is defined as i-property (P, W) where $W = \{w | w \in U \ or \ \in V\}$ and for any two variants w', $w \in W$ if w' subsumes w'' then w'' should be removed from the result of union.

4 Decomposition and update of inconsistent information

A large number of variants and the possibility of overlapping attributes in the specification of i-property decrease the clarity of object description. It also makes the interpretation of our model more difficult. While an uncontrolled minimalization of i-properties may result in loss of information, some reduction in a number of variants and the elimination of overlaps are desirable. We need to identify basic decomposition schemes of i-properties and to establish the criteria for their nonloss decomposition. Another problem is an update of inconsistent descriptions of the already available objects with newly acquired information.

This chapter introduces the concepts of vertical and horizontal decompositions of i-properties and determines the criteria for their nonloss decomposition. Next, we provide the methods for updating inconsistently specified objects.

Consider a set of all i-properties I definable over the class of objects C. We define a *decomposition schema* as a set of mappings $D = \{d_1, \ldots, d_k\}$ such that $d_i : I \rightarrow I, i = 1, \ldots, k$

We say that D is a *nonloss decomposition scheme* if for all $c \in I$ there exists a mapping $d : I \times \ldots \times I$ such that $d(d_1(c), \ldots, d_k(c)) = c$.

Let c be an i-property defined over sets of properties $X = X_1 \cup \ldots \cup X_k$. A *horizontal decomposition scheme* of i-property c is defined as:
$d = \{\Pi_{X_1}(c), \ldots, \Pi_{X_k}(c)\}$

Let c be an i-property defined over sets of properties X and $\Phi_1, \ldots, \Phi_k$ be the selection formulas valid for i-property selection operation. A *vertical decomposition scheme* of i-property c is defined as:
$d = \{\Sigma_{\Phi_1}(c), \ldots, \Sigma_{\Phi_k}(c)\}$

Nonloss decomposition criterion 1.
A horizontal decomposition scheme is nonloss for a set of i-properties C if for all $c \in C$ the following equality holds:
$$c = \Pi_{X_1}(c) \times \ldots \times \Pi_{X_k}(c)$$

Nonloss decomposition criterion 2.
A vertical decomposition scheme is nonloss for a set of i-properties C if for all $c \in C$ the following equality holds:
$$c = \Sigma_{\Phi_1}(c) \cup \ldots \cup \Sigma_{\Phi_k}(c)$$

The horizontal and vertical decomposition schemes are the basic tools that may be used to reduce the complexity of i-properties. The horizontal decomposition decreases a level of inconsistency in i-property, while the vertical one breaks an information part of i-properties into smaller pieces.

Assume that an object is kept in database b_0 and it has an i-property (P, V). Database b_0 receives from a database b_n a variant v' defined over the same set of properties P and such that t_path $b_n : t_{n'} \to \ldots \to b_1 : t_{1'} \to b_0 : t_0$, describes a history of its transfer to b_0. To update a set of variants V we need to consider the following three cases:

(i) If V contains a variant v with a set of t_paths T_v associated with it and T_v contains a t_path with a starting point in $b_n : t_n$ and $t_{n'} > t_n$ then variant v should be replaced with variant v'. Moreover a site b_0 should compare all t_paths in T_v to detect the sites that should be informed about such modification.

(ii) If V contains no variant v with a set of t_paths T_v associated with them such that T_v contains a t_path with a starting point in $b_n : t_n$ then the systems should append a variant v' to V and make $\{b_n : t_{n'} \to \ldots \to b_1 : t_{1'} \to b_0 : t_0\}$ its set of t_paths.

(iii) If variant $v' = v$ then $b_n : t_{n'} \to \ldots \to b_1 : t_{1'} \to b_0 : t_0$ should be appended to T.

5 Object calculus and its interpretation

A declarative query language proposed for the object-oriented environment described above is based on the notation of the first-order logic and, per analogy to the other languages based on the same formalism, we call it an *object calculus*. Adopting syntactical constructions from Ullman 1988, we define a well formed expression of object calculus as $\{x : C \mid \phi(x)\}$ where x is an object variable of class C and $\phi(X)$ is a formula built from atoms and collection of operators defined below. Atoms of the formulas are as follows:

(i) *true, false;*
(ii) $x.a \ominus const,$
$const \ominus x.a,$
$x.a \ominus y.b,$

where x, y are object variables, a,b are properties and Θ is one of the comparison operators;

(iii) $const \in x.s$,

$y \in x.r$,

where s is a repeating attribute and r is a reference attribute in x to object y.

Formulas of the object calculus and their evaluation in the object database may now be defined in a recursive manner using the atomic formulas and the logical symbols: *and, or, not,* $\forall, \exists,(,)$, similarly to the evaluation of tuple calculus given in Ullman 1988. Sample query such as "find all managers employed later than at least one employee they manage or who manage employees employed prior to 1994" takes the following form when expressed in the object calculus:

$\{v : MANAGER \mid \exists x : EMPLOYEE \ v.is\_manager\_of \ and$

$(v.date\_employed > x.date\_employed \ or \ x.date\_employed < 1994)\}$

Interpretation of queries in a database with inconsistent information is very similar to evaluation of query formulas in databases with incomplete information. In some sense inconsistent information may be understood as incomplete or imprecise information. According to Lipski 1979, there exist two essentially different ways of interpreting the queries in the databases with incomplete information - the external interpretation and the internal interpretation. Under the external interpretation, the queries are evaluated directly in the representation of the real world modelled by the contents of the database, while the internal interpretation uses for evaluation a system information about the world only. We use the external interpretation of the formulas of object calculus in the imprecisely specified contents of the database.

We now demonstrate an example of external interpretation of an object calculus formula in an inconsistently specified environment. Consider an object instance of the class $MANAGER$ and the following i-property associated with its identifier (Figure 7):

oid		
attribute	$\{b_0 : t_0\}$	$\{b_1 : t_1 \rightarrow b_0 : t_{0'}\}$
phone_number	214339	214859

Figure 7. Sample i-property

Consider the query:

$\{x : MANAGER \mid x.phone\_number =' 214339' \ or$

$x.phone\_number =' 214859'\}.$

In the internal interpretation, as e.g. used in the relational databases, the two conditions of the above query will be computed separately and then the union of the results will lead to the rejection of this object from the query result. This is not satisfactory because it is obvious from Figure 7 that the i-property represents the information: *phone_number of the manager is either 214339 or*

214859 . Hence, the object should be included in the answer and this is exactly what the external interpretation achieves. More formal definition of the external representation follows.

A result of the computation of a query $\{x : C|\phi(x)\}$ is defined as a set of object identifiers ID such that the external interpretation of the formulas is true i.e. $\{OID : I(\phi(x \leftarrow OID))\}$ where $I(\phi(x \leftarrow OID))$ means the interpretation of ϕ where all occurrences of the object variable x are replaced with the object identifier OID.

Interpretation of the formula ϕ is defined as follows:

(i) if ϕ is $\exists x : C\psi(x)$ then $I(\phi)$ is true if there exists at least one object of class C identified uniquely by OID such that $I(\psi(x \leftarrow OID))$ is true, otherwise $I(\phi)$ is false.

(ii) if ϕ is $\forall x : C\psi(x)$ then $I(\phi)$ is true if for every object of class C $I(\psi(x \leftarrow OID))$ is true, otherwise $I(\psi)$ is false.

(iii) if ϕ is a quantifier free formula where all instances of object variable were replaced with object identifiers i.e. $\phi(x_1 \leftarrow OID_1, \ldots, x_k \leftarrow OID_k)$ then its interpretation is performed as follows: if for all variants existing in the specification of i-properties of objects identified by $OID_1, \ldots, OID_k$ the evaluation of the expression $\phi(x_1 \leftarrow OID_1, \ldots, x_k \leftarrow OID_k)$ is true then $I(\phi(x_1 \leftarrow OID_1, \ldots, x_k \leftarrow OID_k))$ is true, otherwise $I(\phi(x_1 \leftarrow OID_1, \ldots, x_k \leftarrow OID_k))$ is false (the evaluation of an expression is performed in the usual way by the evaluation of atoms of the formulas and the evaluation of Boolean expressions).

6   Summary

In this paper we extended the descriptive power of the object database model in the following ways:

(i) We proposed an environment of federated database system satisfying the main principles of object-orientedness and capable of representing a wide class of inconsistent information.

(ii) We included the definition of a theoretical model of a declarative query language for inconsistently specified object databases and we explained its interpretation.

(iii) We defined the basic operations on the properties of inconsistently described objects.

(iv) We defined the concepts of decomposition of the inconsistent information and elimination of contradictory information using the tools (an algebra of i-properties) and the criteria for nonloss decomposition.

References

Ahlsen, M., Johanesson, P.: Contracts in Database Federations, Working Conference on Cooperating Knowledge Based Systems, 3-5 October, University of Keele, 1990.

Ahrens, Y., Knoblock, C.: Planning and Reformulating Queries for Semantically-Modeled Multidatabase Systems, Proceedings of the 1st International Conference on information and Knowledge Management, 1992, pp. 92-101.

Atkinson, G. et al.: Object-OrientedDatabase Manifesto, Proceedings of the First Internat. Conference onDeductive and Object-Oriented Databases, Kyoto, 1989, pp.233-240.

Bowan, M., Johanesson, P.: Epistemic Logic as a Framework for Federated Information Systems, Working Conference on Cooperative Knowledge Based Systems, 1990, Lecture Notes in Computer Science.

Farquhar, A., Dappert, A., Fikes, R., Pratt, W.: Integrating Information Sources Using Context Logic, On-Line Working Notes of the AAAI Spring Symposium Series on Inf. Gathering from Distributed Heterogeneous Environments, Worl Wide Web, http://www.isi.edu/sims/knoblock/sss95/proceedings.html, 1995

Getta, J.R., Maciaszek, L.A.: Representation of Imprecise Information in Object Databases, Atelier d'Ingenierie des Connaissances et des Donnees AICD'93, Strasbourg, France, 1993, pp.21-39.

Heimbinger, D., McLeod, D.: Federated Architecture for Information Management, ACM Transactions on Office Information Systems, vol. 3 no. 3, 1985, pp. 253-278.

Jakobson, G., Piatetsky-Shapiro, G., Lafond, C., Rajinikanth, M., Hernandez, J.: CALIDA: A System for Integrated Retrieval from Multiple Heterogeneous Databases, Proceedings of the Third Intl. Conf. on Data and Knowledge Engineering, Jerusalem, 1988, pp. 3-18.

Johanesson, P. Wangler, B.: The Negotiation Mechanisms in Decentralized Autonomous Cooperating Information Systems Architecture, Proceedings of the X World Computer Congres, San Francisco, 1989.

Landers, T., Rosenberg, R.: An Overview of Multidatabase, in Distributed Data Bases, North Holland, 1982 pp. 153-183.

Lenat, D.B., Guha, R.V., Pittman, K., Pratt, D., Shepherd, M.: Cyc: Towards Programs with Common Sense, Communications of the ACM, 33(8), 1990, pp. 30-49.

Lipski W.: On Semantic Issues Connected with Incomplete Information Databases, ACM Trans. on Database Systems, vol. 4, no. 3, 1979, pp. 262-296.

Maciaszek, L.A., Dampney, C.N.G., Getta, J.R.: Behavioural Object Clustering, Future Databases'92, Proc. 2nd Far-EastWorkshop on Future Database Systems, Kyoto, Japan, eds. Q.Chen, Y.Kambayashi, R.Sacks-Davis, World Scientific, 1992, pp.186-193.

Maier, D.: A Logic for Objects, Workshop on Foundations of Deductive Databases and Logic Programming, 1986, pp.6-26.

The Object Database Standard: ODMG-93. Release 1.1, ed. R.G.G. Cattell, Morgan Kaufmann, 176p.

Sheth, A., Larson, J.: Fedarated Database Systems for Managing Ditstributed Heterogeneous Autonomous Databases, ACM Computing Surveys, vol. 22, no. 3, 1990, pp. 183-236.

Siegel, M., Madnick, S., Gupta, A.: Composite Information Systems: Resolving Semantic Heterogeneities, Workshop on Information Technology Systems, Cambridge, MA, 1991, pp. 125-140.

Ullman, J.,D.: Principles of Database and Knowledge-Base Systems, Volume 1, Computer Science Press, 1988

Resolving Structural Conflicts in the Integration of Entity-Relationship Schemas

Mong Li LEE   Tok Wang LING

Department of Information Systems & Computer Science
National University of Singapore
{leeml, lingtw}@iscs.nus.sg

Abstract. Schema integration is essential to define a global schema that describes all the data in existing databases participating in a distributed or federated database management system. This paper describes a different approach to integrate two Entity-Relationship (ER) schemas. We focus on the resolution of structural conflicts, that is, when related real world concepts are modelled using different constructs in different schemas. Unlike previous works, our approach only needs to resolve the structural conflict between an entity type in one schema and an attribute in another schema and the other structural conflicts are automatically resolved. We have an algorithm to transform an attribute in one schema into an equivalent entity type in another schema without any loss of semantics or functional dependencies which previous approaches have not considered.

1. Introduction

Schema integration involves merging several schemas into one integrated schema. Recently, with the research into heterogenous database, this process finds an important role in integrating export schemas into a federated schema in a federated database system. There has been a large amount of work in the integration area: a comprehensive and detailed survey by [2] discussed twelve methodologies for view or database integration (or both), and new contributions continously appear in the literature [3, 6, 8, 11, 13, 16, 17] and many more in [10]. Most of these approaches do not provide an algorithmic specification of the integration activities. They provide only general guidelines and concepts on the integration process.

The schema integration process can be divided into five steps: preintegration, comparison, conformation, merging, and restructuring. The schema comparison step involves analysing and comparing schemas to determine correspondences among objects and detect possible conflicts in the representation of the same objects in different schemas. In the integration of ER schemas, we need to resolve the following conflicts: (1) naming conflict, (2) structural conflict, (3) identifier (primary key) conflict, (4) cardinality conflict, (5) domain mismatch or scale differences.

In this paper, we will focus on the resolution of structural conflicts in the integration of two ER schemas. Structural conflict occurs when related real world concepts are modelled using different constructs in the different schemas. We take a different approach to resolve such conflicts. Previous approaches [1, 13, 18] suggest the following types of structural conflicts in the integration of ER schemas:
(1) an entity type in one schema is modeled as an attribute of an entity type or a relationship set in another schema,
(2) an entity type in one schema is modeled as a relationship set in another schema,
(3) a relationship set in one schema is modeled as an attribute of an entity type or a relationship set in another schema,
(4) an attribute of a relationship set is modeled as an attribute of an entity type.

We find that only the first type of conflicts is meaningful. We have a precise algorithm to transform an attribute in one schema into an equivalent entity type in another schema without any loss of semantics or functional dependencies [15]. We advocate and show in this paper that the rest of the conflicts are automatically resolved after we have resolved the first type of conflict. This paper is organized as follows. Section 2 describes the ER model. Section 3 explains the terms and concepts we use in the integration of ER schemas. Section 4 presents our approach to resolve structural conflicts. Section 5 compares our approach with related works.

2. The Entity-Relationship Approach

The ER model, first introduced by Chen [4] incorporates the concepts of *entity type* and *relationship set*. An entity type or relationship set has *attributes* which represent its structural properties. An attribute can be *single-valued* (cardinality 1-1 or m-1) or *multivalued* (cardinality 1-m or m-n), or *composite*. A minimal set of attributes of an entity type E which uniquely identifies E is called a *key* of E. An entity type may have more than one key and we designate one of them as the *identifier* of the entity type. A minimal set of identifiers of some entity types participating in a relationship set R which uniquely identifies R is called a key of R. A relationship set may have more than one key and we designate one of them as the identifier of the relationship set. If the existence of an entity in one entity type depends upon the existence of a specific entity in another entity type, then such a relationship set and entity type are called *existence dependent relationship set* and *weak entity type*. A special case of existence dependent relationship occurs if the entities in an entity type cannot be identified by the values of their own attributes, but has to be identified by their relationship with other entities. Such a relationship set is called *identifier dependent relationship set*. A relationship set which involves weak entity type(s) is called a *weak relationship set*. An entity type which is not a weak entity type is called a *regular entity type*. *Recursive relationship sets* and special relationship sets such as *ISA, UNION, INTERSECT* etc, are allowed. A relationship set which is not weak or special is called a *regular relationship set*. For more details, see [14].

3. Schema Integration

Different approaches to the schema integration problem have been chosen in view integration and database integration. The majority of the view integration papers attempt to establish a semi-automated technique for deriving an integrated schema from a set of integration assertions relating equivalent constructs in the views [7, 18]. On the other hand, database integration methodologies aim at providing a tool allowing the DBA to build manually, by himself, the integrated schema, as a view over the initial schemas [6, 16]. In our integration of ER schemas, we will use the semi-automatic assertion based approach to resolve structural conflicts.

Two entity types E_1 and E_2 from two different schemas are equivalent, denoted by $E_1 \equiv E_2$, if they model the same real world concept. Real world concepts may be involved in a variety of associations called relationships. Two relationship sets R_1 and R_2 from two different schemas are equivalent, denoted by $R_1 \equiv R_2$, if they model the same relationship involving the same real world concepts. Both R_1 and R_2 have the same number of entity types and each of the participating entity type in R_1 has a corresponding equivalent participating entity type in R_2. Two attributes A_1 and A_2

from two different schemas are equivalent, denoted by $A_1 \equiv A_2$, if they model the same property of some real world concept or relationship.

A declarative statement asserting that a modelling construct in one schema is somehow related to modelling construct in another schema is called an *inter-schema correspondence assertion* (*integration assertion* for short). To ensure uniqueness of names, we adopt a full naming convention
`schemaname.objectname` for objects (entity types or relationship sets) and
`schemaname.objectname.attributename` for attributes.

There are three types of integration assertions:
(1) **Object equivalence**: These are assertions which state that two entity types, two relationship sets or two attributes are equivalent.
(2) **Structure equivalence**: These are assertions which state that a real world concept in one modelling construct is equivalent to a real world concept in a different modelling construct.
(3) **Generalization**: These are assertions which state that an entity type in one schema is a generalization of an entity type in the other schema.

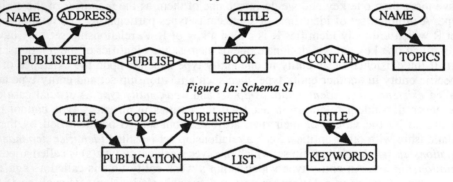

Figure 1a: Schema S1

Figure 1b: Schema S2

Example 1   Consider the two schemas S1 and S2 in Figure 1. The DBA can declare that entity types `TOPICS` and `KEYWORDS` are equivalent as they model the same real world concept: `S1.TOPICS` $\equiv$ `S2.KEYWORDS`
Theit attributes `NAME` and `TITLE` are equivalent since they model the same property of the same real world concept: `S1.TOPICS.NAME` $\equiv$ `S2.KEYWORDS.TITLE`
The DBA can assert that entity type `PUBLISHER` in S1 is equivalent to the attribute `PUBLISHER` in S2, that is, the concept publisher in the real world has been modelled as an entity type `PUBLISHER` in one schema and as an attribute `PUBLISHER` in another schema: `S1.PUBLISHER` $\equiv$ `S2.PUBLICATION.PUBLISHER`
The DBA can declare that `PUBLICATION` in S1 is a more general concept than `BOOK` in S2: `S1.BOOK ISA S2.PUBLICATION`
Finally, if we have `S1.BOOK.TITLE` $\equiv$ `S2.PUBLICATION.TITLE`, then the attribute `TITLE` of the entity type `BOOK` is an **inherited** attribute.

The following example explains why an attribute of a relationship set in one schema cannot be equivalent to an attribute of an entity type in another schema unless one of them is a derived attribute of the other schema.

Example 2   Consider the two schemas shown in Figure 2. The entity type EMPLOYEE in Figure 2a is equivalent to the entity type EMPLOYEE in Figure 2b.

DEPT in Figure 2a is equivalent to DEPT in Figure 2b. The relationship set WORKFOR in Figure 2a is equivalent to WORKFOR in Figure 2b. The attributes EMPNO, NAME, SALARY and DNAME in Figure 2a are equivalent to EMPNO, NAME, SALARY and DNAME in Figure 2b.

If the attribute JOINDATE in Figure 2a is equivalent to the attribute JOINDATE in Figure 2b, then one of them is a derived attribute. Suppose JOINDATE in Figure 2a is a derived attribute, it is obtained from the schema in Figure 2b by joining the entity type EMPLOYEE with the relationship set WORKFOR over the attribute EMPNO. On the other hand, if JOINDATE in Figure 2a is not equivalent to JOINDATE in Figure 2b, then they are homonyms. We could have JOINDATE in Figure 2a model the date which an employee joins a department while JOINDATE in Figure 2b model the date an employee joins the organization. This is a naming conflict which can be easily resolved by renaming one of the attributes.

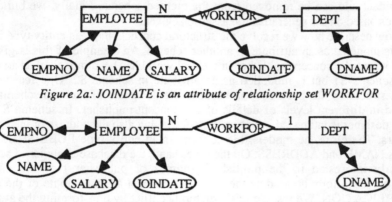

Figure 2a: JOINDATE is an attribute of relationship set WORKFOR

Figure 2b: JOINDATE is an attribute of entity type EMPLOYEE

We advocate that an attribute of a relationship set in one schema cannot be equivalent to an attribute of an entity type in another schema unless one of them is a derived attribute of the other schema. This is because conceptually, the semantics of these two attributes are inherently different. An attribute of an entity type is a property of the entity type. For example, EMPNO, ADDRESS and SALARY are properties of the entity type EMPLOYEE. These attributes are not related in any way to the other entity types or relationship sets in the schema. On the other hand, an attribute of a relationship set is meaningful only when it is associated with all the participating entity types in the relationship set. For example, suppose neither one of the attributes JOINDATE in Figure 2 are derived attributes. In Figure 2a, JOINDATE is meaningful only when it is associated with EMPNO and DNAME together since it models the date on which an employee assumes duty in a department of a company. This is the actual meaning of the relationship construct in the ER approach. The value of JOINDATE does not make sense with just the value of either EMPNO or DNAME only. Furthermore, the value of JOINDATE will need to be updated whenever the value of DNAME of a particular employee is updated. This is not so for JOINDATE in Figure 2b as JOINDATE is a property of the entity type EMPLOYEE and models the date an employee joins the company. The value of JOINDATE in Figure 2b need not be updated if an employee is transfered from one department to another. Therefore, if neither one of the attributes JOINDATE is a derived attribute and both of them are supposed to have the same meaning, then one of them has been designed wrongly.

4. Resolution of Structural Conflicts

In this section, we will discuss our approach to resolve structural conflicts in the integration of two ER schemas. We assume that all naming conflicts have been resolved.

First, we resolve the structural conflicts involving an entity type and an attribute. We have an algorithm to transform an attribute in one schema into an equivalent entity type in another schema [15]. This algorithm takes into consideration the cardinality of the attribute and therefore the transformation is done without any loss of semantics or functional dependencies. Next, we obtain a first-cut integrated schema by merging the two schemas together. Common entity types and relationship sets are superimposed. After the schemas are merged, we look for cycles in the merged ER schema. We interact with the DBA to determine which relationship sets in the cycle are redundant and can be removed from the merged schema. Finally, we build ISA hierarchies based on the generalization assertions given.

We now describe how we resolve the structural conflict where an entity type in one schema is modeled as an attribute in another schema. An example of this is given in Figure 1 where the concept publisher in the real world has been modelled as an entity type in schema S1 but is modelled as an attribute in schema S2. One reason why different structures has been used is because the designers of the two schemas are interested in different levels of details of the concept publisher. In schema S1, the database designer is interested in not only the name, but also the address of the various publishers. Therefore, he models this concept as an entity type PUBLISHER with attributes NAME and ADDRESS. On the other hand, the database designer of schema S2 is only interested in the publishers (names of publishers) of the various publication. Therefore, he models the publisher concept as an attribute of the entity type PUBLICATION. We resolve this structural conflict by transforming the attribute into an entity type. Our transformation takes into consideration the following factors:

(1) whether the attribute belongs to an entity type or a relationship set,
(2) whether the attribute is part of an identifier, a key or a composite attribute,
(3) the cardinality of an attribute, and
(4) the cardinality of the new entity type in the relationship sets it participates in.

These factors are not taken into consideration in previous approaches. It can be easily shown that our transformation is semantics-preserving and dependency-preserving [5, 9, 12]. Note that the cardinalities of the participating entity types in a relationship set R indicates the functional dependencies in R. Suppose R is a ternary relationship set with participating entity types A, B and C with identifiers A#, B# and C# respectively. If the cardinalities of A, B and C in R are n, m, 1 respectively, then we have the functional dependency A#, B# $\rightarrow$ C# in R. That is, if the identifier of a participating entity type of a relationship set R appears on the left hand side of a functional dependency of R, then it has a cardinality of n in R. Otherwise, it has a cardinality of 1 in R. However, note that if all the participating entity types of a relationship set have cardinality 1, then their identifiers are functionally equivalent.

We will give a sketch of our transformation algorithm here. The details of the algorithm can be found in [15]. The algorithm first considers if an attribute A belongs to an entity type E, then there are four basic scenarios when we transform A to an entity type E_A with identifier A:

Case 1: A is not part of a key and not part of a composite attribute.

E_A is connected to E by a new relationship set R.

Case 2: A is part of the identifier of E and there is no other key.

      E becomes a weak entity type which is identifier dependent on E_A.

Case 3: $A \cup B$ is a key of E and there is another key (or identifier), or

      $A \cup B$ is a composite multivalued attribute, where B is a set of attributes.

      Transform B to an entity type E_B with identifier B.

      E_A and E_B are connected to E by a new relationship set R.

Case 4: $A \cup B$ is a composite m-1 attribute, B is a set of attributes.

      E_A is connected to E by a new relationship set R.

      B becomes a m-1 attribute of R.

    These various scenarios and their respective transformations are shown in Figure 3. Note that the relationship set R is not restricted to binary relationships only.

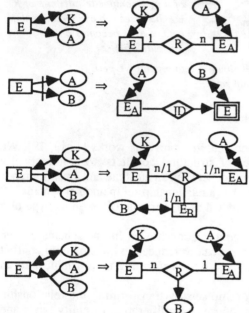

Figure 3a: Case 1 - A is not part of a key & not part of a composite attribute. Entity type E_A is connected to E by R.

Figure 3b: Case 2 - A is part of the identifier and there is no other key. E becomes a weak entity type which is identifier dependent on E_A.

Figure 3c: Case 3 - A is part of a key and there is another key (or identifier). New entity types E_A and E_B are connected to E by R. $K \rightarrow A, B$ & $A, B \rightarrow K$

Figure 3d: Case 4 - A is part of a m:1 composite attribute. New entity type E_A is connected to E by R. B becomes an attribute of R.

Figure 3: Transformations of an attribute A to an entity type E_A .
A belongs to an entity type E.

On the other hand, if an attribute A belongs to a relationship set R, then there are three basic scenarios when we transform A to an entity type E_A with identifier A:

Case 1: A is not part of a composite attribute of R.

      E_A becomes a participating entity type of R.

Case 2: $A \cup B$ is a composite multivalued or 1-1 attribute of R, B is a set of attributes.

      Transform B to an entity type E_B.

      E_A and E_B become participating entity types of R.

Case 3: $A \cup B$ is a composite m-1 attribute of R, B is a set of attributes.

      E_A becomes a participating entity type of R.

      B becomes a m-1 attribute of R.

    These various scenarios and their respective transformations are shown in Figure 4.

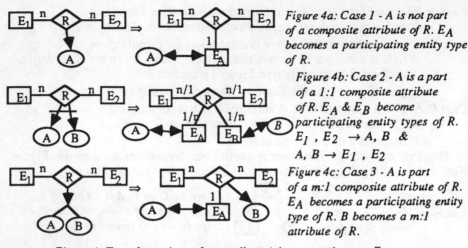

Figure 4a: Case 1 - A is not part of a composite attribute of R. E_A becomes a participating entity type of R.

Figure 4b: Case 2 - A is a part of a 1:1 composite attribute of R. E_A & E_B become participating entity types of R. E_1, $E_2 \rightarrow A$, B & A, B $\rightarrow E_1$, E_2

Figure 4c: Case 3 - A is part of a m:1 composite attribute of R. E_A becomes a participating entity type of R. B becomes a m:1 attribute of R.

Figure 4: Transformations of an attribute A into an entity type E_A
A belongs to a relationship set R.

5. Comparison with Related Works

In this section, we will compare our approach with previous works [1, 13, 19]. We will also show that the following types of structural conflicts are automatically resolved after we resolve the structural conflict between an attribute and an entity type:
(1) an entity type in one schema is modeled as a relationship set in another schema,
(2) a relationship set in one schema is modeled as an attribute of an entity type or a relationship set in another schema.

Note that the structural conflict between a relationship set in one schema and an attribute of an entity type or a relationship set can be reduced to the structural conflict between a relationship set and an entity type by transforming the attribute into an equivalent entity type.

[1] resolves conflict involving relationship sets by transforming the relationship set into an entity type. However, this introduces a proliferation of entity types and relationship sets which increases the complexity of integration. The approach in [19] is not satisfactory because it will result in loss of semantics in the integrated schema. Our investigation into the resolution of structural conflicts have led us to conclude that these conflicts are actually avoidable once we have resolved any structural conflicts between an entity type in one schema and an attribute in another schema.

Example 3   Consider the two schemas shown in Figure 5. Using the approach in [1] to integrate these two schemas S3 and S4, they would reconcile the relationship set OWNS in Figure 5a and the entity type OWNERSHIP in Figure 5b. [1] would transform the relationship set OWNS in Figure 5a into an entity type called OWNS-E. This new entity type OWNS-E is connected to PERSON and VEHICLE in Figure 5a by two new relationship sets R_1 and R_2. Figure 5c shows the schema obtained. There are several problems with this approach. First, we do not know the semantics of R_1 and R_2 or the cardinalities of the entity types participating in these two relationship sets. We should not merge the schemas of Figure 5b and 5c just because structurally

431

they are identical. This is because we can have more than one relationship sets which have distinctly different meanings between the same entity types. Second, the new entity type OWNS-E in Figure 5c has no identifier. Even if we give an identifier for OWNS-E, say O#, we do not know whether CERT# in Figure 5b and O# are equivalent. Third, it is not known how we can populate R_1 and R_2 from the original relationship set OWNS. Finally, there may be loss of information if we arbitrary split a relationship set into two or more relationship sets.

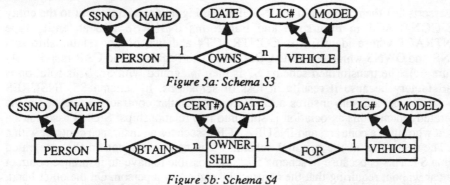

Figure 5a: Schema S3

Figure 5b: Schema S4

In our approach, we first resolve any structural conflicts between an entity type in one schema and an attribute in another schema; in this example there is none. Then, we proceed to merge the two schemas S3 and S4 (Figure 5d). We observe that there is a cycle. We check with the DBA if the relationship set OWNS is actually derived from a join of the two relationship sets OBTAINS and FOR over the common entity type OWNERSHIP and the attribute CERT# has been projected out. If it is, this implies that OWNS is redundant. Therefore we drop OWNS from the integrated schema. The integrated schema is S4. Otherwise, if OWNS is not a derived relationship set and therefore it is not redundant, then the integrated schema is shown in Figure 5d. Note that any conflict between the attributes DATE in S3 and S4 can be easily resolved (see discussion in Example 2).

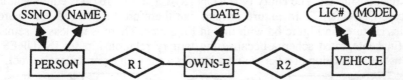

Figure 5c: Relationship set OWNS in S3 transformed to entity type OWNS-E by [Bati84].

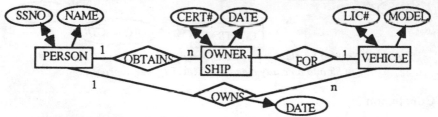

Figure 5d: Schema obtained by merging S3 and S4 by our approach.

Example 4   Consider the following schemas S5 and S6 which is given in [19].

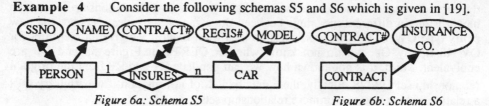

Figure 6a: Schema S5   Figure 6b: Schema S6

[19] asserts that the relationship set INSURES in Figure 6a is equivalent to the entity type CONTRACT in Figure 6b and transforms INSURES into an entity type CONTRACT whose identifier is CONTRACT# and two binary relationship sets SIGNS and OWNS which connects CONTRACT to PERSON and CAR respectively (Figure 6c). The transformed schema S7 is then integrated with S6. This solution is unsatisfactory because it results in loss of semantics. In schema S5, INSURES associates a person who insures a car with a particular contract. However, in the integrated schema, this association is split into two relationships: SIGNS associates a person who signs a contract, and INSURANCE associates an insurance contract with a car. The semantics in the original schema S5 is not maintained in the integrated schema S7. This is because in schema S7, it is possible to have an insurance contract for a car without requiring that the contract by signed by a person. On the other hand, in schema S5, we require a person to be associated (or sign a contract) to insure a car.

Figure 6c: Schema S7 transformed from S5 by [Spac92].

In our approach, we observe that the attribute CONTRACT# in schema S5 has been modeled as an entity type CONTRACT in schema S6. We transform the attribute into an entity type. The new entity type CONTRACT simply becomes another participating entity type in INSURES (Figure 6d). Therefore INSURES becomes a ternary relationship set. The entity type CONTRACT in Figure 6b is equivalent to the entity type CONTRACT in Figure 6d and can therefore be merged. Compare the semantics captured in Figure 6d with that in Figure 6c. There is no loss of semantics in our final integrated schema because the ternary relationship set INSURES still maintains the association of a person who insures a car with a particular contract.

Figure 6d: Schema S8 obtained by transforming the attribute CONTRACT#
in S5 into an entity type CONTRACT by our approach.

6. Conclusion

In this paper, we have presented a different methodology to integrate ER schemas. We have focus on the resolution of structural conflicts and have given a detailed algorithm to transform an attribute into an entity type without any loss of semantics. This algorithm takes into consideration whether the attribute belongs to an entity type or a relationship set, whether the attribute is part of an identifier, a key or a composite attribute, and the cardinality of the attribute. Unlike previous works, we have shown that our approach needs to resolve only one type of structural conflict, which is the structural conflict between an entity type in one schema and an attribute in another schema, and the other types of structural conflict are automatically resolved.

References

[1] Batini, C. and Lenzerini, M., A Methodology for Data Schema Integration in the Entity-Relationship Model, IEEE Trans. Software Engineering, vol 10, 6, 1984.

[2] Batini, C., Lenzerini, M. and Navathe, S.B., A Comparative Analysis of Methodologies for Database Schema Integration, ACM Computing Surveys, Vol 18, No 4, December 1986, pp 323-364.

[3] Bouzenhoub and Commyn-Wattiau: View Integration by Semantic Unification and Transformation of Data Structures, Proc. of the Int. ER Approach, 1990.

[4] Chen, P.P., The Entity-Relationship Model: Toward a Unified View of Data, ACM Transactions on Database Systems vol 1, no 1, 1976, pp 166-192.

[5] D'Atri, A., Sacca, D., Equivalence and Mapping of Database Schemas, in Proc. 10th VLDB Conf., 1984.

[6] Dayal, U. and Hwang, H., View Definition and Generalization for Database Integration in Multibase: A System for Heterogenous Distributed Databases, IEEE Transaction on Software Engineering Vol 10, 6, 1984, pp 628-644.

[7] Effelsberg, W. and Mannino, M.V., Attribute equivalence in global schema design for heterogenous distributed databases, Information Systems 9(3), 1984.

[8] Elmasri, R. and Navathe, S., Object integration in logical database design, IEEE First Int. Conf. on Data Engineering, 1984, pp 426-433.

[9] Hainaut, J.-L., Entity-Generating Schema Transformations for Entity-Relationship Models, 10th Int. Conf. on Entity-Relationship Approach, 1991.

[10] Kambayashi, Y., Rusinkiewicz, M. and Sheth, A., First Int. Workshop on Interoperability in Multidatabase Systems, Kyoto, 1991.

[11] Kaul, M. et. al, ViewSystem: Integrating Heterogenous Information Bases by Object-Oriented Views, IEEE 6th Int. Conf. on Data Engineering, LA, 1990.

[12] Kobayashi, I., Losslessness and Semantic Correctness of Database Schema Transformation: another look at Schema Equivalence, Information Systems Vol 11 No 1, 1986.

[13] Larson, J., Navathe, S. and Elmasri, R., A Theory of Attribute Equivalence in Database with Application to Schema Integration, IEEE Trans. on Software Engineering, 15:449-463, 1989.

[14] Ling, T.W., "A Normal Form for Entity-Relationship Diagrams", Proc. 4th International Conference on Entity-Relationship Approach, 1985.

[15] Lee, M.L. and Ling, T.W., A Methodology for Structural Conflict Resolution in the Integration of Entity-Relationship Schemas, Technical Report, August 1995.

[16] Motro, A., Superviews: Virtual integration of multiple databases, IEEE Trans. on Software Engineering, 13(7), 1987, pp 785-798.

[17] Navathe, S.B. and Gadgil, S., A Methodology for View Integration in Logical Database Design, 8th International Conference on VLDB, 1982, pp 142-152.

[18] Spaccapietra, S., Parent, C, and Dupont, Y., View Integration: A step forward in solving structural conflicts, Technical Report, 1990.

[19] Spaccapietra, S., Parent, C., and Dupont, Y., Model independent assertions for integration of heterogenous schemas, VLDB Journal, (1), 1992, pp 81-126.

Use and control of data models: a repository approach

H.E. Michelsen

Manager Data Administration, AMP Society, NSW, Australia

The Problem

What do you do with the data models once they are created? How do you store them and make them available to the entire organisation in a practical manner? How can such models be reused for further systems development, MIS systems, BPR, maintenance etc.? How does a data architecture assist the system development life cycle and influence the tools controlling data models?

The speaker will outline an approach employed by the AMP Society in trying to answer these non-trivial problems.

The Company

The Australian Mutual Provident Society is a major group of insurance companies with approx $ AU 100 Billion under management world wide. AMP employs some 7000 staff. It spans all forms of insurance including Superannuation, General insurance and Personal insurance.

Discussion

In this age of model driven design methodologies, data models must be able to be stored, displayed, cross references and maintained in a central location. PC CASE tools are not repositories. The valuable information inherent in data models should be available to other development tools through standard APIs. Mappings, supporting documentation and more should form part of integrated model management.

The purpose of this paper is to explain a data architecture within which standards and tools support each other. The AMP Data Architecture is based on the Zachman architecture which specifies different types of data models: Enterprise, Business, Application, Technology (Logical and Physical) data models.

The AMP Data Architecture further groups the models into two levels: The Corporate Level and the Project level.

The Corporate Level consists of the Corporate Enterprise Model and the Corporate Business Models. The Project Level consists of the Project Business Model, the Project Application Model and finally the Project Technology (Logical and Physical) Model. The reason for this break-up is to be found in the nature of the models at each level:

The Corporate level models (Enterprise and Business) reflect a business perspective of Business Unit data. They are based on the organisational structure of the BU as well as the organisational objectives, and are usually preceded by a strategic planning task. They are created by business experts (not computer experts) and are independent of any application system considerations. They are thus stable, long term assets that document business knowledge.

The Project Level Models consist of three models:

1. The Project Business Model is simply a copy of parts of the Corporate Business Model relevant to a new project and not a new model
2. The Project Application Model is created by business analysts based on the Project Business Model. It contains additional information that does not belong to in a business model.
3. The Technology models (Logical and Physical).

These models change more frequently the lower in the hierarchy they are.

AMP has developed a set of inter-connected repositories to control all models for the Society from the highest levels to the lowest. Data naming standards are enforced through an automatic Data Naming System. Other systems developed by AMP interact with the repositories to form a comprehensive set of Data Administration tools. Furthermore, PC CASE tools can interact with the repositories where special functions are required.

These systems will be explained together with discussions of the pros and cons of the various approaches taken over the years.

Contact address: H.E. Michelsen
Manager Data Administration,
AMP Society Information Systems Division,
33 Alfred Street,5th Floor,
Sydney, NSW 2000, Australia
Phone: +61 2 257 5000

The seven habits of highly effective data modellers (and object modellers?)

Daniel Moody

Simsion Bowles and Associates, 1 Collins St., Melbourne, Victoria 3000, Australia

What makes A "good" data modeller?

Data modelling, as a skill, is very difficult to learn, and generally takes years to master. It is not possible to be a good data modeller by following a recipe, reading a textbook or mechanically applying the rules of normalisation. Studies in practice have found that there is a large gulf between "average" data modellers and "expert" data modellers, both in the processes they use and the results they produce. A similar situation has been found in the Object Oriented field, where it has proven difficult to find people with the required abstraction skills.

Anatomy of a habit

This article provides some insights into what separates expert data modellers from the rest. Based on discussions with colleagues in the Object-Oriented field, most of these apply equally to Object Modellers. The characteristics of expert data modellers are identified as "habits", following Stephen Covey's best selling book "The Seven Habits of Highly Effective People". Covey defines a habit as the intersection between knowledge, skill and motivation:
1. Knowing what to do (knowledge)
2. Knowing how to do it (skill)
3. Having the desire to do it (motivation)
In order to make something a habit, you have to have all three. For example, you may know that it is important to be organised (knowledge), but you may not have learned techniques for managing time effectively (skill). Further, knowing you need to be organised and knowing how to manage your time is not enough unless you also have a strong desire to put it into practice (as many people who have attended time management courses can attest). Before you can become organised, you must really want to manage your time better and be prepared to change the way you operate on a day to day basis. Creating a habit thus requires work in all three directions.

The seven habits

Based on observations in practice, the author has identified seven "habits" which characterise successful data modellers:

LISTEN TO THE USER The most common mistake in practice is to concentrate too much on the technical aspects of data modelling, and fail to properly understand the user requirements. A data model can only be as good as the business input used in developing it. However just asking the user what they want is not enough, and other, more effective techniques need to be used.

GENERATE ALTERNATIVES In practice, often the first model proposed which meets user requirements is adopted as the final solution. However usually the most obvious model is the one which most closely reflects the concepts of the existing system, and there may be a much simpler and elegant solution. A characteristic of expert data modellers is the ability to "think outside the square" and consider innovative solutions to problems.

KEEP IT SIMPLE Large, complex models alienate users and are expensive to implement and maintain. Strategic breakthroughs in systems development are most often as a result of finding simpler and more powerful representations. A major focus of the data modeller's job should be to look for simpler ways of representing the data.

LEARN FROM EXPERIENCE Expert data modellers can adapt models developed in one problem domain to new and different situations. One of the distinguishing characteristics of experts in many domains is the ability to recognise patterns and adapt previously used solutions to new problems. Over time expert data modellers develop a large "library" of models that they can adapt to any situation that they might encounter in practice.

KNOW WHEN TO STOP A major problem with data modelling in practice is the "analysis paralysis" syndrome. Any data modelling task can expand to fill the time available - if you let it. The nature of the task is such that there always seems more work to be done. However the cost of gathering requirements beyond a certain point is enormously high. The best data modellers know how to apply the 80/20 rule to achieve as much as possible in a limited time.

KEEP YOUR EYE ON THE BIG PICTURE In practice, the requirements for different system are often modelled in isolation of each other, with little thought as to how they fit together. It is important to consider how each system fits into the overall corporate plan or architecture. Major savings (through reuse) and business benefits (through integration) can be achieved by recognising the synergies between separate projects.

FOLLOW THE JOB THROUGH TO COMPLETION The job is not over when the data model is complete. However in practice, data modellers often "walk away" once the data model has been handed over to the developers. The data modeller should remain involved all the way through to implementation to ensure that the "voice of the customer" is carried through.

This will be a highly interactive session, and will be illustrated by numerous real life examples of data modelling in practice.

Object responsibility categories in support of top-down object discovery

Dan Tasker

Consultant, Cremorne, NSW, Australia

Four object/class categories are presented which have proved most useful during object-oriented requirements analysis efforts. The categories are:

Information/Object/Classes equate virtually 1:1 to entity types in traditional ER modelling. They include things like Customer, Invoice, and Account. These are the 'things' of interest to the problem space that represent the information to be managed, and must therefore be persistent.

Value Set Object/Classes instances are similar to the concept of Domains in ER. These 'virtual' object/classes, such as Name, Phone Number, Salary, not only define the membership or intention of the set, but are intended to include functionality for both formatting values and transformation between related units of measure (e.g. conversion of temperatures form C to F).

Interface Object/Classes instances represent things like screens, report producers, and batch interfaces. Their responsibility is to 'know' things appropriate to the type of interface (e.g. page breaks, window control types) and act as an intermediate 'holding' area for values on their way to or from persistent storage (i.e. input or output fields).

Event Object/Classes instances have the responsibility for understanding the 'unit of work' involved in a business transaction. When a business event effects two or more objects (e.g. a debit/credit transaction), an Event Object/Classes is defined to gather all appropriate information and send all necessary messages. It is also responsible for understanding the concept of 'unit of commit', and perform rollback if required.

This categorisation scheme addresses issues such as "What is an object?" and "Objects are more than just entities with function added." The separation of responsibilities has made it possible to perform top-down object discovery using a technique similar to a Level Zero Context Diagram from Dataflow Diagrams.

The presentation will include both explanation and examples of the categories, and examples of the top-down object discovery technique that has been applied successfully to various industry segments (e.g. banking, telecommunications, manufacturing).

Contact address: Dan Tasker,Consultant
37/9 Hampden Avenue
Cremorne, NSW 2090
Australia
Phone/Fax: +61 2 909 8961
Email: 100241.2337@compuserve.com

Denormalisation as an OO extension

Don Tonkin

ADC Consulting Pty Ltd, NSW Australia

The theory of normalisation results in a set of rules for designing a data model in a manner which eliminates the possibility of data anomalies due to inserting, updating or deleting records. The creation of such a normalised model was considered essential to accurately capture the data component of business requirements. This model is referred to as the 'logical' data model in this paper.

Frequently the implementation of a highly normalised model resulted in the need for some denormalisation in order to meet the performance or capacity requirements of the target platform. This denormalised model is referred to as the 'physical' data model. In some cases, due to the specific usage of data, no data anomalies were possible in the physical model. For example, violation of second and third (but not first, fourth or fifth) normal forms may not introduce any anomalies for data which will never be updated.

In other situations where an anomaly could occur, the data integrity must be maintained by the use of normalised updatable views of the data, or by the use of database triggered procedures, or finally by the use of a program which ensures integrity. In other words, integrity can no longer be guaranteed at the data level and it is essential to associate processes or methods with the data to ensure integrity when data is normalised. The object oriented paradigm meets this requirement.

Given that denormalisation frequently involves data from more than one entity, the scope of integrity has to be widened to include some aspects of more than one entity. This broadening may assist in object classification.

This paper examines some mechanisms used in the denormalisation of data. For primary key denormalisation subtypes are collapsed upwards or downwards. The types of denormalisation are classified as follows:

1. Primary Key
2. Foreign Key
3. Parent Child
4. Derived Data
5. Row Column Interchange
6. Duplication
7. Split
8. Total
9. Domain
10. Relational

Each type of denormalisation has quantifiable benefits for performance, maintainability and flexibility and quantifiable costs in terms of storage space, additional code and understandability. These cost benefit tradeoffs are examined in the light of industrial experience for each type of denormalisation for a relational platform (DB2) and for an OODBMS (Object Store)

Contact address: Don Tonkin
Managing Director, ADC Consulting Pty Ltd
165 Walker Street, suite 2, level 5
North Sydney, NSW 2060
Australia
Phone: +61 2 955 9998; Fax: +61 2 955 9707

Development of a financial markets analytical product: a MOSES casestudy

Bhuvan Unhelkar

Dy. Product Development Manager Dow Jones Telerate, Asia Pacific

1 Introduction

Dow Jones Telerate provides real-time data to the financial markets on its proprietary network. In order to add value to the data they developed TELAN, a global currency and market analytical product comprising a suite of financial applications. TELAN was developed using VC++ / MS Windows and followed MOSES, [Henderson-Sellers and Edwards,1994], a development life-cycle methodology for object-oriented software engineering. TELAN followed the successful development of the Telerate Currency Options (COPS) product which launched last year.

TELAN reuses a large amount of design and code produced during the earlier COPS development. It therefore can be thought of as an augmentation of the COPS class library. The TELAN project by using a recognised OO development methodology gained advantages from reuse, quality assurance, and timely delivery. The parallel team structure and iterative development process provided by MOSES were important factors in gaining these advantages. These effort were recognised when the TELAN development won the Computerworld Object Developer's Award (CODA) in 1995.

This is a presentation on TELAN's development.

2 MOSES background

MOSES is a full life cycle methodology and uses the *fountain model* [Henderson-Sellers and Edwards, 1993] which is an iterative development process. It comprises (1) a product lifecycle which describes three, largely waterfall-based business stages of a system development project, (2) a process lifecycle which describes five technically-oriented iterative phases, and (3) twenty activities which provide the detailed guidance for OO development across these phases.

Embedded within the *Build Stage* of the product lifecycle are the five phases of the process lifecycle which cover technical, managerial and customer involvement issues. Development is also defined by the *Deliverables*, or the documentation collected from each phase.

Within each phase development occurs iteratively as described by the *Activities* which define the final documents to be delivered, and provide purpose, techniques, guidelines and heuristics. There are eight textual deliverables and five graphical models specified in MOSES; the main deliverables being the class specification, subsystem responsibility specification (SRS), object/class (O/C) model, Event Model, Objectcharts, Inheritance Model and Service Structure Model. In most commercial system developments, it is unlikely that all the 13 deliverables will be required - TELAN used only 9.

3   TELAN life cycle

While subsystems are not formally part of the object-model and are not supported by any major Object-Oriented Programming Language, their identification is an important 'divide and conquer' technique. MOSES offers specific directions in an activity to manage this. Minimal coupling between the modules enables parallel development to takes place, ensuring we could take full advantage of the object-oriented approach.

The *Iteration plan* was put in place whilst the teams were organised TELAN was produced in 4 iterations, each lasting about 3 months. The first iteration concentrated on the elicitation of the user requirement, mainly by going through the functionality of the existing system followed by a prototype and its demonstration throughout the company. This was followed by the second iteration which included in-depth analysis and design of overall reuse architecture, and implementation of the Graphics User Interface with its "Views". The third iteration related to the market watch subsystem, as well as co-ordinating with overseas development sites for the underlying database functionalities. Finally, the fourth iteration included the remaining two subsystems (historical analysis and portfolio management - both initial), as well as charting and printing modules.

The TELAN design was conceived as a suite of object-oriented applications which could be put together within short time spans, as requirement specification evolved. The actual design of TELAN followed the reuse architecture, and produced the main graphical deliverable, the O/C model, with its associated Inheritance model. Reusing our own classes as well as classes from third parties is an important aspect of design in MOSES. This activity is expressed by Activity: Library Class Incorporation, and is a very well defined activity in MOSES, stressing the need for the "reuse mindset".

The Instrument subsystem was generalised after investigating all possible instruments that the design team could think of, abstracting the common services to the top Instrument O/C, and then following down from there for specific instruments. It is also a fine granular design, as suggested by the small average size of classes in the system. This is a result of deriving the persistent and the manipulative aspect of the Instrument from two separate smaller sized classes.

All the database ODBC type interfaces form part of the persistent O/C, thereby protecting the design from changes in the underlying databases. The overall design ensures that various financial instruments in the markets are placed in the most generalised inheritance hierarchy, resulting in large scale and efficient reuse in all the subsystems in TELAN, and, we believe, future projects.

TELAN development conforms to the Australian Standards for Software Quality Assurance (AS3563.1 based on ISO9001) and Test Documentation (AS4006). The MOSES methodology helped the team follow the standards easily, since many of the deliverables (for example *Test Report* and *Review Report*) conform to the clauses of the AS3563.1 SQA standard. Quality specific activities (for example *Activity: Quality Evaluation* and *Activity: Testing*) in MOSES provide guidance to achieve these deliverables. Test Designs followed the AS4006 requirements, and together with their test cases were thoroughly reviewed before actual tests were carried out.

4 Conclusion

The approach described in this paper has resulted in iterative development and incremental releases. It enabled analytics to be developed for markets that are of prime importance from a marketing viewpoint, leaving the finer (niche) markets for subsequent iterations. Using a full lifecycle quality specific methodology to develop our software has resulted in the reuse and quality benefits that object-oriented developments claims.

5 Acknowledgement

This is Contribution no 95/20 of the Centre for Object Technology Applications and Research of the University of Technology, Sydney.

Contact address: Mr B. Unhelkar
Dow Jones Telerate,
Level 11, 309 Kent Street
Sydney NSW 2000
AUSTRALIA

The practice of nuclear integrated design and engineering database establishment using object-oriented DBMS

Jaejoo Ha, Kwangsub Jeong, Seunghwan Kim, Sunyoung Choi

Nuclear Information System Development Korea Atomic Energy Research Institute
Korea

In nuclear power plant design, there are hundred of thousands of equipment components to be designed and configured with detailed engineering specifications which satisfy complicated engineering process requirements. Data life can be extended up to 50 years from design to decommissioning of the nuclear power plant. To manage the large amount of complicated engineering data and design processes, Korea Atomic Energy Research Institute is establishing the Nuclear Integrated Design and Engineering Database (NUDB). The database is part of a nuclear design advancement system (NUIDEAS: Nuclear Integrated Database and Design Advancement System).

In the nuclear power plant, often there is only one or a few records (or instance) of a specific component type, but it has a very complicated data structure such as a large amount of associated information and parts that can be also treated as a special kind of component. In such a situation, the object-oriented data model can be more suitable in modeling than the traditional relational data model. In accordance with practice, user-defined class, inheritance, and set (or list) data type are extensively used and found as useful concepts in modeling.

Since engineering data should be also linked into project and document information with revision control, NUDB consists of three top classes including physical object, project, and document, and all objects of the classes are interlinked for a comprehensive information search.

It has been pointed out that the lack of industry standards of object-oriented database hinders an efficient development cycle and information exchange. This has lead to the necessity of more cooperative development for the more active utilisation of object-oriented technology.

Contact address: Jaejoo Ha, Kwangsub Jeong, Seunghwan Kim, Sunyoung Choi
                   Nuclear Information System Development
                   Korea Atomic Energy Research Institute
                   P.O. Box 105, Yusung, Taejeon
                   Korea
                   Phone: +82 42 868 2755; Fax: +82 42 868 8372

Application of "consistent dependency" to corporate and project information models

C N G (Kit) Dampney and Michael Johnson

Macquarie Research Limited, Macquarie University, NSW, Australia

Introduction

Information Architecture encompasses the purpose, structure and function of information needed to support an organisation. Its description takes many different forms. Typically enterprise level analysis uses data models, process models, and various matrices matching organisational characteristics with system components. More detailed analysis uses event models, work-flow models, and various forms of object models.

The search is to find a common basis for information systems architecture. At the same time an information architecture must provide focus for the various distinct processes in the organisation. These two aims represent the essential difficulty in any enterprise - balancing common cause with specific focus in different areas.

At Macquarie, we have developed new methods based on the consistent dependency that observation shows are endemic in Entity Relationship models of information structure. These methods have been applied in two major corporate data modelling projects and numerous smaller projects.

The methods are realised around an information model which uses the conventions of the Entity-Relationship diagram enhanced by shading and highlighting over regions of the model to show the scope of consistent dependencies. This enables meaning to be interpreted both in terms of business purpose and process.

Application

This paper illustrates application of these methods to practice, the additional understanding they deliver, and the challenge of communicating sophisticated concepts concerning semantics into the business domain.

An enterprise-wide approach to information has the potential for providing substantial benefits to an organisation, and has attracted significant investment by major companies over the past 10 years. Common generic classifications of information entities are becoming accepted by industry groups. This could be considered a first phase which is providing efficiencies for organisations developing information systems strategy and information infrastructure. In particular, it recognises the significance of the data asset.

The new methods we use offer a second phase of emerging enterprise-wide information architecture methodology. They offer for example data structures that provide a coherent base on which to build the work-flow loops that can describe business processes. This shifts the emphasis from data to objects, where objects are defined as an amalgam of both data and process.

The methods provide a means of assessing the semantics of large corporate information models. For example, corporate information models tend to contain structures that support management control of activities and other structures that support the transactions themselves. Analysis of existing corporate models reveals that constraints relating transactions to management controls are extant, but require highlighting to make them explicit. Furthermore analysis of project data models shows that processes tend to be confined by data structures which have consistent dependency. Finally, a sophisticated analysis of the mapping from project data models to corporate information models illustrates how consistent dependency can be applied to checking compliance between project and corporate..

Consistent Dependency can be applied in the following ways:-

1. Together with a generic information model, the methods can be used to refine an enterprise-wide information architecture.
2. The methods can be used as an audit and enhancement tool for existing enterprise-wide information architectures.
3. The methods can identify process-coherent regions within a data model, and use that to develop a federated information systems architecture that reflects the desired degree of autonomy between business processes.
4. Process specific data models that define the underlying database schema can be flexed to match the actual automated support required by business processes. The same process in different companies will vary in support required according to the skills, scale of operation and management style in place.
5. Major constraints, expressing desired business, legislative or physical constraints on actions performed can be inferred. These have major implication for the cost of application development.
6. The methods are object-oriented with an emphasis on describing the "application objects" that capture the structure and behaviour of the reality being addressed. In essence the object model is recognised as an enhanced entity-relationship model.

Finally the methods are underpinned by the rigour of Category Theory which provides confidence in the underlying soundness of the methods.

Contact address: Dr.C N G Dampney
Associate Professor in Computing
School of MPCE, Building E6A
Macquarie University, NSW 2109
Australia
Phone: +61 2 850 9520; Fax: +61 2 850 9551
Email: cdampney@mpce.mq.edu.au

The use of agglomerative categorisation to build a conceptual view of statistical data

Clare Atkins

Massey University, Palmerston North, New Zealand

Introduction

This paper describes a strategy that arose spontaneously out of systems practice within the Statistics Division of the Inland Revenue of the United Kingdom during the period 1988 - 1992. The strategy was successfully employed to migrate statistical data from flat files to a relational database. The data supported over 40 major applications The strategy adapted object-oriented and entity-relationship modelling techniques to create a form of conceptual data model using agglomerative categorisation rather than traditional, hierarchical concepts and properties.

Issues

The Statistics Division undertakes statistical analysis relevant to tax assessment and collection. Approximately 60 IS staff in 1988 were responsible for developing applications that collected, stored and manipulated a wide range of data.

Most of the data was held in flat files holding either large samples of confidential taxpayer data or the results of statistical analysis. A decision to migrate all the data to a relational database and re-write the applications where necessary, within three years, was made in 1988. As a result the Division had to face several issues particularly in the area of data modelling.

Realising the potential benefits of migrating to relational technology data models was essential. This required overcoming the difficulties that there were
* an almost complete lack of data modelling skills within the Division;
* no data models for the existing systems;
* an incomplete corporate model for the Inland Revenue; and
* duplicated and redundant data and processing within the Division.

The creation of an agglomerated "Divisional Model"

Initially two exercises were undertaken. An external consultant was brought in to create a "corporate view" of the data at the Divisional level and one member of staff began to create normalised logical database designs for each application. Neither of these approaches was completely satisfactory.

To overcome the shortcomings a "Divisional Model" was devised. This used the constructs of E-R diagramming extended to include the O-O concepts of supertypes, subtypes and inheritance. It provided a new conceptual understanding of the Division's data and a template for all the logical application models. It thus satisfied three objectives:

1. to minimise the inconsistencies inherent in a process effected by different people with different skill levels and understandings;
2. to provide a consistent starting point for all application development; and
3. to provide a conceptual view of all the data handled by the Division.

This model identified eleven agglomerate entities which represented groupings of all the application entities. Several application entities and the relationships between them could map to one agglomerate. Relationships between application entities mapping to different agglomerates had to conform to those between their agglomerates. Each agglomerate had a set of constraints associated with it which were inherited by the application entities and effectively became the rules by which membership of the agglomerate was determined.

A completed application model would typically have entities in most if not all of the agglomerates and in many cases would have several entities in the more significant ones.

Benefits realised from the Divisional Model

As part of the normal development life cycle each application project was required to create an application conceptual model which conformed to the Divisional model. As more application models were completed, the number of new entities required dropped considerably so that entity re-use became a natural part of the development process.

As application models were developed, a CASE tool system made them available for general use throughout the Division. For example, a copy of the agglomerates populated with the application entities previously created became the working model for developing new application

A number of benefits were realised through the use of this approach:

Consistency Application models were consistent with each other and provided an excellent basis for the development of logical database designs.

Completeness The Divisional model provided an accurate, accepted, readily understood, and complete view of the Division's data.

Identification of common areas of data It was discovered that certain agglomerates consistently held entities that were common to a number of applications, while others consistently held only application-specific information.

Identification of duplicated data It became increasingly easy to uncover data previously duplicated across applications, as it was no longer necessary to investigate every attribute or even every entity for each application.

Reuse of models or parts of models Data constructs could be re-used and the identification of duplicated data made possible the elimination of duplicated processing.

Ability to answer new questions For the first time it was possible to accurately and speedily answer questions concerning the Division's data as a whole.

Conclusion

The creation and use of the Divisional model provided a means to record the data components of the Division's systems. This made it easier for the data analysts and designers:

- to develop new application data models rapidly,
- to learn and remember the overall structure of the Division's conceptual data,
- to enforce centralised modelling constraints,
- to train new developers
- to participate effectively in data modelling activities,
- to identify reusable data structures, and
- to identify and eliminate duplicated data structures and related processing.

Although it was developed primarily to assist in the migration process it was also used effectively in the development of new systems and has continued to be used in this way to the present day.

If this principle of agglomeration is portable to other domains then the experience of Statistics Division suggests that it could be used to speed up the development of corporate or enterprise models, improve their effectiveness, utilise the skills of less experienced modellers and significantly increase productivity.

Contact address: Clare Atkins
Department of Information Systems
Massey University
Private Bag 11222
Palmerston North
New Zealand
Phone: +64 6 350 4206
Email: C.Atkins@massey.ac.nz

Index

Springer-Verlag
and the Environment

We at Springer-Verlag firmly believe that an international science publisher has a special obligation to the environment, and our corporate policies consistently reflect this conviction.

We also expect our business partners – paper mills, printers, packaging manufacturers, etc. – to commit themselves to using environmentally friendly materials and production processes.

The paper in this book is made from low- or no chlorine pulp and is acid free, in conformance with international standards for paper permanency.

Lecture Notes in Computer Science

For information about Vols. 1–945

please contact your bookseller or Springer-Verlag

Vol. 981: I. Wachsmuth, C.-R. Rollinger, W. Brauer (Eds.), KI-95: Advances in Artificial Intelligence. Proceedings, 1995. XII, 269 pages. (Subseries LNAI).

Vol. 982: S. Doaitse Swierstra, M. Hermenegildo (Eds.), Programming Languages: Implementations, Logics and Programs. Proceedings, 1995. XI, 467 pages. 1995.

Vol. 983: A. Mycroft (Ed.), Static Analysis. Proceedings, 1995. VIII, 423 pages. 1995.

Vol. 984: J.-M. Haton, M. Keane, M. Manago (Eds.), Advances in Case-Based Reasoning. Proceedings, 1994. VIII, 307 pages. 1995.

Vol. 985: T. Sellis (Ed.), Rules in Database Systems. Proceedings, 1995. VIII, 373 pages. 1995.

Vol. 986: Henry G. Baker (Ed.), Memory Management. Proceedings, 1995. XII, 417 pages. 1995.

Vol. 987: P.E. Camurati, H. Eveking (Eds.), Correct Hardware Design and Verification Methods. Proceedings, 1995. VIII, 342 pages. 1995.

Vol. 988: A.U. Frank, W. Kuhn (Eds.), Spatial Information Theory. Proceedings, 1995. XIII, 571 pages. 1995.

Vol. 989: W. Schäfer, P. Botella (Eds.), Software Engineering — ESEC '95. Proceedings, 1995. XII, 519 pages. 1995.

Vol. 990: C. Pinto-Ferreira, N.J. Mamede (Eds.), Progress in Artificial Intelligence. Proceedings, 1995. XIV, 487 pages. 1995. (Subseries LNAI).

Vol. 991: J. Wainer, A. Carvalho (Eds.), Advances in Artificial Intelligence. Proceedings, 1995. XII, 342 pages. 1995. (Subseries LNAI).

Vol. 992: M. Gori, G. Soda (Eds.), Topics in Artificial Intelligence. Proceedings, 1995. XII, 451 pages. 1995. (Subseries LNAI).

Vol. 993: T.C. Fogarty (Ed.), Evolutionary Computing. Proceedings, 1995. VIII, 264 pages. 1995.

Vol. 994: M. Hebert, J. Ponce, T. Boult, A. Gross (Eds.), Object Representation in Computer Vision. Proceedings, 1994. VIII, 359 pages. 1995.

Vol. 995: S.M. Müller, W.J. Paul, The Complexity of Simple Computer Architectures. XII, 270 pages. 1995.

Vol. 996: P. Dybjer, B. Nordström, J. Smith (Eds.), Types for Proofs and Programs. Proceedings, 1994. X, 202 pages. 1995.

Vol. 997: K.P. Jantke, T. Shinohara, T. Zeugmann (Eds.), Algorithmic Learning Theory. Proceedings, 1995. XV, 319 pages. 1995.

Vol. 998: A. Clarke, M. Campolargo, N. Karatzas (Eds.), Bringing Telecommunication Services to the People – IS&N '95. Proceedings, 1995. XII, 510 pages. 1995.

Vol. 999: P. Antsaklis, W. Kohn, A. Nerode, S. Sastry (Eds.), Hybrid Systems II. VIII, 569 pages. 1995.

Vol. 1000: J. van Leeuwen (Ed.), Computer Science Today. XIV, 643 pages. 1995.

Vol. 1002: J.J. Kistler, Disconnected Operation in a Distributed File System. XIX, 249 pages. 1995.

Vol. 1004: J. Staples, P. Eades, N. Katoh, A. Moffat (Eds.), Algorithms and Computation. Proceedings, 1995. XV, 440 pages. 1995.

Vol. 1005: J. Estublier (Ed.), Software Configuration Management. Proceedings, 1995. IX, 311 pages. 1995.

Vol. 1006: S. Bhalla (Ed.), Information Systems and Data Management. Proceedings, 1995. IX, 321 pages. 1995.

Vol. 1007: A. Bosselaers, B. Preneel (Eds.), Integrity Primitives for Secure Information Systems. VII, 239 pages. 1995.

Vol. 1008: B. Preneel (Ed.), Fast Software Encryption. Proceedings, 1994. VIII, 367 pages. 1995.

Vol. 1009: M. Broy, S. Jähnichen (Eds.), KORSO: Methods, Languages, and Tools for the Construction of Correct Software. X, 449 pages. 1995. Vol.

Vol. 1010: M. Veloso, A. Aamodt (Eds.), Case-Based Reasoning Research and Development. Proceedings, 1995. X, 576 pages. 1995. (Subseries LNAI).

Vol. 1011: T. Furuhashi (Ed.), Advances in Fuzzy Logic, Neural Networks and Genetic Algorithms. Proceedings, 1994. (Subseries LNAI).

Vol. 1012: M. Bartošek, J. Staudek, J. Wiedermann (Eds.), SOFSEM '95: Theory and Practice of Informatics. Proceedings, 1995. XI, 499 pages. 1995.

Vol. 1013: T.W. Ling, A.O. Mendelzon, L. Vieille (Eds.), Deductive and Object-Oriented Databases. Proceedings, 1995. XIV, 557 pages. 1995.

Vol. 1014: A.P. del Pobil, M.A. Serna, Spatial Representation and Motion Planning. XII, 242 pages. 1995.

Vol. 1015: B. Blumenthal, J. Gornostaev, C. Unger (Eds.), Human-Computer Interaction. Proceedings, 1995. VIII, 203 pages. 1995.

Vol. 1017: M. Nagl (Ed.), Graph-Theoretic Concepts in Computer Science. Proceedings, 1995. XI, 406 pages. 1995.

Vol. 1018: T. Little, R. Gusella (Eds.), Network and Operating Systems Support for Digital Audio and Video. Proceedings, 1995. XI, 357 pages. 1995.

Vol. 1019: E. Brinksma, W.R. Cleaveland, K.G. Larsen, T. Margaria, B. Steffen (Eds.), Tools and Algorithms for the Construction and Analysis of Systems. Selected Papers, 1995. VII, 291 pages. 1995.

Vol. 1020: I.D. Watson (Ed.), Progress in Case-Based Reasoning. Proceedings, 1995. VIII, 209 pages. 1995. (Subseries LNAI).

Vol. 1021: M.P. Papazoglou (Ed.), OOER '95: Object-Oriented and Entity-Relationship Modeling. Proceedings, 1995. XVII, 451 pages. 1995.

Vol. 1022: P.H. Hartel, R. Plasmeijer (Eds.), Functional Programming Languages in Education. Proceedings, 1995. X, 309 pages. 1995.

Vol. 1023: K. Kanchanasut, J.-J. Lévy (Eds.), Algorithms, Concurrency and Knowlwdge. Proceedings, 1995. X, 410 pages. 1995.

Vol. 1024: R.T. Chin, H.H.S. Ip, A.C. Naiman, T.-C. Pong (Eds.), Image Analysis Applications and Computer Graphics. Proceedings, 1995. XVI, 533 pages. 1995.

Vol. 1025: C. Boyd (Ed.), Cryptography and Coding. Proceedings, 1995. IX, 291 pages. 1995.